WATERFALLS OF MICHIGAN

GUIDEBOOK SERIES

PHIL STAGG

Book 4 West	Book 3 West Central	Book 2 Central	Book 1 East
*Gogebic Ontonagon * Porcupine Mtn.*	*Baraga Houghton Iron Keweenaw*	*Dickinson Marquette Menominee*	*Alger Chippewa Delta Luce Manistee Presque Isle*

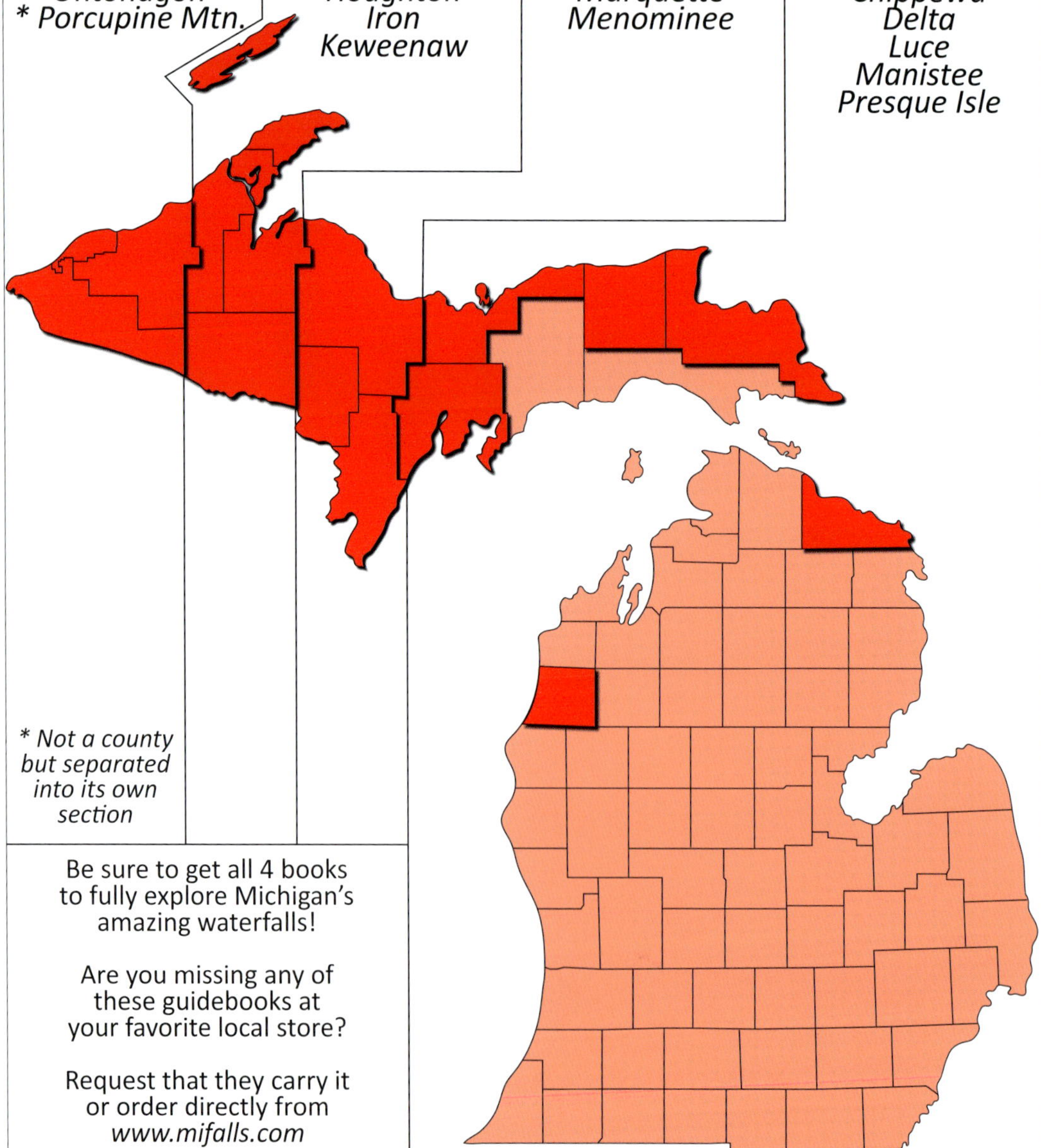

** Not a county but separated into its own section*

Be sure to get all 4 books to fully explore Michigan's amazing waterfalls!

Are you missing any of these guidebooks at your favorite local store?

Request that they carry it or order directly from *www.mifalls.com*

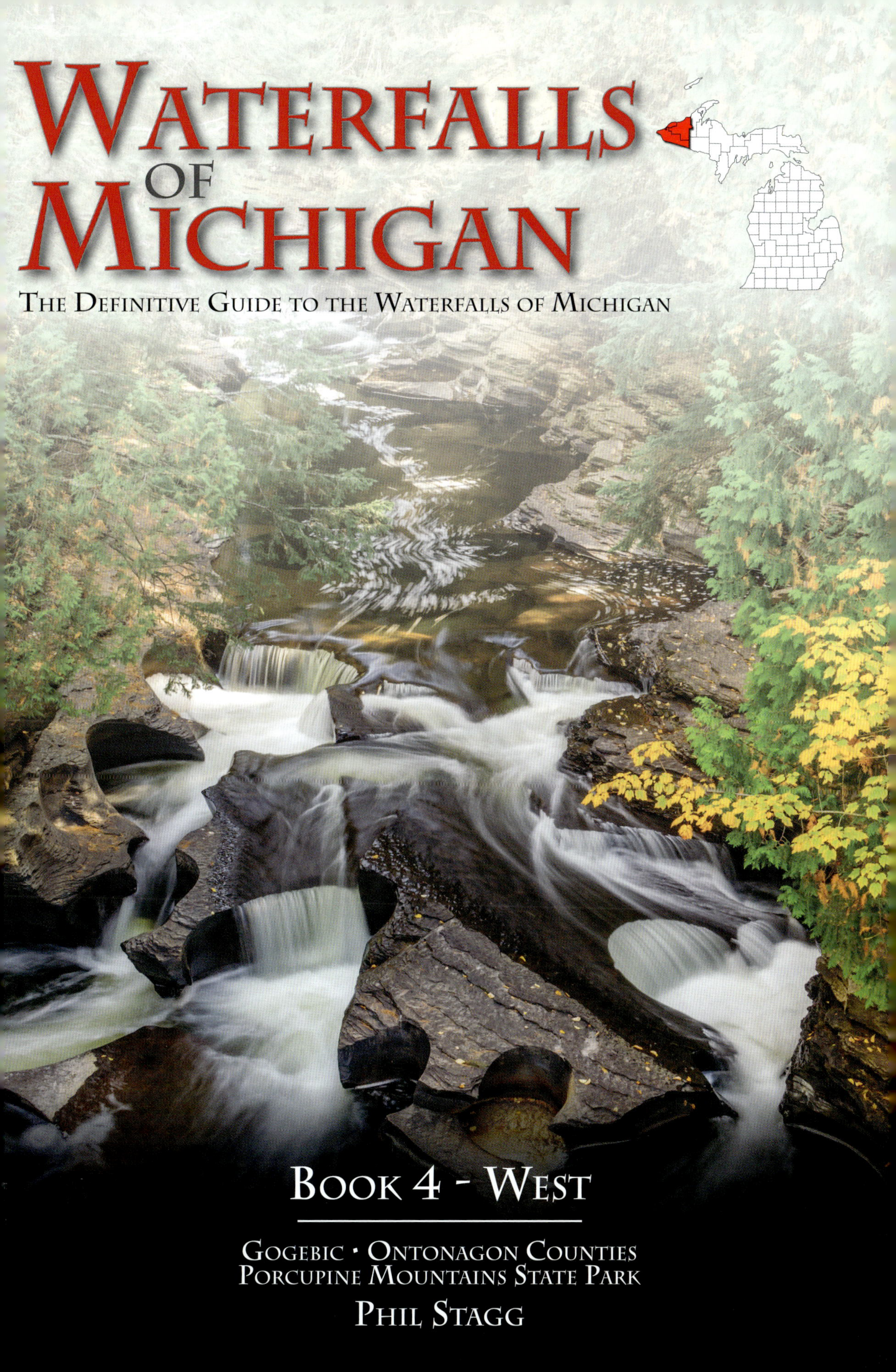

Waterfalls of Michigan

The Definitive Guide to the Waterfalls of Michigan

Book 4 - West

Gogebic · Ontonagon Counties
Porcupine Mountains State Park

Phil Stagg

Waterfalls of Michigan
Book 4 - West

Published by:

MI Falls Publishing
11765 West Cadillac Rd.
Cadillac, MI 49601
231•920•8416

www.mifalls.com

ISBN: 978-0-9971346-3-6
LCCN: 2016900613

Photography: Phil Stagg
Text: Phil Stagg
Design: Phil Stagg

Printed in the United States of America

First Printing: May 2016

I have had the pleasure of meeting countless helpful people during the making of this guidebook series. Some have encouraged me to press on. Others have given me the whereabouts of little known waterfalls. Whether it was the smiling face of a waitress in a small diner or a polite "You're welcome!" from a gas station attendant, I've run across some of the best people on this planet that we call "Earth" while crisscrossing a narrow peninsula at the northern edge of the United States of America.

Let me acknowledge a small number of these most helpful people:

Tracey Barrett, the face of the Baraga County Convention & Visitors Bureau, has provided a treasure trove of information about the Huron Mountains and their watery secrets.

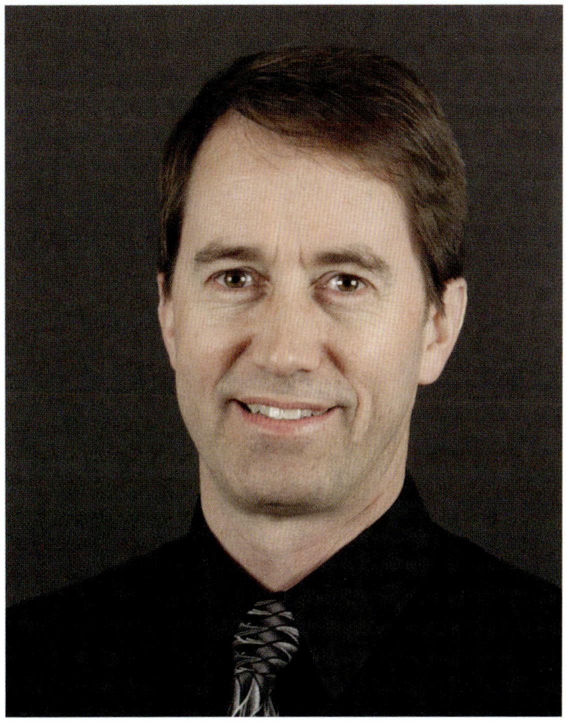

Phil Stagg

Shane Miller, a young man near the Dead River in Marquette guided me to several waterfalls that I had no knowledge of.

Douglas Feltman has been an inspiration and encouragement to me ever since I met him at Alder Falls near Big Bay. It's been a blessing to get to know him better.

Although I've never met Jacob Emerick in person, we've conversed over the internet about some of Michigan's most obscure waterfalls. His online information has helped Michigan waterfall hunters for years.

John and Barbara Gerlach gave me professional technical photography lessons at their workshops in Munising. They have also inspired and encouraged me to see the project through to completion.

Robert Witting rescued me and my son after we had become stuck near the Firesteel River and had hiked for miles in the dark. His selfless help was beyond belief.

Bob Hansen gave me information about a local, lower peninsula waterfall. He, along with Steve Playter, Tim and Dave Fekete and Matt Bendelow have been a source of support for years.

Thank you.

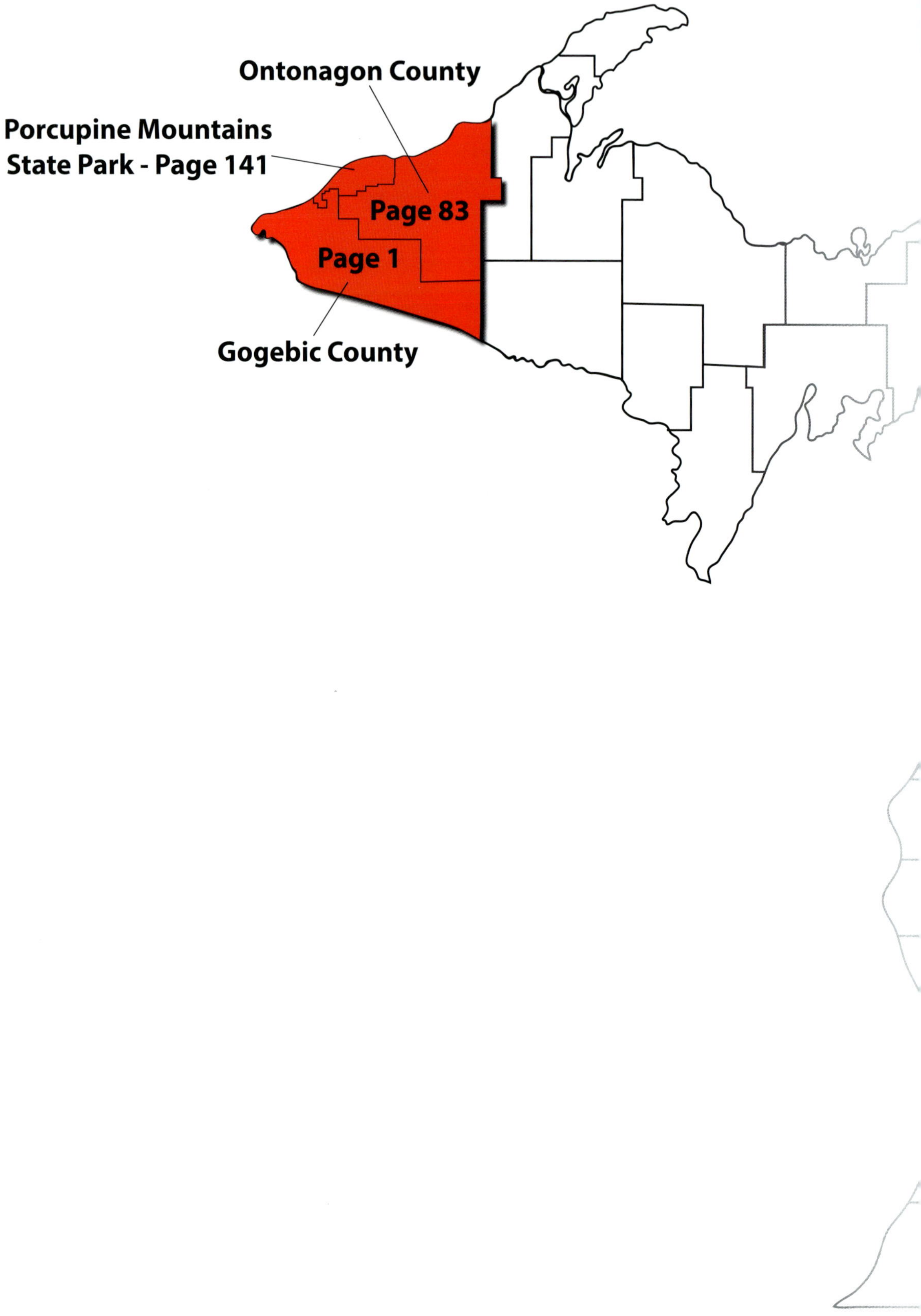
Ontonagon County
Porcupine Mountains
State Park - Page 141
Page 83
Page 1
Gogebic County

TABLE OF CONTENTS

Full Color **County Maps** *have Area Map Breakdowns.*

How to use the Maps and Data Clusters

(A) Pick a County Map
(B) Decide on an Area to check out
(C) Turn to the associated Area Map
(D) Find a waterfall to explore
(E) Review the Data Table for that waterfall

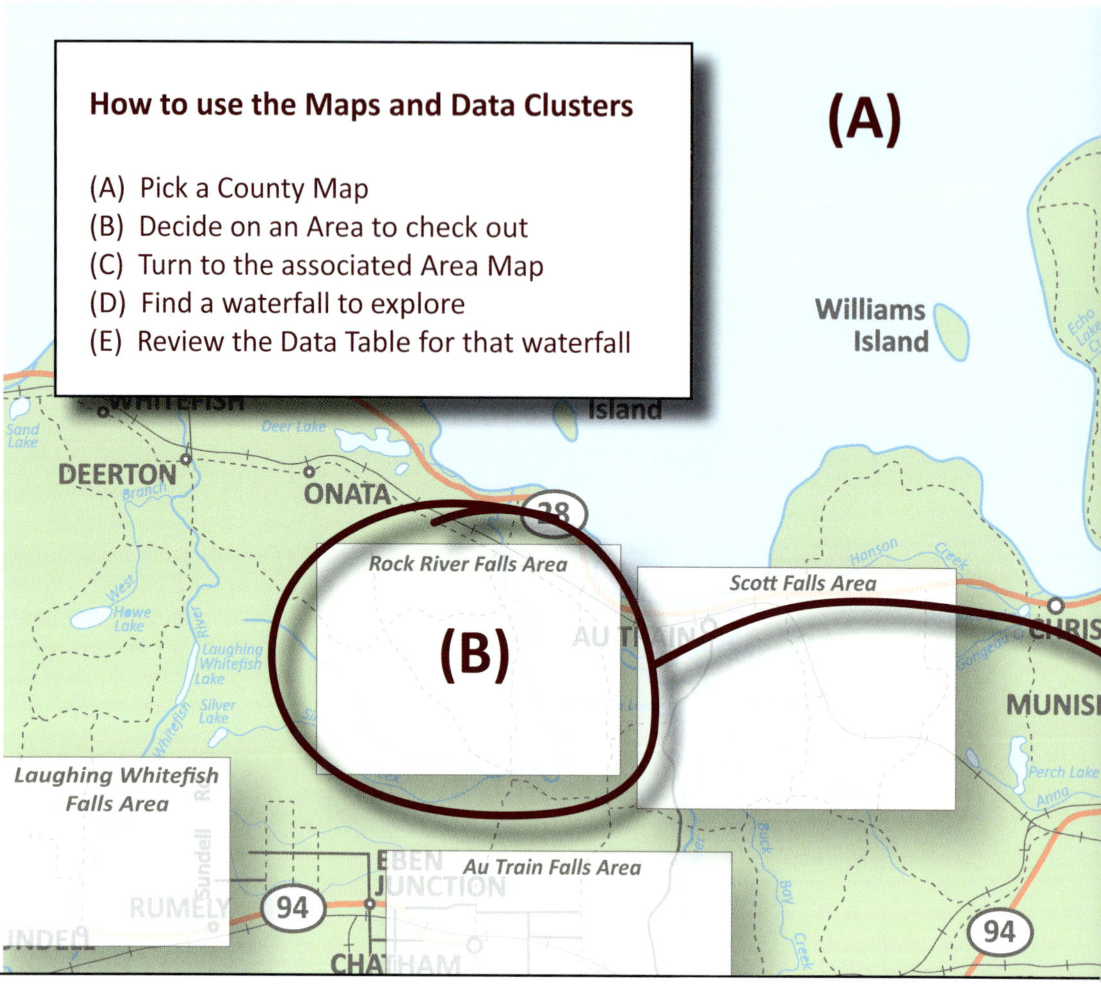

Data Table *is supplied for EVERY waterfall!*
Packed full of VITAL information. **(E)**

(1) (2) **ROCK RIVER FALLS** (3) (Rock River) (12)

(4) 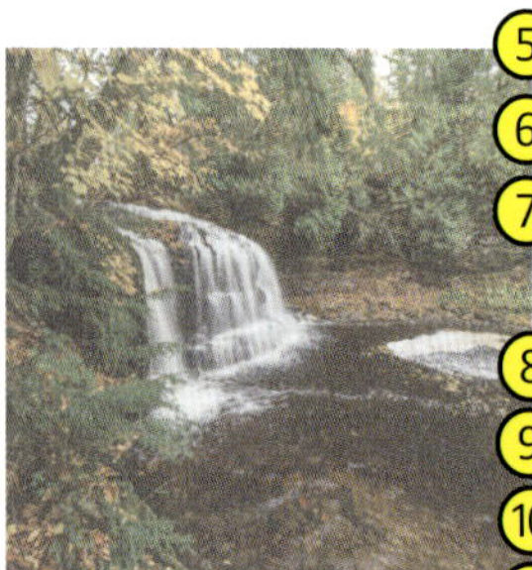

(5) Must See: 9
(6) Height: 18 feet
(7) Time: 60-90 minutes

Driving Information
(8) Signs: None
(9) Road: Dirt Road
(10) Access: Somewhat Difficu
(11) 4WD: Helpful

(13) GPS: N46 24.663 W86 58.583

Hiking Information
(14) Path: Footpath
(15) Length: 7/8 mile
(16) Elev. Change: Slight
(17) GPS: Helpful
(18) Danger: Slight
(19) WP Boots: Required

(20) There is a small parking area large enough for about 6 or 7 vehicles at the trail head. The trail is .86 miles long with the first 2/3 of the walk on a nice footpath. The last 1/4 mile is muddy and there are several places that the trail becomes a little difficult to follow.

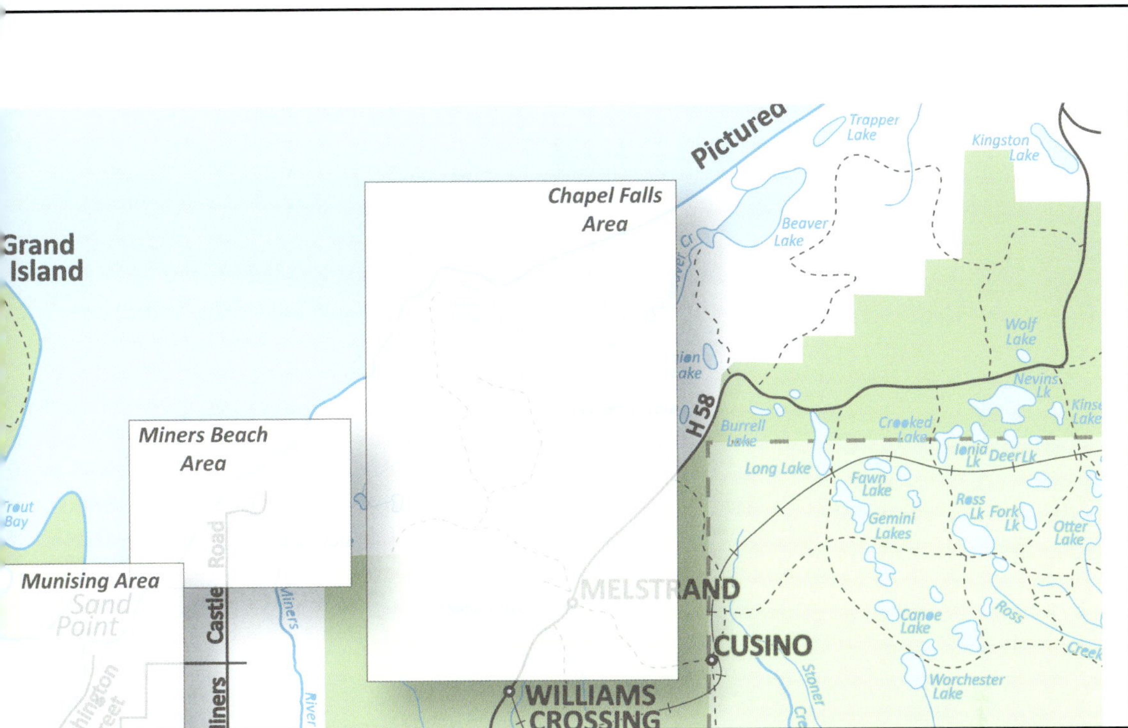

Area Maps

Display roads and trails to ALL waterfalls - each waterfall has GPS coordinates!

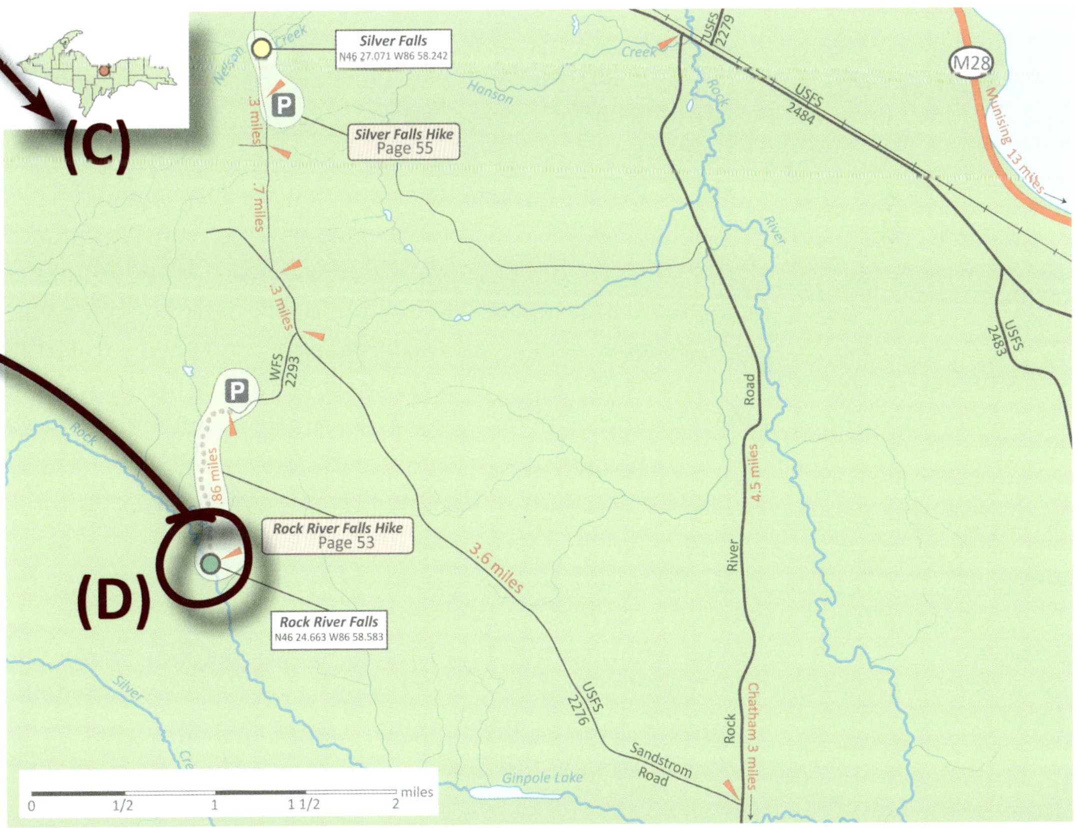

Data Table
Definitions

Must See Swatch (1)

The colored square in the upper, left corner of the Waterfall Data Tables corresponds with the color in the Waterfall Area Map for each particular waterfall and is derived from the "Must See" rating. Those waterfalls with a "Must See" rating of 1-3 are "Red" waterfalls. "Yellow" waterfalls have ratings of 4-6, and "Green" waterfalls are rated 7-10. Think of the "Must See Colors" as you would a standard traffic light.

Green: GO!! You've got to check these out!
Yellow: SLOW DOWN!! These are OK waterfalls, perhaps it'll be nice to visit once or twice.
Red: STOP!! These are waterfalls, or at least considered waterfalls by some, but unless you are a die-hard waterfall fan, you probably won't enjoy them.

Waterfall Name (2)

"Where did you get the names from?" Good question! Most waterfalls were named many years ago and those names were incorporated into the USGS maps which are the basis for most of the maps that we have today. These resultant maps bear those names which are now commonly recognized. In the cases where waterfalls were not named on the USGS maps, the naming of the falls becomes more interesting. I typically have named "unnamed" waterfalls by the area of the river or creek on which they are found. An example of this would be "Carp River Falls - Upper #3". Also, just because a waterfall doesn't have a published name doesn't mean that the residents of an area don't have a name for it. I have tried to use the locally accepted names whenever possible.

You will also find that I rarely start a waterfall name with "Upper", "Middle", or "Lower". For ease of indexing, the name of the fall typically comes first, followed by the locational modifier and/or number if applicable.

③ *Waterway Name*

Most of the waterways on which waterfalls are found have long established names. Just like waterfalls, there are some small creeks that have no published names, but do have locally accepted names. I have used these names whenever known.

④ *Waterfall Picture*

A small picture of each waterfall is attached. Some waterfalls are on posted, private land. If I wasn't able to receive permission to photograph the waterfall, there is obviously no picture.

⑤ *Must See Rating*

Each waterfall is rated on a 1-10 scale, with one being the least desirable and 10 being the most. The following is the guideline I use:

10. Gorgeous! Great eye appeal! Inspiring! One of the best waterfalls in Michigan.
9. Excellent waterfall! You will want to make many repeat visits.
8. Very nice waterfall! Very popular!
7. Nice waterfall. Worth coming back to see several times.
6. An above average waterfall. Might want to see it again.
5. A nice all-around waterfall. Perhaps worth a repeat visit.
4. An OK waterfall. Probably not worth coming back to.
3. Don't have your hopes too high - it's not that good.
2. Avid waterfall enthusiasts may want to check it out just to say that they did.
1. It's water. It's falling. Who cares?

The "Must See" rating is my attempt at describing only the visual desirability of each waterfall. It doesn't take into account the difficulty in getting to the waterfall. There are some very nice waterfalls that require a substantial hike over rough terrain. The difficulty in reaching the waterfall doesn't figure into "Must See" rating.

Everyone has their own taste in waterfalls. What I am looking for in a waterfall is a visually pleasing setting combined with water that is falling at angles and with rates in keeping with the overall genre of the waterfall. Consistency and lack of obvious flaws is also important.

There may be times when you disagree with my rating. Keep in mind that water level, season, temperature, weather conditions, sun position, and even frame of mind affect the visual desirability of any waterfall at any point in time.

I have included the "Must See" rating to offer you a standardized method of comparing waterfalls so that you have some idea of which waterfalls you may wish to view.

Waterfall Height (6) This is an estimate of the height of the waterfall in feet. This is a potentially poor piece of information. Let me explain. If a waterfall has a free drop of 20 feet, flattens out for 20 to 30 feet of river length and then it has small cascading drops of 4 to 6 inches per drop for another 20 feet of accumulated drop, there would be a total drop of 40 feet. When viewing the waterfall, some people may consider just the free drop as the waterfall height, while others may include the additional 20 feet of cascades downstream. I tried to include the "normal" waterfall portion of the falls in my height estimates. I think of most waterfalls as viewable from one location. If a portion of the waterfall is not photogenic, then I may not have included that part in the overall height of the waterfall.

Hike Time (7) How much time should you plan for a hike? I have included an estimated amount of minutes or hours to plan for a hike. I am assuming that a hike entails a leisurely walk to and from the waterfall and includes an "appropriate" amount of time for viewing the waterfall.

Is there a Sign? (8) Most waterfalls have no signs announcing their presence. The waterfalls that do, have signs that are made by the Federal Government, the State of Michigan, counties, and some by private individuals.

Worst Road Type (9) In the process of driving to a waterfall the roads typically go from good to worse. So the road that a waterfall is accessed from will tell you what to expect for the worst driving conditions on your waterfall quest.

Accessibility (10) There is a wide variety of difficulty when it comes to finding a particular waterfall. A waterfall on a main road with signs announcing its presence is very easy to find. The more turns that are required off of a main road, the more difficult or complicated it becomes to find.

Is a 4WD needed? (11) You will find it easier to drive to some waterfalls with a 4WD vehicle. High clearance vehicles are sometimes needed.

⑫ *Quick Reference*

Ghosted Symbols Private
Activated Symbols Private

The "activated symbols" are the ones (if any) that apply to this particular waterfall.

Private This waterfall is on private land and more often than not the land is posted and the waterfall is not accessible to the public. *Note that this information is to the best of my knowledge. There very well may be more waterfalls on private land, but since it was not posted I was unaware. Be respectful of property owners and follow their wishes.*

The waterfall can be viewed from a vehicle.
A particularly kid-friendly waterfall.
Wheelchair accessible
Bathroom facilities are available, normally at the beginning of the hike. There will be flush, composting, or vault toilets.

⑬ *GPS Coordinate*

The GPS coordinate for the waterfall is written in degrees and minutes.

⑭ *Type of Path*

There are a variety of hiking trails that you will encounter. Expect everything from graded and paved trails to narrow dirt footpaths to no paths at all! Note that sometimes there will be one type of path at the beginning of the hike and another one entirely by the end. The worst type of path to the waterfall is listed here.

⑮ *Hike Length*

This is the length of the hike to the falls. Remember to double the length for a round trip estimate. Some hikes have a number of waterfalls along the route. The length for any particular waterfall along that hike is the distance from the vehicle to that waterfall, typically including the previous waterfalls found along the way.

⑯ *Elevation Change*

Many waterfalls involve a change in elevation, either along the hike or climbing down into a ravine to the waterfall.

⑰ *GPS Needed?*

Do you need a handheld GPS to find this waterfall? If so, make sure that you are using a reliable GPS and are familiar with its functions and use. Don't forget to take spare batteries. Having a compass with you is a great backup as well.

Danger (18) Viewing waterfalls has some inherit danger. Walking along potentially wet or icy paths or boardwalks, hiking over uneven ground and climbing into and out of ravines and gorges, standing at the brink of a fifty foot waterfall, navigating moss covered rocks near swift moving waters. Yes, caution is always important. But some waterfalls are more difficult to view or get to, so I trust this "Danger" category will help you to decide which waterfalls are right for you to view.

Waterproof Boots? (19) I prefer to keep my feet dry on waterfall hikes. If there are muddy trails or rivers or creeks that need to be forded I recommend wearing waterproof boots. I wear calf high boots when needing something more than my waterproof hiking shoes that are only ankle high.

Description (20) Find out a little more about the waterfall or hike in this brief description.

Waterfall Etiquette

Proper waterfall etiquette begins with a proper attitude toward people and the environment. Many waterfalls in the Upper Peninsula are on private land. Fortunately for us, many of the land owners allow individuals to drive on their property, park on it, and hike across it.

1) NEVER trespass on posted property. Obey all signs. The private property rights of all land owners must be respected.

2) Don't invade someone's personal space. Just because there isn't a "No Trespassing" sign doesn't mean that you can drive up next to their house, park your vehicle, and walk across their back yard to a waterfall just behind their house. Use common sense. Have proper waterfall etiquette. Do unto others as you would want them to do unto you. This timeless principle always holds true.

There are some waterfalls that are "OK" to view, but they are also quite close to residences. Be quiet and considerate. Be courteous and respectful.

3) Clean up after yourself. I know of a land owner that doesn't allow waterfall enthusiasts onto his land because every year he removes several bags of garbage from around the waterfall on his property. We must do better. Don't leave anything behind on your hikes. In fact, help clean up after others. If we all would do our part, I believe that more land owners would allow us to view the beauty that resides within their estates.

Respecting land owners and the environment in which the wonderful waterfalls of Michigan reside must be our top priority. Forsaking these principles will result in the loss of access to more and more waterfall locations. We must not let that happen.

CHAPTER 1
GOGEBIC COUNTY

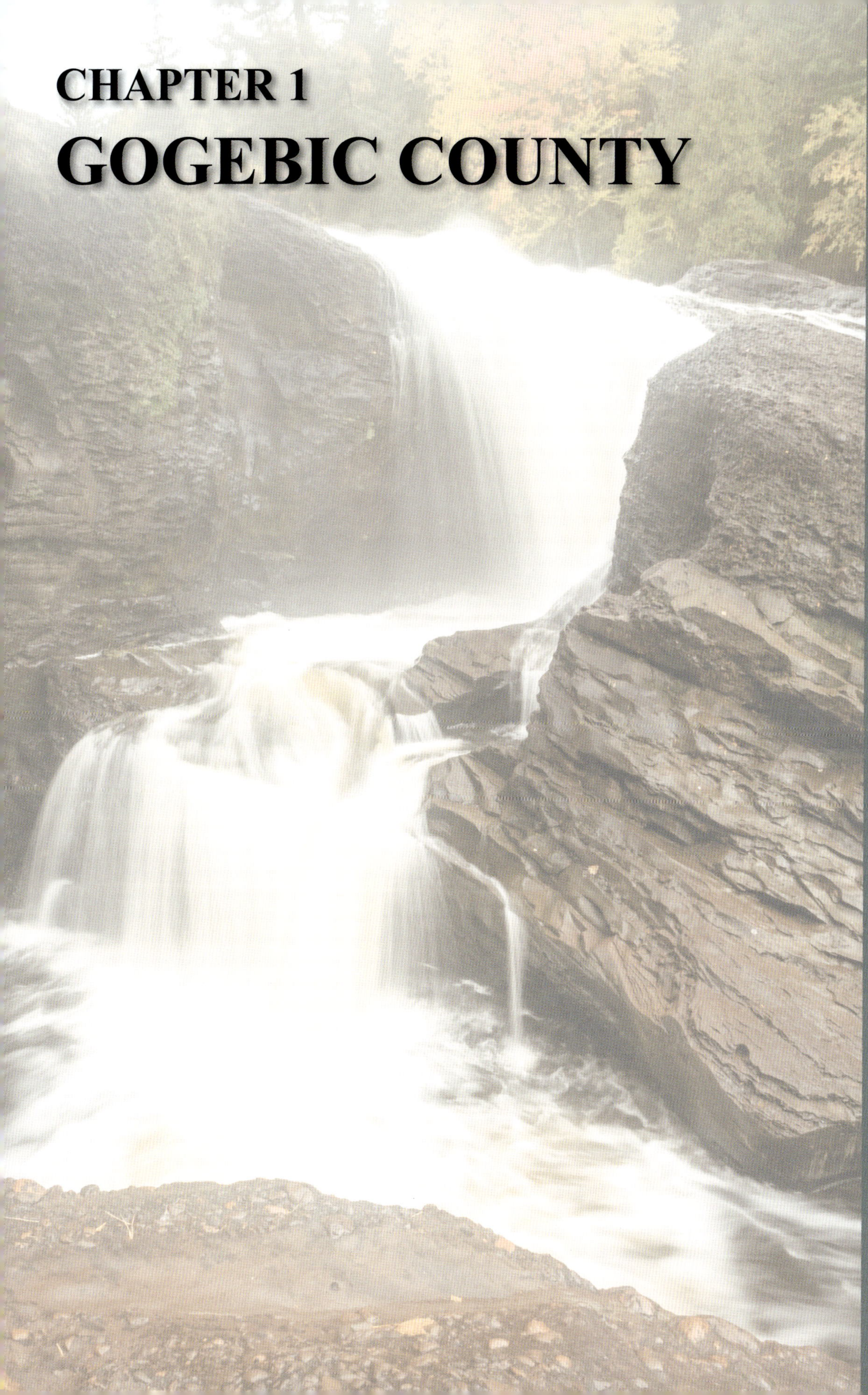

GOGEBIC COUNTY CONTENTS

NOTE: I have separated the waterfalls that lie within Porcupine Mountains State Park into their own chapter since the park contains portions of both Ontonagon and Gogebic Counties.

MAPS........
HIKES........
WATERFALLS........

TABLE OF CONTENT KEY

NOTE: I have separated the waterfalls that lie within Porcupine Mountains State Park into their own chapter since the park contains portions of both Ontonagon and Gogebic Counties.

MAPS............
HIKES............
WATERFALLS............

TABLE OF CONTENT KEY

NOTE: I have separated the waterfalls that lie within Porcupine Mountains State Park into their own chapter since the park contains portions of both Ontonagon and Gogebic Counties.

MAPS.....
HIKES.....
WATERFALLS.....

TABLE OF CONTENT KEY

GOGEBIC COUNTY FACTS

Founded:	1867
Size:	1101 square miles
Population (2010):	16,427
County Seat:	Bessemer

Gogebic County, from the busy US-2 corridor generously sprinkled with motels and restaurants near the Wisconsin border, to the popular Black River waterfalls and the western end of the Porcupine Mountains, embraces its rugged past as a mining and lumber area.

The county derived its name from the largest lake in the Upper Peninsula of Michigan - Lake Gogebic. The ancient Chippewas called it *Agogebic*. Most experts believe it meant, "body of water hanging on high". The lake is at 1,290 feet above sea level. By the time it empties into Lake Superior down the mighty Ontonagon River, it has fallen nearly 700 feet. The water truly does "hang on high" - or perhaps "fall from on high"!

Gogebic County was carved out of the then much larger Ontonagon County in 1867. Iron mining was becoming a major economic force in the southern corridor of Ontonagon County known as the Gogebic mining area. It was taking a week to travel from to Ontonagon, the county seat, in the north. It was thus decided to divide the county in half, creating the county aptly named *Gogebic*.

Iron was discovered in Gogebic County in the latter 1800's and mines starting springing up shortly thereafter. It is interesting to note that the mines are located on a generally east to west route roughly following US-2 in Ironwood, passing through Bessemer, continuing on to Wakefield and then heading eastward nearly to Lake Gogebic. The mining activity was its greatest in the late 1800's to the 1920's. The Great Depression curtailed many of the mines and although there was a bit of resurgence afterwards, the last of the Gogebic Range Mines ceased operations in 1967.

Copper Peak, the world's largest man-made ski jump, is located near the Black River north of Bessemer. The view from the top is breath taking, especially in autumn. For a small fee you can see it for yourself!

Gogebic County Map

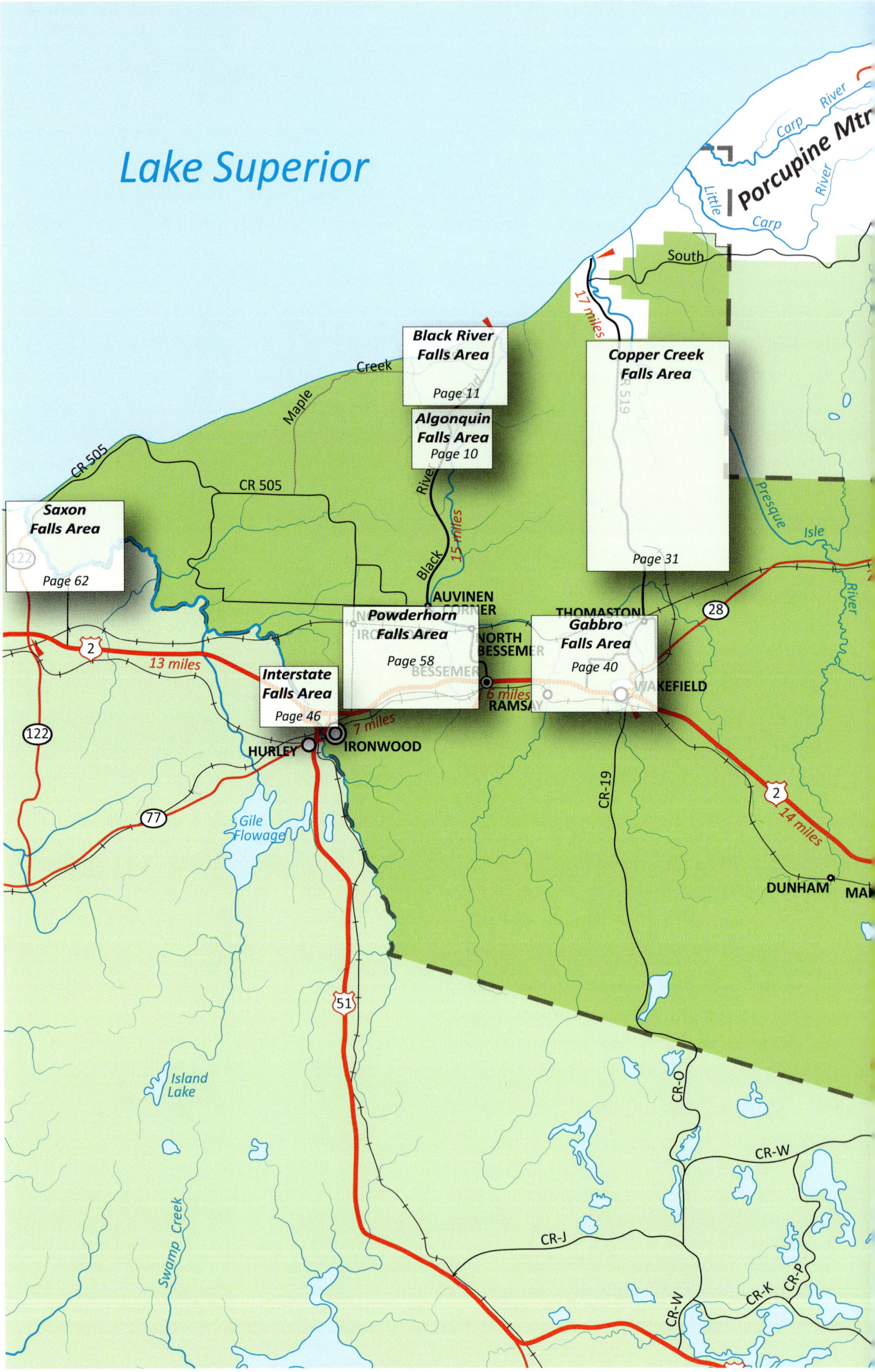

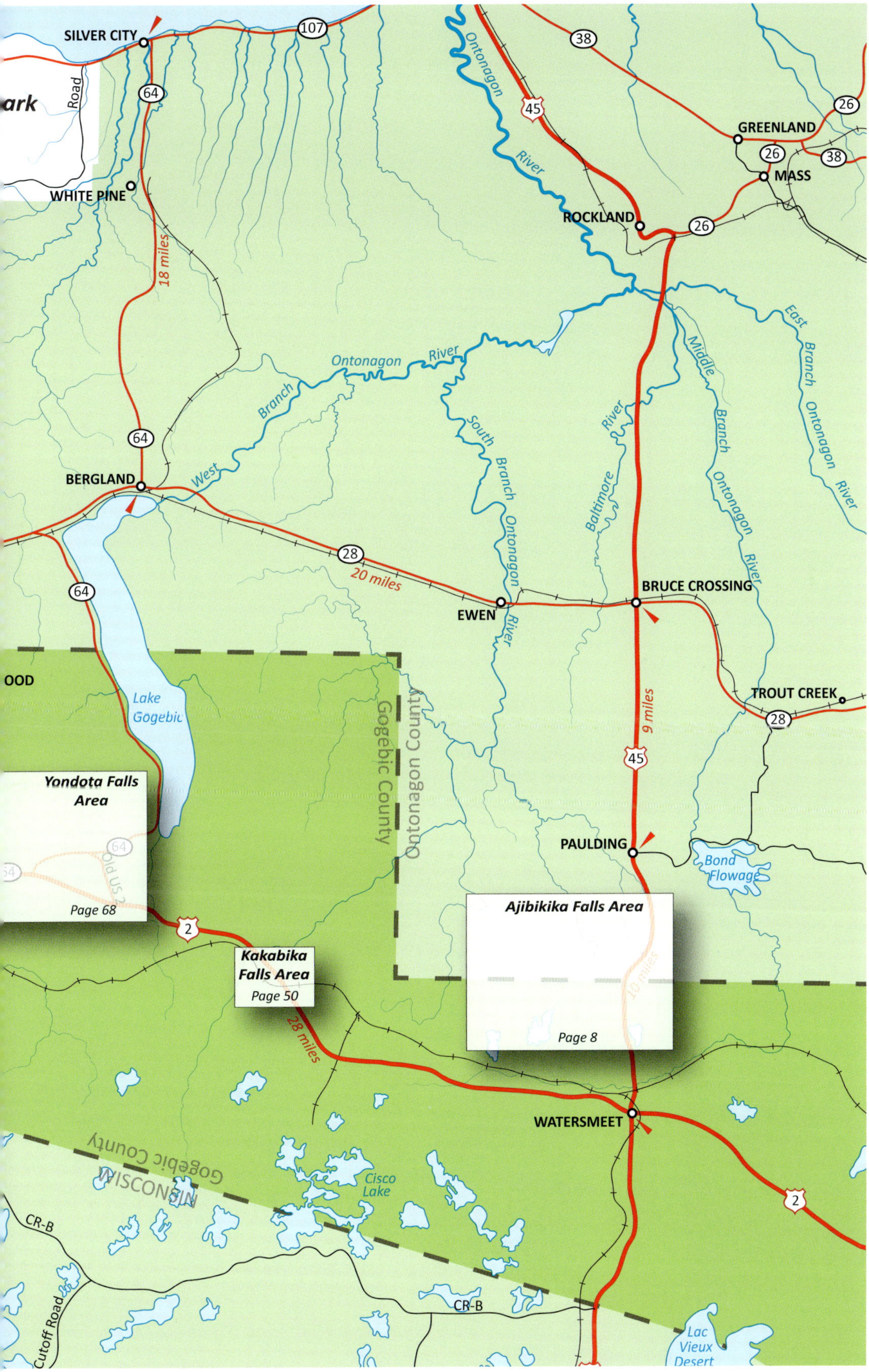
SILVER CITY
107
64
Road
ark
WHITE PINE
18 miles
64
BERGLAND
West
Branch
Ontonagon
River
South
Branch
Ontonagon
River
28
20 miles
EWEN
64
Lake
Gogebic
OOD
Yondota Falls
Area
Page 68
Old US 2
2
Kakabika
Falls Area
Page 50
28 miles
Gogebic County
Ontonagon County
Ontonagon
River
45
38
26
GREENLAND
26
38
MASS
ROCKLAND
26
East
Branch
Ontonagon
River
Middle
Branch
Ontonagon
River
Baltimore
River
BRUCE CROSSING
TROUT CREEK
28
9 miles
45
PAULDING
Bond
Flowage
Ajibikika Falls Area
18 miles
Page 8
WATERSMEET
2
Gogebic County
WISCONSIN
Cisco
Lake
CR-B
Cutoff Road
CR-B
Lac
Vieux
Desert

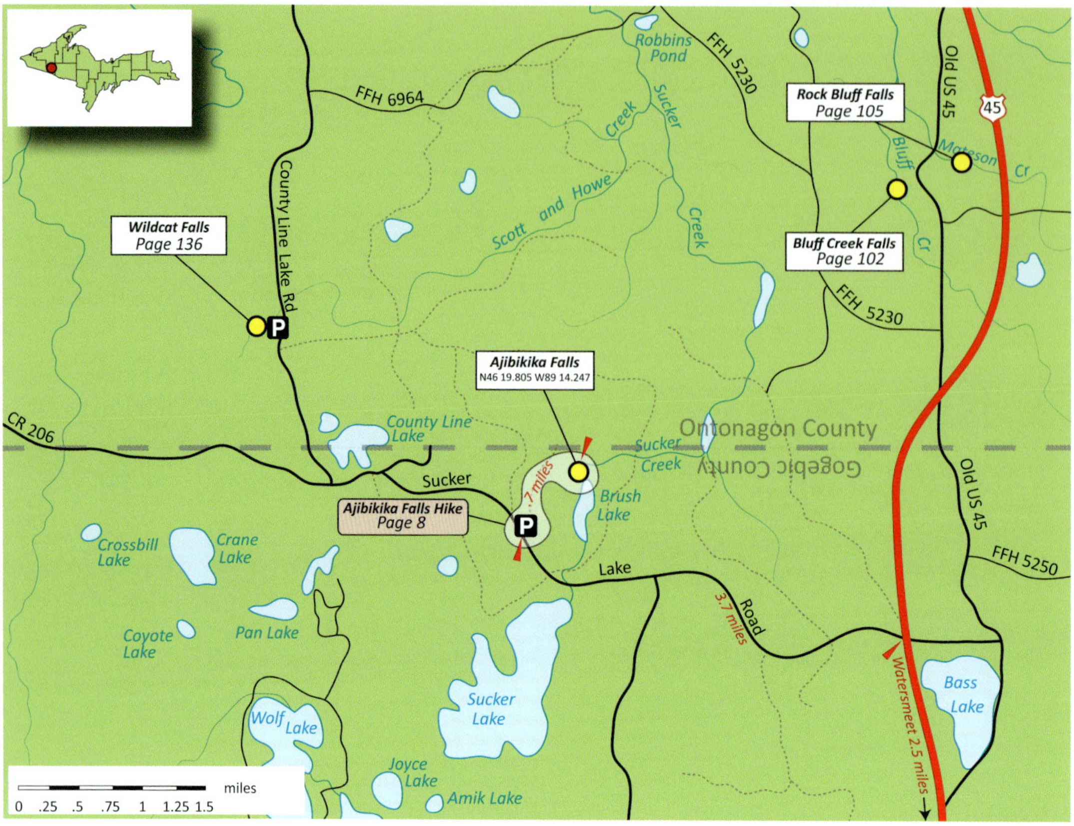

Ajibikika Falls Hike

Brush Lake empties into Sucker Creek, crossing a short stretch of flat ground before tumbling down with alternating slides and drops to a large marshy area. Delicate ferns, thickly matted moss and black stone overlook the falls. A second drop, just upstream from the falls, is almost completely hidden beneath a jumble of mossy boulders. This drop is 7' tall.

Directions: About 2.5 miles north of Watersmeet, turn west on Sucker Lake Road (gravel) off of US-45. Follow the gravel road for 3.7 miles to a the 2-track that is blocked off at N46 19.446 W89 14.860. Park. Hike in on a narrow, old 2-track until perpendicular to the falls. Bushwack through mostly open and dry forest to the waterfall.

AJIBIKIKA FALLS (SUCKER CREEK)

Private

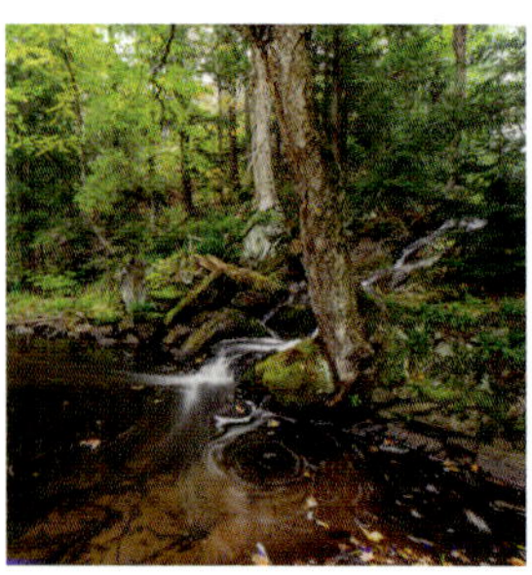

Must See:	6	GPS:	N46 19.805 W89 14.247
Height:	12		
Time:	60-90 minutes	Hiking Information	
		Path:	Old 2-track then None
Driving Information		Length:	.7 miles
Signs:	None	Elev. Change:	Moderate
Road:	Gravel	GPS:	Required
Access:	Somewhat Difficult	Danger:	Minor
4WD:	N/A	WP Boots:	Recommended

This waterfall is rarely visited. Be sure you have a good GPS with spare batteries. There are MANY acres of land and swamps to wander around in out here.

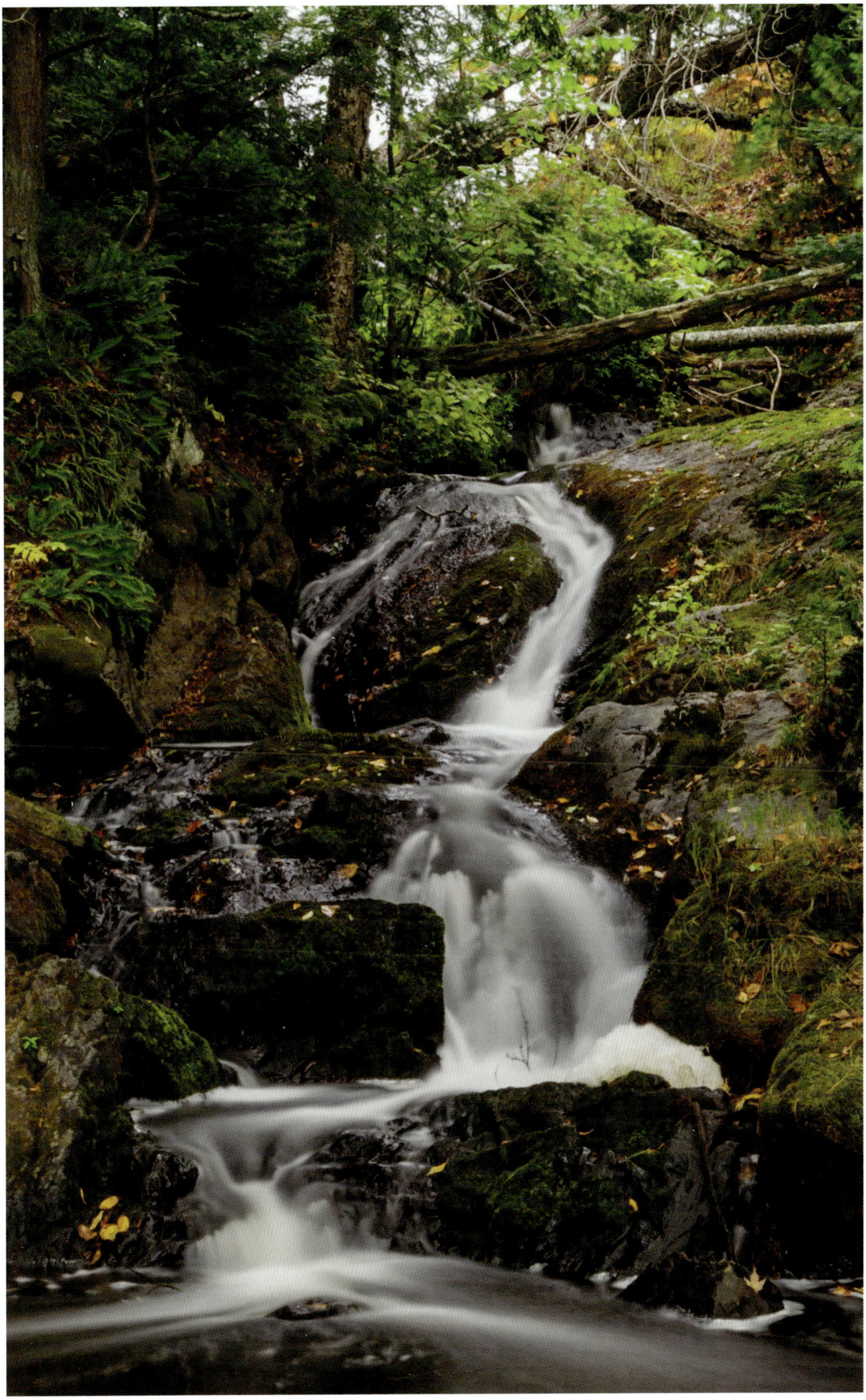

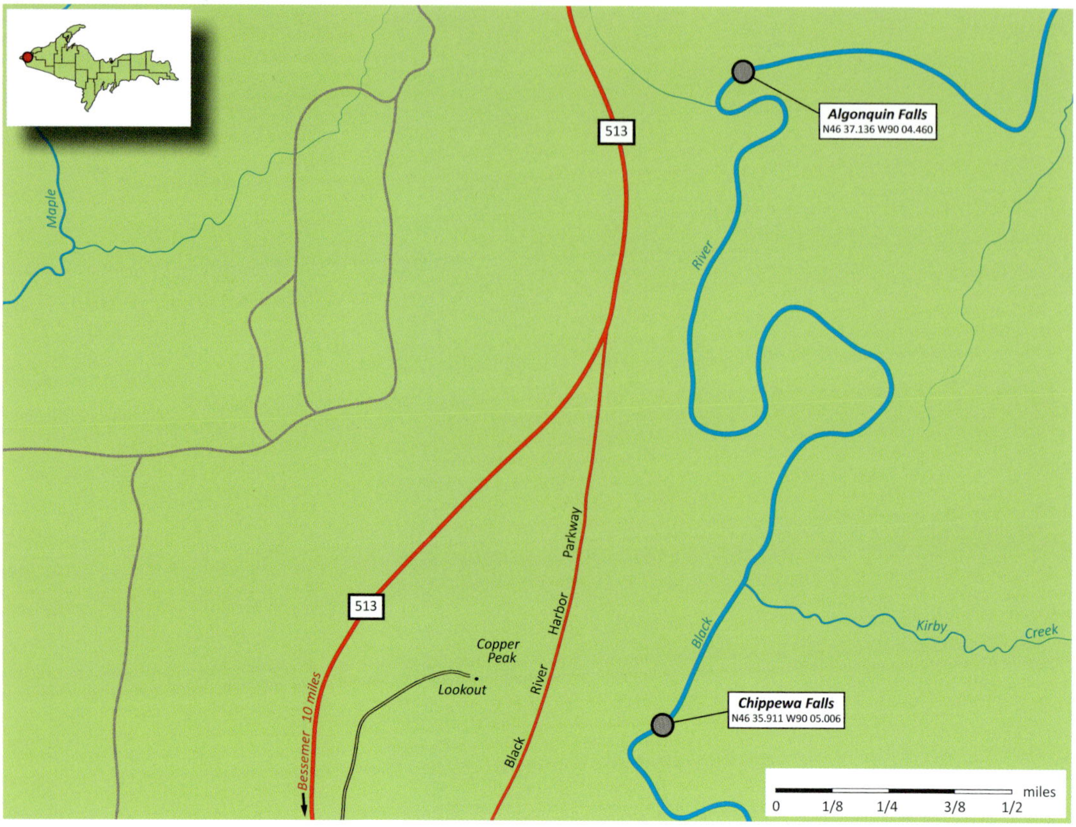

Copper Peak Area Hikes

Algonquin Falls and ***Chippewa Falls:*** I have not hiked in to either of these falls. It is my understanding that they are both a series of aggressive rapids, and nothing like the wonderful waterfalls further down river. There may be a trail to Chippewa Falls but I don't think that there is one to Algonquin Falls. Timing and weather have kept me from making the hike to these yet. Hopefully this next summer I'll have better information on these waterfalls!

The Black River waterfalls toward the mouth of the river are excellent, but the attraction here is Copper Peak, the highest ski flying hill that man has ever made and the ONLY ski flying hill in the western hemisphere! Constructed in 1969, it has hosted ten competitions.

Rising 241 feet above the crest of Chippewa Hill, the top of the superstructure is one of the highest points in Michigan at 1782 feet above sea level. From that vantage point, it provides the highest, most unobstructed vantage point in the Midwest. Portions of Michigan, Wisconsin, Minnesota, and sometimes even Canada can be seen from the viewing deck at the top. Tourists can ride the 800 foot chair lift to the crest of the hill and then travel up some 18 stories to an observation deck. It is possible to continue to climb another 8 stories to the very top for an awe inspiring view and to try to imagine what runs though skiers' minds just before hurtling themselves at nearly 70 MPH down the slope. I've been to the top of Copper Peak to take some pictures. The structure sways in the breeze. It can be a bit disconcerting. But what a view!

These tours are available in Summer and Fall. For more information visit their website at www.copperpeak.com or call (906) 932-3500.

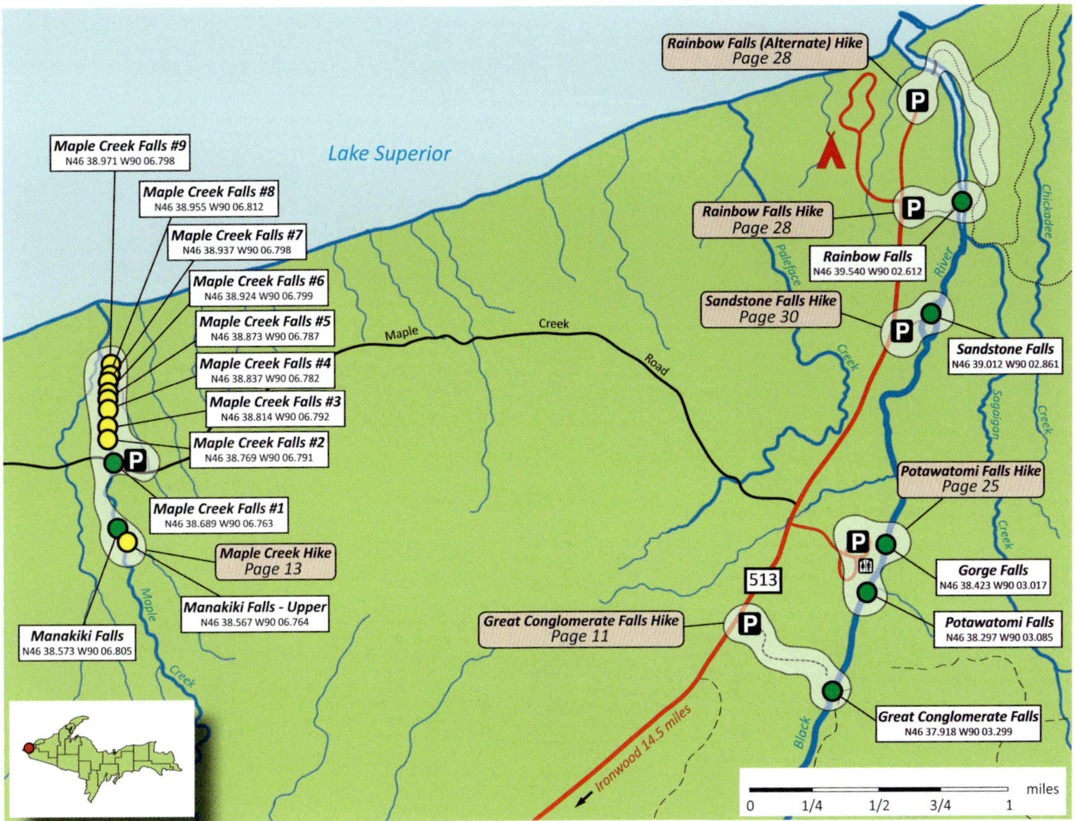

Great Conglomerate Falls Hike

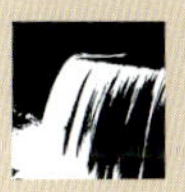

Great Conglomerate Falls: A large protruding section of conglomerate divides the waterfall into two distinct drops. A wooden guardrail was strategically placed around a natural observation area, but tree growth is starting to hinder an unobstructed view.

Directions: Follow CR-513 northerly toward Lake Superior. Turn right (east) at the sign for the waterfall. Park in the small parking lot. A very nice footpath leads 3/4 mile to the waterfall.

GREAT CONGLOMERATE FALLS (BLACK RIVER)

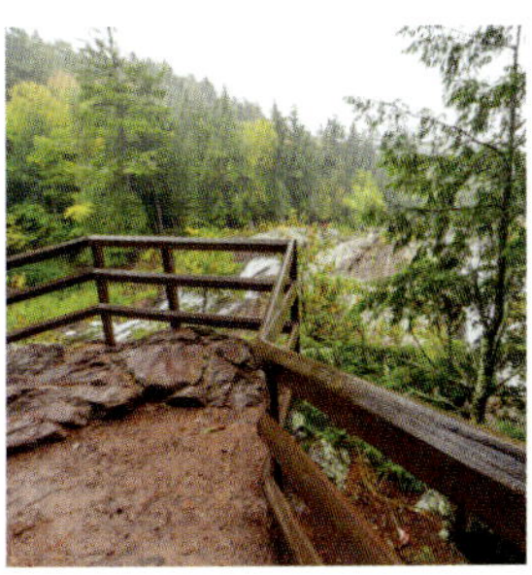

Must See:	7	GPS:	N46 37.918 W90 03.299
Height:	30 feet		
Time:	30-60 minutes	**Hiking Information**	
		Path:	Improved Footpath
Driving Information		Length:	3/4 mile
Signs:	Good Sign	Elev. Change:	Moderate
Road:	Secondary	GPS:	N/A
Access:	Very Easy	Danger:	Slight
4WD:	N/A	WP Boots:	N/A

The hike is fairly flat until right at the end and then around 40 steps lead down to the observation area. There are some benches along the way to give your feet a rest. The North Country Trail intersects the trail near the waterfall. Follow the NCT a short distance upstream and you will find a place where it is possible to scramble down to the river's edge near the base of the falls.

The scene from the viewing platform. Notice how the evergreens are encroaching on the clear vision area. This site has a wooden rail and original bedrock for the platform.

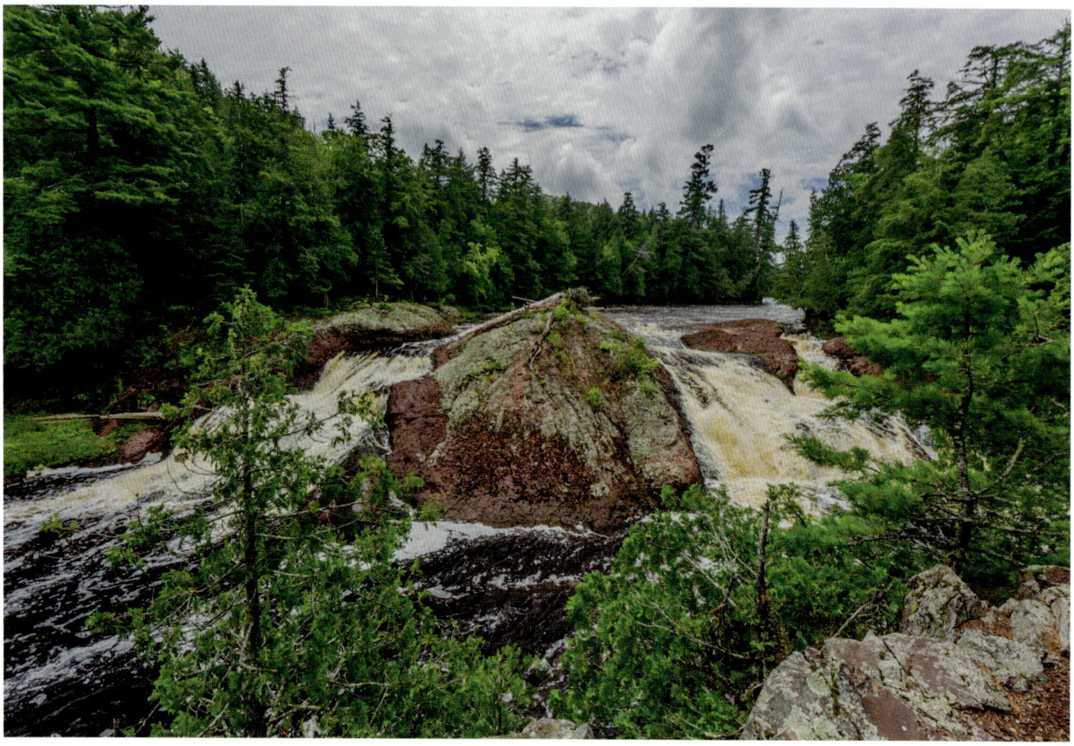

This is the view from the river's edge at the base of the waterfall. The mass of rock jutting out of the water on the left is where the viewing area is located.

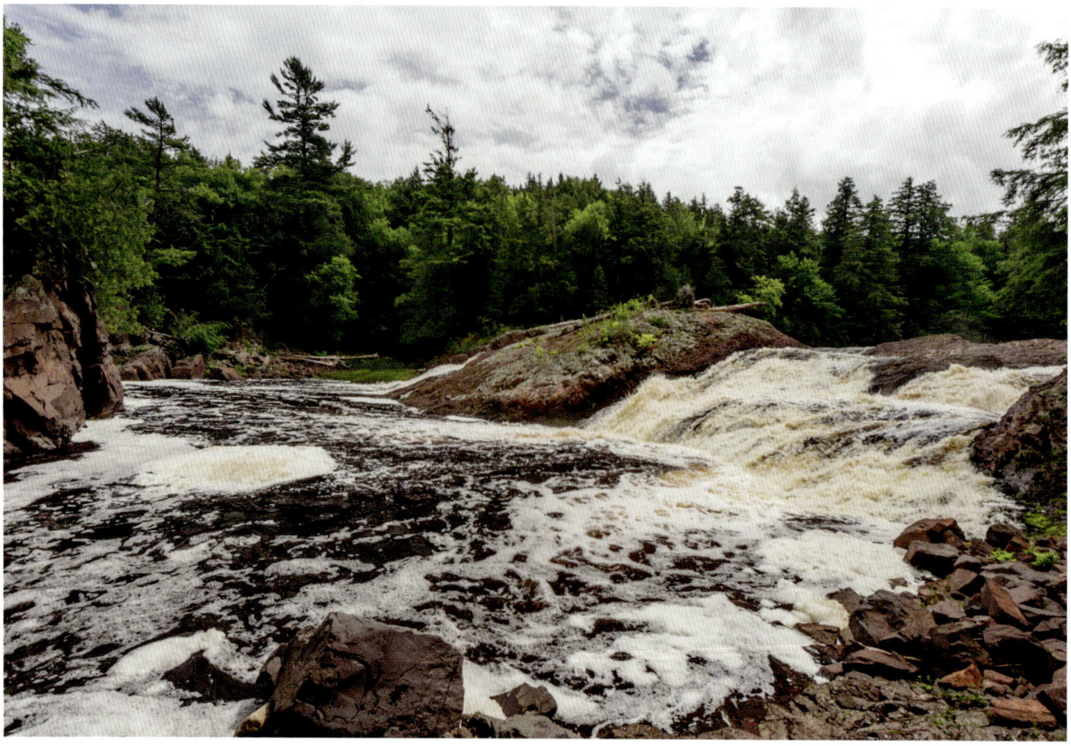

Maple Creek Hike

Maple Creek flows northward to Lake Superior, roughly paralleling the Black River which is about 3 miles to the east. This small creek passes through a gorge, areas with rocky outcroppings, as wells as some calmer terrain. This easily accessed, though seldom traversed strip of land has become one of my favorite hikes in Michigan. There are some sheer drops and steep hillsides, some of which are water saturated and muddy. Be very careful!

Manakiki Falls: Climbing, sometimes slipping down a wet, steep leaf covered hillside is the best means of getting down into the gorge. The other side of the creek is a sheer rock wall which provides a nice backdrop for the waterfall that slides down along the sharply angled riverbed.

Manakiki Falls - Upper: The upper falls are just 150 feet up the creek. Climb up the riverbed next to the waterfall or climb back up the hillside and continue upstream. The upper falls gently slide over several slanted sections. The openness of the area contrasts greatly with Manakiki Falls which is down at the base of the gorge.

(This is the end of the waterfalls on the south side of the road. Head back to the bridge and continue following the creek to the north.)

Maple Creek Falls #1: Just north of the bridge, work your way down to the bottom of the gorge. Wade through the 1 foot deep creek that fills the gorge from wall to wall. Hike upstream and around a turn in the gorge to view the falls.

Maple Creek Falls #2: The creek passes through the gorge, slides down the falls into an orange-tinged pool, then tentatively passes between two, 20 foot tall sentinels of conglomerate, one of which is barely supporting three large cedar trunks.

Maple Creek Falls #3: A series of small cascades and slides continues for over 100 feet. The peaceful babbling can be enjoyed for a soothing break.

Maple Creek Falls #4: A gap in the angular bedrock chutes the creek into a triangular spill pool. Orange lichen accentuates the green mossy rocks that frame the area.

Maple Creek Falls #5: A log-jam with some large tree trunks blocks the view of this "sliding" waterfall from downstream.

Maple Creek Falls #6: Several cascades bring the creek down to a deep pool below the falls.

Maple Creek Falls #7: The creek tumbles over and around slabs of rock tilted up at awkward angles. A nice spill pool is located at the base of the falls.

Maple Creek Falls #8: The creek runs down solid bedrock through a 2 feet wide gouge.

Maple Creek Falls #9: A 1 foot wide slit in the rock forces the creek to slide down at an angle.

Directions: Follow CR-513 northerly toward Lake Superior. Turn left (west) onto Maple Creek Road (dirt). Follow it for 3.1 miles to the bridge that crosses over Maple Creek. Park on the right (north) just before the bridge. There is room for several vehicles here. Hike across the bridge. While crossing the bridge, look down to the left. Maple Creek Falls #1 can be seen falling into a deeper section of the gorge. After crossing the bridge there are faint footpaths that lead both ways along the river. I typically head upstream (left) first, travelling to the Manakiki Falls before backtracking, crossing the road and then following the creek to the north to see the numerous drops on the way to Lake Superior. (There are times when Maple Creek Road is gated. You can park at the gate and hike is. Just keep in mind that this will greatly increase the hiking distance.)

MANAKIKI FALLS (MAPLE CREEK)

Private

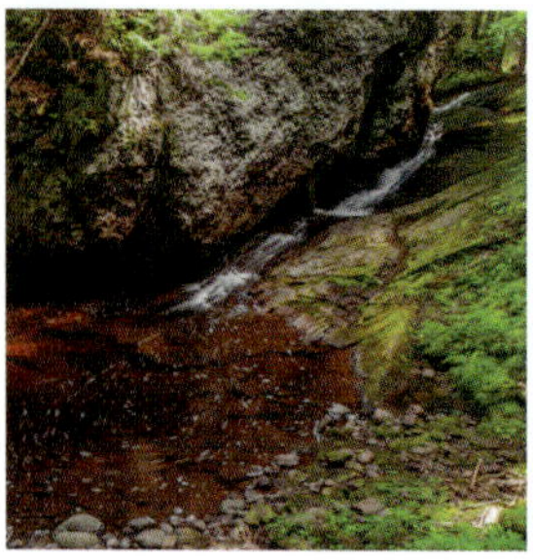

Must See: 7
Height: 25 feet
Time: 30-45 minutes

Driving Information

Signs:	None
Road:	Dirt
Access:	Easy
4WD:	N/A

GPS: N46 38.573 W90 06.805

Hiking Information

Path:	Slight Footpath
Length:	.3 miles
Elev. Change:	Moderate
GPS:	Helpful
Danger:	Moderate
WP Boots:	Required

From the vehicle, cross the bridge to the west. Don't be too concerned with following a path. There is just the faintest of footpaths along the creek. Follow the creek upstream (south) for about 1/3 mile. Climb down the steep ravine to the base of Manakiki Falls. The hillside is made up of moist, spongy, leaf covered soil with sticks and other obstacles to avoid. Manakiki Falls is a nicely sloped slide waterfall with solid rock for a backdrop. What a pleasant surprise to stumble onto this beautiful waterfall tucked away. The splash pool at the bottom of the falls quietly swirls as the water takes its rest from the rapid descent it has just made. Then, gravity takes over again, drawing the creek downward towards its next drop 1/4 mile later.

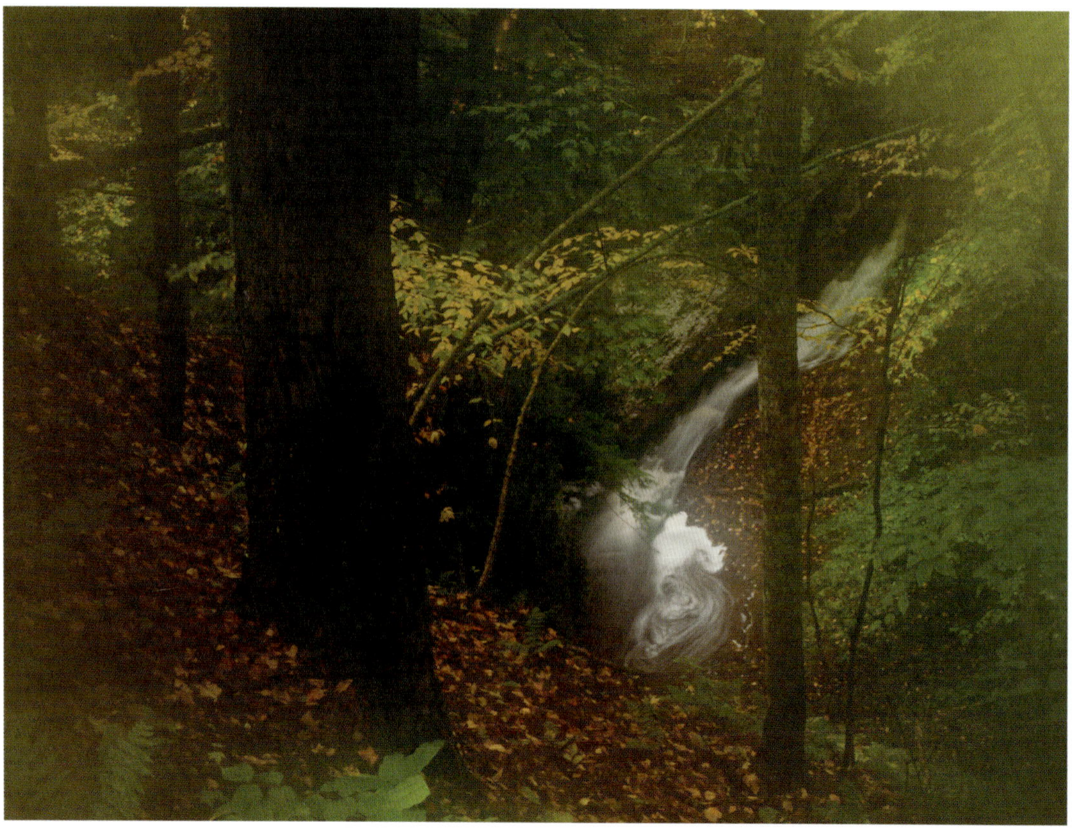

MANAKIKI FALLS - UPPER (MAPLE CREEK)

Private

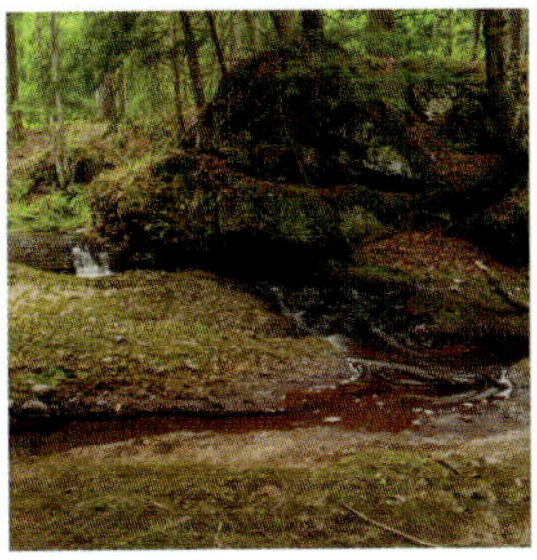

Must See:	4	GPS:	N46 38.567 W90 06.764
Height:	12 feet		
Time:	45-60 minutes	Hiking Information	
		Path:	Slight Footpath
Driving Information		Length:	.3 miles
Signs:	None	Elev. Change:	Moderate
Road:	Dirt	GPS:	Helpful
Access:	Easy	Danger:	Moderate
4WD:	N/A	WP Boots:	Required

Just before Maple Creek enters the gorge (at Manakiki Falls) several gentle drops end in small spill pools before gathering together to run down to the next one. Sunlight filters in through the thin canopy up here above the gorge. After climbing down the steep and often slippery sides to the base of Manakiki Falls the difference can be quite noticeable.

These drops are not nearly as impressive as the long slide just downstream, but they are in a bright and airy setting. It's a perfect picnic area with solid, dry, and clear space for sitting on the ground.

I have not explored further upstream from here, but would not at all be surprised to find more waterfalls in that direction.

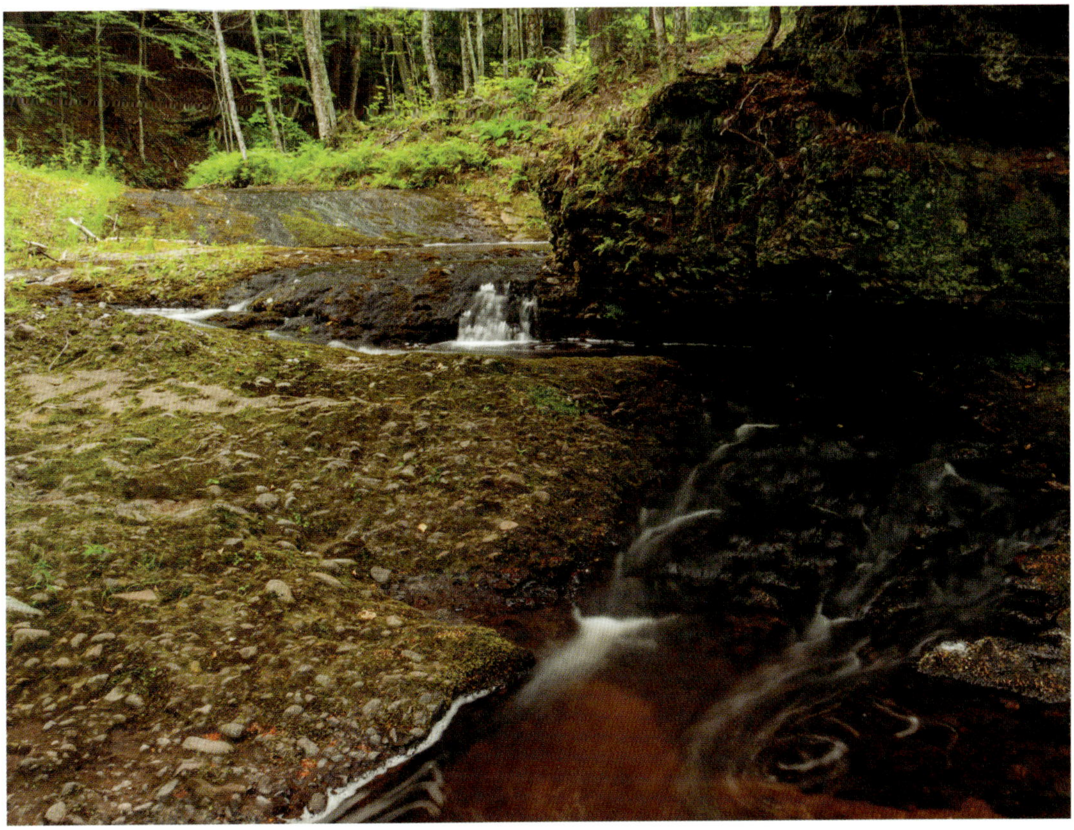

MAPLE CREEK FALLS #1 (MAPLE CREEK)

Private

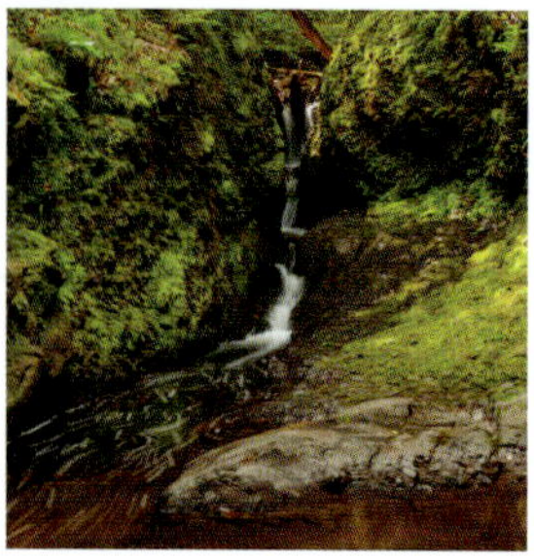

Must See:	7	GPS:	N46 38.689 W90 06.763
Height:	15 feet		
Time:	15-30 minutes	**Hiking Information**	
		Path:	Slight Footpath
Driving Information		Length:	50 yards
Signs:	None	Elev. Change:	Moderate
Road:	Dirt	GPS:	N/A
Access:	Easy	Danger:	Moderate
4WD:	N/A	WP Boots:	Required

This is the first waterfall heading north from the vehicle. Maple Creek Falls #1 can be seen while crossing the bridge. In fact, it is nearly under the bridge, slightly upstream! Take the faint footpath to the north and climb carefully down to the bottom of the gorge. The waterfall is not visible from here because of the rock formation that blocks the view of the falls. To get to the base of the falls, follow the creek back upstream and around a corner in the gorge. The creek takes up the entire width of the gorge, so the only way to follow it back upstream is to walk in the water. Wade through the approximately one foot deep creek to view the falls.

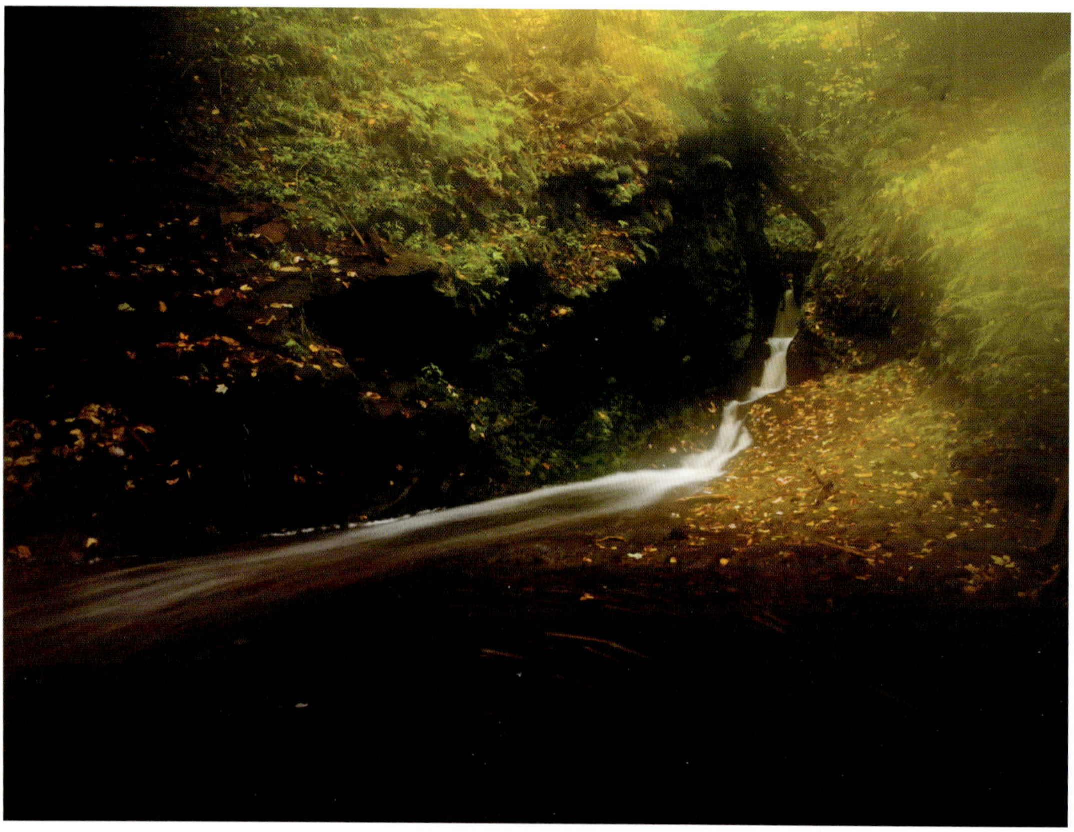

MAPLE CREEK FALLS #2 (MAPLE CREEK)

Private

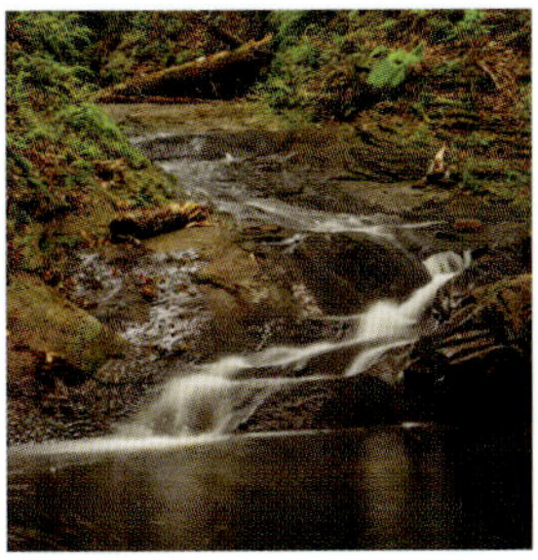

Must See:	5	GPS:	N46 38.769 W90 06.791
Height:	12 feet		
Time:	25-40 minutes	**Hiking Information**	
		Path:	Slight Footpath
Driving Information		Length:	.10 miles
Signs:	None	Elev. Change:	Moderate
Road:	Dirt	GPS:	Helpful
Access:	Easy	Danger:	Moderate
4WD:	N/A	WP Boots:	Required

The massive conglomerate has been eroded over time, leaving a small pool at the base of the slide. Climb to the top of the overlooking rock to view the waterfall from an entirely different vantage point. I love the "secret passage" that was created by the fallen trees propped up on the harder stone. It fairly screams, "Enter, if you dare!"

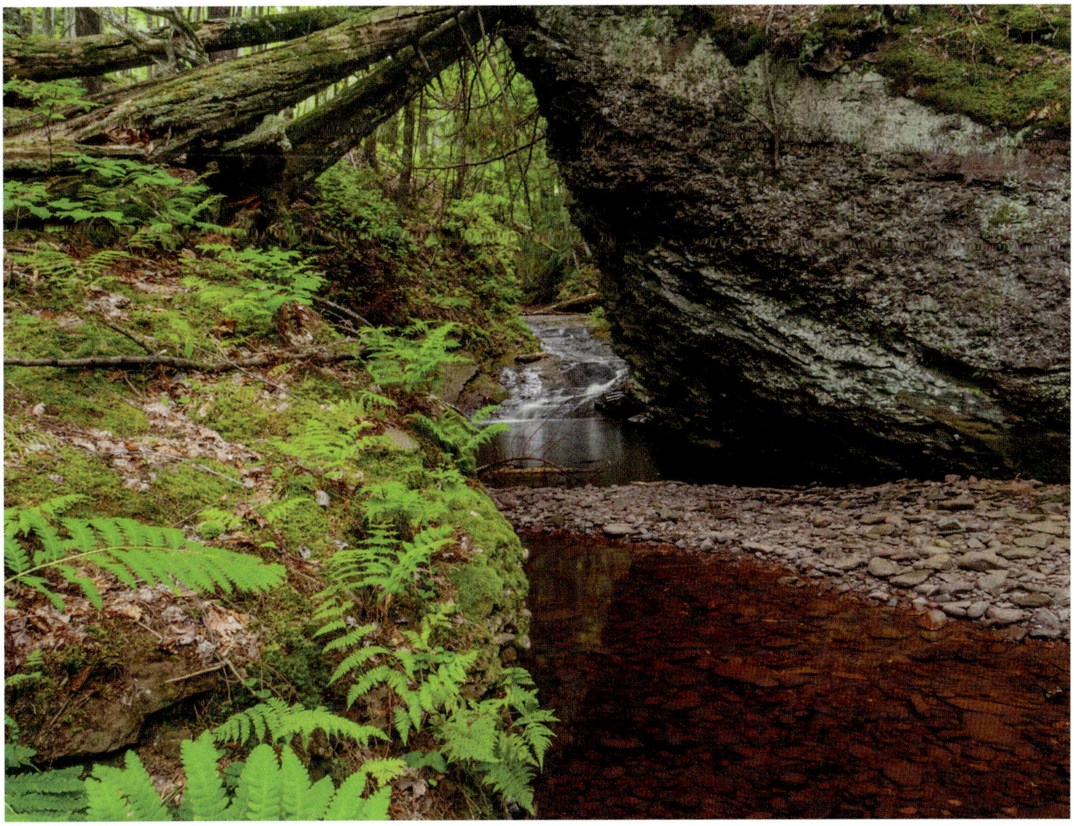

MAPLE CREEK FALLS #3 (MAPLE CREEK)

Private

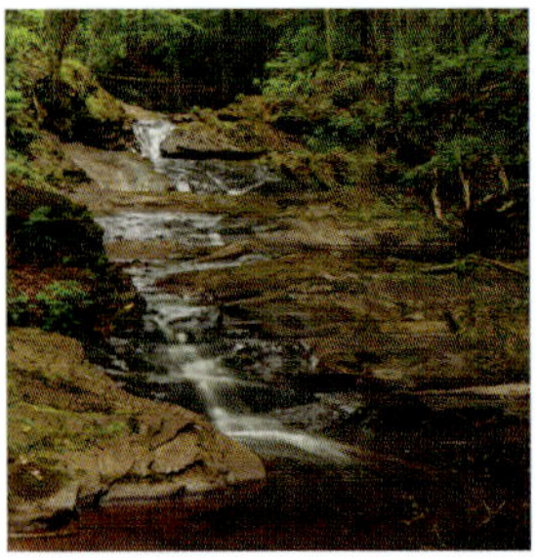

Must See:	5	GPS:	N46 38.814 W90 06.792
Height:	15 feet		
Time:	35-50 minutes	Hiking Information	
		Path:	Slight Footpath
Driving Information		Length:	.15 miles
Signs:	None	Elev. Change:	Moderate
Road:	Dirt	GPS:	Helpful
Access:	Easy	Danger:	Moderate
4WD:	N/A	WP Boots:	Required

The long, constantly dropping creek bed sits in a pastoral setting, nestled in forested rolling hills, with bedrock solid underfoot.

You may have noticed some of the "dreamy" looking pictures I am including along Maple Creek. On this particular hike in early October it was drizzling, very humid and warm. I couldn't keep my camera from fogging up. Although not my goal, it made for some interesting pictures!

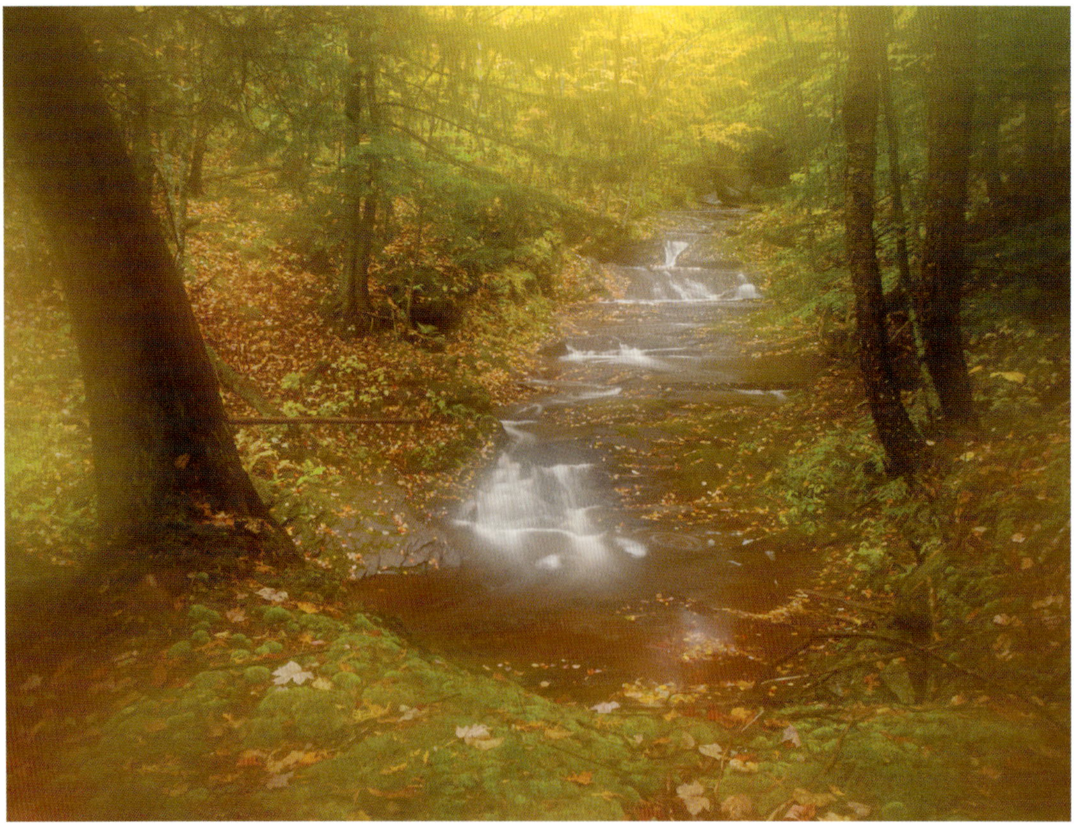

MAPLE CREEK FALLS #4 (MAPLE CREEK)

Private

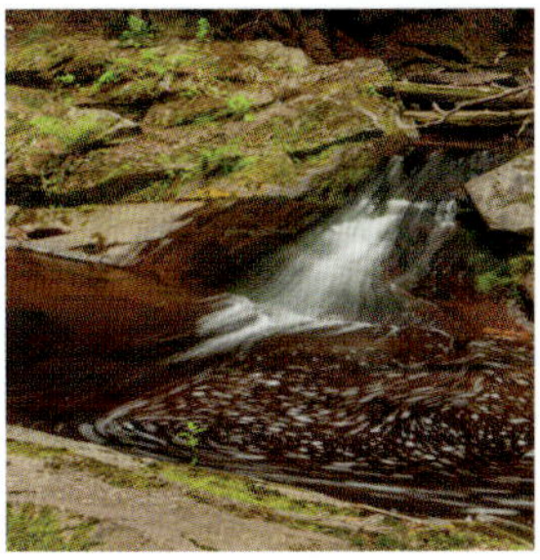

Must See:	6	GPS:	N46 38.837 W90 06.782
Height:	3 feet		
Time:	45-60 minutes	**Hiking Information**	
		Path:	Slight Footpath
Driving Information		Length:	.20 miles
Signs:	None	Elev. Change:	Moderate
Road:	Dirt	GPS:	Helpful
Access:	Easy	Danger:	Moderate
4WD:	N/A	WP Boots:	Required

This is only a 3 foot waterfall slide, but I was intrigued by the way that the creek broached the angled bedrock "dam", pouring through the resulting narrow chute.

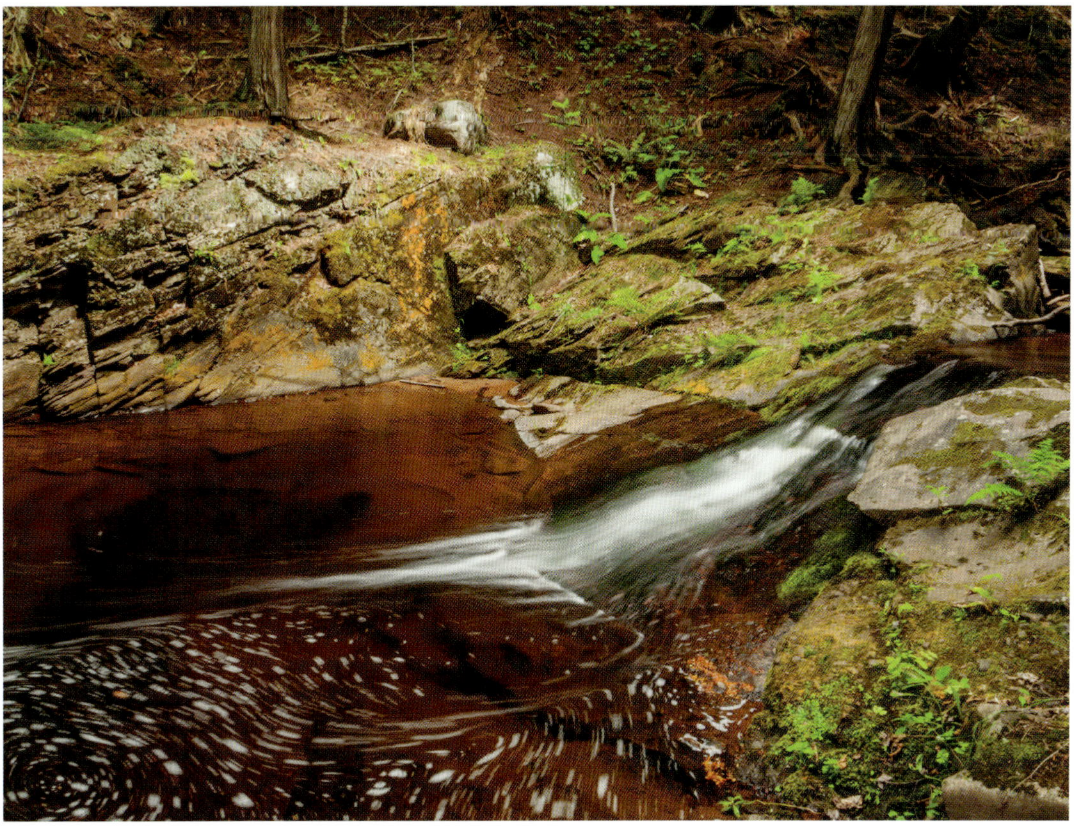

MAPLE CREEK FALLS #5 (MAPLE CREEK)

Private

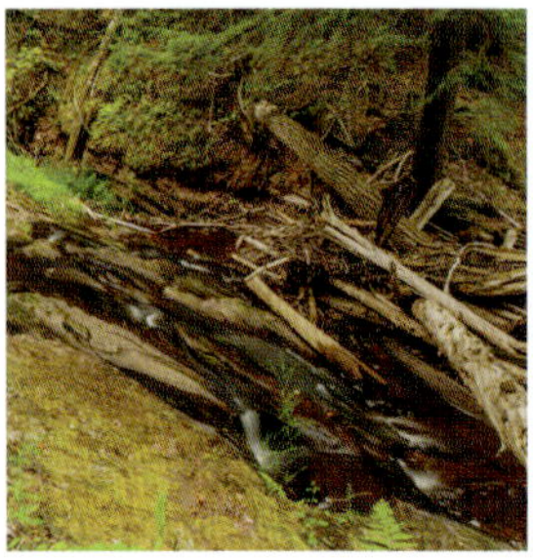

Must See:	5	GPS:	N46 38.873 W90 06.787
Height:	7 feet		
Time:	50-70 minutes	**Hiking Information**	
		Path:	Slight Footpath
Driving Information		Length:	.24 miles
Signs:	None	Elev. Change:	Moderate
Road:	Dirt	GPS:	Helpful
Access:	Easy	Danger:	Moderate
4WD:	N/A	WP Boots:	Required

Here we find another of the "vacuum cleaner" waterfalls. What a tangle of fallen trees! Maybe someday soon they will be cleared out, either naturally, or with some help. The waterfall will look much nicer then! This is a good time to remind us that waterfalls are constantly changing. Erosion, water levels, and yes, toppled trees change the look of waterfalls everywhere!

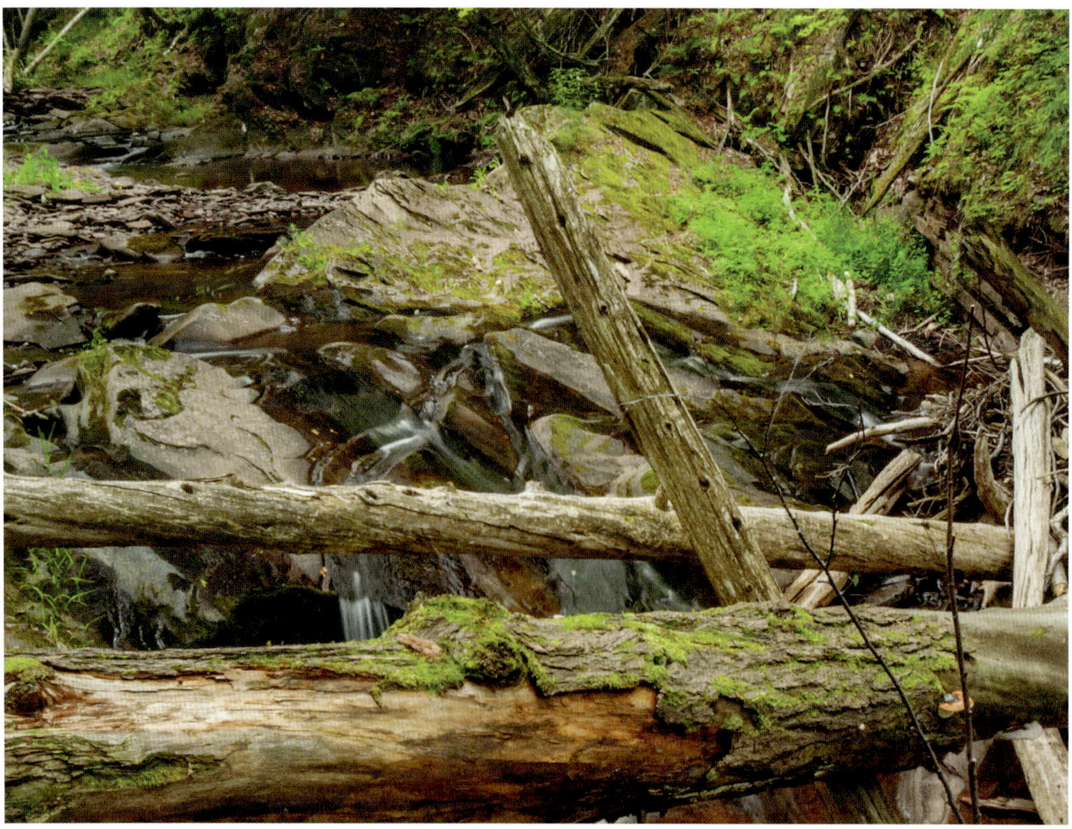

MAPLE CREEK FALLS #6 (MAPLE CREEK)

Private

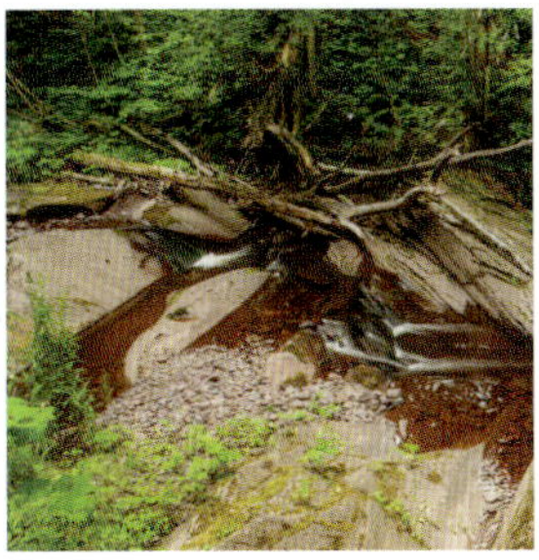

Must See:	4	GPS:	N46 38.924 W90 06.799
Height:	5 feet		
Time:	60-80 minutes	Hiking Information	
		Path:	Slight Footpath
Driving Information		Length:	.28 miles
Signs:	None	Elev. Change:	Moderate
Road:	Dirt	GPS:	Helpful
Access:	Easy	Danger:	Moderate
4WD:	N/A	WP Boots:	Required

Radically tilted layers of bedrock provide a dramatic landscape for the small creek through which to wind its way. This reminds me of the same tilted bedrock that is found in the Porcupine Mountains just to the north of here. The layers angle toward Lake Superior so that they provide a nature slide for the waterways. There is also a "hole" drilled in the rock as seen in the lower photo. This is just like the holes found on the Black River and Presque Isle River, both flowing nearby.

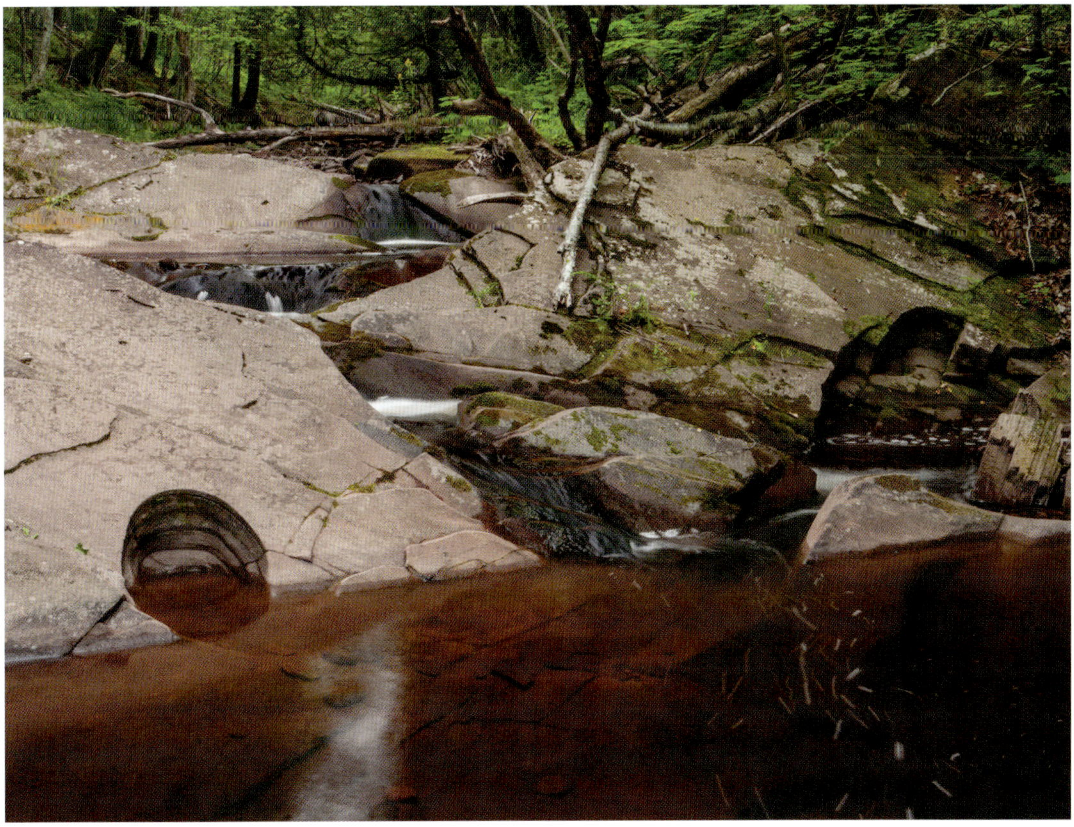

MAPLE CREEK FALLS #7 (MAPLE CREEK)

Private

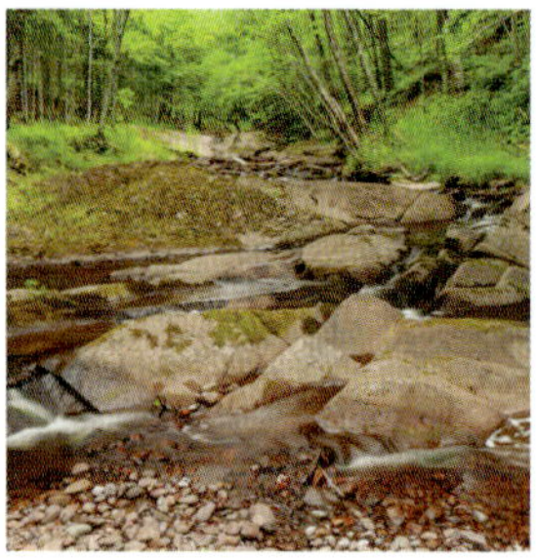

Must See:	4	GPS:	N46 38.937 W90 06.798
Height:	4 feet		
Time:	70-90 minutes	Hiking Information	
		Path:	Slight Footpath
Driving Information		Length:	.32 miles
Signs:	None	Elev. Change:	Moderate
Road:	Dirt	GPS:	Helpful
Access:	Easy	Danger:	Moderate
4WD:	N/A	WP Boots:	Required

Smooth formed rocks bend and twist the waterway. The creek finds a way over and around these blockades. What a serene setting.

The taller, more significant drops are further upstream, but one of the fun aspects of Maple Creek is being able to find a number of these small waterfalls, one right after the other as you head down toward Lake Superior.

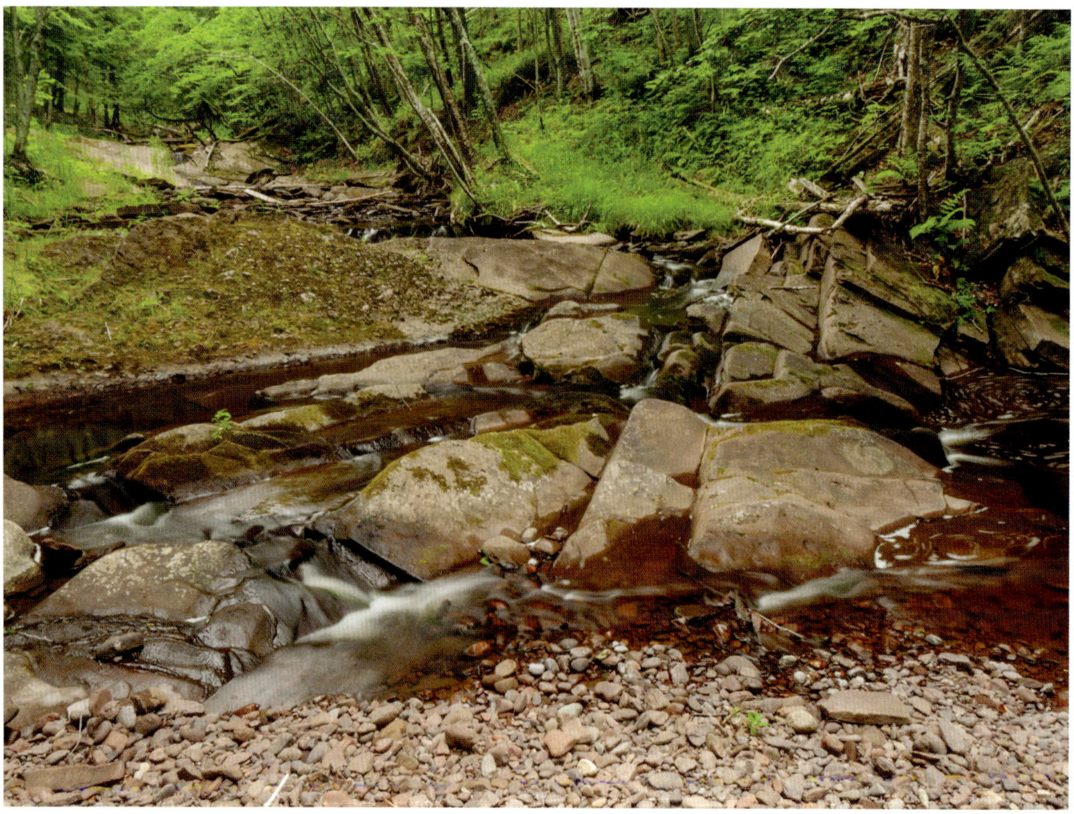

MAPLE CREEK FALLS #8 (MAPLE CREEK)

Private

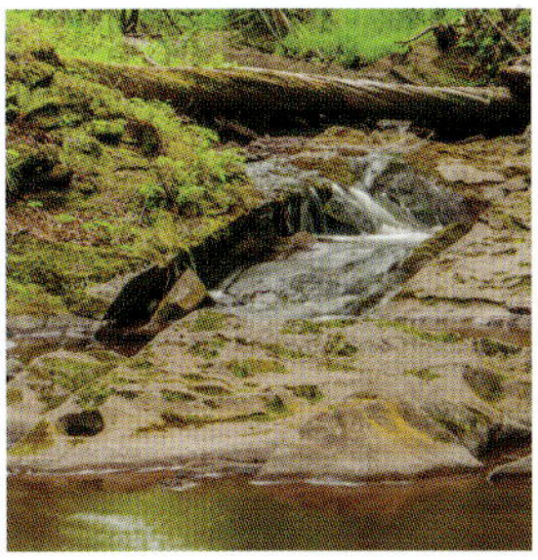

Must See: 4
Height: 3 feet
Time: 60-80 minutes

Driving Information
Signs: None
Road: Dirt
Access: Easy
4WD: N/A

GPS: N46 38.955 W90 06.812

Hiking Information
Path: Slight Footpath
Length: .34 miles
Elev. Change: Moderate
GPS: Helpful
Danger: Moderate
WP Boots: Required

The natural bedrock that is found all along this creek is a pleasure to be able to examine closely! The creek is small enough to be manageable, and yet there is enough water flow to make for interesting drops.

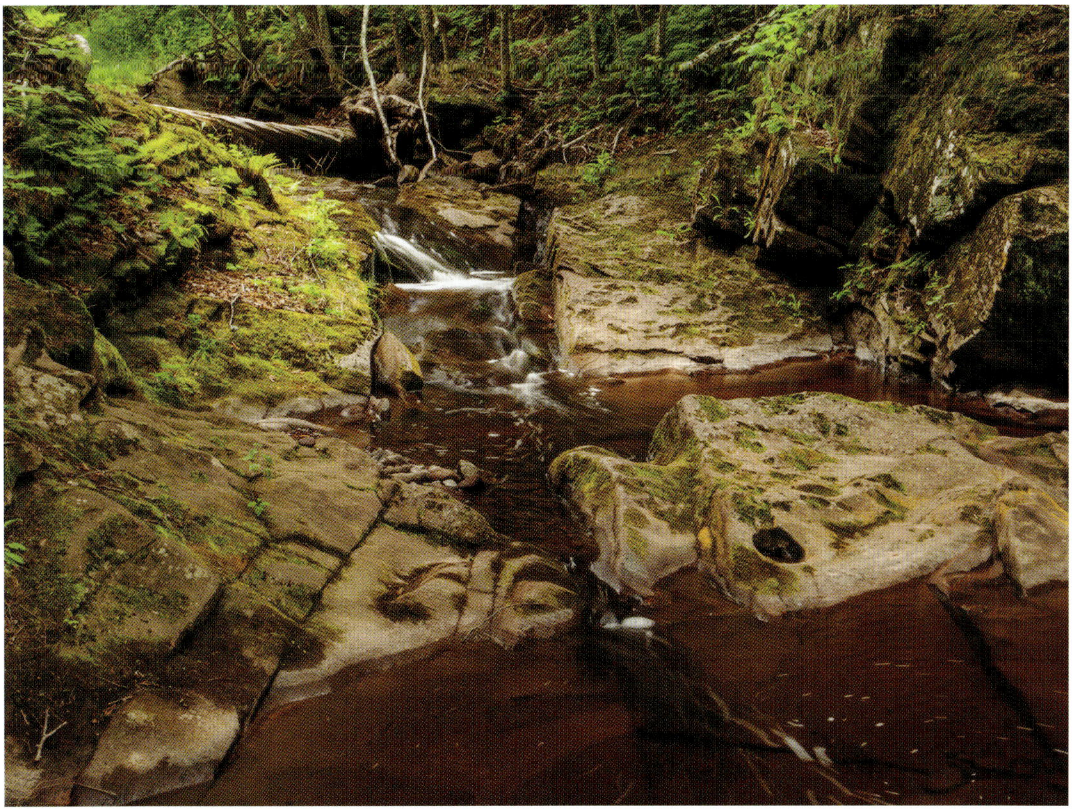

MAPLE CREEK FALLS #9 (MAPLE CREEK)

Private

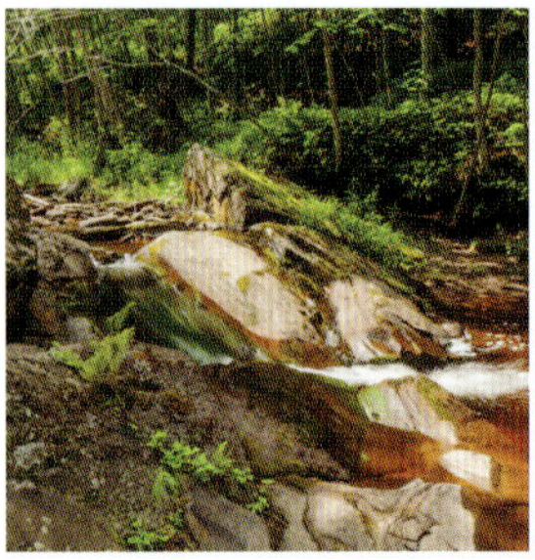

Must See:	4	GPS:	N46 38.971 W90 06.798
Height:	4 feet		
Time:	70-90 minutes	**Hiking Information**	
		Path:	Slight Footpath
Driving Information		Length:	.35 miles
Signs:	None	Elev. Change:	Moderate
Road:	Dirt	GPS:	Helpful
Access:	Easy	Danger:	Moderate
4WD:	N/A	WP Boots:	Required

Algae tinged water flows over a smooth face and between boulders to a wider portion of the creek. It is wonderful to have so many little drops to explore in such a short distance. This is only about 1/3 mile from the vehicle, and yet there are 9 drops to explore between here and there!

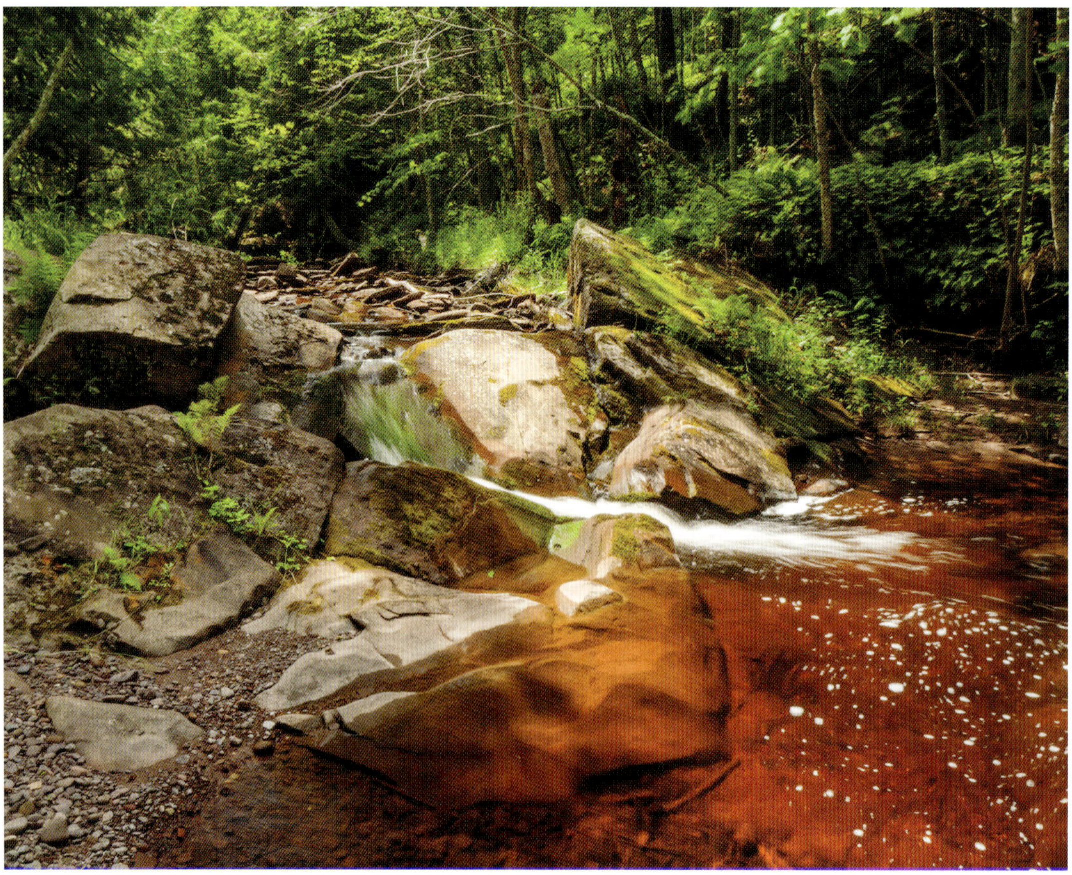

Potawatomi Falls Hike

The most visited waterfalls on the Black River are Potawatomi and Gorge Falls. They also happen to be the closest waterfalls to the parking lots. I wonder if this is coincidental? Nice paved driveways and parking areas greet visitors. A paved path runs next to pit toilets on its way to the wheelchair accessible viewing deck for Potawatomi Falls.

Potawatomi Falls: The falls are 1/8 mile from the parking lot. The main viewing area is barrier free. There are 58 wooden steps to the lower viewing platform. This waterfall feels a bit distant from the platforms, but the majesty of the falls, especially when it is running strong with spring runoff or fall rains, makes this a wonderful waterfall to view. The riverbed is very wide above the falls but is seldom covered edge to edge.

Gorge Falls: Like Potawatomi Falls, Gorge Falls is 1/8 mile from the left (north) end of the parking lot. There are 76 steps down to the main wooden viewing deck. The tiered waterfall is made up of three cascading drops and the viewing deck is at the perfect angle for appreciating all three cascades at once!

Directions: Heading north on CR-513 (toward Lake Superior) turn right (east) into the Gorge/ Potawatomi Falls driveway. The parking lots for these two waterfalls is connected by this common drive. The parking lot to the left is my favorite and is marked by an arrow directing you to Gorge Falls. Park at the far end (south) of the blacktopped parking lot to be centered between the two falls.

POTAWATOMI FALLS (BLACK RIVER)

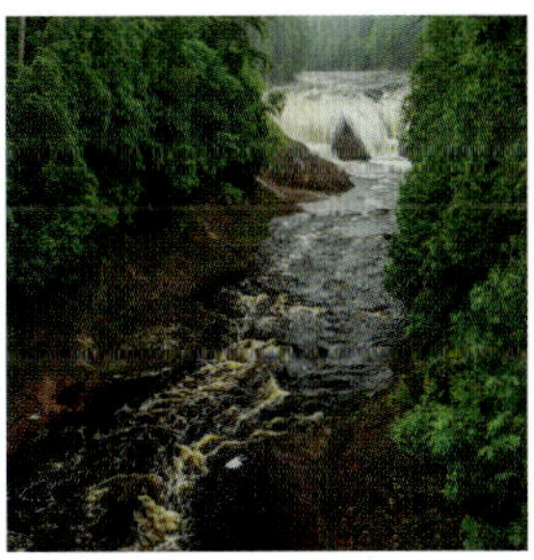

Must See:	8	GPS:	N46 38.297 W90 03.085
Height:	40 feet		
Time:	15-30 minutes	**Hiking Information**	
		Path:	Improved Path
Driving Information		Length:	1/8 mile
Signs:	Good Sign	Elev. Change:	Slight
Road:	Secondary	GPS:	N/A
Access:	Very Easy	Danger:	Slight
4WD:	N/A	WP Boots:	N/A

The Potawatomi were a tribe of Indians, cousins to the Ojibwe that lived in various portions of Michigan as well as Wisconsin. Potawatomi means "People of the place of the fire", referring to a fire kept burning perpetually, or perhaps to their place of honor in intertribal powwows. It is a privilege to have such a wonderful waterfall named after these proud inhabitants of our state.

This area of the U.P. ranks as one of my favorites! The waterfalls on the Black River hold a special place in my heart. Perhaps my winter hike into the five waterfalls in this stretch has something to do with it. The ruggedness of the land along the Black River has been tamed by improved trails and wooden boardwalks and viewing decks. But lest you think that this area is void of raw, natural beauty, a short drive over to Maple Creek will set you straight. This creek has the slightest of footpaths, and the multiple clambers down to the creek require agility and care.

The Potawatomi/Gorge Waterfall Scenic Area is perfect for family outings. Picnic tables and charcoal grills are strategically placed amongst old growth pines near the parking area. Well defined paths, with stairs when needed, lead to Potawatomi and Gorge Falls. Wooden guard rails line the cliff edges to provide protection. There is even a paved, wheelchair accessible path to the main overlook at Potawatomi Falls. A set of pit toilets is also located nearby.

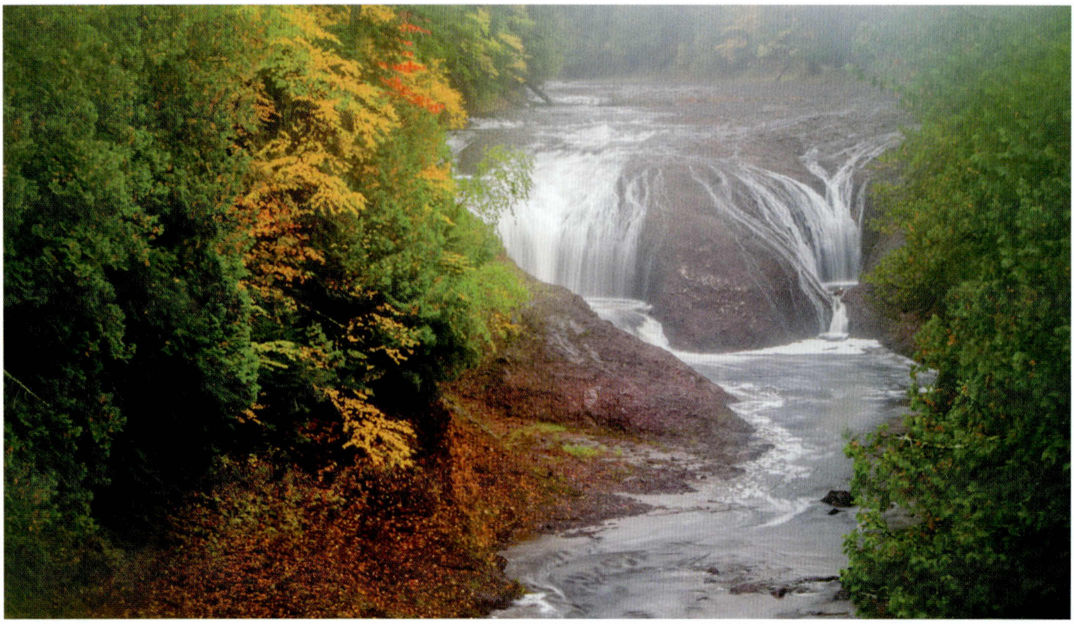

The beautifully maintained walkway to the falls

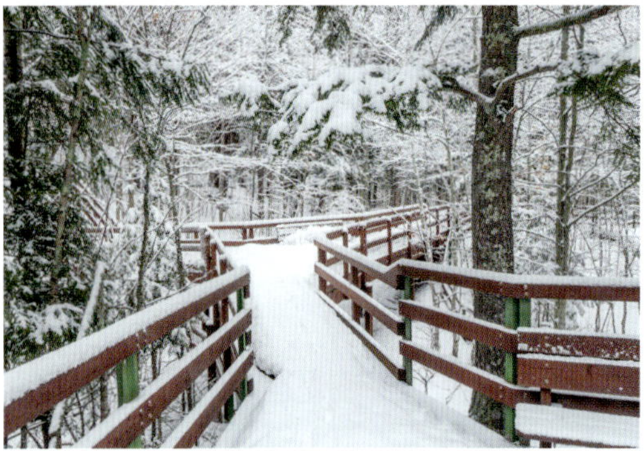

Several interpretive signs are set along the way

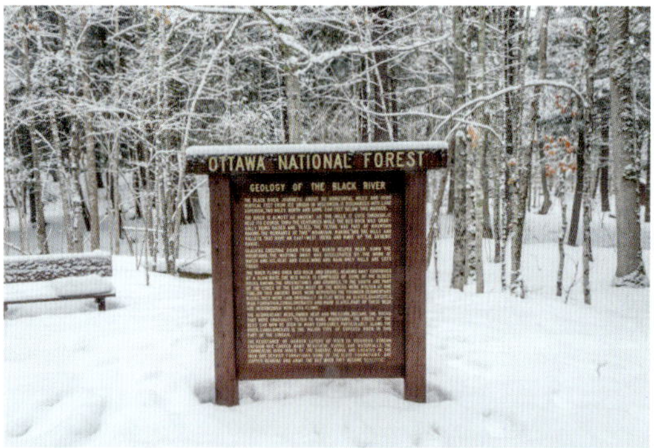

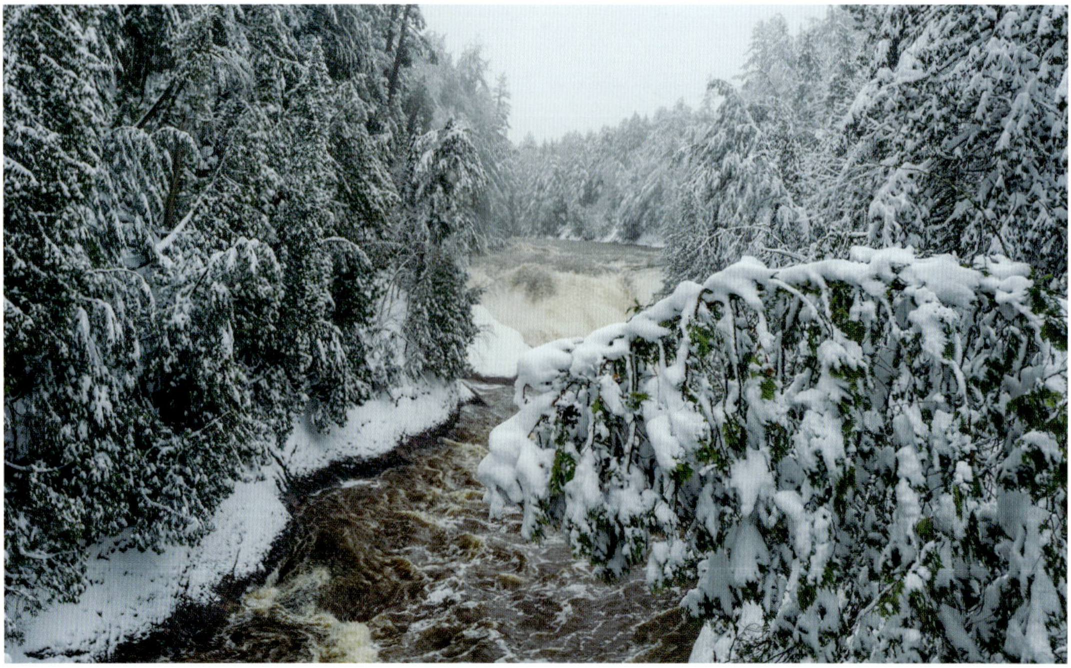

GORGE FALLS (BLACK RIVER)

Private

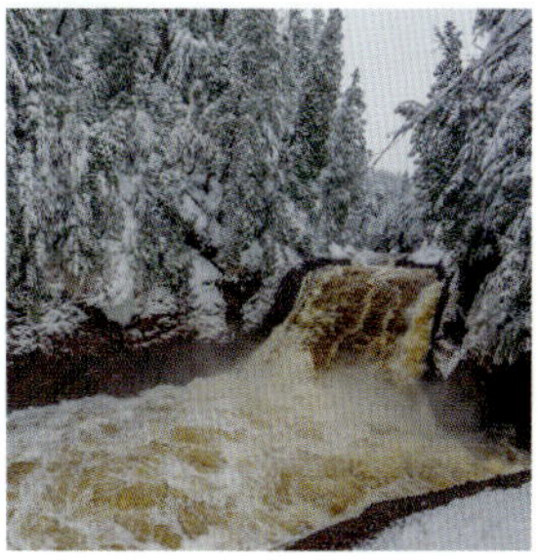

Must See:	8	GPS:	N46 38.423 W90 03.017
Height:	34 feet		
Type:	Series	Hiking Information	
		Path:	Improved Footpath
Driving Information		Length:	1/8 mile
Signs:	Good Sign	Elev. Change:	Moderate
Road:	Secondary	GPS:	N/A
Access:	Very Easy	Danger:	Slight
4WD:	N/A	WP Boots:	N/A

This is a nicely presented waterfall from the viewing deck that is furthest downstream. Don't be confused with the deck upstream that doesn't show the main drop.

The area between Potawatomi and Gorge Falls has been tastefully built up with wooden walkways, stairways, benches, vault toilets and the like. Continuing both up and downstream however, the North County Trail, here a primitive footpath, quietly beckons adventurers to follow it on its 4,600 mile long journey.

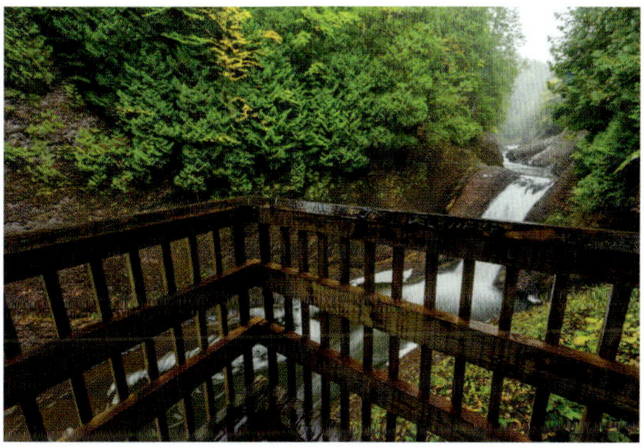

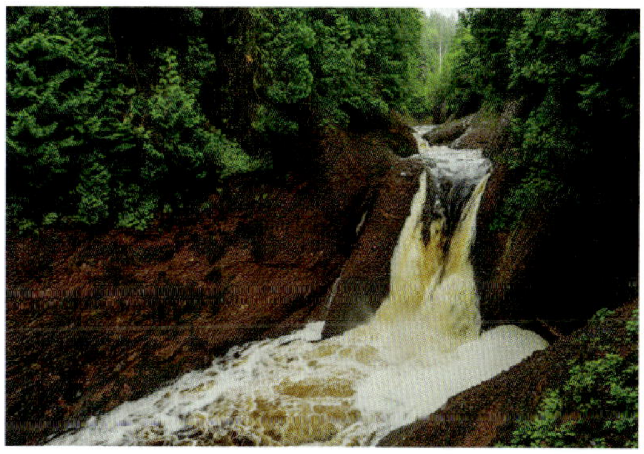

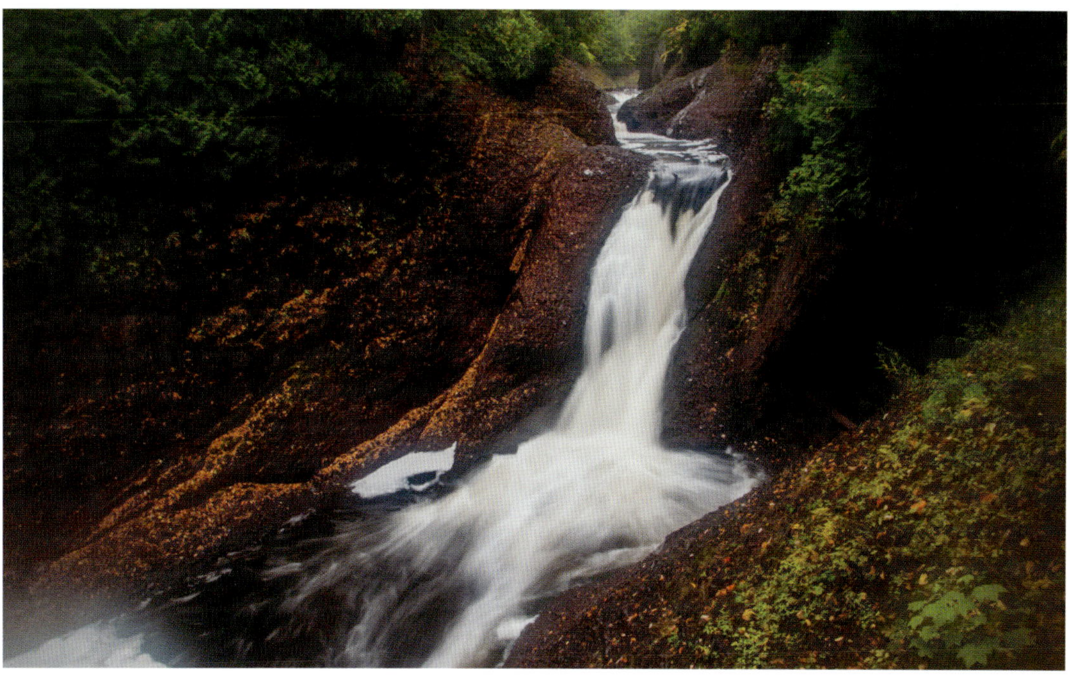

Rainbow Falls Hike

There are two ways to get to Rainbow Falls. The easiest, most common route is from the Rainbow Falls parking area. A footpath leads from there to a wooden overlook. The second option follows the North Country Trail, crossing the Black River near its mouth, and then following the river back upstream to the falls. This route is much longer, and there are no guard rails to protect from falling into the river gorge. I only recommend this route for highly experienced hikers during ideal conditions.

Rainbow Falls: Rainbow Falls plunges into a narrow gorge that quickly widens out as it heads down river. On sunny days, rainbows can sometimes be seen in the mist that rises from the base of the falls.

Directions:

(Standard) The most common and easiest hike to Rainbow Falls starts at the parking lot off of CR-513. Follow the well groomed trail. A sign at the trail head says that it is a 1/2 mile walk from the parking area (it's actually only .19 miles). At the end of the trail there are 159 steps down to the wooden viewing deck.

(Alternate) Viewing from the other side of the river is best. To get there, park in the Harbor Parking Lot where the Black River empties into Lake Superior. Walk across the suspension bridge that spans the river. Follow the North Country Trail back upstream from there. It about a 3/4 mile hike with some decent elevation changes and lots of steps!

RAINBOW FALLS (BLACK RIVER)

Private

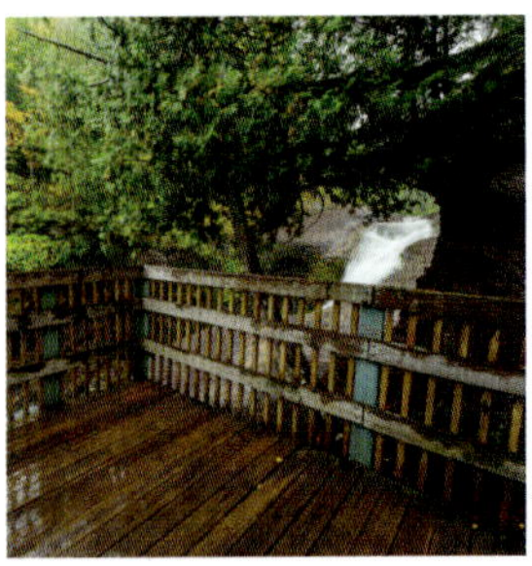

Must See:	8	GPS:	N46 39.540 W90 02.612
Height:	45 feet		
Time:	1/2 to 2 hours	**Hiking Information**	
		Path:	Improved Footpath
Driving Information		Length:	1/5 or 3/4 mile
Signs:	Good Sign	Elev. Change:	Moderate
Road:	Secondary	GPS:	N/A
Access:	Very Easy	Danger:	Slight to moderate
4WD:	N/A	WP Boots:	N/A

The view from the wooden platform located on the west side of the river offers a limited view of the waterfall. The river has cut a narrow groove back from the original precipitous edge. Now the river plunges down into the slit, with little of the drop left visible from this side.

A better view is had from the far side of the river, but getting close to the drop from the top side requires walking on a mass of rock that slants down toward the gorge and the swirling waters below. Use extreme caution if venturing over to the east side of the falls. It is possible to get down to the river's edge. I have seen trout fishermen working the river below the falls. I'm not sure if there is enough of a bank to walk along to view the falls from down there. It may be necessary to wade up the river to get to the base of the waterfall.

The waterfall splits into two separate drops when the river is higher and shrinks back to a single drop during low water conditions.

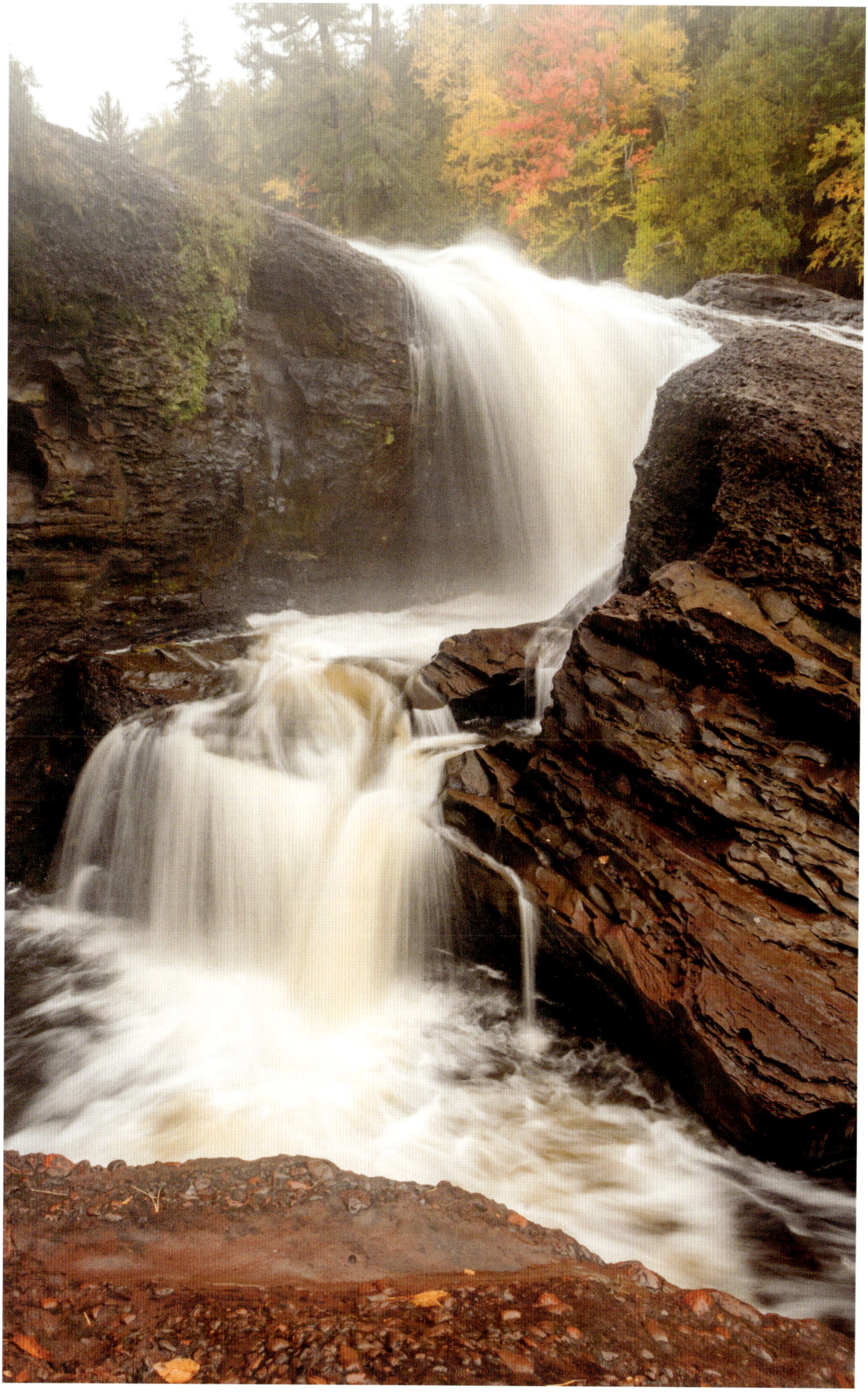

Rainbow Falls

Sandstone Falls Hike

Sandstone Falls: The waterfall is full of conglomerate stone. You can walk all around the falls for an up-close and intimate experience with this less frequently visited waterfall. Be careful of stepping in holes created by the swirling water. Some are quite deep, and all could cause a nasty fall or twisted ankle.

Directions: Between Potawatomi Falls and Rainbow Falls is a short drive marked "Sandstone Falls". Park at the trail head. There are 138 steps down to the river at the end of the 1/4 mile long, nicely maintained trail.

SANDSTONE FALLS (BLACK RIVER)

Private

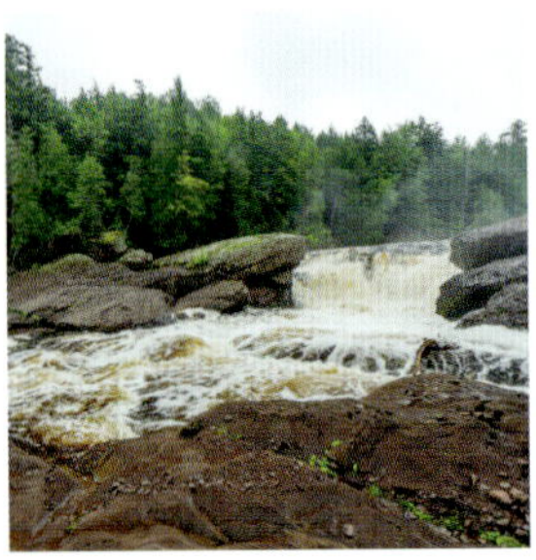

Must See:	7	GPS:	N46 39.012 W90 02.861
Height:	15 feet		
Time:	30-60 minutes	Hiking Information	
		Path:	Improved Path
Driving Information		Length:	1/4 mile
Signs:	Good Sign	Elev. Change:	Moderate
Road:	Secondary	GPS:	N/A
Access:	Very Easy	Danger:	Slight
4WD:	N/A	WP Boots:	N/A

Of all the popular Black River waterfalls, this is the only one that can be viewed from the riverbed. The trail ends at the river, with no overlook or guard rails. The shortest of the waterfalls, it cascades over a sandstone waterway, with interesting, heaved up bedrock layers bordering either side of the falls. The sandstone is quite pitted, and there are a number of circular impressions below the falls. Pebbles and stones swirling in eddies ground their way down through the somewhat softer material, creating these sometimes dry, sometimes water filled holes.

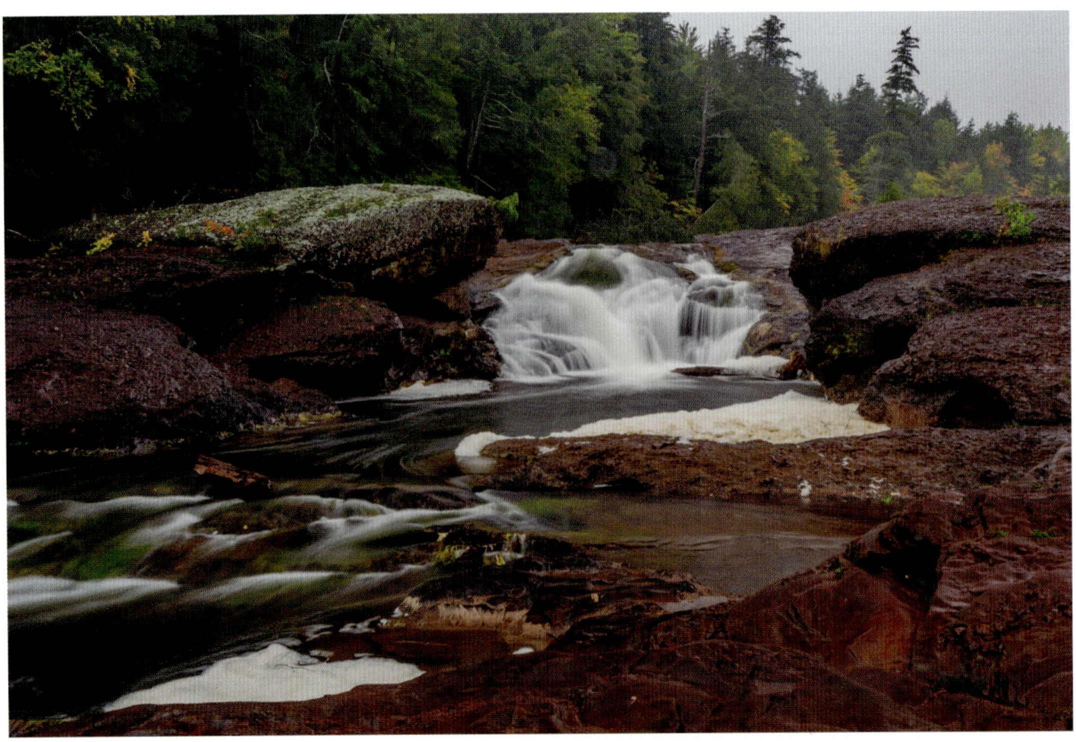

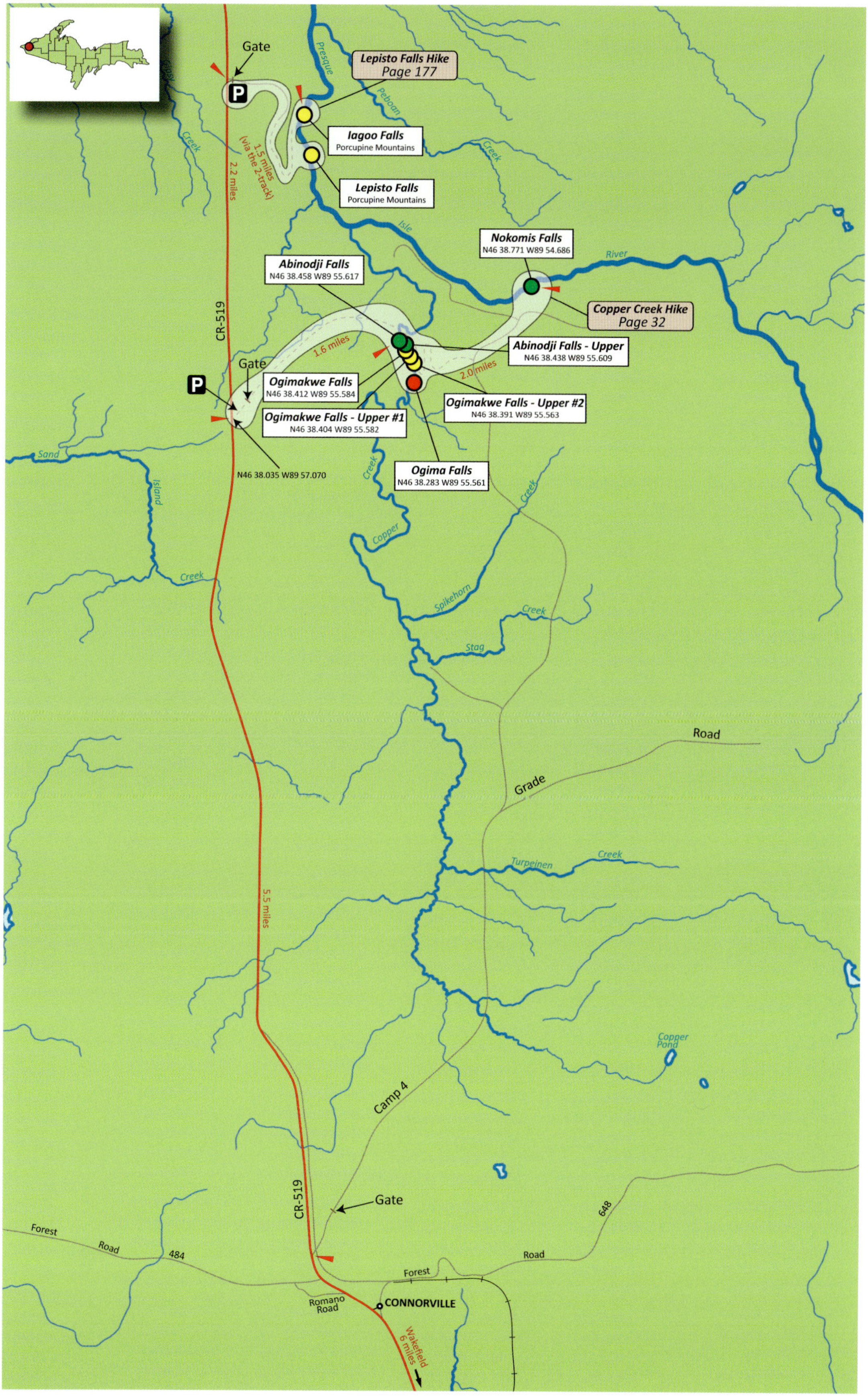
Gate
P
Lepisto Falls Hike
Page 177
Iagoo Falls
Porcupine Mountains
Lepisto Falls
Porcupine Mountains
1.5 miles
(via the 2-track)
2.2 miles
Presque
Peboan
Creek
Isle
River
Nokomis Falls
N46 38.771 W89 54.686
Copper Creek Hike
Page 32
Abinodji Falls
N46 38.458 W89 55.617
Abinodji Falls - Upper
N46 38.438 W89 55.609
CR-519
1.6 miles
2.0 miles
Gate
P
Ogimakwe Falls
N46 38.412 W89 55.584
Ogimakwe Falls - Upper #1
N46 38.404 W89 55.582
Ogimakwe Falls - Upper #2
N46 38.391 W89 55.563
Ogima Falls
N46 38.283 W89 55.561
N46 38.035 W89 57.070
Sand
Island
Creek
Copper
Creek
Spikehorn
Creek
Stag
Road
Grade
Turpeinen
Creek
5.5 miles
Copper Pond
Camp 4
CR-519
Gate
648
Forest
Road
484
Forest
Road
Romano Road
CONNORVILLE
Wakefield
6 miles

Copper Creek Hike

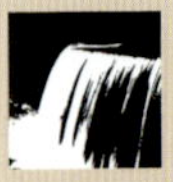

The waterfall names along Copper Creek are all derived from Ojibwa Indian terms. This is the progression of names, starting upstream: *Ogima* "Chief", *Ogimakwe* "Woman Chief", and *Abinodji* "Child".

Abinodji Falls: The first of the waterfalls can be seen near the end of the ATV trail. It is a 4 foot drop with stair-stepping cascades ending in a deep spill pool.

Abinodji Falls - Upper: Just 100 feet upstream from Ogimakwe Falls is a series of 3 to 4 inch high cascades. A moss covered viewing area is tastefully situated below the falls.

Ogimakwe Falls: Another 100 feet upstream this small waterfall can be seen. The river narrows down to 6 feet wide near an 8 foot high sheer rock face.

Ogimakwe Falls - Upper #1: Continuing the trend, follow the creek upstream another 100 feet. Jagged rocks stick out of this cascading waterfall that lacks much definition.

Ogimakwe Falls - Upper #2: This multi-tiered cascading waterfall is stretched out over a 30 foot length of the creek. Moss and wildflowers grow on some of the taller rocky sections that rise up above the flowing water.

Ogima Falls: This is the closest waterfall that I found from where Ogima Falls was "supposed to be" further upstream. Upstream from the falls for over .4 miles the creek runs slowly with dense undergrowth on either side. As the creek nears Ogima Falls it makes a sharp bend and begins it descent. Numerous small drops mixed in with waterfalls continue for a long stretch downstream. Here, the creek drops over a slanted rock that spans the creek.

Nokomis Falls: We leave Copper Creek and head over to the Presque Isle River for this waterfall. The river drops in a series of mega-rapids to form Nokomis Falls. No single cascade is higher than 5 feet, but as that is the last main drop, it leaves a lasting impression with the viewer. The waterway is split by islands of stone repeatedly throughout this stretch of river. A concluding island, just below the last drop has an assortment of greenery growing on it, almost looking like a cultivated rock garden! The river runs through a 60' deep gorge. Use extreme caution attempting to get to the river's edge.

Directions: From County Road 519, turn east onto dirt road at N46 38.035 W89 57.070. Drive a short distance to the gate. Park to the left of the gate and out of the way. Walk around the gate and toward the Copper Creek waterfalls. Stay left at the 1st road. Turn right at the next 2-track. The hike is about 1.6 miles to Abinodji Falls. The trail follows Copper Creek for a short way, ending near the Abinodji Falls. Continue along the river bank to the rest of the falls. After viewing the Copper Creek Falls follow the creek back north. ***(The rest of these directions are for those that want to add the Nokomis Falls spur to the hike)*** After starting back toward the parking spot heading away from Copper Creek, a side 2-track heads to the right, back toward Copper Creek, north of the Copper Creek waterfalls. Follow the 2-track to the creek. Ford the creek. The 2-track continues on the far side. Continue to follow the 2-track. It rises quickly out of the Copper Creek Gorge with a good sized set of switchbacks. Continue to a "main" dirt road. Follow it to the left. This will eventually approach the Presque Isle River. Another good dirt road parallels the river along the top of the gorge. Turn to the right. There is no trail down to the waterfall from here. Head down toward the river, picking as smooth a route through the trees as possible. The grade starts dropping after leaving the road, but it becomes extremely steep just before the river. This is a very dangerous descent. I climbed down just below the falls. This is a very desolate location. Use extreme caution.

ABINODJI FALLS (COPPER CREEK)

Private

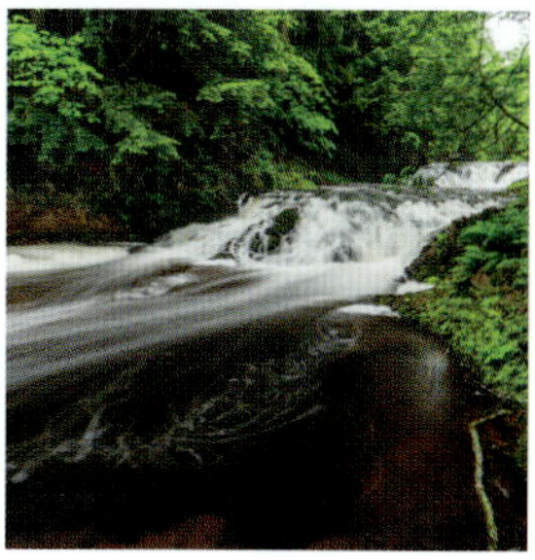

Must See:	7	GPS:	N46 38.458 W89 55.617
Height:	4 feet		
Time:	1 1/2 to 2 hours	**Hiking Information**	
		Path:	2-track most of the way
Driving Information		Length:	1.8 miles
Signs:	None	Elev. Change:	Moderate
Road:	Secondary	GPS:	Required
Access:	Somewhat Difficult	Danger:	Moderate
4WD:	Helpful	WP Boots:	Recommended

The mounded center of the waterfall separates the creek during all but the highest water levels. Notice the difference in these two shots. The top one was taken in June and the lower one in September. *Note: The upper falls can be seen in the background.*

While hiking along Copper Creek you may feel like you've stepped back in time to the days when there was little human influence, and nothing but rocks, trees, water, shrubbery and wild animals were to be found throughout much of Michigan.

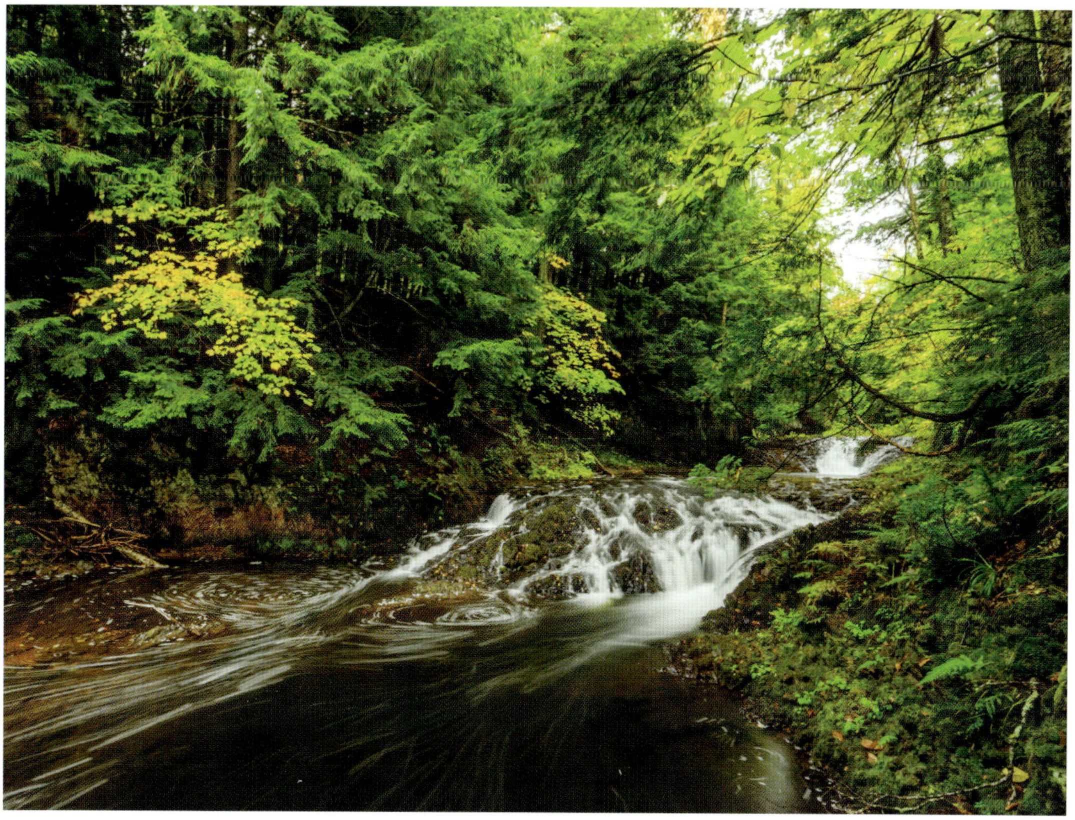

ABINODJI FALLS - UPPER (COPPER CREEK)

Private

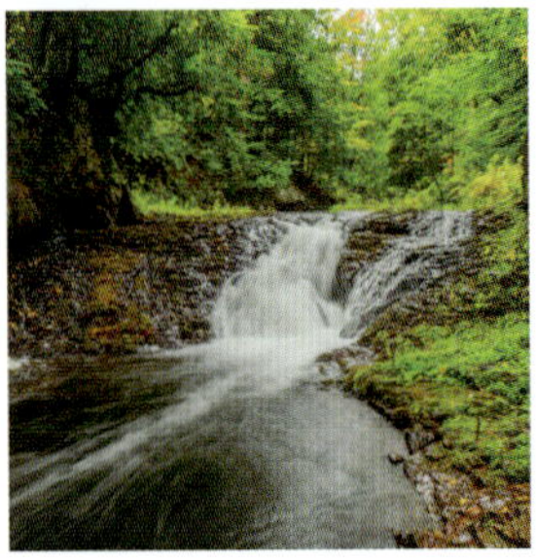

Must See:	7	GPS:	N46 38.438 W89 55.609
Height:	5 feet		
Time:	1 1/2 to 2 hours	Hiking Information	
		Path:	2-track most of the way
Driving Information		Length:	1.9 miles
Signs:	None	Elev. Change:	Moderate
Road:	Secondary	GPS:	Required
Access:	Somewhat Difficult	Danger:	Moderate
4WD:	Helpful	WP Boots:	Recommended

A sheer rock wall rises on the far side of the creek. During high water, the creek runs right up to the edge. The "ripply" effect seen here is caused by numerous thin layers of bedrock broken off in a staggered "stair-step" pattern.

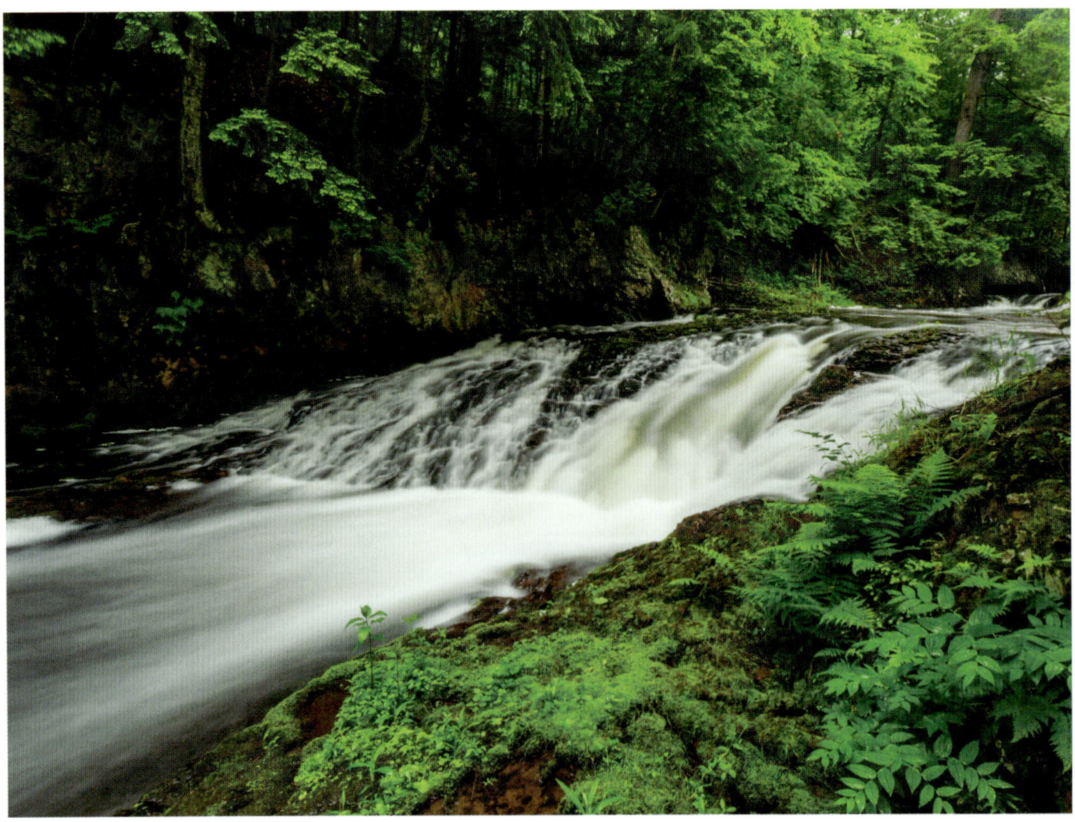

OGIMAKWE FALLS (COPPER CREEK)

Private

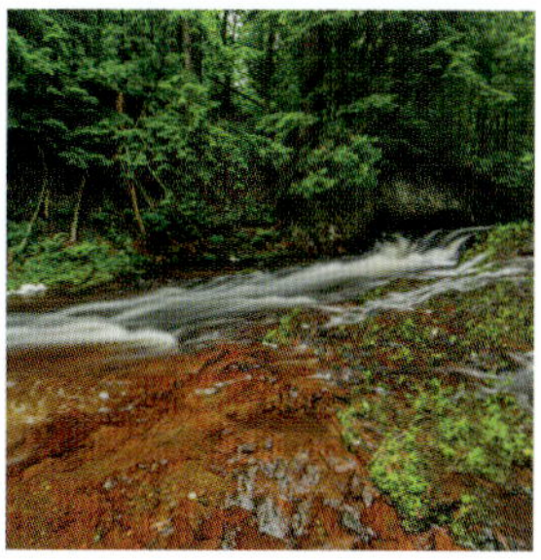

Must See:	6	GPS:	N46 38.412 W89 55.584
Height:	2 feet		
Time:	1 3/4 to 2 1/4 hours	Hiking Information	
		Path:	2-track then none
Driving Information		Length:	1.9 miles
Signs:	None	Elev. Change:	Moderate
Road:	Secondary	GPS:	Required
Access:	Somewhat Difficult	Danger:	Moderate
4WD:	Helpful	WP Boots:	Recommended

Upper #1 can be seen in the distance as the creek makes a bend. This scenery along Copper Creek is rugged, gorgeous, and remote. So many of the falls along here sport cliffs on the opposite side of the creek.

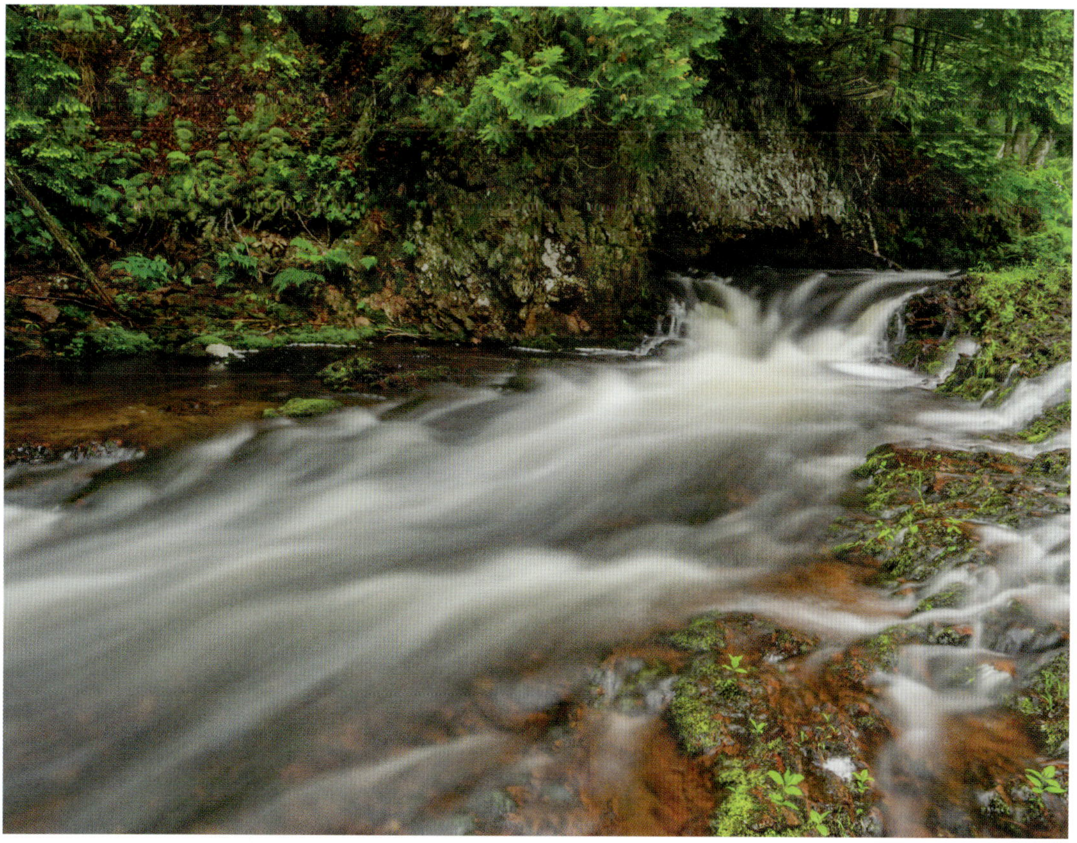

OGIMAKWE FALLS - UPPER #1 (COPPER CREEK)

Private

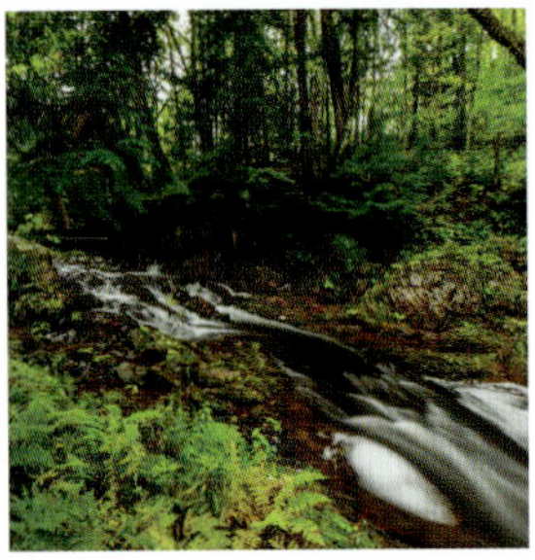

Must See: 5
Height: 4 feet
Time: 2 to 2 1/2 hours

Driving Information
Signs: None
Road: Secondary
Access: Somewhat Difficult
4WD: Helpful

GPS: N46 38.404 W89 55.582

Hiking Information
Path: 2-track then none
Length: 1.9 miles
Elev. Change: Moderate
GPS: Required
Danger: Moderate
WP Boots: Recommended

Upper #1 is found about 100 yards upstream from Upper #2. This waterfall has a less well defined cascade but it does have a nice viewing area on the near side of the creek. Jagged black rocks protrude out of the waterfall during normal water levels.

A fascinating natural occurrence found periodically at waterfalls are these "foam donuts" seen in the picture below. Foam from the waterfall sometimes gets caught in an eddy and if the foam has the proper consistency it can grown into these perfectly formed rings.

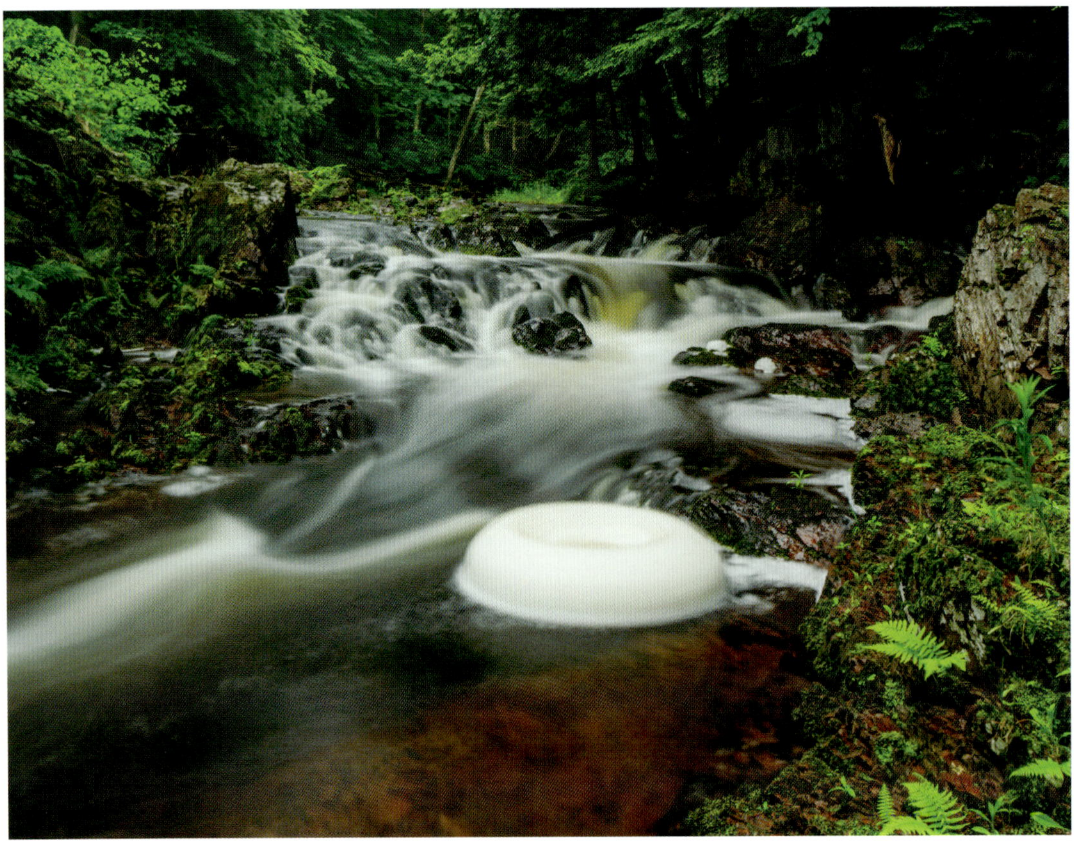

OGIMAKWE FALLS - UPPER #2 (COPPER CREEK)

Private

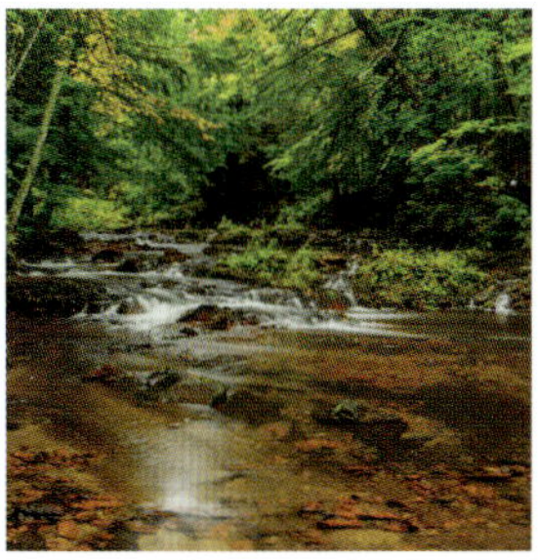

Must See:	4	GPS:	N46 38.391 W89 55.563
Height:	4 feet		
Time:	2 1/4 to 2 3/4 hours	Hiking Information	
		Path:	2-track then none
Driving Information		Length:	2.0 miles
Signs:	None	Elev. Change:	Moderate
Road:	Secondary	GPS:	Required
Access:	Somewhat Difficult	Danger:	Moderate
4WD:	Helpful	WP Boots:	Recommended

Copper Creek widens out over a course of rapids. Some of the taller rocky portions even have grasses and wild flowers growing on them, suggesting that they remain above even the highest water levels. Conifers and deciduous trees grow together in this old forest providing year round color.

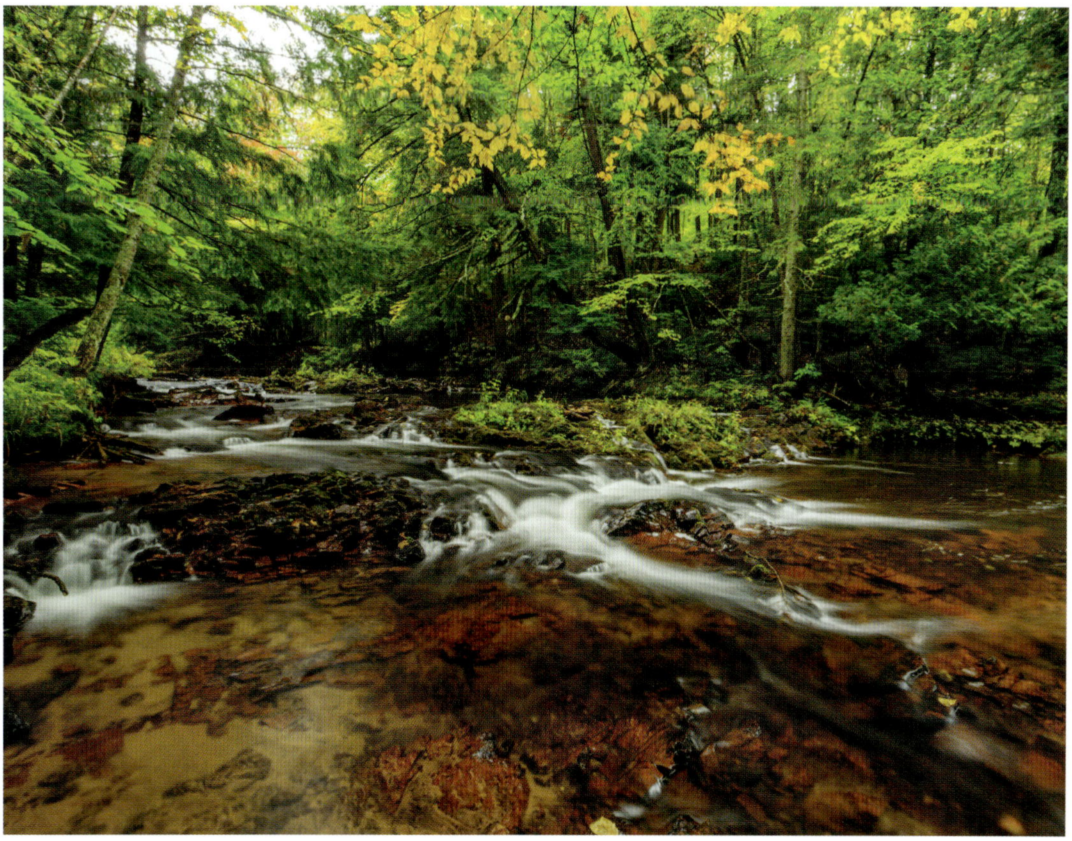

OGIMA FALLS (COPPER CREEK)

Private

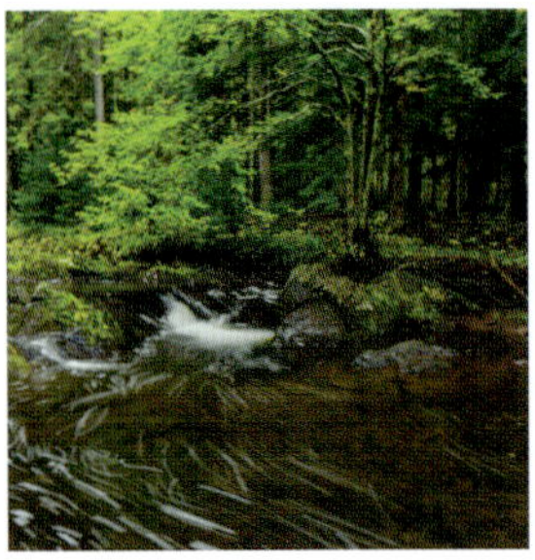

Must See:	3	GPS:	N46 38.283 W89 55.561
Height:	2 feet		
Time:	2 3/4 to 3 1/4 hours	Hiking Information	
		Path:	2-track then none
Driving Information		Length:	2.2 miles
Signs:	None	Elev. Change:	Moderate
Road:	Secondary	GPS:	Required
Access:	Somewhat Difficult	Danger:	Moderate
4WD:	Helpful	WP Boots:	Recommended

According to my information Ogima Falls should be quite a ways further south from here. But after a grueling hike along Copper Creek from nearly 1/2 mile upstream, this is the first drop that I found. Thick undergrowth, fallen trees, steep hillsides and wet lowlands make following the creek much further upstream difficult.

"Ogima", the Ojibwa name for "Chief", hardly seems right for this minor waterfall and makes me wonder if there has been some sort of mix-up in the naming sequence of the falls on the creek over the course of time.

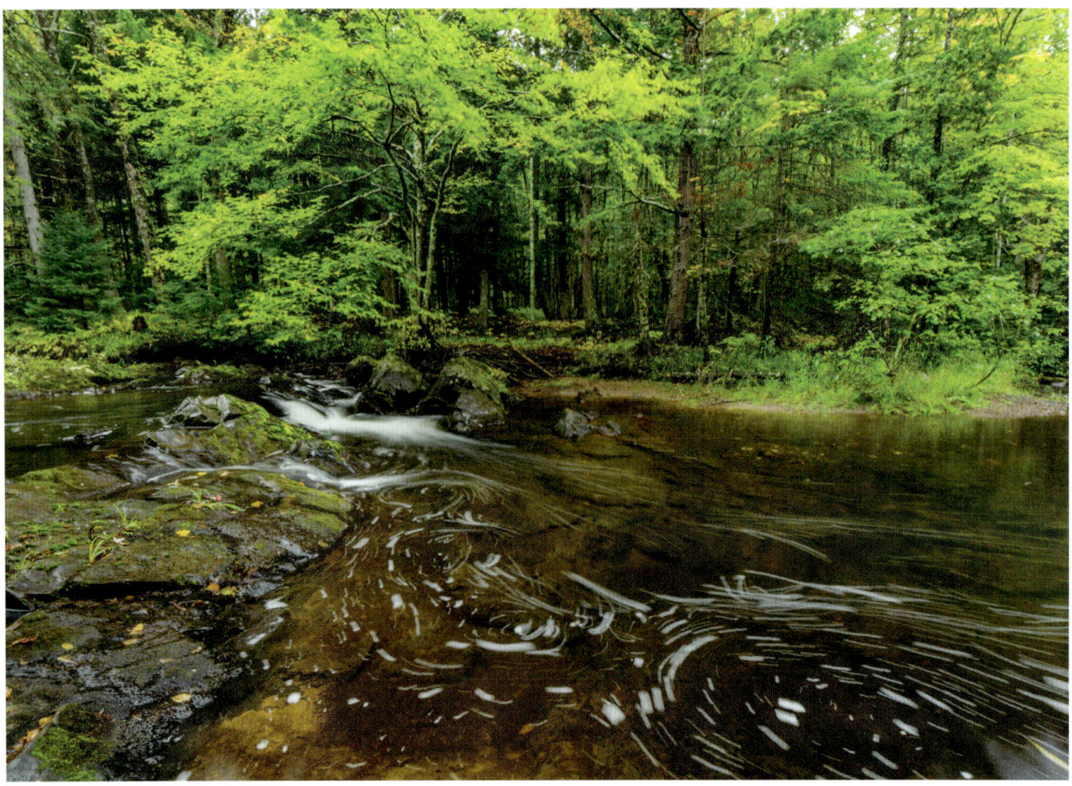

NOKOMIS FALLS (PRESQUE ISLE RIVER)

Private

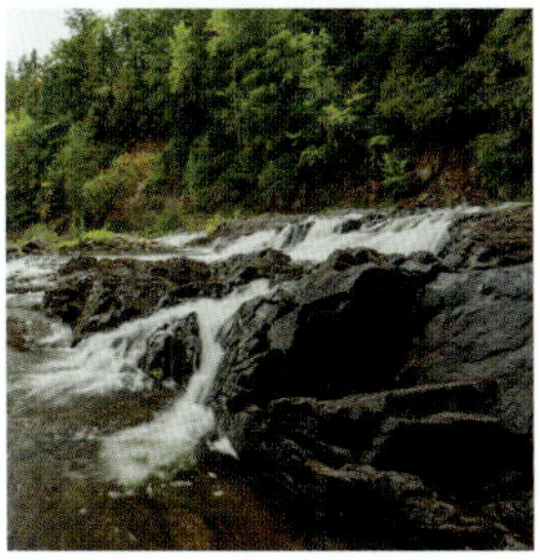

Must See:	7	GPS:	N46 38.771 W89 54.686
Height:	15 feet		
Time:	2 to 3 hours added	**Hiking Information**	
		Path:	2-track then none
Driving Information		Length:	2.0 mile spur additional
Signs:	None	Elev. Change:	High & Steep
Road:	Secondary	GPS:	Required
Access:	Somewhat Difficult	Danger:	Extreme
4WD:	Helpful	WP Boots:	Recommended

The ***Time*** and ***Length*** information provided above are in addition to the hike to and from Copper Creek. There is a decent length switchback that rises out of the Copper Creek Gorge between Copper Creek and Presque Isle River. Cutting cross country can shorten the length of the hike, but it is more strenuous. At the end of the hike, the descent into the Presque Isle River Gorge can be VERY DANGEROUS. It is helpful to scout along the top edge of the cliff to find the best place to climb down.

It was very fulfilling to finally see Nokomis Falls. I had tried every 2-track that seemed promising from South Boundary Road, but they were all gated. I couldn't find any trails from the east either. I finally discovered a route from the west. Even so, it wasn't easy. After many miles of hiking, with a difficult start bushwacking through rugged terrain along Copper Creek, I finally made it to the top of the gorge high above Nokomis Falls. I really wondered if there was a safe way down. A long, steep descent ended about 6 feet above the river bank. I had to jump that final distance since it was basically straight down. I figured that I would be able to find a better way back up after I was done taking pictures. Fortunately, I did! Of course, it's always easier to climb up than to climb down. If you have the privilege to hike in to Nokomis Falls, respect the area. It is rugged and untamed. Of course, that is a great part of the allure. It's like a step back in time to a more primitive day, with the terrain most likely looking very much the same as it has for millennia!

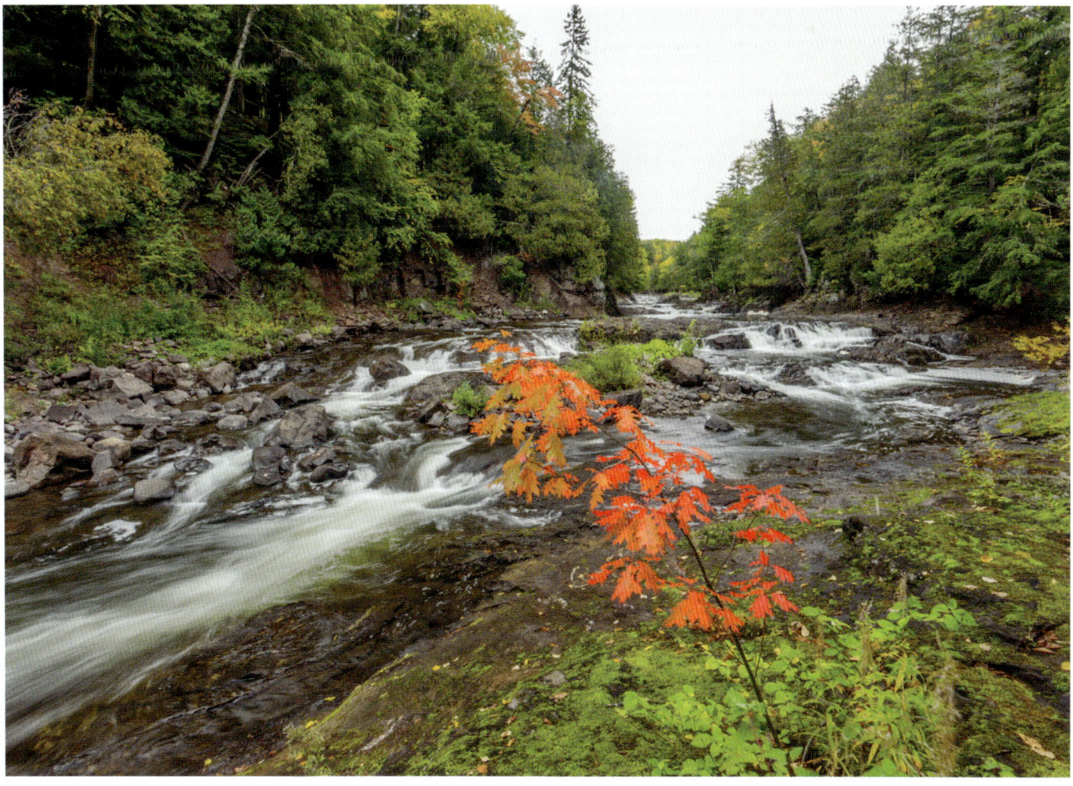

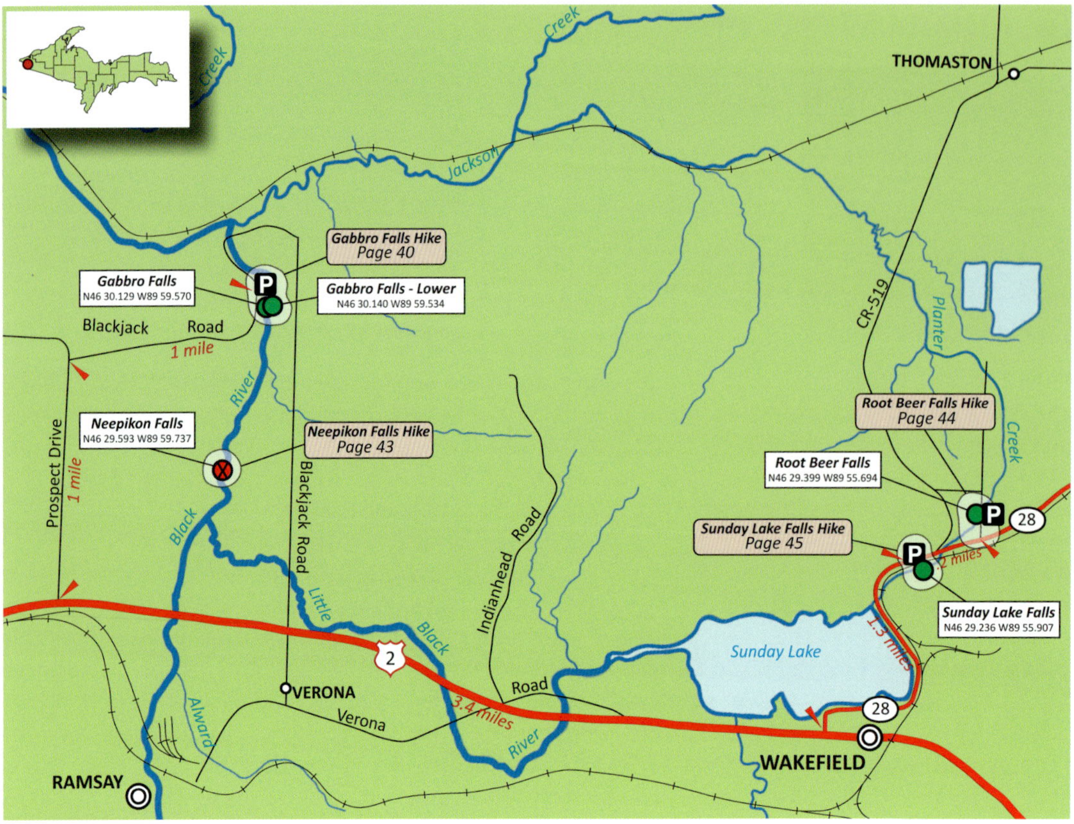

Gabbro Falls Hike

Gabbro Falls: I had one of those "heart stopping" moments here when I almost slid off of a narrow finger of rock that juts out into the gorge and faces the falls. A light rain and my wife slipping into me at just the wrong moment sent the adrenaline pumping! But hey, I did get a frontal shot after I carefully set up the tripod and camera on the precarious perch!

Gabbro Falls - Lower: Are the rivers in the area running high? If so, there is a good chance that the lower falls will be flowing nicely.

Directions: Turn north onto Prospect Drive from US-2. Drive 1 mile. Turn right onto Black Jack Road. The road turns to the left and very soon there will be a yellow metal gate on the left. There is a place on the right to pull over. Park here. A couple of foot trails lead away into the forest. Both of the trails are quite short; two to three minute walks at the most. The trail to the left heads to the bottom of the gorge. The lower falls are seen from down here. However, when the river is low, all the water flows over the upper falls. The upper falls are down here, but are not viewable without wading through the river around a mass of rock. It was deeper than I wanted to attempt. There was also a rope hanging from the top of the large rock. From that vantage point I suspect that there is a GREAT view of the falls, but once again, I did not attempt (and would not recommend) the climb. The second path from the parking area leads to the right and stays to the top of the gorge. From up here, the upper waterfall can be seen dropping down into the deep crevasse. There are no guard rails, and children should not be brought to this waterfall. The drop is about 40 feet straight down into water and solid rock. Use extreme caution, especially when the ground is wet.

GABBRO FALLS (BLACK RIVER)

Private

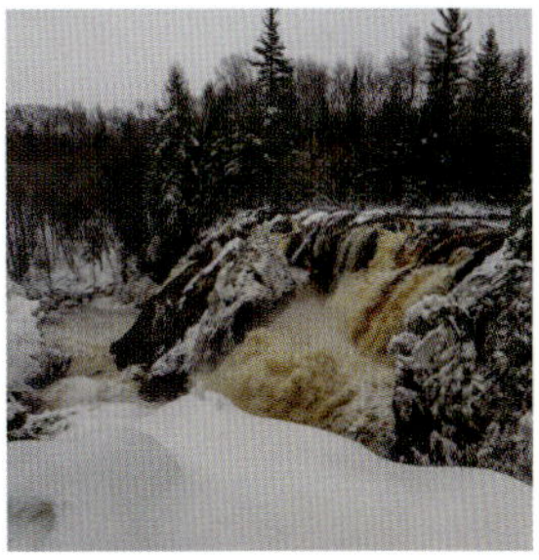

Must See:	8	GPS:	N46 30.129 W89 59.570
Height:	40 feet		
Time:	5 to 20 minutes	**Hiking Information**	
		Path:	Unimproved Footpath
Driving Information		Length:	100 yards
Signs:	None	Elev. Change:	Moderate
Road:	Secondary	GPS:	N/A
Access:	Somewhat Easy	Danger:	Moderate
4WD:	N/A	WP Boots:	Recommended

This is a breathtaking waterfall! The power of the drop and the sheer energy shown are magnified by the rugged terrain and intriguing topography that makes this waterfall possible. The water falls into a split in the rock and then immediately is forced to the right as there is nothing but solid rock straight ahead and to the left. The water then drops again, not so far as the first cascade. Only then does the river become calm again as it continues is journey toward Lake Superior.

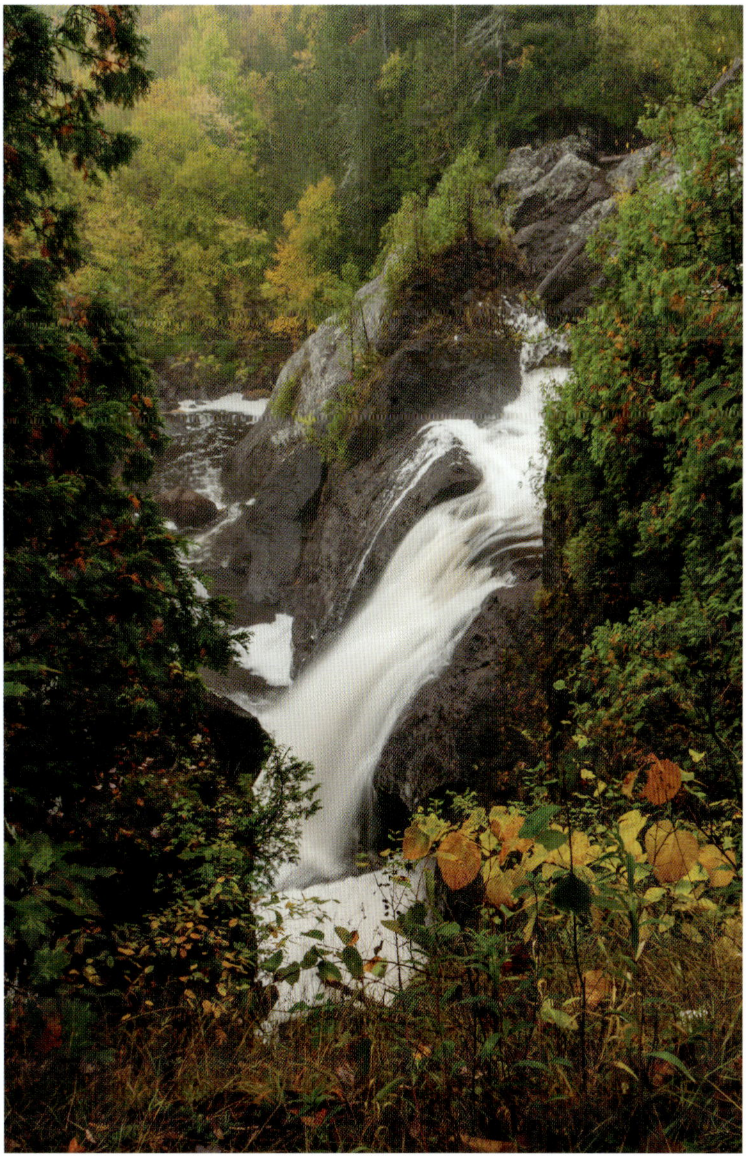

GABBRO FALLS - LOWER (BLACK RIVER)

Private

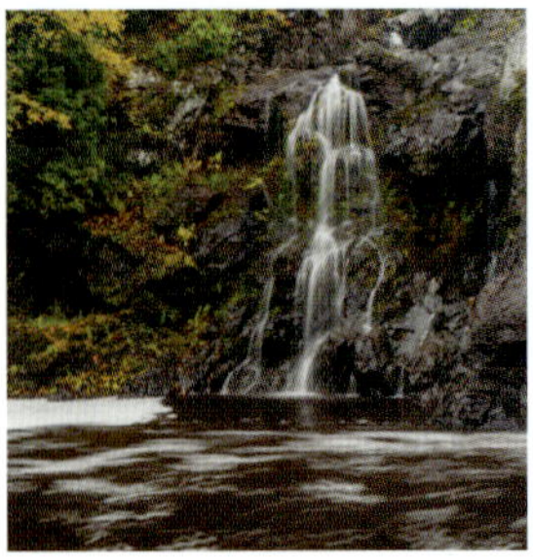

Must See:	8	GPS:	N46 30.140 W89 59.534
Height:	30 feet		
Time:	10-30 minutes	Hiking Information	
Driving Information		Path:	Unimproved footpath
Signs:	None	Length:	100 yards
Road:	Secondary	Elev. Change:	Moderate
Access:	Somewhat Easy	GPS:	N/A
4WD:	N/A	Danger:	Moderate
		WP Boots:	N/A

The level of the river greatly affects this waterfall since it is an overflow of Gabbro Falls. Only excess water flows to this side of the river. Due to the nature of the terrain, there is no easy way to view both waterfalls at the same time. Gabbro Falls is most easily viewed from the top of the gorge and the lower falls is most easily viewed from the river's edge at the bottom of the falls.

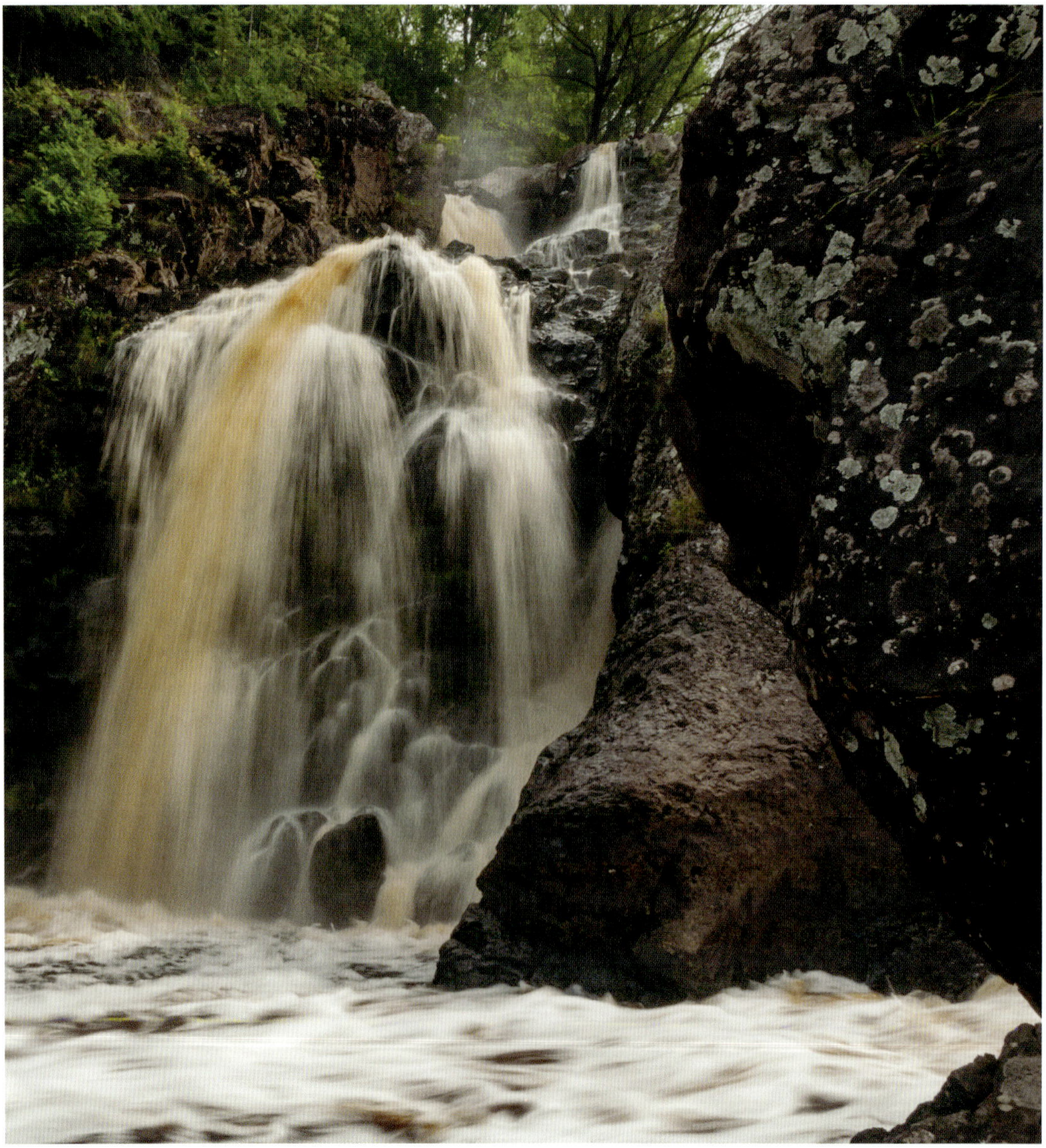

Neepikon Falls Hike

Neepikon Falls: I hiked from near Gabbro Falls, following the river upstream, sometimes bushwacking my way through thick undergrowth, other times following a slightly used fisherman's path. After passing the area that should have contained the falls and finding nothing more than the slightest of rapids, I cut cross country to the east, heading toward Blackjack Road. I ended up in a gentleman's backyard. He was gracious enough to drive me back to my vehicle. He said that Neepikon Falls is nothing more that a couple of rocks sticking out of the river near the bend that I had found earlier. Since there is nothing to look at, I am not including directions to get to the "falls".

X NEEPIKON FALLS (BLACK RIVER)

Private

Must See:	N/A	GPS:	N46 29.593 W89 59.737
Height:	0 feet		
Time:	N/A	**Hiking Information**	
Driving Information		Path:	N/A
Signs:	N/A	Length:	N/A
Road:	N/A	Elev. Change:	N/A
Access:	N/A	GPS:	N/A
4WD:	N/A	Danger:	N/A
		WP Boots:	N/A

There is nothing but a slight ripple in the river to indicate that there is anything here at all. I really don't know why there is an "official" waterfall labeled at this place.

Root Beer Falls Hike

Root Beer Falls: A promontory splits the waterfall in two. The river cascades along either side of the bedrock, presenting itself nicely as it rushes down the clean face to a nice sized spill pool. A large smooth boulder sits in the middle of the spill pool where it collects colorful autumn leaves in October.

Directions: Take M-28 north out of Wakefield. Follow it along the side of Sunday Lake. It then bends hard to the right (northeast). It will quickly cross Planter Creek. The next road on the left (north) is Wertanen Road. Turn left (north). Park on the side of the road near the bridge that once again crosses Planter Creek. It will be an obvious parking area along the dirt road. The waterfall can be seen through the trees. A well worn trail leads from the road down through an 8 foot high steep ditch to the floodplain.

ROOT BEER FALLS (PLANTER CREEK)

Private

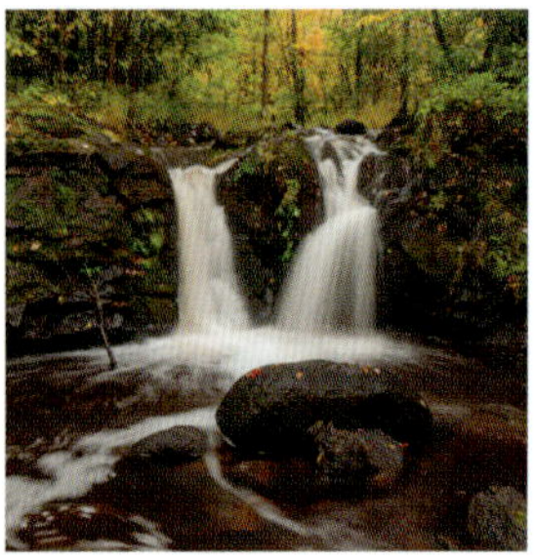

Must See:	7	GPS:	N46 29.399 W89 55.694
Height:	8 feet		
Time:	10 to 20 minutes	Hiking Information	
		Path:	None
Driving Information		Length:	100 yards
Signs:	None	Elev. Change:	Slight
Road:	Secondary	GPS:	N/A
Access:	Somewhat Easy	Danger:	Slight
4WD:	N/A	WP Boots:	Helpful

The falls are segmented by a large boulder planted at the top of the falls. The best viewing angle is on the near side of the creek. This is a nice place for a picnic and playing in the spill pool on a hot summer's day. Make sure the river isn't raging, however. Notice the difference between the two shots shown here. The river was overflowing its banks in the picture below. In the spring, the river overflows its banks and can flood the entire area over to the road.

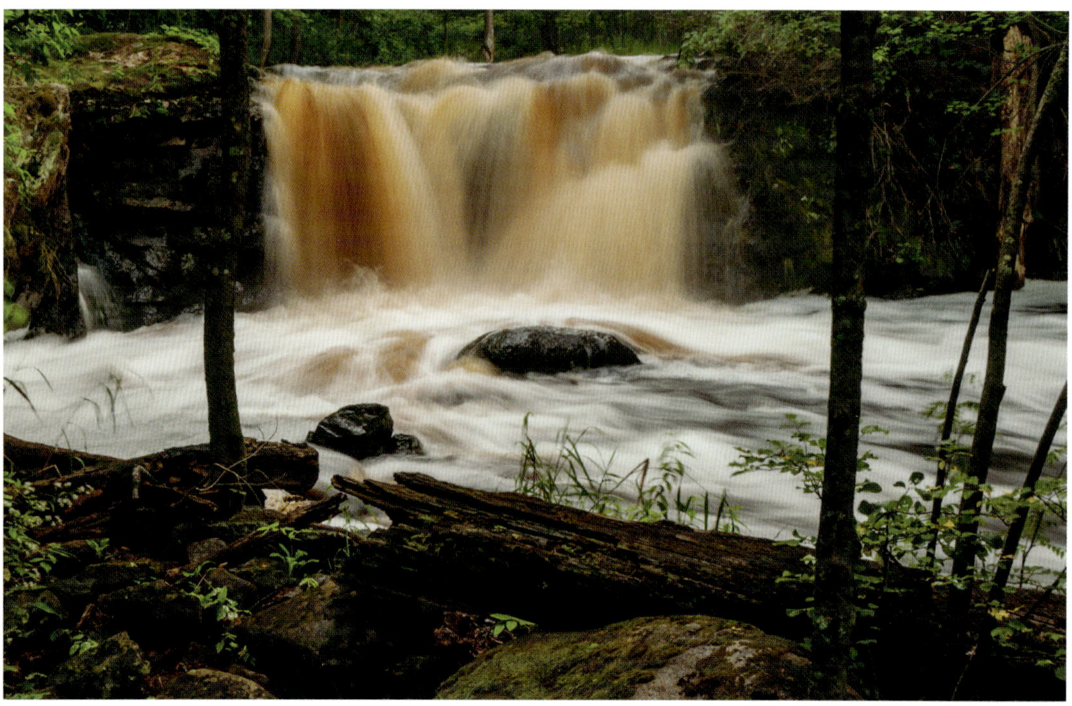

Rootbeer Falls

Sunday Lake Falls Hike

The Sunday Lake Mine operated from 1885 to 1961. It was located not far from the shores of Sunday Lake in Wakefield and extracted over seventeen million tons during its lifetime. For some reason I have not yet discovered, the mine blasted an underground tunnel from Sunday Lake northeasterly for about 1/3 mile to a ravine. Perhaps this was to regulate the height of the Lake, as this ravine seems to be much lower than the natural flow of the lake out of Little Black River on the western end of the lake. Whatever the reason, a gaping hole in solid rock spews out a creek that tumbles and falls through a rock strewn ravine.

Directions: Take M-28 north out of Wakefield. Follow it along the side of Sunday Lake. It then bends hard to the right (northeast). It will quickly cross Planter Creek. Find a safe place to park off either side of the road. Hike upstream along the creek (I prefer the southern side).

SUNDAY LAKE FALLS (PLANTER CREEK)

Private

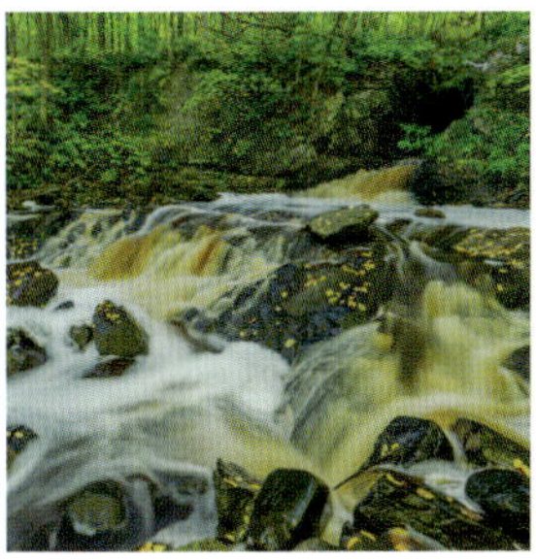

Must See:	7	GPS:	N46 29.236 W89 55.907
Height:	10 feet		
Time:	15 to 30 minutes	Hiking Information	
		Path:	None
Driving Information		Length:	100 yards
Signs:	None	Elev. Change:	Moderate
Road:	Main	GPS:	N/A
Access:	Somewhat Easy	Danger:	Moderate
4WD:	N/A	WP Boots:	Helpful

The creek emerges from a cavernous tunnel in the rock face. It cascades down 4 feet to a roundish spill pool encircled by a 15 foot high rocky embankment. The creek continues to cascade down the black boulder strewn creek bed, sweeping around a teardrop shaped island where several hardwood trees have matured, fed by the ever present water source.

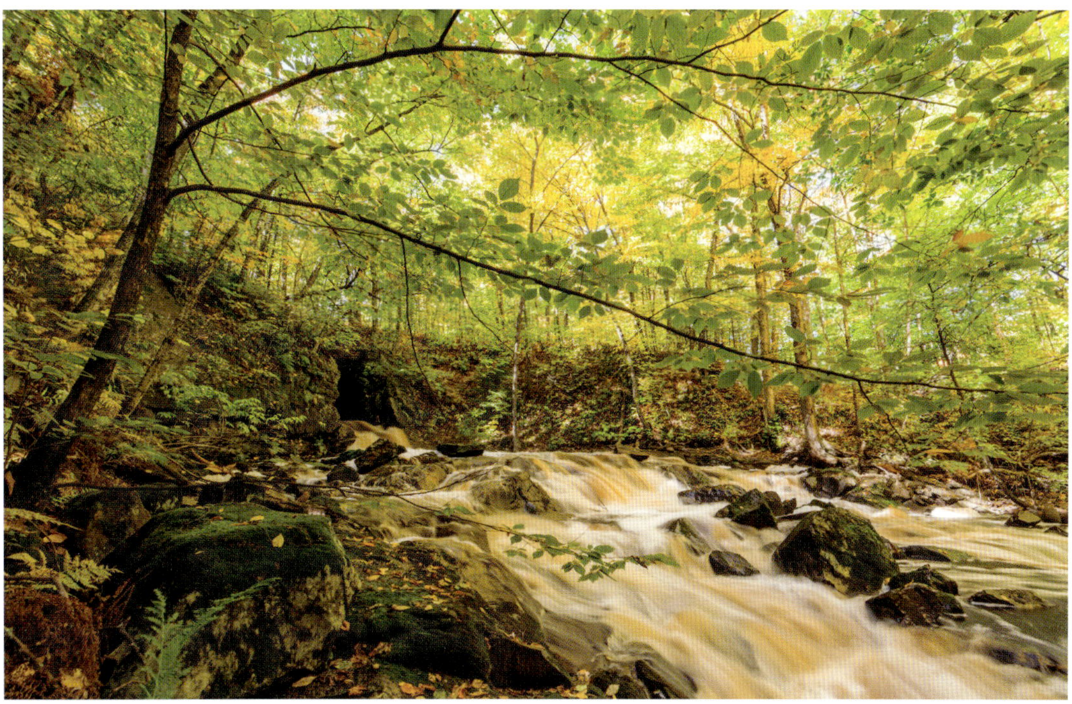

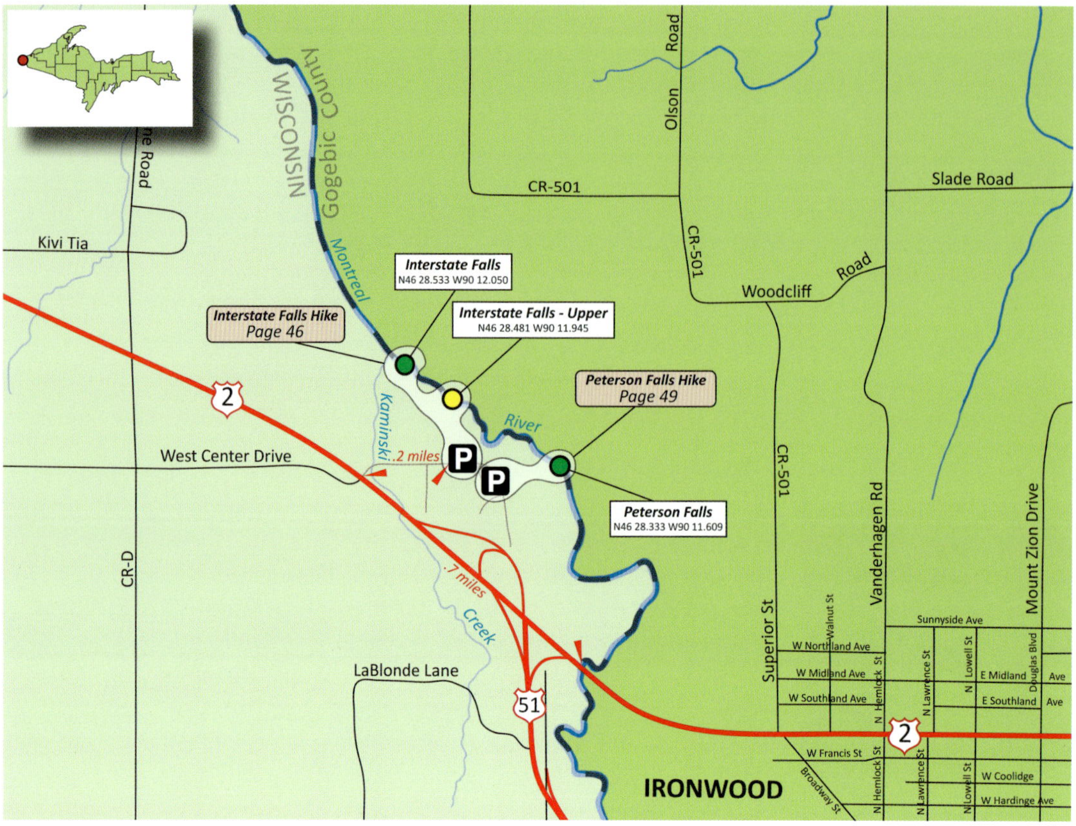

Interstate Falls Hike

Interstate Falls: This classic cascading waterfall is displayed wonderfully with mist rising up from the force of the pounding water when the river is running well. The trail to the falls is obvious. The hike is easy. The waterfall is gorgeous. But the viewing area is somewhat limited. Be careful near fast moving water.

Interstate Falls - Upper: A series of drops and spills clutter a section of the river between Peterson Falls and Interstate Falls. These oversized rapids are interesting, but not spectacular.

Directions: Drive just into Wisconsin on US-2. Turn right just before "The Country Store". There is a wooden sign - "Peterson Falls" - on the corner. Continue straight ahead on the dirt road that becomes a 2-track until you see a trailhead on the left. Park. Hike northwest to the falls. On the way back to the vehicle listen for the upper falls. There is a faint path leading to the upper falls.

Remember that this is private land. Be courteous and respectful of the land.

INTERSTATE FALLS (MONTREAL RIVER)

Private

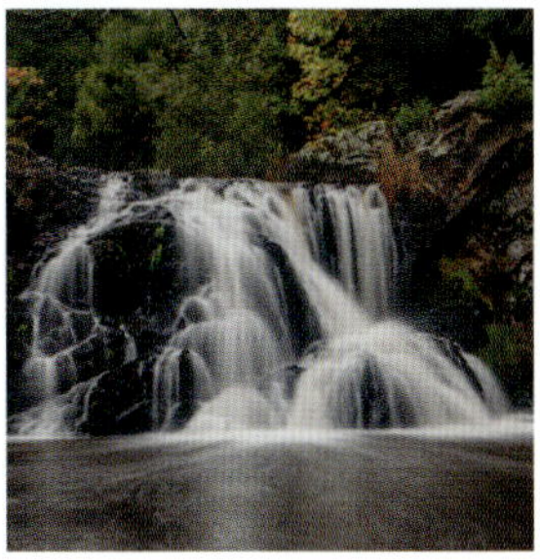

Must See:	9	GPS:	N46 28.533 W90 12.050
Height:	20 feet		
Time:	20 to 40 minutes	Hiking Information	
		Path:	Good footpath
Driving Information		Length:	1/4 mile
Signs:	Wooden	Elev. Change:	Slight
Road:	Dirt	GPS:	N/A
Access:	Somewhat Difficult	Danger:	Slight
4WD:	Helpful	WP Boots:	Helpful

This is best viewed from the Wisconsin side of the river. Not only is there signage to help you find the waterfall, a small parking spot, and a trail to the falls, but there is a house just above the waterfall on the Michigan side.

The look from the top (a house on the Michigan side of the river can be seen peeking through the trees).

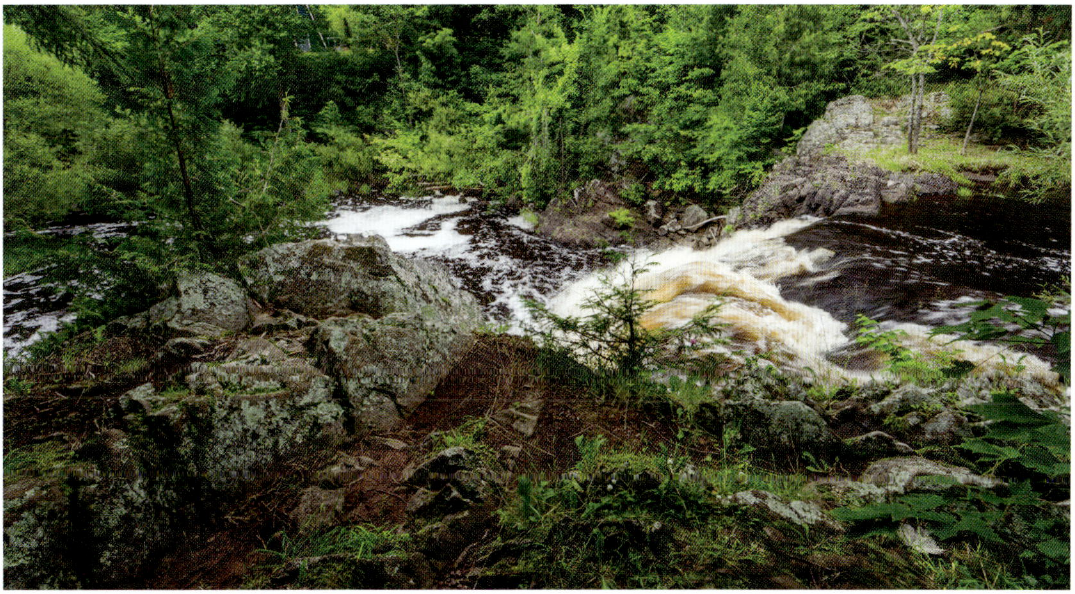

The river level changes radically. Note the difference from the thumbnail shot to this one!

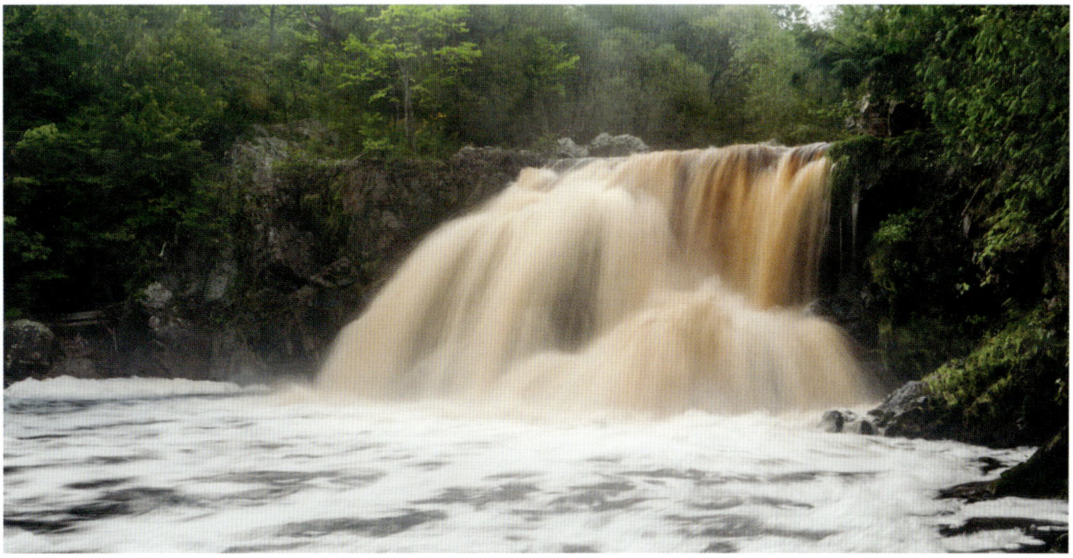

INTERSTATE FALLS - UPPER (MONTREAL RIVER)

Private

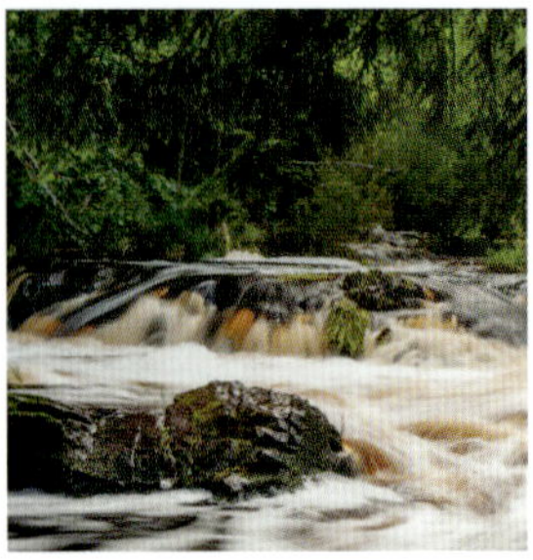

Must See:	5	GPS:	N46 28.481 W90 11.945
Height:	5 feet		
Time:	20 to 40 minutes	**Hiking Information**	
		Path:	Footpath
Driving Information		Length:	1/4 mile
Signs:	Wooden	Elev. Change:	Slight
Road:	Dirt	GPS:	N/A
Access:	Somewhat Difficult	Danger:	Slight
4WD:	Helpful	WP Boots:	Helpful

Turbulent drops fill this section of the river just upstream from Interstate Falls. Although it lacks the pizzazz of the main featured waterfall, there are many interesting drops to explore.

A gnarled old tree clutters the lower portion of the waterfall (for now)

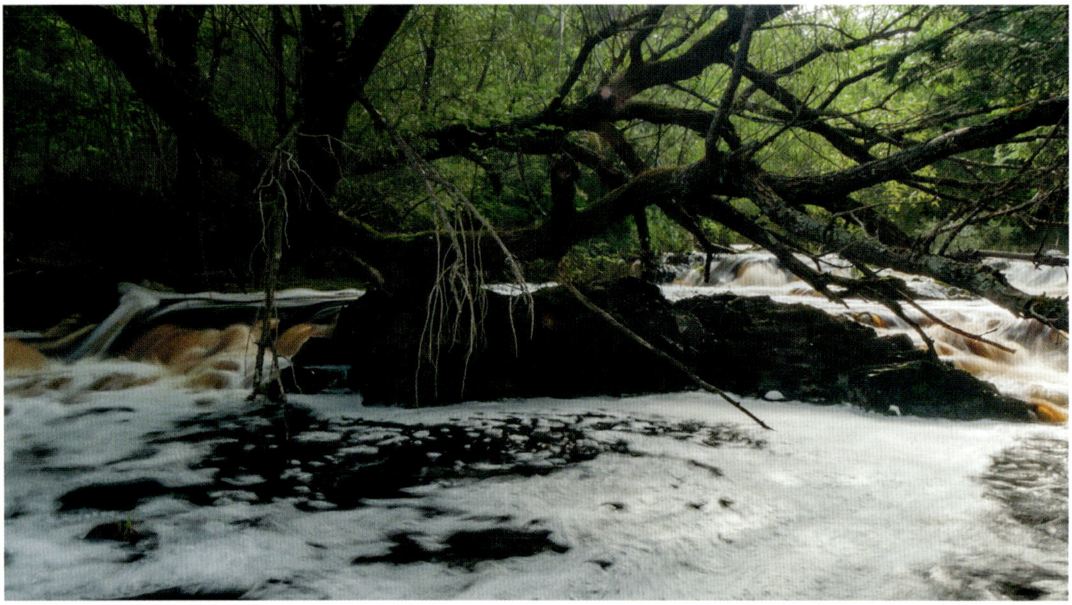

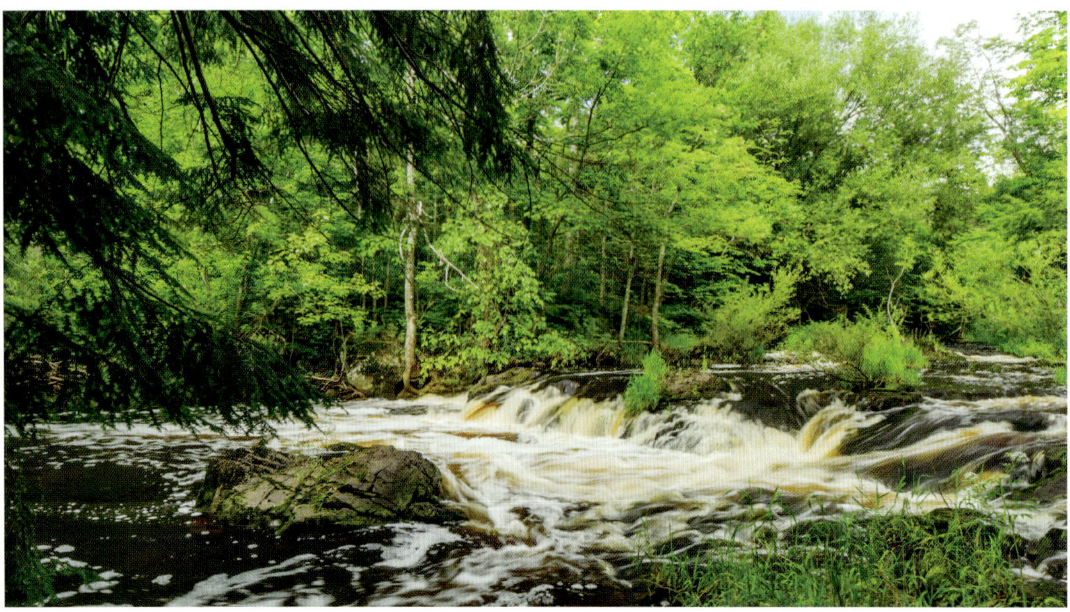

Peterson Falls Hike

Peterson Falls: An island splits the river at the head of the falls. Grasses and trees grasp for footing on the rocky, water-slick outcropping. As the river flows around the island, it pours down over the rock-filled river, merging together again halfway down the falls.

Directions: These instructions are nearly identical to the directions for Interstate Falls Hike. The Peterson Falls trailhead is not that far past the trailhead to Interstate Falls. Heading west on US-2, turn to the right just after entering Wisconsin and just before "The Country Store". There is a wooden sign marked "*Peterson Falls*" on the corner. Continue straight and park at GPS location N46 28.309 W90 11.842. An unimproved foot trail starts here. Walk 1/8 mile to the falls.

Peterson Falls is also on private property, but the owners allow for waterfall visitors. Be respectful of their property.

PETERSON FALLS (MONTREAL RIVER)

Private

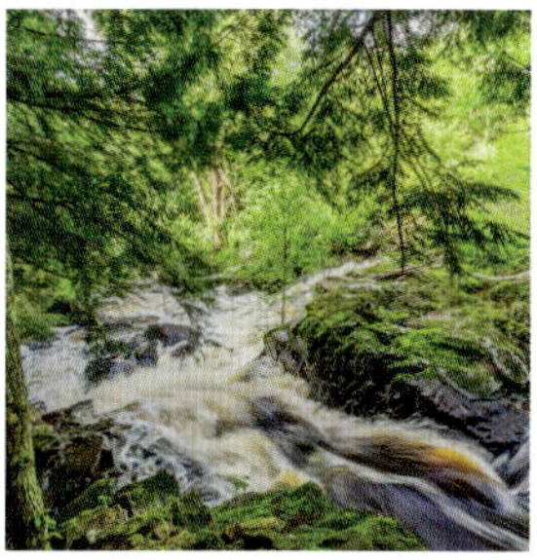

Must See:	8	GPS:	N46 28.333 W90 11.609
Height:	15 feet		
Time:	20 to 40 minutes	Hiking Information	
		Path:	Unimproved footpath
Driving Information		Length:	1/8 mile
Signs:	Wooden	Elev. Change:	Slight
Road:	2-track	GPS:	Helpful
Access:	Somewhat Difficult	Danger:	Slight
4WD:	Helpful	WP Boots:	Helpful

This is on private property. Be respectful.

Sweeping branches arch over the river as though to protect it from prying eyes, or perhaps to soak up some of the water mist that sometimes plays about the falls. The island divides the river, so the level of water here really makes a large difference in the appearance of the waterfall.

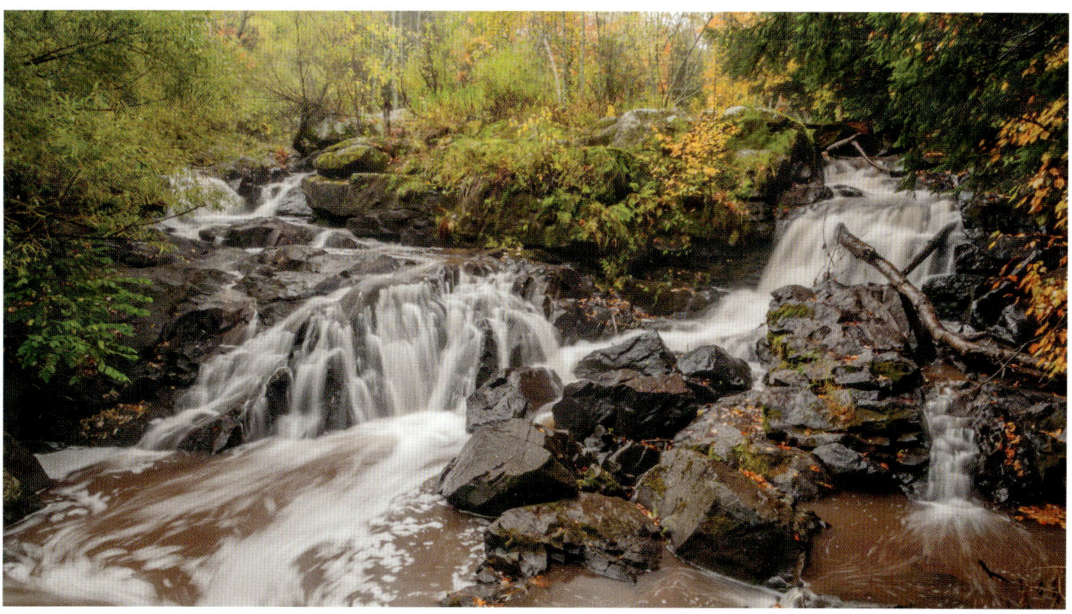

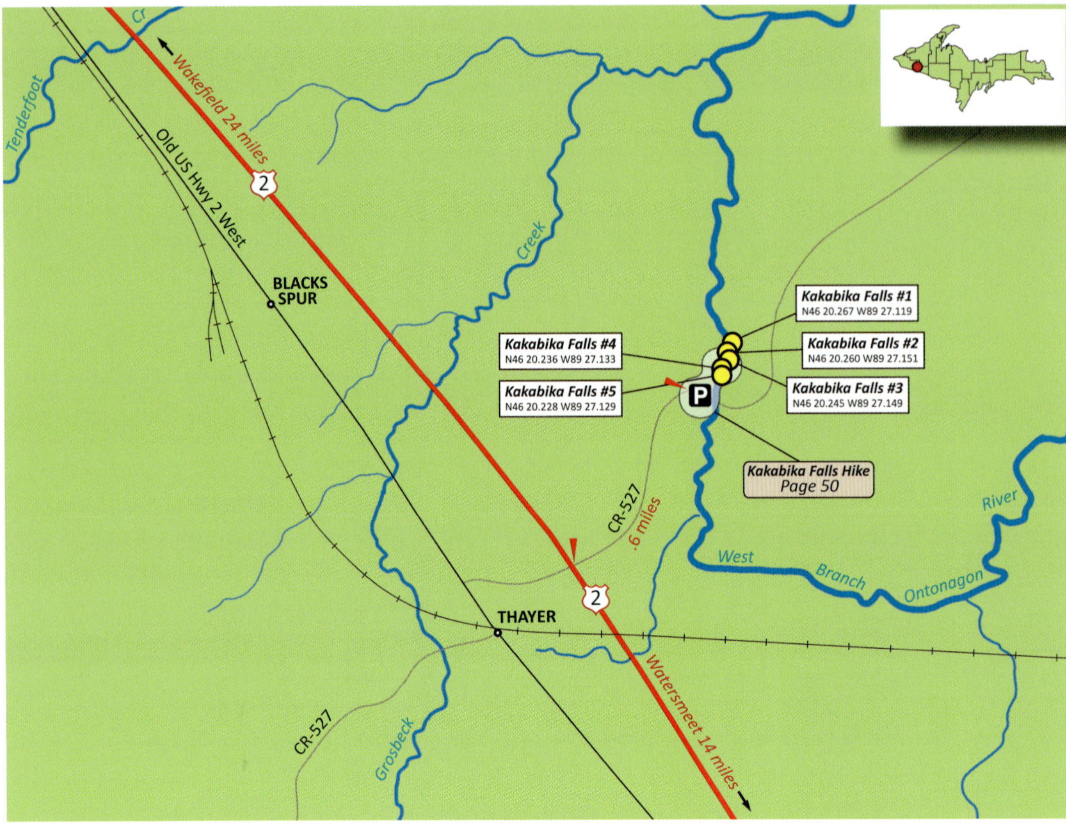

Kakabika Falls Hike

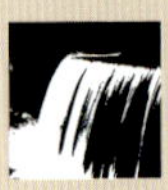

Kakabika Falls: A thunderstorm was brewing as I checked out Kakabika Falls for the first time. Mosquitoes were buzzing around in abundance, as though they knew this was to be their last chance to feed for some time. I was pleasantly surprised when Kakabika Falls turned out to be a series of waterfalls over several hundred yards and not just a single drop!

Why not follow up a thunderstorm with a snowstorm? My next stop did just that! A freak May snowstorm dumped a foot of snow in Wakefield, and just less than that here. A beautiful combination of snow capped trees and water rushing down the river from the annual spring melt met me for an amazing experience on the swollen West Branch of the Ontonagon River.

Directions: Turn east off of US-2 onto County Road 527. Just before the road crosses the West Branch of the Ontonagon River there is a circular turnoff on the left (north) with a sign announcing Kakabika Falls. Park. Hike down the well-worn footpath along the river to the series of waterfalls.

KAKABIKA FALLS #1 (ONTONAGON RIVER - WEST BRANCH)

Private

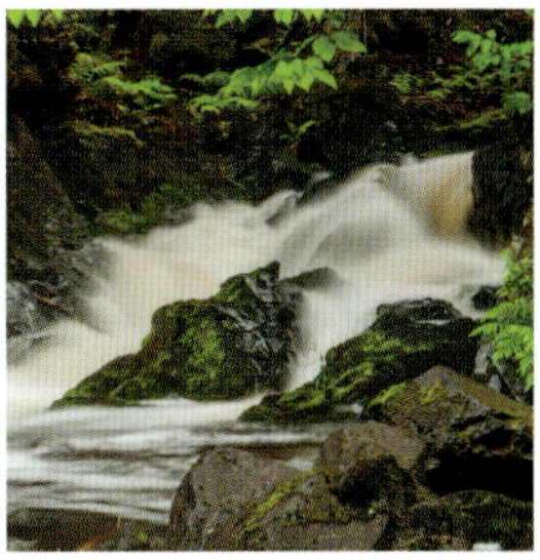

Must See:	6	GPS:	N46 20.267 W89 27.119
Height:	10 feet		
Time:	10 to 30 minutes	**Hiking Information**	
		Path:	Unimproved footpath
Driving Information		Length:	1/8 mile
Signs:	Wooden Sign	Elev. Change:	Slight
Road:	Dirt	GPS:	N/A
Access:	Somewhat easy	Danger:	Moderate
4WD:	N/A	WP Boots:	Helpful

A tree shrouded shallow canyon funnels the river between rugged lichen covered rocky banks. The river quickly descends in the canyon, exiting in a final burst over sharp jagged bedrock. As the river has completed its Kakabika descent it slows down and meanders through a gorgeous mature forest.

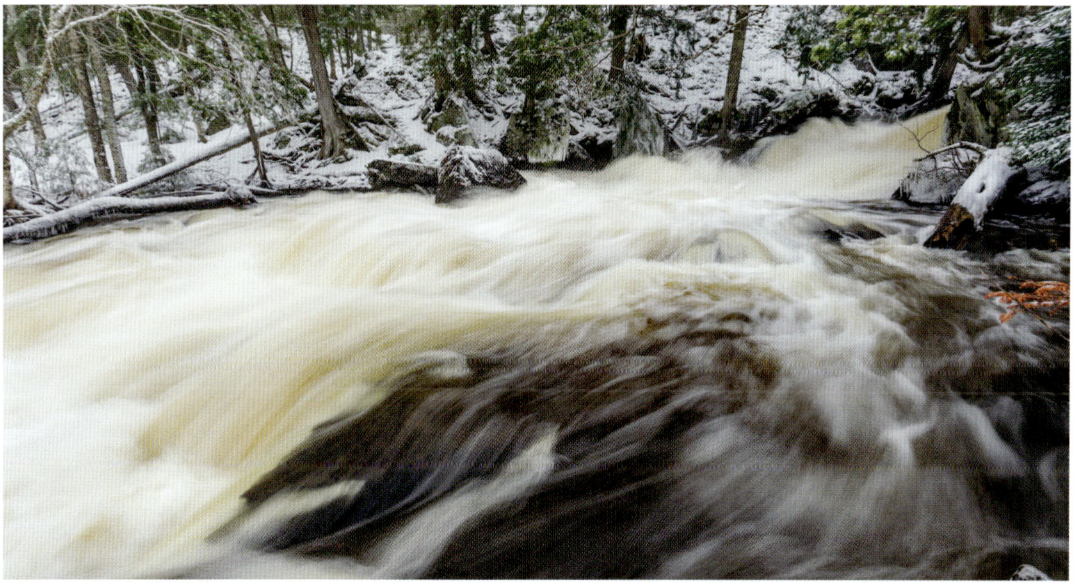

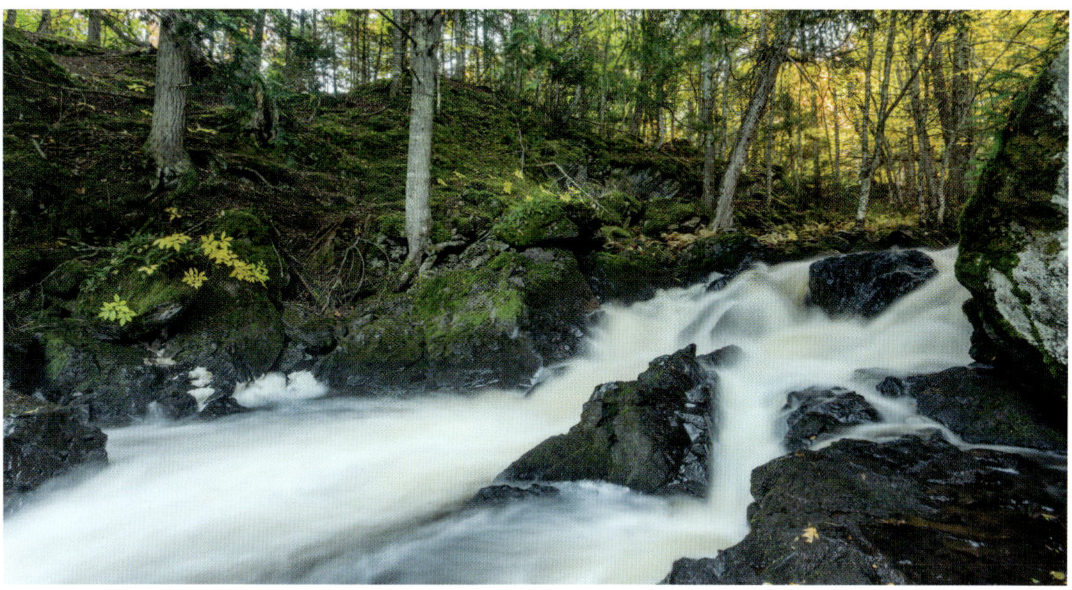

KAKABIKA FALLS #2 (ONTONAGON RIVER - WEST BRANCH)

Private

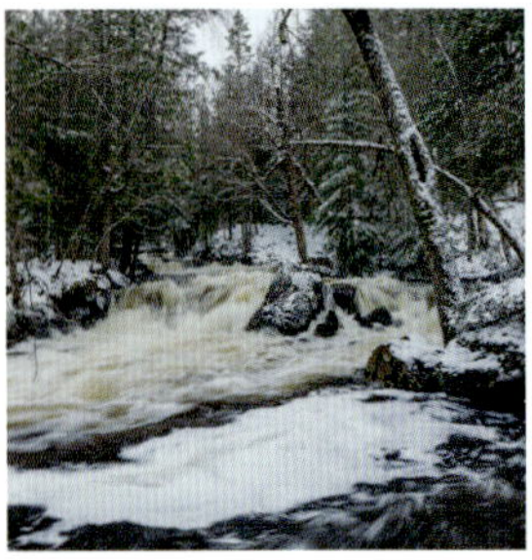

Must See:	5	GPS:	N46 20.260 W89 27.151
Height:	5 feet		
Time:	10 to 30 minutes	Hiking Information	
		Path:	Unimproved footpath
Driving Information		Length:	1/8 mile
Signs:	Wooden Sign	Elev. Change:	Slight
Road:	Dirt	GPS:	N/A
Access:	Somewhat easy	Danger:	Moderate
4WD:	N/A	WP Boots:	Helpful

The river makes a hard turn back on itself between #2 and #1. Just before the turn, #2 tumbles down over sharp black rocks. Birch, cedar, and maple trees line the rocky river's edge.

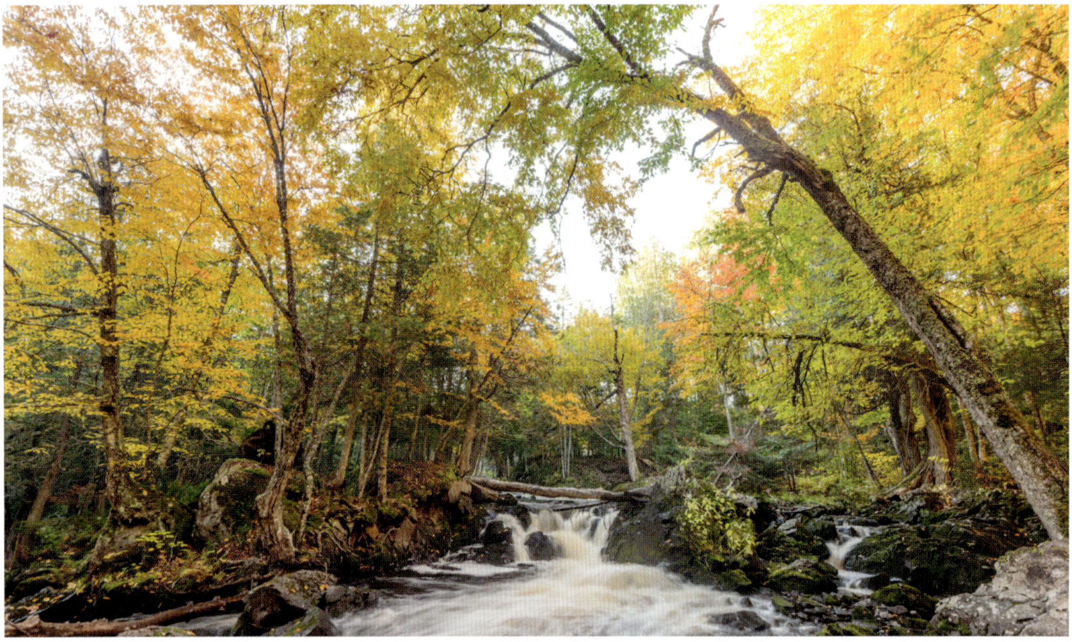

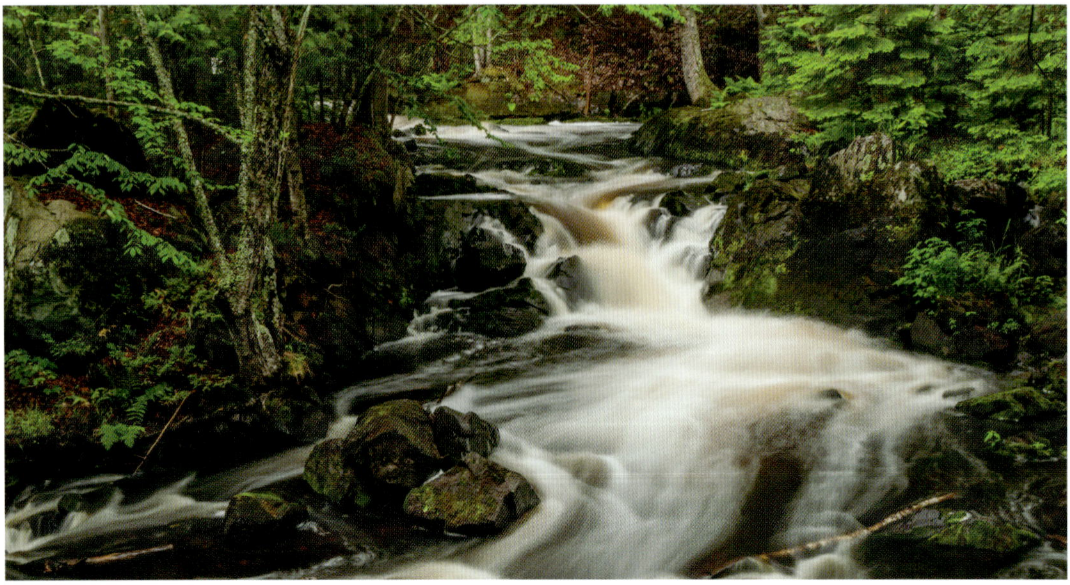

KAKABIKA FALLS #3 (ONTONAGON RIVER - WEST BRANCH)

Private

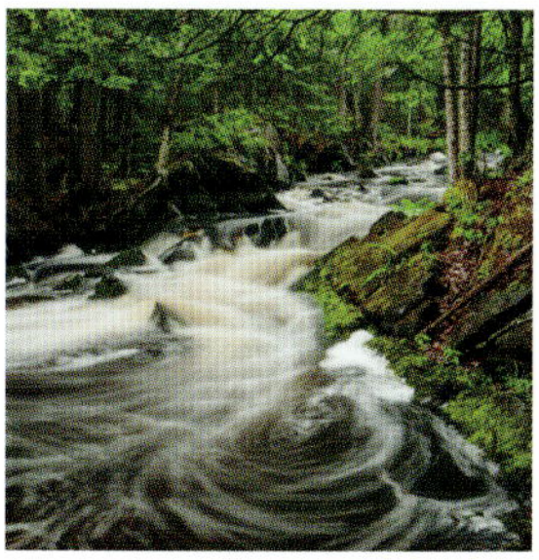

Must See:	5	GPS:	N46 20.245 W89 27.149
Height:	3 feet		
Time:	10 to 20 minutes	**Hiking Information**	
		Path:	Unimproved footpath
Driving Information		Length:	1/8 mile
Signs:	Wooden Sign	Elev. Change:	Slight
Road:	Dirt	GPS:	N/A
Access:	Somewhat easy	Danger:	Moderate
4WD:	N/A	WP Boots:	Helpful

The river has turned and runs through a shallow gorge filled with rapids. A river-level viewing area below the falls is tucked into a corner of an oblong spill pool.

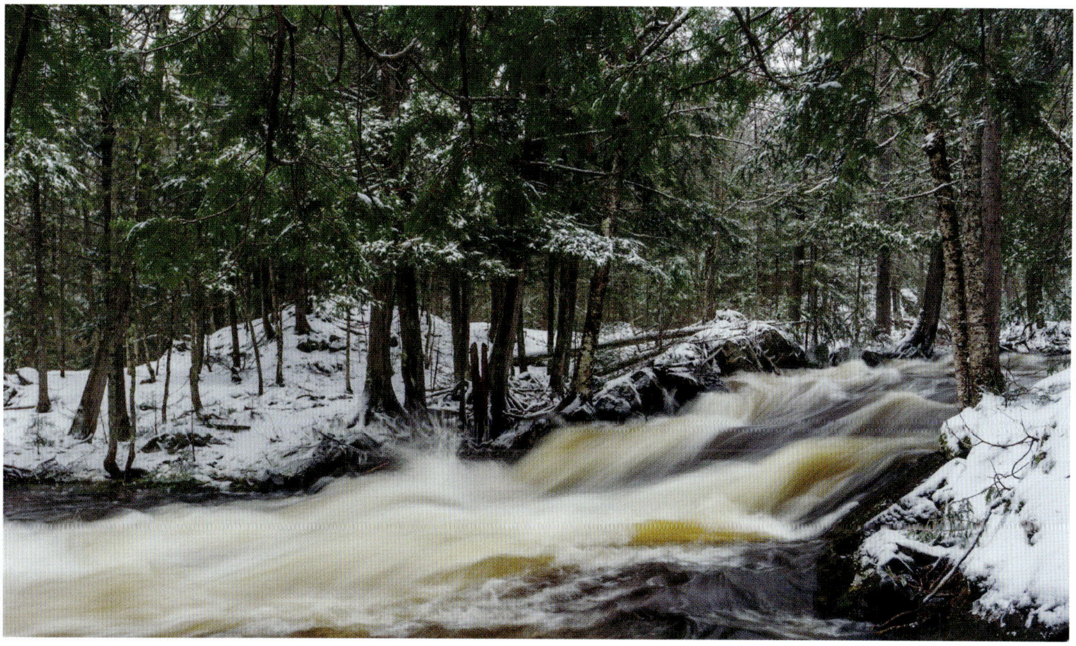

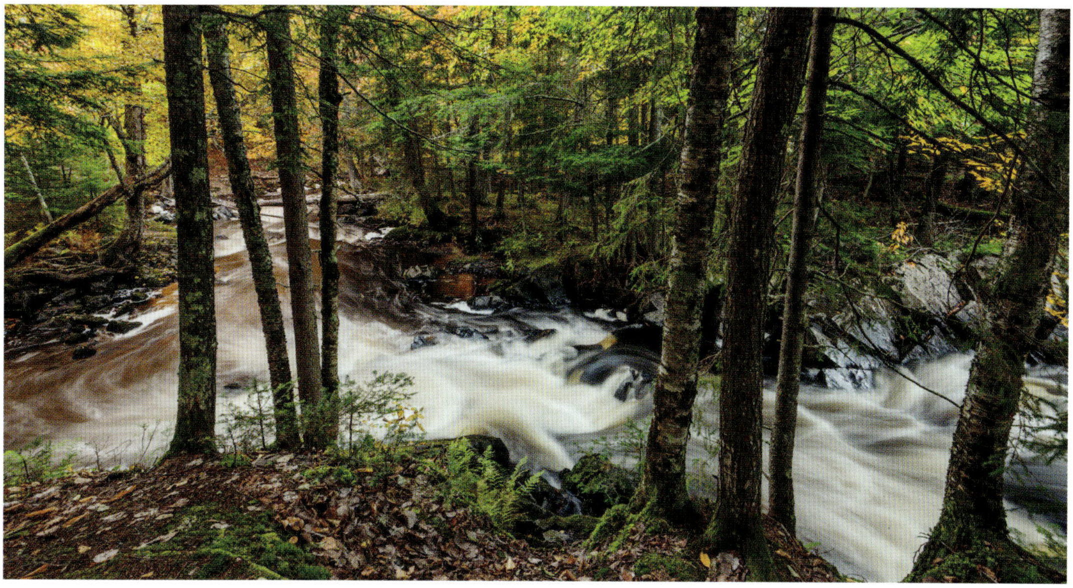

KAKABIKA FALLS #4 (ONTONAGON RIVER - WEST BRANCH)

Private

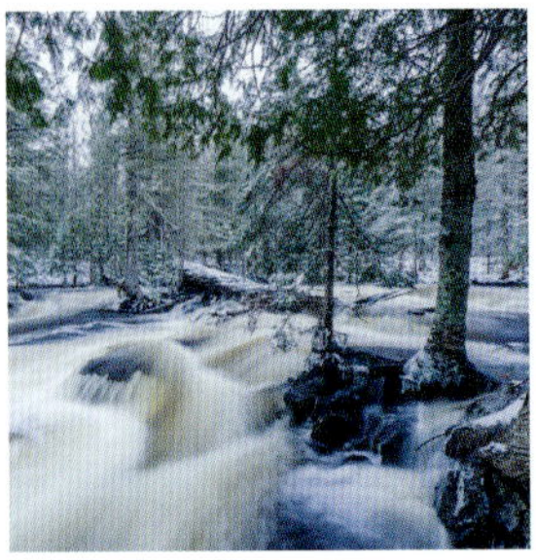

Must See:	4	GPS:	N46 20.236 W89 27.133
Height:	3 feet		
Time:	5 to 15 minutes	**Hiking Information**	
		Path:	Unimproved footpath
Driving Information		Length:	1/8 mile
Signs:	Wooden Sign	Elev. Change:	Slight
Road:	Dirt	GPS:	N/A
Access:	Somewhat easy	Danger:	Moderate
4WD:	N/A	WP Boots:	Helpful

A massive pine fell across the near branch of the river years ago. Accumulating debris has forced most of the water to flow around the back side of the island where it is partially hidden from view. These two falls (#4 & #5) are easily viewed from fairly level and brush free terrain.

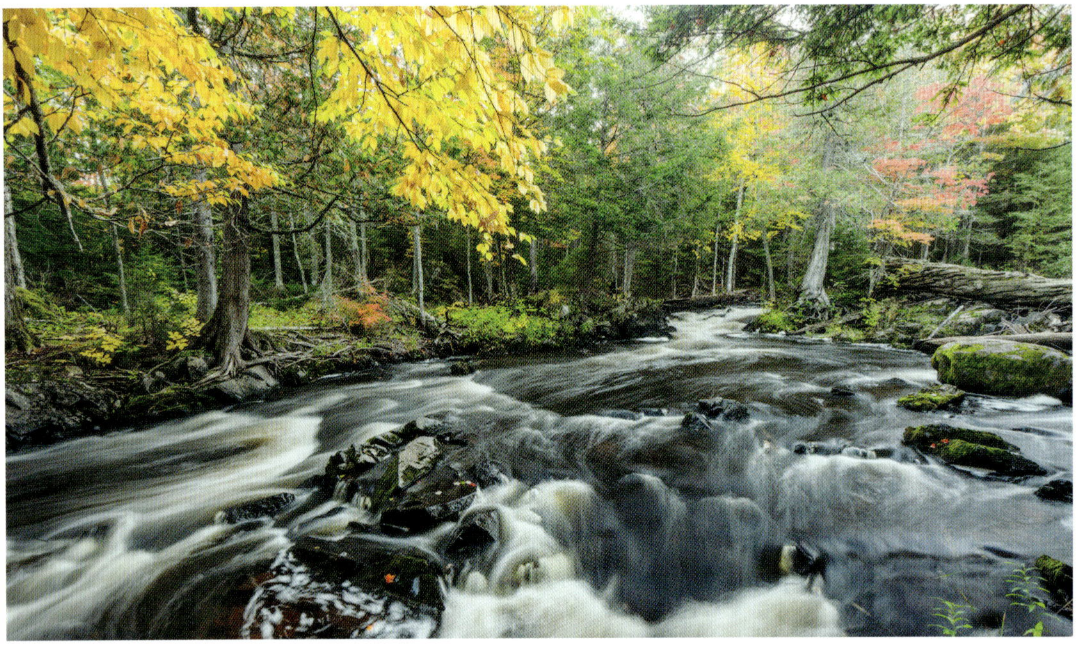

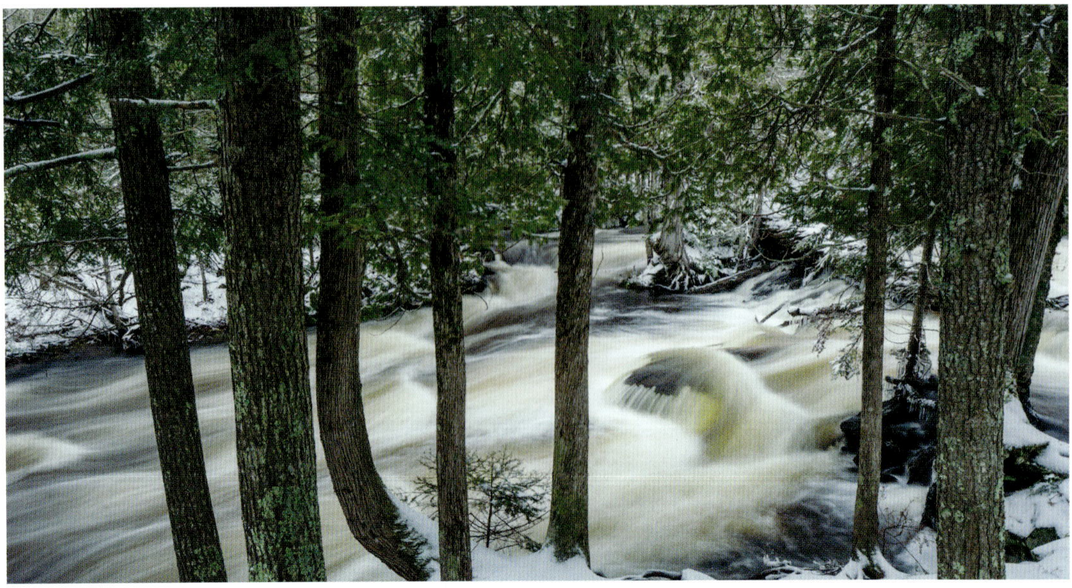

KAKABIKA FALLS #5 (ONTONAGON RIVER - WEST BRANCH)

Private

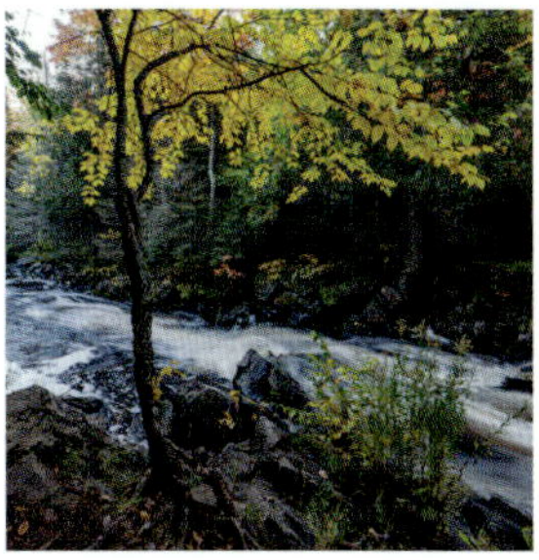

Must See:	4	GPS:	N46 20.228 W89 27.129
Height:	3 feet		
Time:	5 to 15 minutes	**Hiking Information**	
		Path:	Unimproved footpath
Driving Information		Length:	100 feet
Signs:	Wooden Sign	Elev. Change:	Slight
Road:	Dirt	GPS:	N/A
Access:	Somewhat easy	Danger:	Moderate
4WD:	N/A	WP Boots:	Helpful

This waterfall is the first that you come to as you leave your vehicle. It is easily in sight of the road bridge. Squarish boulders add character to the waterfall. The river narrows between rocky banks, dropping over this short waterfall as the river begins its descent over the Kakabika Falls. A small, gnarly birch sits above the waterfall accompanied by a woodpecker favored cedar.

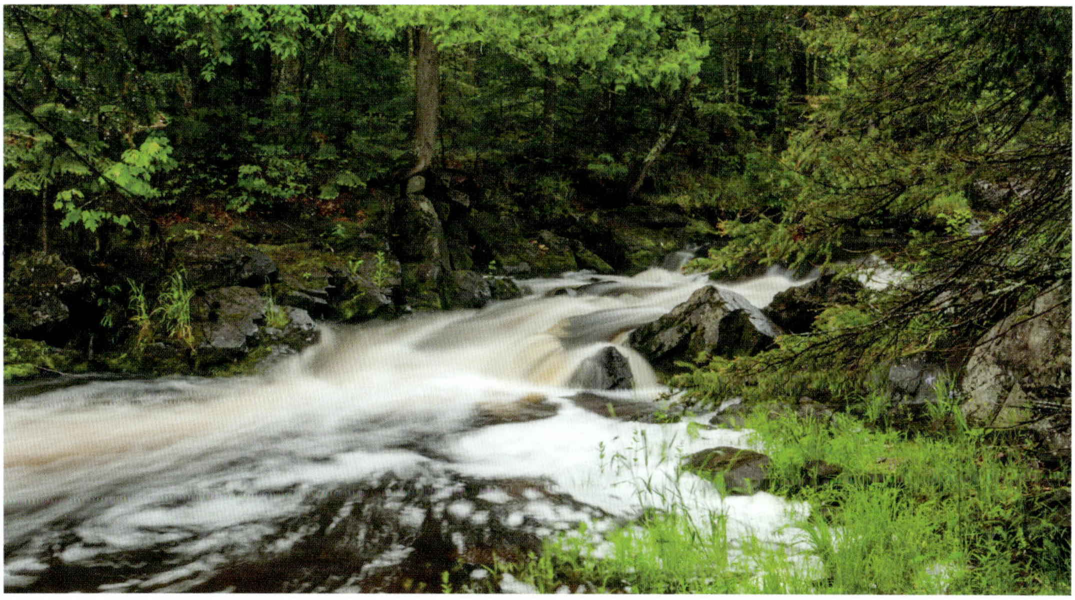

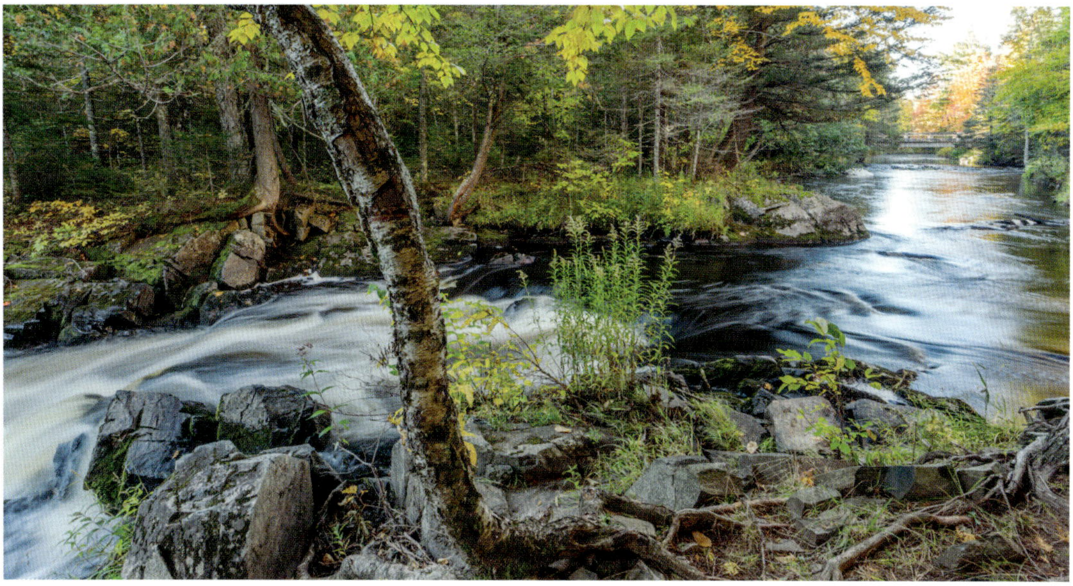

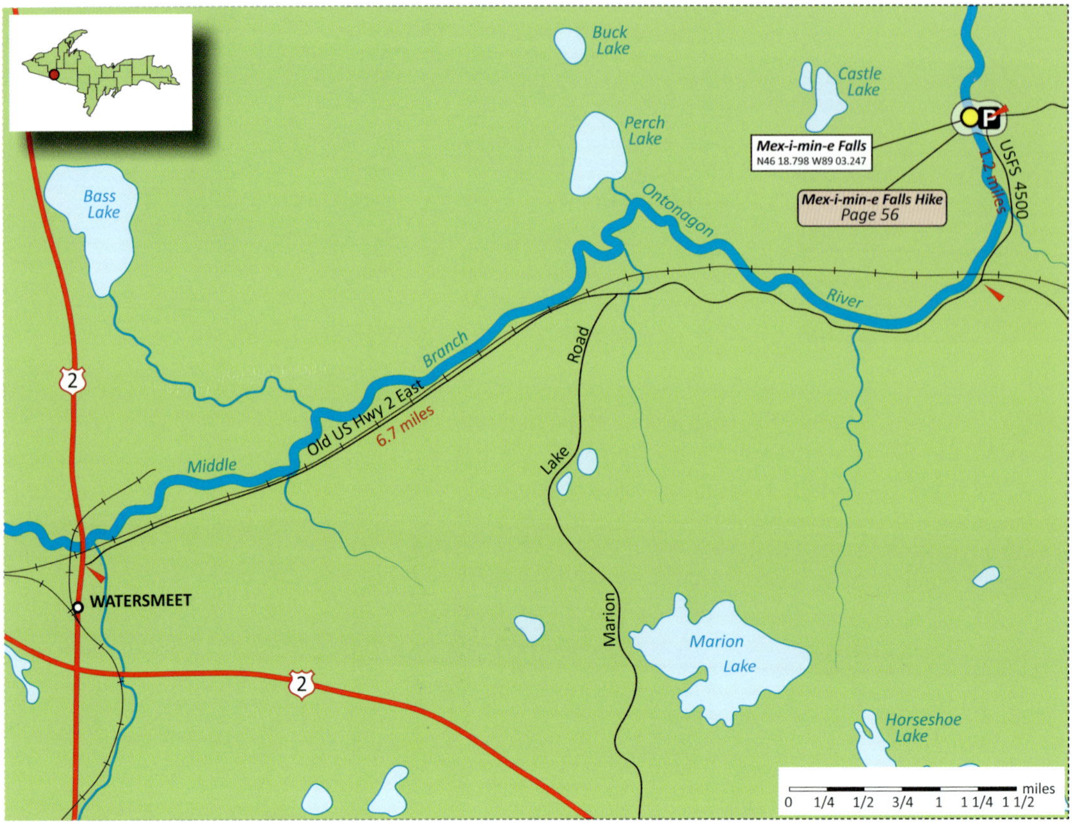

Mex-i-min-e Falls Hike

Mex-i-min-e Falls is also known as *"Burned Dam Falls"*. At the end of the 1800's logging was a major industry in this area. A dam was constructed on the river here, and logs floated from upstream were gathered in the backwaters and then transported overland to Interior, a small logging community near Bond Falls. Around 1900 a fire burned through the area, greedily consuming the bone dry slash left from clear cutting and subsequently destroying the dam.

Now, a lightly used rustic Federal Forest campground occupies the grounds. The no fee campground has a pit toilet, but no other facilities.

Directions: From Watersmeet, turn north onto US-45 from US-2. In .6 miles, turn right (east) onto Old US-2. Follow it for 6.6 miles to US Forest Road 4500. Turn left (north) and continue for 1.1 miles to the entrance of Burned Dam Camp. Drive around to the back of the campground and look for a sign that describes the history of the area. The river is on the left, and a short 200 foot long hike ends at the falls.

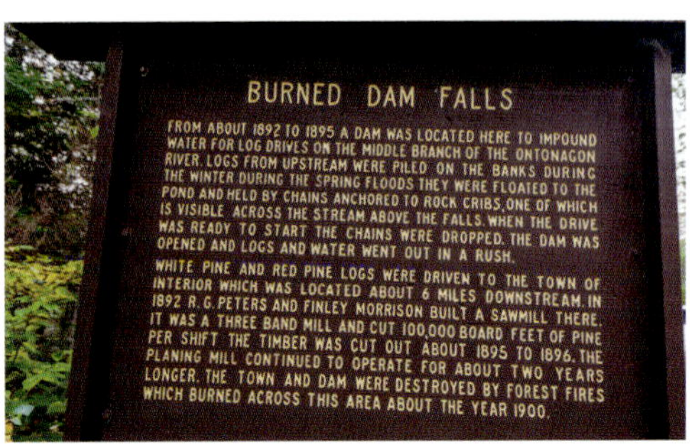

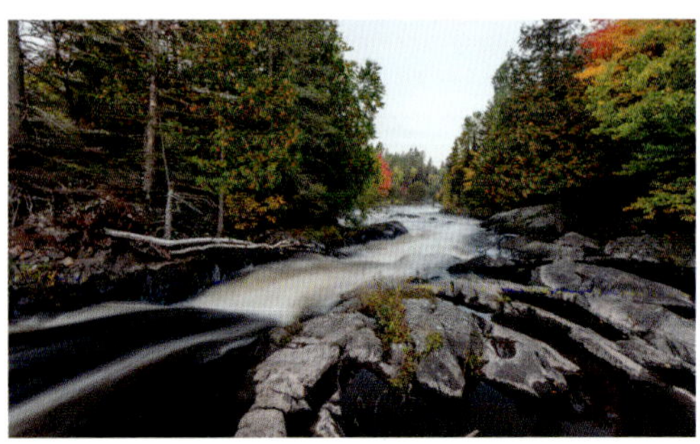

MEX-I-MIN-E FALLS (ONTONAGON RIVER - MIDDLE BRANCH)

Private

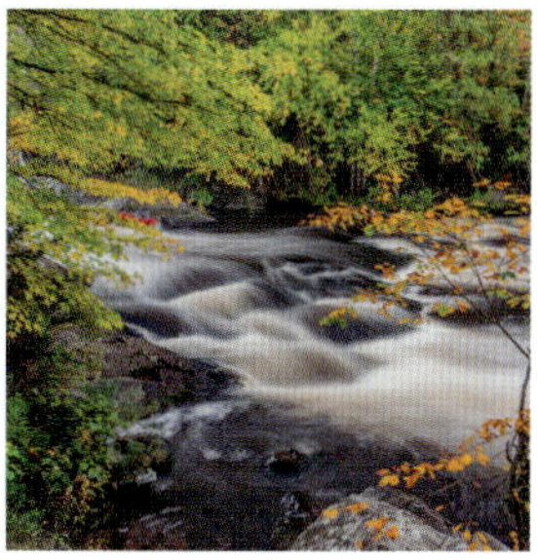

Must See:	6	GPS:	N46 18.798 W89 03.247
Height:	12 feet		
Time:	10 to 20 minutes	Hiking Information	
		Path:	Unimproved Footpath
Driving Information		Length:	200 feet
Signs:	None	Elev. Change:	Slight
Road:	Dirt	GPS:	N/A
Access:	Somewhat difficult	Danger:	Slight
4WD:	N/A	WP Boots:	N/A

A nice Federal Forest Campground has been built along the Middle Branch of the Ontonagon River with Mex-i-min-e Falls as its main attraction. A short walk through small pines is reminiscent of the hike to Whitefish Falls in Alger County.

The water flows around bedrock and tumbles over and around some misshapen black rocks. A lot of water flows here. In the middle of the falls it is only about twelve feet wide. Below the falls is a rapids area. The total waterfall area is about 150 feet long, with numerous small cascades and four larger drops. The tallest cascade is toward the top of the falls and has one arching trough of water that dumps into the middle of the river. As is quite typical of Michigan waterfalls, rootbeer colored water flows over the falls.

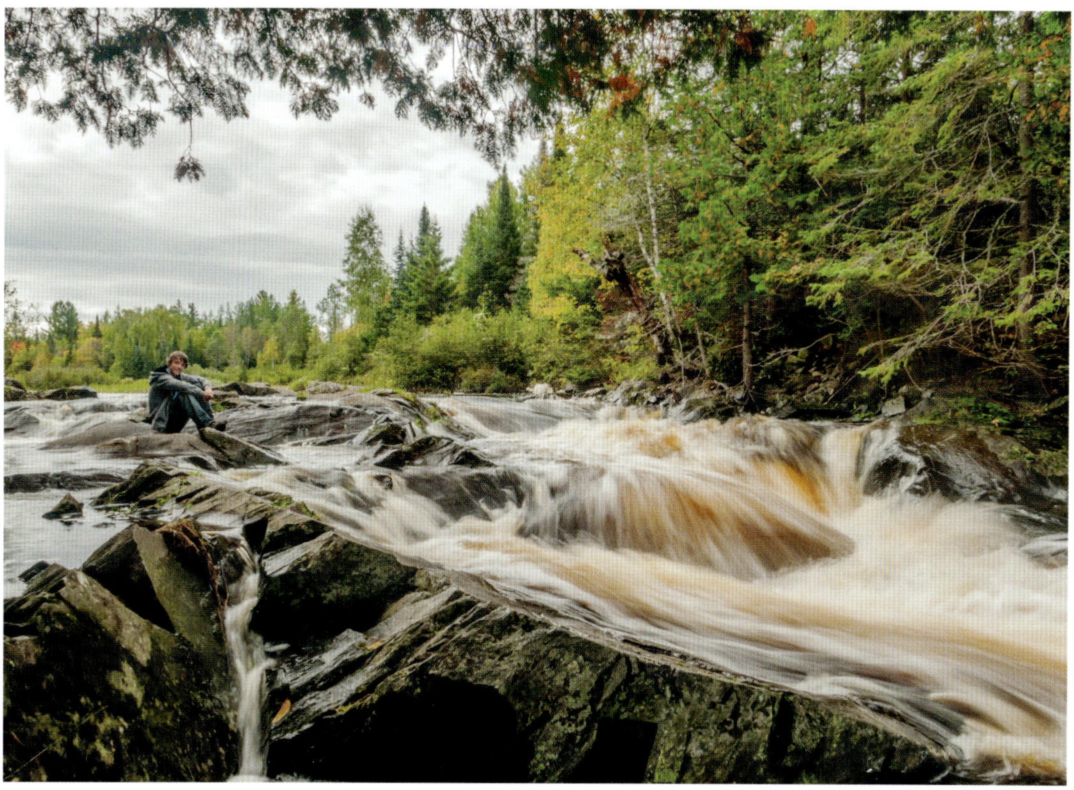

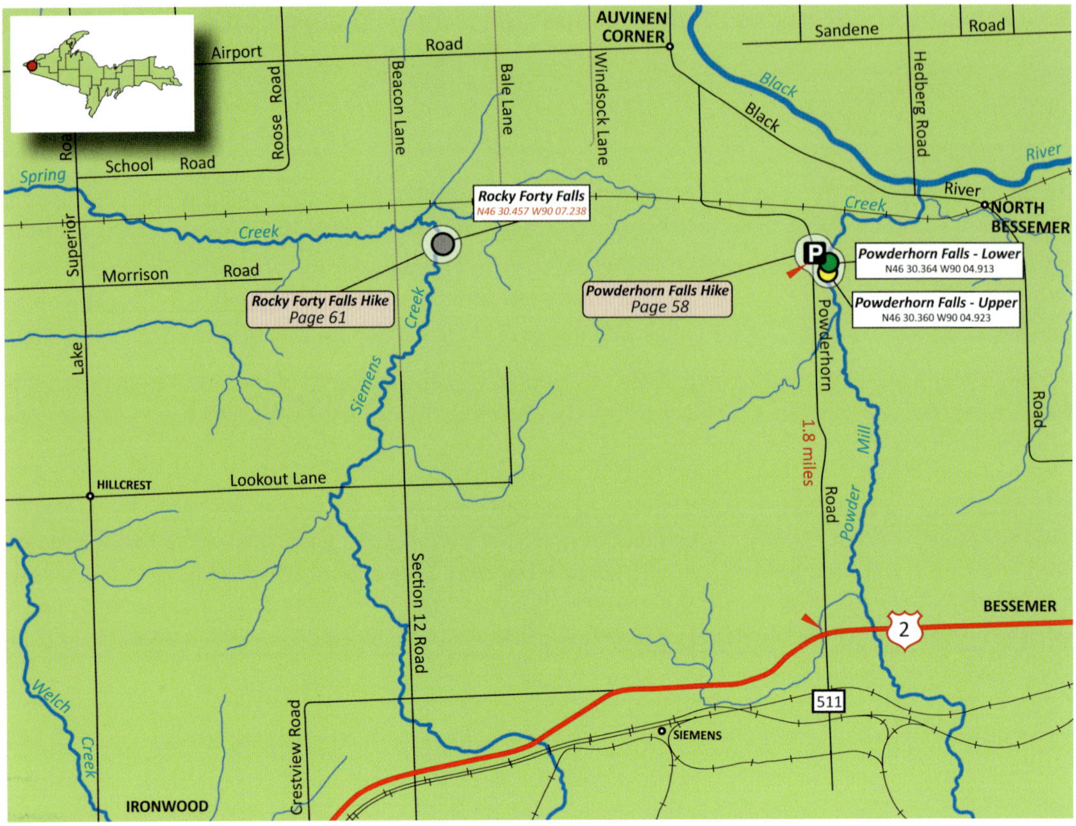

Powderhorn Falls Hike

Downhill skiing has become an integral part of the tourism industry for the western end of Michigan's Upper Peninsula. Porcupine Mountains Ski Area in the Porcupine Mountains State Park, Indianhead Mountain Resort in Wakefield, along with Blackjack Ski Resort and Big Powderhorn Mountain in Bessemer provide a variety of options for downhill skiers. In the 1960's, Big Powderhorn was considered to be the premier skiing destination in Michigan. Just 2/3 mile to the east of the Big Powderhorn Mountain peak, Powder Mill Creek plunges down into a ravine over a couple of drops know as the Powderhorn (or Powder Mill) Falls.

Two parallel strings of mountains run in an arc with the northern portion being more dominant and starting basically near Copps Creek by Lake Gogebic and running westerly, swinging gently toward the west/southwest as it crosses the Michigan/Wisconsin line and finally fades out near Mellen, WI. The southern string begins between Wakefield and Bessemer and ends just past Mellen, WI. A smooth valley sits between the slopes for the roughly 40 miles that these parallel ridges interrupt an otherwise flat terrain. Michigan engineers, taking advantage of the relatively level conditions, ran US-2 through the valley. The cities of Wakefield, Bessemer, and Ironwood all lie in this corridor, as well as Hurley, Montreal, Pence, Iron Belt, Upson, and Mellen on the Wisconsin side. Big Powderhorn Mountain is at the northern apex of the arc with the Black River cutting across the countryside just north of the mountain. Nestled between Big Powderhorn Mountain on the west and an unnamed, slightly less steep mountain on the east, Powder Mill Creek runs from the south to the north, joining forces with the much larger Black River less than a mile downstream from the waterfalls.

Directions: Turn north onto Powderhorn Road off of US-2 just to the west of Bessemer. In 1.8 miles, just before the road sweeps to the left is a parking spot on the right. Park. Hike the well worn footpath 100 yards to the top of a rocky expanse overlooking Powdermill Creek.

POWDERHORN FALLS - UPPER (POWDER MILL CREEK) Private

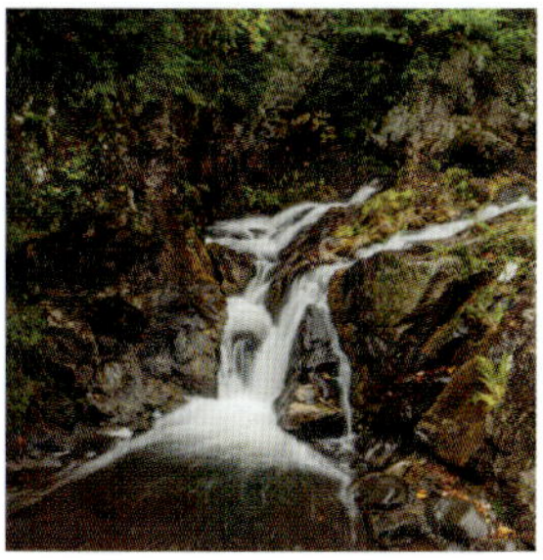

Must See:	5	GPS:	N46 30.360 W90 04.923
Height:	15 feet		
Time:	10 to 20 minutes	Hiking Information	
		Path:	Unimproved Footpath
Driving Information		Length:	100 yards
Signs:	None	Elev. Change:	Moderate
Road:	Secondary	GPS:	N/A
Access:	Fairly Easy	Danger:	Moderate
4WD:	N/A	WP Boots:	N/A

Hike from the vehicle to a large rocky area. The upper falls are straight ahead and can be seen from the outcropping. To get a more intimate view requires climbing down to a small landing by the spill pool. The last time that I was at the falls there was a decent rope attached to a tree to aid in descending through a slit in the rocks.

The upper falls can be viewed from the top of the rocky knob, but it is most nicely viewed from the small carved out niche near the base of the falls. It is a short, but not easy climb. Be careful.

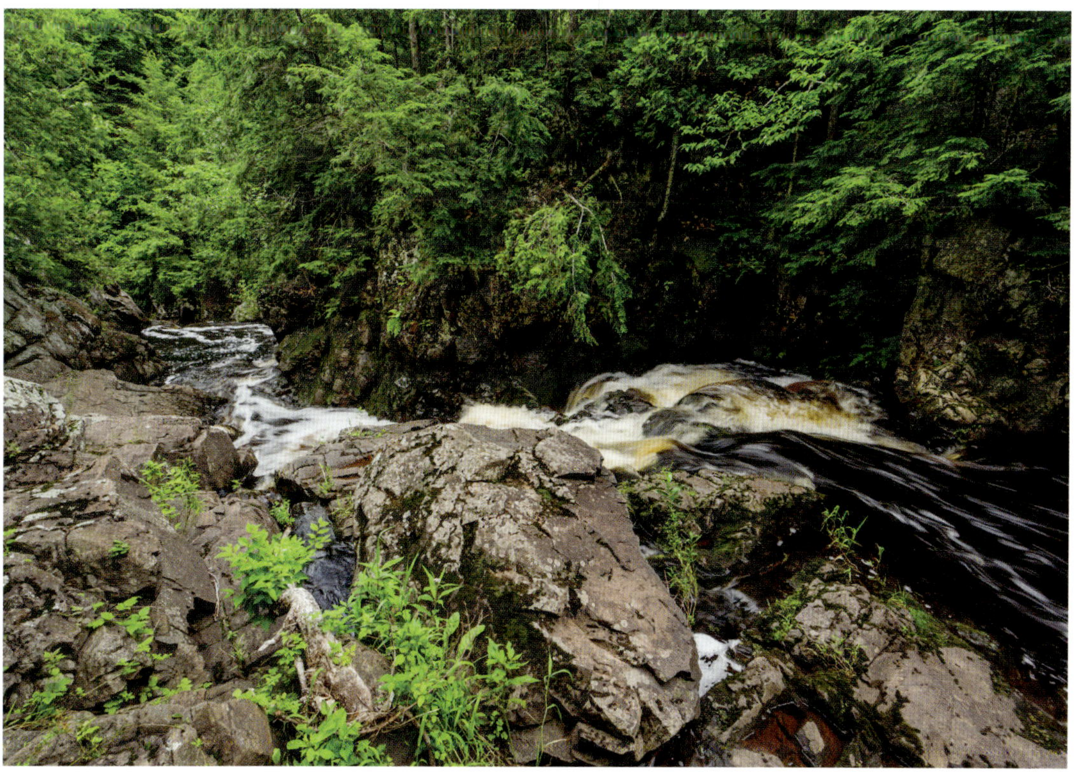

POWDERHORN FALLS - LOWER (POWDER MILL CREEK) Private

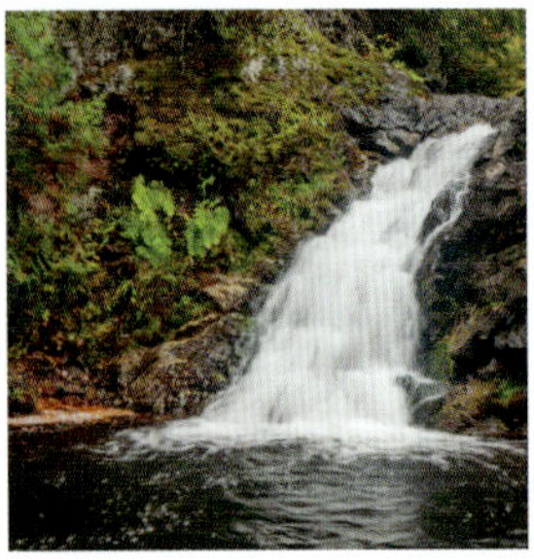

Must See: 8
Height: 20 feet
Time: 25-40 minutes

Driving Information
Signs: None
Road: Secondary
Access: Fairly Easy
4WD: N/A

GPS: N46 30.364 W90 04.913

Hiking Information
Path: Unimproved Footpath
Length: 100 yards
Elev. Change: Moderate
GPS: N/A
Danger: Moderate
WP Boots: Required

The upper falls drop into a nice, little pool then quickly drop over the lower falls. There is no good way to view them from the top. A rope with knots strategically spaced for hand-holds was stretched between two trees; one at the top of the knob and the other near the base. The creek falls on the far side of the knob, with the spill pool tucked into a partially hidden corner and then cutting sharply back to the "footpath". To fully appreciate the lower waterfall, wade across the one to two foot deep creek. Bedrock slopes up steeply on the far side, so walking along the "bank" is not an easy feat.

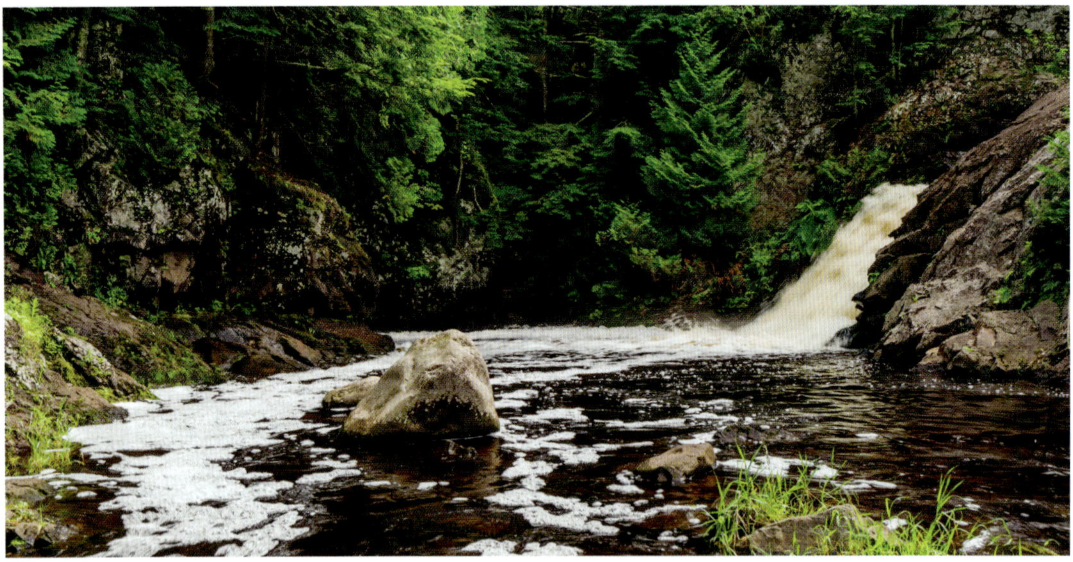

One of the knotted ropes tied between trees at the falls, helpful for climbing!

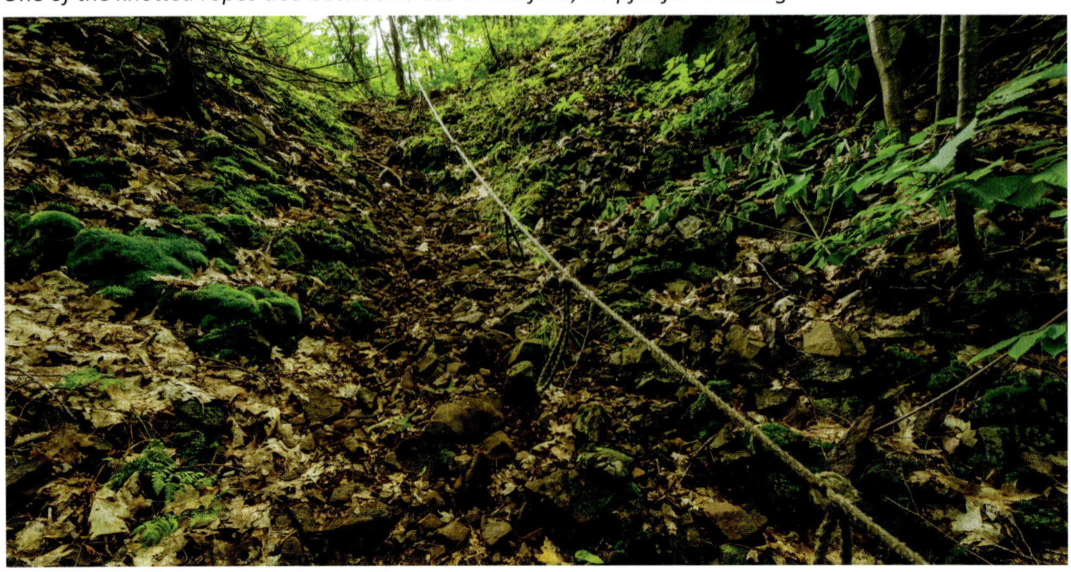

Rocky Forty Falls Hike

Rocky Forty Falls: An intriguing name for a waterfall. Is it a forty foot drop? Are there forty little cascades? Did a landowner have a forty acre parcel that was referred to as the "Rocky Forty" and the name was then applied to a waterfall on that tract? Knowing the terrain in this area, I seriously doubt that there is a forty foot drop! But whatever is the case, I haven't been able to find the waterfall. Coming in from Section 12 Road there is private, posted land. From the north, Beacon Lane dead ends at some rail road tracks. South of the tracks in a long east-west swath is a large swampy area where Siemens Creek and Spring Creek meet. And I haven't found any obvious access points from the east either.

I recently was given some directions to the falls from a fisherman who loved this area decades ago. I will be checking the accuracy of the directions and the availability of access.

ROCKY FORTY FALLS (SIEMENS CREEK)

Private

Must See:	?	GPS:	*N46 30.457 W90 07.238* *Not Confirmed*
Height:	? feet	Hiking Information	
Type:	?	Path:	?
Driving Information		Length:	?
Signs:	?	Elev. Change:	?
Road:	?	GPS:	?
Access:	?	Danger:	?
4WD:	?	WP Boots:	?

There are a couple of drops along Siemens Creek. I have yet to verify...

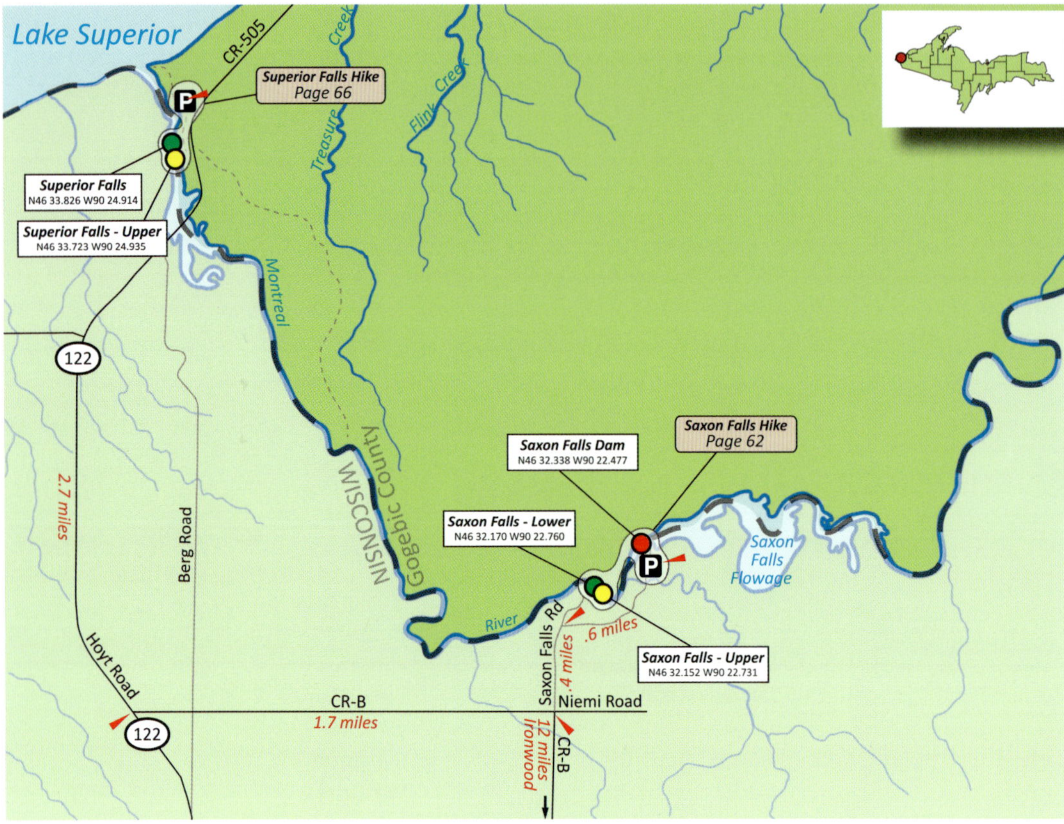

Saxon Falls Hike

I must say that access to Saxon Falls is one of the strangest that I have run across. Saxon Falls Road ends at a small parking area with a portable pit toilet. A heavy chain link fence blocks access to a steep metal stairway that descends many feet to a bridge that spans the river. No trespassing signs make it clear that there is no public access here. However, back down Saxon Falls Road a short way is an access road that heads east to the hydroelectric plant's dam, another port-a-jon and the Saxon Falls Flowage above the dam. Signage here shows exactly how to get to the waterfalls from the Michigan side! Go, MICHIGAN!

Directions: From Ironwood, drive west on US-2 into Wisconsin. Turn right (north) onto CR-B and follow it until it turns to the left. Continue on straight on Saxon Falls Road (dirt road). Follow it for .36 miles. Turn right (east) and follow the dirt access road for .6 miles to the end. Park. The dam is nearby and is easily seen from the parking area. Hike on top of the large steel tube that carries water from the dam to the hydroelectric plant. The tube runs across the river, taking you to the Michigan side of the river and the viewing areas for the waterfalls.

SAXON FALLS DAM (MONTREAL RIVER)

Private

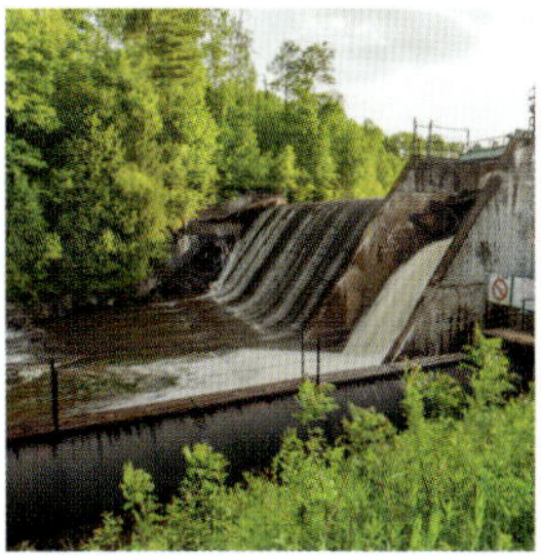

Must See:	3	GPS:	N46 32.338 W90 22.477
Height:	18 feet		
Time:	5-10 minutes	Hiking Information	
		Path:	Improved Footpath
Driving Information		Length:	50 yards
Signs:	None	Elev. Change:	Moderate
Road:	Dirt	GPS:	N/A
Access:	Fairly Easy	Danger:	Slight
4WD:	N/A	WP Boots:	N/A

A gently sloping spillway allows excess water from the hydroelectric plant dam to course down the riverbed and eventually tumble over the falls downstream. What must the set of waterfalls looked like when ALL the water poured over the impressive drops?

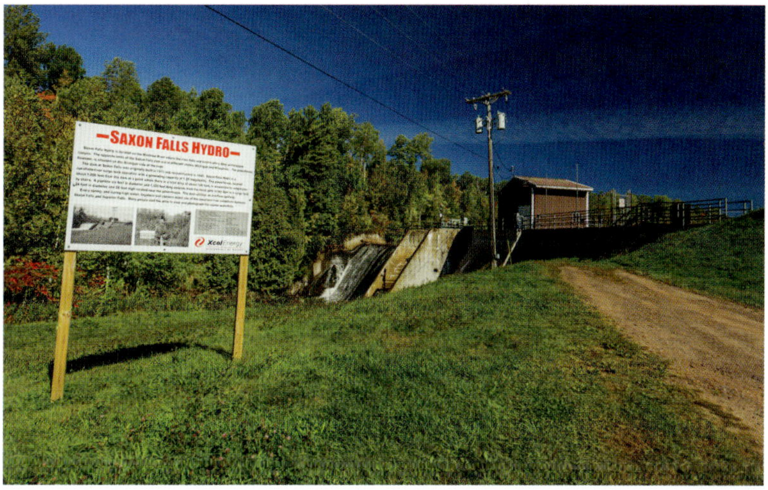

The current dam was built in 1940, although there has been a dam on this site since 1913. A total of 1.25 megawatts of power can be produced when the plant is operating at peak capacity.

Note the wooden catwalk. This is the walkway that bridges the river to Michigan and provides the best viewing of the Saxon waterfalls.

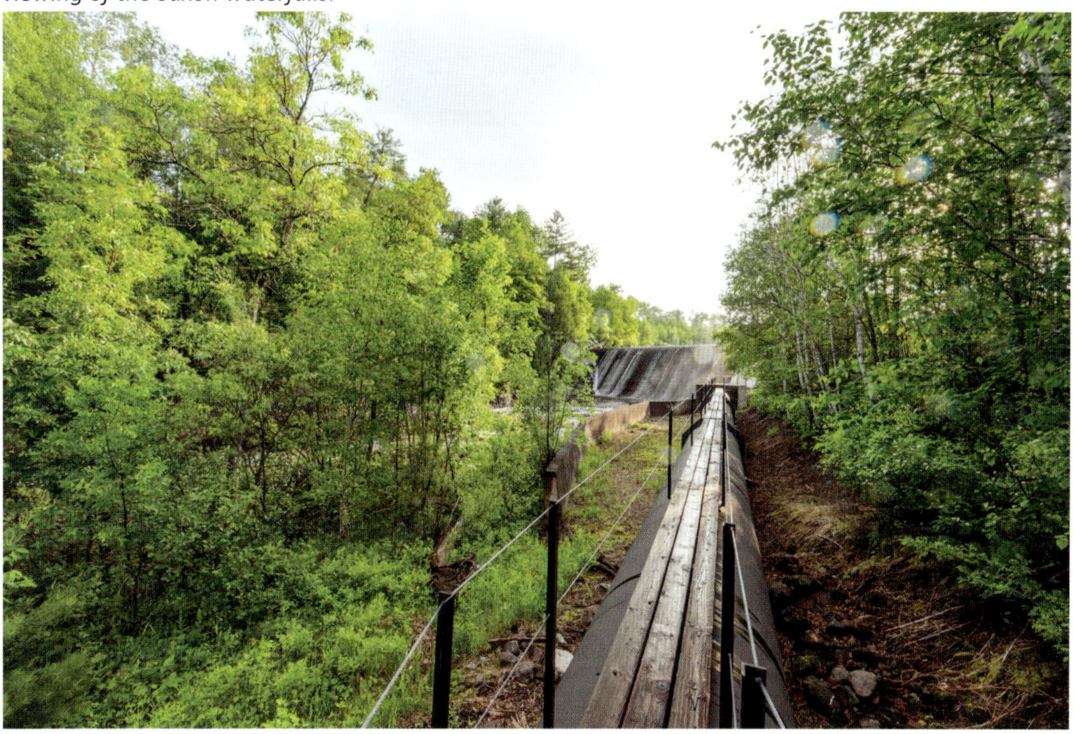

SAXON FALLS - UPPER (MONTREAL RIVER)

Private

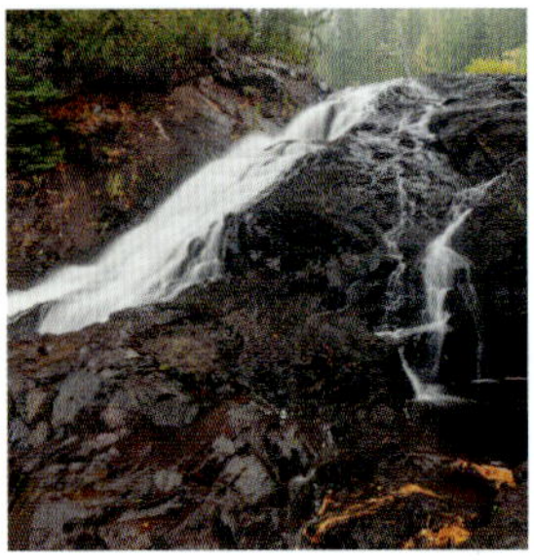

Must See:	6	GPS:	N46 32.152 W90 22.731
Height:	20 feet		
Time:	20 to 40 minutes	Hiking Information	
		Path:	Unimproved Footpath
Driving Information		Length:	.33 miles
Signs:	None	Elev. Change:	Moderate
Road:	Dirt	GPS:	N/A
Access:	Fairly Easy	Danger:	Moderate
4WD:	N/A	WP Boots:	N/A

From the parking area at the dam, hike over to the large steel tube that begins at the dam. A wooden catwalk with cable handrails is fastened to the top of the tube. Use this walkway to cross the river and then...

1) Stay on the catwalk to the surge tank. Climb down the short steel ladder (watch out for hornets - they like to build nests here) and then down a long steel stairway to the power plant. Walk around to the east side of the building. Another short metal ladder mounted to the concrete base leads down to the riverbed. The upper falls can be viewed from the bridge, but the riverbed juts out too far to be able to see them from down at the base of the lower falls.

2) Follow the tube a short distance to an exit. Follow a footpath through the woods to the top of the falls. This path also winds around to the top of the lower falls as well. Be careful as this trail skirts the top of the very deep ravine. There are no guard rails, and the drop could easily be fatal.

I have climbed down to the riverbed from the Wisconsin side above the upper falls. It is a steep climb and I don't really recommend it.

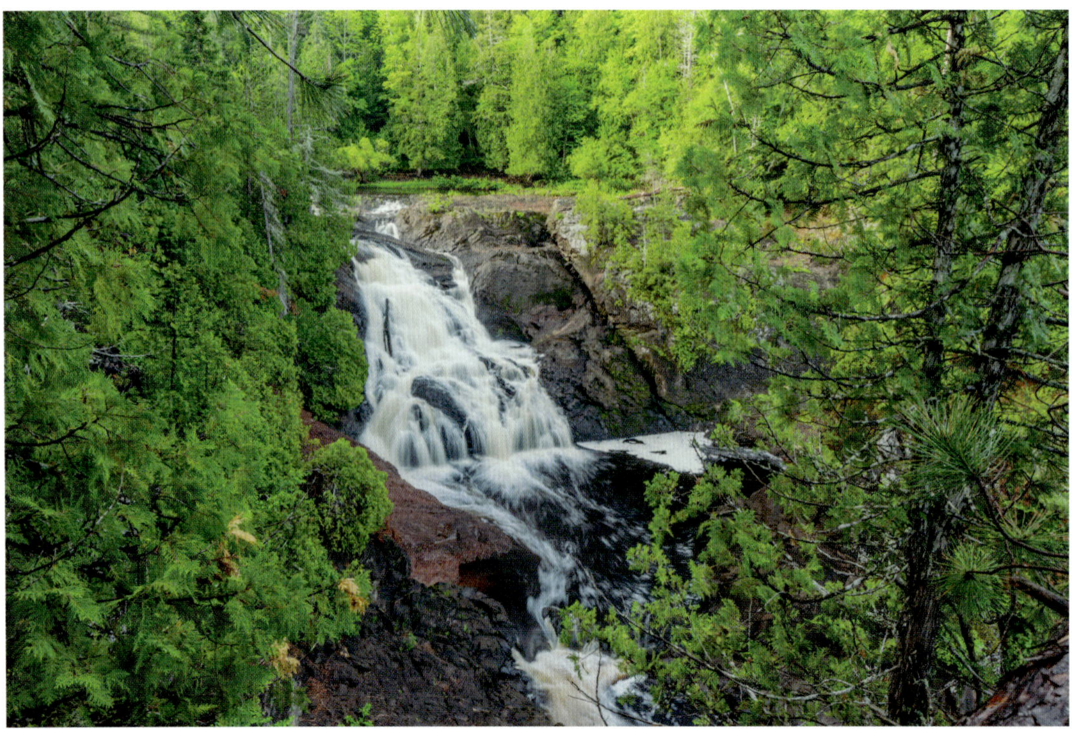

SAXON FALLS - LOWER (MONTREAL RIVER)

Private

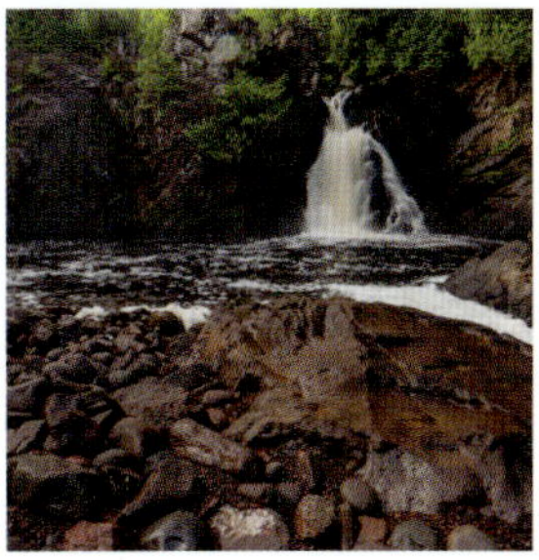

Must See:	7	GPS:	N46 32.170 W90 22.760
Height:	40 feet		
Time:	5 to 15 minutes	Hiking Information	
		Path:	Footpath
Driving Information		Length:	.43 miles
Signs:	None	Elev. Change:	Moderate
Road:	Dirt	GPS:	N/A
Access:	Fairly Easy	Danger:	Moderate
4WD:	N/A	WP Boots:	Helpful

Use the same directions as given for the upper falls on the previous page. This can be viewed from the top of the ravine or from down at the riverbed.

In the spring and after very heavy rains the lower waterfall flows over 3 separate sections of the riverbed. It always flows on the southern side of the river. As the river rises, it also pours over the center section and when the river is at its highest it will also cascade down the northern side as well.

I really recommend viewing this waterfall from the Michigan side. On the Wisconsin side the gorge is VERY deep. Respect it. A wrong step along the edge could be deadly.

The access to the waterfalls from Michigan

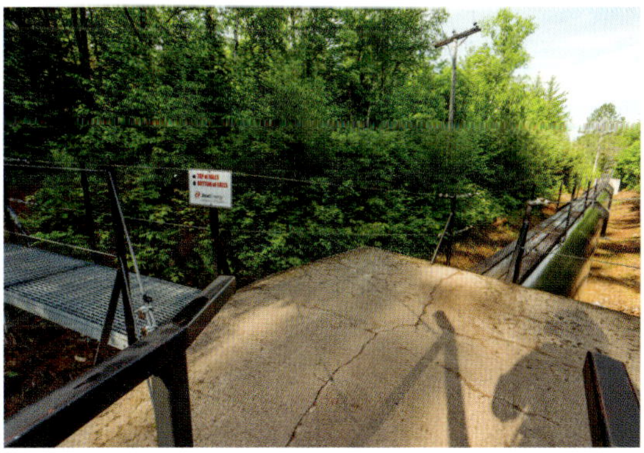

Looking downstream from the base of the fall

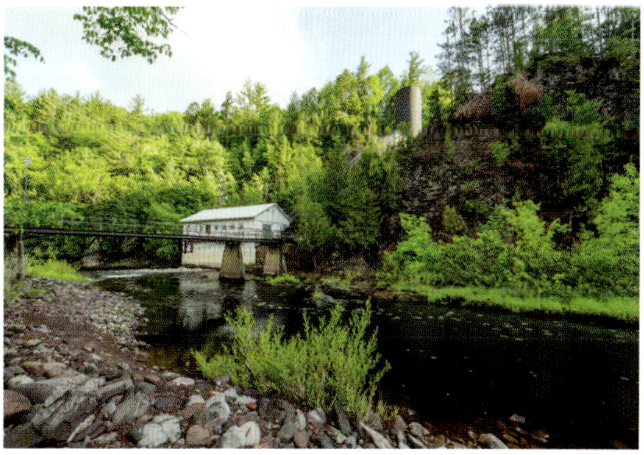

This shot shows the Upper and Lower Falls together

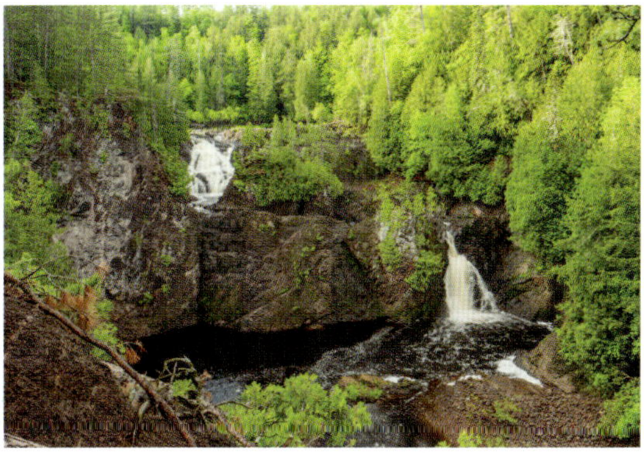

The signage on the Wisconsin side

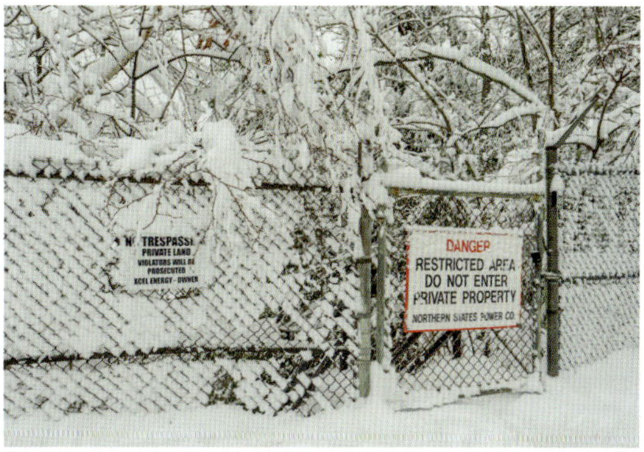

Superior Falls Hike

There is a path that heads back up the road to the right (south). Cross the cable and walk about 100 feet. A foot path wanders through the woods on the right. Follow it along a fence for about 100 feet to a viewing area. To get to the top of the falls, go back on the foot path to the trail. Follow the trail to the right (away from the parking area) for another 100-150 feet to another foot path on the right. The path is steep and slippery when wet, but worth the view!

Directions: From the Saxon Falls area, continue west on CR-B. It will end at CR-122. Turn right (north) and follow CR-122 across the Montreal River and back into the state of Michigan. In about a half mile, a small sign on the left of the road marks Superior Falls. Turn left onto the dirt road and drive to the Power Plant. Park.

SUPERIOR FALLS (MONTREAL RIVER)

Private

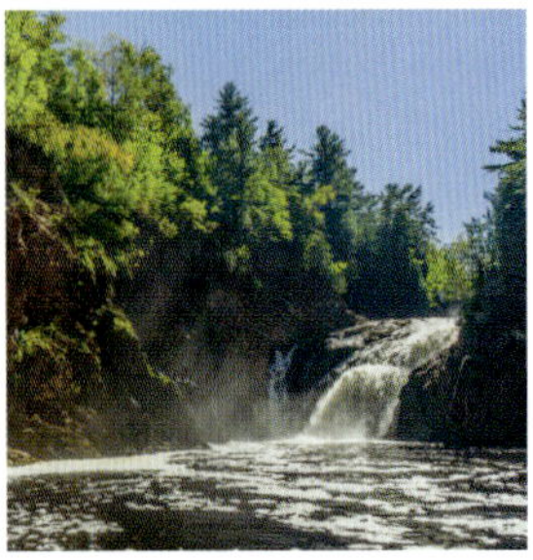

Must See:	8	GPS:	N46 33.826 W90 24.914
Height:	70 feet		
Time:	15 to 30 minutes	Hiking Information	
		Path:	Unimproved Footpath
Driving Information		Length:	100 yards
Signs:	Small Sign by Road	Elev. Change:	Moderate
Road:	Dirt	GPS:	N/A
Access:	Fairly Easy	Danger:	Moderate
4WD:	N/A	WP Boots:	N/A

The waterfall slides into a channel that feeds directly into Lake Superior just a couple hundred yards down river. The upper falls can just be seen in the picture below. The thumbnail picture was taken from the river's edge while the lower shot was from the top of the gorge.

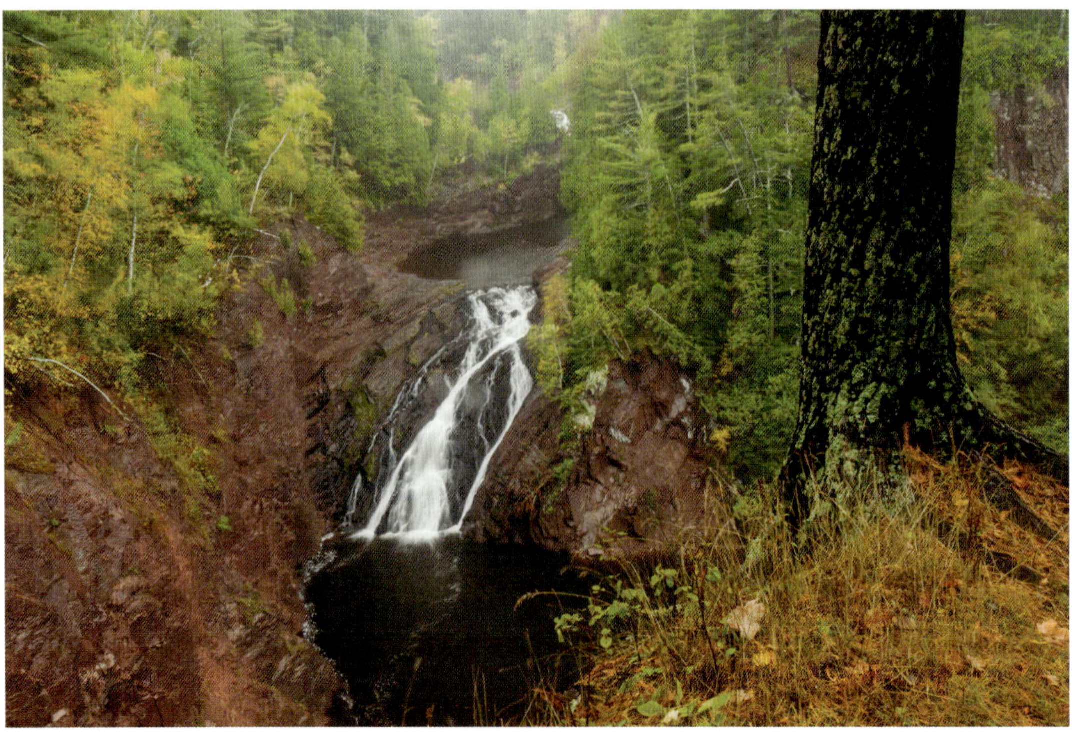

SUPERIOR FALLS - UPPER (MONTREAL RIVER)

Private

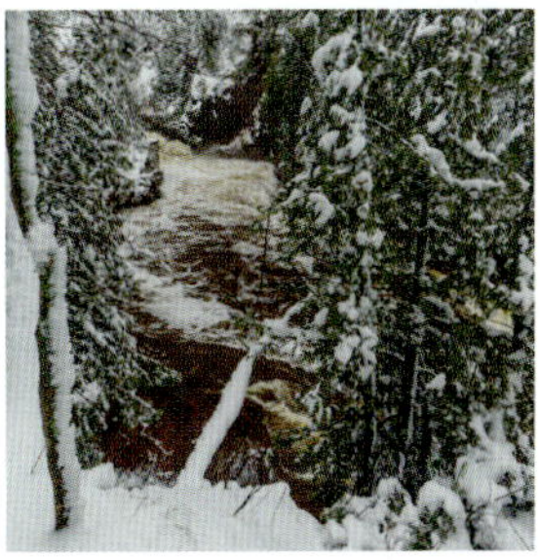

Must See:	6	GPS:	N46 33.723 W90 24.935
Height:	20 feet		
Time:	20 to 40 minutes	**Hiking Information**	
		Path:	Unimproved Footpath
Driving Information		Length:	200 yards
Signs:	Small Sign by Road	Elev. Change:	Increased and steep
Road:	Dirt	GPS:	N/A
Access:	Fairly Easy	Danger:	Moderate
4WD:	N/A	WP Boots:	N/A

From the fence overlook of the lower falls follow a path up river. It runs along a 2-track and then dives down the fairly steep hillside to a vantage point. These pictures were taken from that location. If you turn and look downstream, Lake Superior can be seen in the distance.

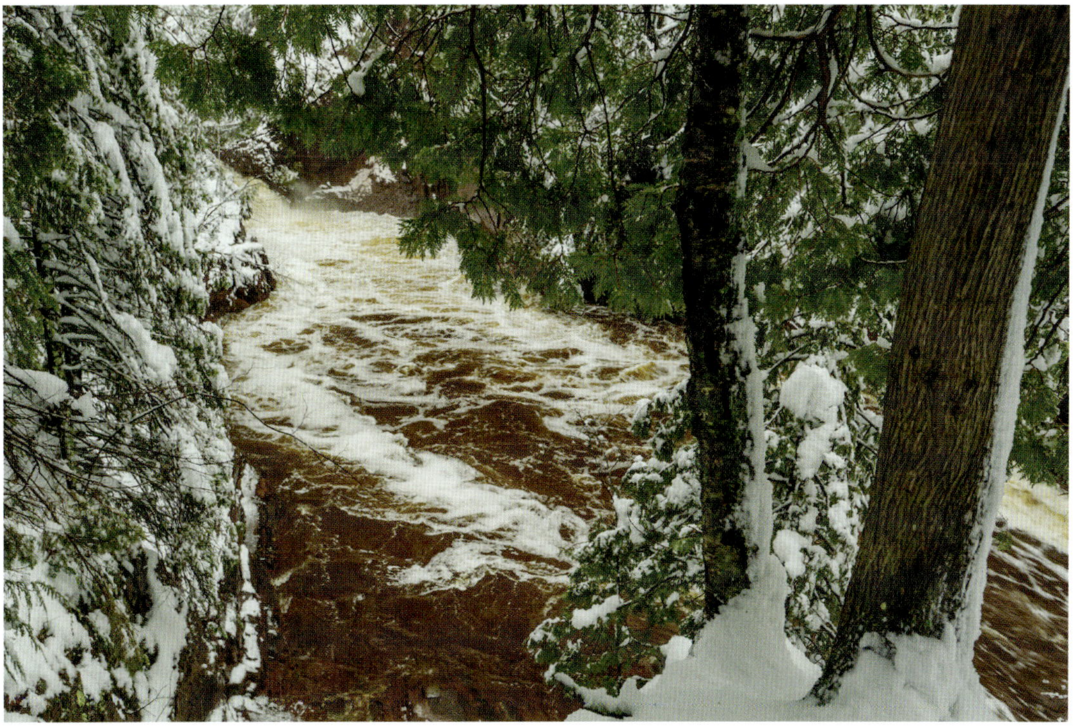

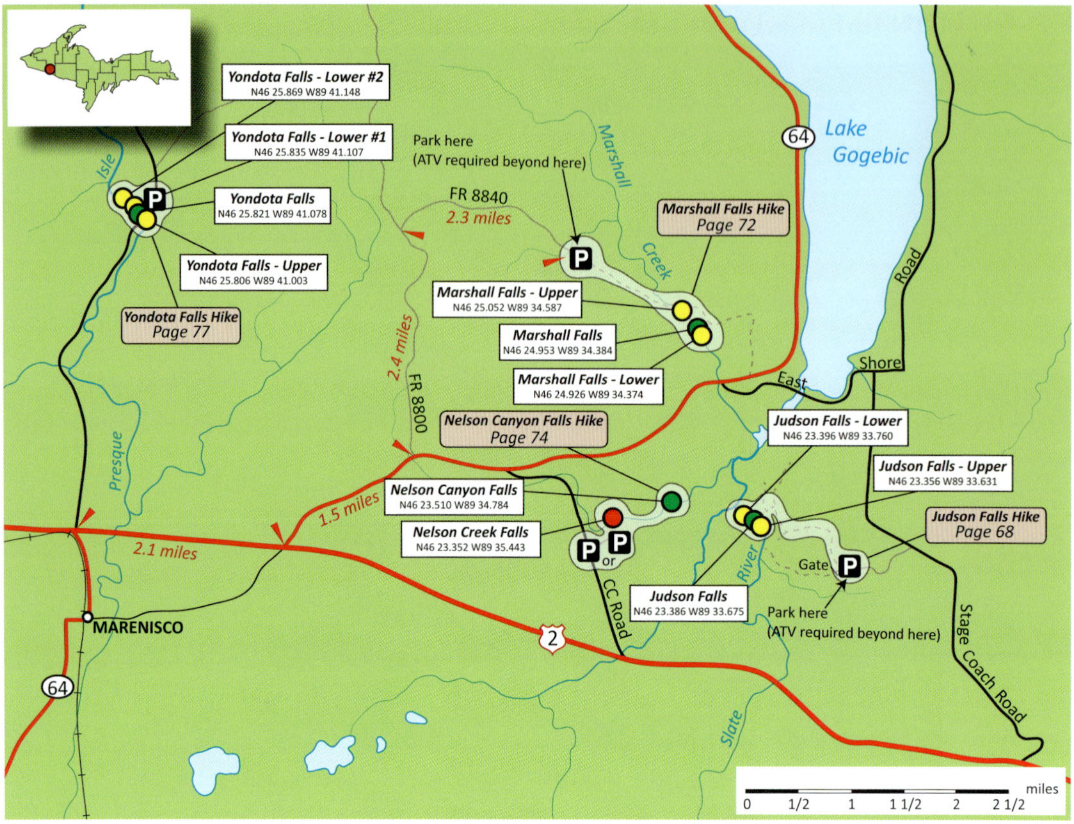

Judson Falls Hike

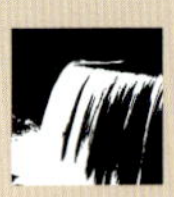

Prepare for a rugged hike! This is in keeping with the historical context of the area. The eastern shore of Lake Gogebic, one of Michigan's largest inland lakes, didn't begin to be developed until the 1960's. The last stagecoach robbery recorded in US history took place on Stage Coach Road on August 16, 1889. It fits that there should be a wild, untamed feel here near the headwaters of the Ontonagon and Presque Isle Rivers.

Judson Falls - Upper: This is a three-tiered drop. It's nicely displayed with moss and ferns growing amongst the cascades.

Judson Falls: This classic, nearly vertical drop has multiple cascades frothing white into a large spill pool ringed with rocks of basalt. The main falls are ten feet wide with a smaller, possibly seasonal one foot wide fall on the right side. Ancient cedar trees overlook the falls, conforming to the solid rock out of which it appears they are growing.

Judson Falls - Lower: This is a nine foot drop scattered over six smaller drops. The river drops amongst misshapen moss-covered exposed bedrock. The Slate River runs through a mature forest with very little human interaction. Enjoy the primitive surroundings!

Directions: Turn north on Stagecoach Road off of US-2. In 2.8 miles turn left (southwest) onto dirt road (N46 23.176 W89 31.801). This requires an ATV. Plan on hiking 2 miles in otherwise. In .98 miles there is a fork in the road. The left hand trail is gated. Take the right trail at N46 23.012 W89 32.605. Turn right at N46 23.292 W89 33.365. Turn hard left at N46 23.358 W89 33.488. Turn left at N46 23.383 W89 33.581. This will take you to the river and the falls.

JUDSON FALLS - UPPER (SLATE RIVER)

Private

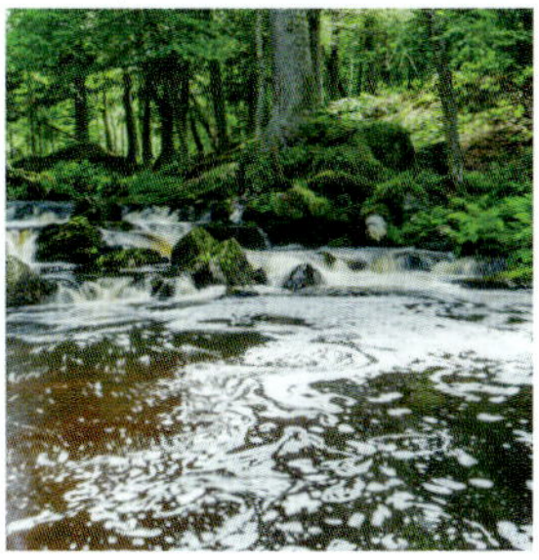

Must See:	6	GPS:	N46 23.356 W89 33.631
Height:	5 feet		
Time:	10-20 minutes	Hiking Information	
		Path:	None
Driving Information		Length:	100 yards
Signs:	None	Elev. Change:	Slight
Road:	ATV trail	GPS:	Required
Access:	Very difficult	Danger:	Moderate
4WD:	ATV required	WP Boots:	Recommended

I was surprised to find a trail that led all the way to Judson Falls. Waterfalls in the middle of nowhere often require a lot of legwork, but I was able to drive my ORV nearly to the river! It was obvious that others had done the same, but not often.

Rugged terrain, rushing water, flitting butterflies, green moss, earthy smells, lichen covered rocks, gnarled cedars: surrounded by nature, there is a peace and a calm that flows from the solitude of this place. Take time to absorb the beauty. Listen to the birds as they call overhead. Observe the delicate fiddle heads as they slowly grow into fanned out ferns. Revel in the order and variety of creation.

The upper falls are not far upstream from the end of the ATV trail. The obvious path heads over to Judson Falls. Just follow the river 100 yards the opposite way to see this small set of drops.

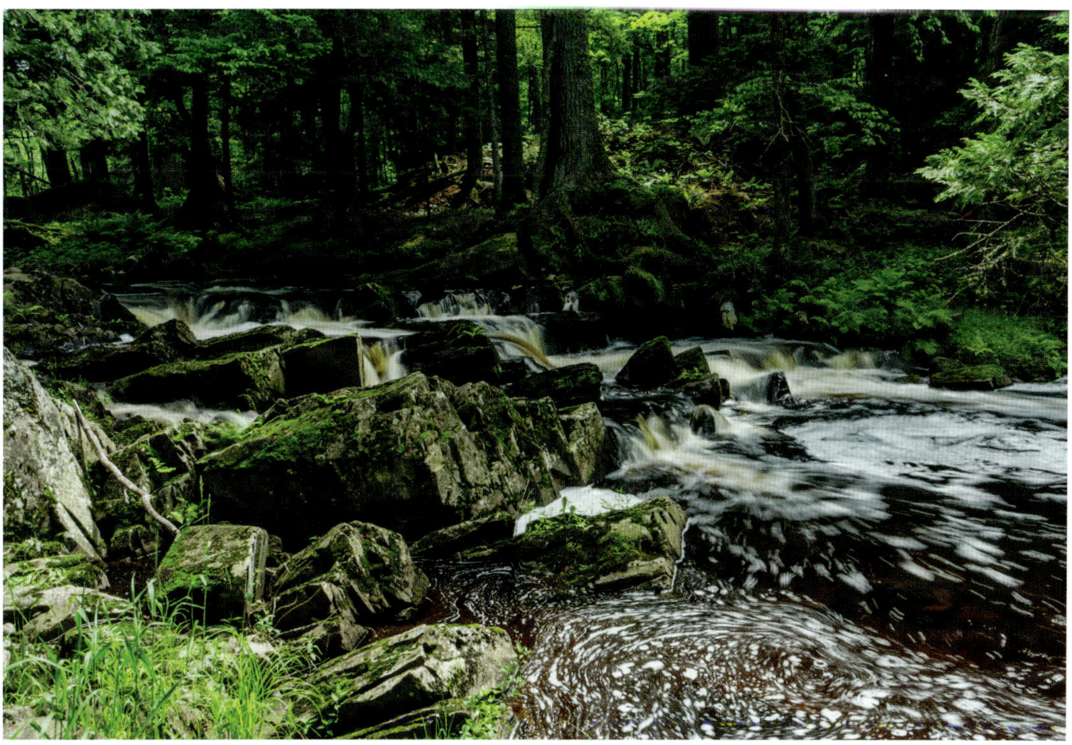

JUDSON FALLS (SLATE RIVER)

Private

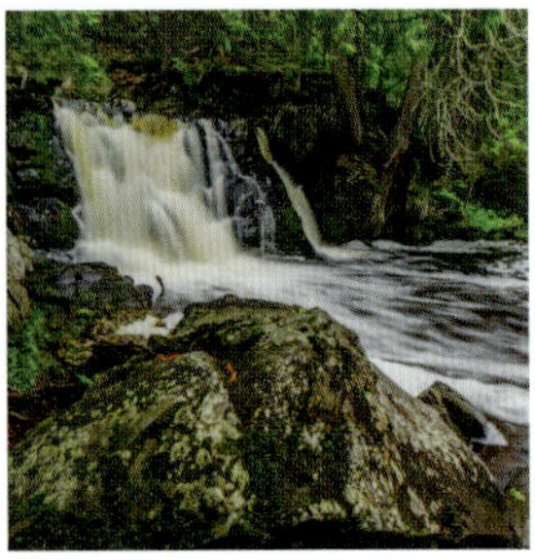

Must See:	9	GPS:	N46 23.386 W89 33.675
Height:	12 feet		
Time:	15-30 minutes	Hiking Information	
		Path:	None
Driving Information		Length:	100 yards
Signs:	None	Elev. Change:	Slight
Road:	ATV trail	GPS:	Required
Access:	Very difficult	Danger:	Moderate
4WD:	ATV required	WP Boots:	Recommended

Expectations are funny things. I really didn't know what to expect at Judson Falls. I had never seen a picture of it. For all I knew, it was a little ripple in the river! What an unexpected blessing to see this wonderful waterfall cascading down a mostly vertical face through a narrow channel and then bursting down into a widened spill pool that then turned and wound its way through scattered rocks in the shallow riverbed.

Although the terrain is rugged, and the trails getting out here are muddy, rutted and overgrown, this is a locally popular destination, and with good cause! The beauty of this waterfall is a magnet, drawing adventurous souls back, time and time again.

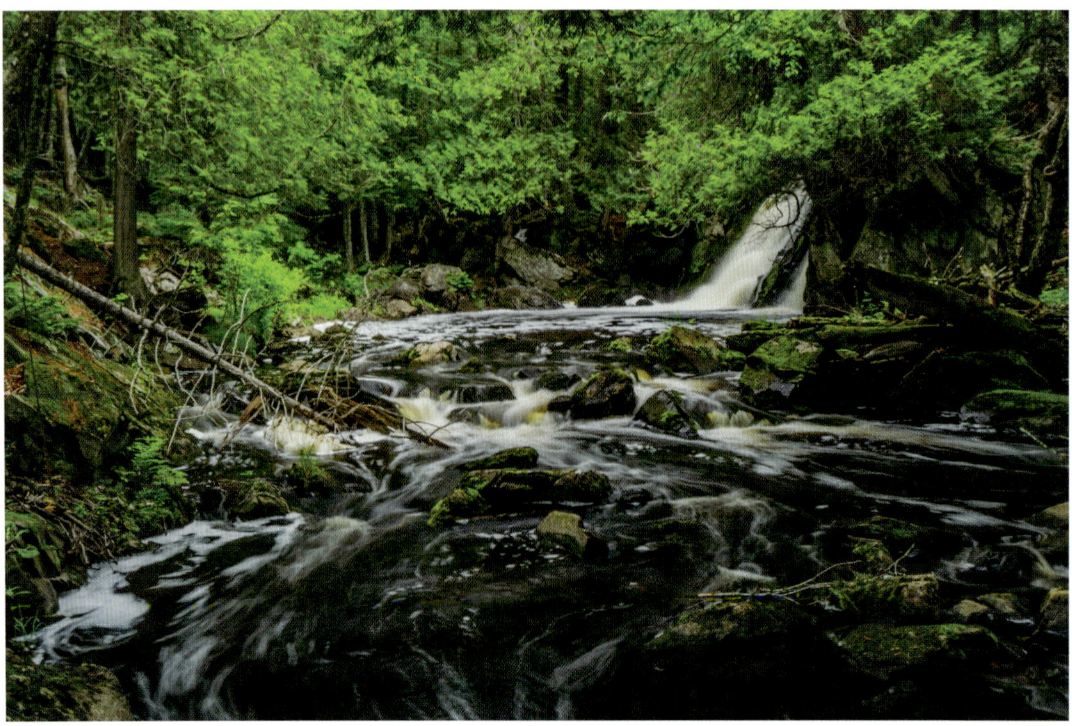

JUDSON FALLS - LOWER (SLATE RIVER)

Private

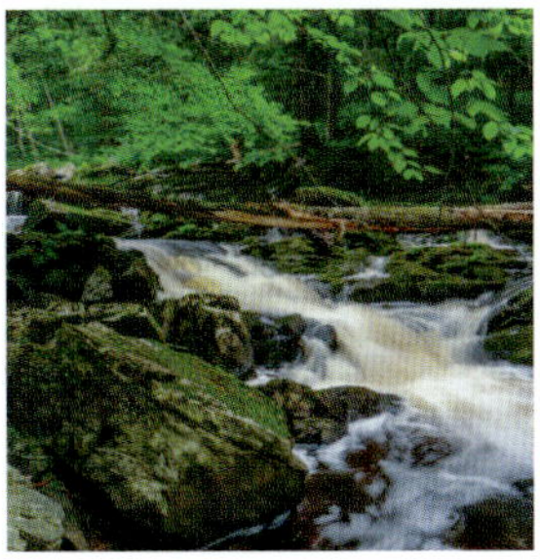

Must See:	5	GPS:	N46 23.396 W89 33.760
Height:	9 feet		
Time:	25-40 minutes	Hiking Information	
		Path:	None
Driving Information		Length:	300 yards
Signs:	None	Elev. Change:	Moderate
Road:	ATV trail	GPS:	Required
Access:	Very difficult	Danger:	Moderate
4WD:	ATV required	WP Boots:	Recommended

Below the spill pool at Judson Falls, the river narrows and picks up speed. Follow it down river for a couple of hundred yards to the lower falls. The river is easily followed. So many of the rivers with waterfalls flow through gorges or steep walled canyons. It's a treat to be able to walk with relative ease along this section of the Slate River. (Don't confuse this with the Slate River in Baraga County.)

I saw the most interesting butterflies flying around and landing on low lying greenery. Perhaps it was mating season. Whatever the case, there was an abundance of iridescent colored wings opening and closing. I wish now that I had taken some photos of them, but at the time I was more interested in the waterfalls!

A faint trail along the river suggests that fishermen may work this area. Roots, rocks and vegetation underfoot require maintaining a vigilant eye on the ground.

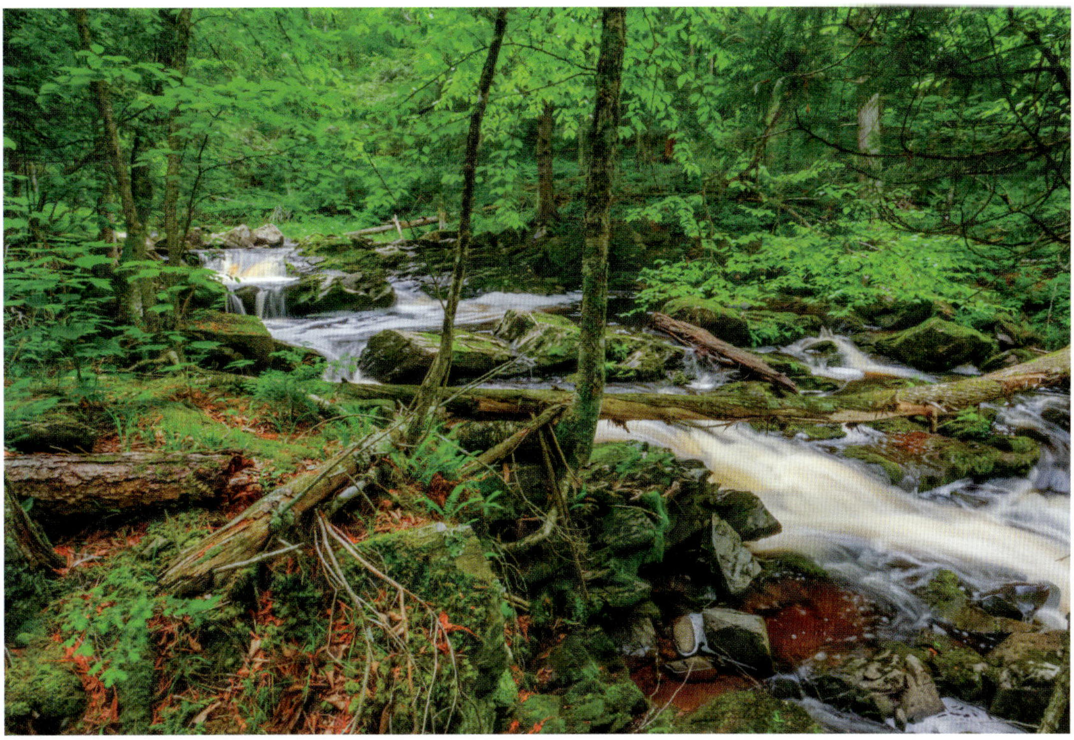

Marshall Falls Hike

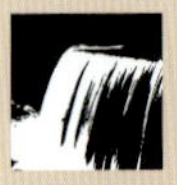

Marshall Falls - Upper: It's not large, but the four foot drop is couched in a small rocky alcove with a quiet spill pool at its base - a soothing place for contemplation.

Marshall Falls: Marshall Falls consists of two drops: first an eight foot cascade followed by a four foot drop. This is not a place for children. The terrain is quite rugged. Look for the upthrust of a large plate of rock just downstream from here.

Marshall Falls - Lower: The final drop, before Marshall Creek levels out, pours over solid bedrock in a series of small drops and slides.

Directions: Follow M-64 south along Lake Gogebic. At the southern end of the lake the road sweeps to the west. About a mile later there is a dirt road to the right (northwest). Follow it to the north and a bit west for 1.0 mile. Park here at the "T". Walk about .3 miles down the snowmobile trail (2-track) to the east. When it crosses the bridge, don't cross the bridge. Walk straight ahead to the upper falls. Head back to the bridge. Cross it and follow the eastern side of the creek down river to Marshall Falls and the lower falls.

MARSHALL FALLS - UPPER (MARSHALL CREEK)

Private

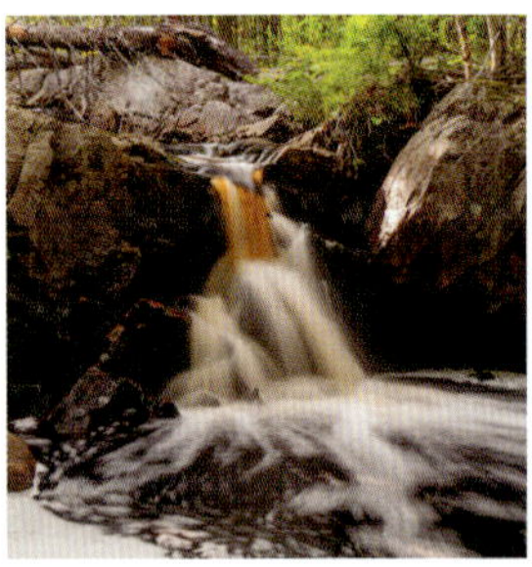

Must See:	4	GPS:	N46 25.052 W89 34.587
Height:	4 feet		
Time:	20 to 40 minutes	Hiking Information	
		Path:	2-track then none
Driving Information		Length:	.4 miles
Signs:	None	Elev. Change:	Moderate
Road:	Dirt	GPS:	Required
Access:	Difficult	Danger:	Moderate
4WD:	Recommended	WP Boots:	Recommended

A GPS is recommended for the Marshall set of waterfalls. They are located in a remote tract of land and there is the potential of becoming disoriented and lost.

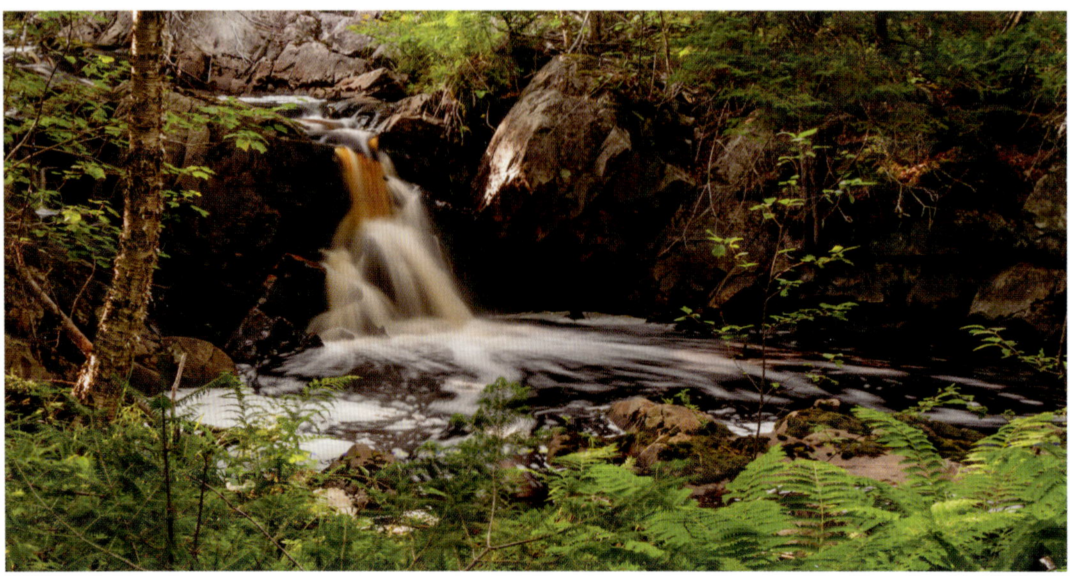

MARSHALL FALLS (MARSHALL CREEK)

Private

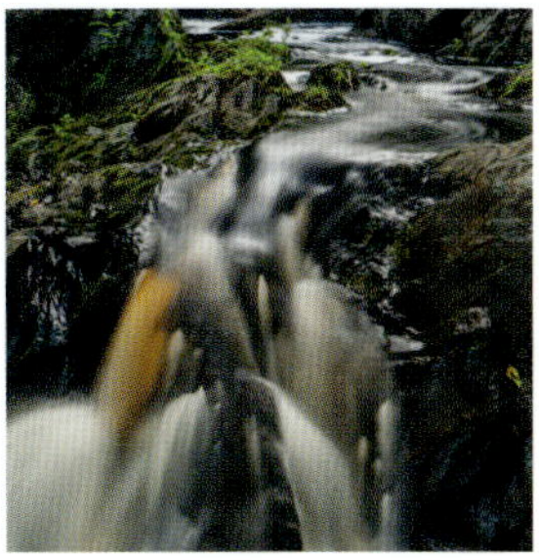

Must See:	7	GPS:	N46 24.953 W89 34.384
Height:	12 feet		
Time:	40 to 60 minutes	Hiking Information	
		Path:	2-track then none
Driving Information		Length:	.66 miles
Signs:	None	Elev. Change:	Moderate
Road:	Dirt	GPS:	Required
Access:	Difficult	Danger:	Moderate
4WD:	Recommended	WP Boots:	Recommended

There is always a sense of excitement mixed with apprehension when getting close to where a waterfall is "supposed to be". Too often I have been engaged in wild goose chases, with either no waterfall anywhere in the area, or else up to 1/2 mile away from the target destination. Sometimes the "waterfall" is nothing more that some aggravated ripples in the water. Other times they are on obviously private property with "No Trespassing" signs posted. Let me tell you how the search for Marshall Falls transpired.

It was August 7, 2010. It had been a long day of waterfall hunting. I had started at the western end of Gogebic County, taking pictures of Interstate, the upper falls and Peterson Falls between 8:51 and 9:48 AM. From there I travelled to Maple Creek and hiked from Manakiki Falls to Maple Creek Falls #9, taking about 2 hours to document those 11 waterfalls (12:50 -2:56 PM). Next I visited Rootbeer Falls between 4:00 and 4:03. Gabbro Falls and its lower brother were next between 4:34 and 4:54. I had already been to 18 waterfalls. Traveling east I really wanted to find Marshall Falls. It had been on my to-do list for some time and now I was at Marshall Creek!

Not only was I fatigued, but mosquitoes were out in force. Oh, and it was soon going to be dark. Driving as far as I dared with my truck down deteriorating 2-tracks, I finally parked when the trail ahead looked like a snowmobile trail. Not daring to risk getting stuck I struck out on foot. After hiking nearly a 1/2 mile I found a small drop. I took some pictures between 7:00 and 7:02 PM. I wasn't sure if this was Marshall Falls. I was 1/4 mile upstream from where I thought Marshall Falls was supposed to be so I plunged on. No trail, and sometimes rugged terrain slowed the progress. But finally, success! The creek dropped down into a lower grade. I had to get to the base of the falls for some shots, but it was tricky going with very uneven footing and slippery rocks throughout the descent. The creek twisted and fell in an interesting S-curve as it started to run down to the lower grade. I took several pictures between 7:15 and 7:16, then headed further down. There was an obvious lower fall. After taking a shot of that drop at 7:20, I headed back up to Marshall Falls for some wider shots. I took another 5 pictures between 7:30 and 7:32. By now I was happy to head back to the truck and drive over to L'Anse for dinner!

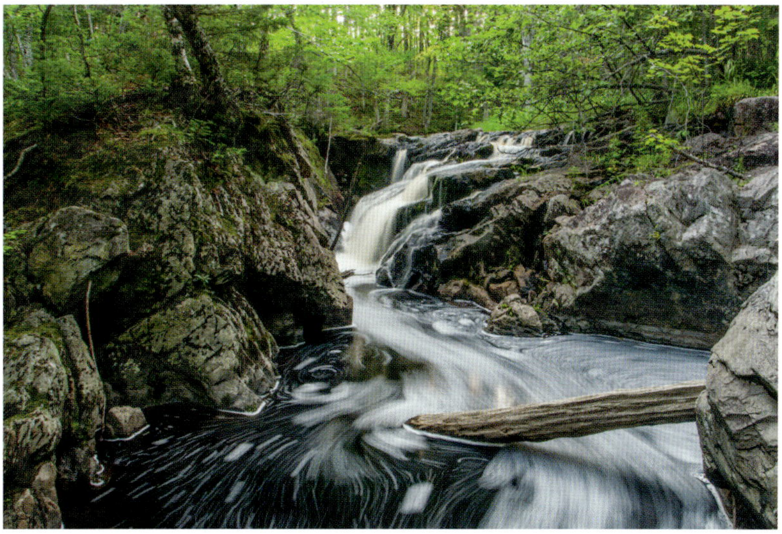

MARSHALL FALLS - LOWER (MARSHALL CREEK)

Private

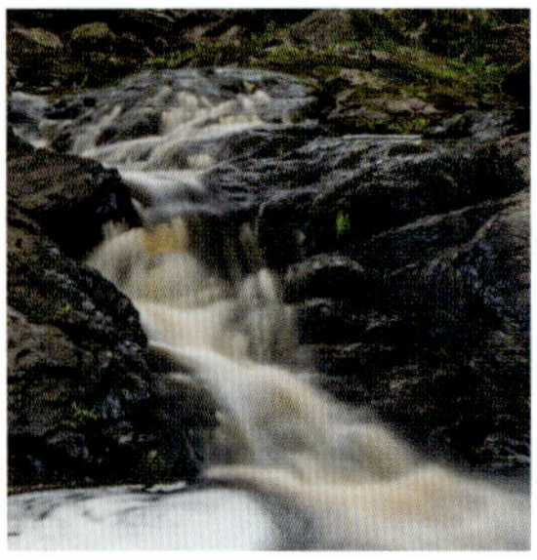

Must See:	6	GPS:	N46 24.926 W89 34.374
Height:	8 feet		
Time:	45 to 70 minutes	**Hiking Information**	
		Path:	2-track then none
Driving Information		Length:	.69 miles
Signs:	None	Elev. Change:	Moderate
Road:	Dirt	GPS:	Required
Access:	Difficult	Danger:	Moderate
4WD:	Recommended	WP Boots:	Recommended

Marshall Creek drops with twists and turns down into a lower plateau. Just before it flattens out is the lower falls. Be careful in climbing down from up above. There isn't a cliff, but near the creek are steep, angled boulders and chunks of bedrock. These woods are rarely visited, and a twisted ankle would make for a very bad day!

Nelson Canyon Falls Hike

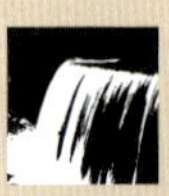

Nelson Canyon Falls: Canyon Falls has been described as the "Grand Canyon of Michigan". If so, Nelson Canyon Falls must be a close runner-up! Twenty to thirty foot sheer rock walls extend for about 100 yards . There are multiple cascades and drops its entire length. As the river enters the canyon, it divides into thirds and drops 15' to the canyon floor. The right-hand third pours onto an outstretched slab of rock, sending out a fan of water to the spill pool below.

Directions: West of Lake Gogebic, turn onto CC Road. This is a shortcut between M-64 and US-2. Go either 1.3 miles south of M-64 or 1.2 mile north of US-2. Either park off the road near the 2-track that heads east and hike down the trail, or, if you have a vehicle that has good clearance and the trail doesn't look too muddy, follow the 2-track until it fades (about .2 miles from CC Road). This is where it gets a bit tricky. There is a VERY FAINT path that continues. As of this writing, the path had sporadically placed faded ribbons tied to trees along it. Try to stay on this trail. If not, bushwack over to Nelson Creek Falls - you need a GPS for this. From Nelson Creek Falls follow the continuing faint footpath that parallels the creek downstream to Nelson Canyon Falls. There is a smaller but very beautiful canyon to be enjoyed along the way.

NELSON CREEK FALLS (NELSON CREEK)

Private

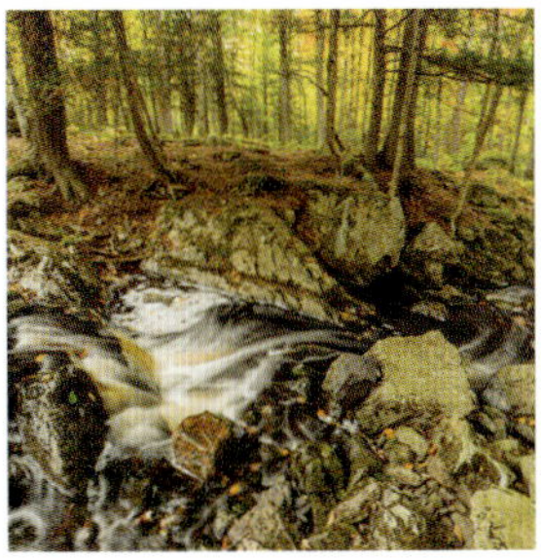

Must See:	3	GPS:	N46 23.352 W89 35.443
Height:	4 feet	Hiking Information	
Time:	20 to 40 minutes	Path:	VERY FAINT
		Length:	.12 to .32 miles
Driving Information		Elev. Change:	Slight
Signs:	None	GPS:	Required
Road:	Secondary	Danger:	Moderate
Access:	Somewhat difficult	WP Boots:	Recommended
4WD:	N/A		

The faint trail from the road intersects the creek here. The creek, filled with small roundish stones suddenly enters a short section of gray-green heavily fractured bedrock. Several small cascades drop the creek level by 4 feet along a 30 foot section of the creek. The angular bedrock on the far side supports birch trees, their root structure contributing to the fracturing.

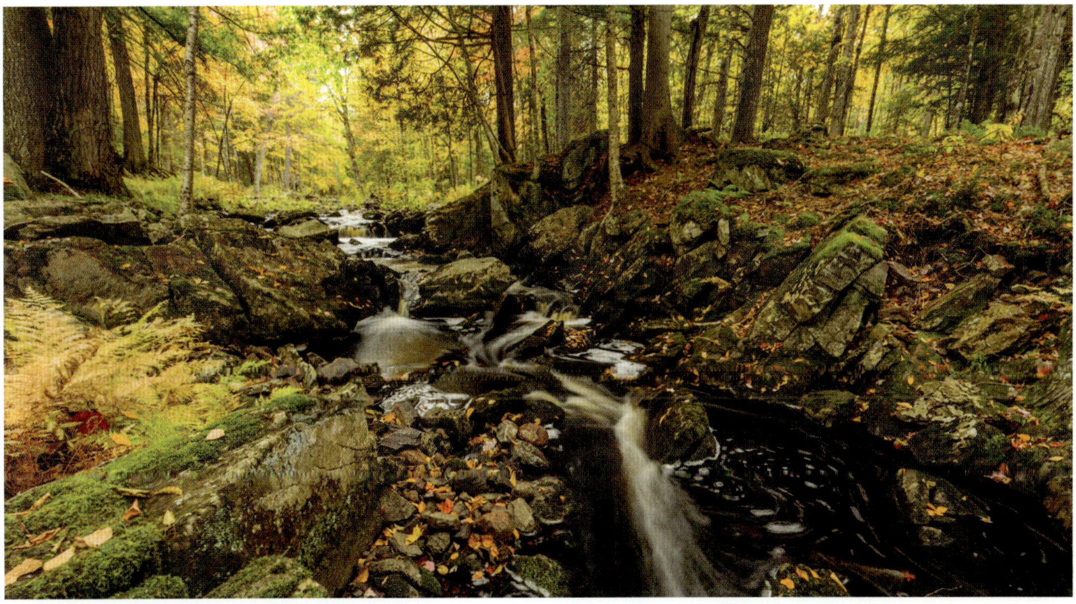

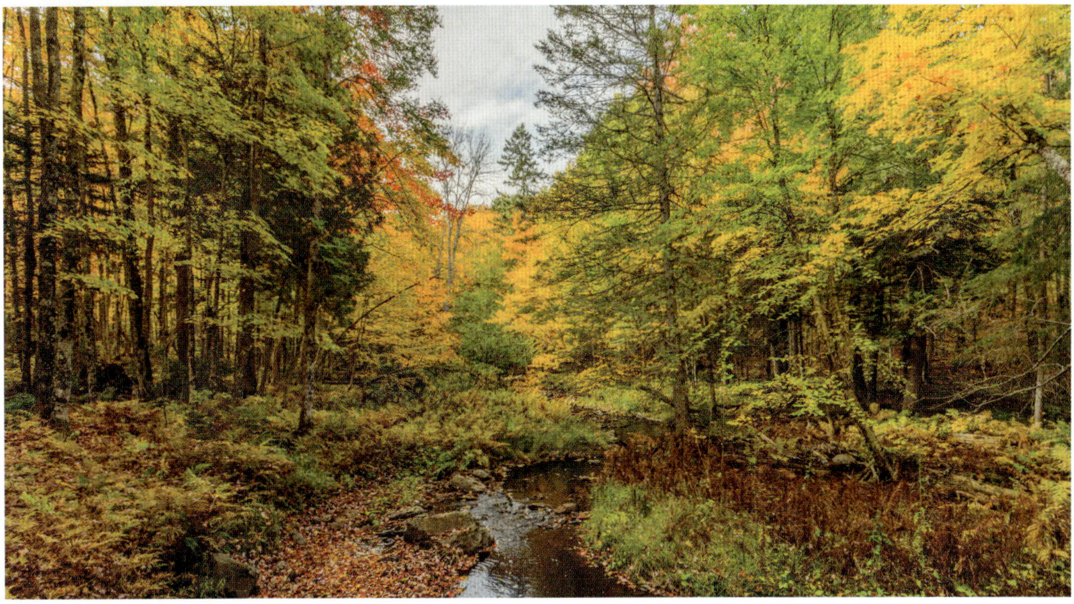

NELSON CANYON FALLS (NELSON CREEK)

Private

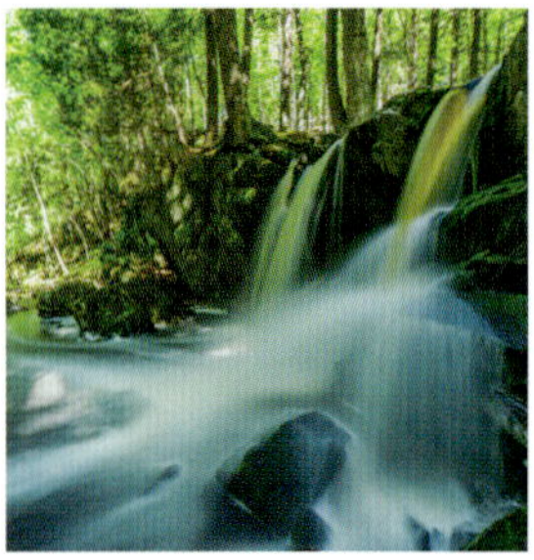

Must See:	9	GPS:	N46 23.510 W89 34.784
Height:	15 feet		
Time:	1.5 to 2 hours	Hiking Information	
		Path:	VERY FAINT
Driving Information		Length:	.64 to .92 miles
Signs:	None	Elev. Change:	Slight
Road:	Secondary	GPS:	Required
Access:	Somewhat difficult	Danger:	Moderate
4WD:	N/A	WP Boots:	Recommended

Nelson Creek meanders to the east-northeast for about a mile after the falls before merging with the Slate River just before an elongated inlet on Lake Gogebic. Also entering Lake Gogebic nearby is Marshall Creek. The Marshall Falls, Judson Falls and Nelson Canyon Falls all occur in this wild land.

The top of the falls

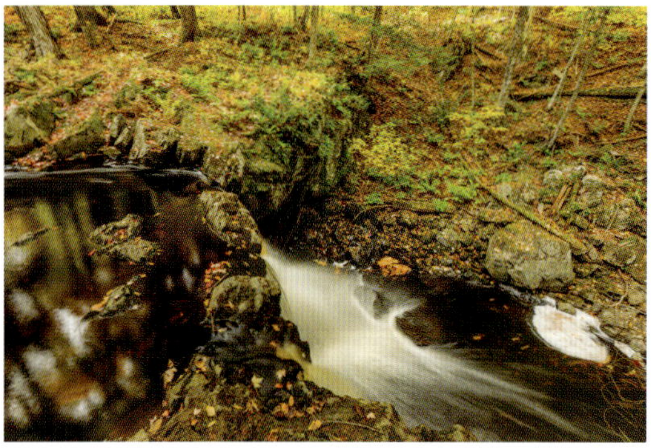

Looking up the canyon

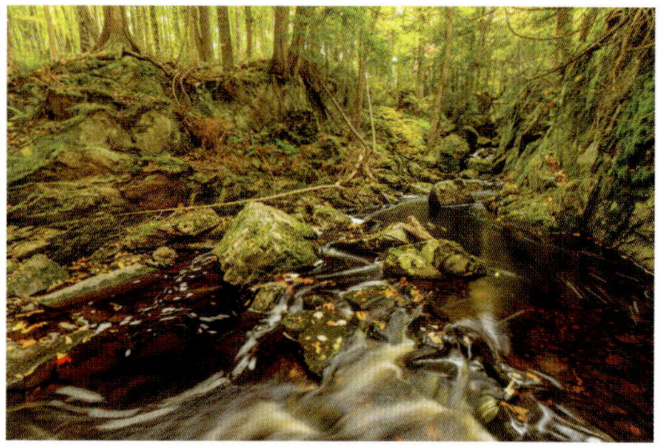

Viewing the falls from the other side of the canyon

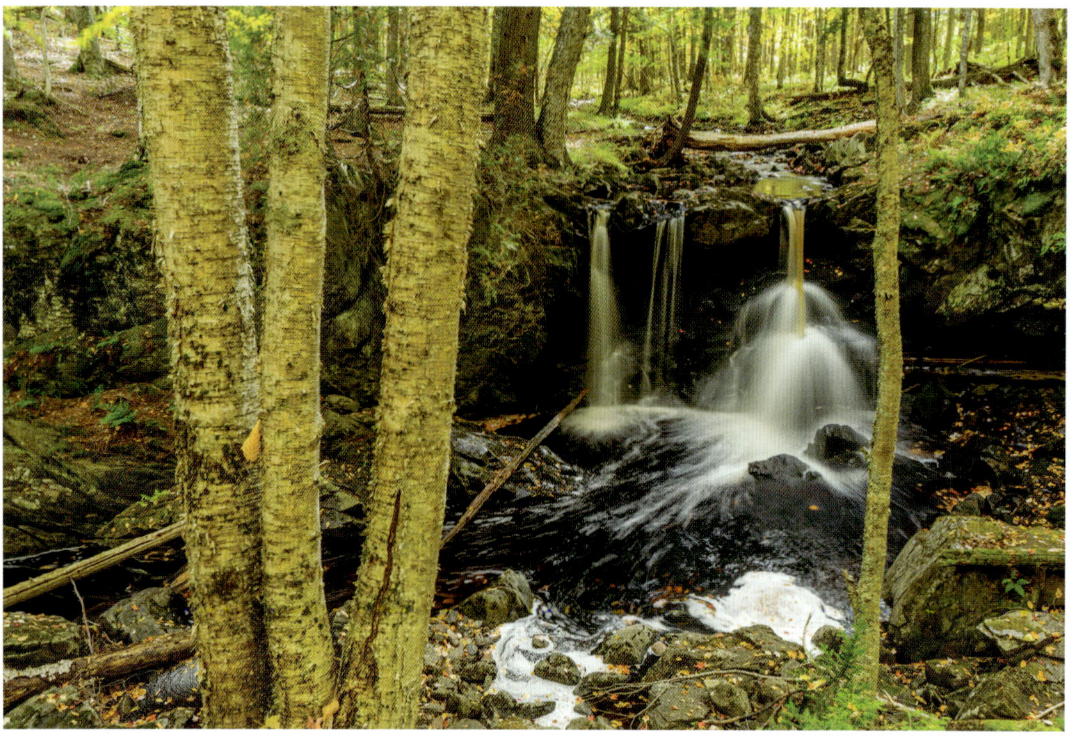

Yondota Falls Hike

Yondota Falls - Upper: A small precursor to Yondota Falls is found above the oval shaped pool above Yondota Falls. It is easy to miss this waterfall. Follow the faint footpath off of the NCT soon after leaving the parking lot to get here.

Yondota Falls: A footpath leads to an outcropping at the top of the falls. Yondota Falls is a nice, clean plunge bordered by basalt masses.

Yondota Falls - Lower #1: This jumbled set of drops is not a well defined waterfall, but rather a series of scattered cascading falls. The path from the road comes directly here. Waterproof boots are recommended.

Yondota Falls - Lower #2: Lower #2 is very similar to Lower #1. This is a series of drops over and around boulders and bedrock.

Directions: At Marenisco, turn north onto County Road 105 from US-2. In 3.3 miles a bridge spans Presque Isle River. Park on the far side of the bridge. The NCT runs along the river here. Spurs off of the trail need to be taken to get to the Upper Falls, Yondota Falls, and Lower #2. There is a lot of uneven terrain along this series of waterfalls. Use caution.

YONDOTA FALLS - UPPER (PRESQUE ISLE RIVER)

Private

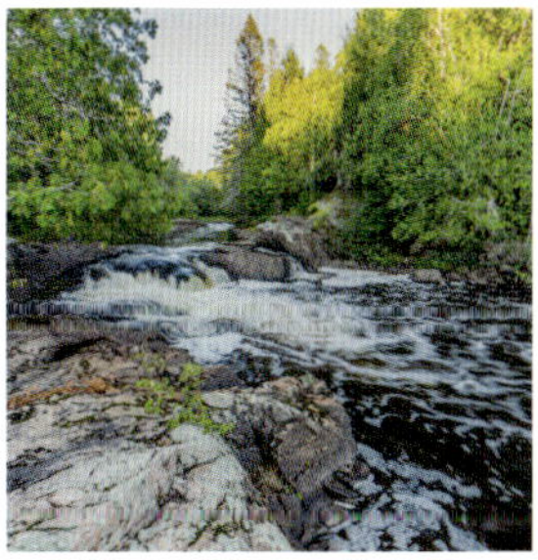

Must See:	4	GPS:	N46 25.806 W89 41.003
Height:	3 feet	Hiking Information	
Time:	10-20 minutes	Path:	Footpath
		Length:	.12 miles
Driving Information		Elev. Change:	Moderate
Signs:	By bridge	GPS:	Helpful
Road:	Dirt	Danger:	Moderate
Access:	Easy	WP Boots:	Recommended
4WD:	N/A		

The NCT skirts past this first drop as you leave the parking spot. Follow the less travelled "Y" toward the beginning of the trail to get to the outcropping along the river to view this initial waterfall.

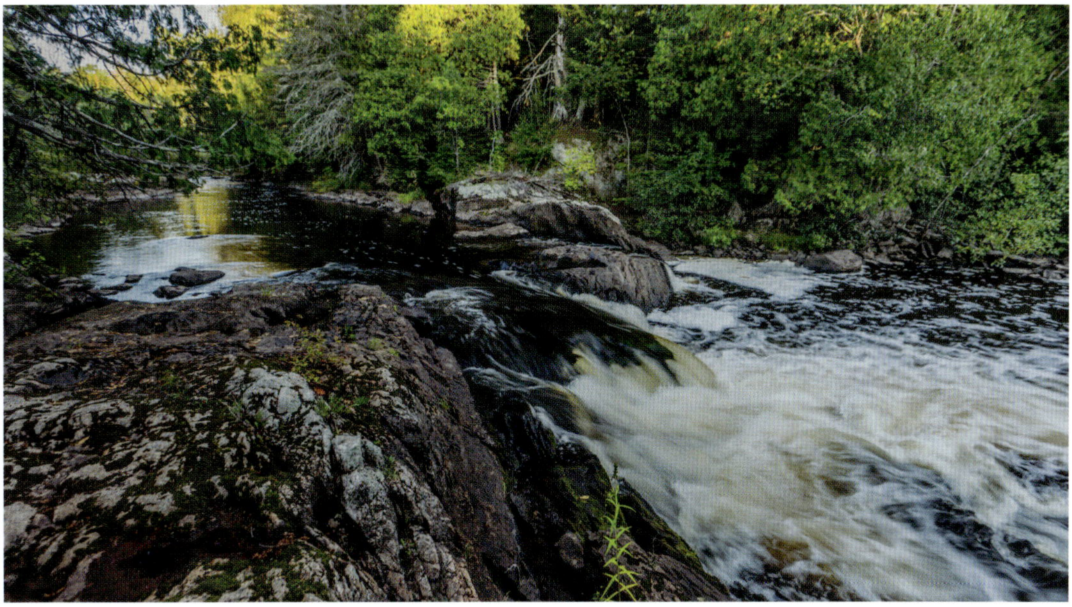

YONDOTA FALLS (PRESQUE ISLE RIVER)

Private

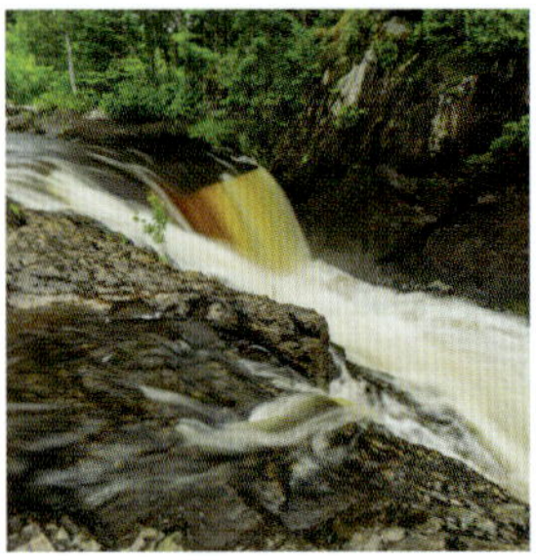

Must See:	8
Height:	6 feet
Time:	15-25 minutes

Driving Information

Signs:	By bridge
Road:	Dirt
Access:	Easy
4WD:	N/A

GPS:	N46 25.821 W89 41.078

Hiking Information

Path:	Footpath
Length:	.14 miles
Elev. Change:	Moderate
GPS:	N/A
Danger:	Moderate
WP Boots:	Recommended

The path to the falls, though well defined, requires climbing around on rocks and over uneven ground. The river above the falls, cradled in the bare rocked riverbed, can appear as a calm enlarged swimming pool. And then, the seemingly serene scene changes to a frothing, turbulent river, churning through a narrow chasm.

Pink and gray stone line the banks that are covered in several hues of green moss and pastel greenish lichen. The rugged banks make viewing the waterfall tricky. A sheer wall on the far side of the top drop makes a great backdrop for the beginning of this 30 yard long waterfall. This plunge is the most spectacular of the drops in the "Yondota" series.

After a sweeping bend, the river narrows to ten feet. It then plunges over a sheer drop into a straight edged slot. This narrows the river even more - down to five feet at its narrowest. Emerging from the short canyon, it widens out and cascades around a number of rocks in Lower #1.

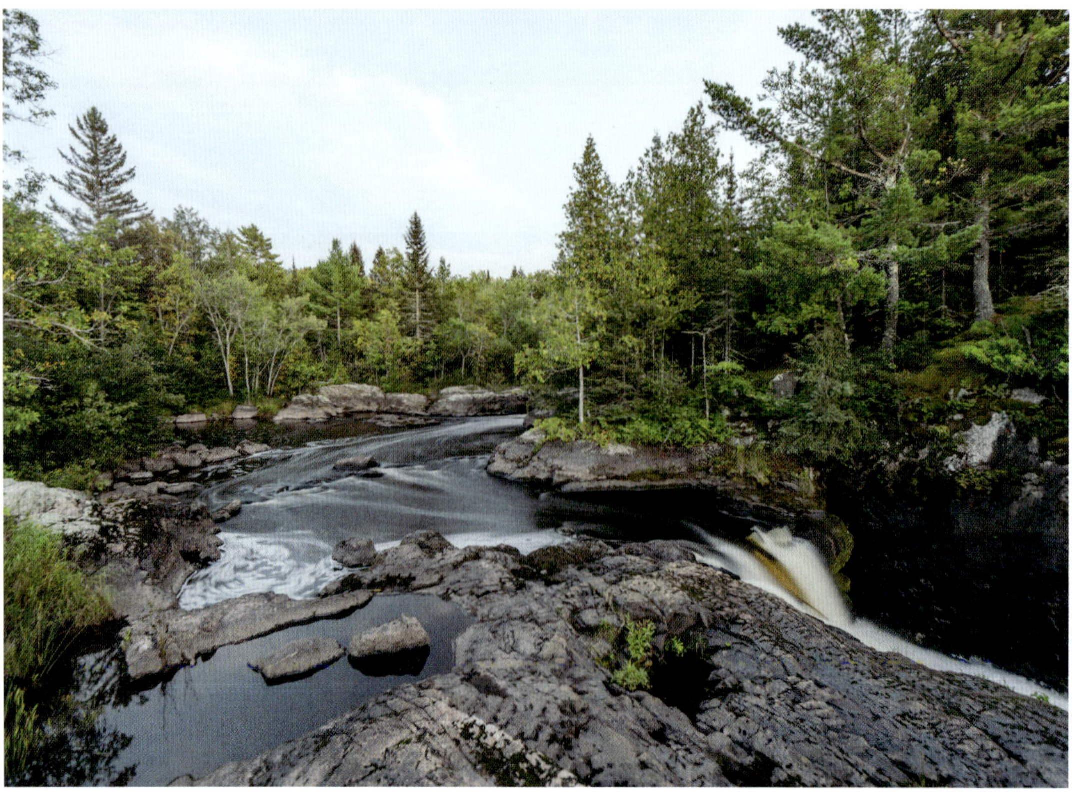

YONDOTA FALLS - LOWER #1 (PRESQUE ISLE RIVER)

Private

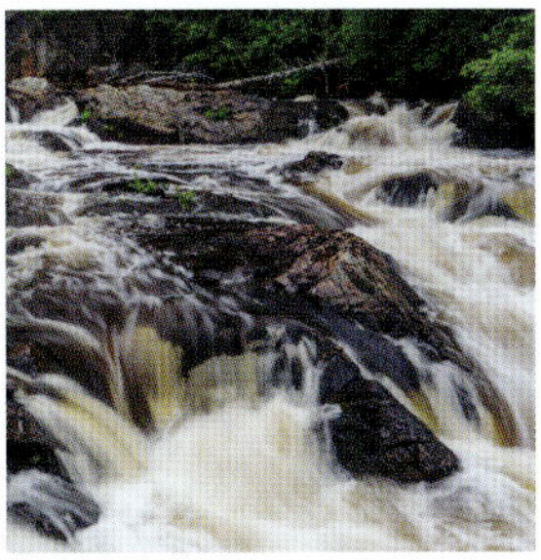

Must See:	6	GPS:	N46 25.835 W89 41.107
Height:	10 feet		
Time:	20-40 minutes	Hiking Information	
		Path:	Footpath
Driving Information		Length:	.18 miles
Signs:	By bridge	Elev. Change:	Moderate
Road:	Dirt	GPS:	N/A
Access:	Easy	Danger:	Moderate
4WD:	N/A	WP Boots:	Recommended

The footpath leads most directly to the bare rock at the base of these falls. Yondota Falls is up river from here. This is not very far below Yondota Falls. In fact, you can see that plunge as a small white spec in the lower picture.

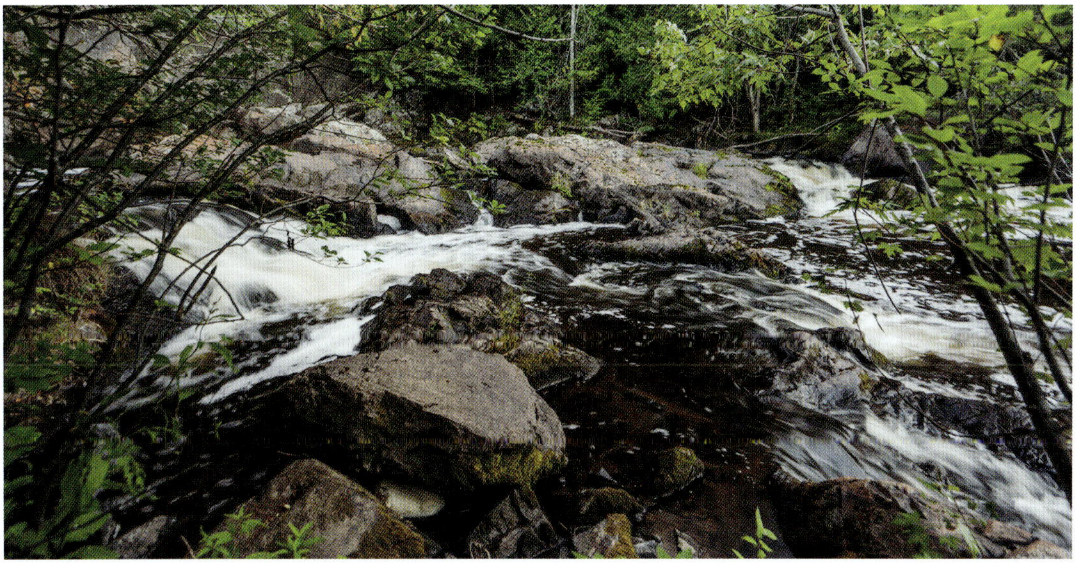

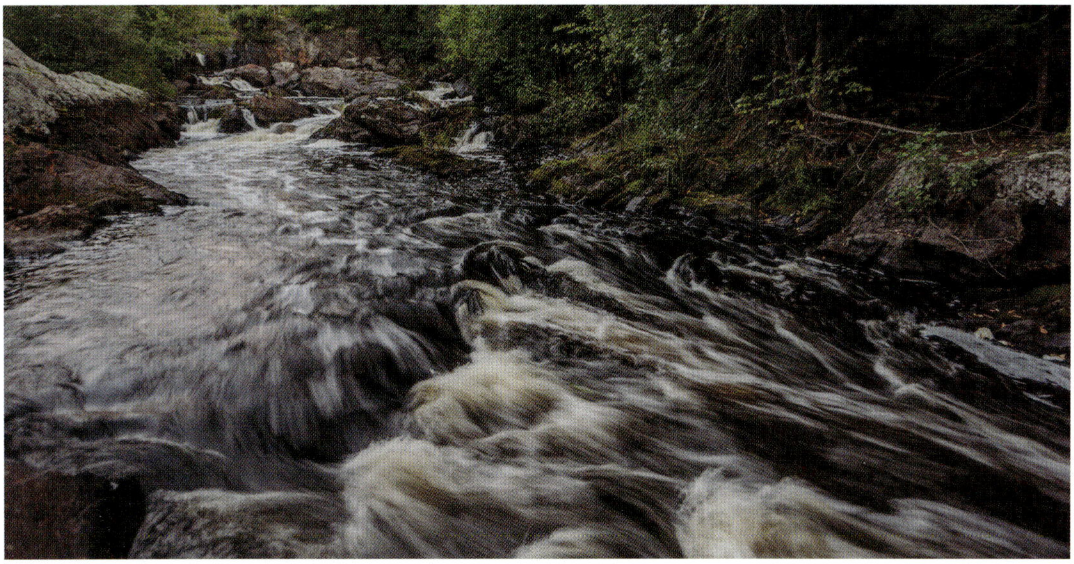

YONDOTA FALLS - LOWER #2 (PRESQUE ISLE RIVER)

Private

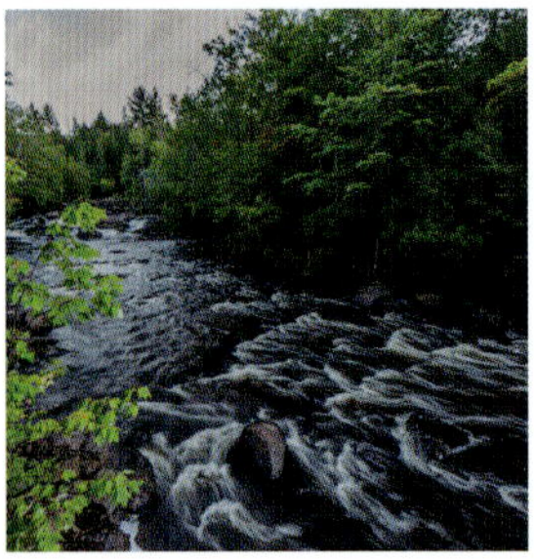

Must See:	5
Height:	5 feet
Time:	25-45 minutes

Driving Information

Signs:	By bridge
Road:	Dirt
Access:	Easy
4WD:	N/A

GPS:	N46 25.869 W89 41.148

Hiking Information

Path:	Footpath
Length:	.22 miles
Elev. Change:	Moderate
GPS:	N/A
Danger:	Moderate
WP Boots:	Recommended

Numerous cascades fill the 50 foot wide riverbed. A large finger of rock pushes over halfway across the river 50 yards downstream. This is a great place to get a good "feel" for the waterfall. Once past the waterfall, the river widens out to nearly 75 yards across as it slows down.

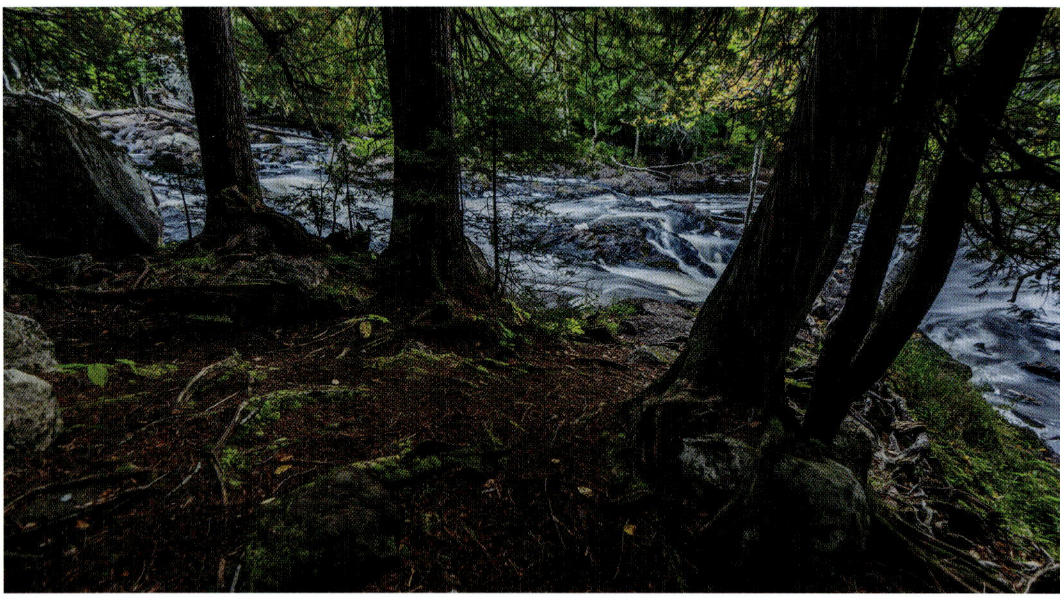

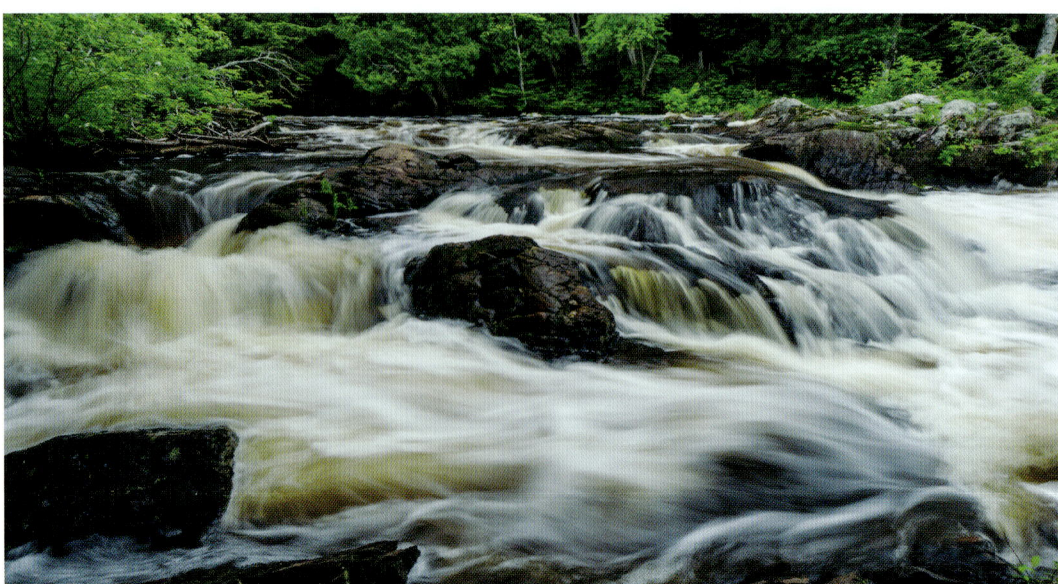

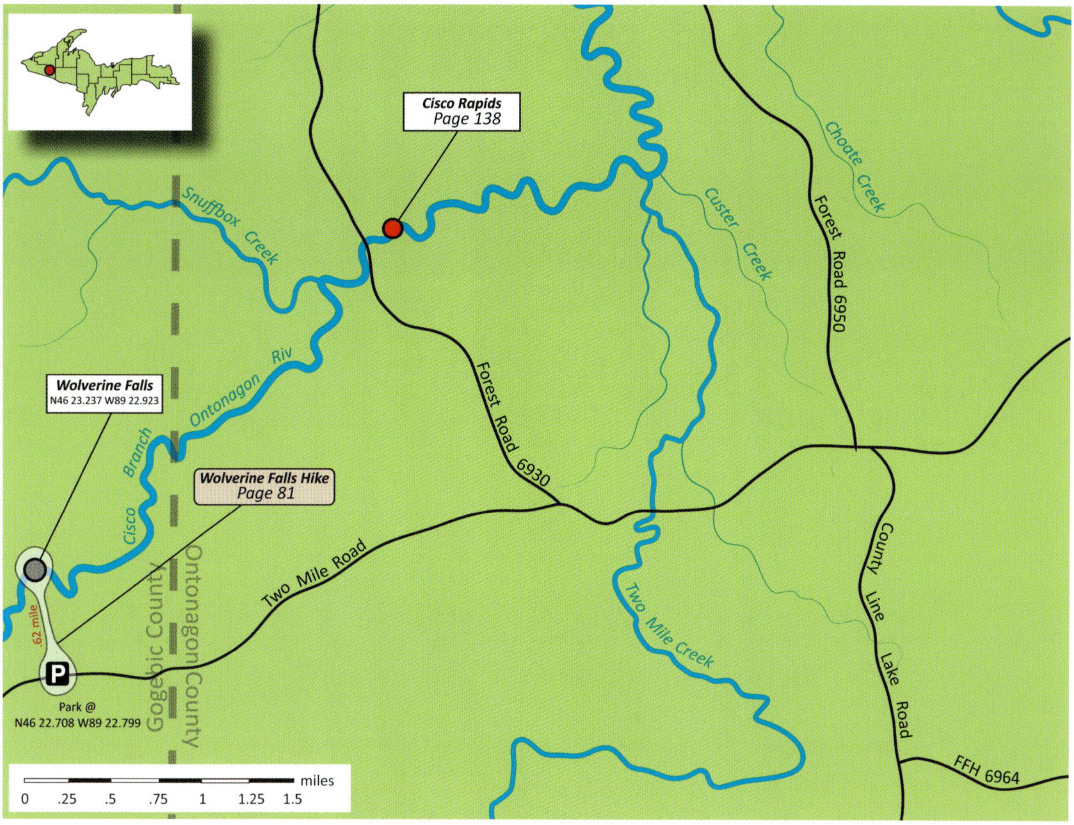

Wolverine Falls Hike

This is one of the waterfalls that is misplaced on atlases. The USGS messed up with the location and that has led to trouble in finding the waterfall. Fortunately, I talked to the knowledgeable folks at Sylvania Outfitters in Watersmeet and they told me about Wolverine Falls being a couple miles further upstream than commonly thought. I am including the information here. I haven't been able to research it yet, but I include the data as unverified for now.

Directions: A good dirt road connects US-2 and US-45. This road goes by several names along the way: CR-527, Two Mile Road and Sleepy Hollow Road. About 5.4 miles from US-2 and 10.6 miles from US-45, park off the side of the road at N46 22.708 W89 22.799. There is no trail. Hike cross-country to the GPS coordinates for the waterfall.

WOLVERINE FALLS (CISCO BRANCH - ONTONAGON RIVER)

Private

Must See:	??	GPS:	*N46 23.237 W89 22.923 (not verified)*
Height:	?? feet		
Time:	N/A	Hiking Information	
		Path:	None
Driving Information		Length:	.62 miles
Signs:	None	Elev. Change:	Minor
Road:	Dirt	GPS:	Required
Access:	Difficult	Danger:	N/A
4WD:	N/A	WP Boots:	N/A

I believe this waterfall might be the mouth of an unnamed tributary dumping into the Cisco Branch of the Ontonagon River. I haven't been here yet, so you get to make this discovery on your own! Enjoy the adventure!

CHAPTER 2
ONTONAGON COUNTY

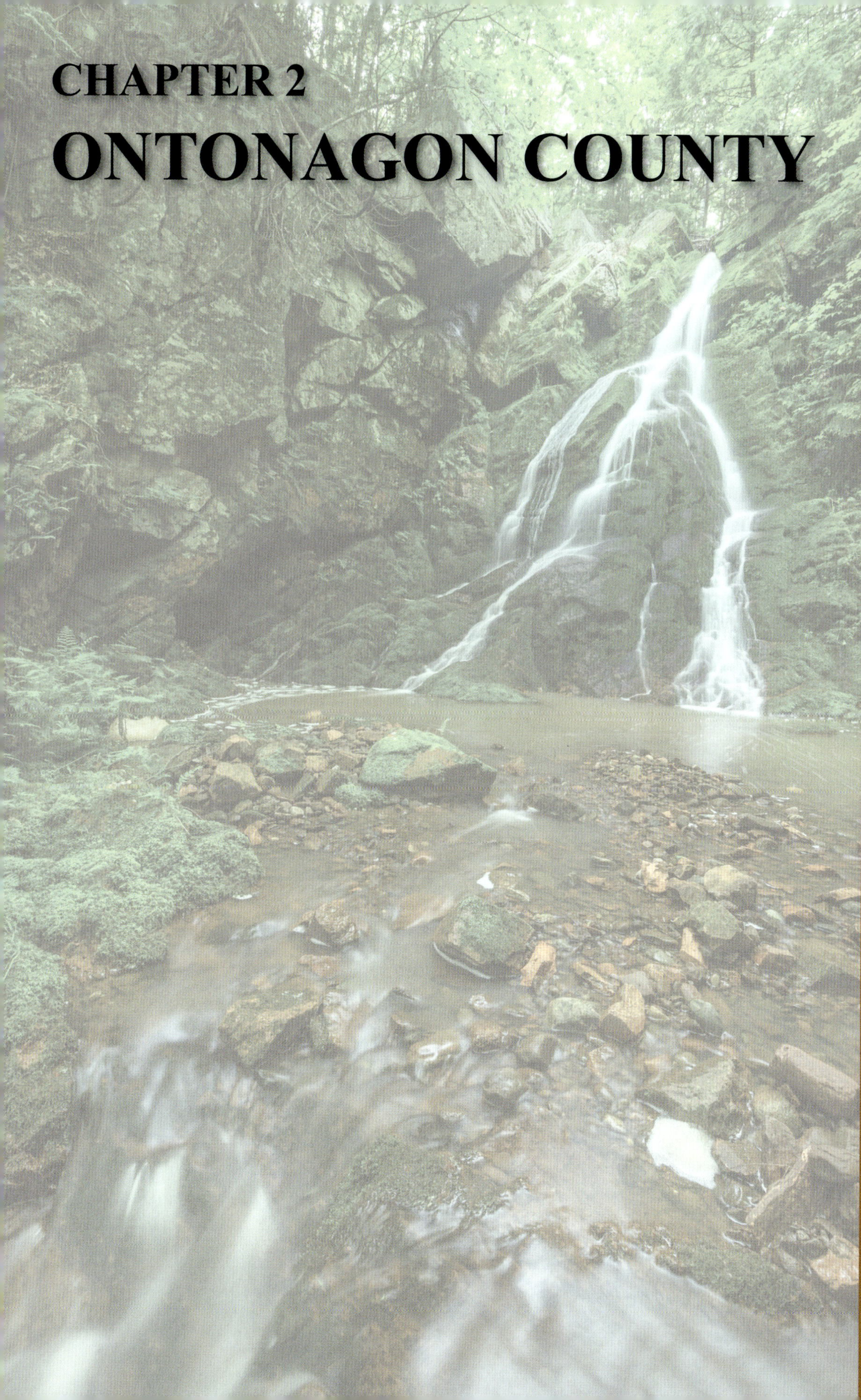

ONTONAGON COUNTY CONTENTS

MAPS........................
HIKES........................
WATERFALLS........................

TABLE OF CONTENT KEY

MAPS .....
HIKES .....
WATERFALLS .....

TABLE OF CONTENT KEY

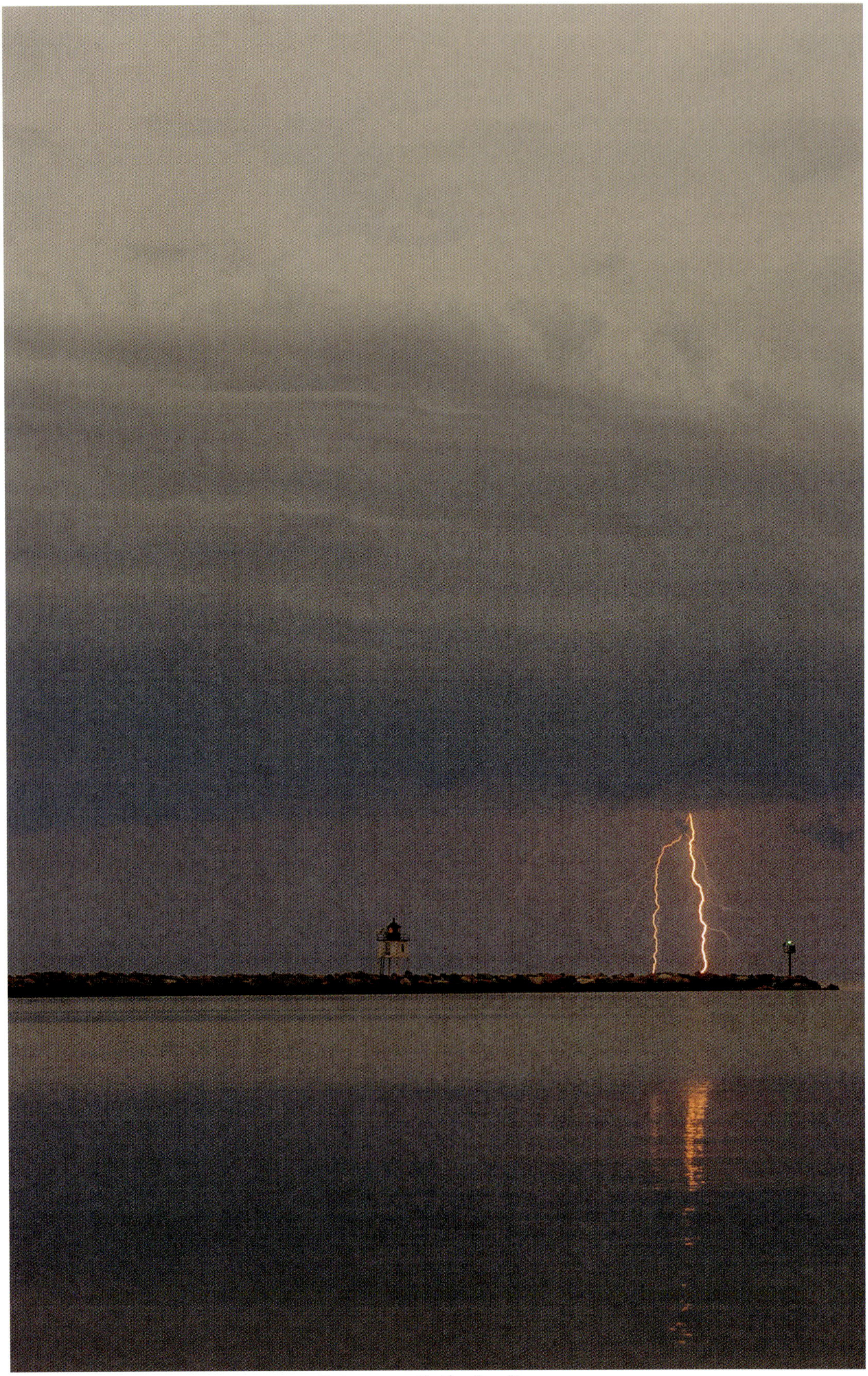

Ontonagon Gathering Storm

ONTONAGON COUNTY FACTS

Founded:	1848
Size:	1311 square miles
Population (2012):	6,413
County Seat:	Ontonagon

"Ontonagon" is the Americanized version of the Chippewa (Ojibwa) phrase, "my dish". Tradition tells us that a squaw went to the river, now known as the *Ontonagon*, dropped her clay bowl in the rushing waters where it quickly sank, much to her distress. She cried out, "My dish, my dish!" Somehow the name stuck, and the name of this river became the name of the village at its mouth and 5 years later, the name of the county. Amazing! All this from the inadvertent dropping of a piece of pottery!

Massive white pines dominated the landscape in the heart of Ontonagon County, while lurking just below the rocky surface were millions of tons of copper. Lumberjacks cut the pine, floating it down river or transporting the huge logs on economically viable rail cars pulled by the newly designed Shay Locomotives. Miners delved deep underground, bringing up ton after ton of the precious red metal. But times changed. The early miners, whose numbers swelled the village of Ontonagon to over 6,000 in the 1850's, ran out of "easy" copper or out of money or the will to look for more. Then the white pine boom ended. The county's premier copper mine, the aptly named *White Pine Mine* started up again in the mid 1950's. Times were great until they also ceased production in 1995 after a dispute with local Indian tribes and ultimately the DNR over environmental issues. As the economy faltered, so did the population. There were over 11,000 people living in the county in the mid 1970's, but since then that number has declined annually.

The county is transitioning to a tourism based economy. Fortunately, Ontonagon County is blessed with amazing natural beauty! The bulk of Porcupine Mountains State Park lies within its borders. Mile after mile of pristine Lake Superior shoreline makes up the northern boundary of the county. The Trap Hills, an increasingly popular hiking destination, offers spectacular overlooks and the North County Trail connects these hills and bluffs for some of the highest elevation hiking in the state!

Ontonagon Lighthouse

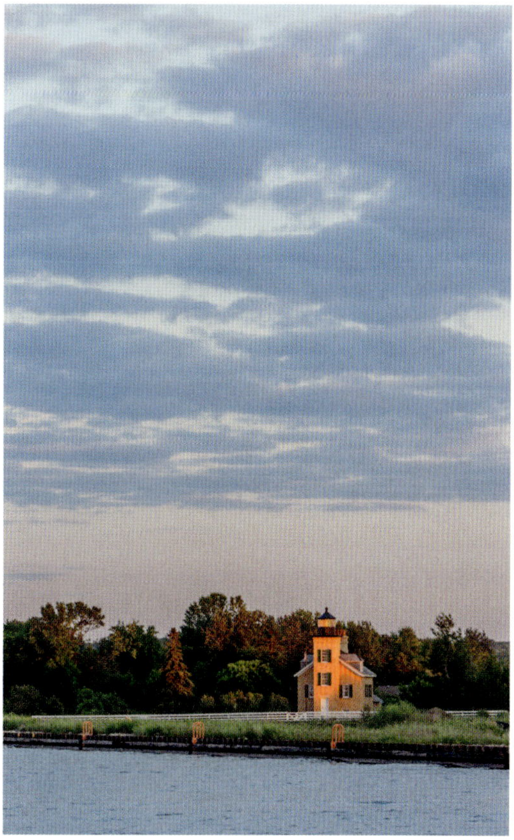

Ontonagon County Map

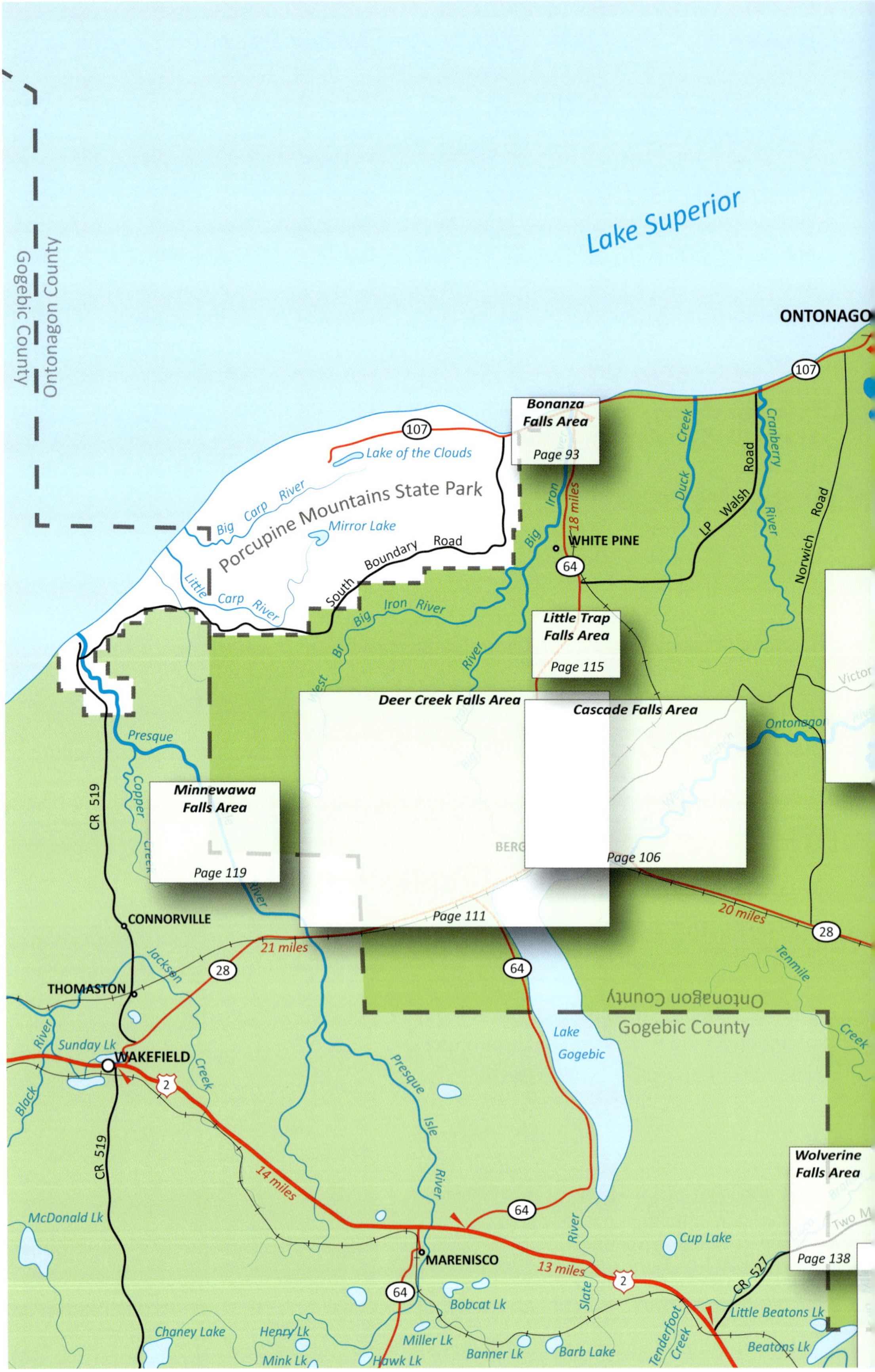

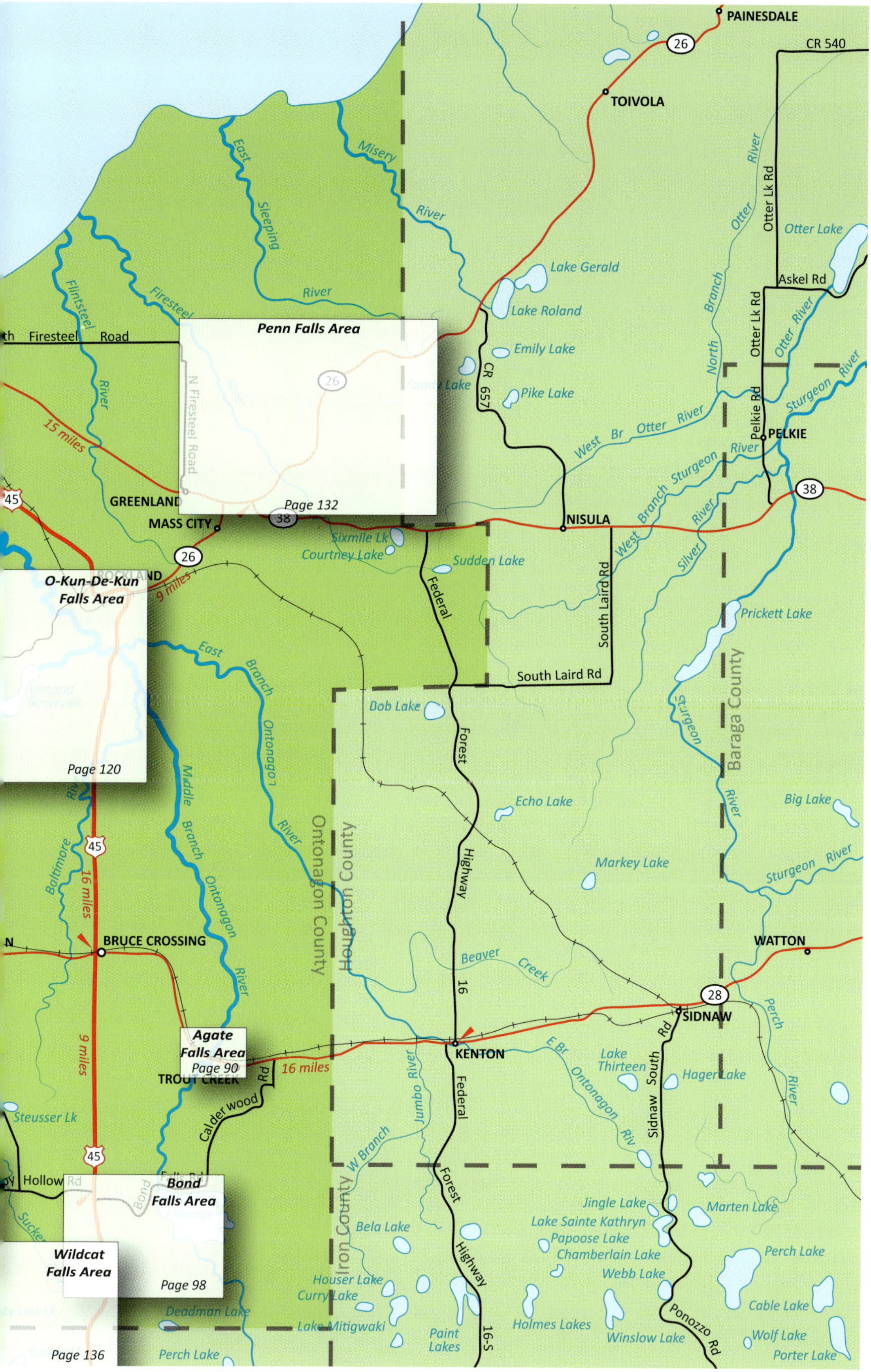
PAINESDALE
26
CR 540
TOIVOLA
East
Sleeping
River
Misery
River
Flintsteel
Firesteel
River
Firesteel
Road
Penn Falls Area
Page 132
15 miles
45
GREENLAND
MASS CITY
38
26
Lake Gerald
Lake Roland
Emily Lake
Sandy Lake
Pike Lake
CR 657
West Br Otter River
NISULA
Otter Lake
Otter Lk Rd
Askel Rd
Otter River
North Branch
Otter River
Pelkie Rd
PELKIE
Sturgeon River
West Branch Sturgeon River
38
Silver River
Sixmile Lk
Courtney Lake
Sudden Lake
O-Kun-De-Kun
Falls Area
Page 120
9 miles
Federal
South Laird Rd
South Laird Rd
Prickett Lake
Baraga County
Sturgeon
River
Dob Lake
Forest
East Branch
Ontonagon
River
Middle
Branch
Ontonagon
River
Ontonagon County
Houghton County
Echo Lake
Highway
Big Lake
Markey Lake
Sturgeon River
45
Baltimore
16 miles
BRUCE CROSSING
Beaver Creek
16
WATTON
28
SIDNAW
Perch River
KENTON
E Br Ontonagon River
Lake Thirteen
Hager Lake
Sidnaw South Rd
Agate
Falls Area
Page 90
TROUT CREEK
16 miles
9 miles
Jumbo River
Federal
Calder wood Rd
Steusser Lk
45
Hollow Rd
W Branch
Forest
Bond
Falls Area
Page 98
Wildcat
Falls Area
Page 136
Iron County
Bela Lake
Jingle Lake
Marten Lake
Lake Sainte Kathryn
Papoose Lake
Chamberlain Lake
Perch Lake
Webb Lake
Highway
Houser Lake
Curry Lake
Deadman Lake
Lake Mitigwaki
Paint Lakes
16-S
Holmes Lakes
Winslow Lake
Ponozzo Rd
Cable Lake
Wolf Lake
Porter Lake
Perch Lake

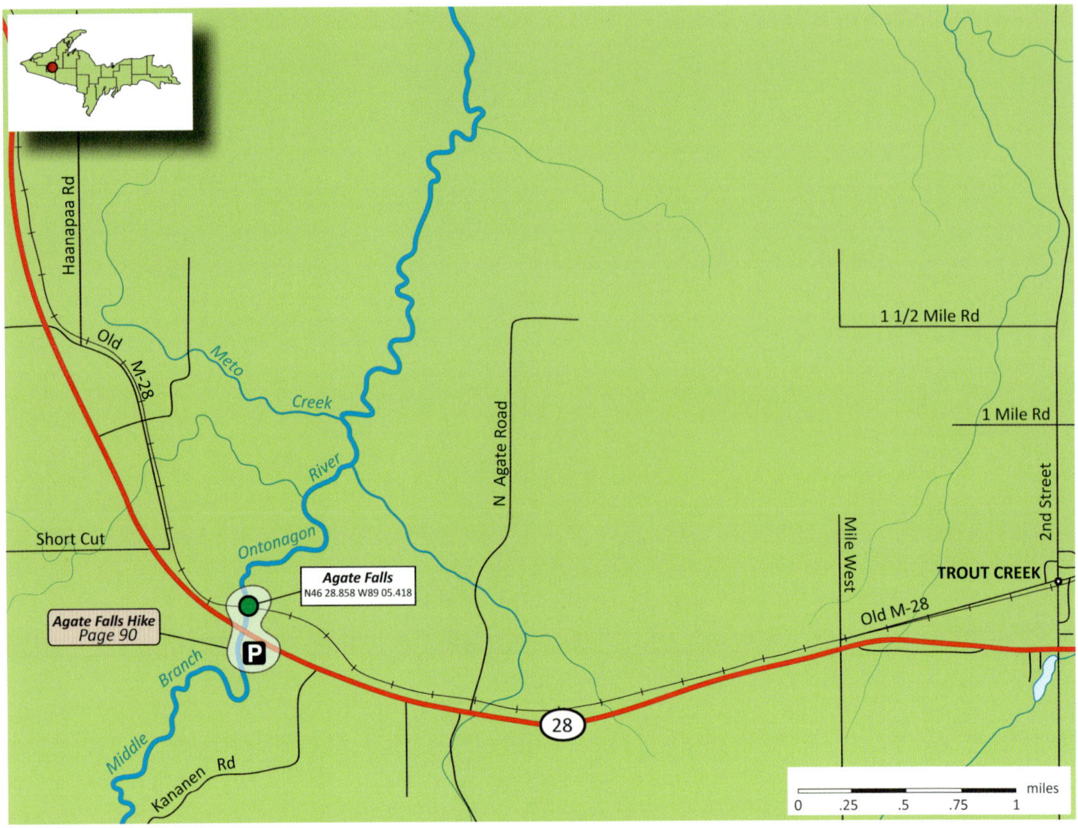

Agate Falls Hike

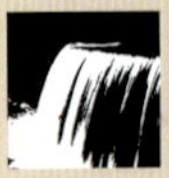

Agate Falls is one of the most beautiful waterfalls in Michigan! And fortunately, it is an easy, short hike to view it from the top. The Middle Branch of the Ontonagon River flows over a multi-stepped sandstone ledge resulting in numerous cascades. The quiet waters below the falls are favored by local fishermen.

The Michigan DNR maintains the Agate Falls Scenic Site which is located on the south side of M-28 while Agate Falls is on the north. A vehicle pass is required at the Scenic Site. It is a tastefully maintained park, with toilets, water and picnic tables available. There are plenty of paved parking spots and a wide sidewalk follows the river to the north, passing beneath the highway and continuing to a waterfall overlook above the falls.

In 1900 a railroad trestle was constructed high above the falls. It has since been converted for snowmobile use. It is a common site in the winter to see snowmobilers stop and peer over the side rail to catch an overhead view of the waterfall.

Directions: About 4 miles west of Trout Creek on M-28 is the Agate Falls Scenic Site on the left (south) side of the road just before the bridge that crosses the Middle Branch of the Ontonagon River. Park (a Recreation Passport is required). Follow the walkway a short distance to the river then turn and continue on the wide path under M-28 and over to the waterfall viewing area. A steep unimproved fisherman's trail continues down into the ravine below the falls. This trail is not easy to navigate and is not recommended for children.

The steep trail down into the ravine

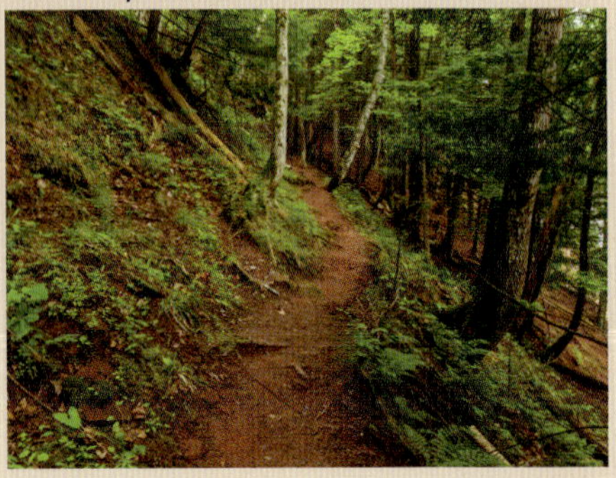

AGATE FALLS (WEST BRANCH - ONTONAGON RIVER)

Private

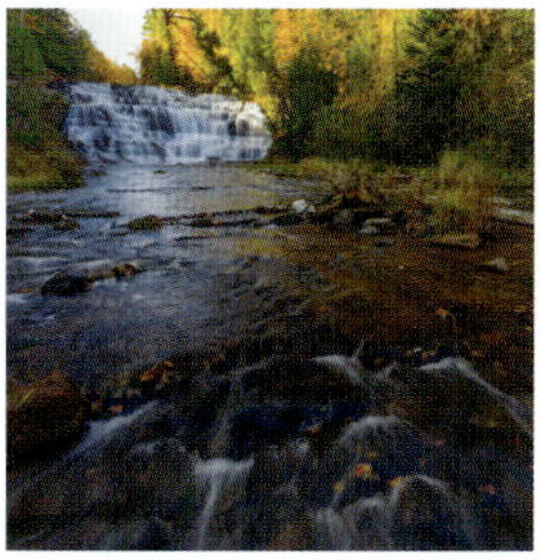

Must See:	10	GPS:	N46 28.858 W89 05.418
Height:	30 feet		
Time:	10-40 minutes	Hiking Information	
		Path:	*Paved then Dirt
Driving Information		Length:	*.15 miles or .25
Signs:	Roadside	Elev. Change:	*Moderate or Elevated
Road:	Main	GPS:	N/A
Access:	Very Easy	Danger:	*Slight or Elevated
4WD:	N/A	WP Boots:	*N/A or Recommended

*The first set of data is to the overlook - the second is to climb down to the base of the falls.

It is my understanding that a large hotel was situated on the site over 100 years ago. Tourists would catch a train from downstate, arriving in the logging community of Trout Creek. Photography was a recent phenomena and men and women would climb down a wooden set of stairs dressed in their finest to have their photographs taken at the base of the falls. The lure and charm of this waterfall remains and many take advantage of the relatively easy access to enjoy Agate Falls to this day!

The historic bridge over the Middle Branch of the Ontonagon River completed in 1929

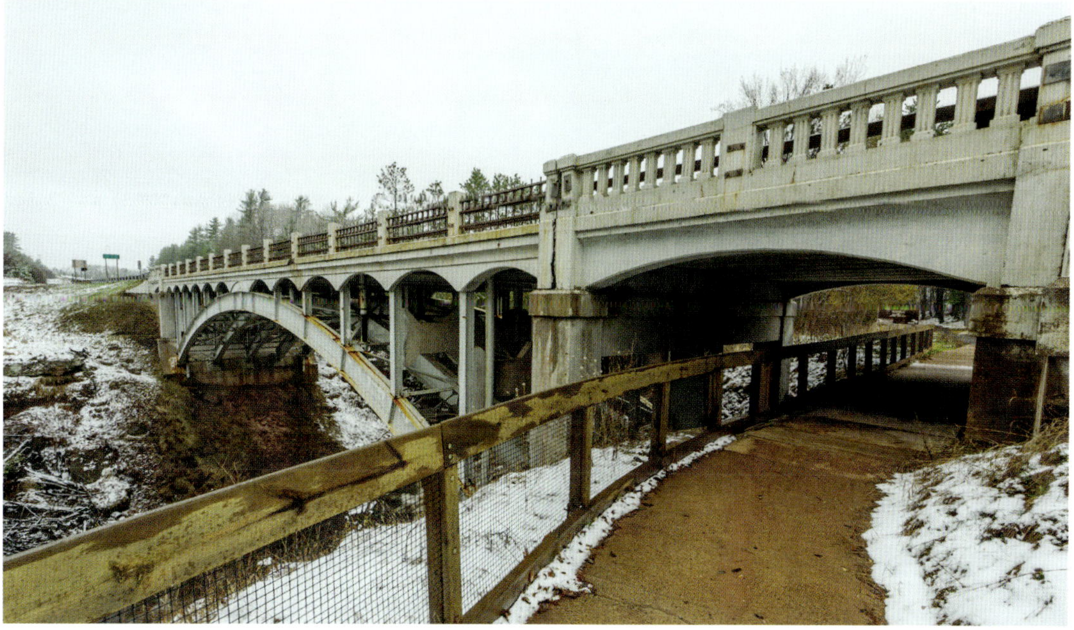

Agate Falls Scenic Site parking area

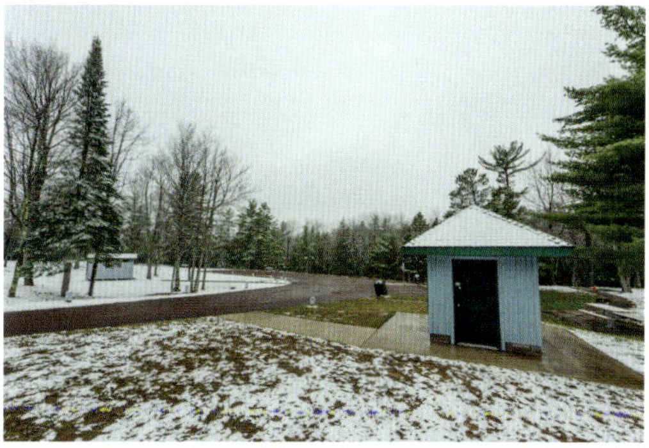

The viewing deck at Agate Falls

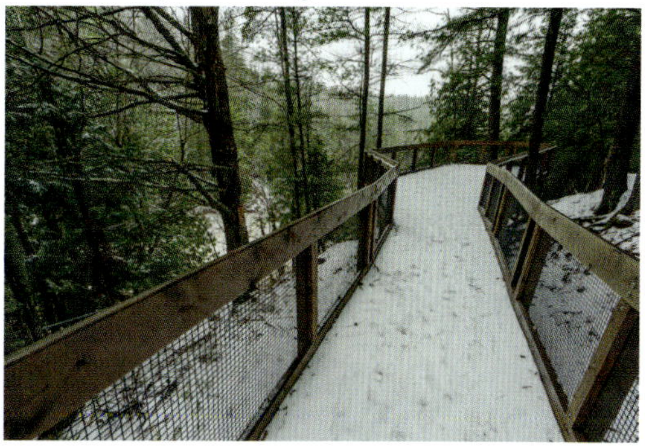

Looking down from the trestle toward M-28

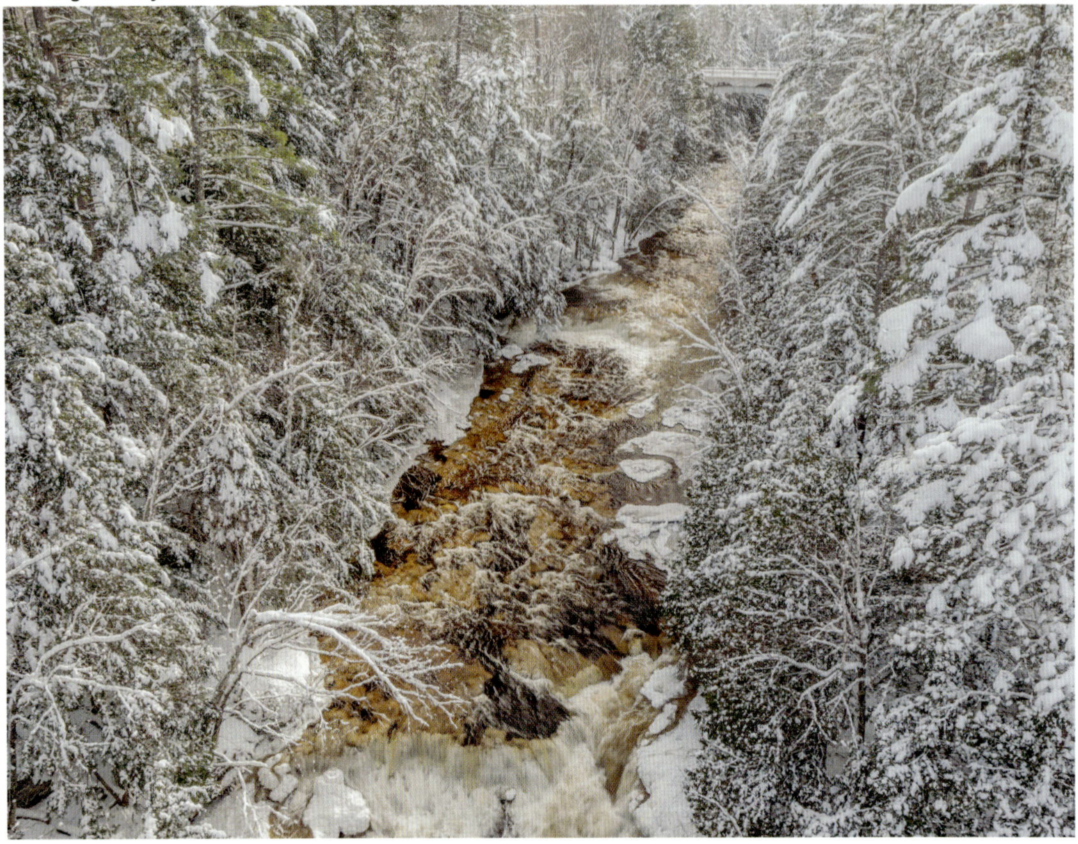

A beautiful view of the river and trestle

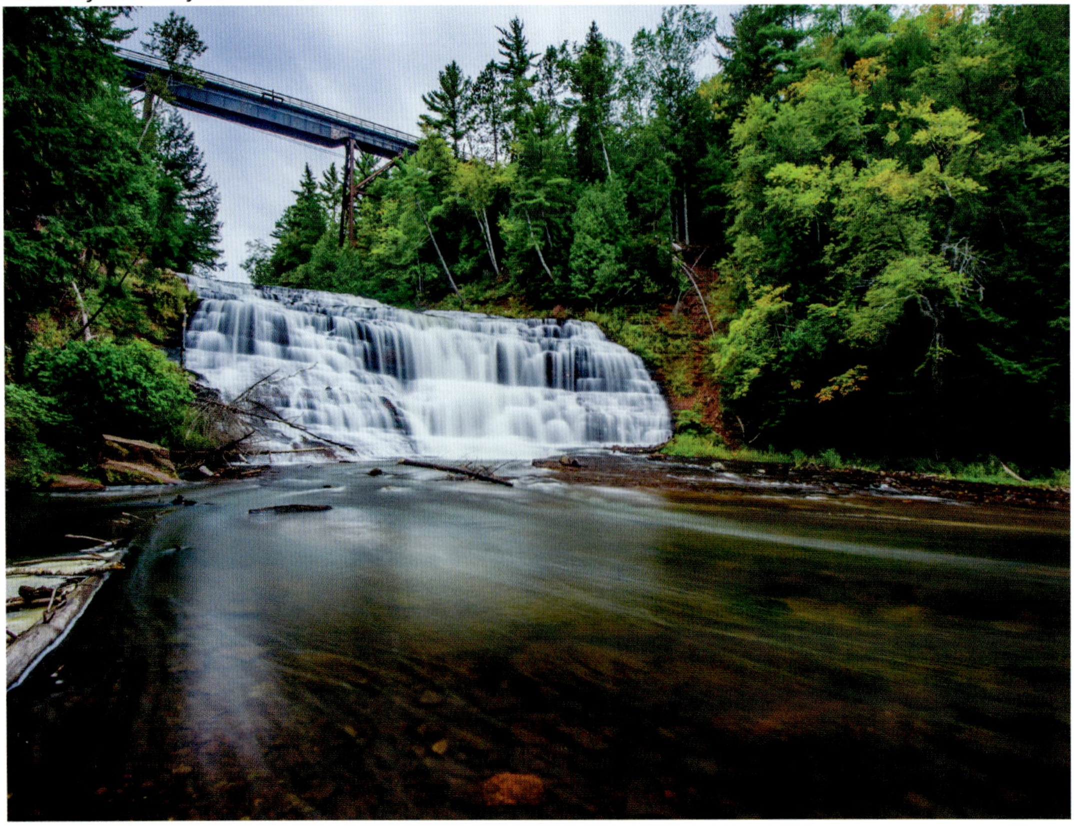

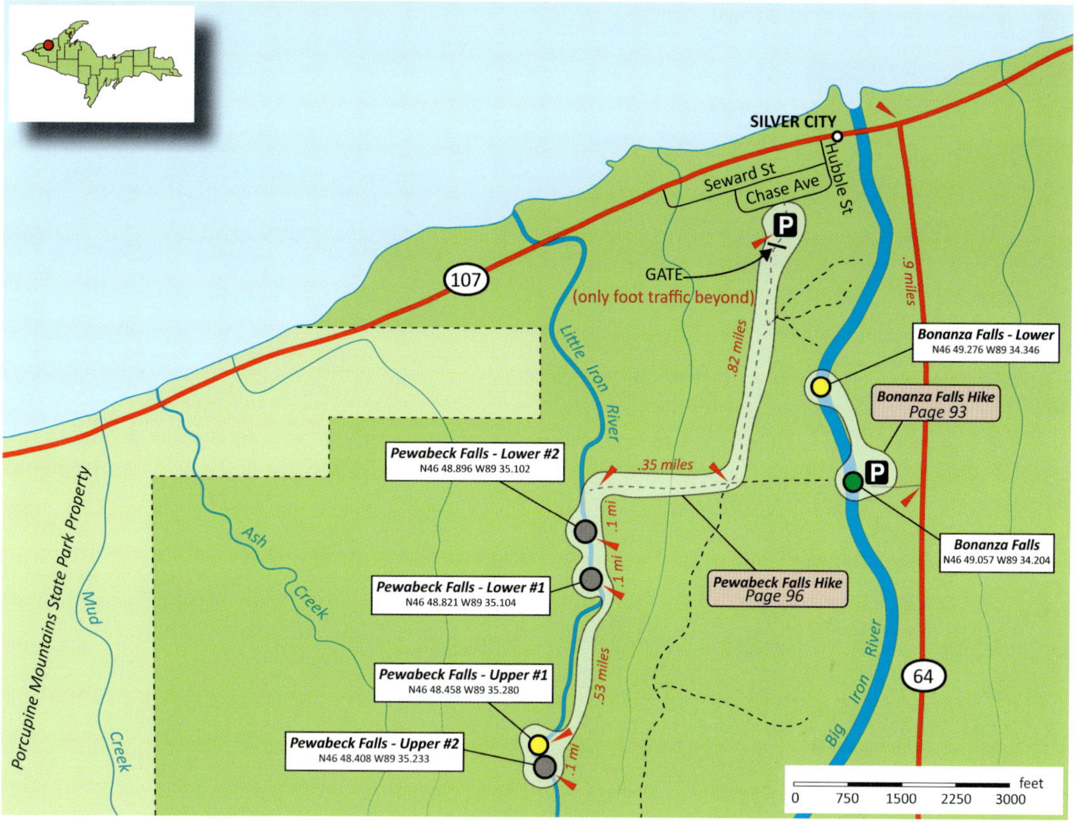

Bonanza Falls Hike

Bonanza Falls, also known as "Greenwood Falls", is not a typical Michigan waterfall. The Big Iron River runs against the grain of the angled rock layers. This forces the river to pool and then drop over the ledges. During periods of lower water it is possible to walk nearly across the river on the exposed rock ridges. There are drops for several hundred yards downstream. The last of them I have designated as the "Lower" falls. This waterfall is at a sharp turn as the river heads to the northeast.

A silver mine was established here in 1872 but was closed by 1876. The initial anticipation for a "Bonanza" of silver gave the nearby waterfall its name. Later on, in the early 1900's, the Greenwood Lumber Company built their headquarters on the premises. The waterfall then started to take on the name "Greenwood Falls". It currently goes by both names, but it is most often referred to as "Bonanza Falls".

The history of Bonanza Falls

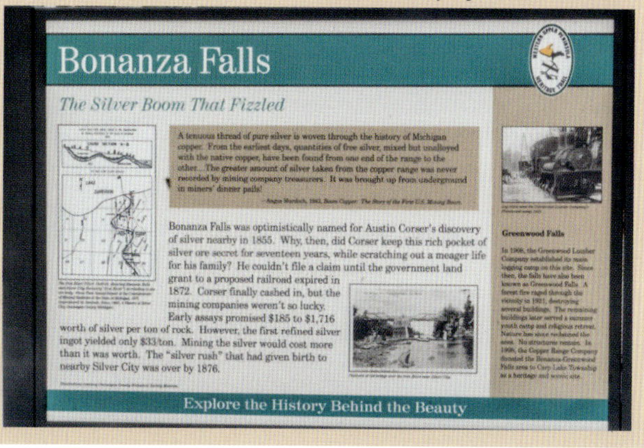

Directions: Drive south on M-64 from the intersection of M-107 for .9 miles. Turn right (west) on a 2-track and follow it to the end. Park. The main drop is nearly straight ahead. Climb down about 6 feet to the river's edge. A fisherman's trail runs along the river. Many small drops can be seen for hundreds of yards, culminating at the "Lower" falls.

BONANZA FALLS (BIG IRON RIVER)

Private

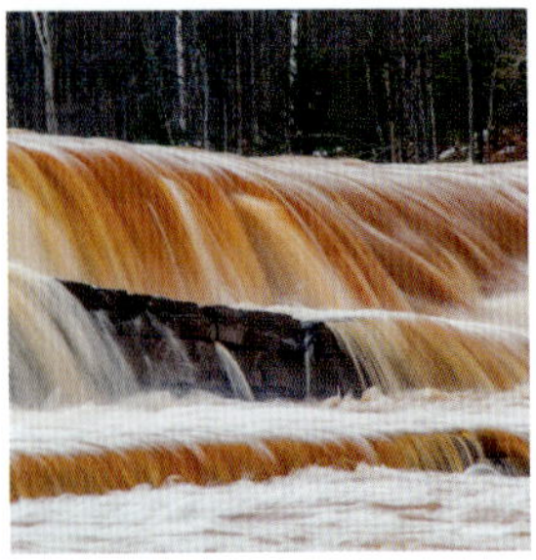

Must See:	7
Height:	14 feet
Time:	5-30 minutes

Driving Information

Signs:	Roadside
Road:	Main
Access:	Very Easy
4WD:	N/A

GPS:	N46 49.057 W89 34.204

Hiking Information

Path:	Unimproved path
Length:	100 feet
Elev. Change:	Slight
GPS:	N/A
Danger:	Slight
WP Boots:	N/A to helpful

Bonanza Falls is a family paradise! The numerous small pools and countless miniature drops can keep an inquisitive individual occupied for hours. What better way to spend a hot summer day than wading in the cool water and listening to the rush of falling water along the Big Iron River. My youngest son loves to slide down the "main" plunge. He typically comes up covered in small leeches, but he thinks half of the fun is pulling them off!

Looking back toward the parking area

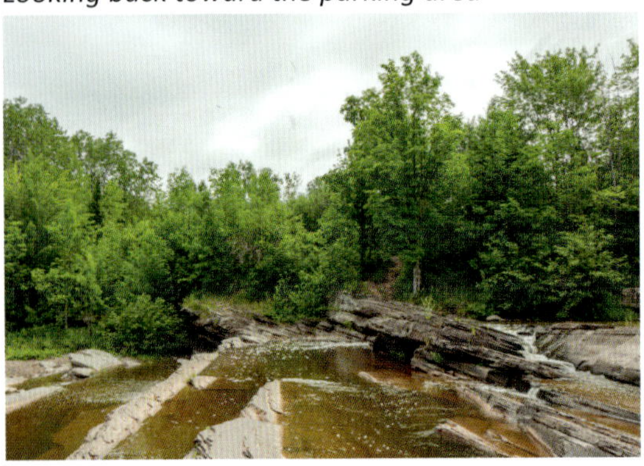

High water in spring

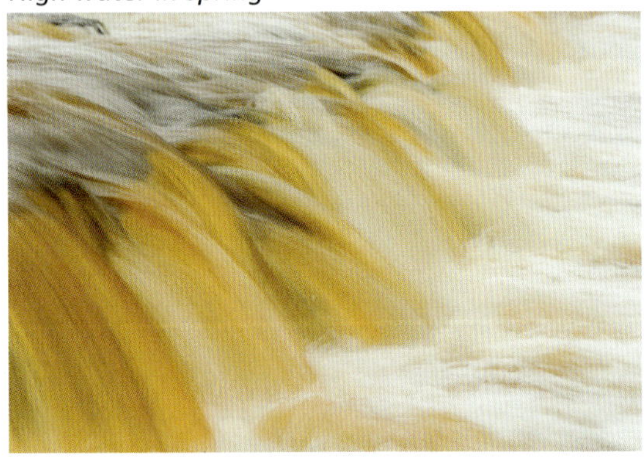

Low water on a gorgeous autumn day

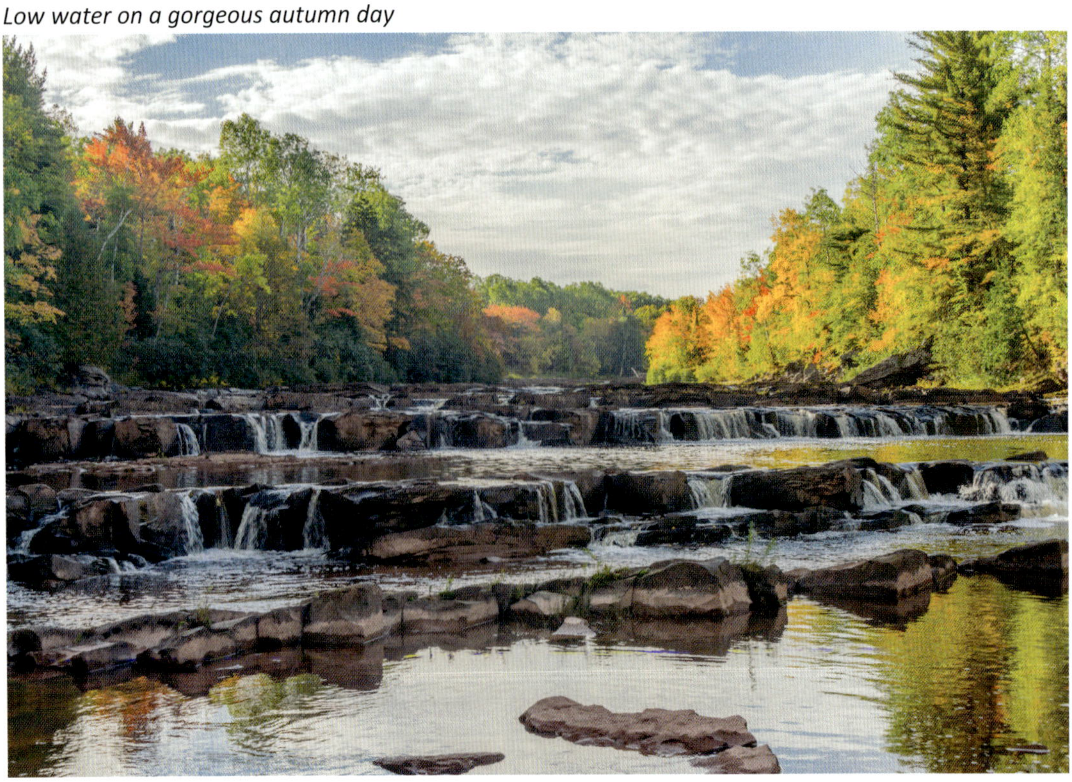

BONANZA FALLS - LOWER (BIG IRON RIVER)

Private

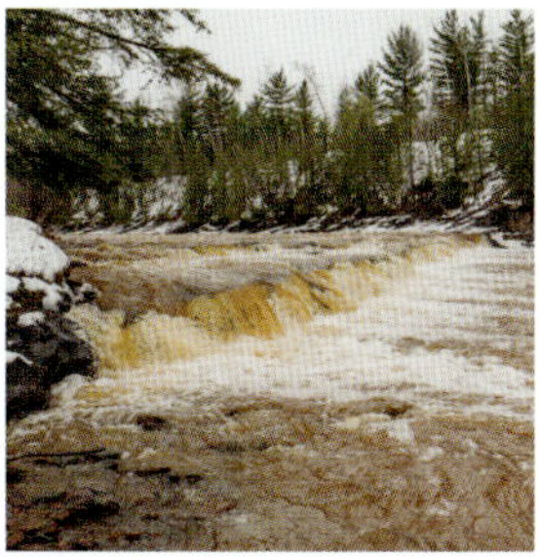

Must See:	5	GPS:	N46 49.276 W89 34.346
Height:	4 feet		
Time:	20-45 minutes	Hiking Information	
		Path:	Unimproved path
Driving Information		Length:	.3 miles
Signs:	Roadside	Elev. Change:	Slight
Road:	Main	GPS:	N/A
Access:	Very Easy	Danger:	Slight
4WD:	N/A	WP Boots:	Helpful

Fishermen frequent this area just below the lowest of the falls on the Big Iron River. Fish congregate here since the river is harder to navigate through the falls area.

The river turns hard to the right as the ravine cuts deeper into the terrain. Now the river starts flowing along one of the layers instead of fighting the uplifts. This waterfall represents the end of the Bonanza Falls.

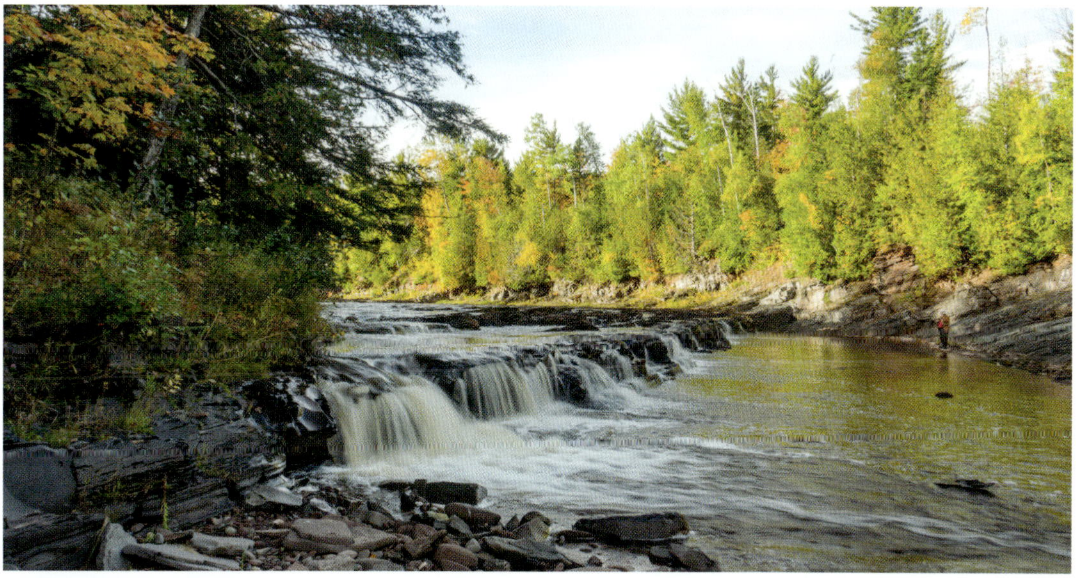

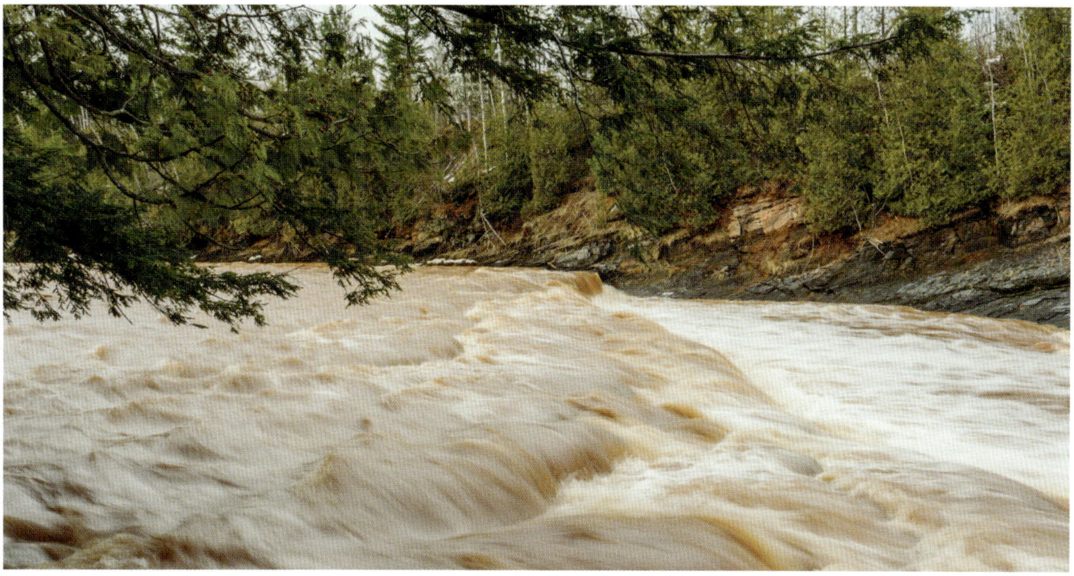

Pewabeck Falls Hike

I have been to "Pewabeck Falls" once so far. Since making that hike, I have reason to believe that there may be 3 more drops along the river. I am including them only as a reference in this edition since I'm not positive that they really exist. I have let you know where I "think" they are so you can do some adventuring of your own!

The Little Iron River pours through broken up blocks of rock. Over time the bedrock at the falls has split into squared off sections. The river dives down between the gaps like sand through a rake's teeth. There is a fair amount of undergrowth on the hike to the falls, as well as along the river. Most waterfalls are found in ravines as rivers and creeks have cut down through soft layers of rock and earth, but Little Iron River defies this trend. The river is nearly at the grade of the surrounding terrain.

Directions: There is a small residential area in Silver City. It consists of a couple of loops directly south of M-107 and is nestled between Little Iron River and Big Iron River. Turn south onto Hubble Street (this is across the street from the AmericInn). In an 1/8 mile the road will turn right and become Chase Avenue. In .15 miles there will be a 2-track to the left (south). Follow the 2-track until it suddenly ends at a gate. Park well off of the trail. Be careful though. There is quite a crown to the roadway and you don't want to get stuck in the tall undergrowth. It is permissible to walk past the gate but not to take motored vehicles. There is signage there to this effect. Follow the 2-track southerly for .82 miles. A less used 2-track will cross the trail. Turn right. Follow it until reaching the Little Iron River (approx .35 miles). Follow the riverbank south for .1 miles. Here you should find the first of the "Lower" Pewabeck Falls. In another .1 miles there should be another one. Continue south along the river for another .53 miles to the first of the "Upper" Pewabeck Falls. The final waterfall should be about another .1 miles south. It may be possible that there is a fisherman's trail along the river, but I don't know as this is my "best guess" as to what you will find on this hike! Remember, it's an adventure! Have fun!

PEWABECK FALLS - UPPER #1 (LITTLE IRON RIVER)

Private

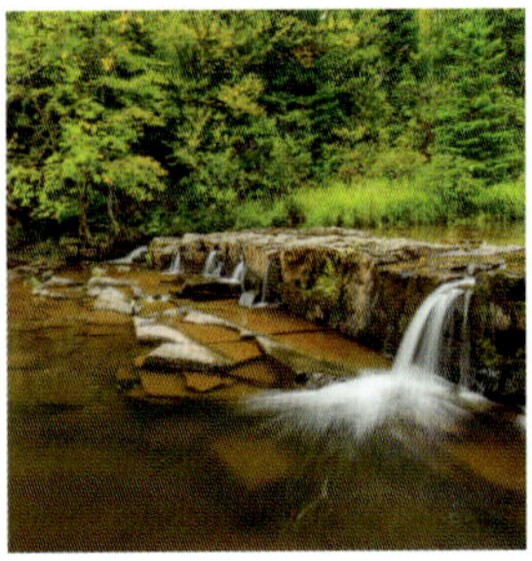

Must See:	6	GPS:	N46 48.458 W89 35.280
Height:	3 feet		
Time:	1.5 to 2.5 hours	Hiking Information	
		Path:	None
Driving Information		Length:	1.8 miles
Signs:	None	Elev. Change:	Slight
Road:	Main	GPS:	Required
Access:	Somewhat Easy	Danger:	Elevated
4WD:	N/A	WP Boots:	Recommended

This is the only one of the Pewabeck Falls that I have been to so far. I think that there are possibly three more drops and I have included the GPS coordinates for them on the area map. I also have given my "best guess" as to where you will find them in the hiking directions above.

Also, this hike is untried. This is how I will be attempting to get to the falls the next time I go. The last time I went, I hiked in from the other side of the river. Although it is a somewhat shorter hike, it requires very tricky navigating to keep from encroaching on private property and there is no trail most of the way. Do not try to access the falls from the west side of the river.

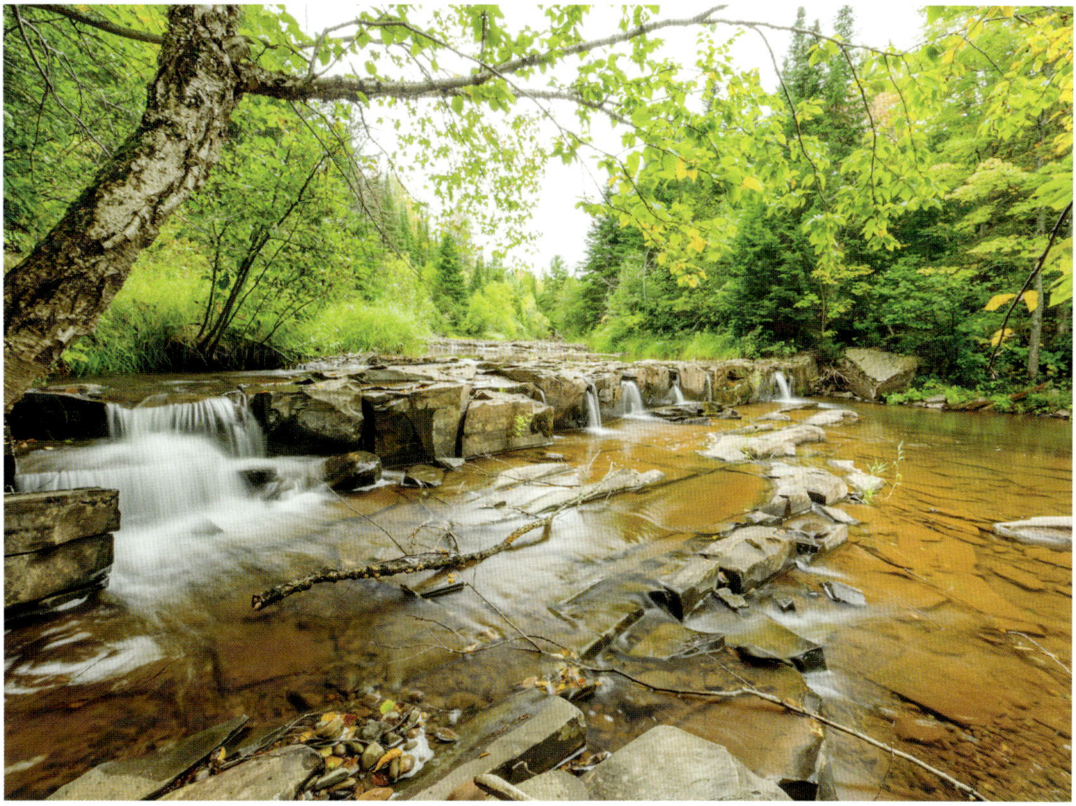

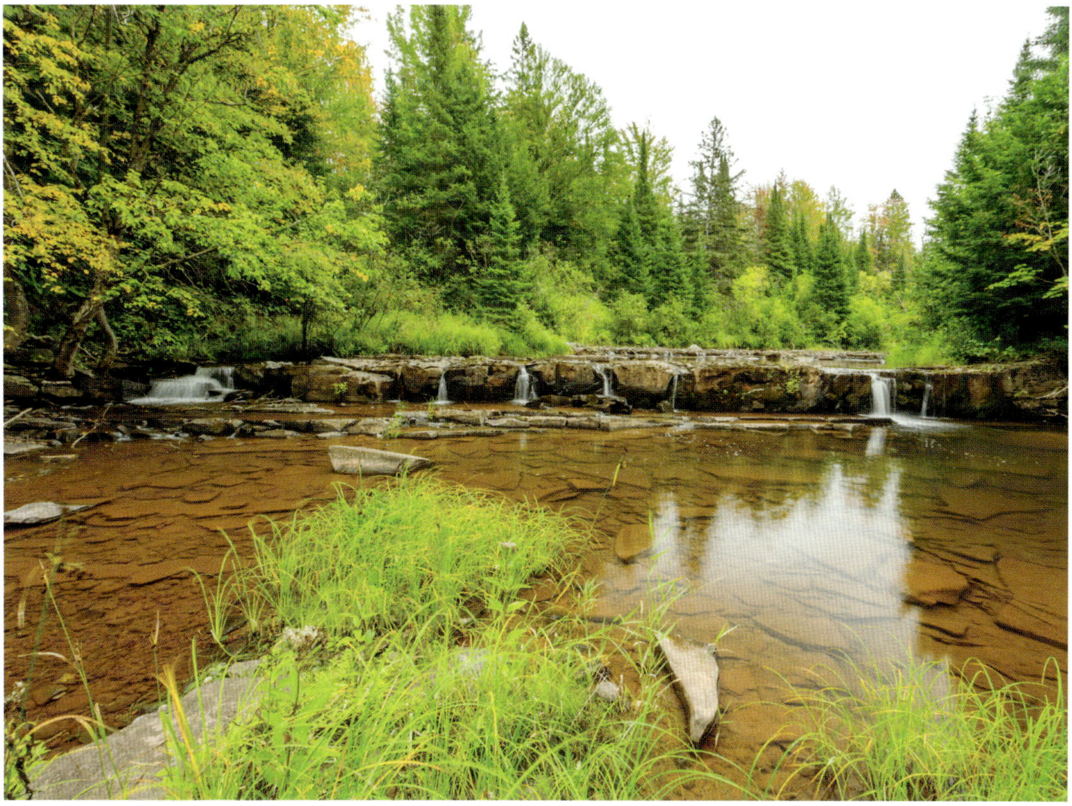

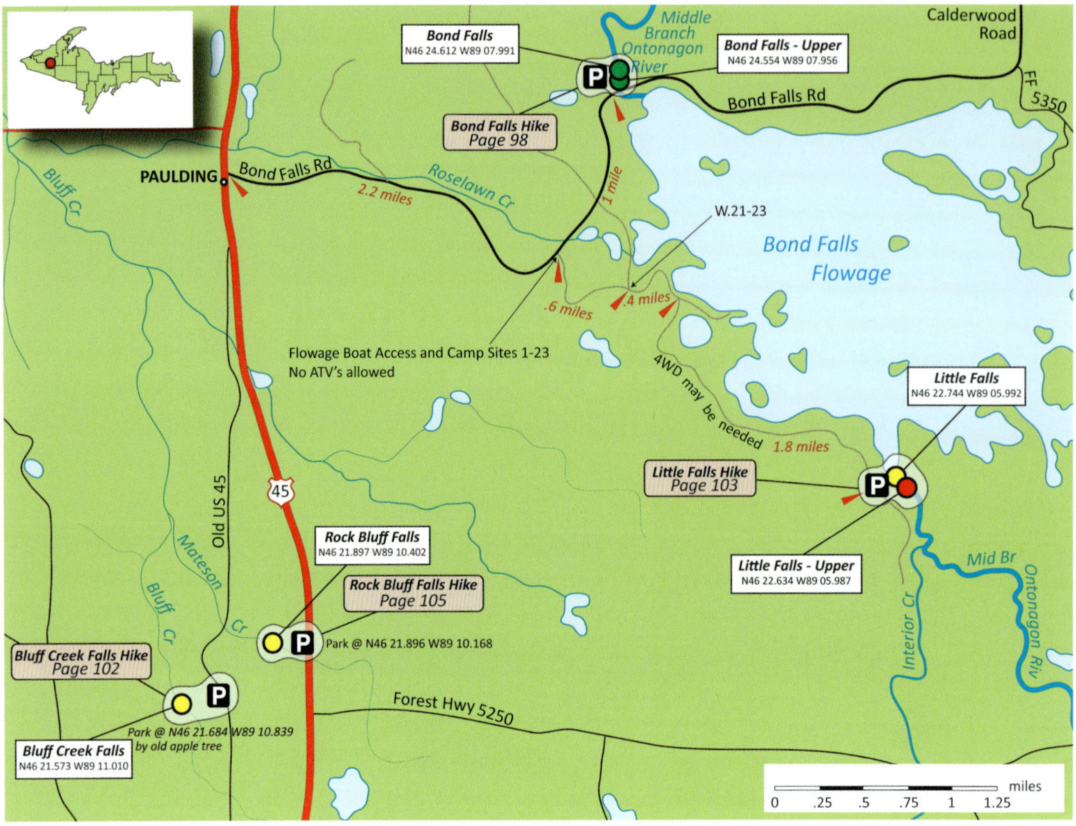

Bond Falls Hike

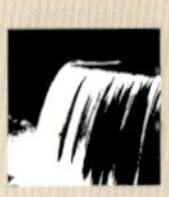

What a waterfall! A number of smaller drops conclude with the main drop that is so well known. About 500 gallons of water flow over the falls every second. This supports a thriving brook trout population.

Six viewing locations along an expansive boardwalk allows for a number of visitors to enjoy a multitude of perspectives of this top-rated waterfall. This is the easiest of the waterfalls with my "10" ratings to hike to. It is only about 200 yards to the falls on a fairly level wheelchair accessible path.

There are more rustic paths leading away from the observation deck along both sides of the waterfall. These lead to the Upper Falls. The trail on the west side is the better of the two and passes by the famous "Z" that is a favorite stopping spot for photographers.

A Recreational Passport is required for access to the site. For current information check the DNR website at http://www.michigandnr.com/parksandtrails/Details.aspx?id=412&type=SPRK or call (906) 353-6558.

Directions: About 10 miles north of US-2 and 9 miles south of M-28 on US-45 is the ghost town of Paulding. A gas station on the corner serves as a landmark for Bond Falls Road. Turn east and follow Bond Falls Road for 3.2 miles to the well marked entrance to Bond Falls on the left (north). A short steep paved drive descends to the base level below the falls. Park in the ample lot. Hike 200 yards to the observation deck. Climb up the trails on either side of the waterfall to access the Upper Falls.

BOND FALLS (MIDDLE BRANCH - ONTONAGON RIVER)

Private

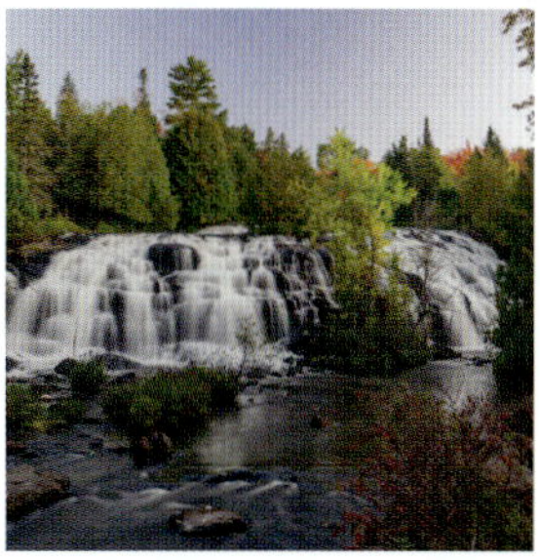

Must See:	10	GPS:	N46 24.612 W89 07.991
Height:	50 feet		
Time:	5-60 minutes	Hiking Information	
		Path:	Boardwalk
Driving Information		Length:	200 yards
Signs:	Large Entrance	Elev. Change:	Slight
Road:	Secondary	GPS:	N/A
Access:	Easy	Danger:	Slight
4WD:	N/A	WP Boots:	N/A to helpful

Bond Falls has been attracting sightseers since the 1800's. In the 1930's the Bond Falls Dam project was begun. The idea was to divert water from the Ontonagon River's Middle Branch to the South Branch by means of Roselawn, Sucker and Bluff Creeks. This would increase the water flow to the Victoria Power Plant by as much as 35 percent, allowing for a decent increase in the amount of electricity produced there. Nearby mines were demanding more and more cheap power and this seemed like the perfect fix. Unfortunately, when the diversion took place in 1937, the ENTIRE Middle Branch was stopped for years as the flowage filled up. This killed all the fish down river and created a huge outcry from fishermen and environmentalists as well as the local population. Plans for several more dams scheduled for construction along the river were scrapped. Finally, in 1940, water was again flowing over Bond and Agate Falls. Much has been done in the years since to restore the public trust. Just recently, a $5 million upgrade to the dam and spillway has improved the safety of the dam and allows for a greater flow of water over the falls.

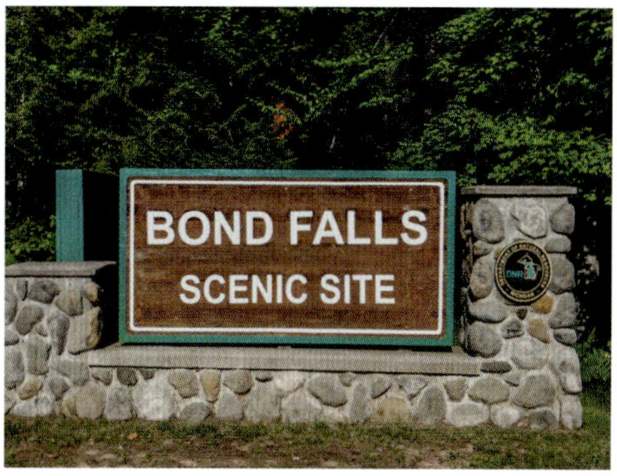

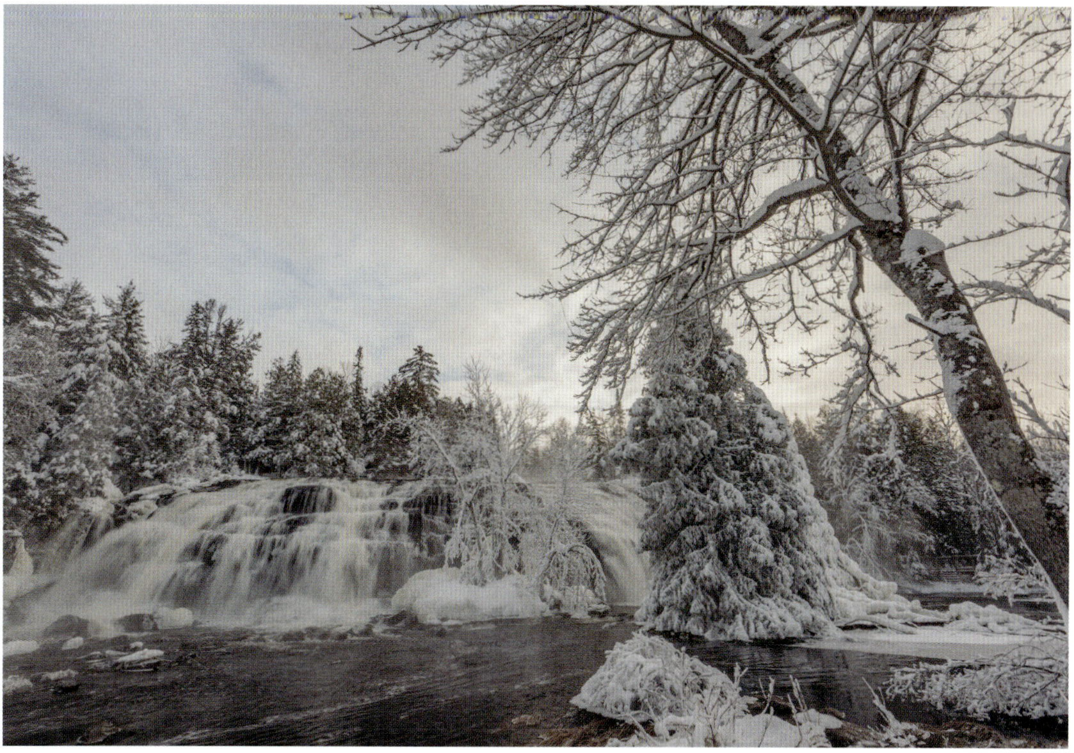

ONTONAGON COUNTY

Bond Falls

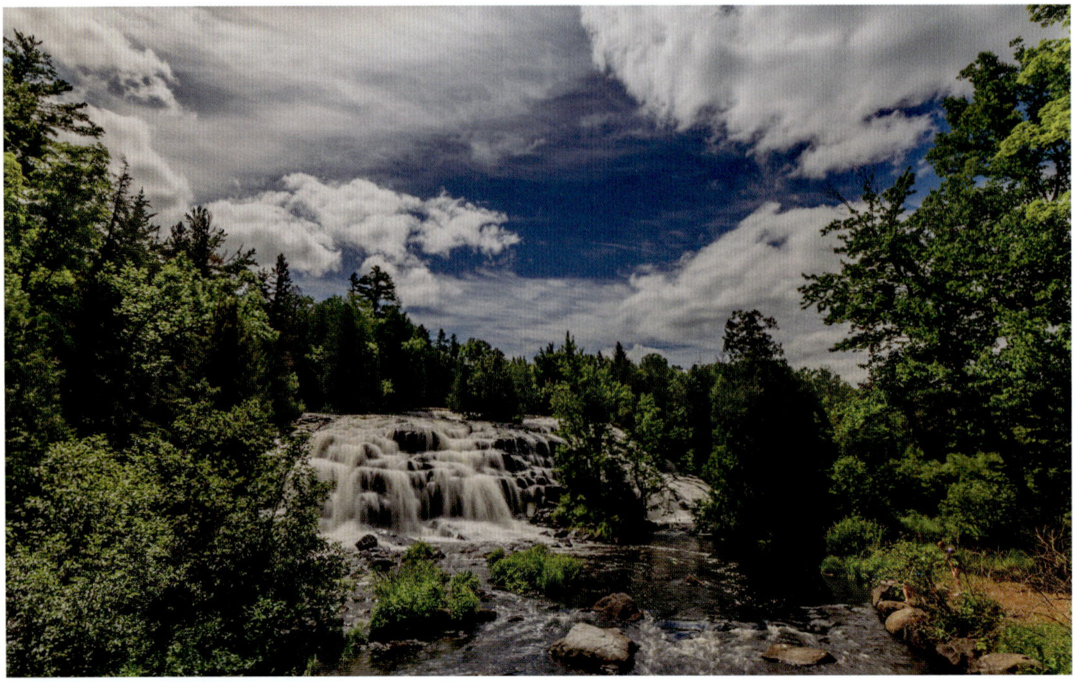

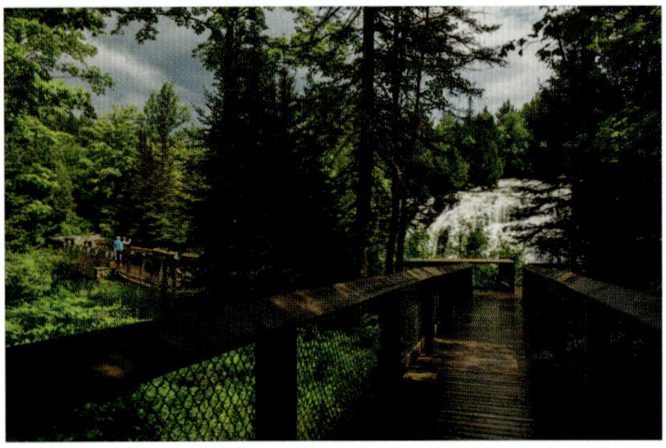

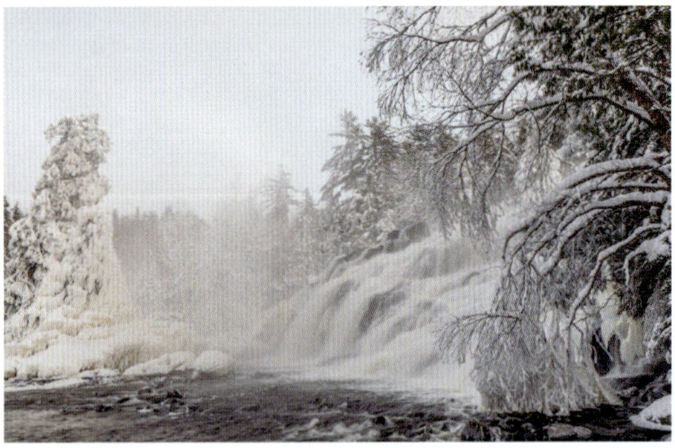

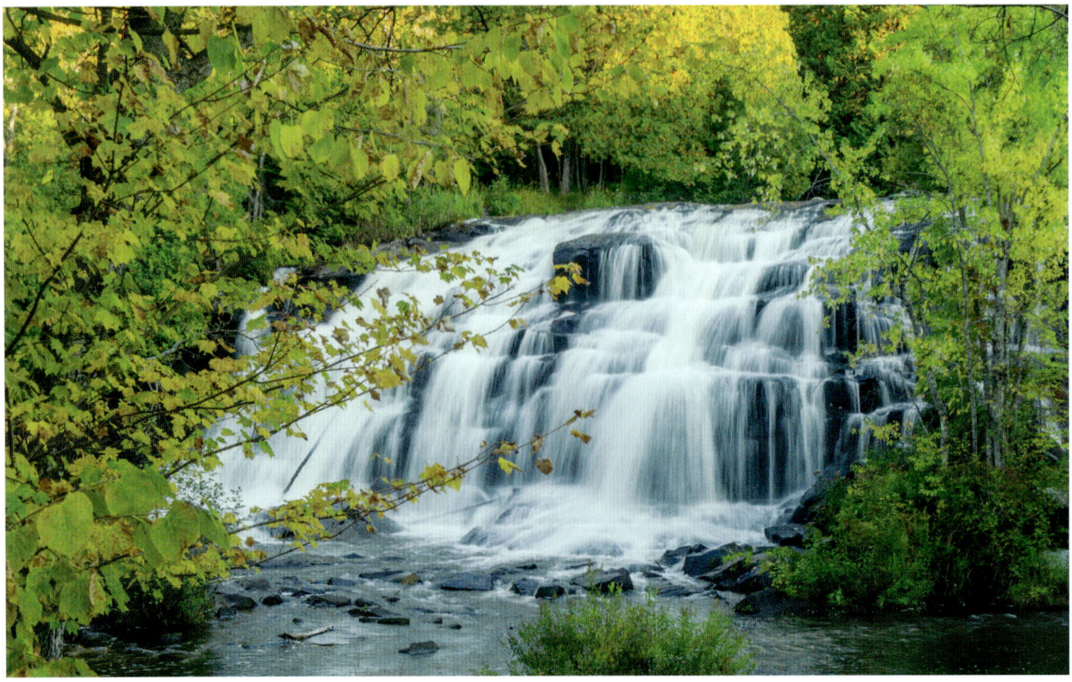

BOND FALLS - UPPER (MIDDLE BRANCH - ONTONAGON RIVER)

Private

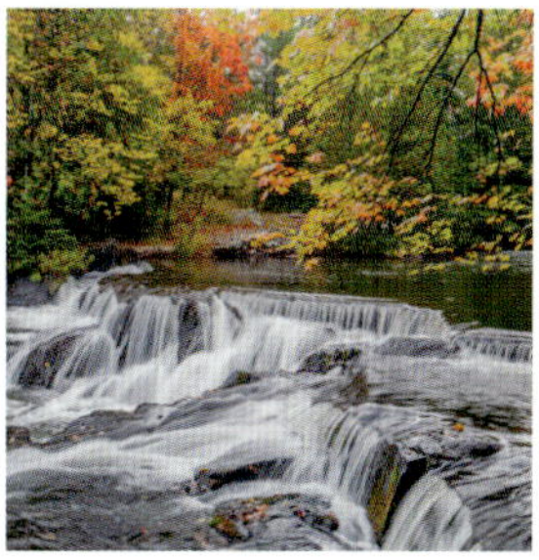

Must See:	7	GPS:	N46 24.554 W89 07.956
Height:	20 feet		
Time:	20-75 minutes	Hiking Information	
		Path:	Boardwalk,Stairs, Path
Driving Information		Length:	300 yards
Signs:	Large Entrance	Elev. Change:	Moderate
Road:	Secondary	GPS:	N/A
Access:	Easy	Danger:	Slight
4WD:	N/A	WP Boots:	N/A to helpful

Climb up the improved side of Bond Falls (west side). Concrete stairways with rails assist in the ascent. Keep in mind that in the winter, spray from the falls ices the stairway, making it extremely dangerous.

Once at the top of Bond Falls, the Upper falls come into view. There are a series of drops that can be seen as you walk along the river's edge. Autumn viewing is iconic and you will likely join other tourists enjoying the breath taking beauty of one of Michigan's most visited waterfalls.

Remember: A Michigan Recreational Passport is required for admittance to Bond Falls. They can be purchased on site.

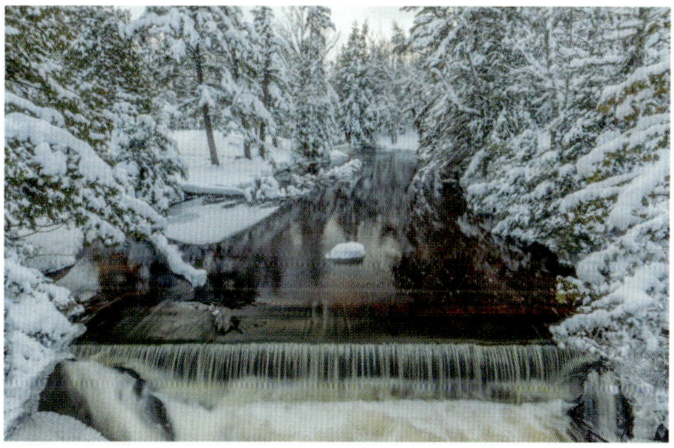

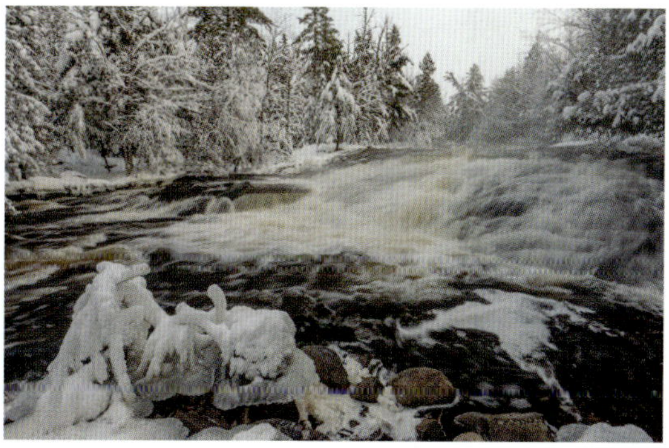

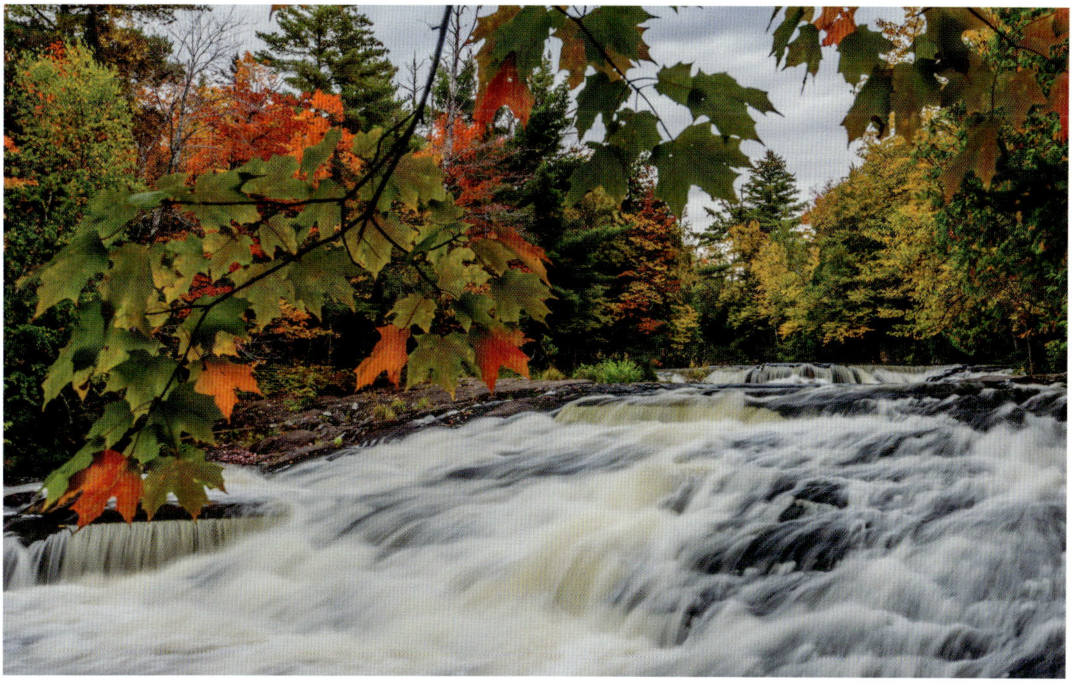

Bluff Creek Falls Hike

I searched for Rock Bluff Falls for years. As things turned out I found this waterfall while looking for that waterfall! So how did I get here? After ending up in a swamp several times, I finally found some new directions *(Still not correct for getting to Rock Bluff Falls!)*. I climbed down into the deep ravine by the "Paulding Lights" parking area. Bluff Creek runs southeast to northwest. I followed the creek down river. The undergrowth along the creek is extremely thick and I found that it was often easier to walk in the creek than on the land. I startled several large trout along the way. The ravine became deeper and steeper before gradually flattening out a little. After about 3/4 mile there was the small waterfall. Unfortunately, a couple of trees had fallen across the creek right at the waterfall. In time they will deteriorate and the waterfall will improve its look.

Since Bluff Creek roughly parallels Old US-45, I am saving you from the longer, more difficult hike along the creek. It is a much shorter and easier hike if you follow the directions below!

Directions: About .3 miles south of Paulding, veer right (south) onto Old US-45. Follow it for about 2.7 miles. Park along side the dirt road at N46 21.684 W89 10.839 by an old apple tree. Hike .18 miles down into the ravine to the falls. There is no trail. USE A GPS.

BLUFF CREEK FALLS (BLUFF CREEK)

Private

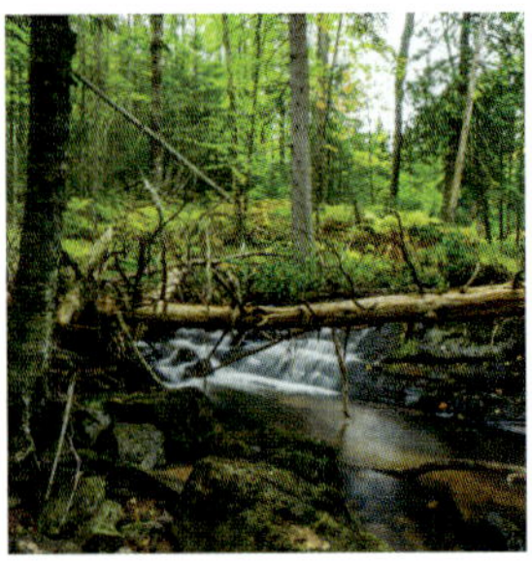

Must See:	4	GPS:	N46 21.573 W89 11.010
Height:	3 feet		
Time:	45-60 minutes	Hiking Information	
		Path:	None
Driving Information		Length:	.18 miles
Signs:	None	Elev. Change:	Major
Road:	Dirt	GPS:	Required
Access:	Somewhat Easy	Danger:	Increased
4WD:	N/A	WP Boots:	Recommended

The creek is at the bottom of a 60 foot deep ravine. Be aware of the need to hike down the steep sides with no trail.

The waterfall is located halfway around the last turn of a zig-zag that the creek makes here. As seen in these photos, several large trees have recently fallen across the creek.

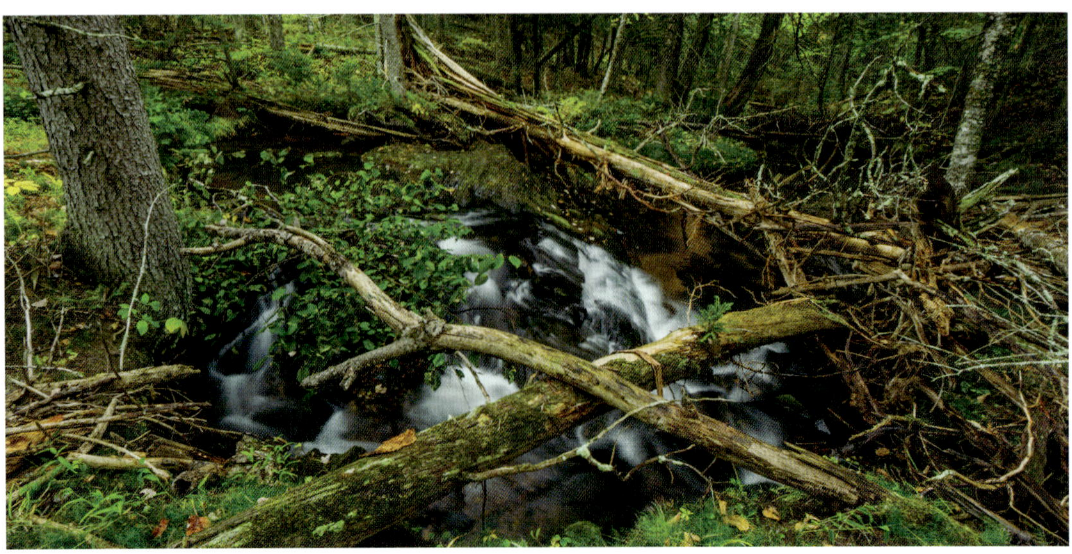

Little Falls Hike

At the entrance to the Bond Falls Flowage is a set of two waterfalls. Warning: If the flowage is too high, Little Falls may be under water. The "Little Falls" name is quite appropriate! The small drops here are "under whelming" after seeing Bond Falls just below the flowage.

Directions: About 10 miles north of US-2 and 9 miles south of M-28 on US-45 is the ghost town of Paulding. A gas station on the corner serves as a landmark for Bond Falls Road. Turn east and follow Bond Falls Road for 2.2 miles. Turn right (south) on a good dirt road. A sign here reads, "Flowage Boat Access and Camp Sites 1-23". Follow this road for .6 miles. Stay to the right where a sign reads, "W.21-23". Continue for .4 miles. Turn right. This road may require a 4WD to navigate. Follow it for 1.8 miles to a 2-track on the left (northeast). The short 2-track ends in about 200 feet. Park. Hike about 400 feet to the falls.

LITTLE FALLS (MIDDLE BRANCH - ONTONAGON RIVER)

Private

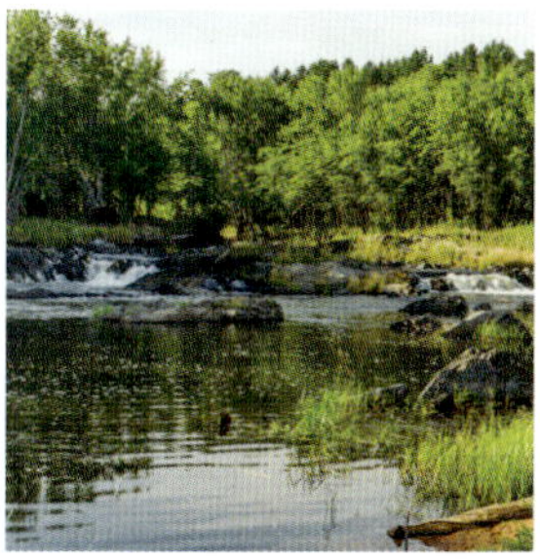

Must See:	5	GPS:	N46 22.672 W89 06.002
Height:	4 feet		
Time:	15-30 minutes	Hiking Information	
		Path:	Minor Footpath
Driving Information		Length:	200 feet
Signs:	None	Elev. Change:	Slight
Road:	Dirt	GPS:	Helpful
Access:	Somewhat Difficult	Danger:	Slight
4WD:	Recommended	WP Boots:	Helpful

As the river enters the Bond Falls Flowage area, the river divides around an island of black rock. The falls on the right side are three feet high, while the falls on the left are four feet. Both sides cascade over rounded rocks, throwing up white water.

Here the waterfall is gone as the flowage is backed up and covering the short rocky drop

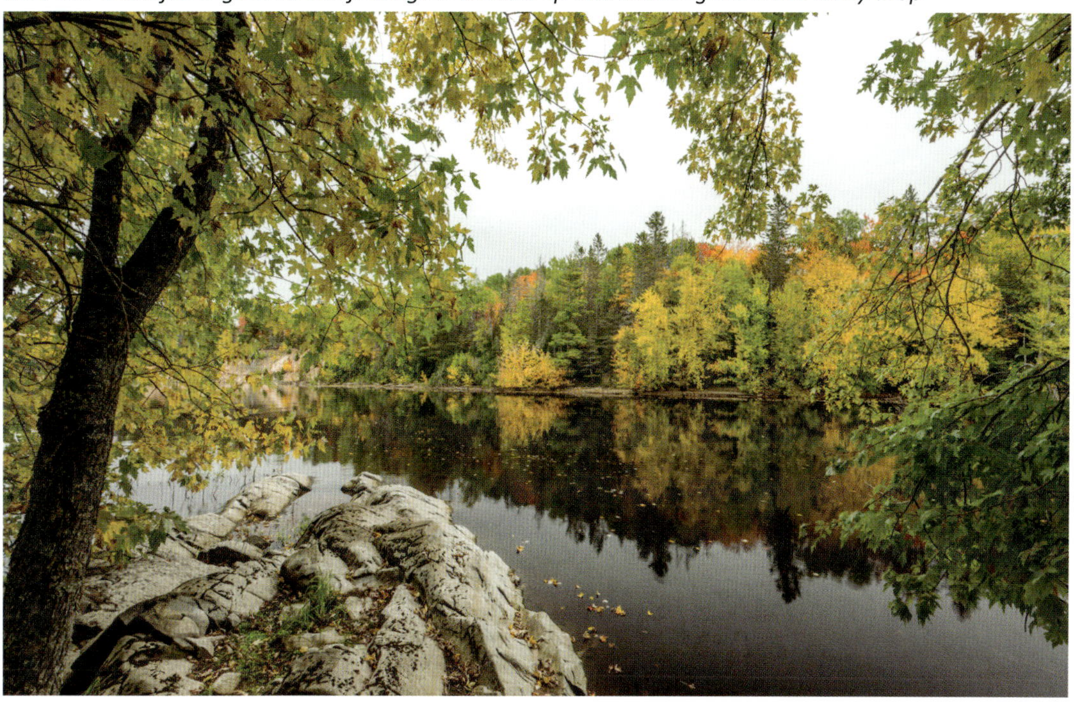

LITTLE FALLS - UPPER (MIDDLE BRANCH - ONTONAGON RIVER) Private

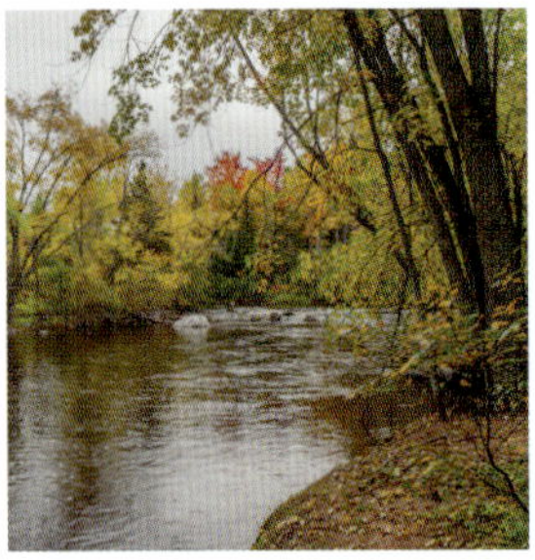

Must See:	3	GPS:	N46 22.634 W89 05.987
Height:	2 feet		
Time:	20-40 minutes	Hiking Information	
		Path:	Minor Footpath
Driving Information		Length:	300 yards
Signs:	None	Elev. Change:	Slight
Road:	Dirt	GPS:	Helpful
Access:	Somewhat Difficult	Danger:	Slight
4WD:	Recommended	WP Boots:	Helpful

Just upriver about 250 yards from Little Falls , this two-tiered cascade spans the entire sixty foot wide river. A nicely beaten footpath from Little Falls follows the shoreline for an easy walk through knee high grass and level terrain!

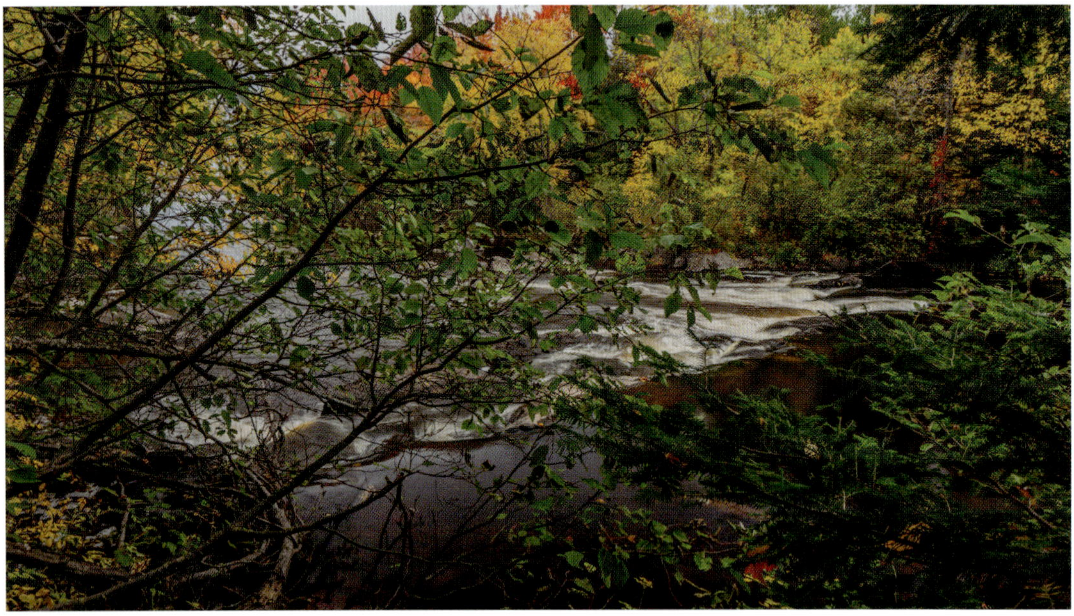

As this waterfall is higher than Little Falls it doesn't get flooded even when the flowage is high

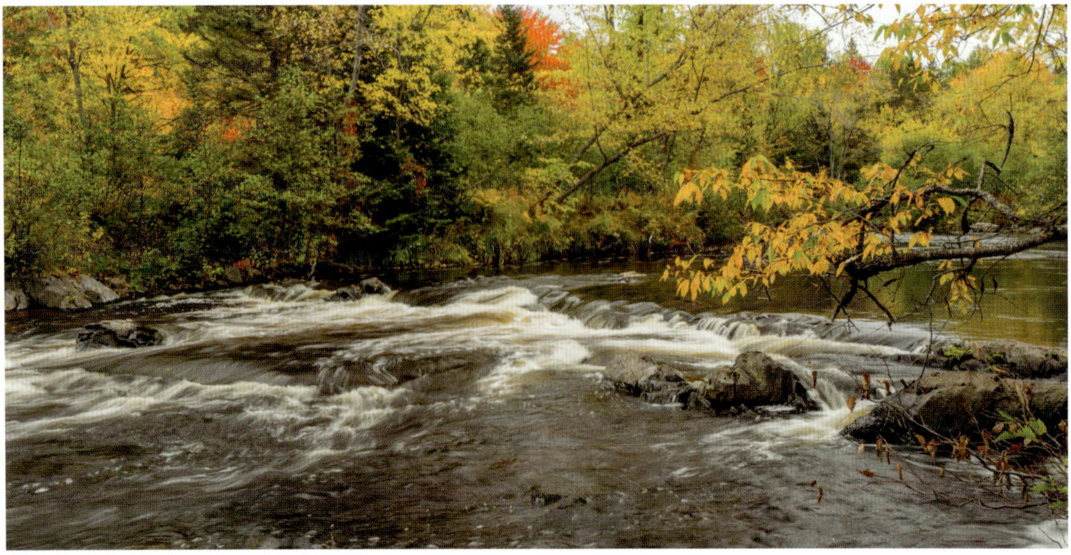

Rock Bluff Falls Hike

This waterfall eluded me for years. My best information seemed to point to some location along Bluff Creek. It made sense with the "Bluff" idea syncing the two names. After talking to the very helpful folks at Sylvania Outfitters in Watersmeet, they informed me of this waterfall and I'm quite sure that this is the "true" Rock Bluff Falls. After all, this waterfall actually falls over a rock bluff!

Directions: About 2.6 miles south of Paulding, park off the side of US-45. You should be at N46 21.896 W89 10.168. There is no trail and you will be taking a short cut to the creek instead of following the creek bed to the waterfall. You must have a GPS for this shortcut hike. Follow the GPS coordinates to the waterfall.

(If you don't have a GPS, park a little further south on US-45 near where the guard rail lines both sides of the road. Follow Mateson Creek downstream (west) for about .25 miles to the waterfall.)

ROCK BLUFF FALLS (MATESON CREEK)

Private

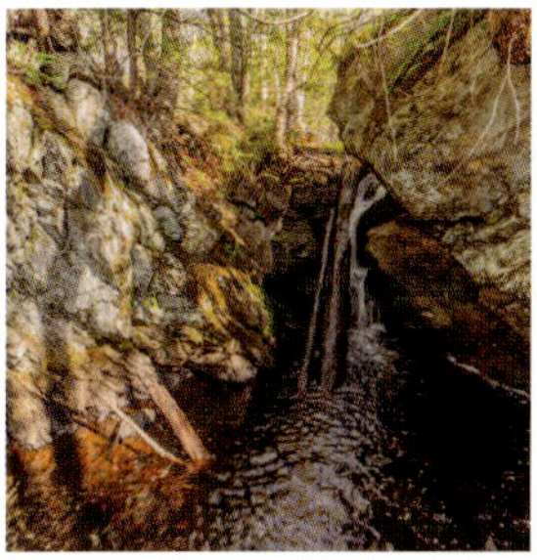

Must See:	4	GPS:	N46 21.897 W89 10.402
Height:	20 feet		
Time:	45-60 minutes	Hiking Information	
		Path:	None
Driving Information		Length:	.19 miles
Signs:	None	Elev. Change:	Minor
Road:	Main	GPS:	Required
Access:	Somewhat Easy	Danger:	Moderate
4WD:	N/A	WP Boots:	Recommended

Rock Bluff Falls begins with a ten foot, fast slide and drop between two sharp overhanging points on the bluff. After passing through a jumble of tree debris, the waterfall continues down a protracted intermittent slide and drop series for another ten feet. The water level can be quite low, hence the lower "Must See" rating. It may be quite impressive when the creek bed is rushing with water during the spring melt. There are some wet spots along the hike so waterproof boots are recommended.

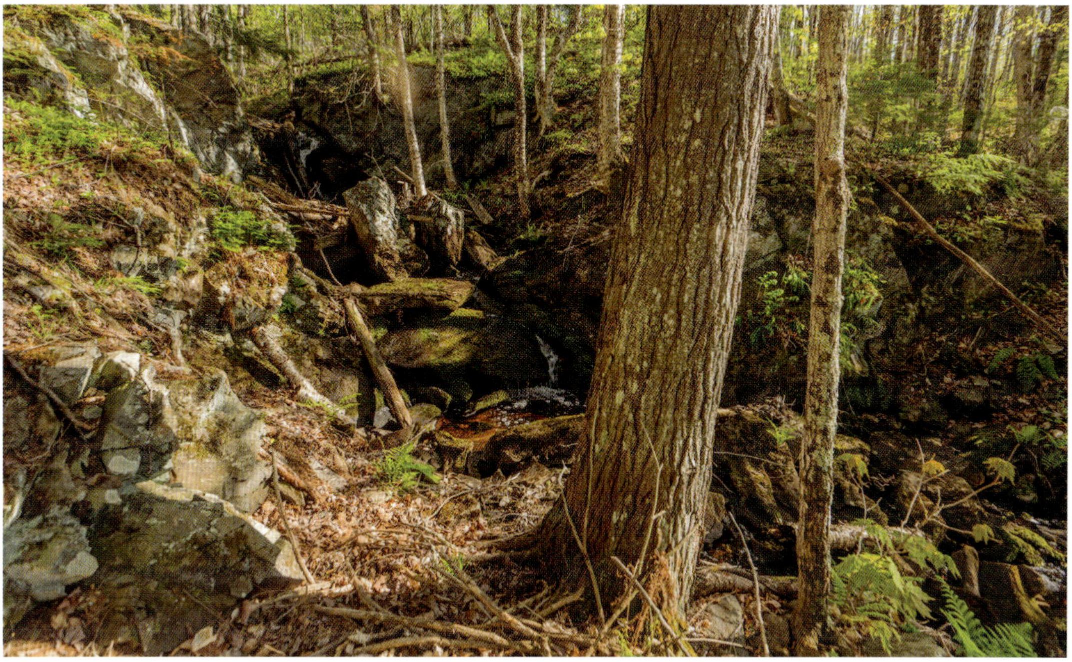

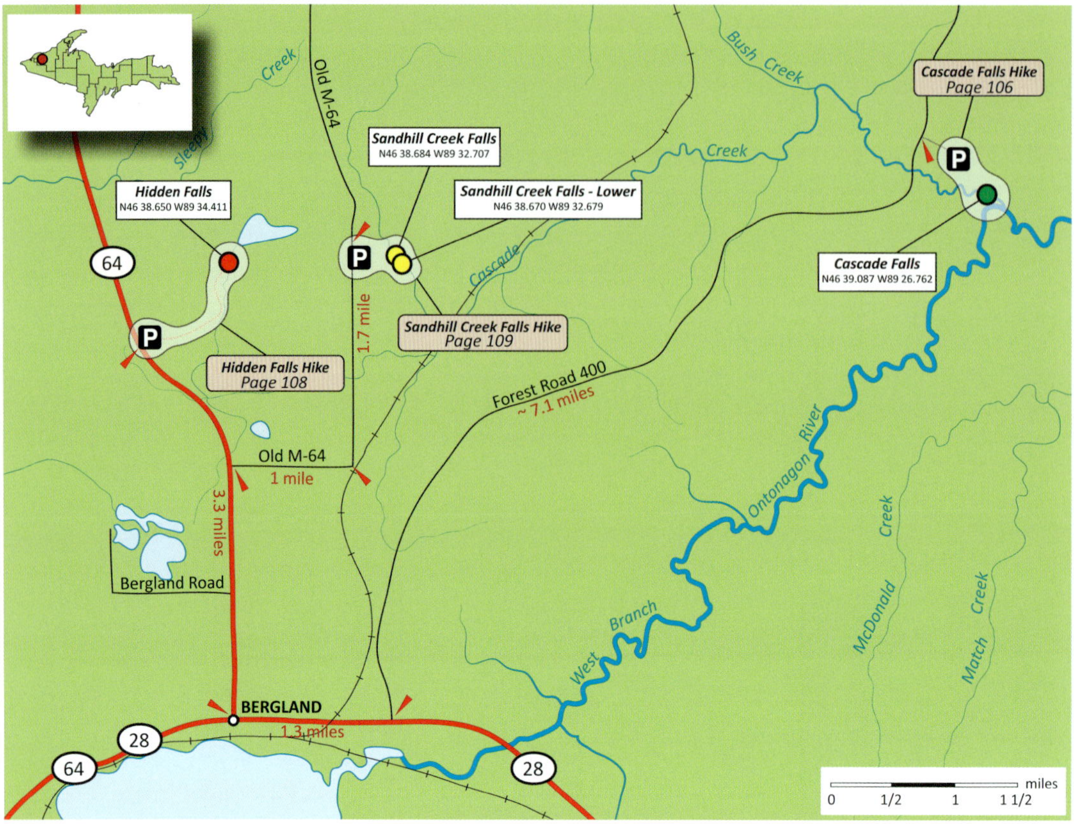

Cascade Falls Hike

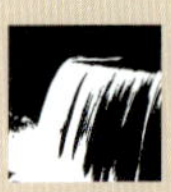

A spur off of the North Country Trail extends southward to Cascade Falls. Take either the "High" or "Low" trail for various looks at the terrain along the hike.

Directions: From Bergland, drive 1.3 miles east on M-28. Turn left (north) onto Forest Road 400 (a dirt road). Follow it for about 7.1 miles. A well marked road to the right ends at the trailhead. There is plenty of room for parking. Hike down the groomed trail to the falls.

CASCADE FALLS (CASCADE CREEK)

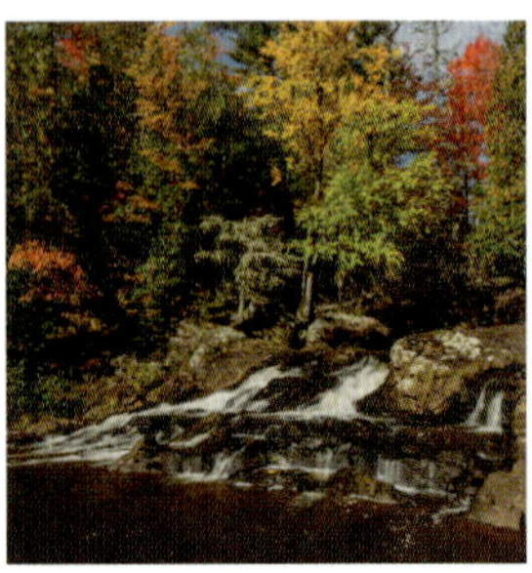

Must See:	7	GPS:	N46 39.087 W89 26.762
Height:	20 feet		
Time:	45-60 minutes	Hiking Information	
		Path:	Well traveled
Driving Information		Length:	1/2 mile
Signs:	Roadside	Elev. Change:	Minor
Road:	Dirt	GPS:	Required
Access:	Somewhat Easy	Danger:	Slight
4WD:	N/A	WP Boots:	Helpful

As the name implies, Cascade Falls is made up of multiple cascades. Wildflowers grow profusely on a multitude of rocks scattered down river from the falls.

One of my most embarrassing waterfall experiences occurred here! I didn't know there was a trail to the falls, so I trekked cross-country with one of my sons along the southern side of the river. The nearly mile long hike led through dense undergrowth, wet areas, briars, and thick pines. We finally made it to this seemingly remote waterfall only to find a family at the top of the falls wearing flip-flops! We were glad to hike the extra mile back to the vehicle via the newly discovered trail!

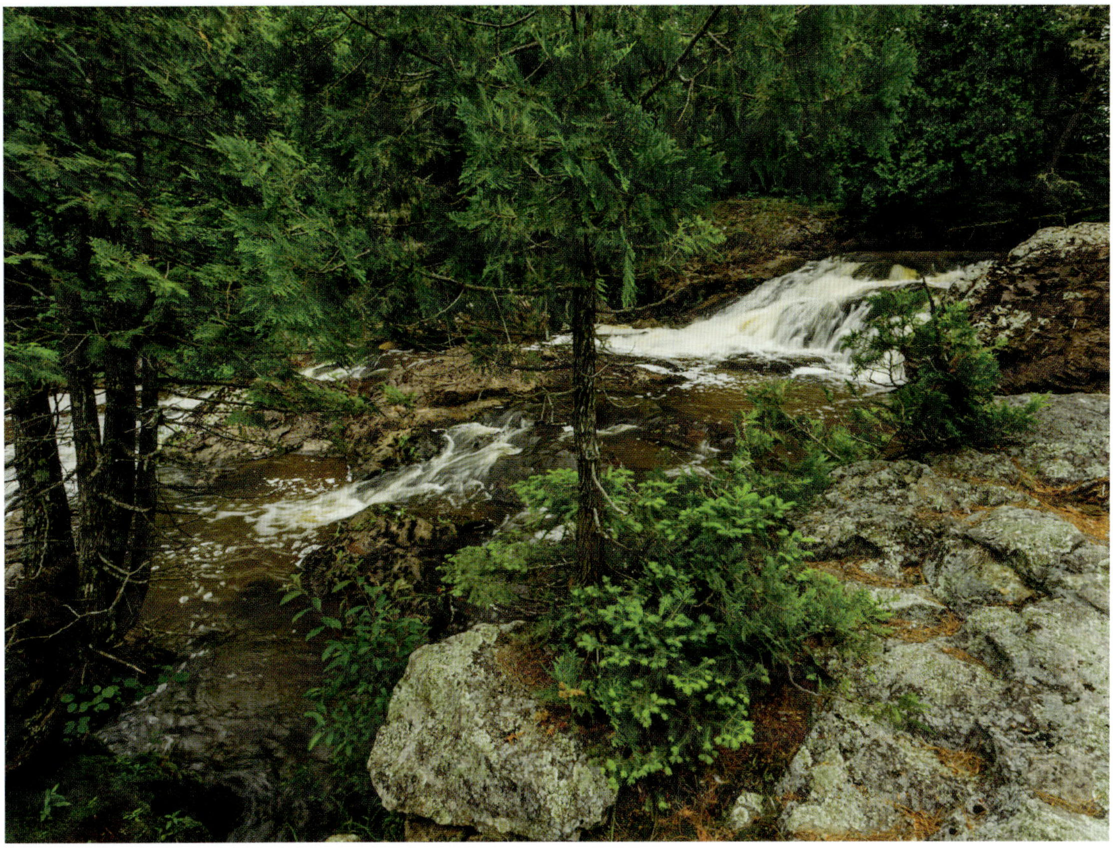

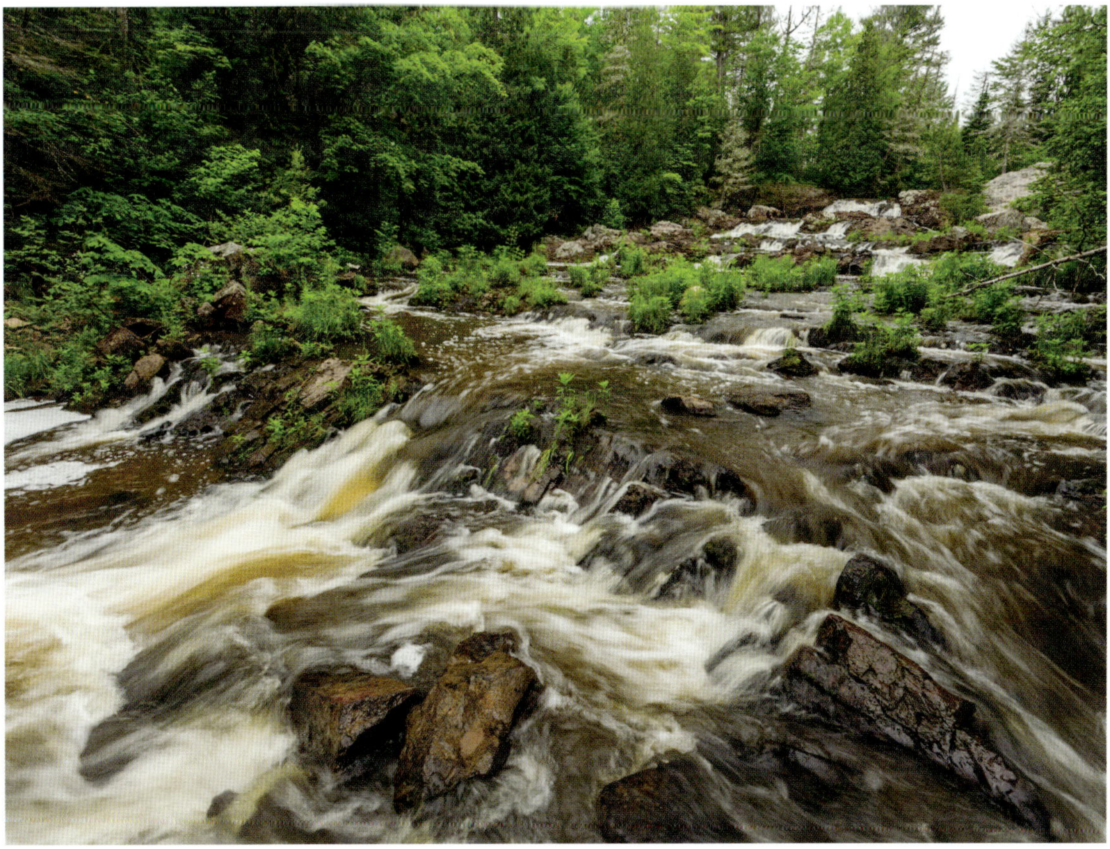

Hidden Falls Hike

Weidman Lake is a fairly high elevation lake for Michigan at 1483 feet above sea level. It is nestled between two peaks that top out at over 1,700 feet each. An unnamed stream exits the lake to the southwest, tumbling down some minor drops before reaching Hidden Falls some 250 yards beyond the lake.

Directions: From Bergland, drive north on M-64 for 3.2 miles. Turn into a small parking area for a trailhead for the Gogebic Ridge Trail at N46 38.119 W89 35.379. Hike the footpath for about 1 mile. It ends at the creek. Follow the GPS coordinates through some dense undergrowth to the falls.

HIDDEN FALLS (CASCADE CREEK)

Private

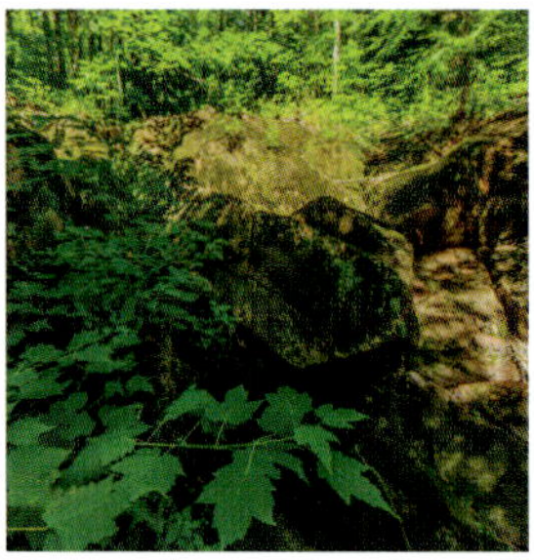

Must See:	2	GPS:	N46 38.650 W89 34.411
Height:	8 feet		
Time:	1 1/2 to 2 hours	Hiking Information	
		Path:	Footpath then none
Driving Information		Length:	1.2 miles
Signs:	None	Elev. Change:	Minor
Road:	Main	GPS:	Required
Access:	Somewhat Easy	Danger:	Moderate
4WD:	N/A	WP Boots:	Recommended

The stream was down to a trickle the one time that I was here (as seen in these pictures). With a good flow this waterfall might rate a 4 or 5. Angular, flat sided rocks channel the creek over patches of moss. The base of the falls has a tangle of downed trees. There are some smaller drops upstream to explore as well. This waterfall is truly "Hidden"!

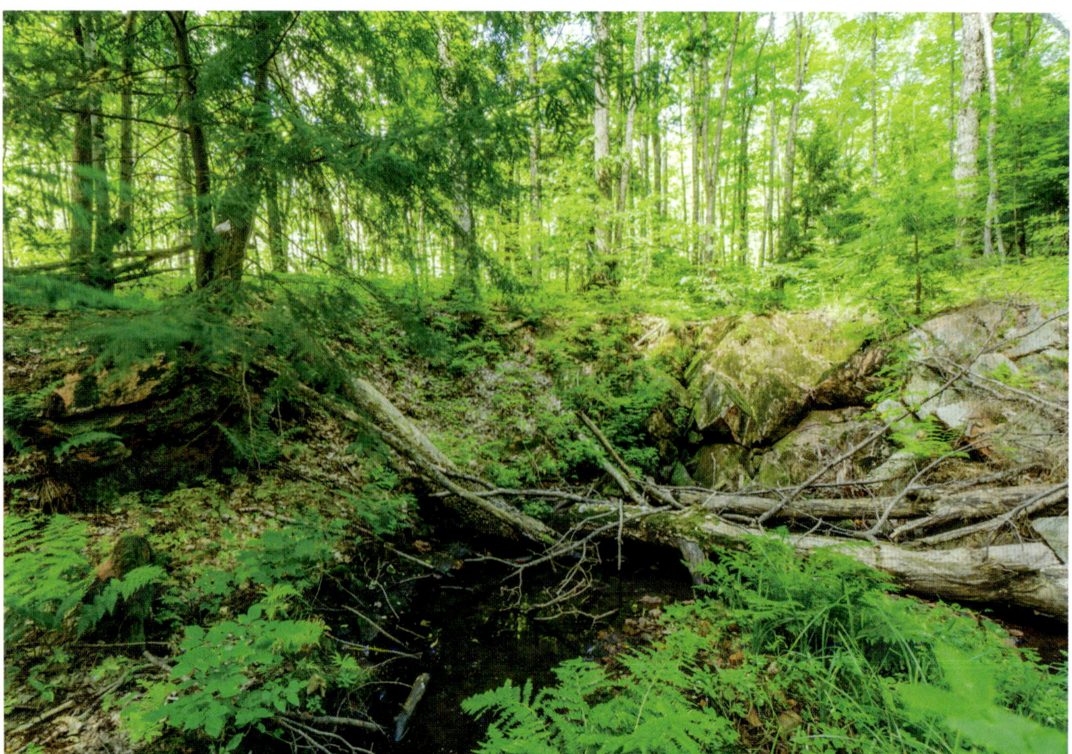

Sandhill Creek Falls Hike

The North Country Trail meanders from peak to peak through some of Michigan's highest country, the spectacular Trap Hills. The trail hairpins three hundred feet above the joining of Sandhill Creek and Cascade Creek. About .9 miles upstream from the mouth of Sandhill Creek is the waterfall.

Directions: Drive 2 miles north of Bergland on M-64. Turn right (east) on Old M-64. In 1 mile the road bends left (north). Follow it for 1.7 miles to an old Forest Road 320H. It's overgrown and is found at N46 38.637 W89 33.147. Park. Hike along the "road" until it disappears. Head toward the GPS coordinates, slightly to the right. There are several wet areas. Keep them to your left. At a large marshy area, once again stay to the right. Skirt the marsh in a large semi-circle, following the high, narrow strip of ground that runs between the marsh on the left and small, wet ravine on the right. Once past the marsh continue through the hilly forest to the falls.

SANDHILL CREEK FALLS (SANDHILL CREEK)

Private

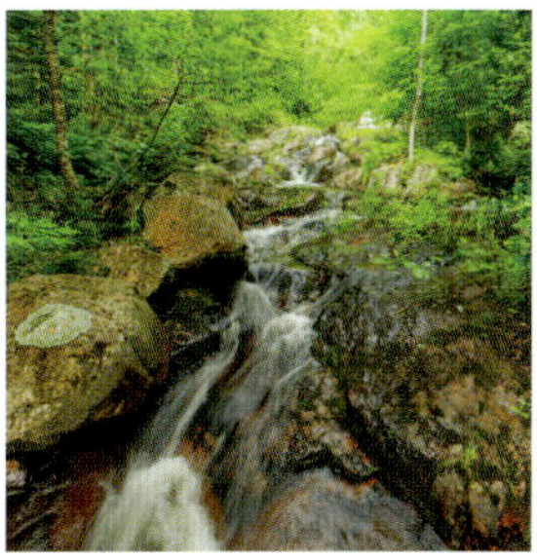

Must See:	6	GPS:	N46 38.684 W89 32.707
Height:	12		
Time:	45-70 minutes	Hiking Information	
		Path:	None
Driving Information		Length:	.35 miles
Signs:	None	Elev. Change:	Moderate
Road:	Dirt	GPS:	Required
Access:	Somewhat Difficult	Danger:	Moderate
4WD:	N/A	WP Boots:	Required

I didn't know about this waterfall until my database was already populated with over 500 drops that I had visited in Michigan. I was excited to add a previously unknown waterfall to this list. All went well until meeting a formidable army of mosquitoes that seemed bent on driving me back out of the woods. I'm sure that the marshy areas passed along this hike served as wonderful breeding grounds for the ever hungry insects.

The waterfall cascades almost constantly for 50 yards with main drops at the start and end of the run. Red and gray basalt lines the creek bed. Slabbed chunks are strewn along the sides.

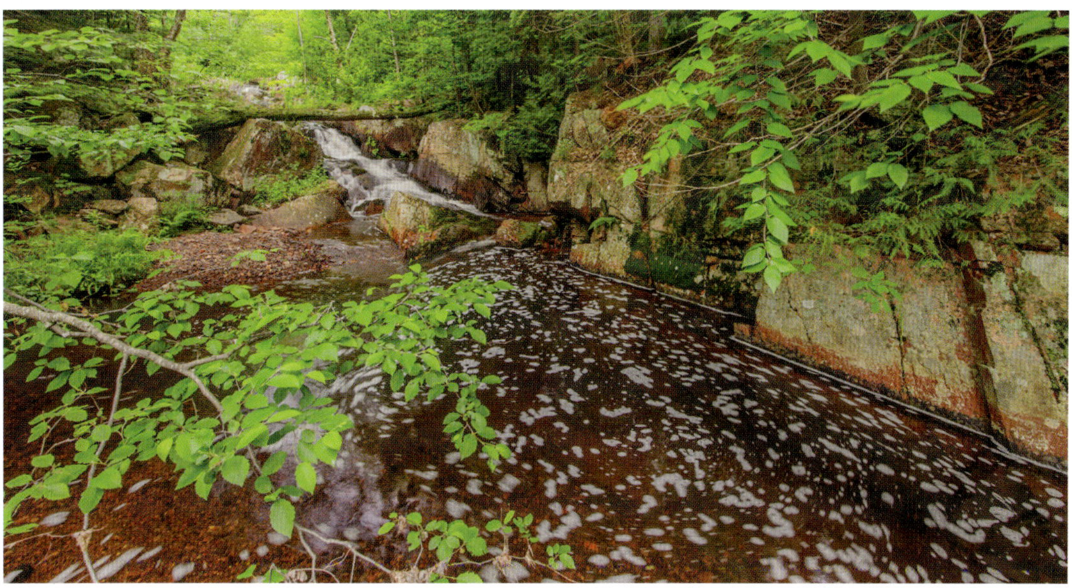

SANDHILL CREEK FALLS - LOWER (SANDHILL CREEK) Private

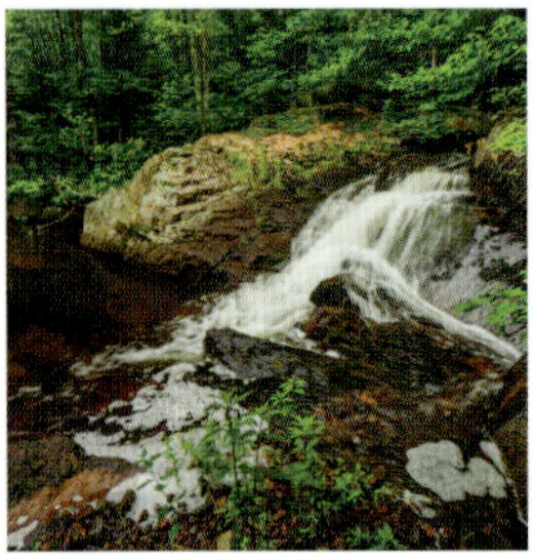

Must See:	5	GPS:	N46 38.670 W89 32.679
Height:	5		
Time:	50-75 minutes	Hiking Information	
		Path:	None
Driving Information		Length:	.35 miles
Signs:	None	Elev. Change:	Moderate
Road:	Dirt	GPS:	Required
Access:	Somewhat Difficult	Danger:	Moderate
4WD:	N/A	WP Boots:	Required

Just 100 feet downstream from Sandhill Creek Falls is this lower drop. It splashes down at an angle to a dammed up spill pool. Several large rocks create this dam. The creek runs around and under the boulders.

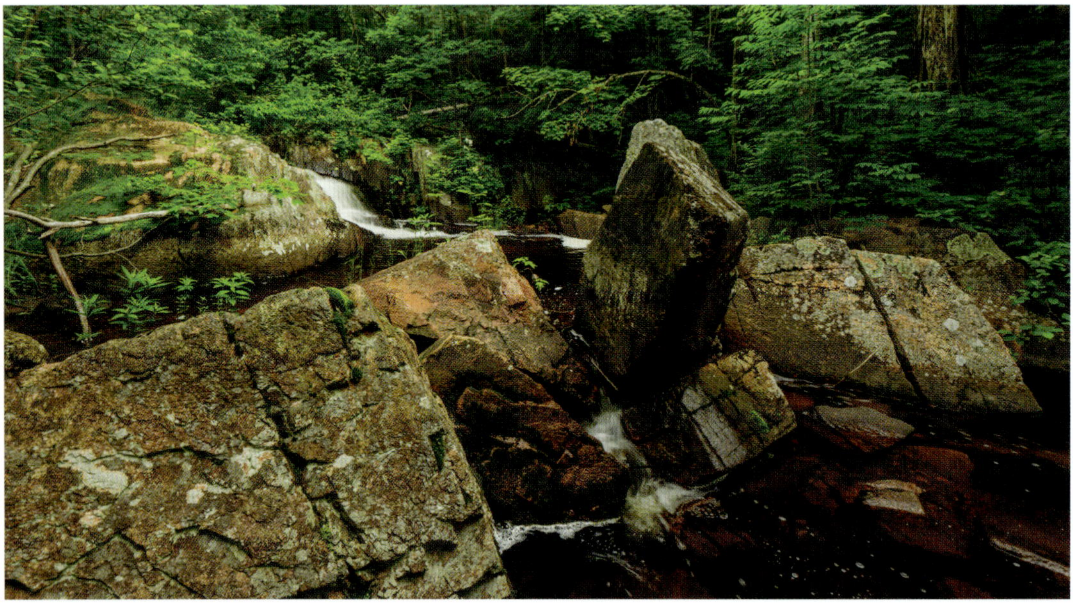

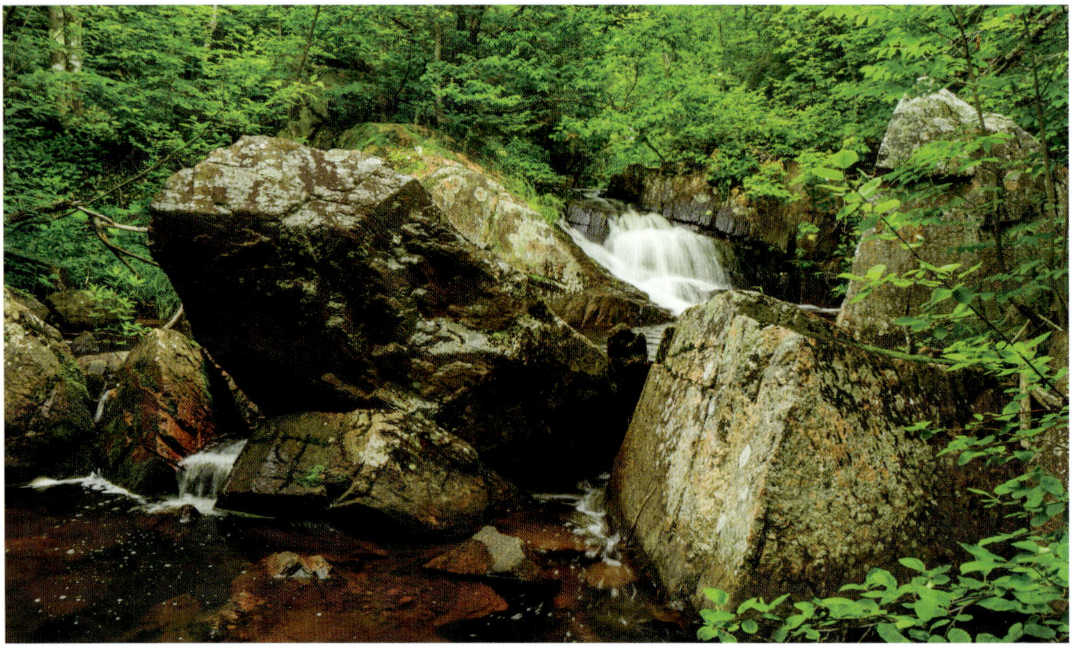

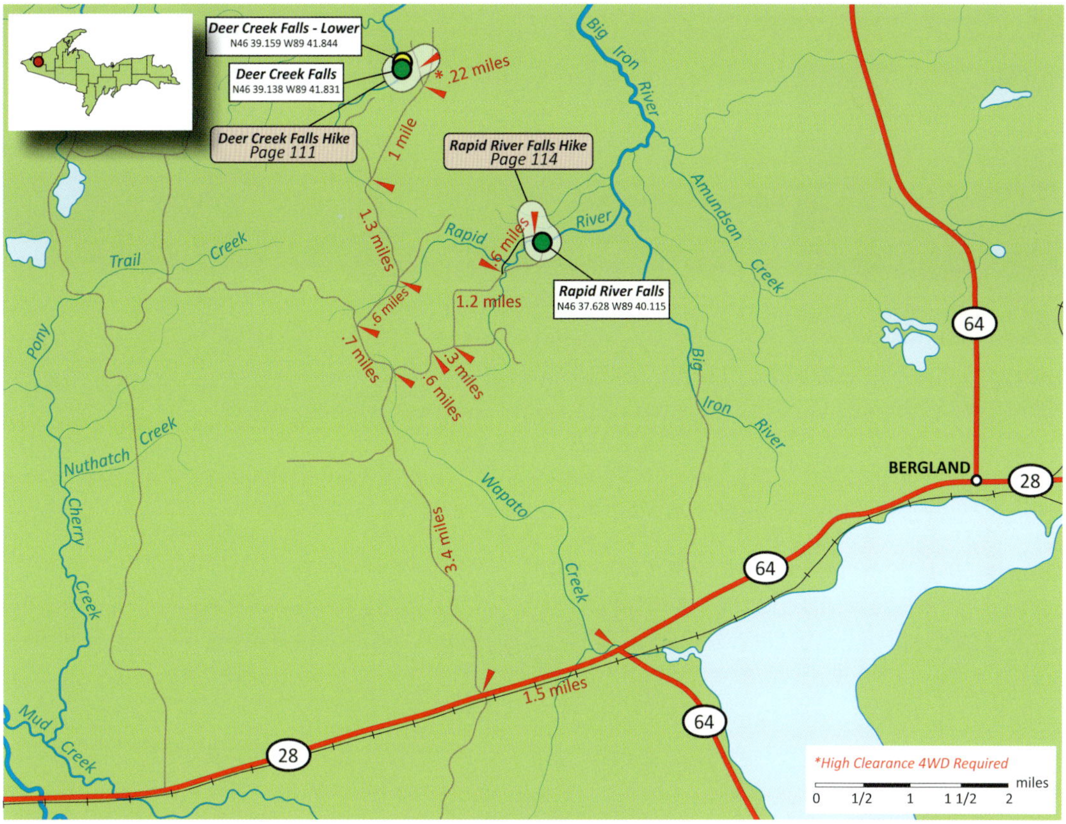

Deer Creek Falls Hike

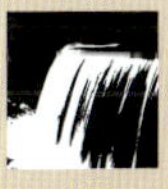

Between M-64 on the east, M-28 to the south, CR-519 to the west and South Boundary Road in the north lies over 240 square miles of Ottawa National Forest. Numerous trails crisscross the land, resulting in a mind-numbing maze. Many 2-tracks dead-end near rivers and creeks, delivering fishermen to their favorite holes. Other promising roads turn out to be nothing more than snowmobile trails, wonderful highways of white in the winter, but dangerous ribbons of green winding through tree filled forests during the warmer months. Three foot high grasses and briars cloak the rocks, stumps, ruts and boggy areas hidden below.

Dissecting this rugged tract roughly into quarters are waterways, most of which run south to north. The Big Iron River is to the east while the Presque Isle River lies to the west. Nearly centered between these two rivers are two lakes a mere 1/4 mile apart. The lake to the north, Clark Lake, empties into the West Branch of the Big Iron River which then flows northerly until it gets close to the Porcupine Mountains State Park boundary. The West Branch then doglegs to the east, meandering a little southwesterly before heading back to the northwest and finally joining the Big Iron River near the village of White Pine. The lake to the south is Bass Lake, which drains into Cherry Creek. This creek defies the norm and flows to the south, eventually meeting up with Mud Creek and shortly thereafter, the Presque Isle River.

Centered between Big Iron River and the West Branch of the Big Iron River is a tributary of Big Iron River, White Deer Creek. After flowing along quietly through scenic woodlands for 2 1/2 miles, the creek suddenly cascades down over a moss covered rock face, turns sharply to the left and continues a bumpy journey downstream.

Directions: From Bergland, drive 5.7 miles west on M-28. Turn right (north) onto a good, dirt road. Follow it for 3.4 miles. Continue for another .7 miles. Turn right for .6 miles. Veer left for 1.3 miles. Continue straight for 1 mile. Turn left (if you have a high clearance 4WD) for .22 miles. Park. Hike (no trail) to the GPS coordinates.

ONTONAGON COUNTY

DEER CREEK FALLS (WHITE DEER CREEK)

Private

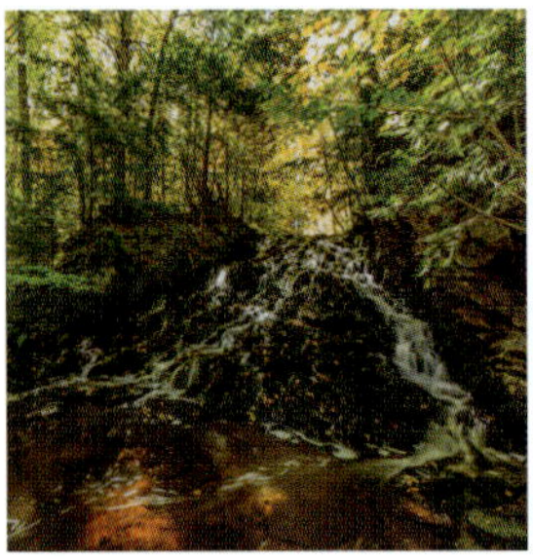

Must See: 7
Height: 16 feet
Time: 20-40 minutes

Driving Information
Signs: None
Road: *Snowmobile or Dirt
Access: Very Difficult
4WD: *Helpful or Required

GPS: N46 39.138 W89 41.831

Hiking Information
Path: None
Length: *.10 or .28 miles
Elev. Change: Minor
GPS: Required
Danger: Moderate
WP Boots: Helpful

During summer the creek dries up. I would love to see the waterfall rushing with spring melt! The "7" rating is an assumption of what this will look like when the creek is running nicely.

Delicate Rivulets cascade down over moss covered rocks. The falls are at the head of a small canyon with 10 to 20 foot walls just downstream. The Lower Falls are found through this stretch.

*The last .22 miles of the drive is on a primitive trail. It requires a high clearance 4WD to navigate the uneven terrain. If you don't have the proper machine for the job just park at the entrance to this trail. Hike along the trail to the northwest before cutting to the west or just head straight for the waterfall. This hike will be about .28 miles, nearly tripling the hike length.

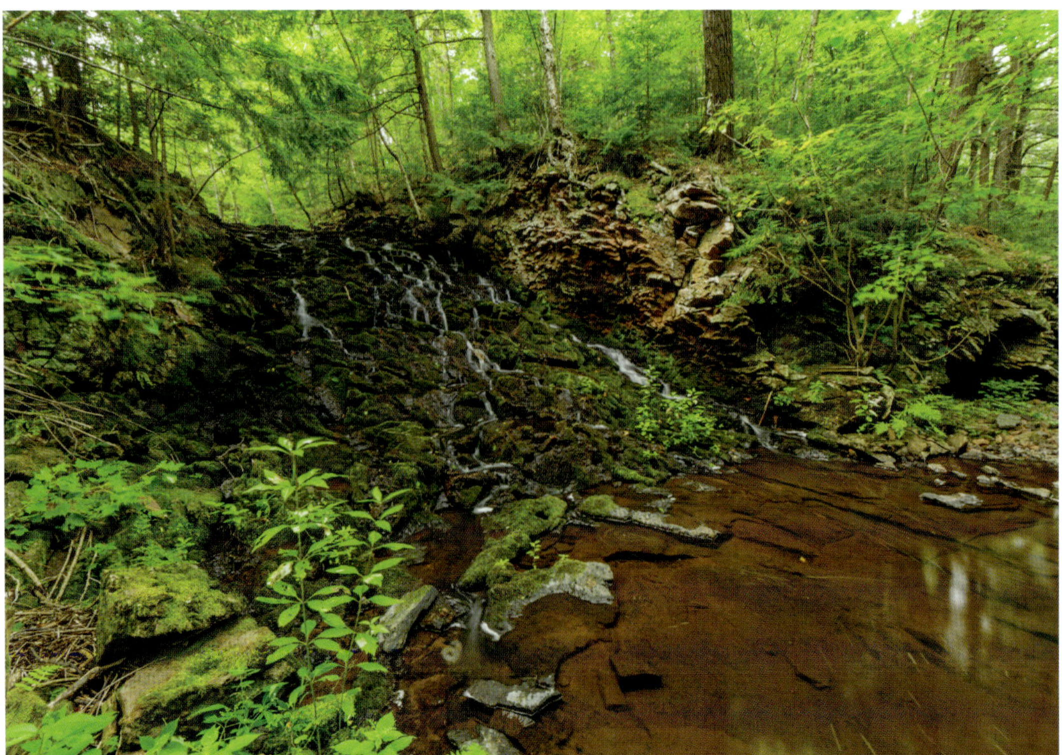

Deer Creek Falls

DEER CREEK FALLS - LOWER (WHITE DEER CREEK)

Private

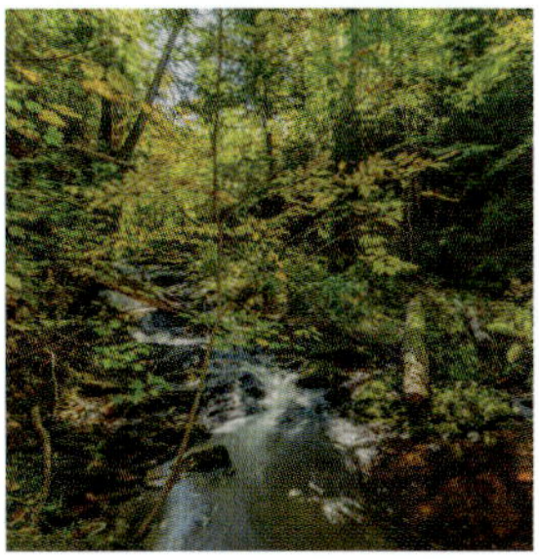

Must See:	4	GPS:	N46 39.159 W89 41.844
Height:	5 feet		
Time:	20-40 minutes	Hiking Information	
		Path:	None
Driving Information		Length:	*.10 or .28 miles
Signs:	None	Elev. Change:	Minor
Road:	*Snowmobile or Dirt	GPS:	Required
Access:	Very Difficult	Danger:	Moderate
4WD:	*Helpful or Required	WP Boots:	Helpful

Fifty yards downstream from Deer Creek Falls the canyon walls are at their highest, rising 20 feet above the creek bed. The fractured bedrock walls tentatively support cedar and birch trees as well as white lichen and thick patches of dark moss. As fate would have it, a couple of trees have fallen into the canyon directly over the waterfall. They will be here until time or a chainsaw move them along. Upstream, a series of rapids hint at the larger waterfall (Deer Creek Falls) lurking around the bend in the creek.

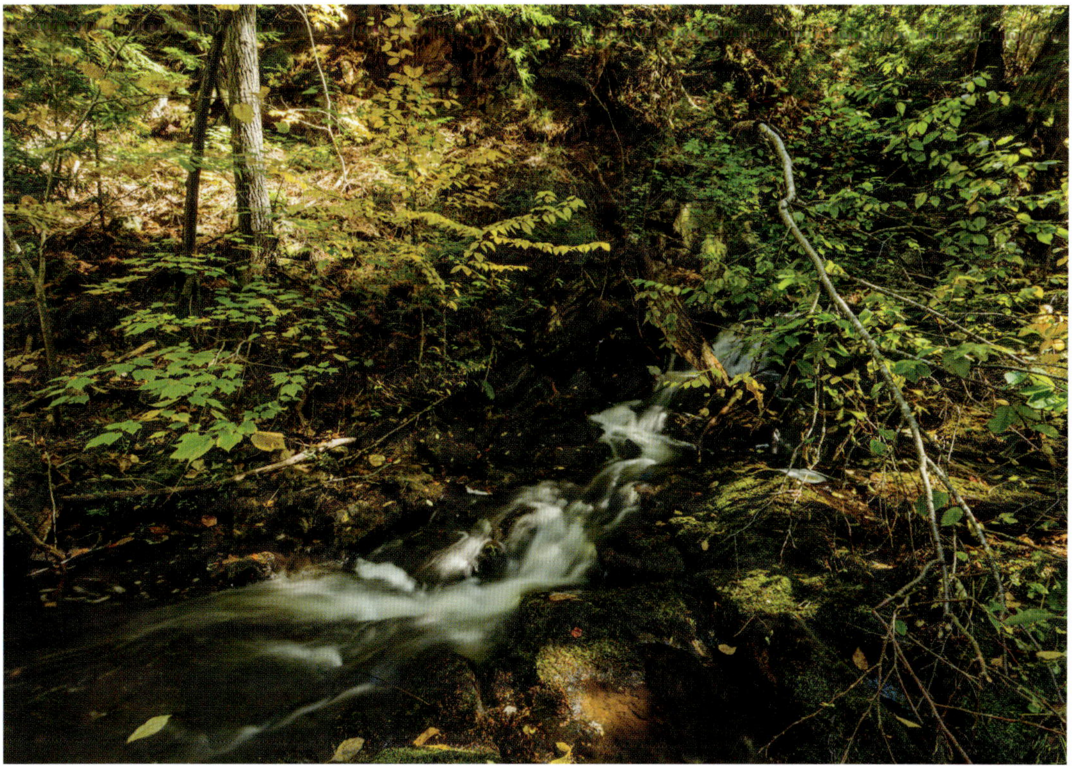

Rapid River Falls Hike

Let's eliminate any confusion right from the start! There is another Rapid River Falls. It is found in Delta County and is much more easily accessed than this one! At the end of the drive, an old bridge crosses over Rapid River. I am not sure it is safe. You might want to hike from here on foot.

Directions: From Bergland, drive 5.7 miles west on M-28. Turn right (north) onto a good, dirt road. Follow it for 3.4 miles. Turn right onto a 2-track and follow it for .6 miles. Turn right. After .3 miles turn left and follow the 2-track for 1.2 miles. Veer left for .6 miles, crossing a very rickety looking bridge and ending in a field within 100 yards of the waterfall.

RAPID RIVER FALLS (RAPID RIVER)

Private

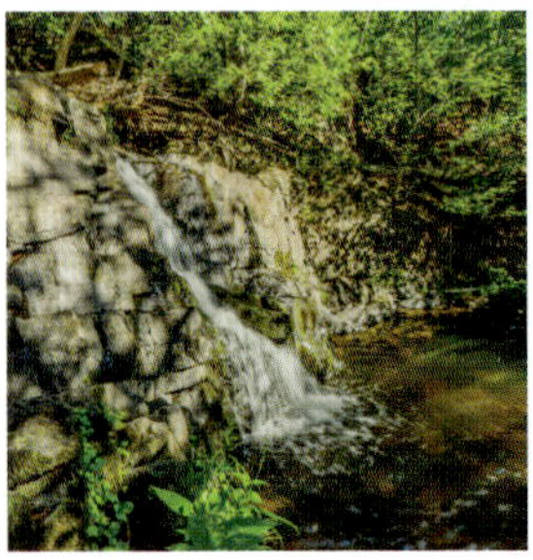

Must See: 8
Height: 17 feet
Time: 10-20 minutes

Driving Information
Signs: None
Road: 2-track
Access: Very Difficult
4WD: Recommended

GPS: N46 37.628 W89 40.115

Hiking Information
Path: None
Length: 100 yards
Elev. Change: Minor
GPS: Recommended
Danger: Minor
WP Boots: Recommended

Warning! Rapid River Falls is on private property. A nice cabin is situated just above the ravine with a good view of the falls. DO NOT ACCESS THE FALLS WITHOUT PERMISSION!

Rapid River narrows to just a couple of feet as it spills down over a 30 foot wide face of rock into a 20 by 30 foot spill pool that is over 6 feet deep. The river then drops another 7 feet out of the center of a second vertical face with a nice stair stepping cascade to a second, smaller spill pool.

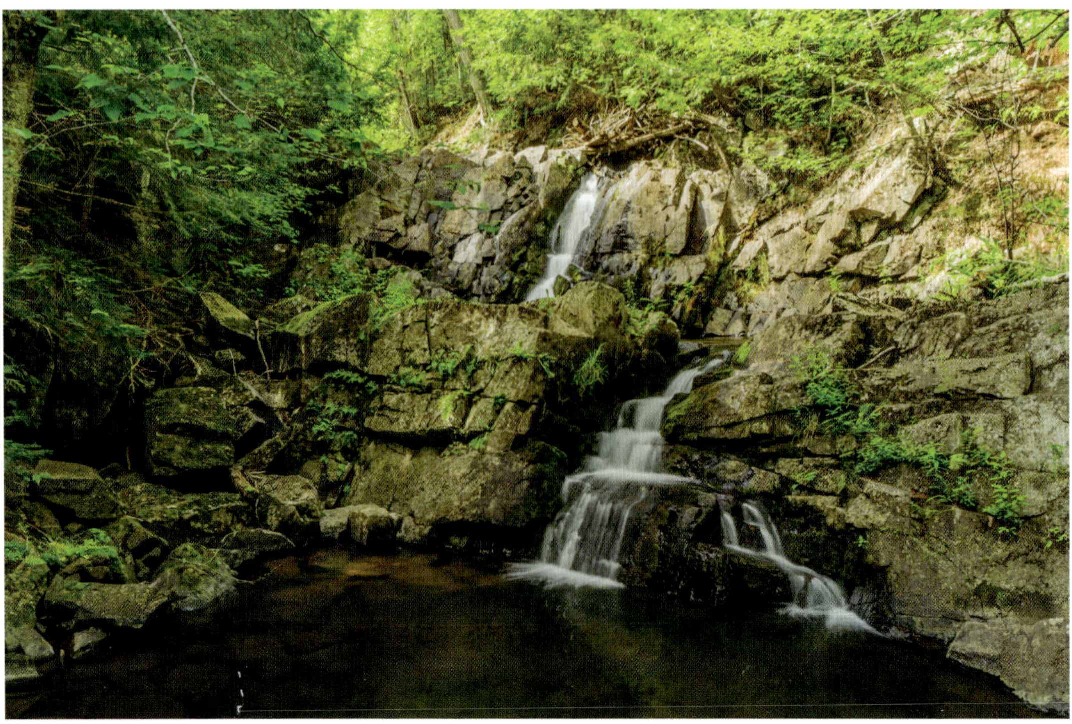

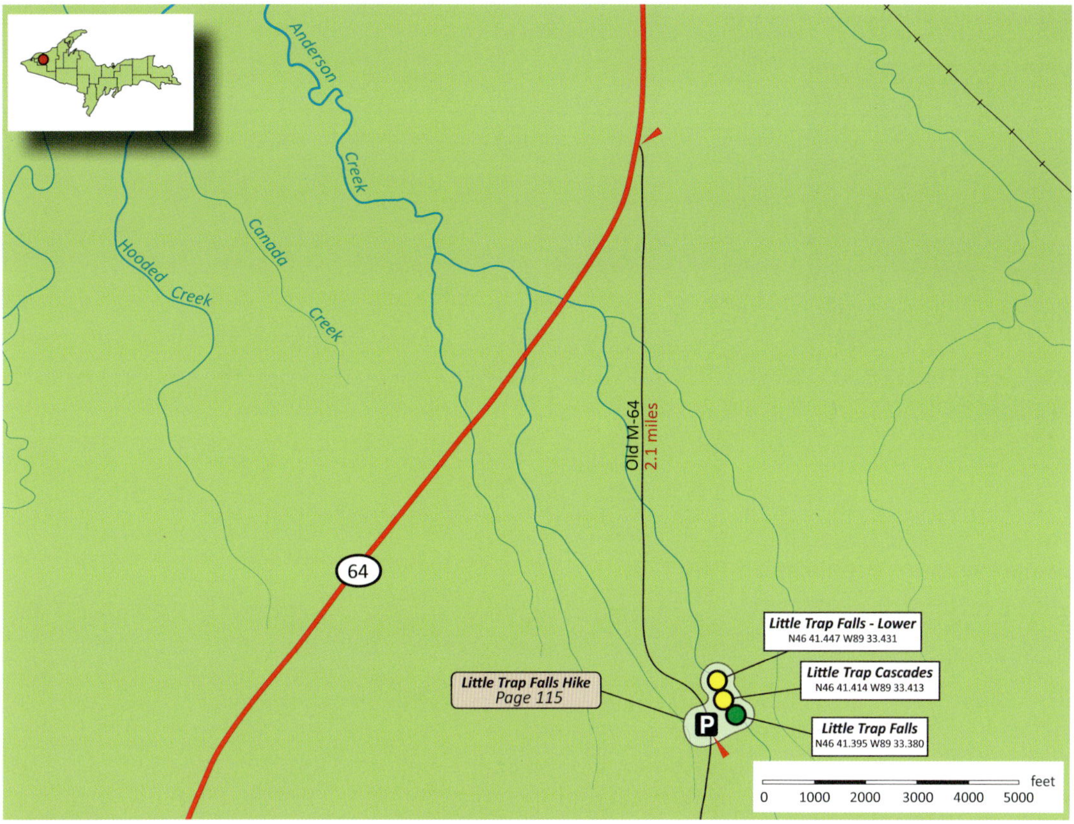

Little Trap Falls Hike

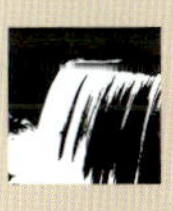

Two thirds of the way north between Lake Gogebic and the shore of Lake Superior lies the settlement of White Pine, created by the owners of the nearby White Pine Mine. The mine began operations in 1955 and was closed in 1995. In its glory days the mine employed over 3,000 workers. Now White Pine is down to less than 500 residents, consisting more and more of retirees looking for affordable solitude in beautiful northern Michigan.

It is just south of White Pine that Old M-64 veers off to the south. Not far off of this dirt road flows the upper reaches of an unnamed tributary of the Big Iron River. Little Trap Falls occurs as the stream pours down a fractured face into a short walled canyon.

Directions: From White Pine, drive south on M-64 for 2.5 miles to Old M-64. Follow Old M-64 (dirt road) for 2.2 miles. Park. Hike 250 yards to the falls using a GPS. Along the short hike you will cross a couple short but steep drainage channels. There is no trail and care needs to be taken in choosing good footing along in the uneven terrain.

LITTLE TRAP FALLS (ANDERSON CREEK)

Private

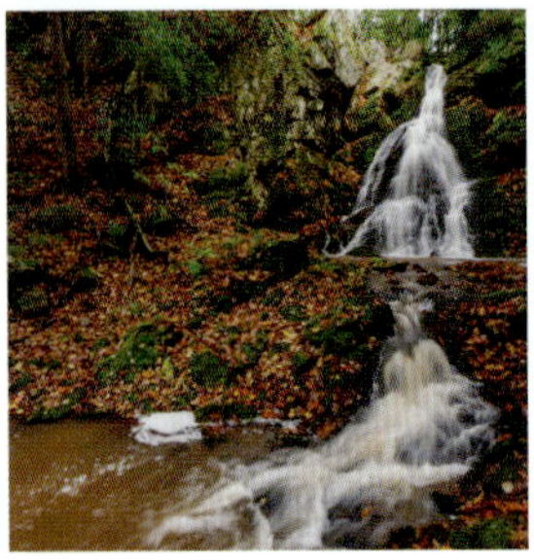

Must See:	7	GPS:	N46 41.395 W89 33.380
Height:	25 feet		
Time:	20-40 minutes	Hiking Information	
		Path:	None
Driving Information		Length:	250 yards
Signs:	None	Elev. Change:	Moderate
Road:	Gravel Road	GPS:	Required
Access:	Somewhat Difficult	Danger:	Minor
4WD:	N/A	WP Boots:	Required

Walk up the creek bed through the canyon with its 30 foot high walls to view the falls from its base. The creek slides down a steep face of moss-covered angular rocks. Various small plants line the sides of the falls.

The volume of water flowing over this waterfall varies greatly during the year. I recommend visiting after a good rain, or early in the spring. One note of caution, however: Old M-64 is not plowed in the winter. In fact, it is used as a snowmobile trail. This packs the snow down and takes a long time to melt. This will delay accessibility via automobile. Don't get stuck trying to push through the slowly melting snow!

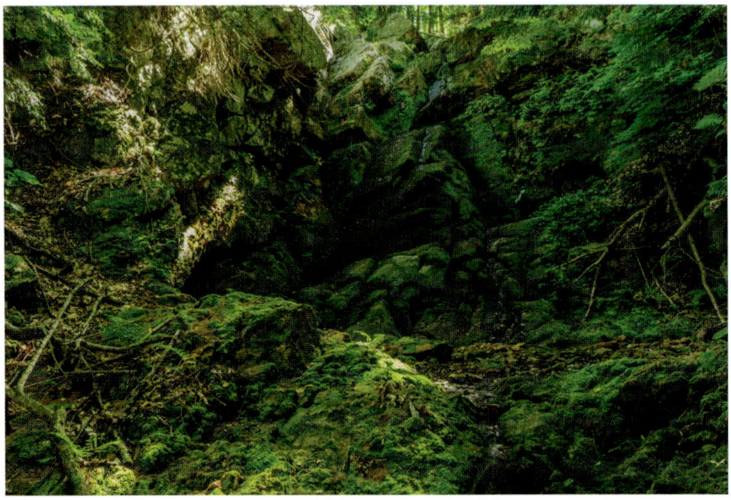

The waterfall can slow to a trickle as seen in this August picture

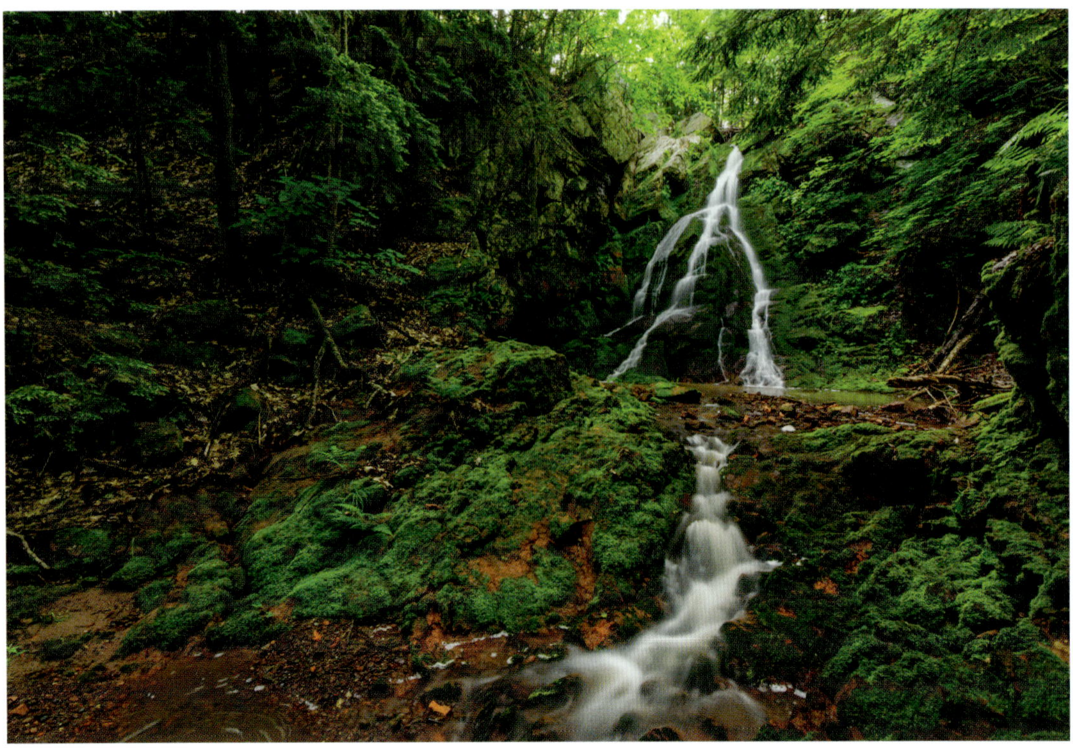

LITTLE TRAP CASCADES (ANDERSON CREEK)

Private

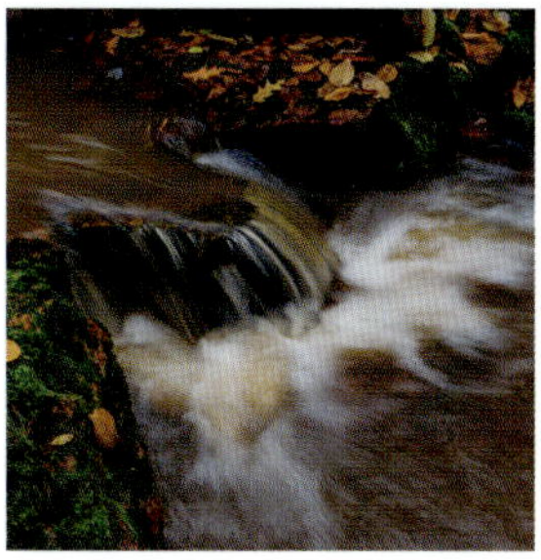

Must See:	5	GPS:	N46 41.414 W89 33.413
Height:	8 feet		
Time:	30-60 minutes	Hiking Information	
		Path:	None
Driving Information		Length:	250 yards
Signs:	None	Elev. Change:	Moderate
Road:	Gravel Road	GPS:	Required
Access:	Somewhat Difficult	Danger:	Minor
4WD:	N/A	WP Boots:	Required

Follow the creek back downstream 75 yards to where the ravine walls start fading down and widening out. Here, numerous small drops cascade down over 25 yards in a slight "S" curve. Moss covered boulders line the creek bed. The oversized rapids are best viewed when the creek is flowing with a good amount of water in it.

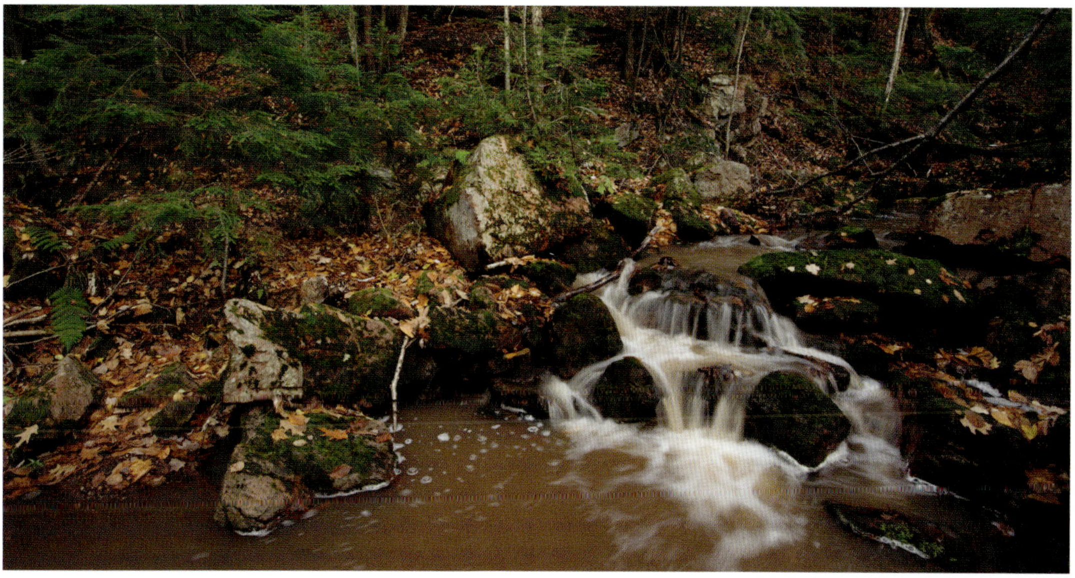

The mossy oversized rocks add to the sense of adventure while visiting Anderson Creek!

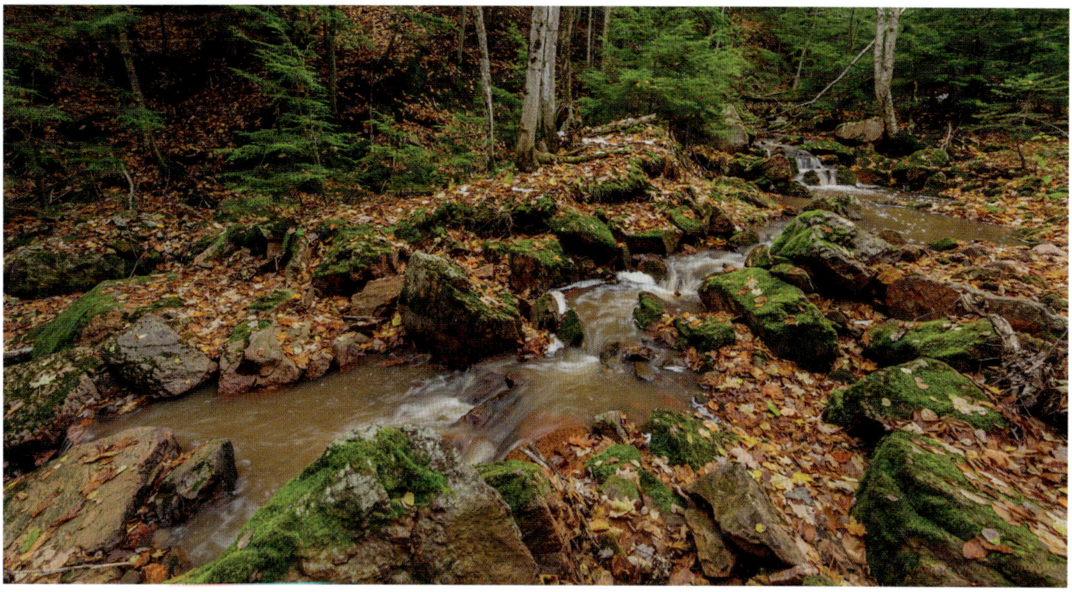

LITTLE TRAP FALLS - LOWER (ANDERSON CREEK)

Private

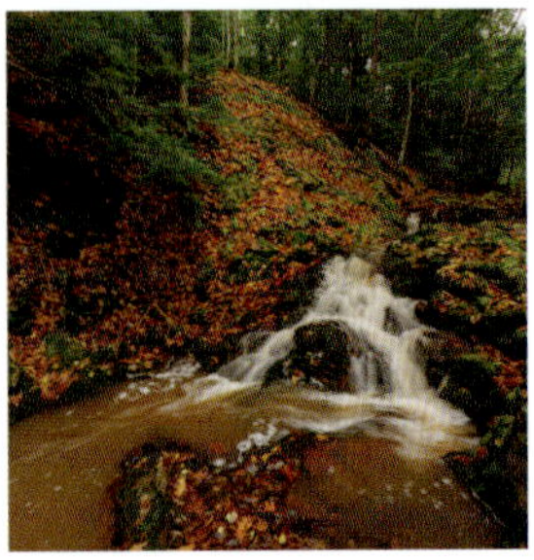

Must See:	5	GPS:	N46 41.447 W89 33.431
Height:	5 feet		
Time:	45-75 minutes	Hiking Information	
		Path:	None
Driving Information		Length:	300 yards
Signs:	None	Elev. Change:	Moderate
Road:	Gravel Road	GPS:	Required
Access:	Somewhat Difficult	Danger:	Minor
4WD:	N/A	WP Boots:	Required

Below the cascades, the ravine tightens up a bit, with the walls steeper and a little closer. But this doesn't last long. As the canyon dwindles away, a last jumble of mossy rocks force the creek into a narrow channel. The water then cascades over several rounded boulders along slanted bedrock on the far side of the creek. Then the main cascade splays down in a widening "V" shape to the somewhat wider creek bed below.

Note the steeper walls upstream. After this final burst of energy, the creek calms down.

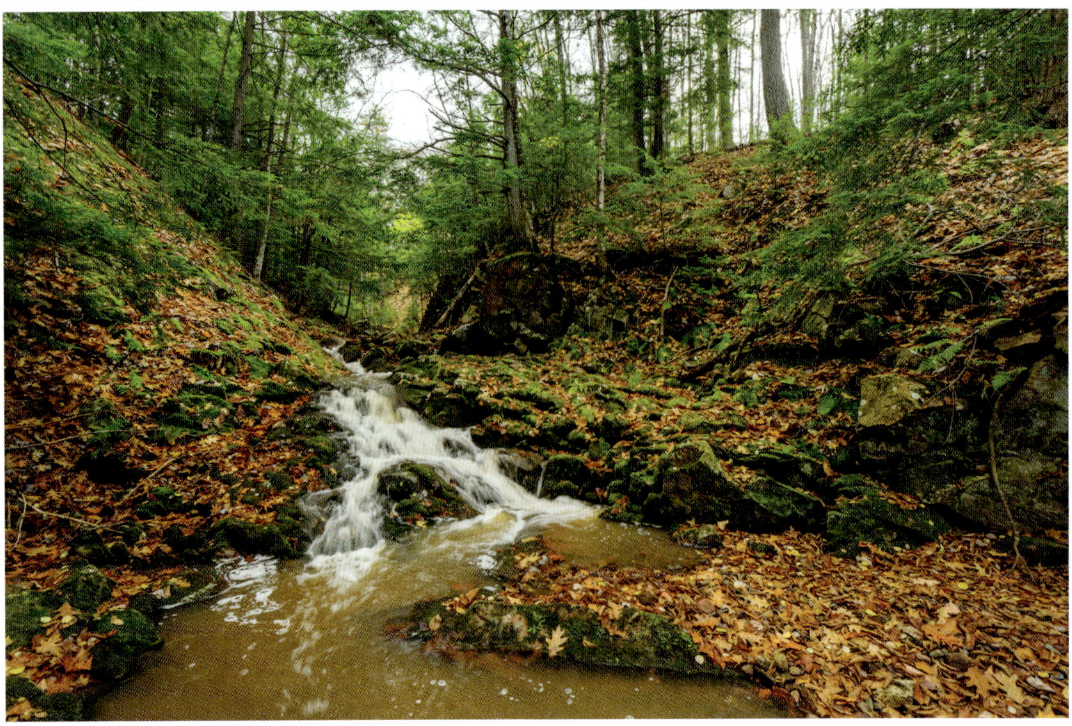

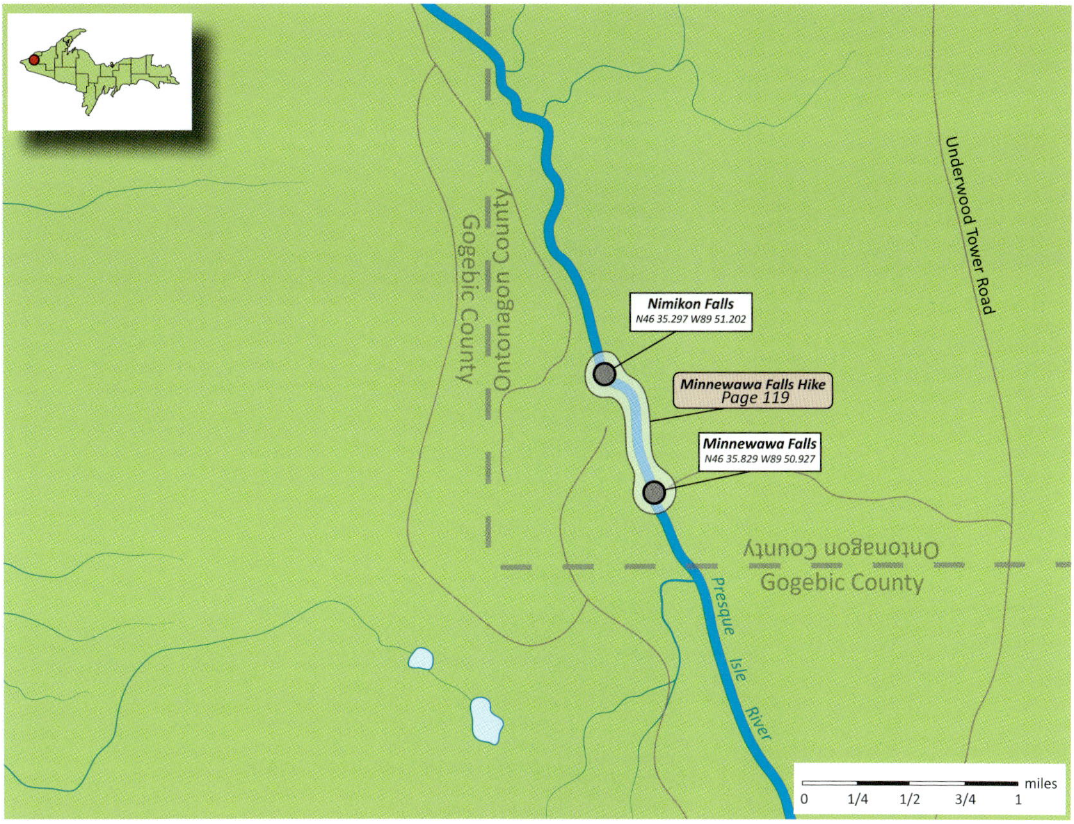

Minnewawa Falls Hike

Nimikon and Minnewawa Falls are on private property along the Presque Isle River. I hope to be able to photograph these waterfalls at some point. It is my understanding that Minnewawa in particular is a very nice waterfall!

WARNING! Get permission before attempting to see these waterfalls.

MINNEWAWA FALLS (PRESQUE ISLE RIVER)

Private

Must See: ??
Height: ?? feet
Time: N/A

Driving Information
Signs: N/A
Road: N/A
Access: N/A
4WD: N/A

GPS: *N46 35.829 W89 50.927 (not verified)*

Hiking Information
Path: N/A
Length: N/A
Elev. Change: N/A
GPS: N/A
Danger: N/A
WP Boots: N/A

NIMIKON FALLS (PRESQUE ISLE RIVER)

Private

Must See: ??
Height: ?? feet
Time: N/A

Driving Information
Signs: N/A
Road: N/A
Access: N/A
4WD: N/A

GPS: *N46 36.297 W89 51.202 (not verified)*

Hiking Information
Path: N/A
Length: N/A
Elev. Change: N/A
GPS: N/A
Danger: N/A
WP Boots: N/A

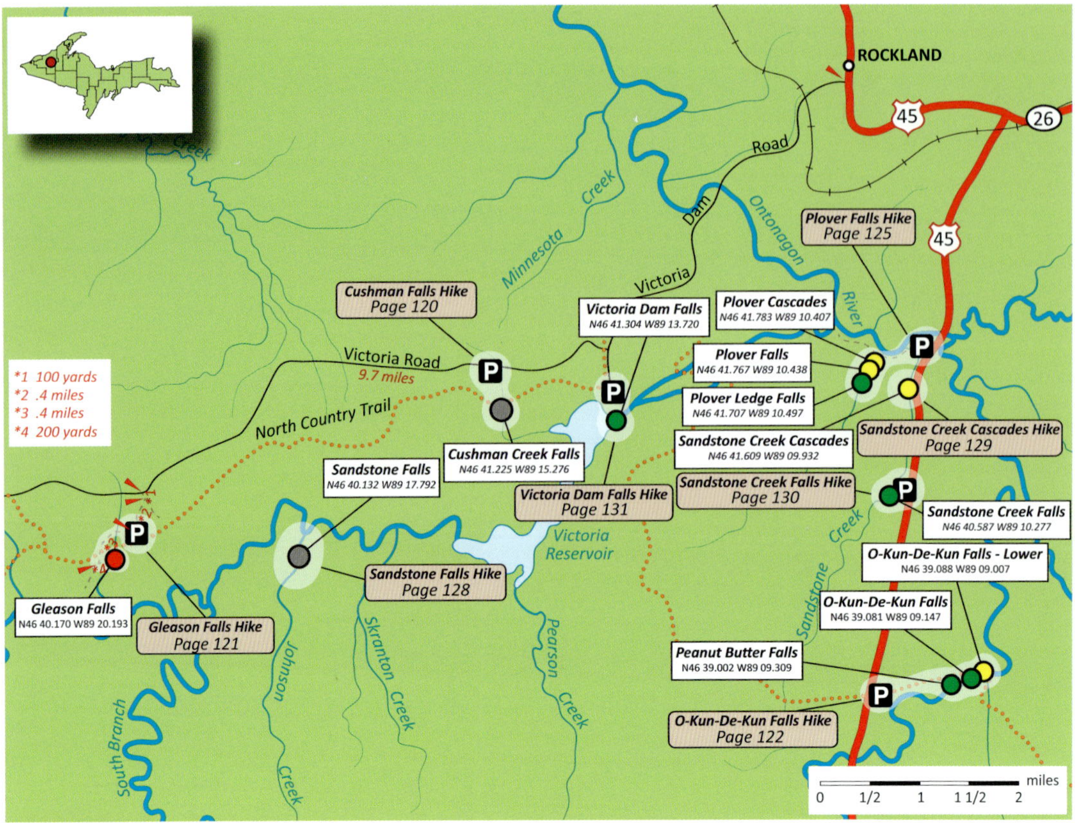

Cushman Falls Hike

I just recently discovered that there is a waterfall along Cushman Creek. I will be exploring it the next time that I am in the area!

Directions: About halfway from I-45 to the turnoff to Gleason Falls, Cushman Creek flows below Victoria Road. Park. Hike the creek downstream to the falls.

CUSHMAN CREEK FALLS (NORTH FORK - CUSHMAN CREEK)

Private

Must See:	??	GPS:	*N46 41.225 W89 15.276 (not verified)*
Height:	?? feet	Hiking Information	
Time:	N/A	Path:	N/A
Driving Information		Length:	N/A
Signs:	N/A	Elev. Change:	N/A
Road:	N/A	GPS:	N/A
Access:	N/A	Danger:	N/A
4WD:	N/A	WP Boots:	N/A

The North Fork of Cushman Creek slides over a moss covered mass of rock on its way down to the Victoria Reservoir. Hike in from Victoria Road to see this little-known waterfall.

Gleason Falls Hike

Original experiences often create lasting impressions, whether accurate or not. My first time to Gleason Falls was after a long day of hiking into waterfalls. The sun was close to setting and I knew I needed to hurry to get some pictures before dark. Having never been here before, I didn't know that there was a 2-track that would get me close, so I started hiking down along the creek from Victoria Road. Eventually I ran across a trail that led me down below the base of the falls. The waterfall occurs at the head of a wedge shaped canyon, a deep and jagged scar partially filled with roughly contoured, moss covered rocks spilled into the canyon as though trying to cover up an inadvertent excavation but running short on fill material. After clambering up the slippery rocks to get a somewhat better look at the waterfall - somewhat better because much of the water runs behind a large boulder wedged into the narrow crevasse that marks the start of the canyon - I took several shots and started heading back to the truck. Now that I knew there was a trail, I backtracked to see where it would come out. It added nearly 1/2 mile to the hike, but was well worth it for the comfort of walking on a trail! When I was about 1 mile from the truck I heard a gunshot. It was followed by more shots, several coming in rapid succession. I thought that it was the beginning of black bear season, and started envisioning a wounded bear racing toward the creek. It was now dusk. I pulled out the only "weapon" that I had at the time, a small multi-tool pocket knife. I'm sure I was quite a sight, running the last mile to the truck; my backpack shifting up and down as with one hand I tried to steady it, wielding my less-than-deadly "bear protection device" in the other! I was terribly winded and relieved to get into the truck. I closed the day, adding yet another waterfall experience to the growing list! Adventures!

Directions: From I-45, drive about 9.7 miles west on Victoria Road (a twisting dirt road). A 4WD with high clearance is required. Turn left (south) onto a 2-track at N46 40.664 W89 19.834. Turn right in about 100 yards. In .4 miles turn right again. To continue driving, an ATV is needed. Follow the narrow trail for another .4 miles along the edge of a ravine. Turn left, heading back to the base of the canyon for another .1 miles. Follow the creek upstream through the canyon a short distance to the falls.

GLEASON FALLS (UNNAMED CREEK)

Private

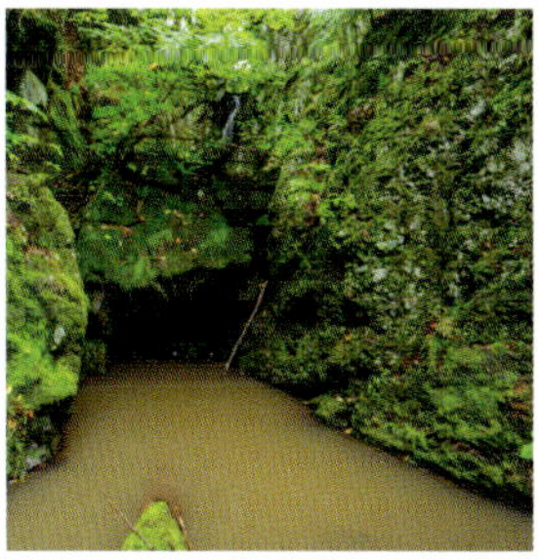

Must See:	3	GPS:	N46 40.170 W89 20.193
Height:	20 feet		
Time:	45-80 minutes	Hiking Information	
		Path:	None
Driving Information		Length:	1/2 mile
Signs:	None	Elev. Change:	Increased
Road:	2-track	GPS:	Required
Access:	Difficult	Danger:	Elevated
4WD:	Required	WP Boots:	Recommended

The rugged terrain and steep ravines add a sense of danger and intrigue.

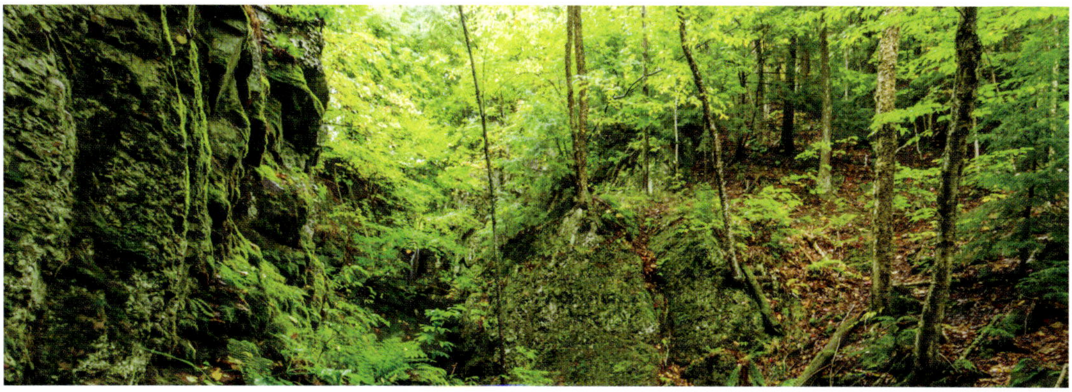

O-kun-de-kun Falls Hike

It is always a joy to be able to hike along a section of the North Country Trail! This hike is no exception. Follow the trail, just wide enough for one person, through briar thickets, over sometimes muddy areas, beneath mature hardwoods, and finally along the Baltimore River to the waterfalls. A well constructed footbridge crosses the river just below O-kun-de-kun Falls. Near the bridge are several primitive campsites within earshot of the falls.

Directions: Drive 6.1 miles south from the junction of M-26 and US-45 or north 8 miles from Bruce Crossing on US-45. Turn east into a short parking area at the trailhead to the falls. Park. Hike to the falls. Peanut Butter Falls is 1.1 miles from the parking area. The main falls is another 300 yards down river. The Lower Falls is just down river from the bridge.

PEANUT BUTTER FALLS (BALTIMORE RIVER)

Private

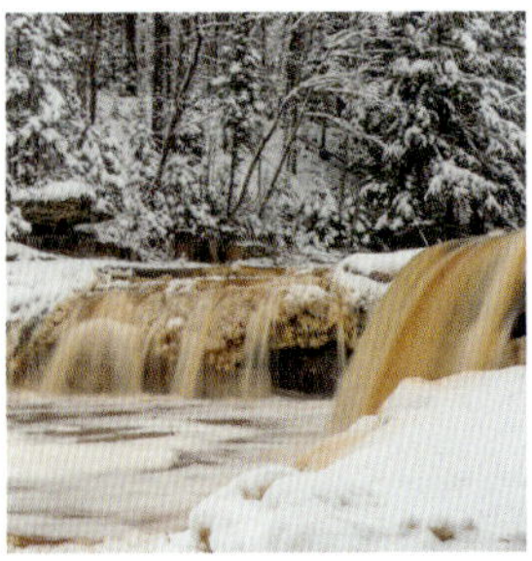

Must See:	7	GPS:	N46 39.002 W89 09.309
Height:	8 feet		
Time:	60-90 minutes	Hiking Information	
		Path:	Narrow but well kept
Driving Information		Length:	1.1 miles
Signs:	None	Elev. Change:	Slight
Road:	Main	GPS:	Helpful
Access:	Easy	Danger:	Slight
4WD:	N/A	WP Boots:	Recommended

Follow the North Country Trail from the parking area. Twelve inch wide boardwalks span wet areas. Rusty gray sandstone bedrock suddenly drops 8 feet with an undercut waterfall and banks down river. The "V" shaped waterfall is slightly lower toward the near bank. Therefore, most of the river pours over the close side of the falls. In low water, it only flows to the near side. Several large, misshapen sandstone chunks are just below the waterfall on the trail side of the river.

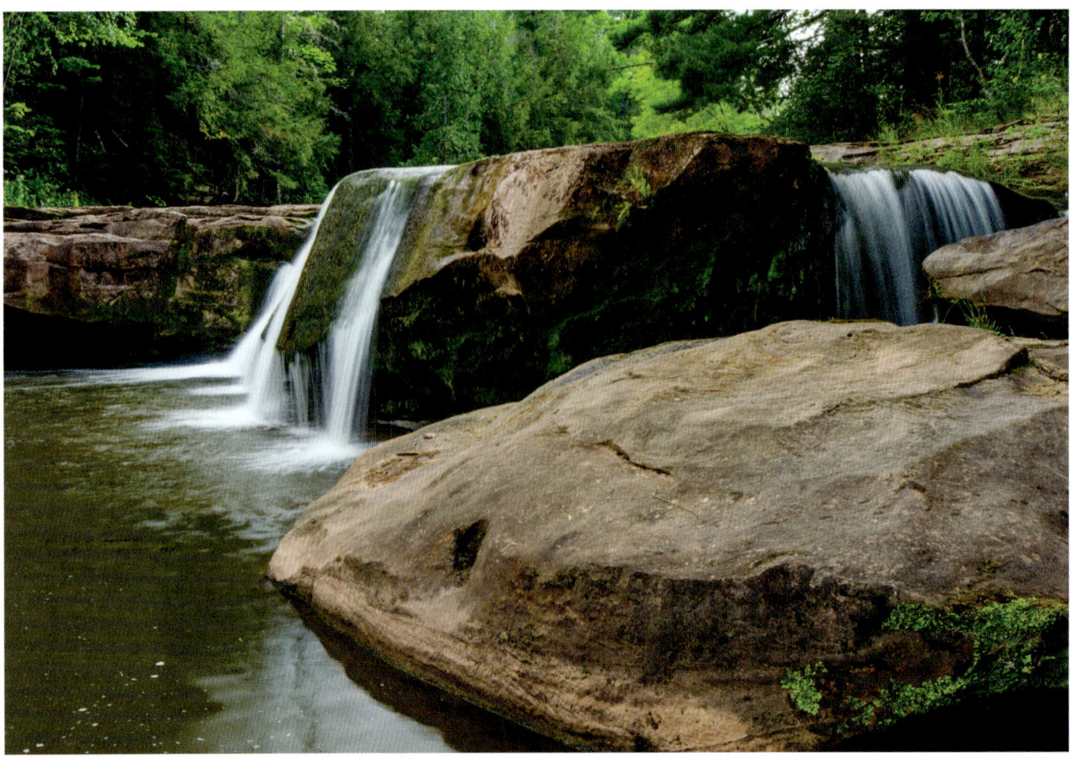

O-KUN-DE-KUN FALLS (BALTIMORE RIVER)

Private

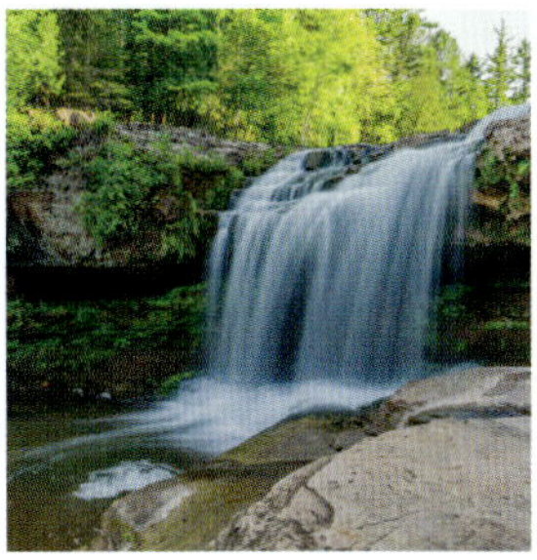

Must See:	9	GPS:	N46 39.081 W89 09.147
Height:	18 feet		
Time:	75-120 minutes	Hiking Information	
		Path:	Narrow but well kept
Driving Information		Length:	1.3 miles
Signs:	None	Elev. Change:	Moderate
Road:	Main	GPS:	Helpful
Access:	Easy	Danger:	Slight
4WD:	N/A	WP Boots:	Recommended

Continue to follow the trail downstream from the Upper Falls about 1/4 mile. As is often the case, the sound of the waterfall will be the first evidence that the waterfall is getting close! And then the wonderful waterfall will come into view. It is easily seen from the North Country Trail bridge that spans the Baltimore River below the falls. The waterfall itself is centered in a 70 foot wide sandstone cliff wall. An undercut, 20 feet deep, angles back behind the falls allowing for an exhilarating, if somewhat dangerous view from behind the falls. A large shelf of rock halfway down the falls provides a close-up and personal experience with the waterfall!

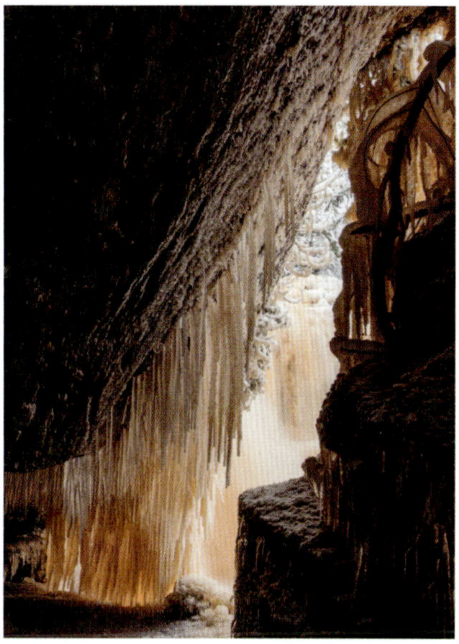

Ice formations in the cave behind the falls

Winter highlights the tannins and sediment in the Ontonagon River watershed

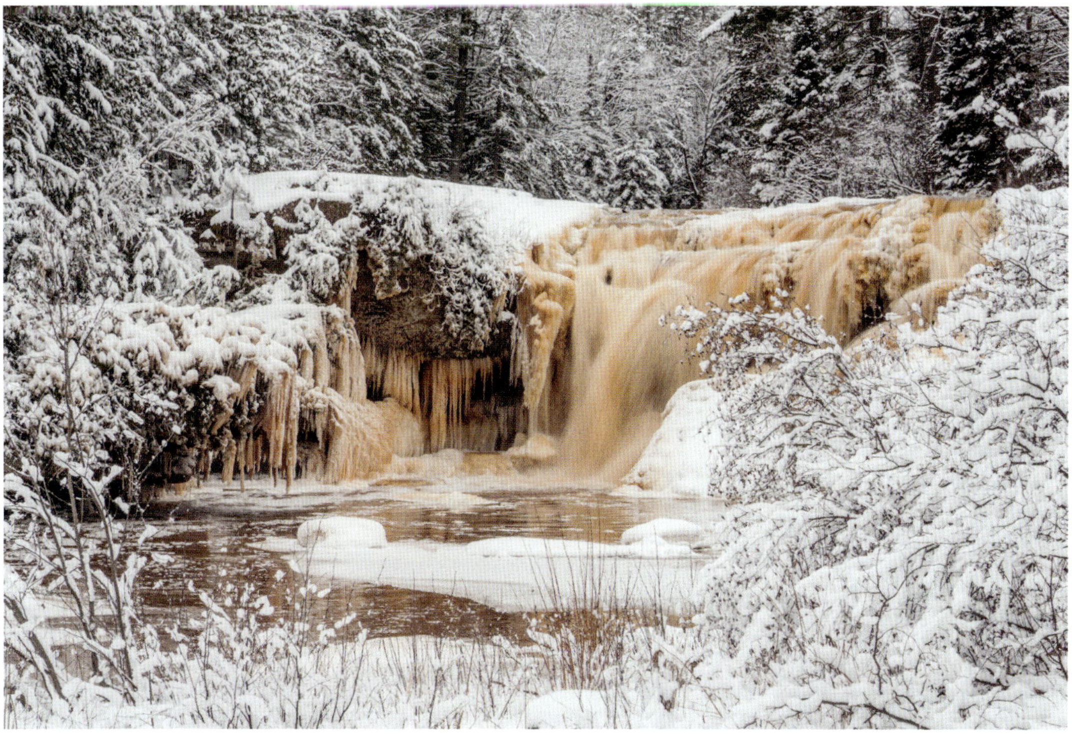

O-KUN-DE-KUN FALLS - LOWER (BALTIMORE RIVER)

Private

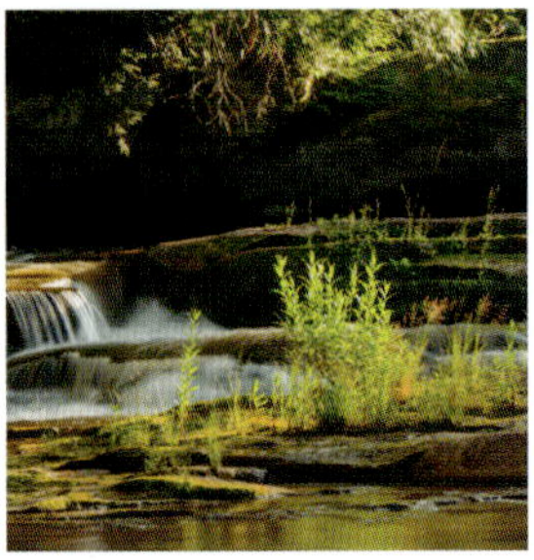

Must See:	4
Height:	10 feet
Time:	75-120 minutes

Driving Information

Signs:	None
Road:	Main
Access:	Easy
4WD:	N/A

GPS:	N46 39.088 W89 09.007

Hiking Information

Path:	Narrow but well kept
Length:	1.4 miles
Elev. Change:	Moderate
GPS:	Helpful
Danger:	Slight
WP Boots:	Recommended

The riverbed widens out to about 70 feet with the river meandering back and forth through the low points in it. Numerous 1/2 to 2 foot drops are found within a 200 foot stretch of the river just down river from the North Country Trail footbridge.

Like a kid in a candy store, you may find yourself racing from one interesting drop to another! Since the river widens out so far at this point, the water is often very shallow, running easily over the bedrock riverbed. Unless the water level is up, there are many dry pathways leading out into the middle of the river, as the water flows along the paths of least resistance.

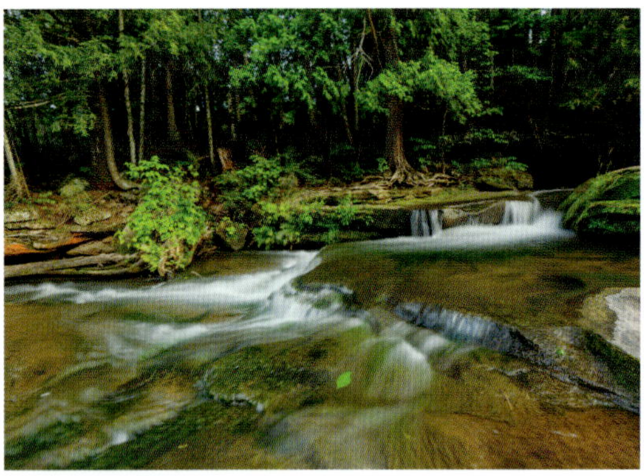

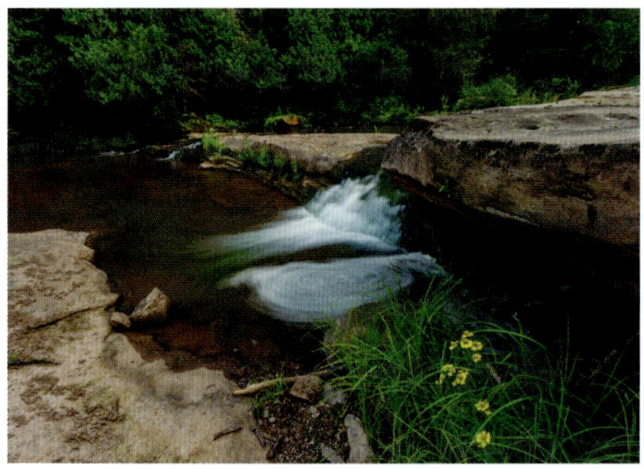

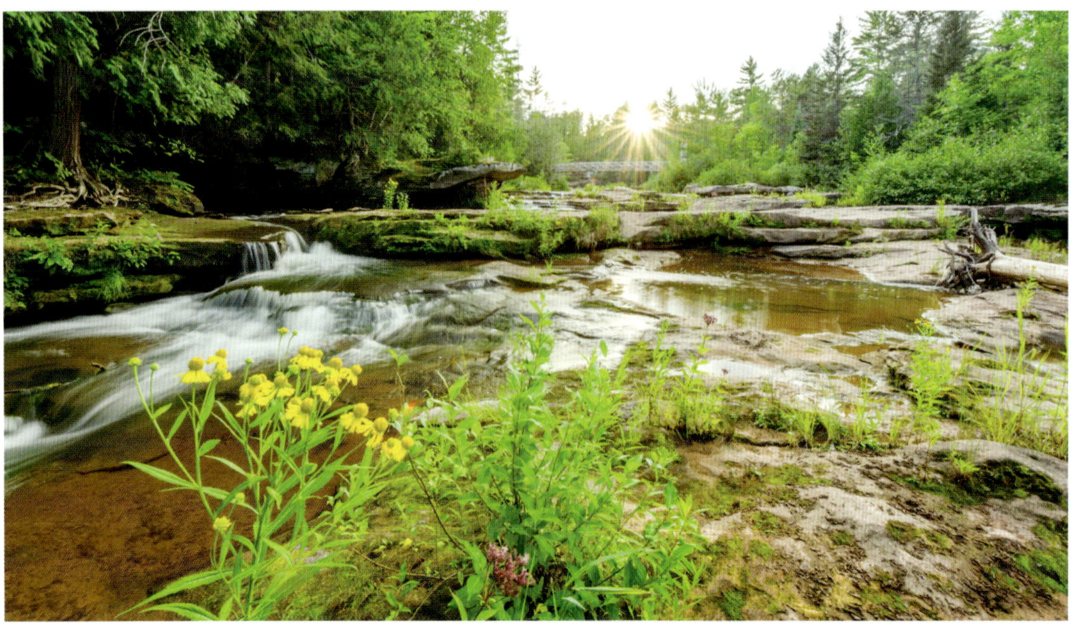

Plover Falls Hike

The East Branch, West Branch and Middle Branches of the Ontonagon River all join together within a 2 mile area to form the Ontonagon River. In the middle of this area, Plover Creek also joins the river. The creek rushes down from 1,000 feet above sea level, cutting a ravine through the terrain to meet the Ontonagon River at 675 feet just 2 miles later. Toward the end of this descent we find the Plover Falls series.

Directions: A snowmobile trail runs west off of US-45 just south of the Ontonagon River. Park well off the road. Hike westerly .3 miles along the sometimes marshy trail. It will lead to the mouth of Sandstone Creek. Ford the creek. There is no bridge and the creek may be deep. An old ATV trail runs along the West Branch of the Ontonagon River. Follow it upstream for .33 miles to Plover Creek. Follow the creek upstream for 75 yards to the Cascades. Another 50 yards upstream is Plover Falls. Climb up above Plover Falls and follow the creek upstream another 150 yards to Plover Ledge Falls.

PLOVER CASCADES (PLOVER CREEK)

Private

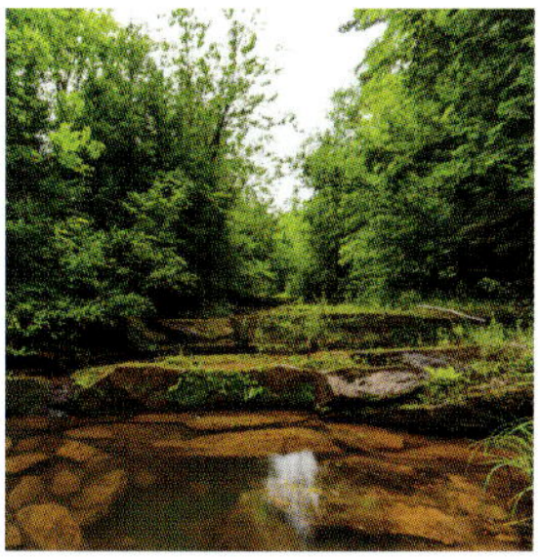

Must See:	5	GPS:	N46 41.783 W89 10.407
Height:	20 feet		
Time:	45-70 minutes	Hiking Information	
		Path:	Primitive/wet/ford
Driving Information		Length:	.64 miles
Signs:	None	Elev. Change:	Moderate
Road:	Main	GPS:	Helpful
Access:	Somewhat easy	Danger:	Elevated
4WD:	N/A	WP Boots:	Required

The cascade is long and drawn out. It starts with several tight stair-stepped cascades with shallow pools between each one. The waterfall ends with two squared off ledges, a 3 foot followed by a 2 foot drop. The creek runs on the left side of the creek bed typically. Clay stained moss covered bedrock is the norm on this waterway.

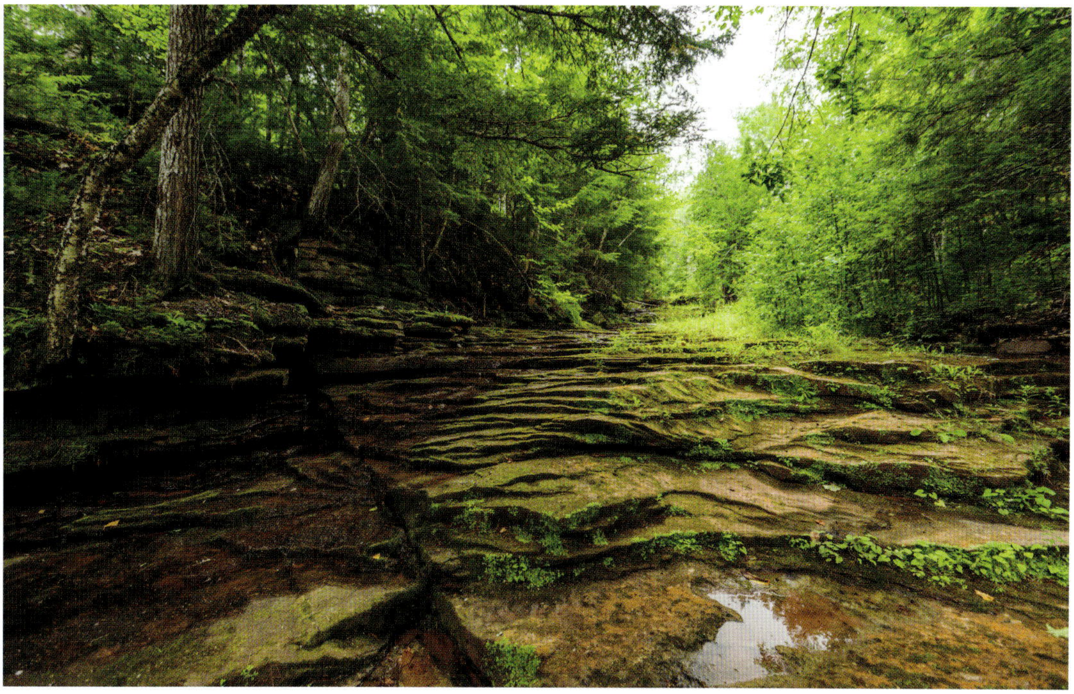

PLOVER FALLS (PLOVER CREEK)

Private

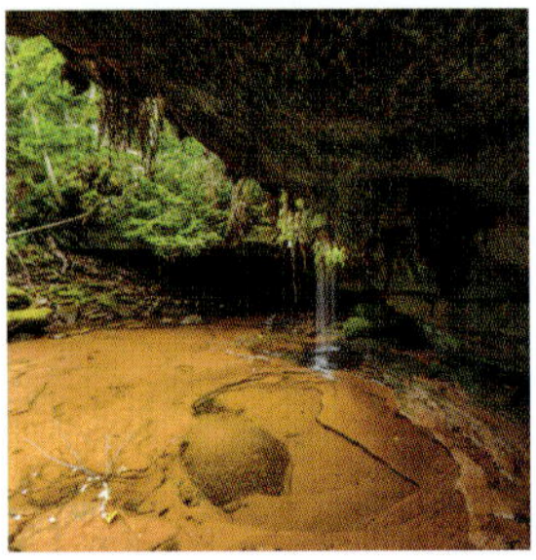

Must See:	5	GPS:	N46 41.767 W89 10.438
Height:	5 feet		
Time:	50-75 minutes	Hiking Information	
		Path:	Primitive/wet/ford
Driving Information		Length:	.69 miles
Signs:	None	Elev. Change:	Moderate
Road:	Main	GPS:	Helpful
Access:	Somewhat easy	Danger:	Elevated
4WD:	N/A	WP Boots:	Required

This is the head of the shallow gorge, just above Plover Cascades. It is so different from the cascades that follow that it needs special recognition. The creek bed is 50 feet wide here with a severe undercut shelf that forms a graceful arc, the creek spilling over the center to a shallow pool below. Duck down to view the waterfall from behind! Cedars, birch, and oak trees are thick all around. This is in a remote portion of Michigan. My first time to these falls a coyote sauntered through the creek, finding me of little interest.

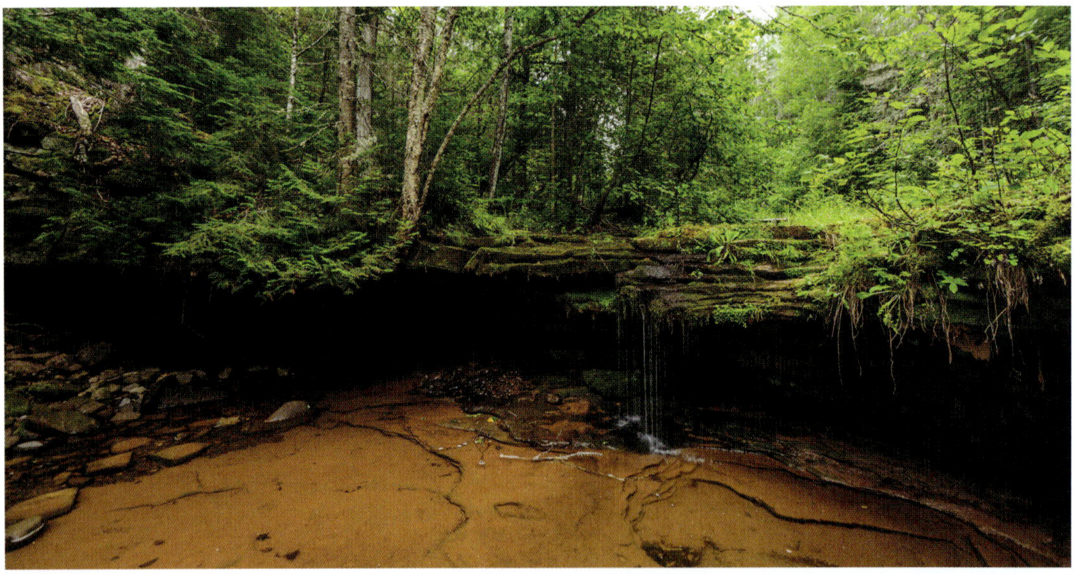

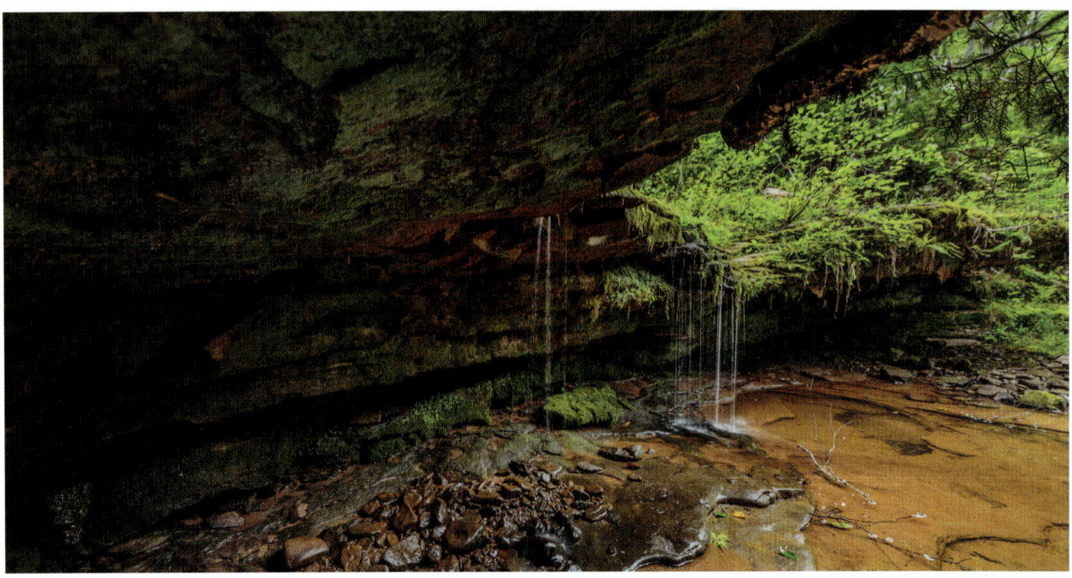

PLOVER LEDGE FALLS (PLOVER CREEK)

Private

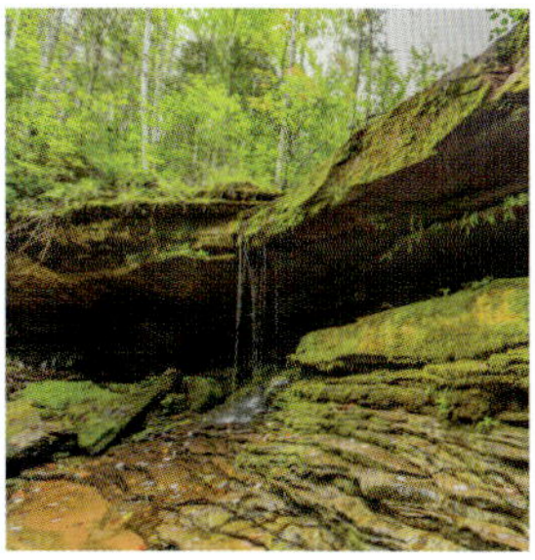

Must See:	7	GPS:	N46 41.707 W89 10.497
Height:	12 feet		
Time:	60-90 minutes	Hiking Information	
		Path:	Primitive/wet/ford
Driving Information		Length:	.76 miles
Signs:	None	Elev. Change:	Moderate
Road:	Main	GPS:	Helpful
Access:	Somewhat easy	Danger:	Elevated
4WD:	N/A	WP Boots:	Required

If you like Plover Falls, you'll lover Plover Ledge Falls! This is like an oversized Plover Falls. It's much higher and has a thicker ledge (at least 2 feet). The undercut is over 6 feet high in places. This must be an amazing waterfall with good water flow. The creek flows over the center of the squared off moss covered sandstone face, falling 9 feet to a numerous tiered cascade that feeds a wide spill pool. A couple small drops are spaced a couple dozen yards apart downstream. Between this and Plover Falls the creek is wild looking, with much of the creek bed full of boulders.

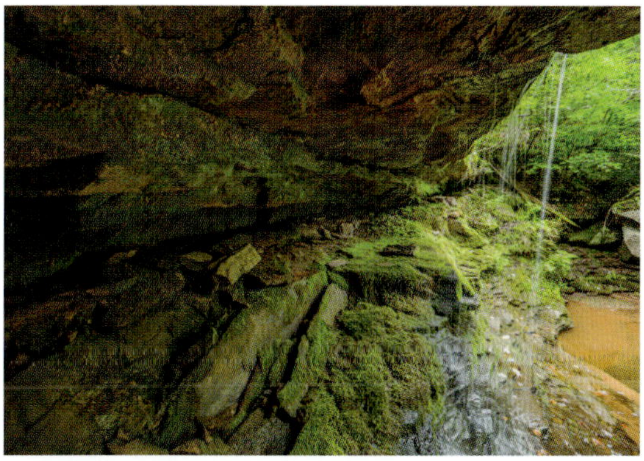

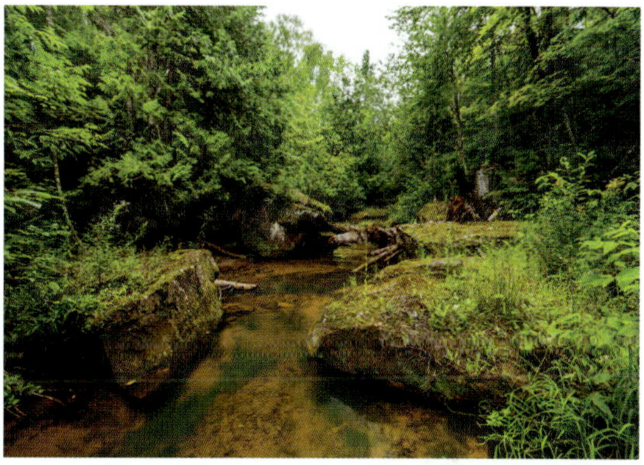

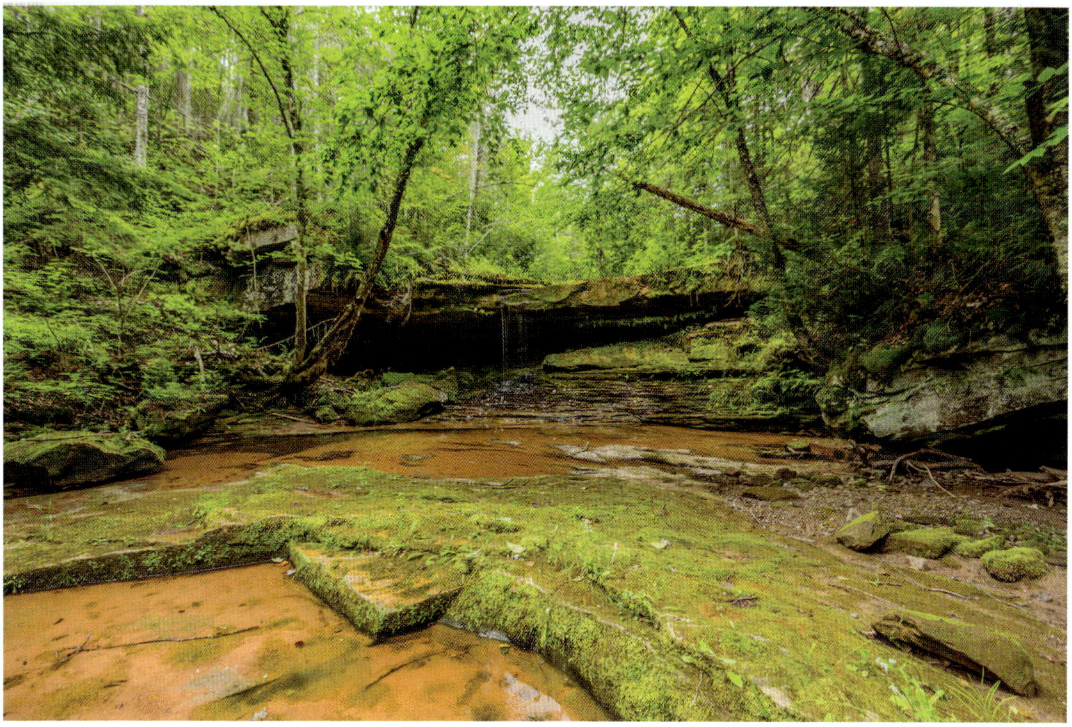

Sandstone Falls Hike

I know nothing about this waterfall. I have not been able to find anyone that has been to it and I have not yet hiked in to this remote waterfall. Johnson Creek (aka: Topp Creek) empties into the West Branch of the Ontonagon River about 2 miles up river of Victoria Reservoir. The USGS data suggests that this waterfall is about 1/4 mile up from the mouth of the creek.

Directions: Turn west onto Forest Highway 730 (located just south of the trailhead to O-Kun-De-Kun Falls off of US-45). Follow it for 5.5 miles. Turn right (north). Follow that trail as far north and slightly west as possible. Hike the rest of the way to the GPS position.

SANDSTONE FALLS (JOHNSON CREEK)

Private

Must See:	??	GPS:	*N46 40.132 W89 17.792 (not verified)*
Height:	?? feet		
Time:	N/A	**Hiking Information**	
		Path:	N/A
Driving Information		Length:	N/A
Signs:	N/A	Elev. Change:	N/A
Road:	N/A	GPS:	N/A
Access:	N/A	Danger:	N/A
4WD:	N/A	WP Boots:	N/A

I've never seen a picture of this waterfall. I've never spoken to anyone that has been here. I HOPE that there really is a waterfall at this location!

I tried to get to this waterfall in 2011. The most promising trail that I could find was blocked while I was still over 3 miles from the waterfall. I was too tired and didn't have enough time for that long of a hike that day.

Sandstone Creek Cascades Hike

Over the years, the various branches of the Ontonagon River and their tributaries have cut a deep swath through the surrounding highlands. The Trap Hills, running in a line just to the north of the West Branch of the Ontonagon River, rise to nearly record heights above an otherwise flat plateau. The plateau, sitting at 950 to 1,100 feet, is furrowed by numerous fingerlets, creeks and the mighty Ontonagon River. These waterways have carved ever deeper and wider, culminating with a wet basin some 300 feet below the surrounding plateau. Engineers, attempting to construct a bridge across the Ontonagon River, picked a spot just to the west of the confluence of the East Branch and Middle Branch. The basin is so wide in this area, that at the narrowest point a bridge would need to be nearly 3/4 mile in length to span the basin. Therefore, US-45 was constructed to run down through a gully from the north, cross the river and then angle to the southwest to snuggle up close to Sandstone Creek, using the path that the creek cut through the landscape as a natural pathway back to the high plateau. It's toward the beginning of this rise out of the basin that the Sandstone Creek Cascades can be found next to US-45.

Directions: Less than 1/2 mile south of Ontonagon River park on the side of US-45 just before the guard rails. Hike down the steep embankment to the falls.

SANDSTONE CREEK CASCADES (SANDSTONE CREEK) Private

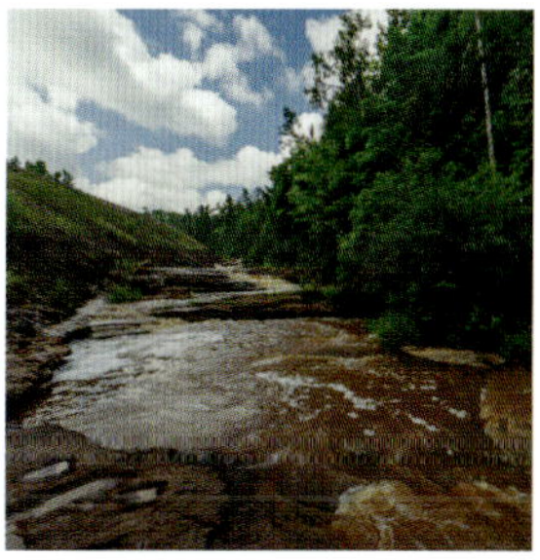

Must See:	6	GPS:	N46 41.609 W89 09.932
Height:	20 feet		
Time:	15-30 minutes	Hiking Information	
		Path:	None
Driving Information		Length:	100 yards
Signs:	None	Elev. Change:	Moderate
Road:	Main	GPS:	Helpful
Access:	Easy	Danger:	Moderate
4WD:	N/A	WP Boots:	N/A

There are numerous cascades stretching out for over 100 yards along the river. The larger drops are 3 to 4 feet high with smaller ones interspersed. The largest are near the lower end of the cascade.

The hike down into the ravine is not easy. There is no trail, so take care navigating the mine tailings that were used as fill for the roadway. Care was taken along the creek to keep the fill from eroding into the waterway with concrete protecting the steepest areas. A profusion of wildflowers coats the steep embankment.

My favorite drop is down toward the end of the long set of cascades.

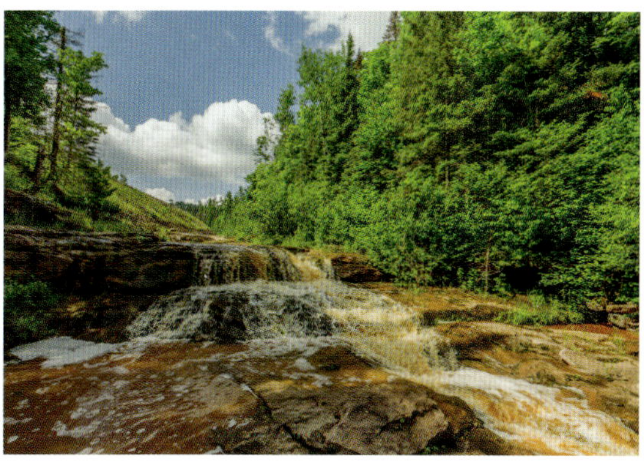

Sandstone Creek can be seen down at the base of the ravine. Note the steep grade down to the creek, around 20 feet high, as viewed from US-45.

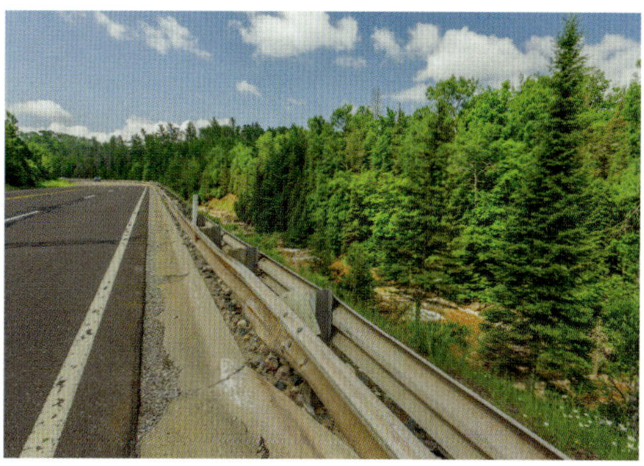

Sandstone Creek Falls Hike

Put on a thick pair of jeans and some good hiking boots. This short hike down to the falls is through some of the thickest saplings and undergrowth I've encountered! Poplars grow tightly together down the steep hillside. Trees that have succumbed to age or wind lay haphazardly along the route as well. The reward for pressing through is a view that few have witnessed in person!

US-45 continues to climb up out of the Ontonagon River Basin after it passes the Sandstone Creek Cascades. As the road nears the top of the plateau, it is no longer right next to the creek. The road has taken a fairly straight path while the creek's upstream route comes in further west.

Directions: (On US-45) About 1 3/4 miles south of the bridge over the Ontonagon River, a thick, tree covered ravine can be seen on the west side of the road. Just past the ravine is a clear, steep embankment rising to a small field. Park here. Climb up the embankment, heading towards the trees in the middle of the west side of the field. The terrain starts to drop, heading for the river. I have found that it's easier to get down to the river up above the waterfall. The trees aren't as thick, and the ravine not as steep.

SANDSTONE CREEK FALLS (SANDSTONE CREEK)

Private

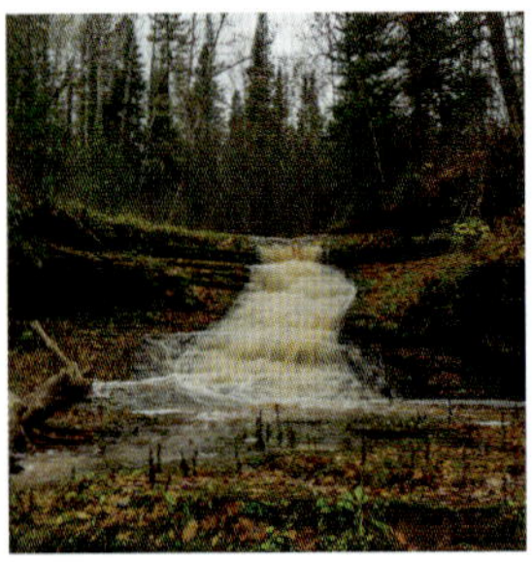

Must See:	7	GPS:	N46 40.587 W89 10.277
Height:	12 feet		
Time:	60-75 minutes	Hiking Information	
		Path:	None
Driving Information		Length:	.23 miles
Signs:	None	Elev. Change:	Elevated
Road:	Main	GPS:	Required
Access:	Easy	Danger:	Elevated
4WD:	N/A	WP Boots:	Recommended

Set amongst some of the thickest undergrowth I have seen, this seldom seen waterfall cascades down over stair-stepped sandstone, widening out below the falls to run wall to wall between rusty brown canyon walls. A small tributary cuts through the rocks on the near side of the creek, forming a small, trickling waterfall.

The shallow "canyon" can be seen in the lower left photo, although the walls are much higher and intimidating in person! This is another reason to come down above, rather than below, the waterfall. The river flows from wall to wall downstream, so there is no easy way to get down to the river down below there.

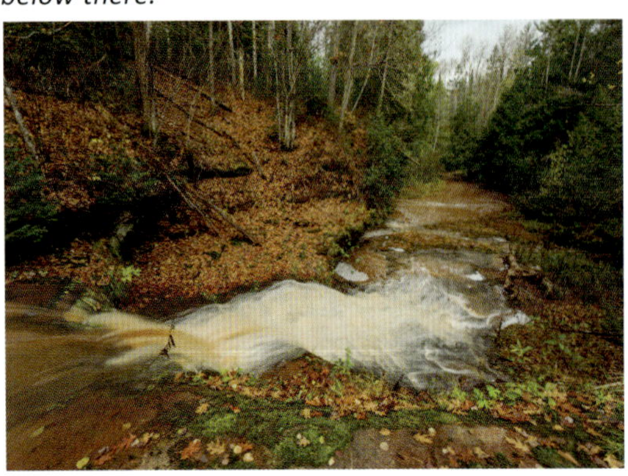

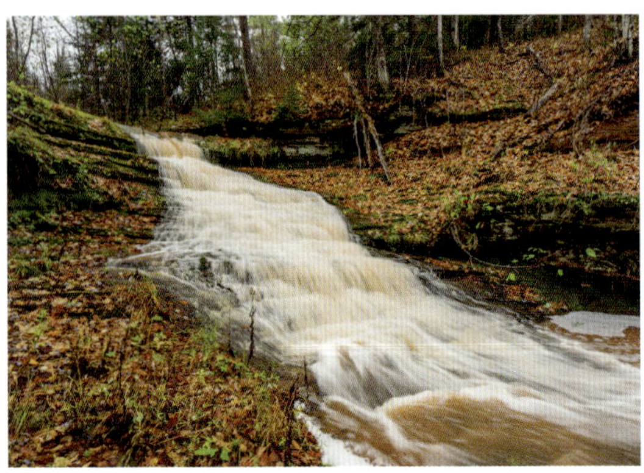

Victoria Dam Falls Hike

Victoria Dam was originally built in the early 1900's at the sight of an impressive waterfall. The river has since provided power to the area. Subsequent upgrades to the dam and hydroelectric plant as well as a partial diversion of the Middle Branch of the Ontonagon River brings the capacity to 850 cubic feet per second with a 215 foot head. It is able to operate at about 80% efficiency per year. When the flow of water coming into Victoria Reservoir exceeds this volume, the excess is diverted over what remains of the falls. There are times when there is NO water running over the falls. This occurs primarily in July and August. For the best chance at seeing a substantial torrent of water, check out the waterfall during the spring melt.

Directions: From Rockland, turn off of US-45 to the west on Victoria Dam Road (AKA: Elm Street). The road winds and twists through the rugged countryside. In 4 miles Victoria Road turns to the left (west). CONTINUE TO THE SOUTH to stay on Victoria Dam Road for another .8 miles to the parking area slightly below the dam and in plain sight of the discharge tube as it runs down the hillside. Park. View the waterfall from up near the dam or hike past the gate (no driving allowed) along the service drive to see the waterfall closer. Respect the dam property and personnel.

VICTORIA DAM FALLS (ONTONAGON RIVER - WEST BRANCH) Private

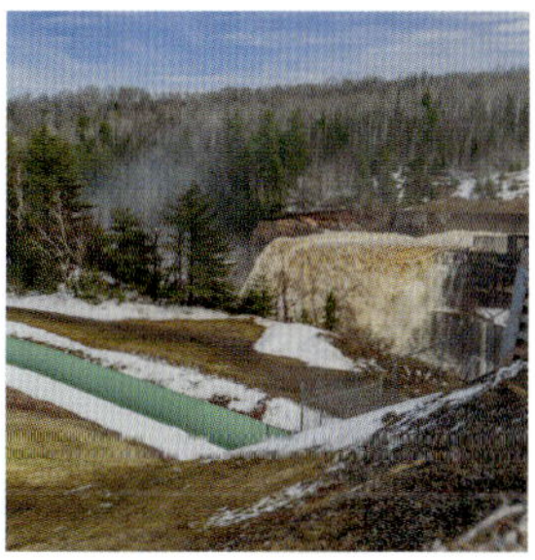

Must See:	9	GPS:	N46 41.304 W89 13.720
Height:	50 feet		
Time:	5-20 minutes	Hiking Information	
		Path:	N/A
Driving Information		Length:	100 yards
Signs:	(For the dam)	Elev. Change:	Moderate
Road:	Dirt	GPS:	None
Access:	Somewhat Easy	Danger:	Slight
4WD:	N/A	WP Boots:	None

Remember that dams hold large amounts of water behind them. In the event you hear a siren, seek high ground immediately! The Must See rating can vary from 2 to 9 depending on water flow. Keep this in mind when deciding to visit the waterfall.

Spring Melt: so much force there is a rainbow

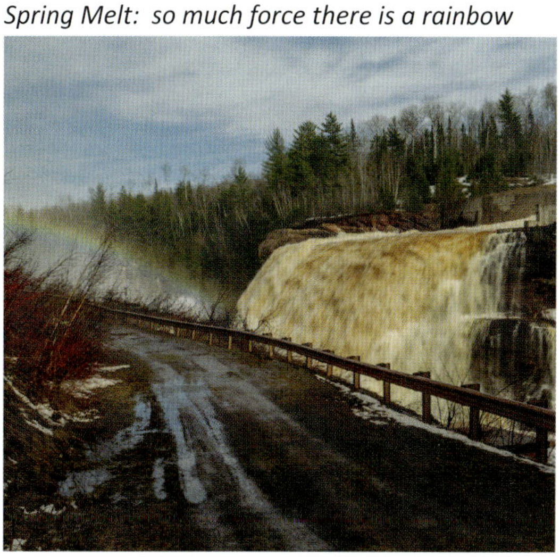

Dry Autumn: barely a trickle runs down the face

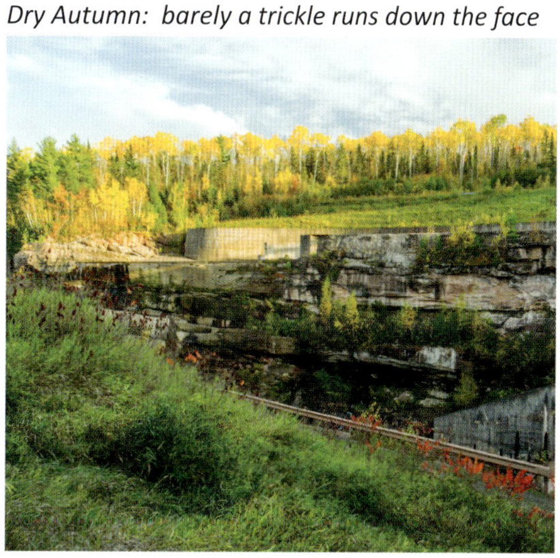

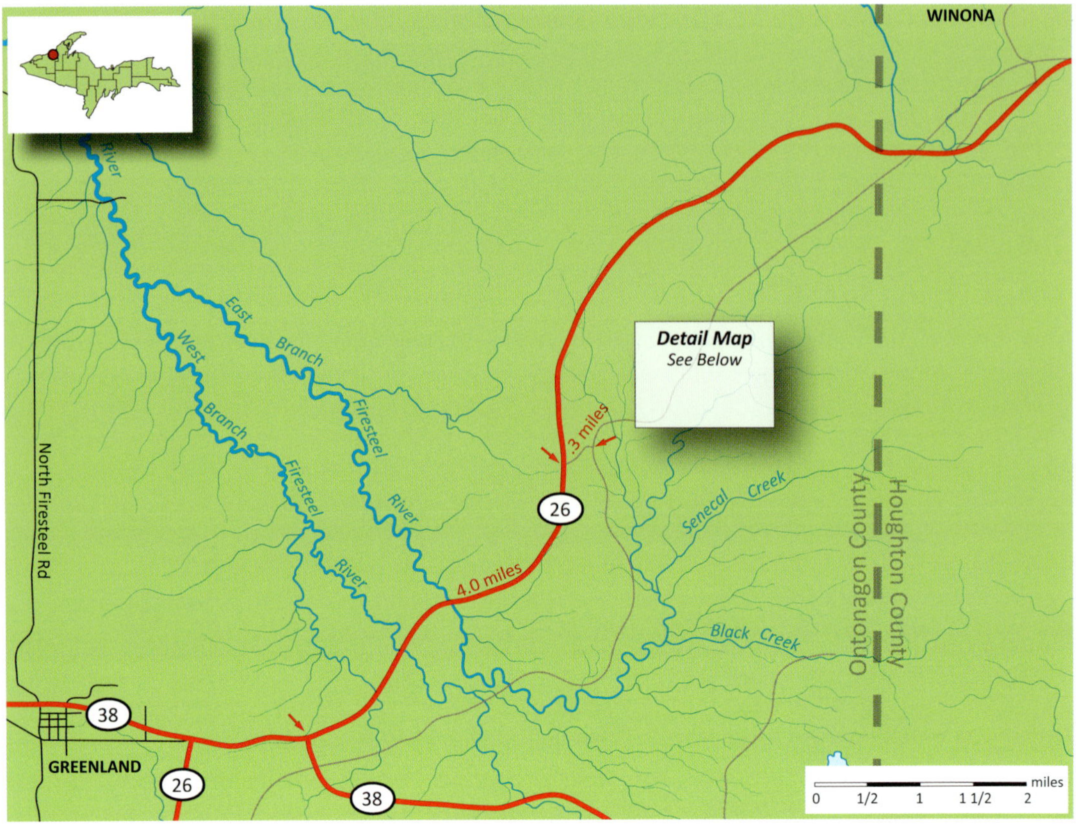
WINONA
Detail Map
See Below
East Branch Firesteel River
West Branch Firesteel River
River
Senecal Creek
Black Creek
.3 miles
4.0 miles
26
38
GREENLAND
North Firesteel Rd
Ontonagon County
Houghton County
miles
0 1/2 1 1 1/2 2

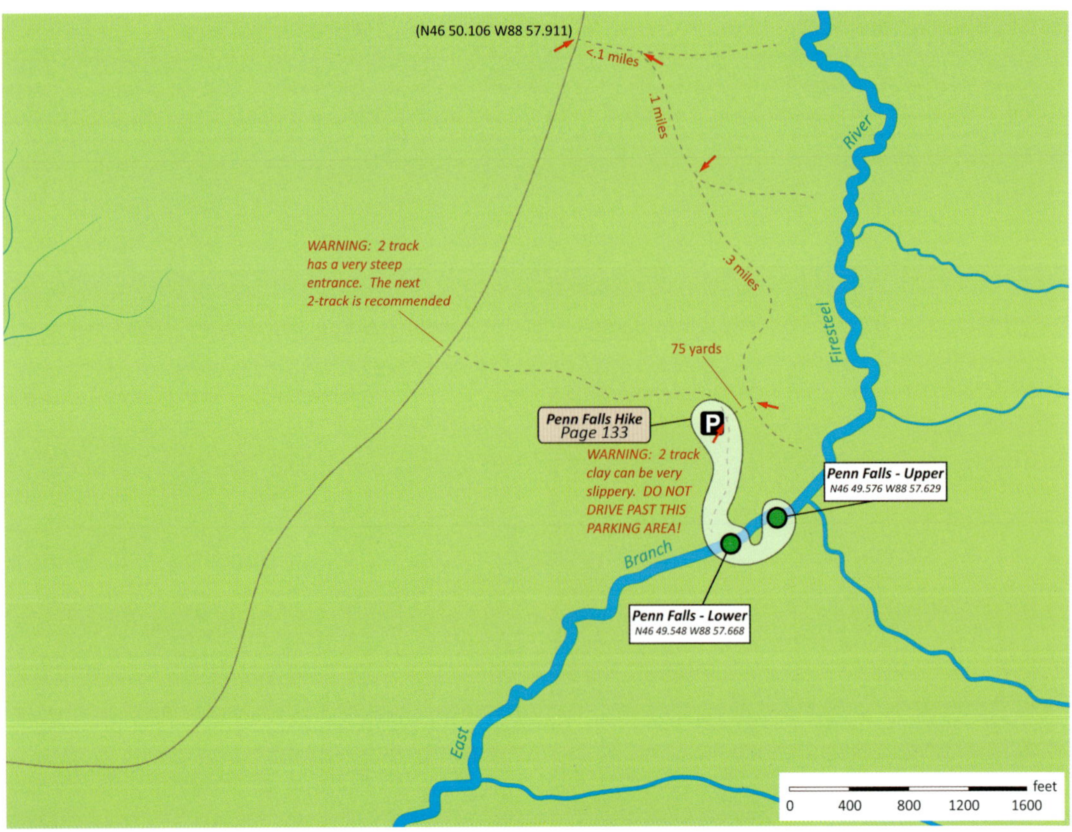
(N46 50.106 W88 57.911)
<.1 miles
.1 miles
.3 miles
75 yards
WARNING: 2 track has a very steep entrance. The next 2-track is recommended
Penn Falls Hike Page 133
WARNING: 2 track clay can be very slippery. DO NOT DRIVE PAST THIS PARKING AREA!
Penn Falls - Upper
N46 49.576 W88 57.629
Penn Falls - Lower
N46 49.548 W88 57.668
East Branch Firesteel River
feet
0 400 800 1200 1600

Penn Falls Hike

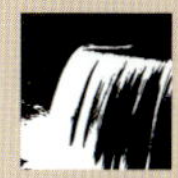

One of my most memorable adventures happened here at the Firesteel River. My oldest son was with me on one of the rare occasions we have had to go hiking together. It was a beautiful October day and we had been to a number of waterfalls. I had never been to Penn Falls. In fact, I didn't even know about them until late into my project. Anticipating a long hike, we were pleasantly surprised to find a 2-track that took us a little upstream from the falls. Noticing that there was a 2-track that ran right down to the river at the lower falls, we looked for it after getting back to the vehicle. It was easy to find. The trail headed downhill toward the river, and before it dropped even more sharply I decided to turn around at a small clearing. That's where the problem really presented itself! This whole area is Ontonagon clay based. A thin layer of October leaves covered the wet, slippery mess below. After several hours of trying to get my 4WD Chevy out of the slimy muck it was obvious that it wasn't going to happen without some help. I called AAA to see what type of assistance they could offer. The cell phone signal was poor, and the agent was not helpful at all. This chewed up the last 1/2 hour of precious daylight. By this time, we were ready for a warm shower, a clean bed and some much needed sleep. So we each quickly made an overnight bag out of our camera backpacks and started hiking out of the woods. The sun had completely set during this time so we had a night hike ahead of us. The village of Ontonagon was about 20 miles away. We really hoped that we could find a kind soul or two to drive us partway there. We hiked about 3 miles back to M-26 and there met a vehicle. We had found our kind soul! Here was a hunter heading out from his hunting camp for some supper. After explaining our plight to him, he gave us a ride to Rockland where we had a wonderful Saturday Pizza Buffet with him. From there we went back to see about getting the truck out. After an hour of futile effort, he took us back to his nearby hunting lodge where we spent the night. In the morning, he went out hunting with his aging dog and let us drive his truck to a rendezvous he had set up the night before with an off-road towing company from Houghton. We led the tow truck to our vehicle. He winched it 100 yards up the 2-track, and then promptly got stuck himself! Now there were two 4WD's in trouble. About this time, our hunter friend and his dog came wandering in. They had hiked the several miles along the river to see how we were doing. Putting all the tow ropes together that we could scrounge up, there were just enough to hook the hunter's truck to the tow truck and pull him out. He then winched me up the rest of the way and we were once again on our way! It's nice to know that there are still helpful people in this world. May we all be like our "guardian angel" yooper!

Directions: Drive 4 miles northeast on M-26 from the eastern intersection of M-38. Turn right (east) on a short connector dirt road. It ends at a "T" junction in .3 miles. Turn left (north) onto the old railroad bed made into a dirt road. Follow it for 1.9 miles. Turn right (east) onto a 2-track at N46 50.106 W88 57.911. (Higher clearance is needed - A 4WD is recommended) Veer right in less than .1 miles. Stay right in .1 miles. Stay right in .3 miles. Stay right and park in 75 yards where the 2-track "V's". Walk down the 2-track to the left to the lower waterfall. (DO NOT drive down this 2-track! This is where I became quite stuck!) Wade across the river, climb the far bank and follow it upstream to the upper falls.

PENN FALLS - LOWER (FIRESTEEL RIVER - EAST BRANCH)

Private

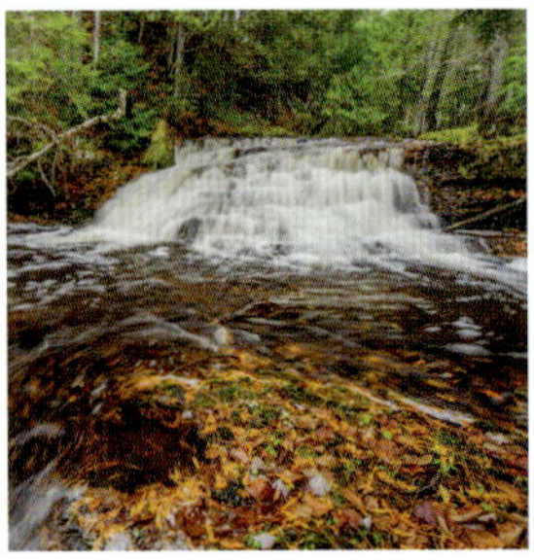

Must See:	7	GPS:	N46 49.548 W88 57.668
Height:	10 feet		
Time:	30-60 minutes	Hiking Information	
		Path:	2-track
Driving Information		Length:	.17 miles
Signs:	None	Elev. Change:	Moderate
Road:	2-track	GPS:	Recommended
Access:	Difficult	Danger:	Slight
4WD:	Recommended	WP Boots:	Recommended

The lower fall is a classic cascading face waterfall occurring as the river exits the short canyon. The setting is so idyllic! Looking at the waterfall from the shoreline the canyon wall rises up far above the waterfall, the river hugging the wall's edge. The far side of the river rises much more gently. On the near river's edge a stone fire ring is centered in a naturally flat space. It is an inviting campsite that I'm sure has seen its share of fishermen!

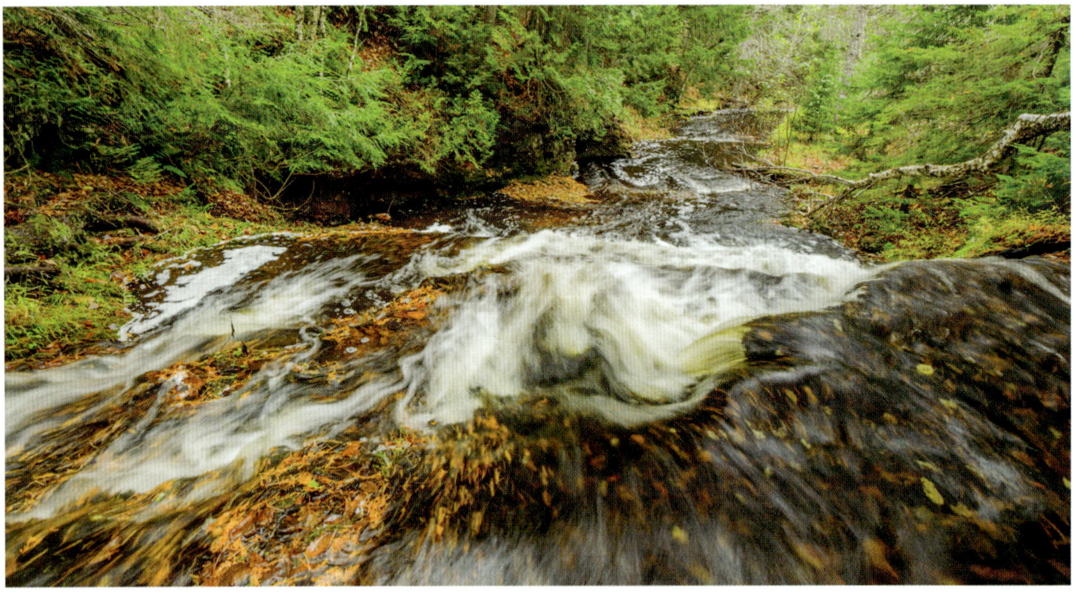

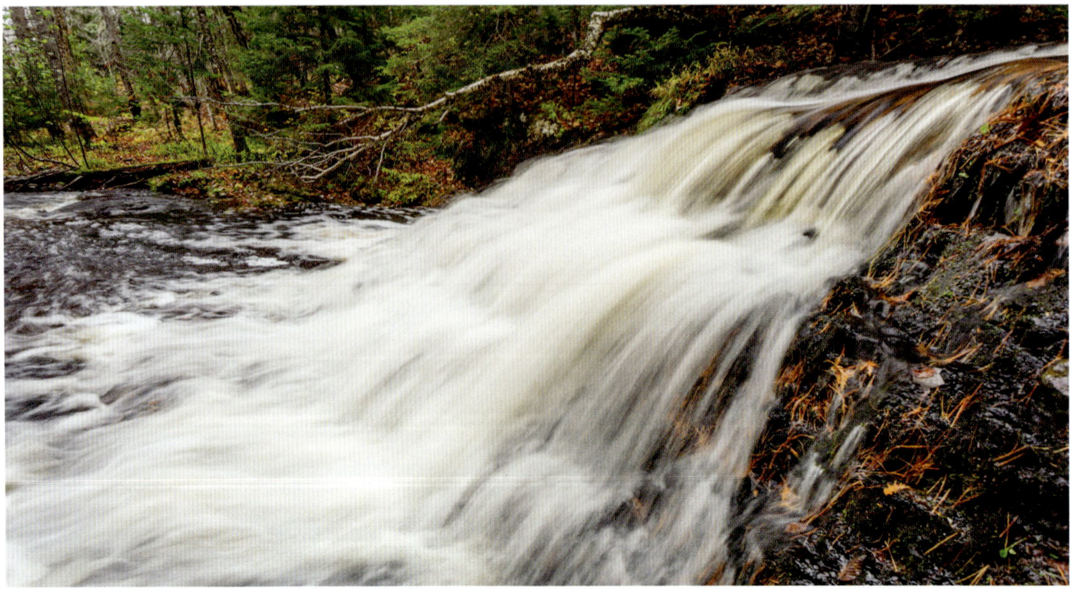

PENN FALLS - UPPER (FIRESTEEL RIVER - EAST BRANCH)

Private

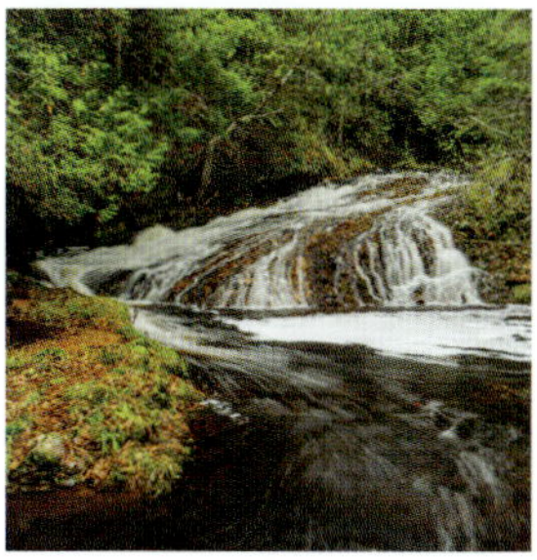

Must See:	7	GPS:	N46 49.576 W88 57.629
Height:	15 feet		
Time:	45-75 minutes	**Hiking Information**	
		Path:	2-track
Driving Information		Length:	.22 miles
Signs:	None	Elev. Change:	Moderate
Road:	2-track	GPS:	Recommended
Access:	Difficult	Danger:	Moderate
4WD:	Recommended	WP Boots:	Required

The steep canyon wall on the northwest side of the river requires crossing the river at the lower falls to be able to get to the upper falls. Once across the river, climb up the embankment to the top of the lower waterfall. The riverbank is easily navigated. There is not much undergrowth and the going is easy.

As the river enters the canyon, a 10 foot drop slides down a steep conglomerate face. An angular spill pool at the base turns hard around a small outcropping, then cascades down another 3 feet to the edge of the canyon wall. Then it bursts down 2 feet to a final black pool beneath the overhanging rock.

The view from the top

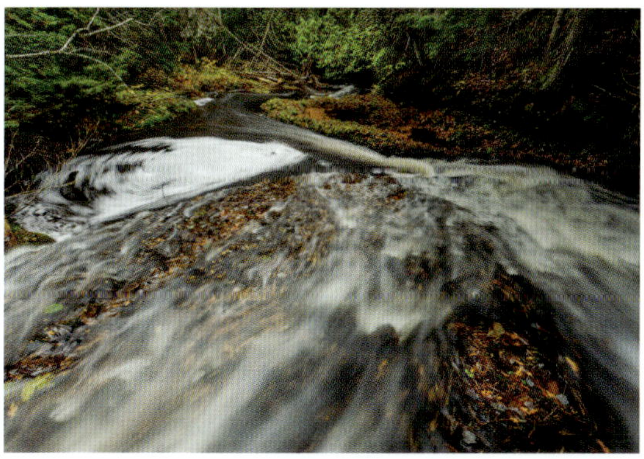

Looking upstream

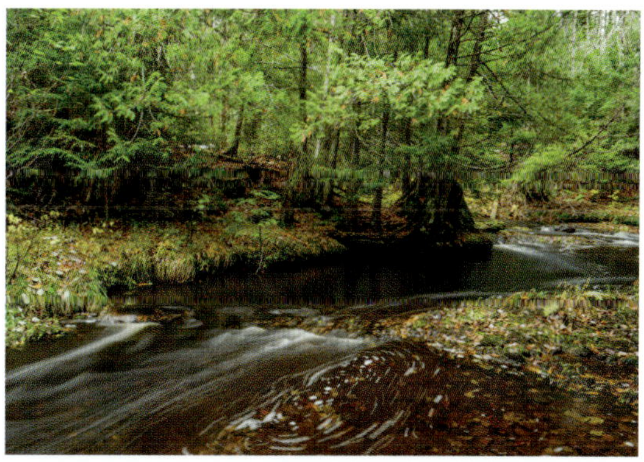

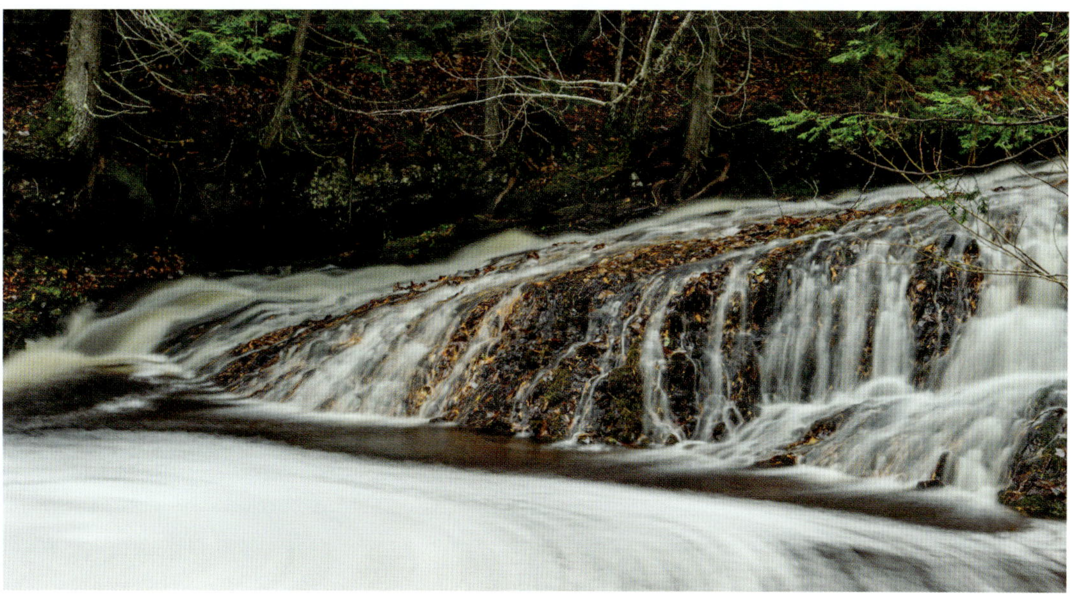

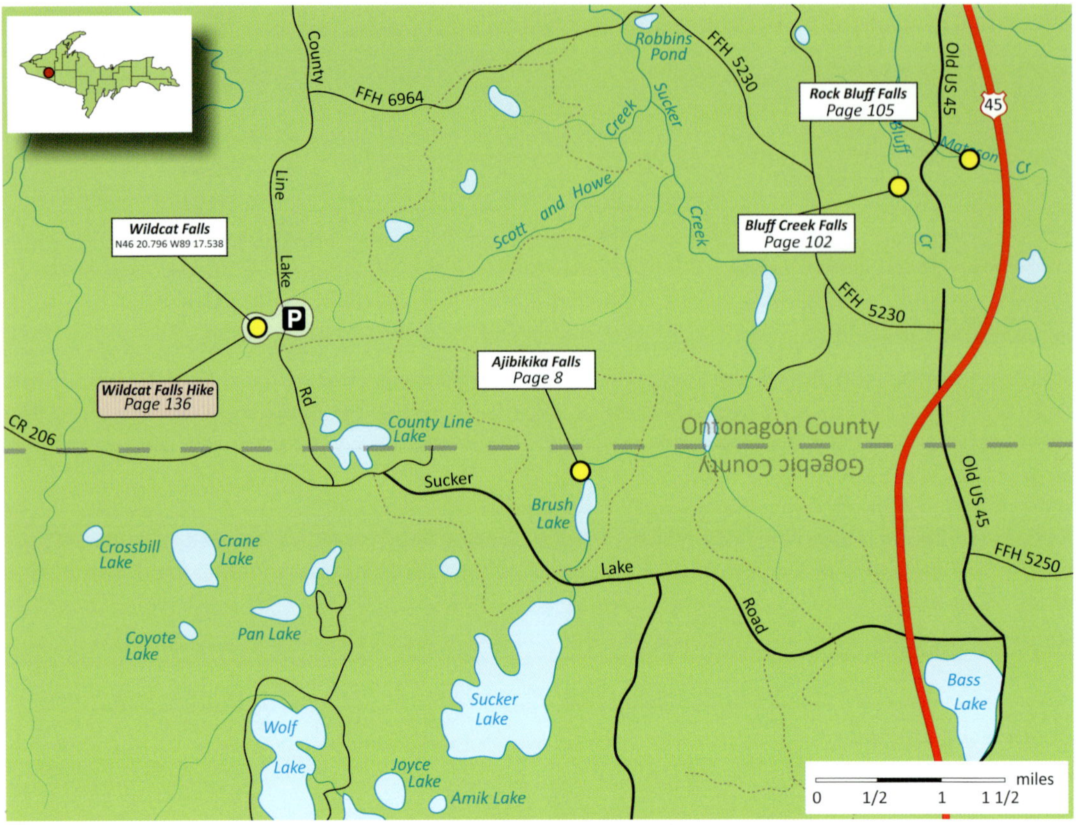

Wildcat Falls Hike

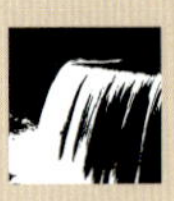

Near the headwaters of the Scott and Howe Creek is a spongy land where much of the creek runs along beneath the woodland floor. The underlying bedrock channels the creek along its way while just above a forest of cedars interspersed with a smattering of hardwoods clings to craggy rocks with gnarled roots seeking a better footing. Mossy clumps grown together carpet the web-like root structure. Everything seems muffled in this enchanted land above Wildcat Falls. Nothing to be heard but the running of water and the soft gurgling of its falling just downstream.

Directions: Drive 3.4 miles north from US-2 on US-45. Turn left (west) on Sucker Lake Road (dirt). Drive 5.5 miles on the twisting road. Turn right (northwest) onto County Line Lake Road (dirt). Follow it for 1.4 miles to N46 20.897 W89 17.237. Park on the side of the road. Stay on the high ground during the hike. Don't be tempted to follow the creek. It is too dense and wet down there. A mass of rock 400 feet from the road must be taken into consideration. Either stay to the right (creek side) and follow the base of the cliff, which requires fighting vegetation, or turn left until you can get to the top of the outcropping and follow the cliff ledge from the top where it is easier walking. This second route is my preferred method. A faint trail leads to the falls. Don't rely on it. It is VERY FAINT and easily lost.

WILDCAT FALLS (SCOTT AND HOWE CREEK)

Private

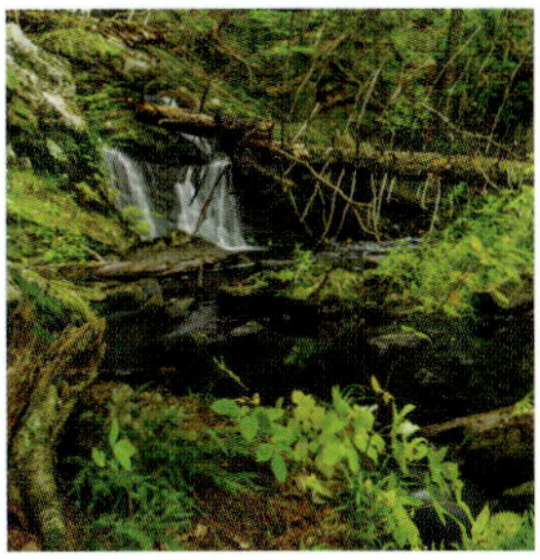

Must See:	5	GPS:	N46 20.796 W89 17.538
Height:	16 feet		
Time:	45-75 minutes	**Hiking Information**	
		Path:	VERY FAINT
Driving Information		Length:	.3 miles
Signs:	None	Elev. Change:	Moderate
Road:	Dirt	GPS:	Required
Access:	Somewhat difficult	Danger:	Moderate
4WD:	N/A	WP Boots:	Recommended

This hike feels longer that the 1/3 mile hike that it is. I suppose that is because the trail is nearly non-existent, the large outcropping of rock requires special navigation, and the spongy forest toward the end of the hike slows down the hiking. All in all, it is the uniqueness of the hikes that brings me back for more!

I would like to see this waterfall when the creek is running better. The water level was quite low when I was there. The waterfall starts with a 6 foot drop. Thirty feet later there is a 4 foot drop and then 3 smaller cascades within the next 20 feet finish off the falls. Below the waterfall is a backed up, low lying area. Stay out of this ravine during the hike.

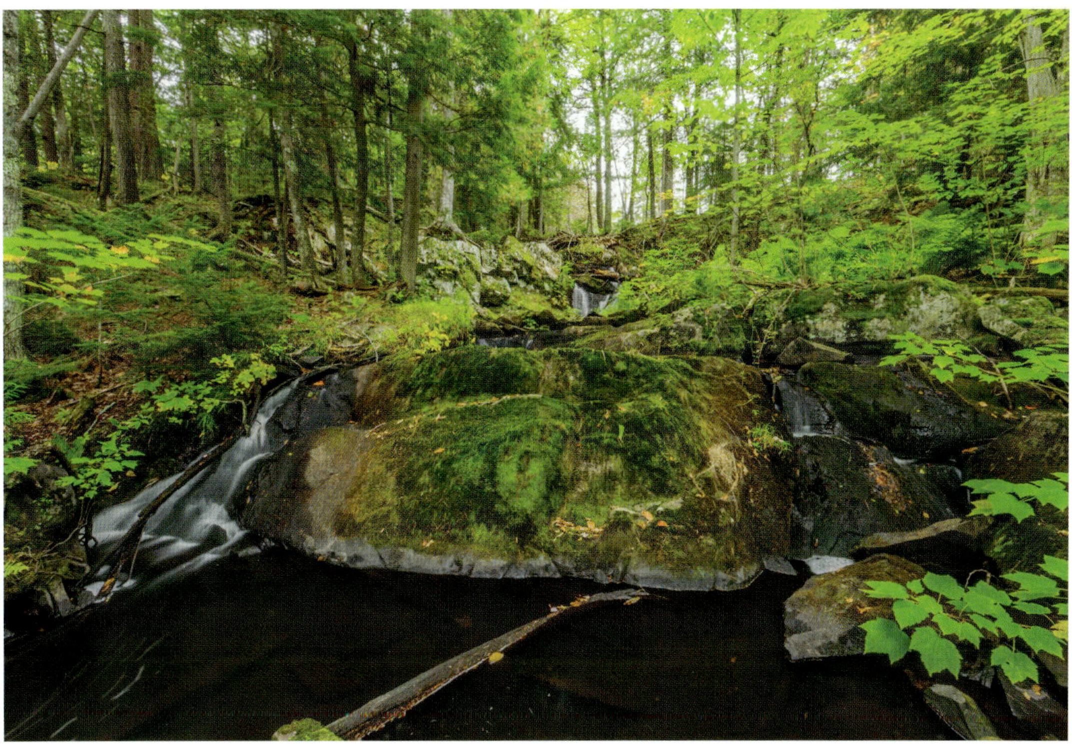

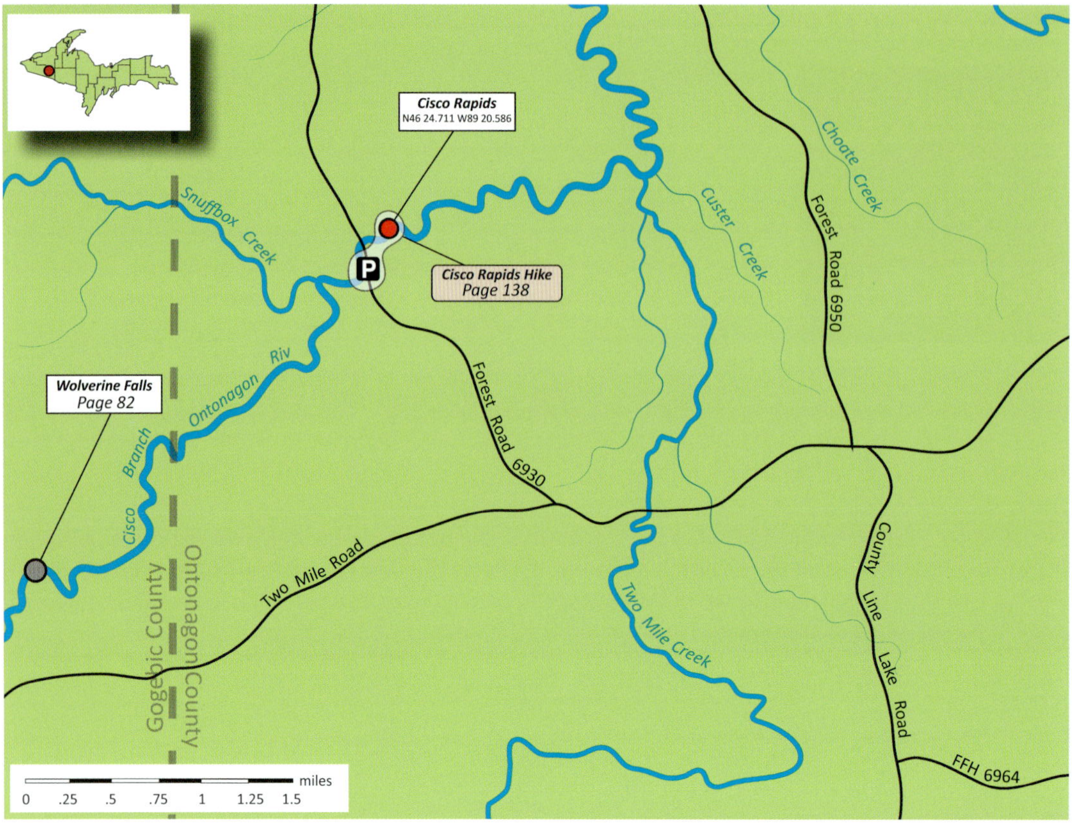

Cisco Rapids Hike

I discovered this small set of drops while looking for Wolverine Falls. The USGS somehow misplaced the waterfall, and so I hiked nearly a half mile along the Cisco Branch of the Ontonagon River to the southwest of Forest Road 6930 before concluding that there was no waterfall to be had in that area. Atlases can't always be trusted! I nearly gave up the search, thinking that this must be one of the "phantom" waterfalls. Instead I hiked on the other side of the road, following the fisherman's trail up a steep embankment that overlooked the river from a good height. Only .2 miles later I was back down to river level and standing alongside the minor drops that I now call Cisco Rapids. At the time I thought that this must be Wolverine Falls, but after talking to the knowledgable folks at Sylvania Outfitters in Watersmeet, they told me that Wolverine Falls is actually several miles further upstream. That puts it into Gogebic County. I will verify it when I get the chance. Meanwhile, we gain a little set of rapids to be enjoyed in Ontonagon County!

Directions: A good dirt road connects US-2 and US-45. This road goes by several names along the way: CR-527, Two Mile Road and Sleepy Hollow Road. About 8.5 miles from US-2 and 7.5 miles from US-45, FR-6930 turns to the northwest. Follow it 1.6 miles to the bridge that crosses over the Cisco Branch. Park off the side of the road. Follow the faint fisherman's trail down river on the south side of the river. The trail climbs up a steep embankment, hugging its edge until it drops back down close to the river.

CISCO RAPIDS (ONTONAGON RIVER - CISCO BRANCH)

Private

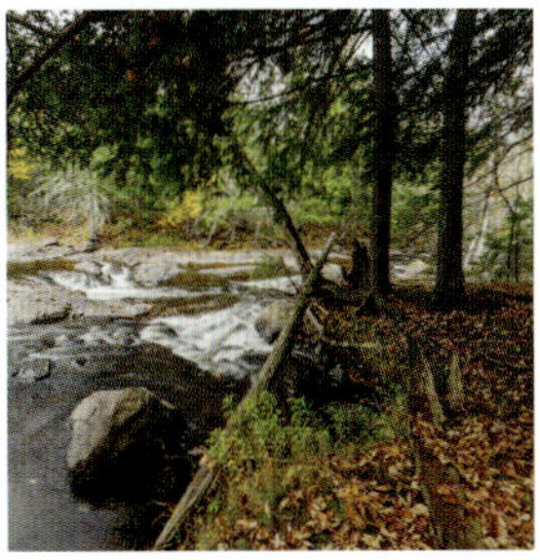

Must See:	3	GPS:	N46 24.711 W89 20.586
Height:	3 feet		
Time:	20-45 minutes	Hiking Information	
		Path:	Slight Footpath
Driving Information		Length:	.2 miles
Signs:	None	Elev. Change:	Moderate
Road:	Dirt	GPS:	Recommended
Access:	Somewhat difficult	Danger:	Slight
4WD:	N/A	WP Boots:	N/A

Small rock outcroppings divert the river's flow in several directions. At the lower points along these rocky masses the river floods down to the next level. The waterfall consists of 5 drops, with 4 of them on the same plane. Various sized boulders, some as large as 4 feet tall, are strewn along the riverbed.

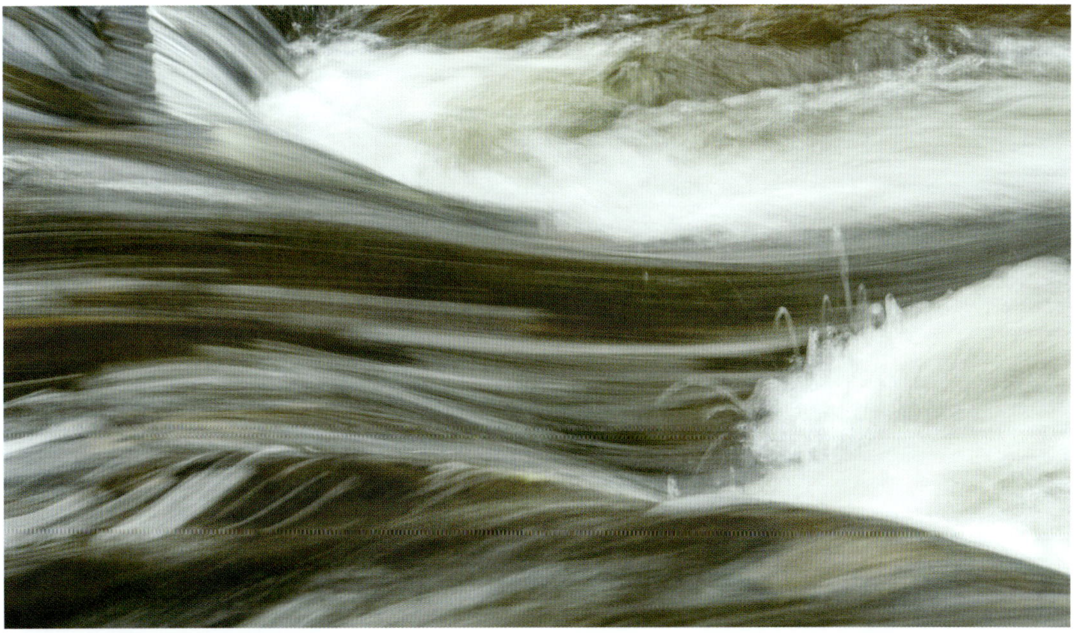

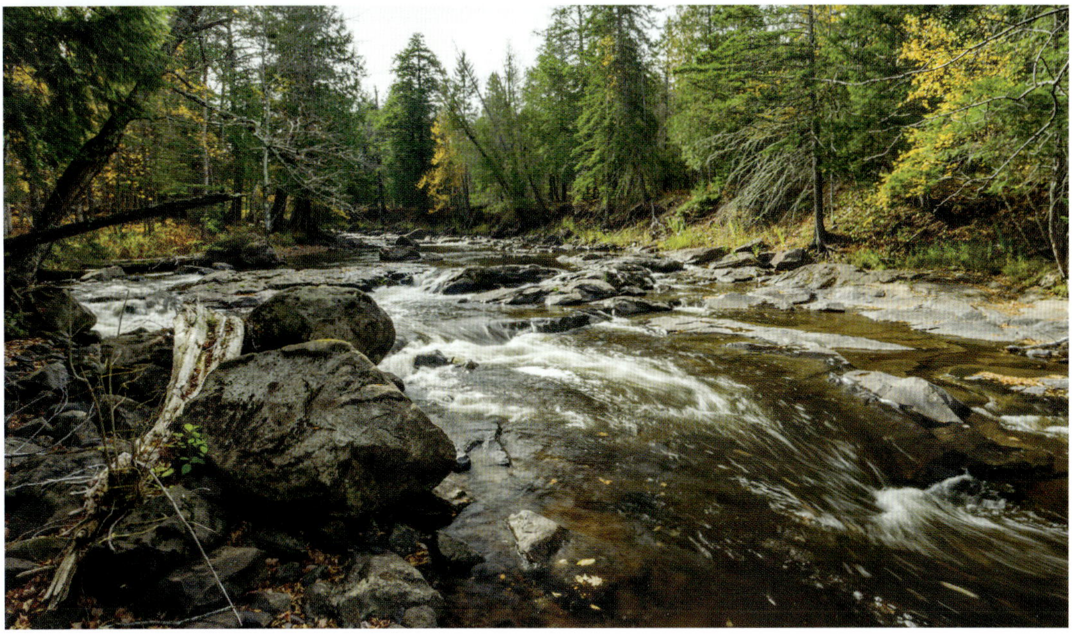

CHAPTER 3
PORCUPINE MOUNTAINS WILDERNESS STATE PARK

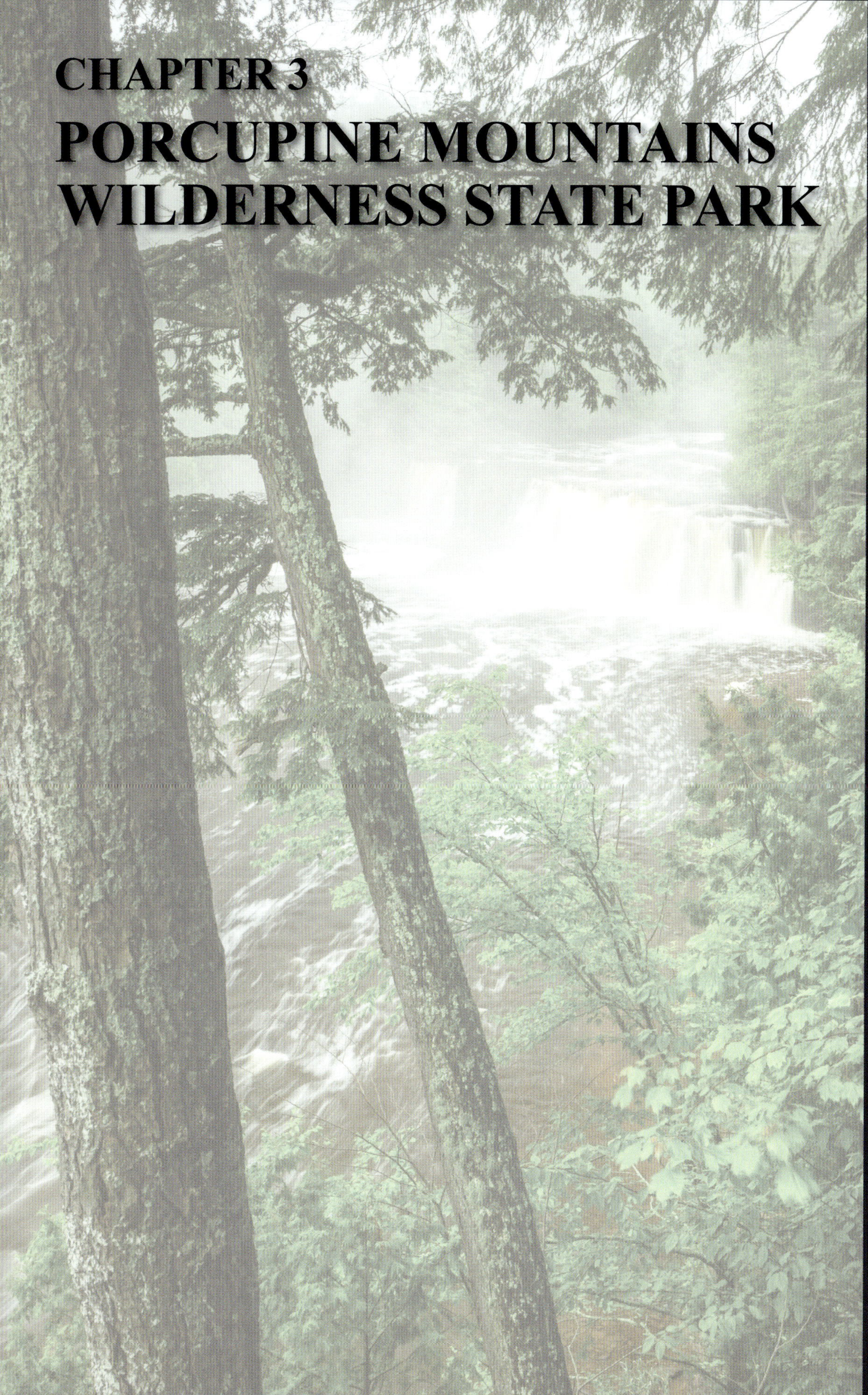

PORCUPINE MOUNTAINS CONTENTS

MAPS
HIKES
WATERFALLS

TABLE OF CONTENT KEY

MAPS..
HIKES..
WATERFALLS........................

TABLE OF CONTENT KEY

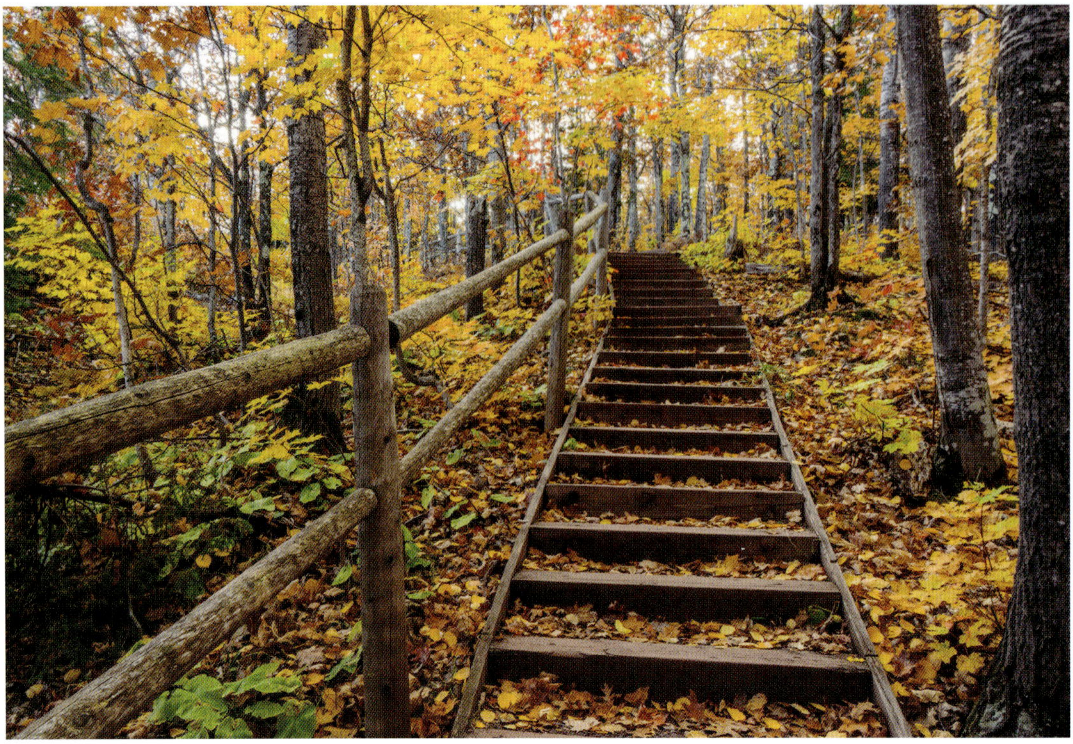

One of the many stairways found within the park

In wet areas there are often narrow, raised boardwalks laid out for your convenience

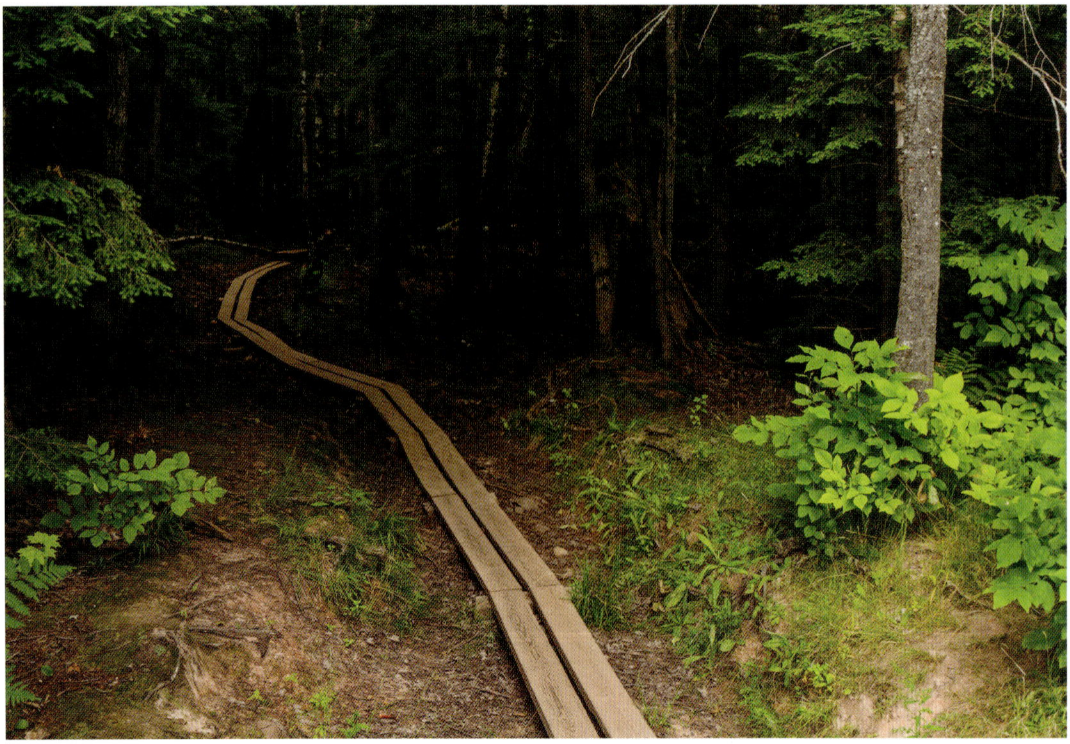

PORCUPINE MOUNTAINS WILDERNESS STATE PARK

Founded: 1945
Size: 59,000+ acres
Population: 0

The Porcupine Mountains Wilderness State Park is not a county of its own, but rather straddles the border between Ontonagon and Gogebic Counties, with the bulk of the part in Ontonagon County. I have decided to separate the Park into its own chapter for the following reasons:

1) Many people travel to the area to visit the park.
2) The park has a number of waterfalls in both counties, and it seemed disjointed to break them up between two separate chapters.
3) The book lines up nicely with the literature that the park hands out by giving the park its own chapter.

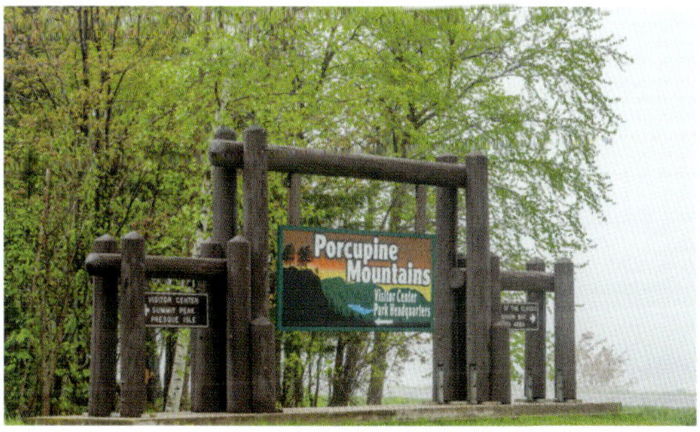

The Porcupine Mountains, affectionately known as the "Porkies", have fortunately been set aside for all to enjoy by the formation of the Porcupine Mountains State Park in 1945 and the subsequent inclusion of "Wilderness" in its name in 1972 when Michigan passed the Wilderness and Natural Areas Act. This has preserved large swaths of old growth forests. From the mid 1800's through the early 1900's there was some copper mining activity in the Porkies. There are still some traces of these mines that can be seen here and there within the park. Today, you'll find modern campgrounds, rustic cabins, miles of pristine Lake Superior shoreline, numerous hiking and mountain biking trails, areas for swimming and boating, park ranger led interpretive programs, downhill and cross country skiing, and of course, wonderful waterfalls!

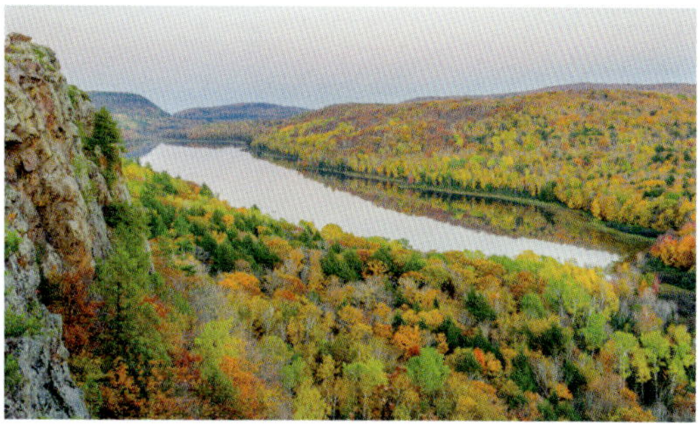

One of Michigan's iconic vistas, the Lake of the Clouds overlook, is easily accessed from M-107. This natural feature draws thousands of visitors annually from around the world.

There are only two main roads within the park. M-107 winds along the Lake Superior shoreline to the north, abruptly ending at a large parking lot near the Lake of the Clouds overlook. South Boundary Road skirts the southern and eastern sides of the park, intersecting CR-519 on the western side near the famous Presque Isle River. A Michigan Recreational Passport is required for admittance into the parking areas along the Presque Isle River. If you don't already have one, they are available for a small fee on site.

For the latest information about the park, visit the DNR's website at *http://www.dnr.state.mi.us/parksandtrails/Details.aspx?id=426&type=SPRK*.

Porcupine Mountains Map

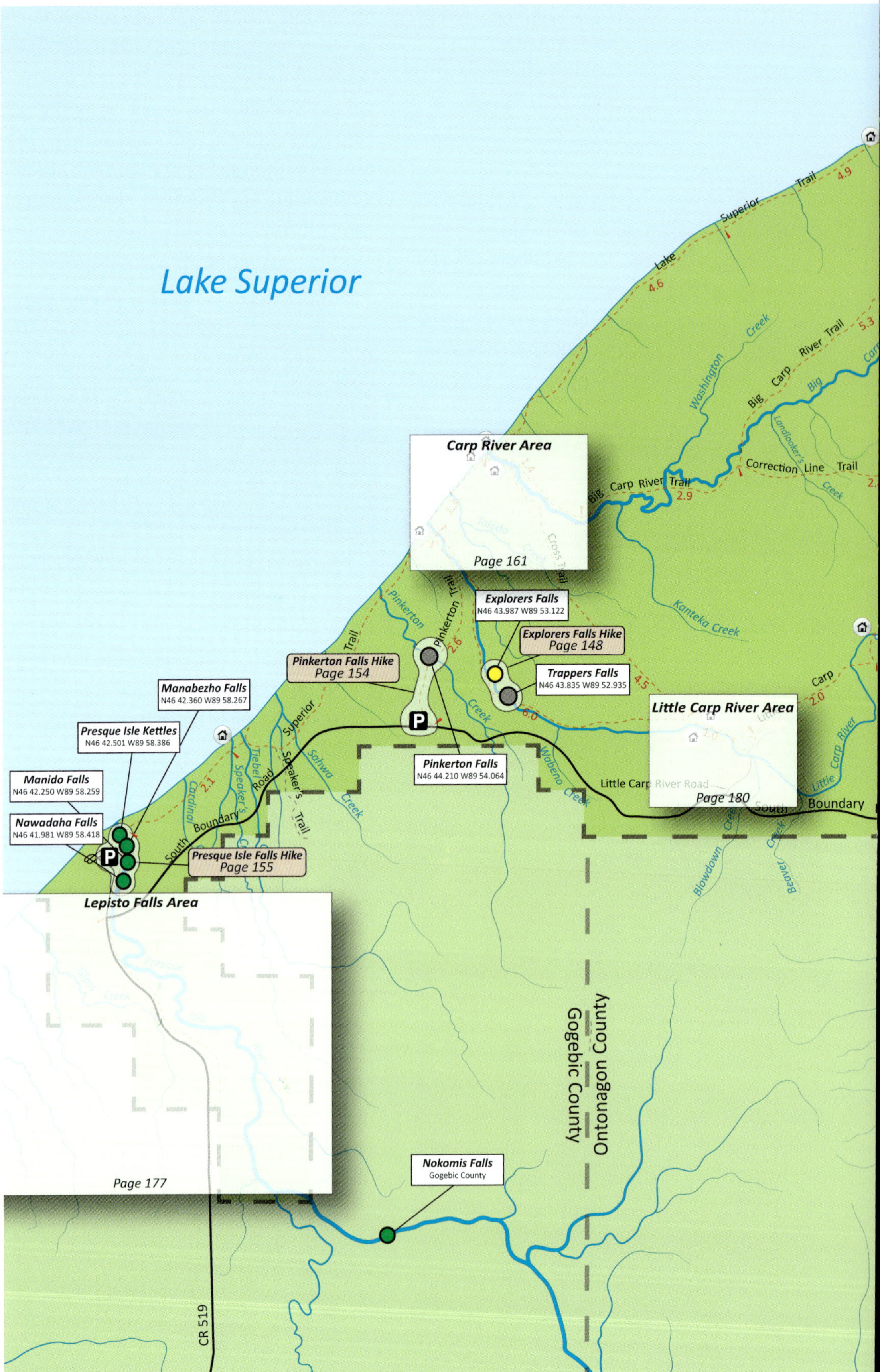

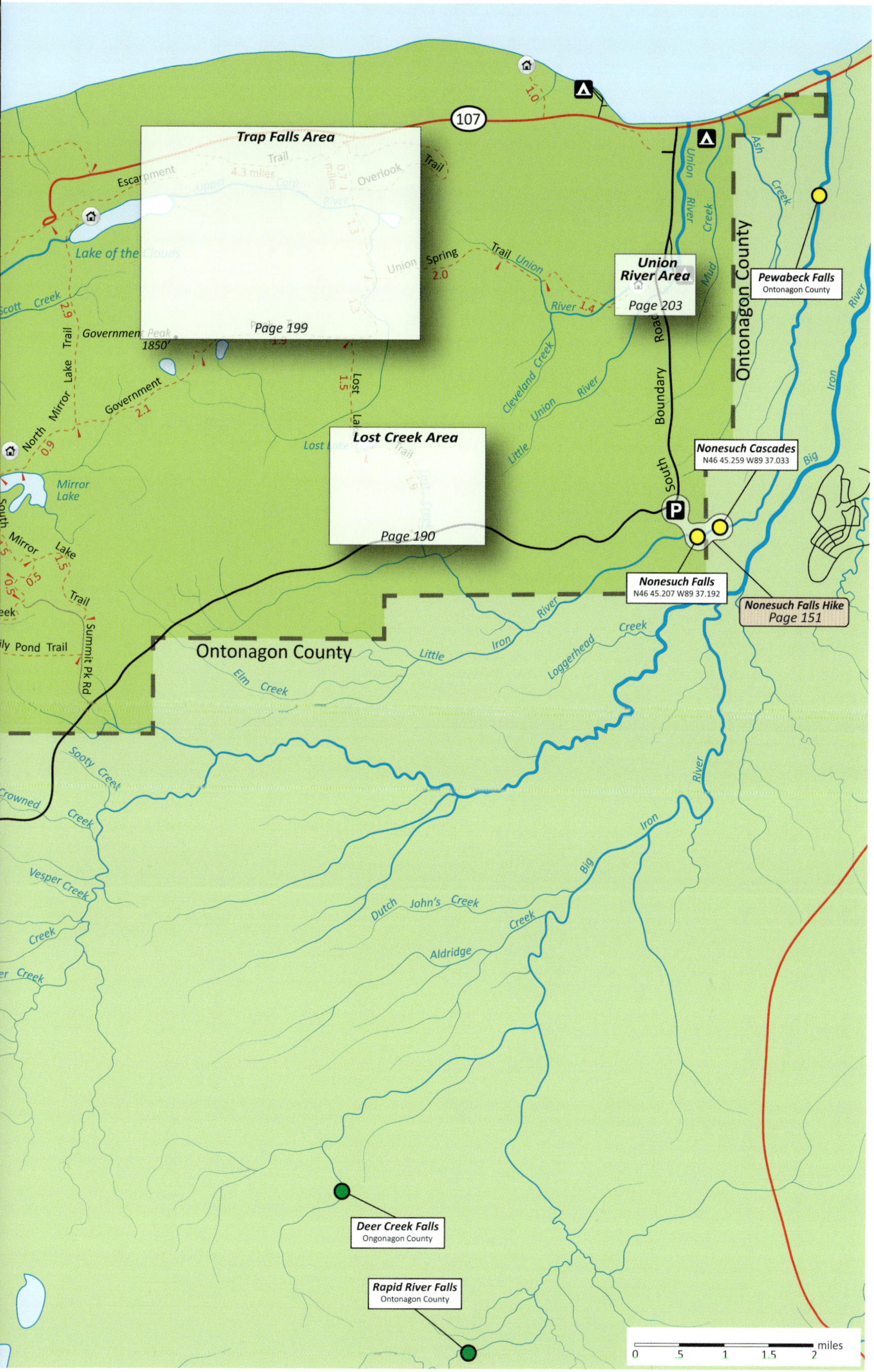
107
Trap Falls Area
Page 199
Lost Creek Area
Page 190
Union River Area
Page 203
Pewabeck Falls
Ontonagon County
Nonesuch Cascades
N46 45.259 W89 37.033
Nonesuch Falls
N46 45.207 W89 37.192
Nonesuch Falls Hike
Page 151
Deer Creek Falls
Ongonagon County
Rapid River Falls
Ontonagon County
Ontonagon County
Ontonagon County
South Boundary Road
Lake of the Clouds
Escarpment
Union Spring Trail
2.0
Union River 1.4
Government Peak
1850'
North Mirror Lake Trail
Government 2.1
Mirror Lake
South Mirror Lake Trail
Lost Lake
Lost Lake Trail
Summit Pk Rd
Scott Creek
Cleveland Creek
Little Union River
Union River
Mud Creek
Ash Creek
Big Iron River
Little Iron River
Loggerhead Creek
Elm Creek
Sooty Creek
Crowned Creek
Vesper Creek
Dutch John's Creek
Aldridge Creek
miles
0 .5 1 1.5 2

Explorers Falls Hike

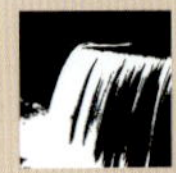

There is some confusion surrounding this set of waterfalls on the Little Carp River. The long slide has often been referred to as Trappers Falls, but I believe that it is actually Explorers Falls. There is no waterfall properly down river from this waterfall and the little waterfall upstream about 1/3 mile more accurately reflects the proper position for Trappers Falls. I hate to fly in the face of tradition, but I want to be as accurate as possible.

Quiet. Peaceful. Hiking through miles of Porcupine Mountains' wilderness typically reveals nothing of man's presence other than a narrow footpath and an occasional wooden bridge over a ravine or creek. In this solitude, the only sounds to be heard are those of nature at work. Small feet scurry, carrying a chipmunk with twitching nose and beady eyes to view the surrounding from atop a fallen tree. A scolding black squirrel, hiding from view as it climbs up the backside of a sugar maple, drowns out the tap-tap-tap of a pileated woodpecker looking for a meal in an old hemlock. The Little Carp River gurgles and splashes, supplying flora and fauna alike with a seemingly endless source of life. Leaves and twigs crunch underfoot, especially during the golden autumn season.

Directions: There is no "obvious" way to these falls. It really depends on what else you are trying to see along the way. Let me describe the 3 "shortest" ways to the falls:

The Simplest Way
Park at the end of Little Carp River Road. Remember that there is no place to turn trailers or RV's around here! Follow the Little Carp River Trail. It basically follows the northern side of the river until it gets close to Explorers Falls. You need to ford the river (there is no bridge) as the trail continues along the southern side to the falls. This hike is about 7 miles (round trip) long.

The Shortest Way
Park on the side of the South Boundary Road between Wabeno Creek and Pinkerton Creek. Hike cross country to the falls. THERE IS NO TRAIL! A GPS is required. I have not hiked this route, so I don't know what conditions to expect. Plan on about a 1.5 mile (round trip) hike.

The Western Route
Park at the trailhead for the Pinkerton Trail on South Boundary Road. Hike the Pinkerton Trail to the Little Carp River. Cross the river on the footbridge that is part of the Superior Trail. This will intersect with the western end of the Little Carp River Trail. Follow it to the east along the northern side of the river to the falls. This route requires about a 9 mile hike to complete.

The advantage to the ***Shortest Way*** is obviously the much shorter distance. The ***Simplest Way*** gives you just one trail to follow and is shorter than the ***Western Route***. It also passes by a number of waterfalls that are found in the Little Carp River Area. The ***Western Route*** provides access to Lake Superior as well as the waterfalls found near the mouth of the Little Carp River, but this hike is the longest of the three.

There are obviously many other hiking routes to take. Take into account your level of experience and ability when planning a hike, especially the longer ones that present themselves in Porcupine Mountains State Park. Enjoy! And be safe!

EXPLORERS FALLS (LITTLE CARP RIVER)

Private

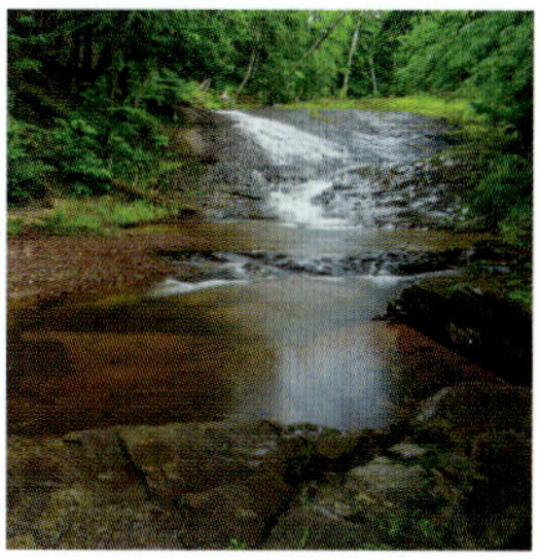

Must See:	6	GPS:	N46 43.996 W89 53.123
Height:	20 feet		
Time:	Varies	Hiking Information	
		Path:	Varies
Driving Information		Length:	Varies
Signs:	None	Elev. Change:	Moderate
Road:	Secondary	GPS:	Varies
Access:	Somewhat easy	Danger:	Moderate
4WD:	N/A	WP Boots:	Recommended

This waterfall has traditionally been referred to as Trappers Falls, but as there is no waterfall down river for a ways and there is a drop upstream, I believe that this is Explorers Falls and the one upstream is Trappers Falls. This follows the USGS pattern.

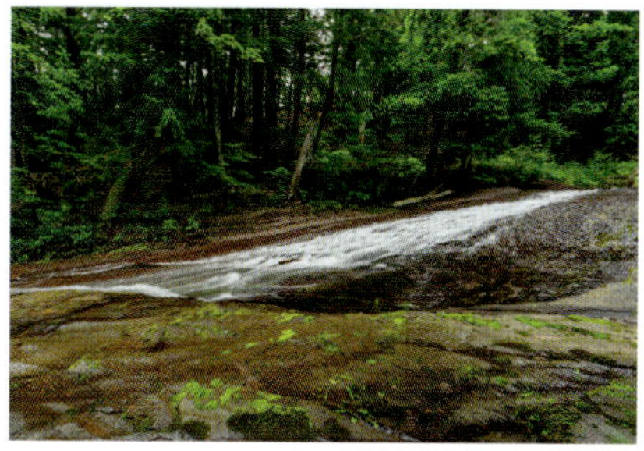

The conglomerate slide follows the pattern so typical at Porcupine Mountains' waterfalls. The tilted bedrock creates these "slides", many of which are found on the Big Carp River to the north.

Looking down from the top of the sliding waterfall you get a good view of the conglomerate bedrock

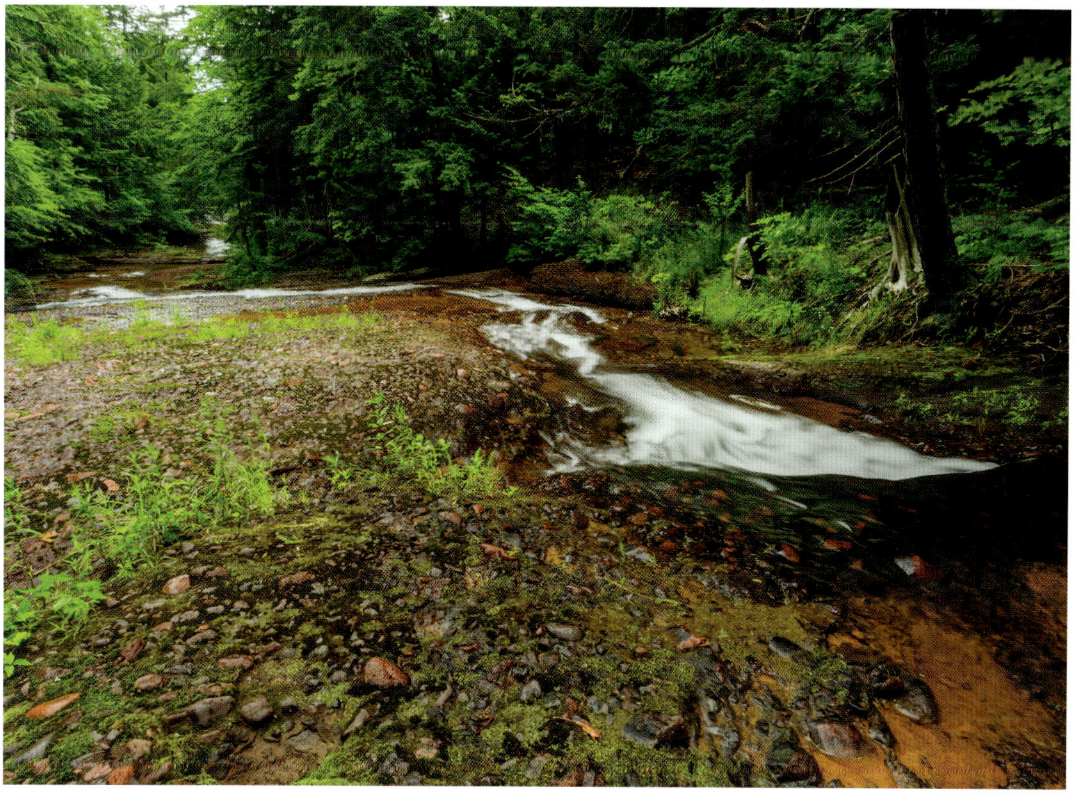

TRAPPERS FALLS (LITTLE CARP RIVER)

Private

Must See:	??	GPS:	N46 43.834 W89 53.024
Height:	?? feet		
Time:	Varies	**Hiking Information**	
		Path:	Varies
Driving Information		Length:	Varies
Signs:	None	Elev. Change:	Moderate
Road:	Secondary	GPS:	Varies
Access:	Somewhat easy	Danger:	Moderate
4WD:	N/A	WP Boots:	Recommended

Read the information regarding the name of this waterfall on the write-up for Explorers Falls several pages back. I believe this to be the "true" Trappers Falls. I have yet to get to this location. I will include my findings in upcoming printings!

Nonesuch Falls Hike

The old birch tree overlooks Nonesuch Falls, its gnarled roots grasping air as the soil, once packed securely around its base, has washed down river over the years during the rush of numerous spring melts. Oh, the countless stories it could tell of when it was but a sapling. The laughter of children splashing below the falls. The sound of steel on rock. The murmur and curses of men's voices as they tried with limited success to wrench stubborn copper from the hard earth. The slowly growing pile of poor rock tailings on the far side of the river. And then... nothing.

The once proud community, lacking the prosperity needed to keep its economic engine running, moved on, its dreams and hopes falling into ruin, much like its buildings would over the years. Slowly the forest reclaimed the land, swallowing up all but the hardiest remnants of the mine.

Now, day after day, the aging birch sits silently, listening to the endless chatter of the falls, interrupted occasionally by the call of a bird, the furtive approach of a white tail deer looking for a drink of water, or the snuffling of a black bear searching out black berries.

My musings are interrupted by the darkening sky leaking a fine mist. I pack away my field notes and take a long last look at the birch. I see that its heart is exposed, foretelling its doom. Any day it will topple over, falling into the river from which it drank these many years.

Directions: South Boundary Road runs along two general corridors. The longer of the two is the east/west route that winds along the park's southern border. The north/south portion begins near the park's visitor's center and heads down along the eastern edge of the park. At the point that these two legs of the road meet in a large sweeping bend (4.25 miles south of M-107), a 2-track runs off to the southwest for a short distance. It ends at a small clearing where a number of vehicles may park near a metal gate. Informational signage provides a historical context for the ruins and clearings that are observed on the way to the falls. Follow the nicely mowed path through the woods and finally into a clearing that was once the site of the mining community. The trail angles to the right at the rear of the clearing and reenters the woods. Immediately the trail splits. Head left. The trail divides again. The left path ends at a point down river from the falls. To the right, the trail ends at the base of the falls. Both paths pass by the mining ruins.

Follow the river downstream from Nonesuch Falls about .2 miles to reach the Nonesuch Cascades. You will likely need to be in the river for some of the hike, so waterproof boots are recommended.

NONESUCH FALLS (IRON RIVER)

Private

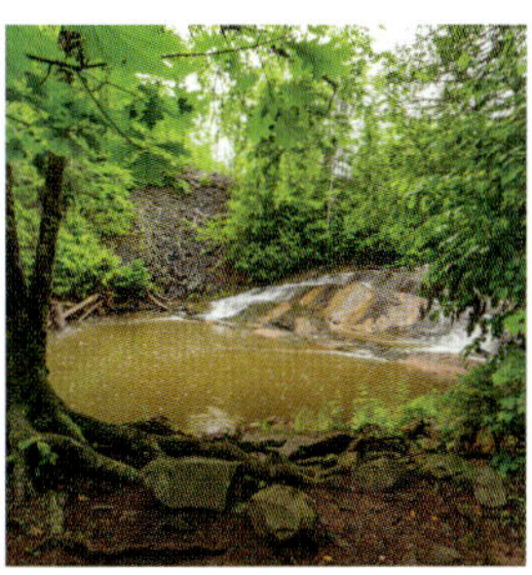

Must See:	5	GPS:	N46 45.207 W89 37.192
Height:	15 feet		
Time:	40-70 minutes	Hiking Information	
		Path:	Footpath
Driving Information		Length:	.47 miles
Signs:	None	Elev. Change:	Slight
Road:	Secondary	GPS:	N/A
Access:	Somewhat easy	Danger:	Slight
4WD:	N/A	WP Boots:	N/A

A rocky riverbed adds an interesting look down river from the angling waterfall. Make sure to spend time at the ruins while here. Imagine what it must have been like living through snowy northern winters, viewing the amazing beauty that was literally just outside the door, working underground for long hours, dragging around heavy steel tools and moving heavier yet stone.

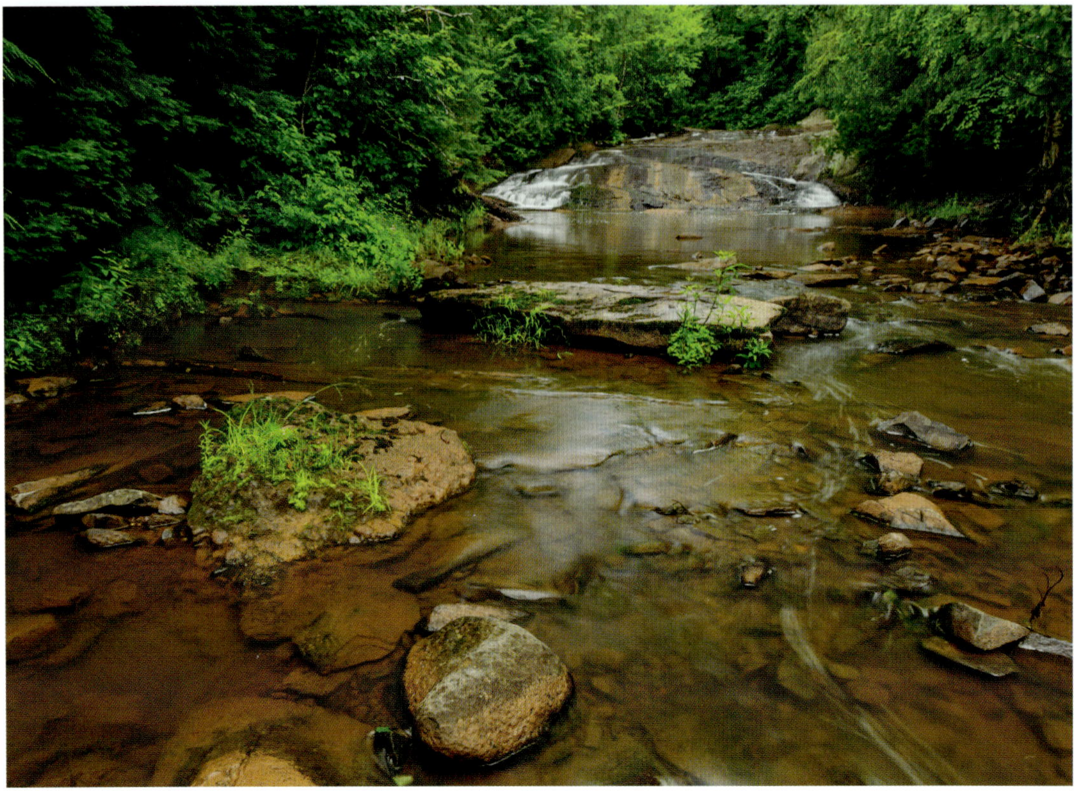

Remnants from the Nonesuch Mine. Enjoy viewing, but don't disturb the increasingly fragile stonework.

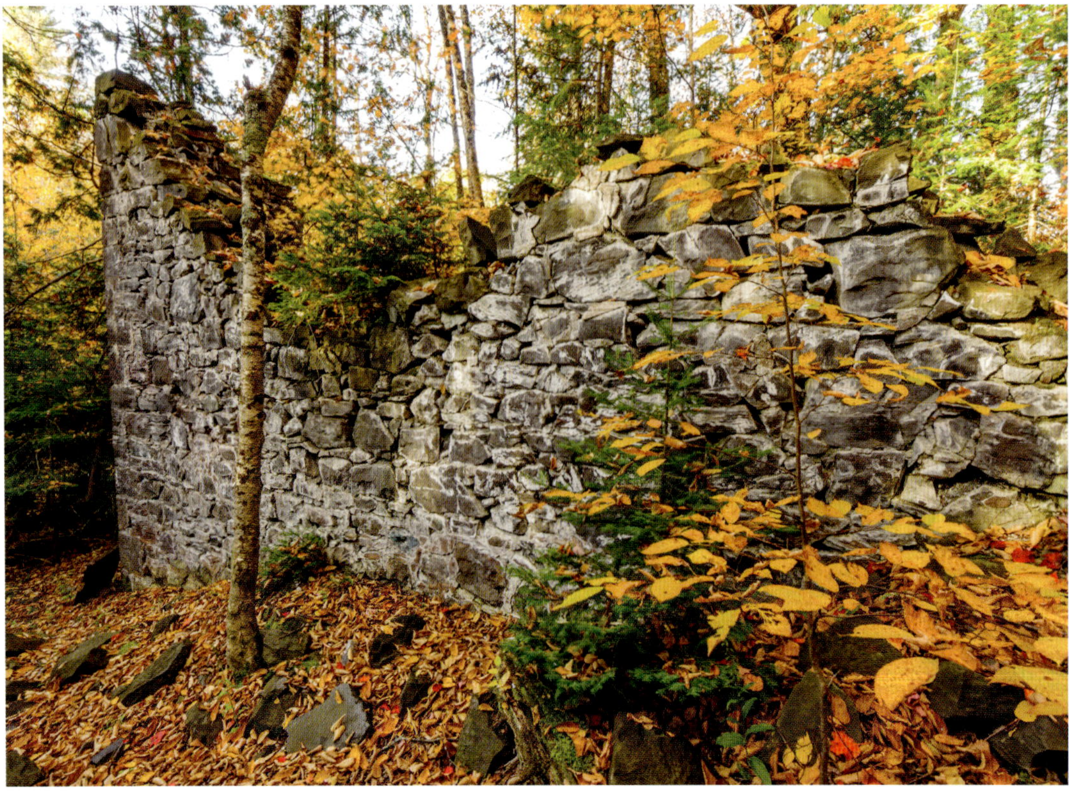

NONESUCH CASCADES (IRON RIVER)

Private

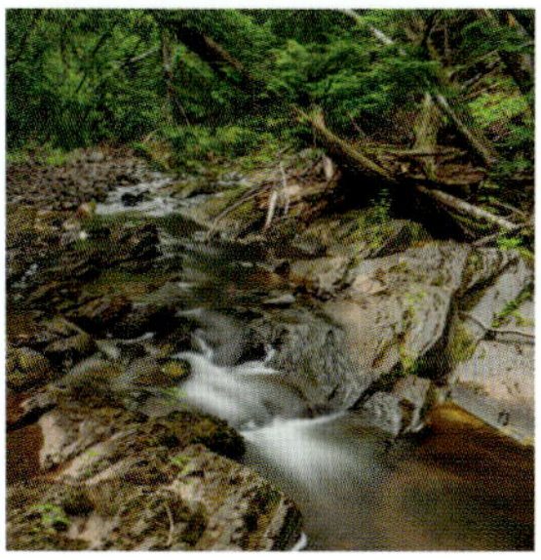

Must See:	5	GPS:	N46 45.259 W89 37.033
Height:	5 feet		
Time:	60-90 minutes	**Hiking Information**	
		Path:	Footpath
Driving Information		Length:	.67 miles
Signs:	None	Elev. Change:	Slight
Road:	Secondary	GPS:	N/A
Access:	Somewhat easy	Danger:	Moderate
4WD:	N/A	WP Boots:	Recommended

The river has carved a path down the center of the river bed, cutting through fine layered shale, leaving bulwarks of chalky gray stone uplifted at an awkward angle. Through the feathered features the river babbles and gurgles, singing a song that minnows love to hear. The two foot wide channel widens out substantially as the river rises. Cedars and birch trees overhang the river, their bows gracefully arching over the rocky river while steep banks on either side add to the sense of seclusion.

Remnants from the Nonesuch Mine. Enjoy viewing, but don't disturb the increasingly fragile stonework.

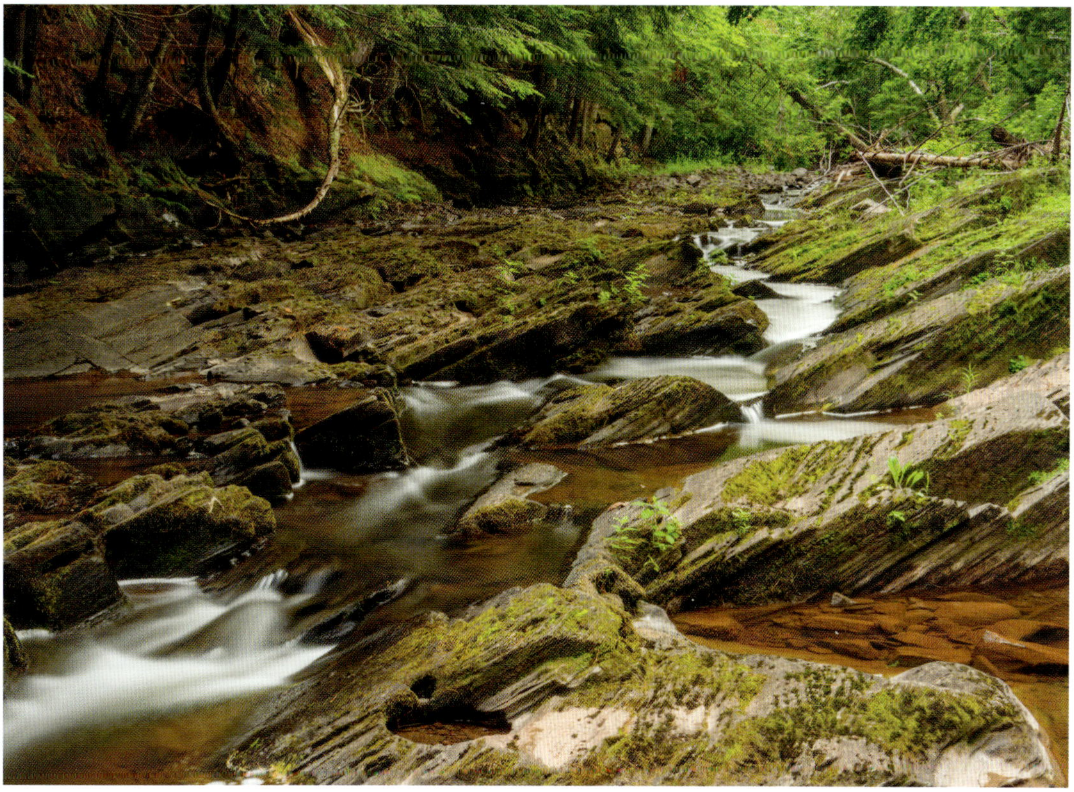

Pinkerton Falls Hike

I went on a wild goose chase the first time I looked for the falls. I overlooked the small falls near the intersection of Pinkerton Trail and Pinkerton Creek. Instead, I hiked upstream along Pinkerton Creek for about 1/2 mile through a light rain, finding nothing but wet pants and socks along the way!

Directions: Park along South Boundary Road at the trailhead for Pinkerton Trail. This is about 4.4 miles east of CR-519. Hike along the Pinkerton Trail (north) for about .7 miles until the trail crosses Pinkerton Creek. The waterfall can be seen from the bridge (I think). You may want to look a little downstream as well.

PINKERTON FALLS (PINKERTON CREEK)

Private

Must See:	??	GPS:	*N46 44.210 W89 54.064 (not verified)*
Height:	?? feet		
Time:	60-90 minutes	**Hiking Information**	
		Path:	Improved trail / NONE?
Driving Information		Length:	About .7 miles
Signs:	None	Elev. Change:	??
Road:	Secondary	GPS:	Recommended
Access:	Somewhat easy	Danger:	??
4WD:	N/A	WP Boots:	??

My research has indicated that Pinkerton Falls is slightly downstream from where the Pinkerton Trail crosses Pinkerton Creek. It may be seen from the bridge. I believe that there are a couple of closely located rocky sliding cascades that make up Pinkerton Falls.

Presque Isle Falls Hike

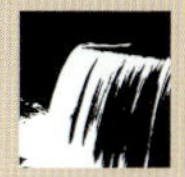

Magnificent waterfalls, coveted camping sites, towering hemlocks, ample paved parking, seemingly tame whitetail deer, boardwalks and well placed viewing decks. These thoughts flit through my mind as I contemplate the popular Presque Isle waterfall area. "Presque Isle", a French term meaning "almost island", refers to the land mass near the mouth of the river which can become a short lived island during a heavy spring melt. At that time, the river divides around the large, wedge shaped area. A waterfall even forms on the seldom used riverbed on the far side of the "island".

I never tire of hiking along this section of the Presque Isle River. The natural features seen in this 3/4 mile hike are spectacular! The four waterfalls are connected by a series of boardwalks and dirt paths. At the northern end, a suspended bridge spans the river close to Lake Superior. This provides access to the east side of the river as well. There is a trail along that side also, but it is primitive and lacks the viewing platforms, stairs and guardrails that are found in abundance on the commonly traveled side.

Fifty primitive camp sites are within walking distance of the river. There are several vault toilets and a couple hand pumps that provide water. The campground is situated along the 100 foot high cliffs that overlook Lake Superior. Sunsets from this vantage point can be stunning! http://www.michigandnr.com/parksandtrails/Details.aspx?id=75&type=SPCG

Although the Presque Isle Campground is easily accessed, RV'ers often prefer the one hundred sites at the Union Bay Campground where there is electricity at every site and four water spigots are strategically located throughout the campground and a modern bathhouse is centered among the campsites. http://www.michigandnr.com/parksandtrails/Details.aspx?id=74&type=SPCG

Directions: At the western end of Porcupine Mountains State Park drive north on CR-519 past South Boundary Road. After passing the small ranger's station (you must confirm that you have a recreational passport here) there are several parking areas to choose from. I prefer the furthest, which is at the end of the road. Park. Signage marks the way to the swinging bridge, which is about 200 yards from the parking lot. The Presque Isle Kettles are located just up river from the bridge. After viewing the "Holes" come back and follow the wooden stairs and walkway up river to the 3 other waterfalls.

PRESQUE ISLE KETTLES (PRESQUE ISLE RIVER)

Private

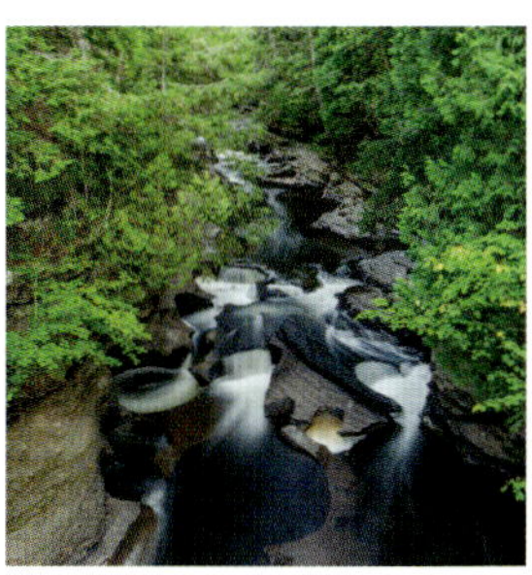

Must See:	8	GPS:	N46 42.501 W89 58.386
Height:	3 feet		
Time:	20-40 minutes	Hiking Information	
		Path:	Footpath
Driving Information		Length:	200 yards
Signs:	None	Elev. Change:	Moderate
Road:	Secondary	GPS:	N/A
Access:	Easy	Danger:	Slight
4WD:	N/A	WP Boots:	N/A

Circular bowls, hollowed out by boulders caught in swirling eddies over the years, display a uniquely beautiful pattern, fashioned as it were by a master artist. When the water level is just right, the river pours from one bowl to the next. During the spring melt and after heavy rainfalls the river may be too high to even see the bowls. When the river is quite low, the riverbed will be dry between some of the bowls.

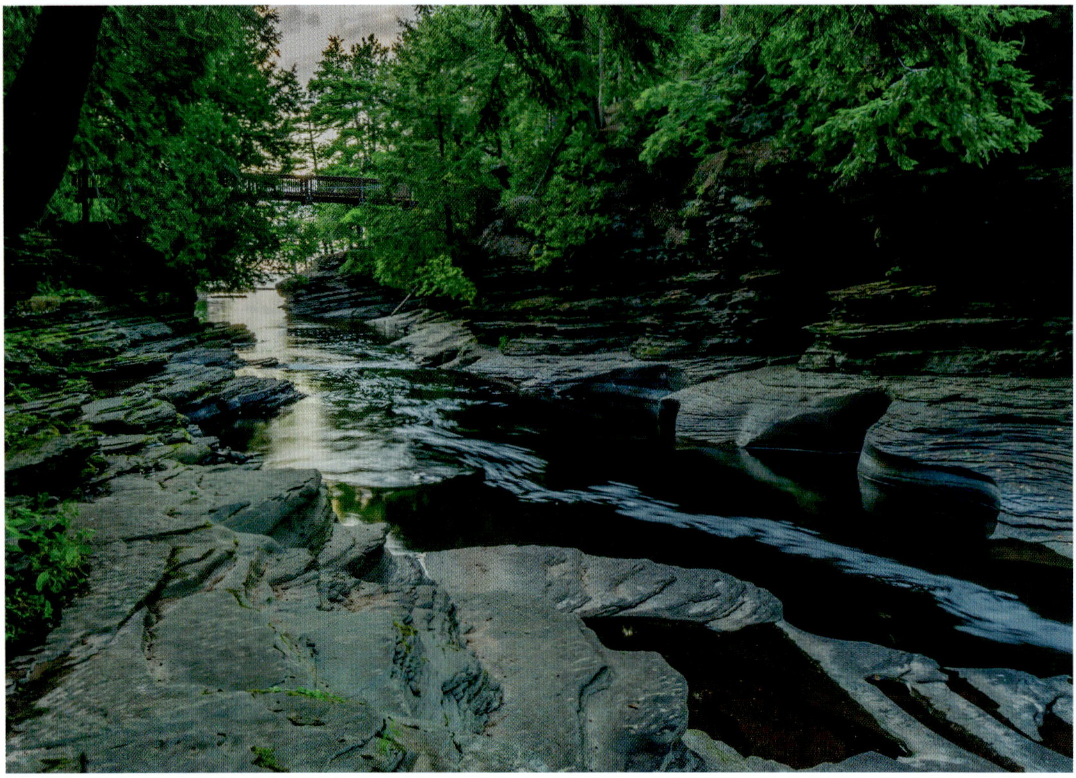

The footbridge can be seen suspended over the river just downstream from the bowls. It is the perfect viewing platform for this unique geological scene.

The scenery cloaks itself with multi-colored splendor as autumn takes hold from late September to early October each year.

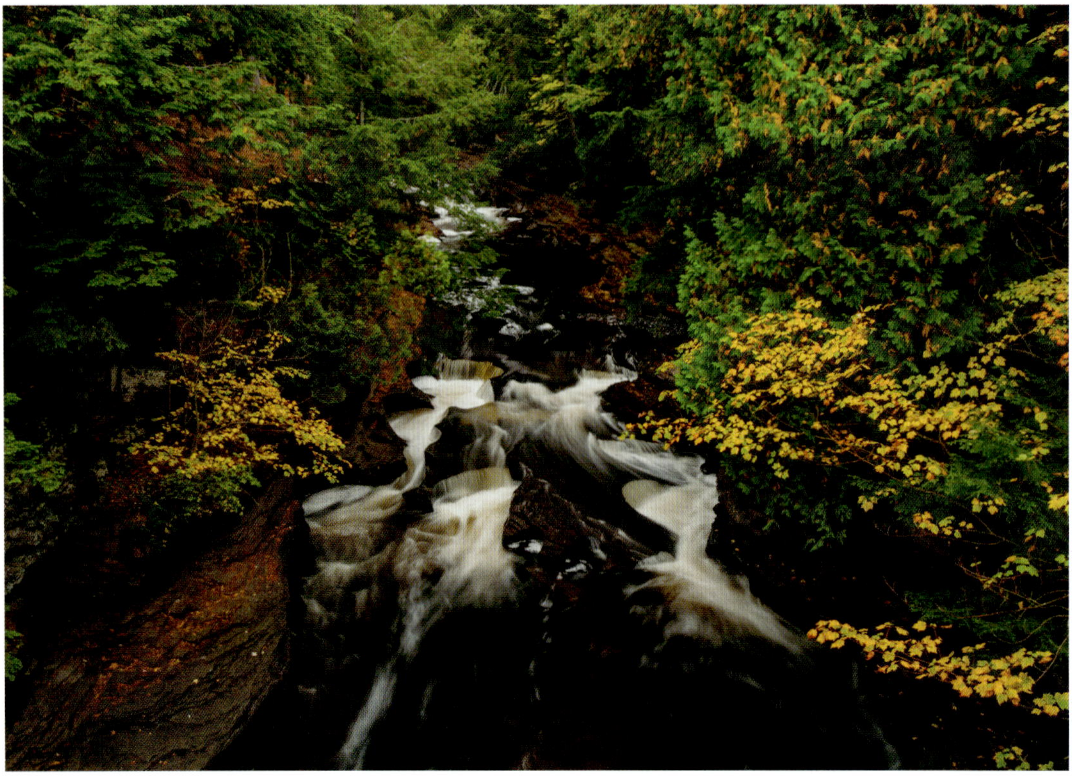

MANABEZHO FALLS (PRESQUE ISLE RIVER)

Private

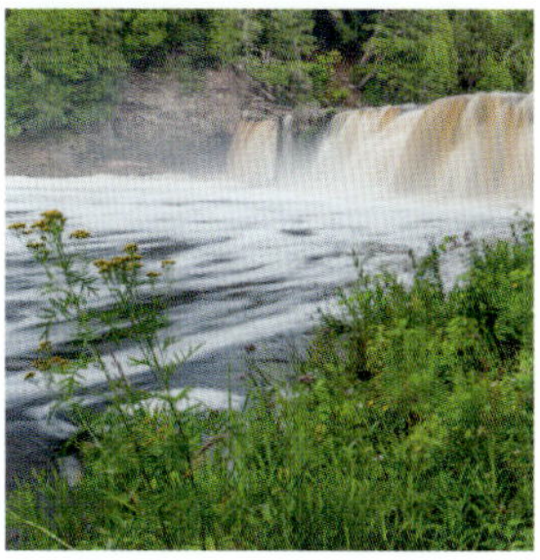

Must See:	10	GPS:	N46 42.360 W89 58.267
Height:	22 feet		
Time:	30-45 minutes	Hiking Information	
		Path:	Footpath
Driving Information		Length:	.25 miles
Signs:	None	Elev. Change:	Moderate
Road:	Secondary	GPS:	N/A
Access:	Easy	Danger:	Slight
4WD:	N/A	WP Boots:	N/A

There are two viewing decks for Manabezho Falls. The main deck is down river from the falls and provides a sweeping view of the falls and river from atop the gorge walls. The other deck is at the brink of the waterfall. There is not much to see from this vantage point. It is possible to climb down the steep embankment to the riverbed although this is discouraged due to the inherent danger and erosion concerns.

Manabezho, the Ojibwa name for a popular spirit-god, thought by some to enjoy playing tricks, lends its name to this, the most majestic of the Presque Isle waterfalls. In fact, I consider this to be one of the finest waterfalls in Michigan! What is the perfect volume of water for ideal viewing conditions? Perhaps this is the "trickiest" aspect of this waterfall! In the driest times, there are large patches of dry rock at the top of the falls, with no water falling on the eastern side of the river. When the river is raging with spring melt or after heavy downpours, the water levels are so high, that no underlying rocks can be seen at all. I prefer something in between. I love it when water is running across the entirety of the river, and yet the rock outcroppings stand out- water pouring around them like sand sifting through outstretched fingers.

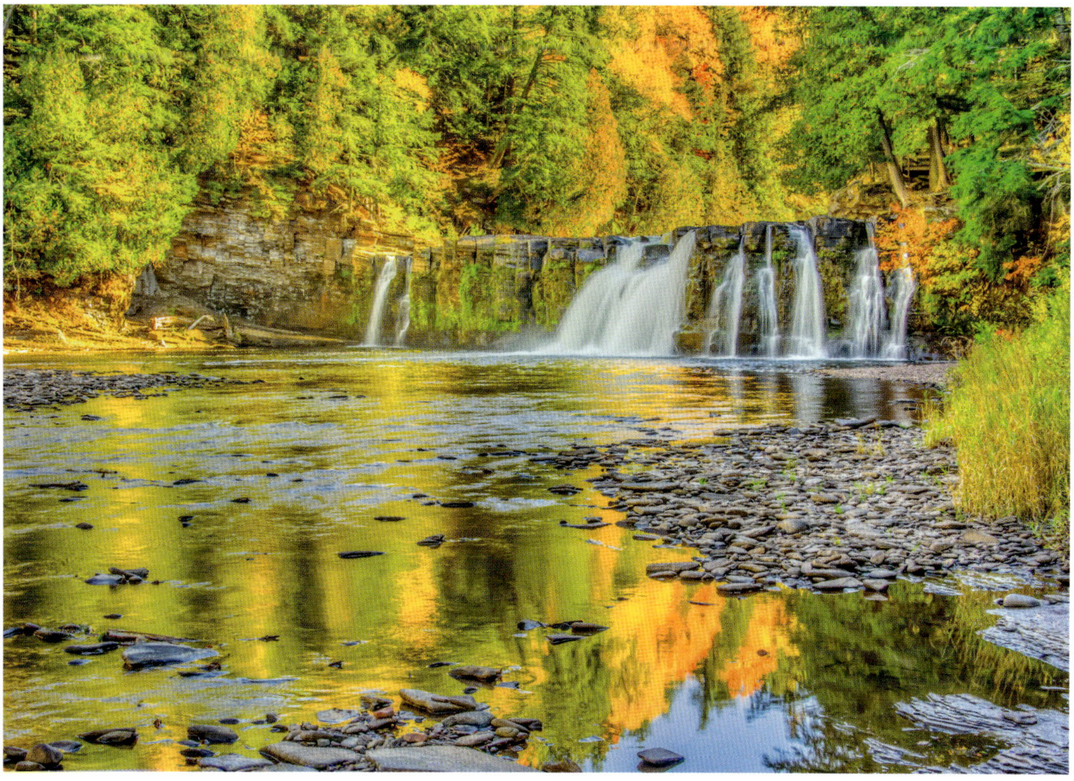

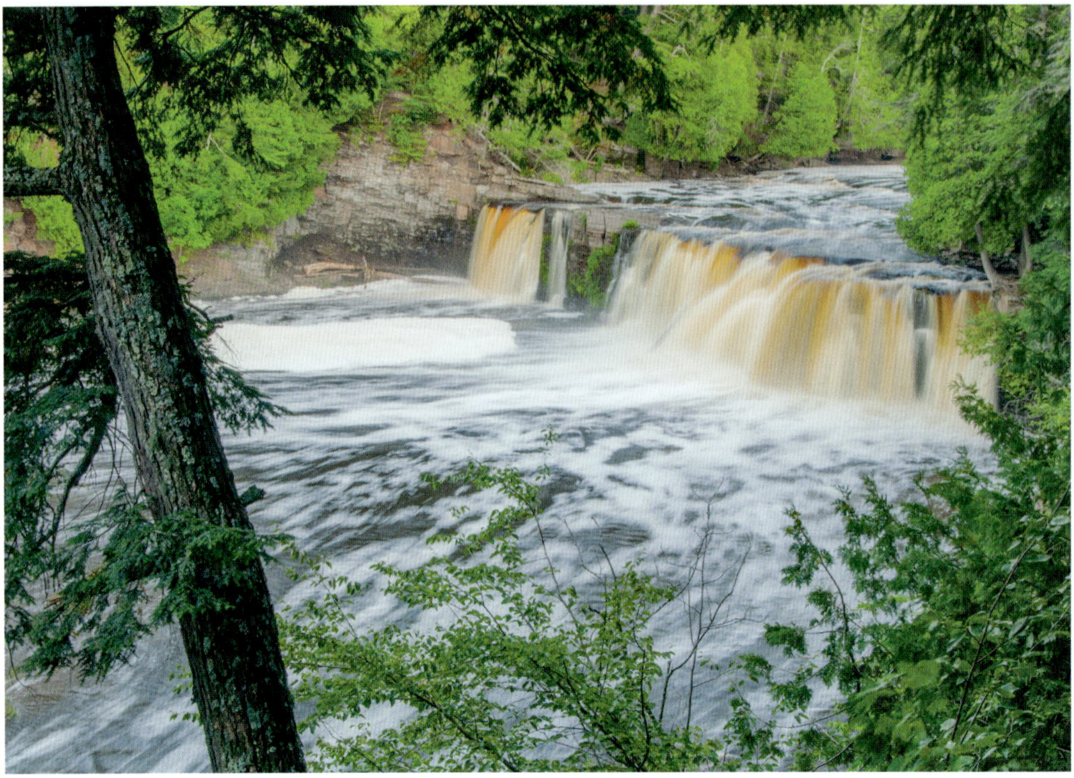

This is the scene from the "main" viewing deck for Manabezho Falls. It's the classic view of the waterfall.

Another, less used viewing deck, is located at the brink of the waterfall.

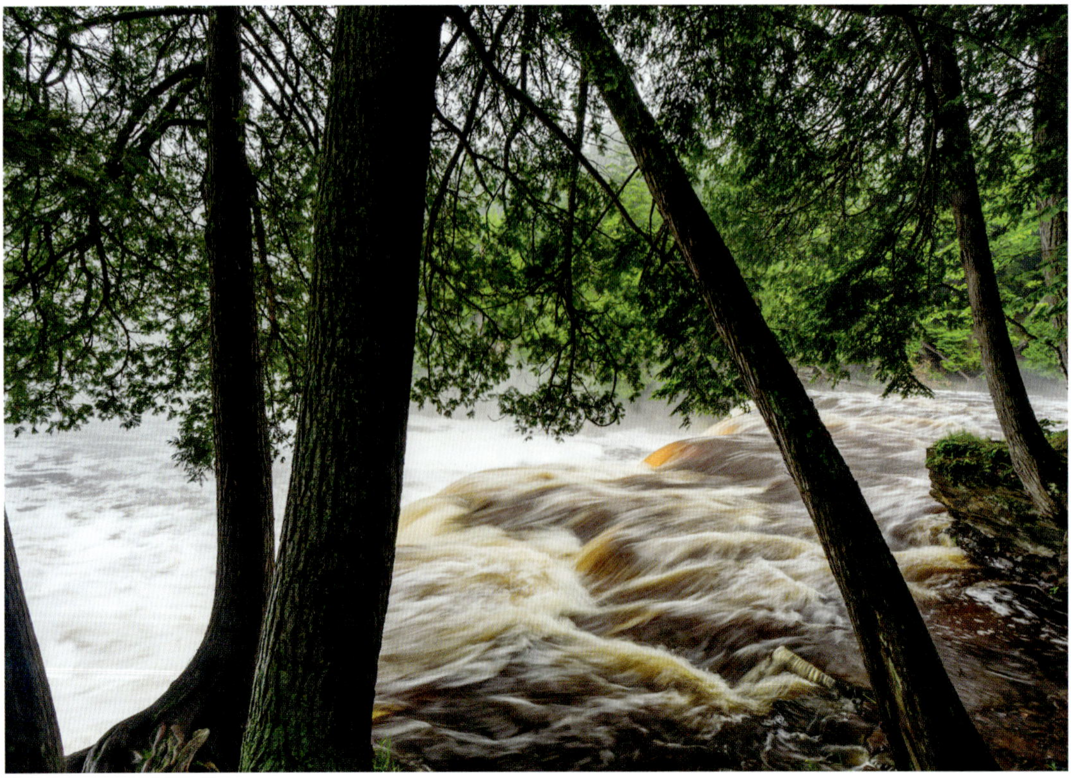

MANIDO FALLS (PRESQUE ISLE RIVER)

Private

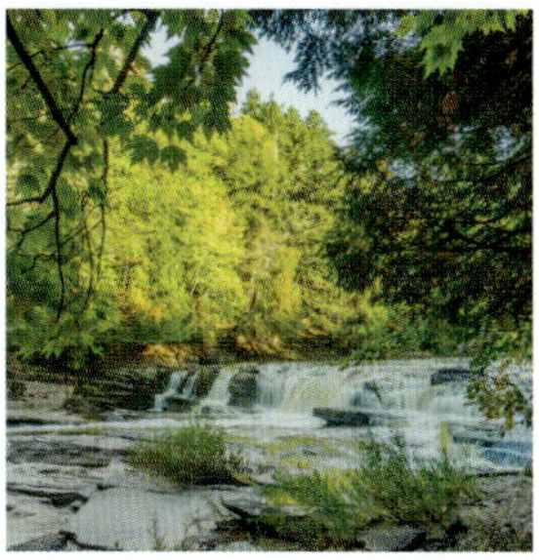

Must See:	7	GPS:	N46 42.250 W89 58.259
Height:	8 feet		
Time:	40-60 minutes	Hiking Information	
		Path:	Footpath
Driving Information		Length:	.50 miles
Signs:	None	Elev. Change:	Moderate
Road:	Secondary	GPS:	N/A
Access:	Easy	Danger:	Slight
4WD:	N/A	WP Boots:	N/A

Smoothly sculpted into intricately shaped holes and pinnacles, the undulating patterns can only be seen when the river runs low enough to leave the western side of the riverbed above water. Looking like an otherworldly landscape, the milk chocolate colored bedrock gives way below the falls to a small debris field filled with splintered off pieces of rock, eroded from the banks of the river and waterfall cascades up river. In the spring, the river runs from bank to bank, completely covering this entire area!

The Ojibwa people were very impressed by this river. The strong currents, swirling eddies and impressive waterfalls made this a dangerous river to cross. This waterfall was named "ghost" or Manido Falls. Try to view the waterfall as an Ojibwa would have several hundred years ago. What an impressive sight! No boardwalks, no handrails, no roads. Just the thundering river, beautiful waterfalls, and no bridges!

A circular polarizer knocks down the glare and reveals the rich colors during this misty morning.

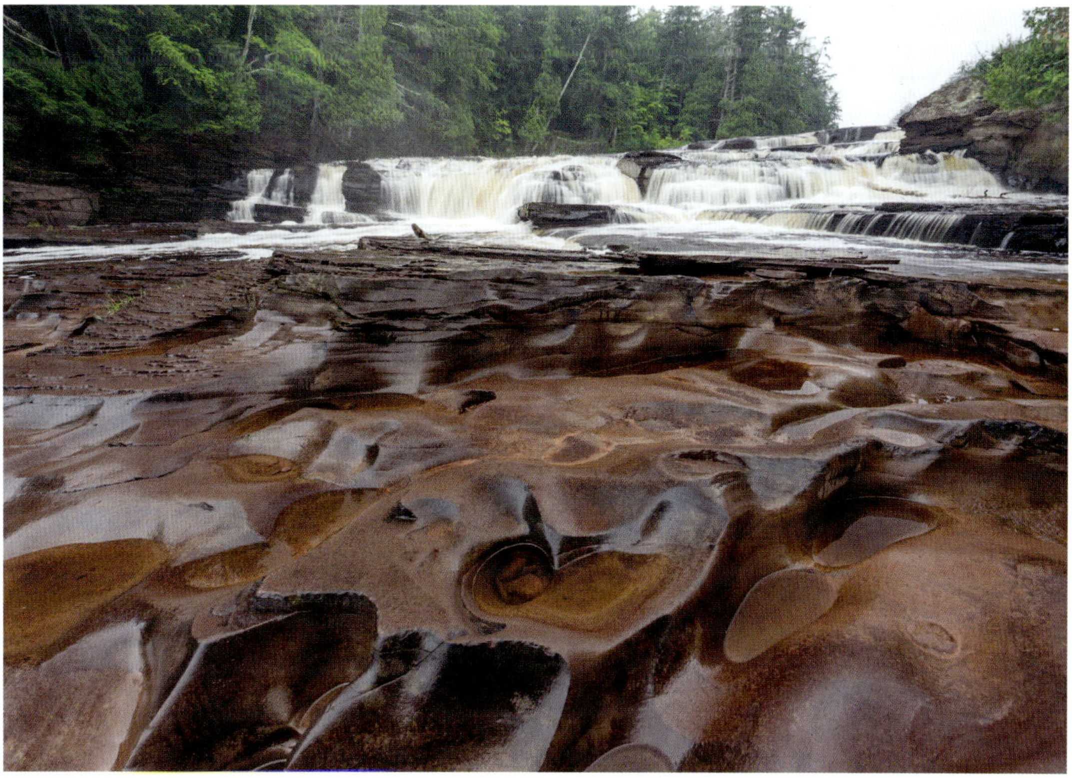

NAWADAHA FALLS (PRESQUE ISLE RIVER)

Private

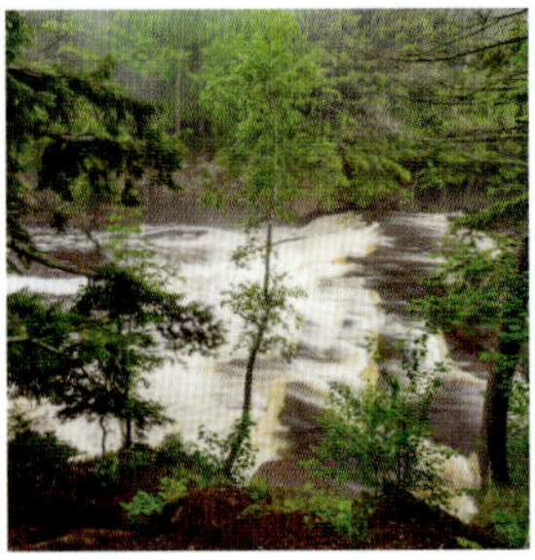

Must See:	8	GPS:	N46 41.981 W89 58.418
Height:	10 feet		
Time:	*60-80 minutes	Hiking Information	
		Path:	Footpath
Driving Information		Length:	.50 miles
Signs:	None	Elev. Change:	Moderate
Road:	Secondary	GPS:	N/A
Access:	Easy	Danger:	Slight
4WD:	N/A	WP Boots:	N/A

The Presque Isle River rushes through a shallow canyon cut through layers of shale and sandstone in the Nonesuch Shale bed. It tumbles over a series of waterfalls in the last mile of its journey to Lake Superior. Nawadaha Falls is the first of these drops, falling about 10 feet, cascading over sheets of bedrock, a haphazardly arranged stair-stepped affair.

Nawadaha, the Ojibwa name meaning "in the midst of the rapids", perhaps marks the beginning of the nearly continuous waterfalls and rapids that stretch down river from here to Lake Superior. This waterfall, like the next one, Manido, are the little kids on the block compared to Manabezho Falls, the spectacular waterfall that many have mistaken for Tahquamenon Falls! Even so, it is a nice waterfall, especially when viewed with a low to medium volume of water flowing.

*Plan on 60-80 minutes if hiking from the far parking lot. This is the furthest of the falls from that spot. There is a parking lot across from the ranger station that provides an easy access to this waterfall. Plan on 10-20 minutes if using this access point.

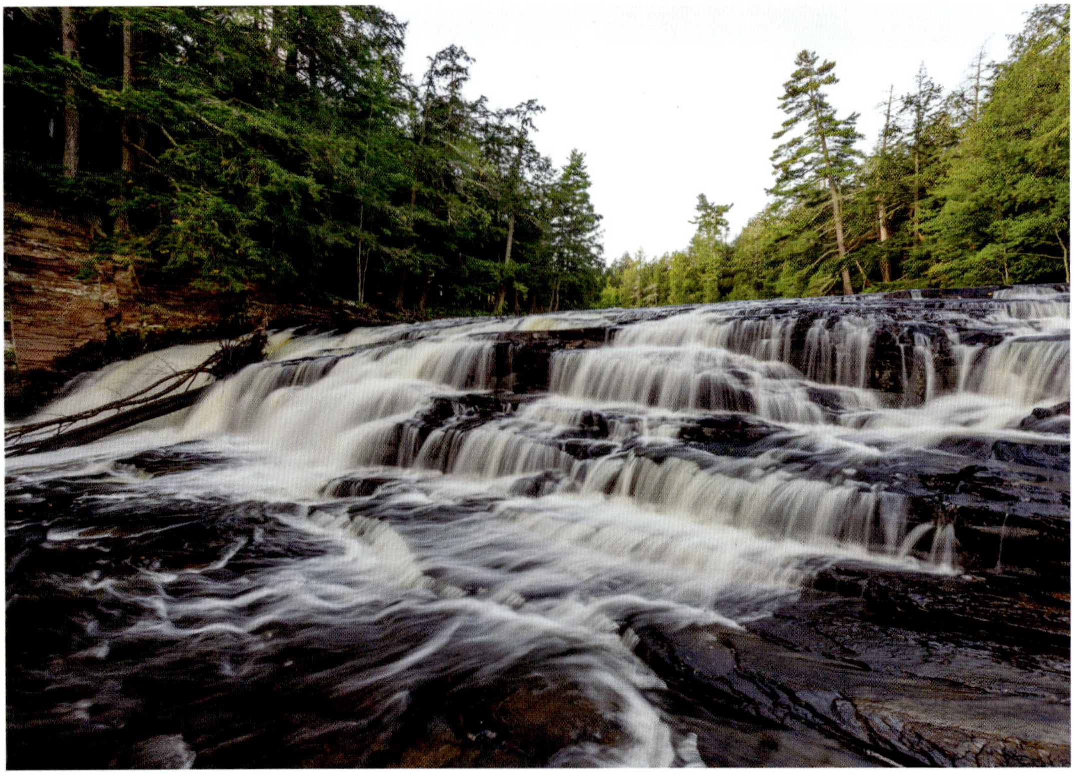

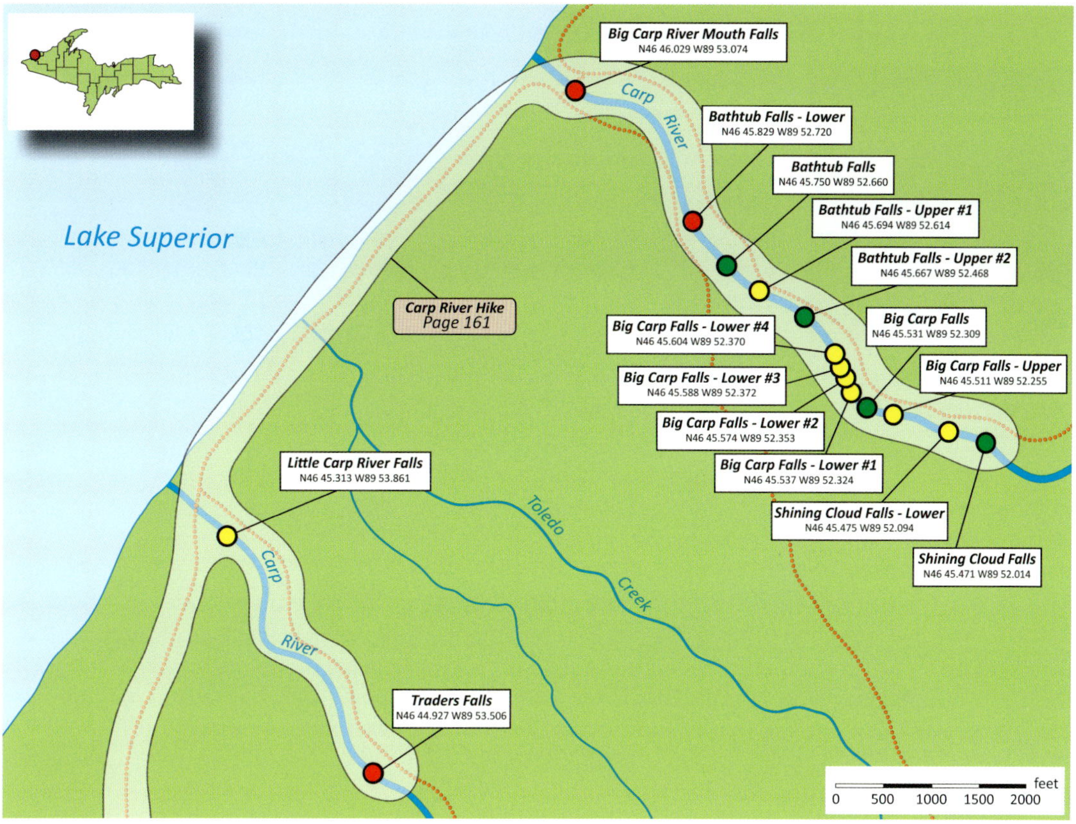

Carp River Hike

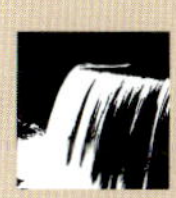

This is the longest of all the hikes that I have in this Michigan waterfall series! The Porcupine Mountains State Park has a very limited number of roadways within its premises. This is seen by some as limiting access, while others relish the primitive trails and rugged nature of the park. I concur with the latter. As much as my feet may ache after a long day of hiking, it is so rewarding to have intimately viewed the scenery, soaking in the sights and sounds of nature that are little changed after thousands of years.

Directions: There are various ways to get to this remote portion of the park. (1)Hike in along the shore from the north or south on the Lake Superior Trail, (2)follow the Carp River from the Lake of the Clouds overlook, (3)hike across the interior of the park on Correction Line Trail from Summit Park Road, (4)follow Little Carp River from the end of Little Carp River Road. (5)The shortest is the one I will describe. Drive along South Boundary Road (northeast) from CR-519 (at the west entrance to the park) about 4.5 miles to the Pinkerton Trailhead. Park off the side of the road on the small gravel parking lot. Hike the well traveled footpath northerly through a mostly flat mature hardwoods forest. Wooden planks attempt to cover wet areas along the way. Eventually the trail bridges Pinkerton Creek and continues cross country to meet up with the Lakeshore Trail and the Little Carp River Trail near the mouth of the Little Carp River. Add the 1.4 mile excursion to view Traders Falls (.7 miles each way) if desired. The 1.3 mile hike between Little Carp River and Carp River parallels the Lake Superior shoreline. Hike to the rhythm of the crashing waves that pound the rock strewn beach 100 yards from the trail. Thimbleberries offer August hikers a treat, their large green velvety leaves shading the sour-sweet delicate berries. After crossing the Big Carp River, the trail follows the northern side of the river past numerous waterfalls, with Shining Cloud Falls making for a wonderful destination point!

PORCUPINE MOUNTAINS

LITTLE CARP RIVER FALLS (LITTLE CARP RIVER)

Private

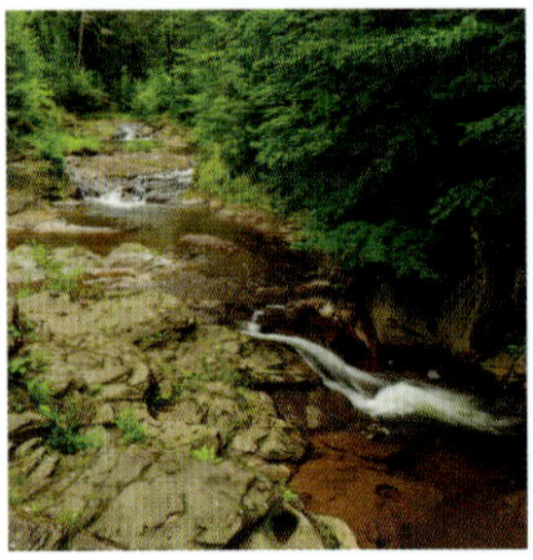

Must See:	5	GPS:	N46 45.313 W89 53.861
Height:	15 feet		
Time:	*Variable	Hiking Information	
		Path:	Footpath
Driving Information		Length:	*Variable
Signs:	None	Elev. Change:	Moderate
Road:	Secondary	GPS:	Recommended
Access:	Fairly Easy	Danger:	Moderate
4WD:	N/A	WP Boots:	Recommended

The waterfall is just upstream from the bridge over the Little Carp River. View from the foot bridge or from the bank on the northeast side of the river.

Three cascades rush down toward Lake Superior as the Little Carp River nears the Great Lake. Several of the Porcupine Mountains State Park trails converge here. Don't get confused and inadvertently take the wrong path.

Most of the southern half of Porcupine Mountains State Park drains into the Little Carp River. About 1/2 mile southwest of Government Peak a small tributary marks the humble beginnings of the Little Carp River. It flows southerly and about 1.5 miles later joins up with a couple more small streams and forms Mirror Lake. After traveling another 1.5 miles it enters the Lily Pond. Five more creeks join the river downstream before it enters Lake Superior, some 15 miles from its humble beginnings.

**Time and distance are determined by hiking options. These can vary greatly in this back country hike.*

What a great place to rest or have a picnic after the long hike through the woods. This is the second of the three waterways that are seen on this hike: Pinkerton Creek, Little Carp River, and the Carp River.

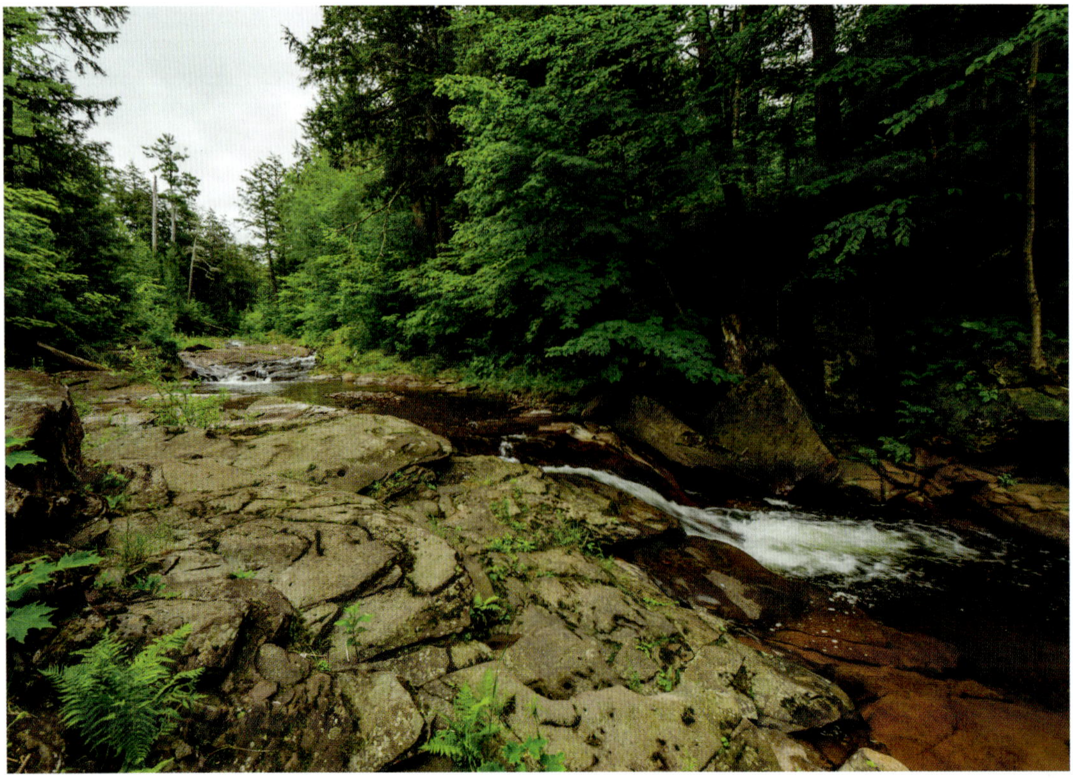

Little Carp River Falls

TRADERS FALLS (LITTLE CARP RIVER)

Private

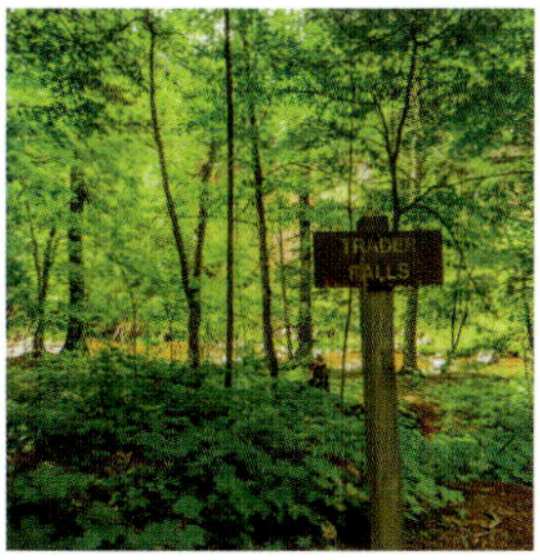

Must See:	3	GPS:	N46 44.927 W89 53.506
Height:	2 feet		
Time:	*Variable	**Hiking Information**	
		Path:	Footpath
Driving Information		Length:	*Variable
Signs:	None	Elev. Change:	Moderate
Road:	Secondary	GPS:	Recommended
Access:	Fairly Easy	Danger:	Moderate
4WD:	N/A	WP Boots:	Recommended

A sign placed by Porcupine Mountains State Park marks this waterfall. There are very few such marked waterfalls in the park.

The bedrock, as is so typical in Porcupine Mountain waterfalls, is sloped at a steep angle. There are some small cascades above and below the falls.

As this is such a small waterfall with no other waterfalls on this stretch of the Little Carp River, it is easy to skip it in search of the more densely packed in waterfalls on the Carp River to the north. This is about .7 miles from the footbridge that is down near the mouth of the Little Carp River.

**Time and distance are determined by hiking options. These can vary greatly in this back country hike.*

Of all the "officially named" waterfalls in the park, this one is the most baffling. Why was this one historically named? Perhaps a trader lived here? Perhaps it was a "landmark" for traders to meet at?

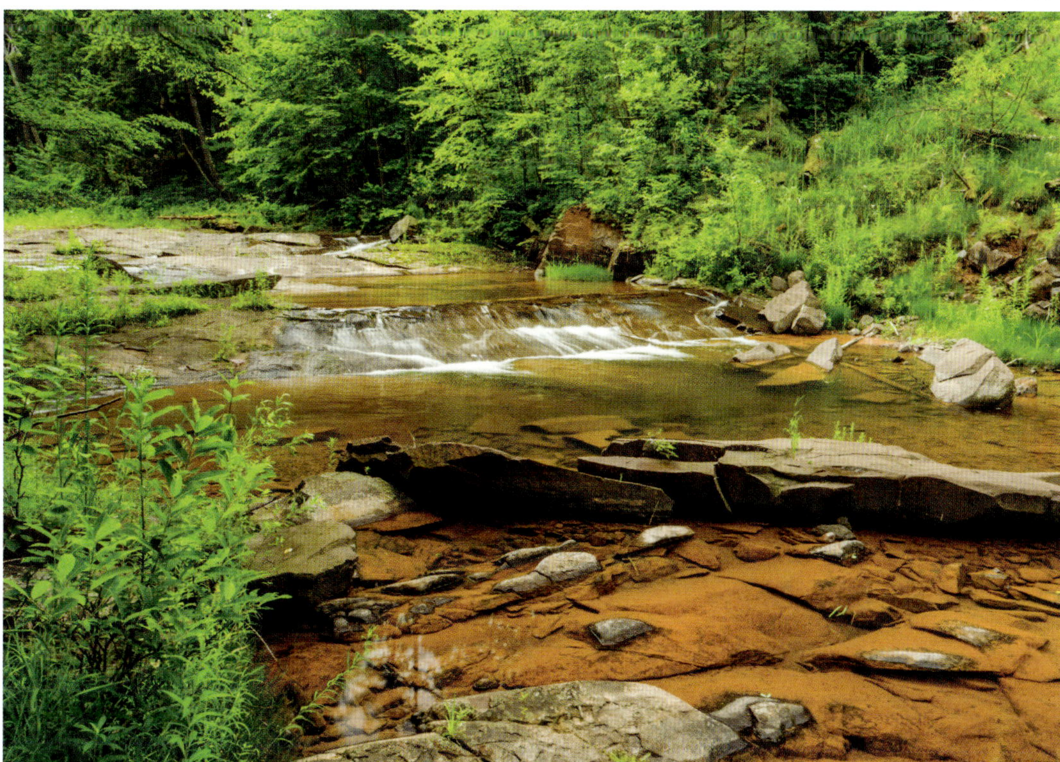

BIG CARP RIVER MOUTH FALLS (CARP RIVER)

Private

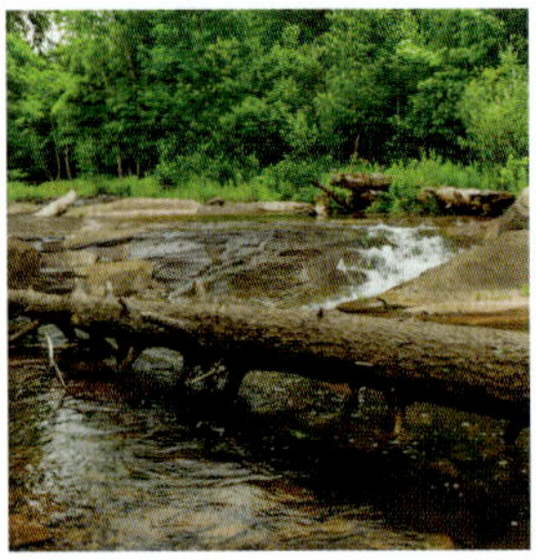

Must See:	2	GPS:	N46 46.029 W89 53.074
Height:	8 feet		
Time:	*Variable		

Driving Information		Hiking Information	
		Path:	Footpath
		Length:	*Variable
Signs:	None	Elev. Change:	Moderate
Road:	Secondary	GPS:	Recommended
Access:	Fairly Easy	Danger:	Moderate
4WD:	N/A	WP Boots:	Recommended

After hiking 1.1 miles along the Superior lakeshore from the Little Carp River, a cabin appears off to the right of the trail through a small field of thimbleberries. A short distance later the Big Carp River comes into view. A footbridge, cleverly engineered to utilize the large rocks along the river's edge as a foundation, spans the river. On the near side of the river is a bronze plaque set in the bedrock celebrating the groundwork that P. J. Hoffmaster did to ensure that the Porcupine Mountains would forever be public land, available for generations of nature enthusiasts to enjoy the beauty of the region, unspoiled by development. A couple more cabins grace this side of the river, one quite near the bridge and the other closer to the mouth of the river.

Just upstream from the bridge are the waterfalls. The small rush down the slanting bedrock is a minor drop, but it does afford a nice location to take a break near the mouth of the Big Carp River for rest and relaxation deep in the heart of the Porcupine Mountains State Park.

**Time and distance are determined by hiking options. These can vary greatly in this back country hike.*

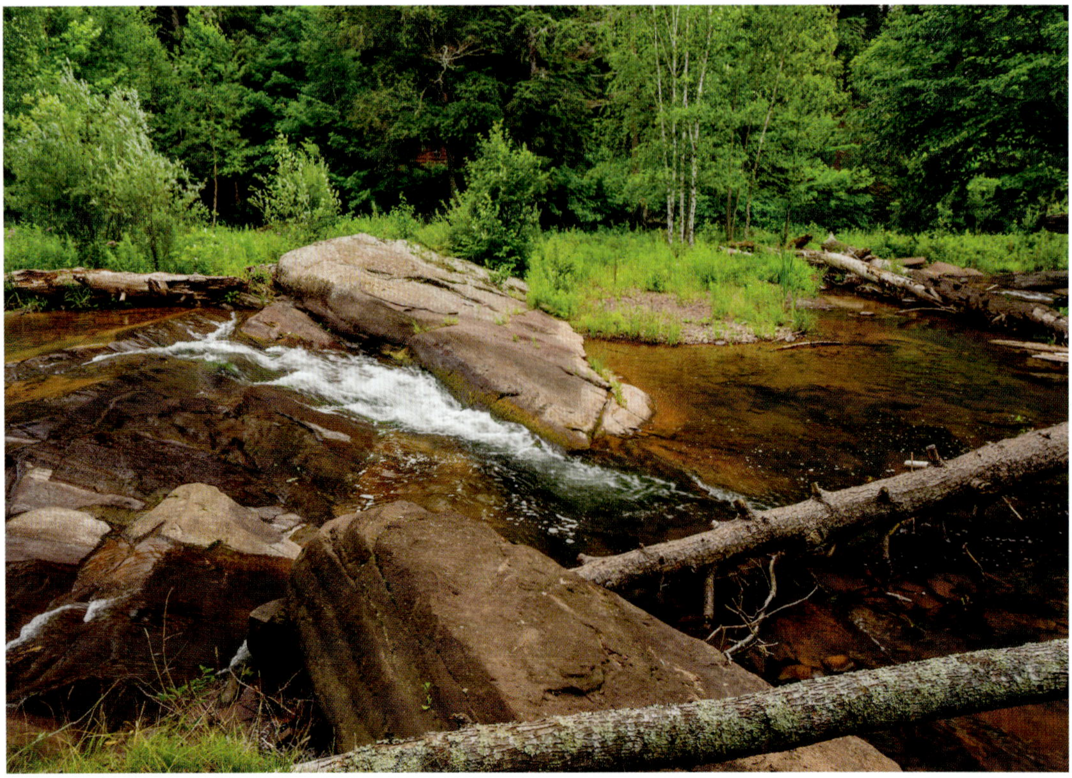

BATHTUB FALLS - LOWER (CARP RIVER)

Private

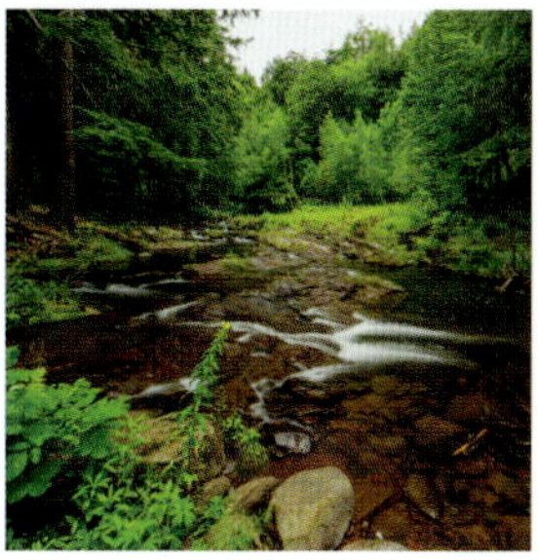

Must See:	3	GPS:	N46 45.829 W89 52.720
Height:	8 feet		
Time:	*Variable	Hiking Information	
		Path:	Footpath
Driving Information		Length:	*Variable
Signs:	None	Elev. Change:	Moderate
Road:	Secondary	GPS:	Recommended
Access:	Fairly Easy	Danger:	Moderate
4WD:	N/A	WP Boots:	Recommended

It's a .4 mile hike from the Mouth Falls before running across these fast rapids. After this stretch of hiking, it's nice to have another waterfall to stop at! This, and the next 3 waterfalls make up the "Bathtub Series". These 4 waterfalls are grouped together over the next .3 miles.

The gently sloping evergreen covered banks give way to the hard rock riverbed with choppy little cascades falling across the slanted layers of bedrock. The river makes a slight "S" curve as it falls.

**Time and distance are determined by hiking options. These can vary greatly in this back country hike.*

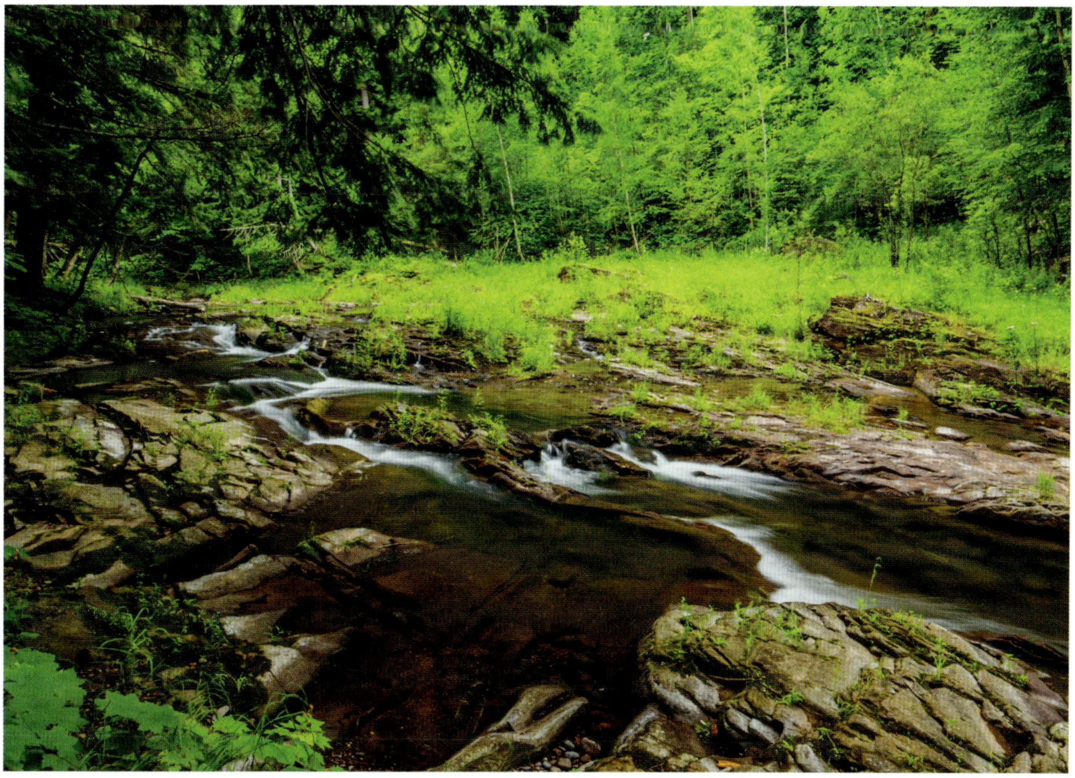

BATHTUB FALLS (CARP RIVER)

Private

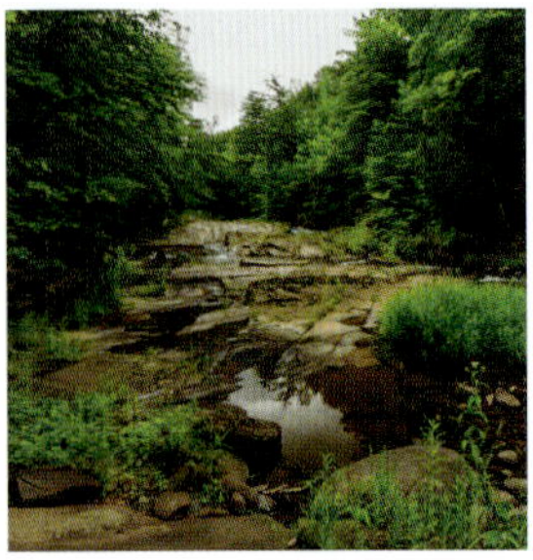

Must See:	7	GPS:	N46 45.750 W89 52.660
Height:	15 feet		
Time:	*Variable	Hiking Information	
		Path:	Footpath
Driving Information		Length:	*Variable
Signs:	None	Elev. Change:	Moderate
Road:	Secondary	GPS:	Recommended
Access:	Fairly Easy	Danger:	Moderate
4WD:	N/A	WP Boots:	Recommended

Bathtub Falls skips and slides down about 15 feet in a series of small cascades. The namesake feature, a hollowed out section of bedrock, looks like it was drilled out with an oversized bit. Actually, it is similar to the Presque Isle Kettles, formed over time by boulders spinning in eddies. I can only imagine that Indians, trappers and miners in days gone by may well have used this as a bathtub!

Looking from downstream, the river falls on the right side of the riverbed, turns 90 degrees to the left and then finishes its drop on the left side. It's a double slanted drop following the angle of the basalt bedrock.

**Time and distance are determined by hiking options. These can vary greatly in this back country hike.*

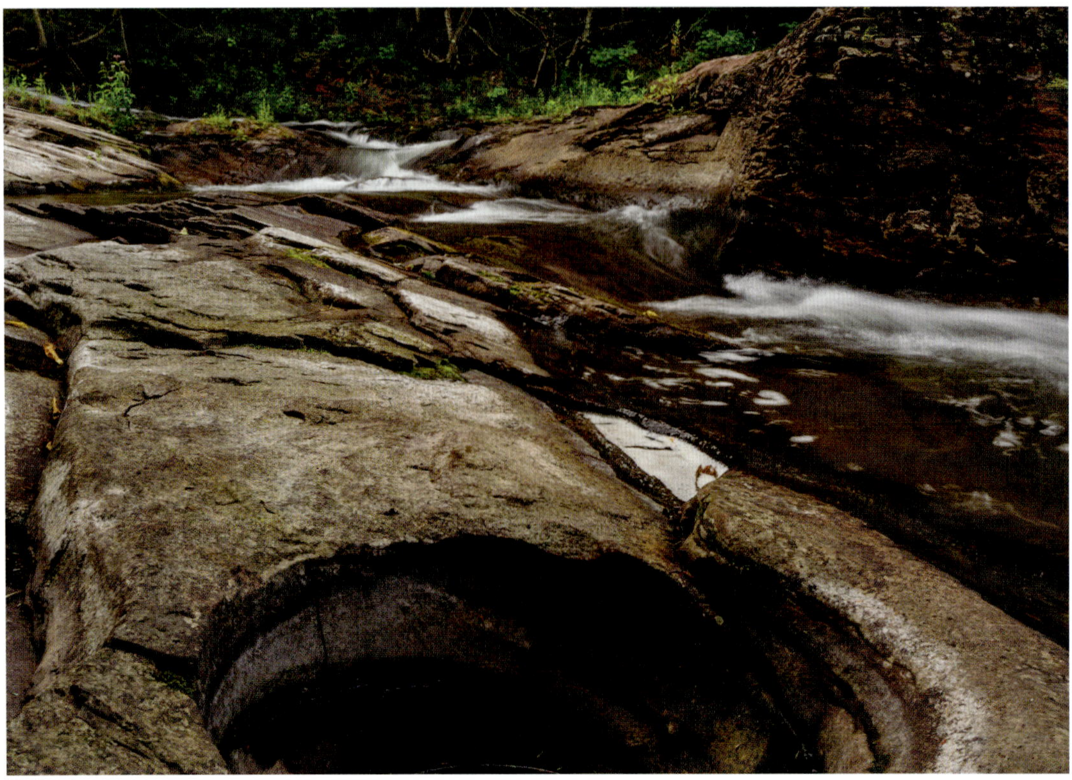

BATHTUB FALLS - UPPER #1 (CARP RIVER)

Private

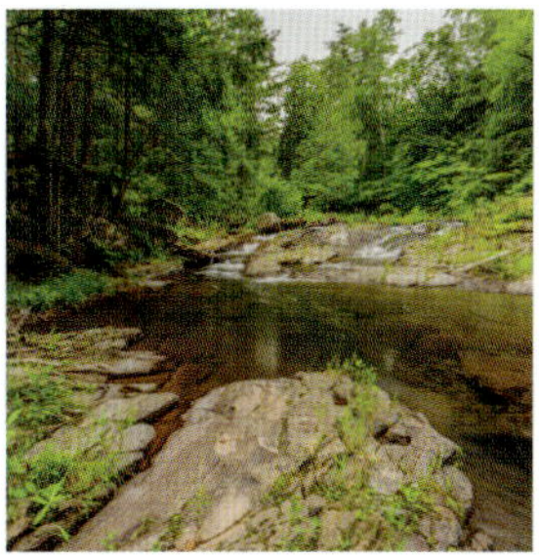

Must See:	5	GPS:	N46 45.694 W89 52.614
Height:	7 feet		
Time:	*Variable	Hiking Information	
		Path:	Footpath
Driving Information		Length:	*Variable
Signs:	None	Elev. Change:	Moderate
Road:	Secondary	GPS:	Recommended
Access:	Fairly Easy	Danger:	Moderate
4WD:	N/A	WP Boots:	Recommended

Just 150 yards upstream from Bathtub is the third of the four "Bathtub" falls. This is a multi-tiered cascade with a 4 foot roundish boulder sitting on the left side of the river halfway down the falls.

**Time and distance are determined by hiking options. These can vary greatly in this back country hike.*

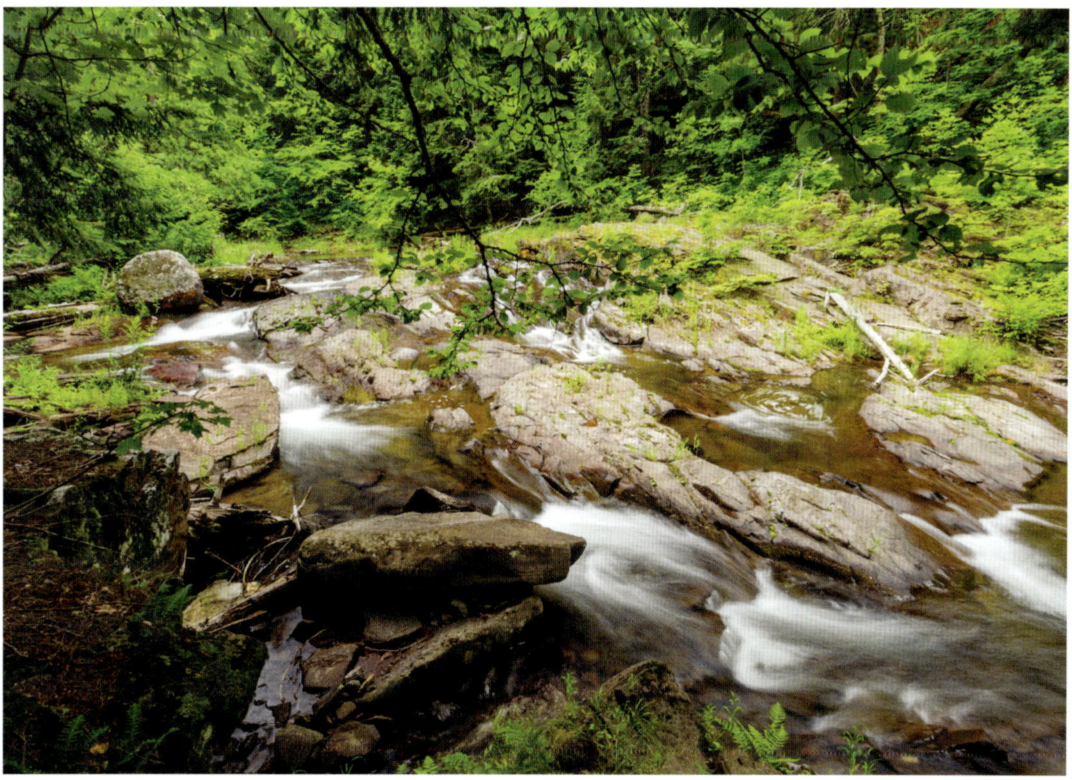

BATHTUB FALLS - UPPER #2 (CARP RIVER)

Private

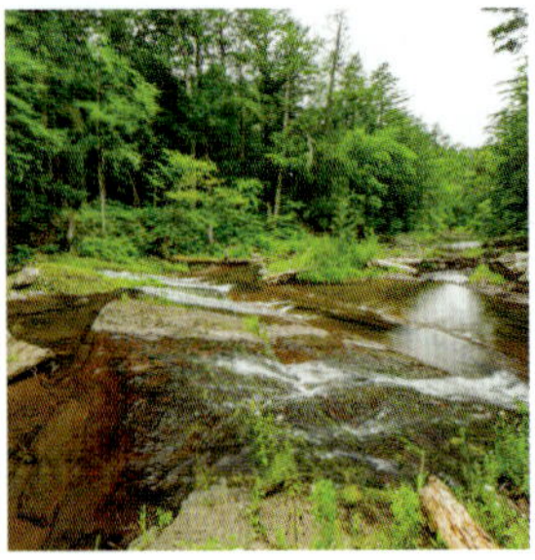

Must See:	7	GPS:	N46 45.667 W89 52.468
Height:	10 feet		
Time:	*Variable	**Hiking Information**	
		Path:	Footpath
Driving Information		Length:	*Variable
Signs:	None	Elev. Change:	Moderate
Road:	Secondary	GPS:	Recommended
Access:	Fairly Easy	Danger:	Moderate
4WD:	N/A	WP Boots:	Recommended

This conglomerate slide consists of three sections when the river is at the low level seen in these shots. It has a nice, consistent look with the rocky mass just above the falls. The impression of design rather than randomness is evident at this waterfall!

As I think of heading back to the Carp River, this waterfall ranks as one that I particularly desire to visit again. Perhaps the setting, or the evenly landscaped slide draw me back? Maybe it was the initial impression of seeing this one for the first time from the dark shadows of the tree shrouded footpath.

**Time and distance are determined by hiking options. These can vary greatly in this back country hike.*

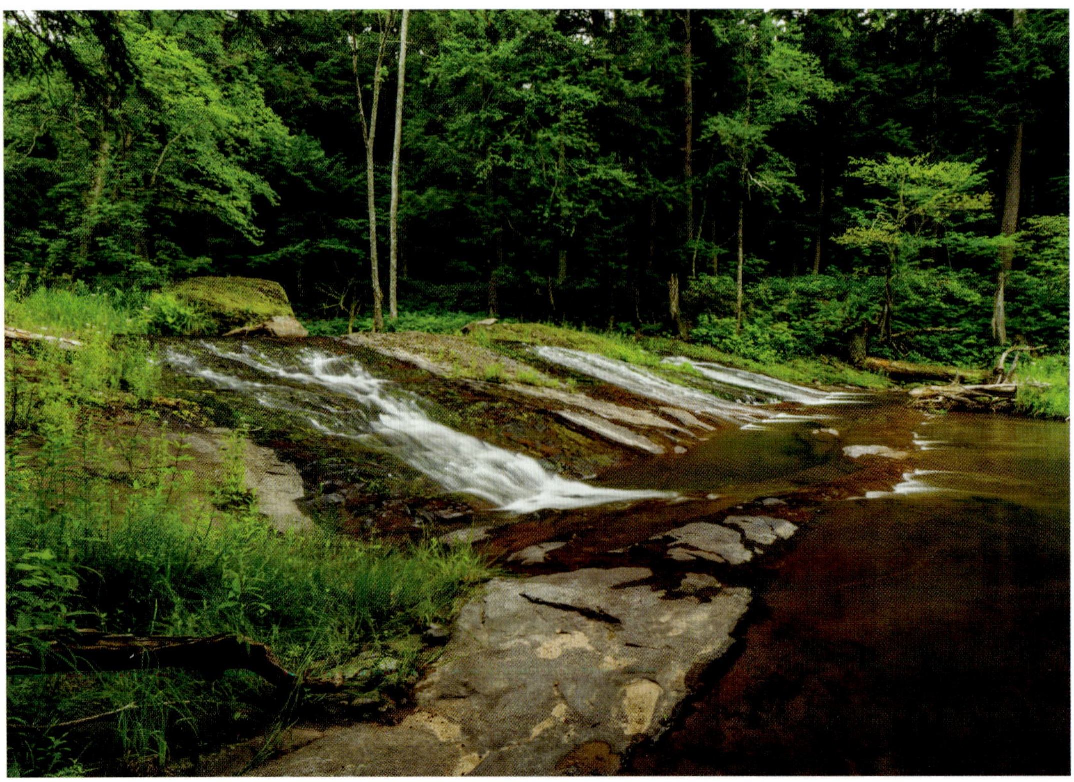

BIG CARP FALLS - LOWER #4 (CARP RIVER)

Private

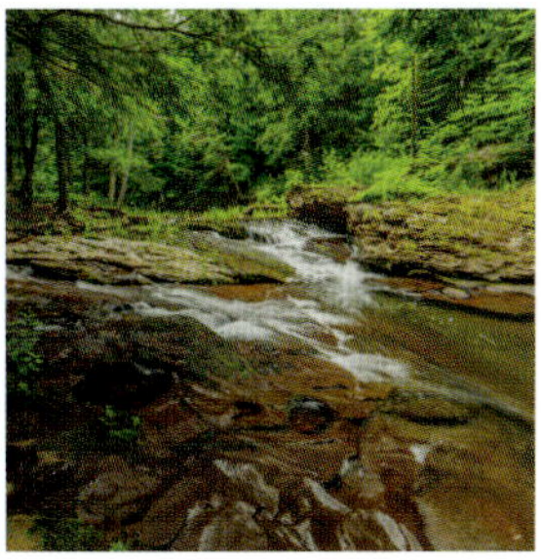

Must See:	5	GPS:	N46 45.604 W89 52.370
Height:	5 feet		
Time:	*Variable	**Hiking Information**	
		Path:	Footpath
Driving Information		Length:	*Variable
Signs:	None	Elev. Change:	Moderate
Road:	Secondary	GPS:	Recommended
Access:	Fairly Easy	Danger:	Moderate
4WD:	N/A	WP Boots:	Recommended

Following the river upstream from the somewhat scattered Bathtub Falls, six waterfalls are packed together in just 300 yards.

This small cascade is carved into the side of the encroaching outcropping on the far side of the river. Overhanging hemlocks on the near side shade the narrow riverbed as is so typical in this secluded and idyllic portion of Michigan!

**Time and distance are determined by hiking options. These can vary greatly in this back country hike.*

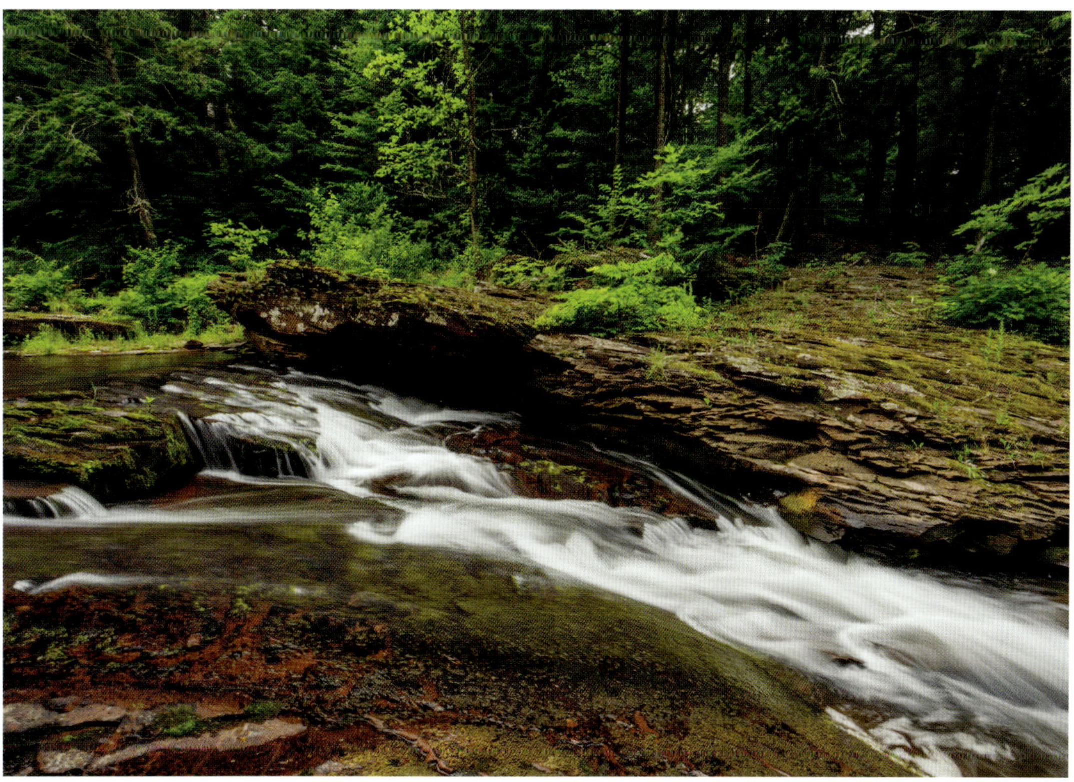

BIG CARP FALLS - LOWER #3 (CARP RIVER)

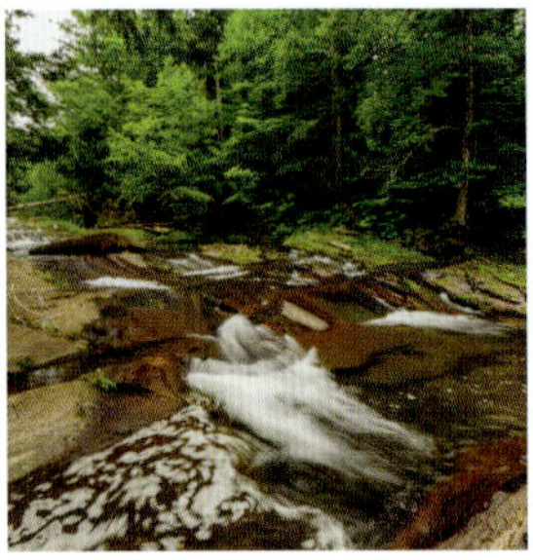

Must See:	4	GPS:	N46 45.588 W89 52.372
Height:	4 feet		
Time:	*Variable	Hiking Information	
		Path:	Footpath
Driving Information		Length:	*Variable
Signs:	None	Elev. Change:	Moderate
Road:	Secondary	GPS:	Recommended
Access:	Fairly Easy	Danger:	Moderate
4WD:	N/A	WP Boots:	Recommended

Just 100 feet up river from Lower #4 Falls the natural slant of the bedrock forces the river to rush down over several short layers of hard rock. Water pools up in the gaps between the layers before pouring down to the next level.

**Time and distance are determined by hiking options. These can vary greatly in this back country hike.*

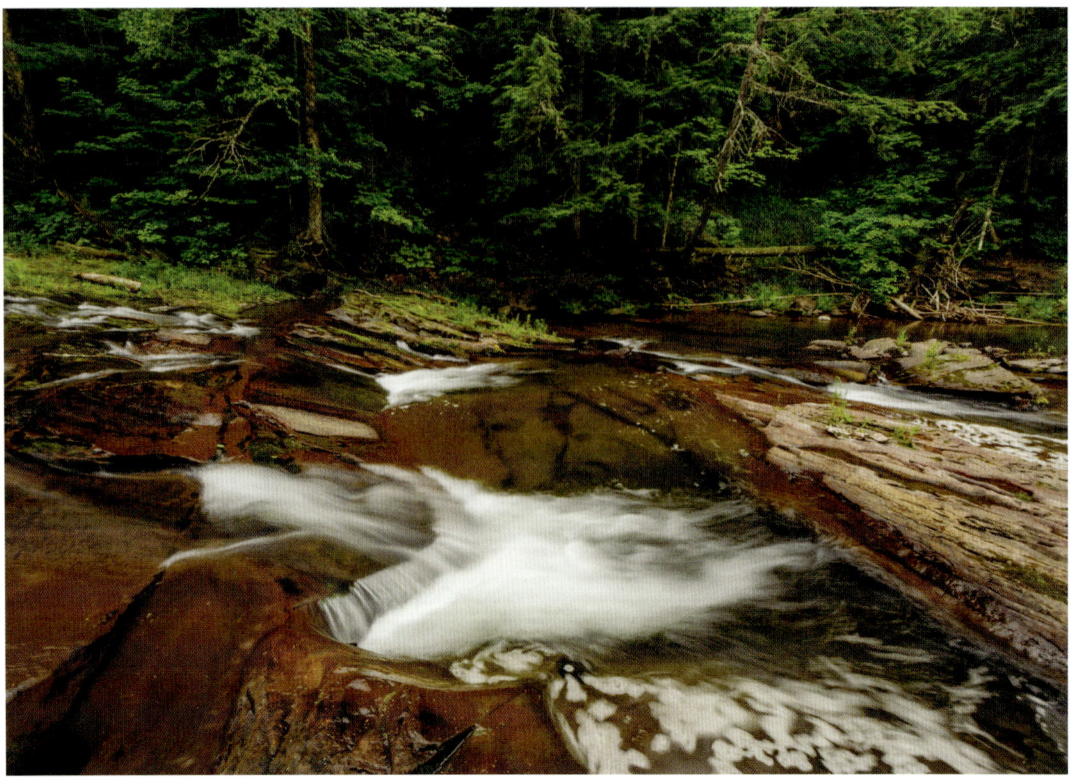

BIG CARP FALLS - LOWER #2 (CARP RIVER)

Private

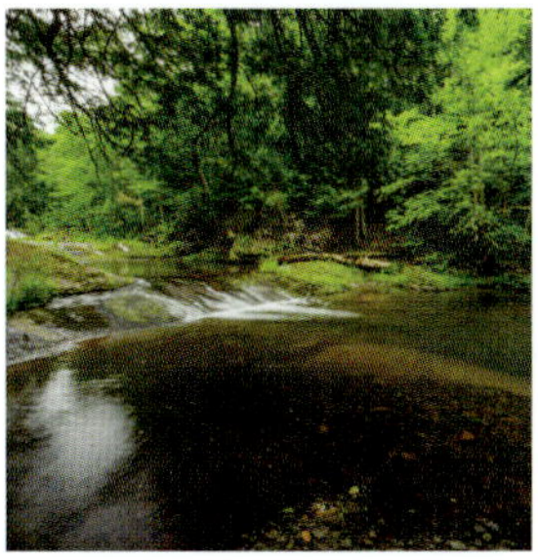

Must See:	5	GPS:	N46 45.574 W89 52.353
Height:	3 feet		
Time:	*Variable	Hiking Information	
		Path:	Footpath
Driving Information		Length:	*Variable
Signs:	None	Elev. Change:	Moderate
Road:	Secondary	GPS:	Recommended
Access:	Fairly Easy	Danger:	Moderate
4WD:	N/A	WP Boots:	Recommended

About 50 yards further up river is this small 3 foot drop. The cute waterfall slides into a large, quiet spill pool. Notice once again the angle of the bedrock - another of the typical Porcupine Mountain slide waterfalls!

**Time and distance are determined by hiking options. These can vary greatly in this back country hike.*

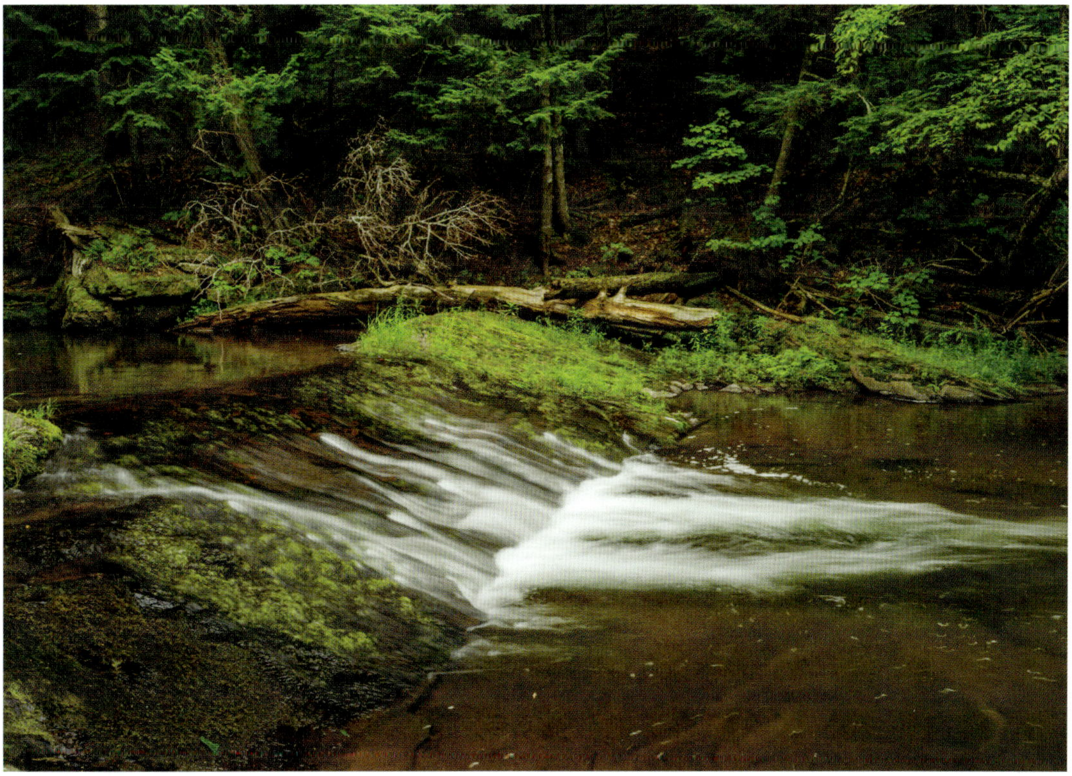

BIG CARP FALLS - LOWER #1 (CARP RIVER)

Private

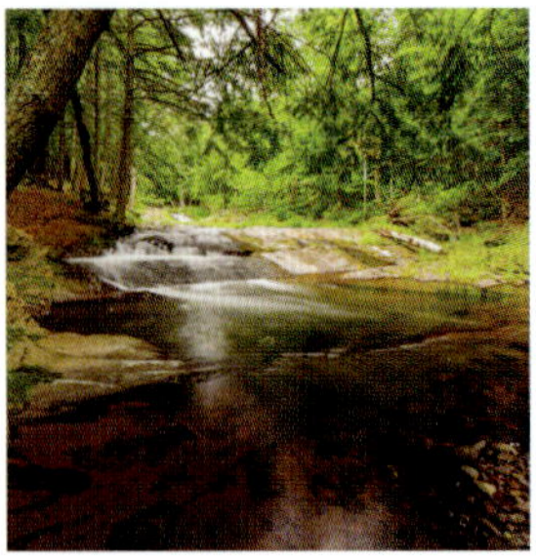

Must See:	5	GPS:	N46 45.537 W89 52.324
Height:	4 feet		
Time:	*Variable	Hiking Information	
		Path:	Footpath
Driving Information		Length:	*Variable
Signs:	None	Elev. Change:	Moderate
Road:	Secondary	GPS:	Recommended
Access:	Fairly Easy	Danger:	Moderate
4WD:	N/A	WP Boots:	Recommended

This two-tiered waterfall slides down a smooth face. Big Carp Falls is just upstream from here! Finally!

The amazingly flat rock surface shows signs of erosion on this side of the river where the constant flow of water has taken its greatest toll.

**Time and distance are determined by hiking options. These can vary greatly in this back country hike.*

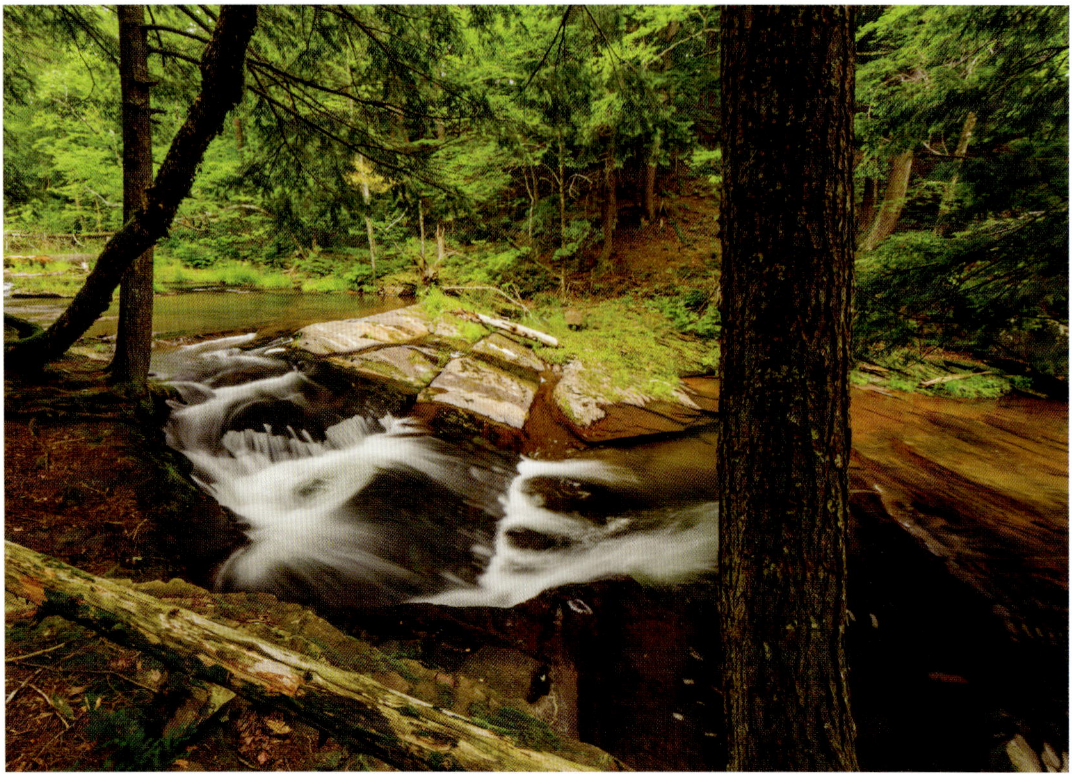

BIG CARP FALLS (CARP RIVER)

Private

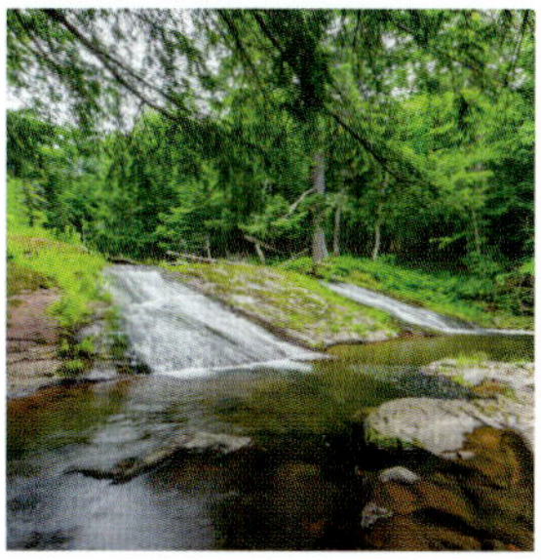

Must See:	7	GPS:	N46 45.531 W89 52.309
Height:	12 feet		
Time:	*Variable	Hiking Information	
		Path:	Footpath
Driving Information		Length:	*Variable
Signs:	None	Elev. Change:	Moderate
Road:	Secondary	GPS:	Recommended
Access:	Fairly Easy	Danger:	Moderate
4WD:	N/A	WP Boots:	Recommended

All the small slides in the "Big Carp" series set the stage for this 12 foot high slide! The river runs down the 30 foot long moss covered decline, divided into two streams unless the water volume is high enough to bring the two together.

At the base of the angled sandstone, the river widens out before surrounding a shallow rock island. This waterfall is 200 yards upstream from the northernmost of the "Big Carp" waterfalls and is 100 yards downstream from the last of the "Big Carp" waterfalls - the Upper Falls.

Time and distance are determined by hiking options. These can vary greatly in this back country hike.

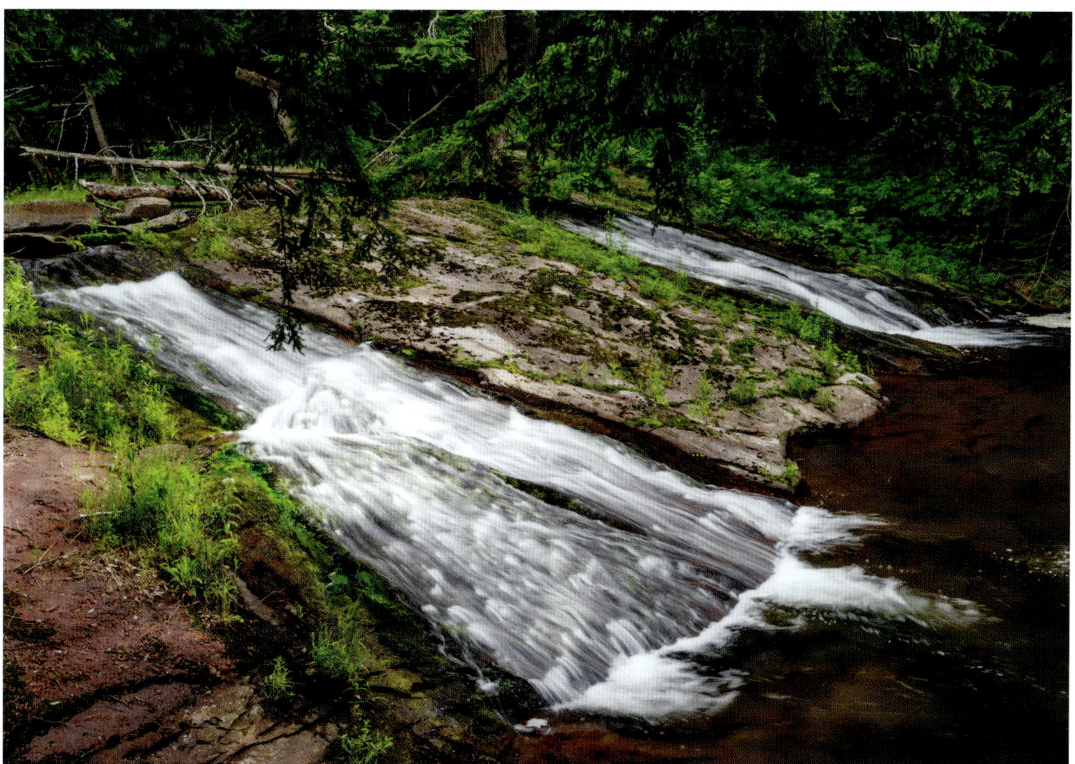

BIG CARP FALLS - UPPER (CARP RIVER)

Private

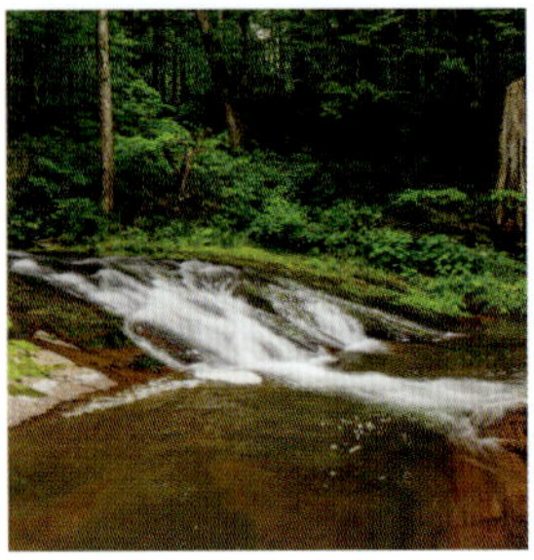

Must See:	5
Height:	8 feet
Time:	*Variable

Driving Information

Signs:	None
Road:	Secondary
Access:	Fairly Easy
4WD:	N/A

GPS:	N46 45.511 W89 52.255

Hiking Information

Path:	Footpath
Length:	*Variable
Elev. Change:	Moderate
GPS:	Recommended
Danger:	Moderate
WP Boots:	Recommended

Hike 100 yards above Big Carp Falls to find the last of the "Big Carp" falls. Here a small, 2 foot rounded slide sits above a 6 foot slanted sandstone slide.

**Time and distance are determined by hiking options. These can vary greatly in this back country hike.*

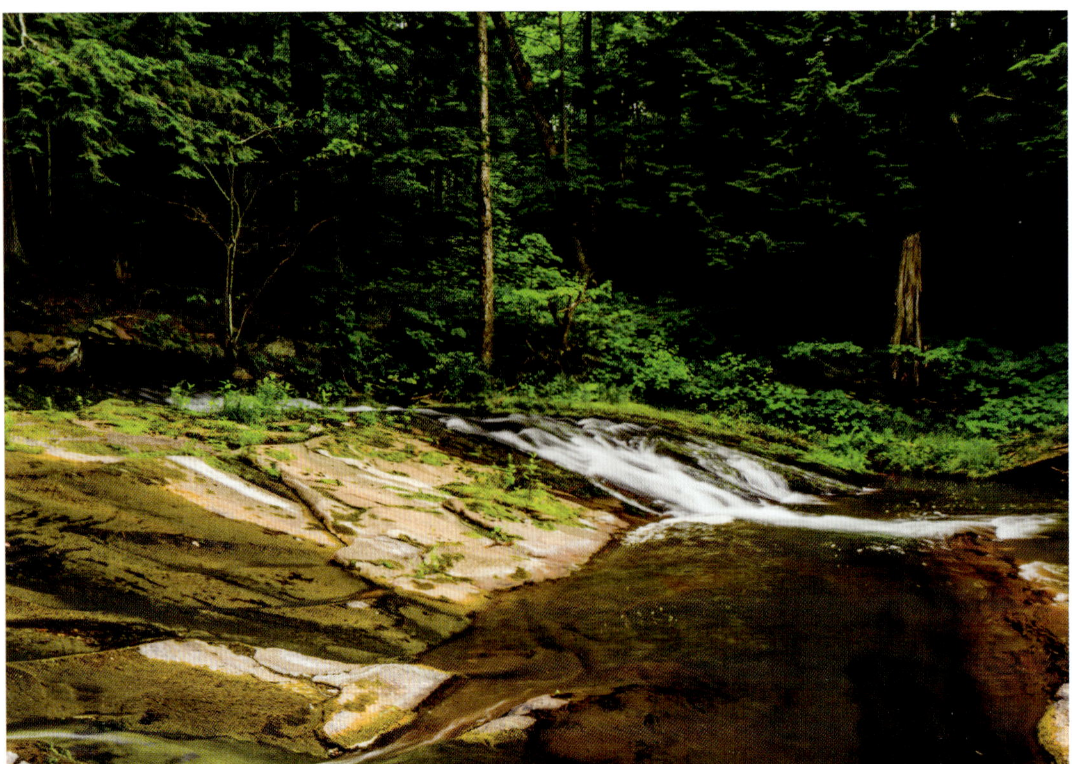

SHINING CLOUD FALLS - LOWER (CARP RIVER)

Private

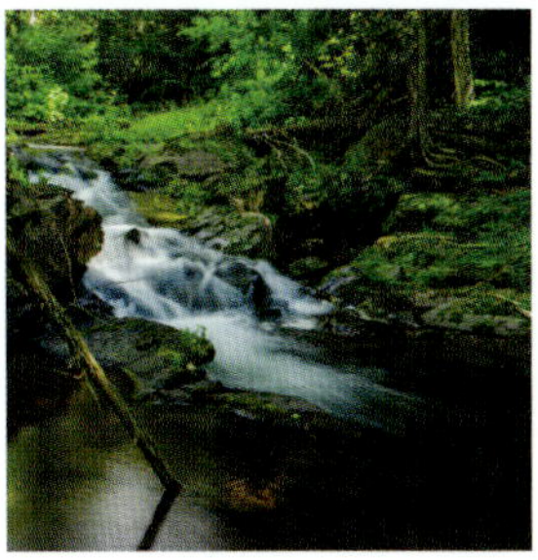

Must See:	6	GPS:	N46 45.475 W89 52.094
Height:	6 feet		
Time:	*Variable	Hiking Information	
		Path:	Footpath
Driving Information		Length:	*Variable
Signs:	None	Elev. Change:	Moderate
Road:	Secondary	GPS:	Recommended
Access:	Fairly Easy	Danger:	Elevated
4WD:	N/A	WP Boots:	Recommended

The "Big Falls" waterfalls are simple to see and photograph. Surprisingly then, both of the "Shining Cloud" falls are just the opposite! They are not easily viewed from the trail and both require a climb down to the river to see the waterfall.

The Big Carp Trail pulls away from the river and climbs up to higher ground after having hugged the river past all of the "Big Falls" waterfalls. So, follow the riverbank up river from Big Falls - Upper. The waterfall is hidden by the rocky walls along the edge of the river, so it is necessary to climb down the steep mossy bank to the rocks below to view the falls.

The river drops into a bit of a ravine here. As the rocky walls pinch together this small waterfall appears! Rugged, moss covered rocks line the sides of the river. It's a mixture of sandstone and conglomerate. Lush green is everywhere in this semi-hidden waterfall setting.

**Time and distance are determined by hiking options. These can vary greatly in this back country hike.*

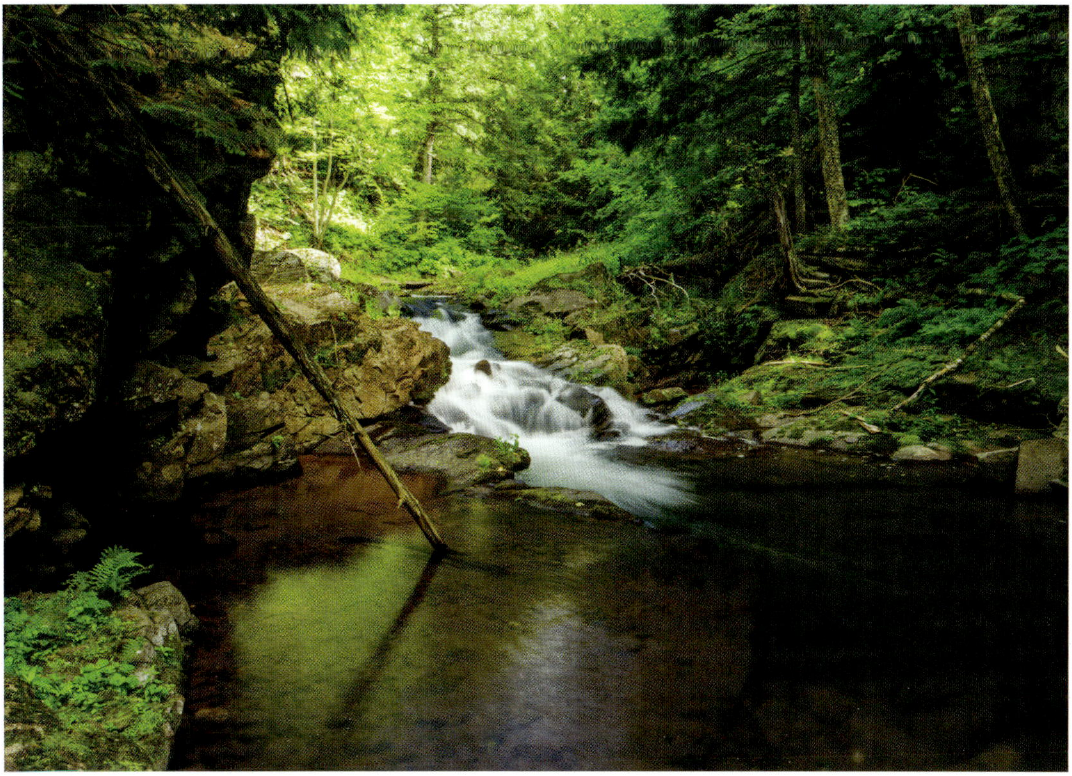

SHINING CLOUD FALLS (CARP RIVER)

Private

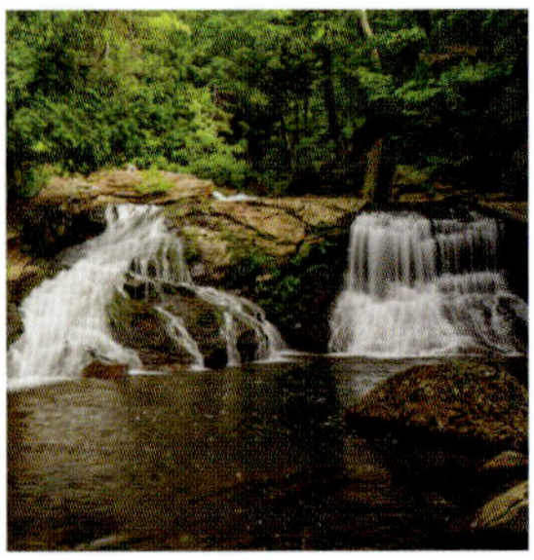

Must See:	9	GPS:	N46 45.471 W89 52.014
Height:	30 feet		
Time:	*Variable	Hiking Information	
		Path:	Footpath
Driving Information		Length:	*Variable
Signs:	None	Elev. Change:	Elevated
Road:	Secondary	GPS:	Recommended
Access:	Fairly Easy	Danger:	Extreme
4WD:	N/A	WP Boots:	Recommended

Porcupine Mountains' premier back country waterfall, Shining Cloud Falls, is tucked away into a gorge with 30 foot walls on either side. Climbing down to the base of the falls is difficult and dangerous. The steep hillside drops about 60 feet down from the trail to the cliff's edge. Then comes the dangerous part. A very narrow ledge angles down the face of the cliff with a short 3 foot drop interrupting its continuous descent. *After climbing back out of the ravine I think it may be easier to access the river by climbing down above the waterfall and carefully sliding down the near edge of the waterfall.*

I love mysteries! Several large conglomerate boulders sit in a riverbed that is made of sandstone. Where did THEY come from?

The waterfall is split in half except during periods of high water. The right side slides down the 1st third of the falls, continues in a sheer drop for the 2nd third, and concludes the drop with another slide. The left side of the falls slides all the way to the river. The main drop is 20 feet high with a smaller, 10 foot double slide just downstream. A large piece of conglomerate sits at the base of the last drop.

**Time and distance are determined by hiking options. These can vary greatly in this back country*

Notice the conglomerate boulder on the right side of the riverbed below the smaller drops.

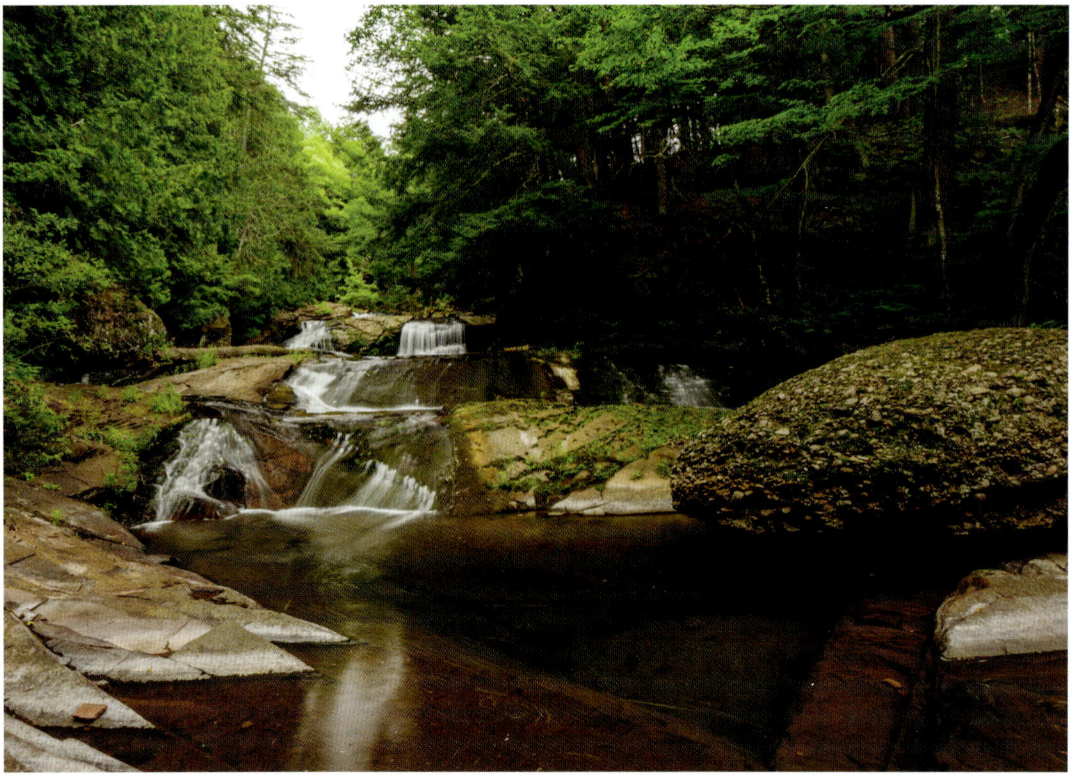

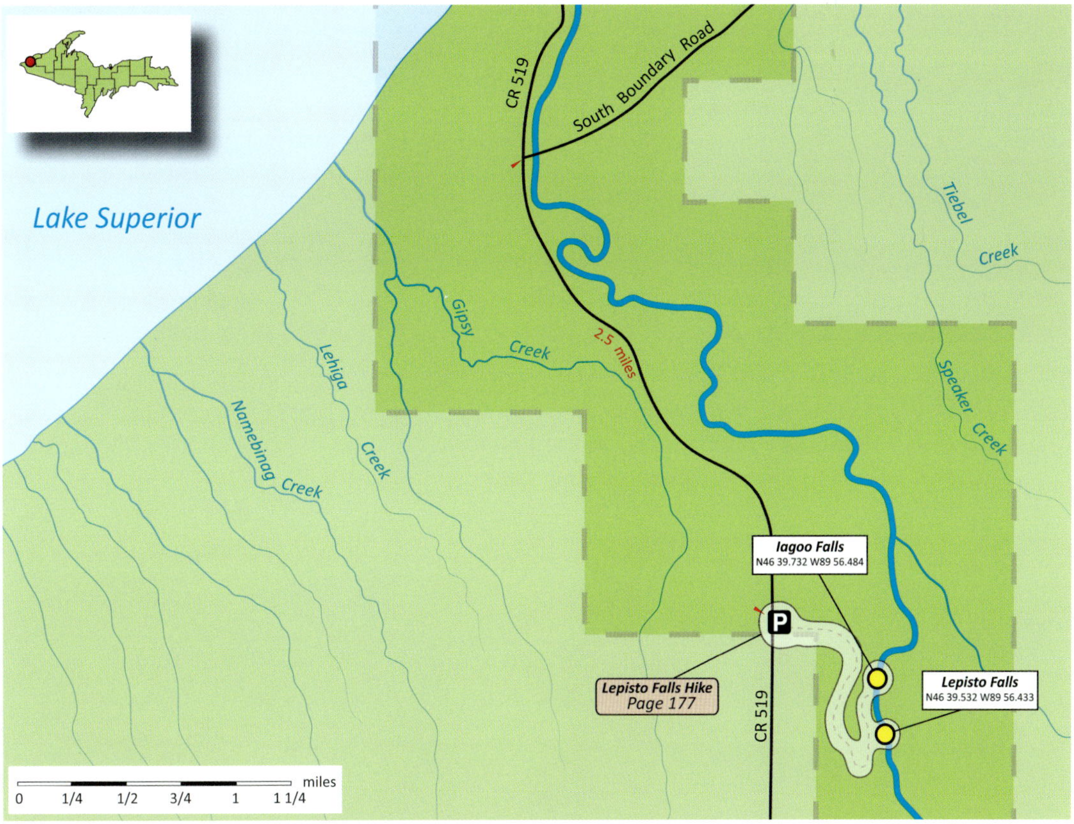

Lepisto Falls Hike

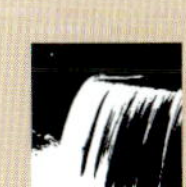

Iagoo Falls: Conglomerate mixed with sedimentary stone forms the bed of the river. The river has formed its way through a tilted shelf of conglomerate. It then fans out while sliding down the remaining angled plateau to create Lepisto Falls.

Lepisto Falls: Mounds of conglomerate rise gently from the riverbed, dividing the river as it slides down the undulating bedrock. Beautiful hardwoods mix with evergreens to line the river's edge with brilliant colors in autumn.

Directions: Drive north from Wakefield on SR-28 for 1.3 miles. Turn left onto Thomaston Road. In 1 mile it becomes CR-519. Stay on CR-519 for 12.2 miles. Turn right on the gravel road with a gate. Park out of the way at the gate and hike in. The road deteriorates and becomes very muddy about 1/4 mile from the falls as it descends quickly down toward the river on a switchback. At the end of the road is a cable spanning the river. A basket is suspended from the cable that allowed items to be shuttled back and forth across the river. Iagoo Falls is 1/8 mile down river. Lepisto Falls is 1/8 mile upriver. There is the faintest of footpaths leading to the falls.

IAGOO FALLS (PRESQUE ISLE RIVER)

Private

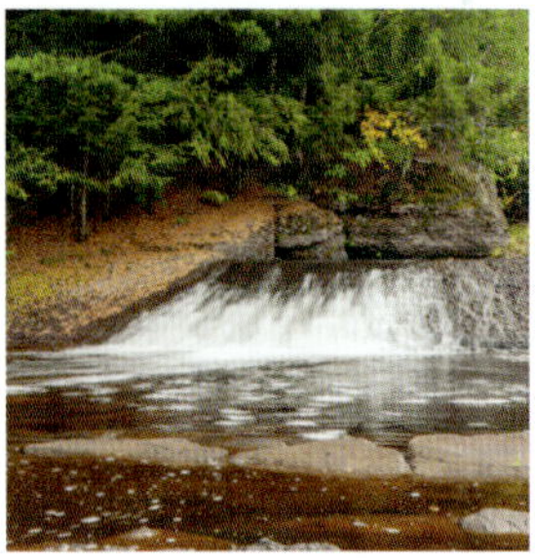

Must See:	5	GPS:	N46 39.732 W89 56.484
Height:	6 feet		
Time:	1 3/4 to 2 1/2 hours	Hiking Information	
		Path:	Dirt road/Slight path
Driving Information		Length:	1 7/8 miles
Signs:	None	Elev. Change:	Moderate
Road:	Secondary	GPS:	Recommended
Access:	Somewhat Easy	Danger:	Moderate
4WD:	N/A	WP Boots:	Required

This stretch of river is now part of Porcupine Mountain State Park and I have heard that the North Country Trail will soon include these waterfalls on its route. This area is full of conglomerate bedrock. I have included a shot of the matrix found at the top of the falls. As its name implies, the rock is a "conglomerate" of smaller stones "cemented" together.

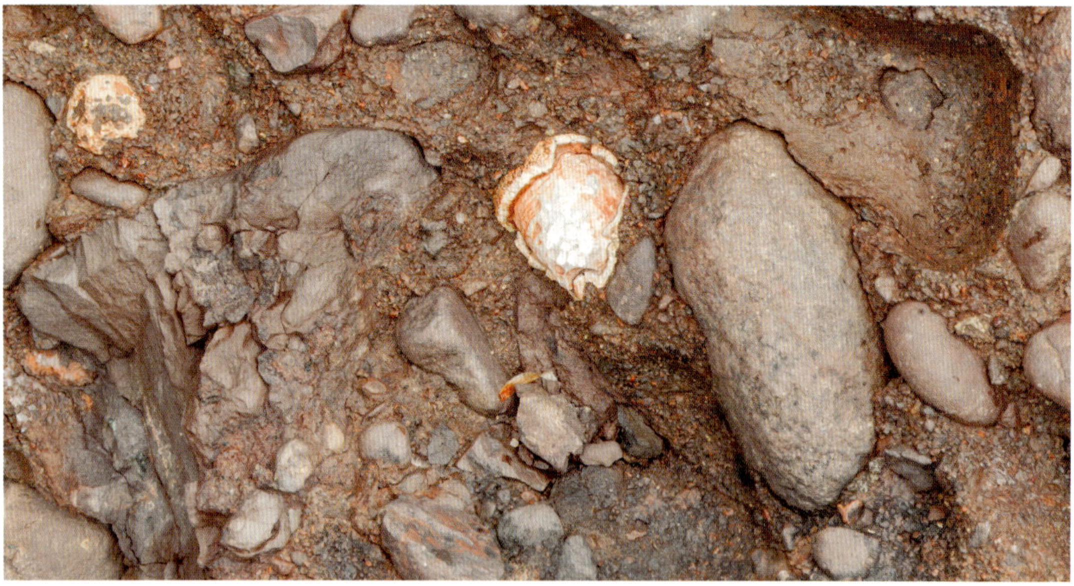

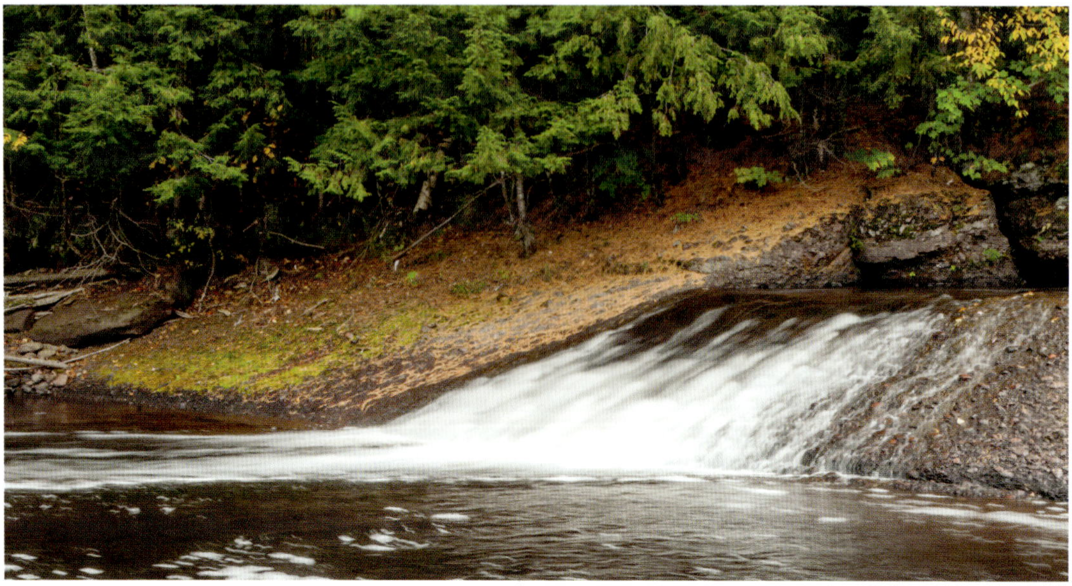

LEPISTO FALLS (PRESQUE ISLE RIVER)

Private

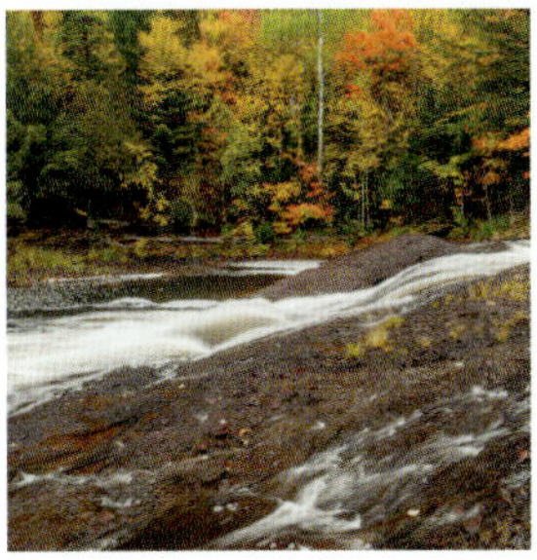

Must See:	5	GPS:	N46 39.532 W89 56.433
Height:	6 feet		
Time:	1 3/4 to 2 1/2 hours	**Hiking Information**	
		Path:	Dirt road/Slight path
Driving Information		Length:	1 7/8 miles
Signs:	None	Elev. Change:	Moderate
Road:	Secondary	GPS:	Recommended
Access:	Somewhat Easy	Danger:	Moderate
4WD:	N/A	WP Boots:	Required

It is possible to cut some hiking distance off by cutting cross country to the west where the last leg of the switchback parallels the river. The ground between the river and the switchback is very soft. Groundwater leaches out of the hillside, working its way down to the river. Be sure to wear waterproof boots if attempting this shortcut.

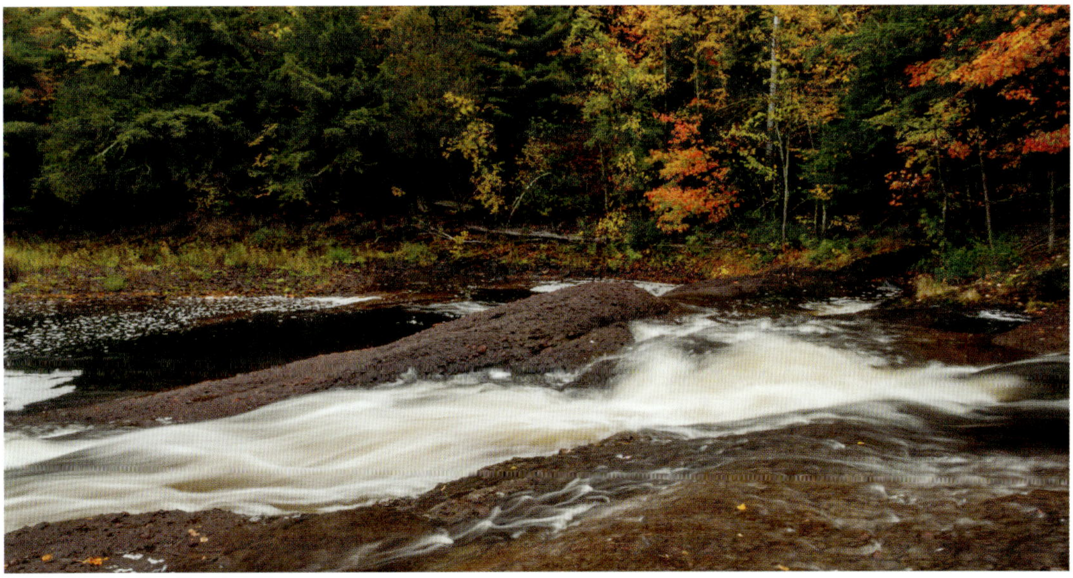

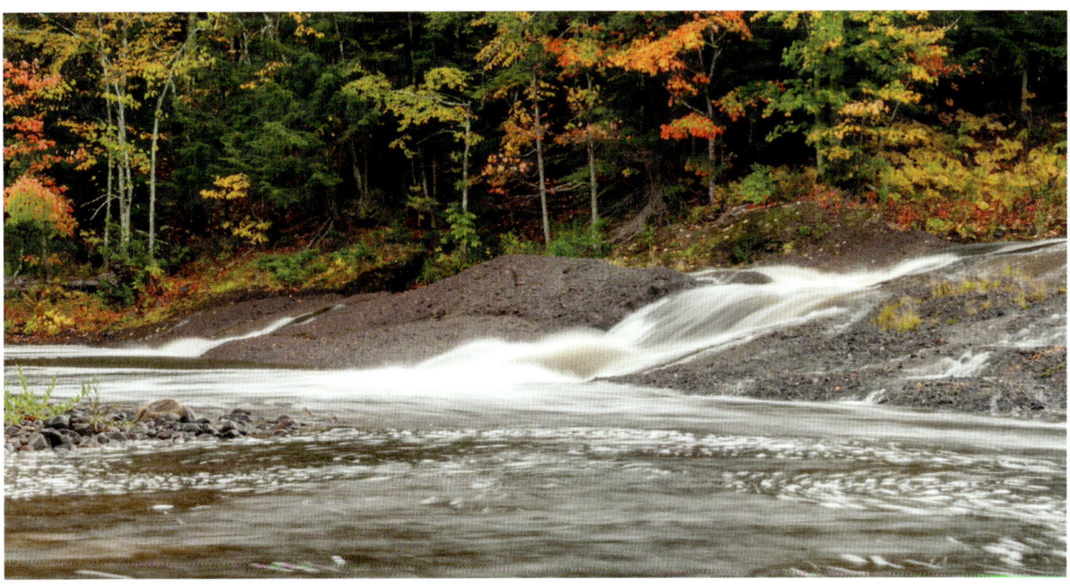

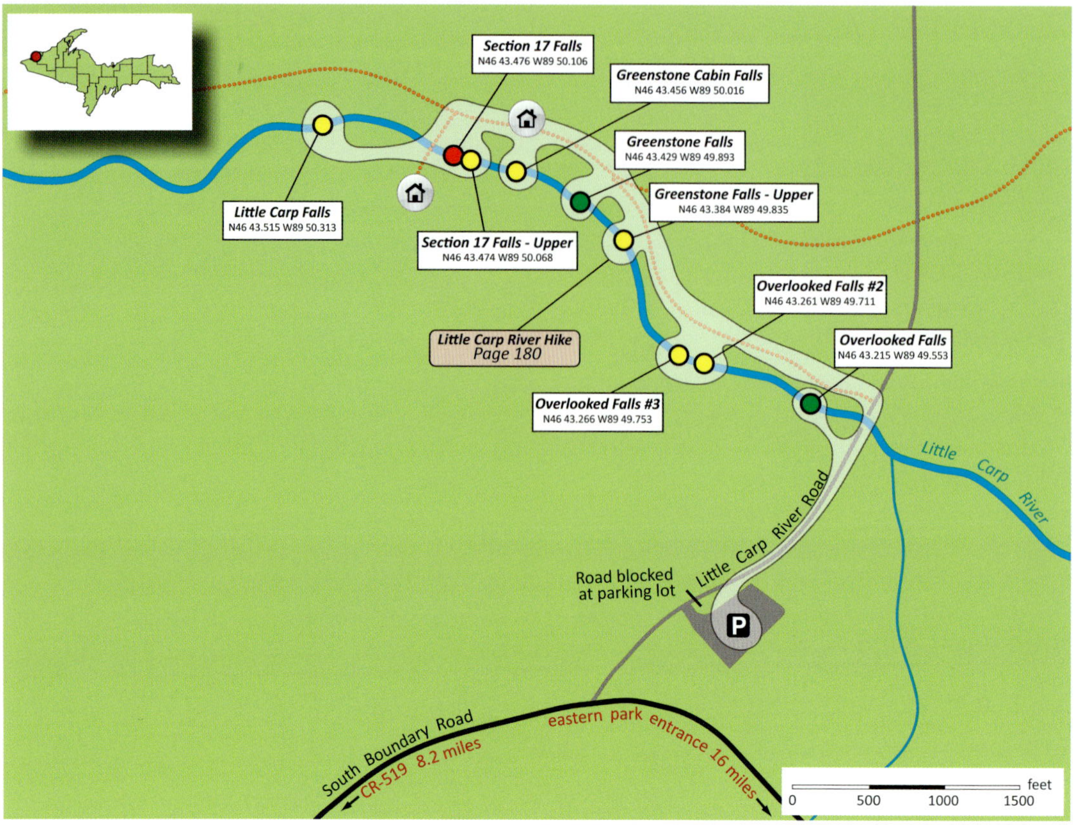

Little Carp River Hike

Drink in the earthen smell on this hike through interspersed white pine, hemlock, maple and aspen. The muted footfalls of spongy earth underfoot are easily covered by the sound of the rushing, falling river that is ever near! Soak it up. Enjoy. Glory.

Overlooked Falls is probably the most viewed waterfall in the park besides the famous ones on the Presque Isle River. In fact, during one of my many stays at the AmericInn in Silver City a gentleman from the Chicago area showed me pictures of a replica of Overlooked Falls he had built in his garden!

The road continues over the Little Carp River but is gated and is only for use by park Rangers. Parking is set back from the river in an ample lot. The hike along the Little Carp River includes some improvements such as footbridges over small ravines and wet areas. But do be prepared to navigate over tree roots and uneven ground at times. The hike is predominantly level, running about 5 to 15 feet above the rivers edge. Climb down earthen banks at some of the waterfalls along the way to get to the base of the falls for ideal viewing.

Directions: Near the western entrance to Porcupine Mountains State Park, at the intersection of CR-519 and South Boundary Road, drive east on South Boundary Road for 8 miles. Turn left (northeast) onto Little Carp River Road (DO NOT ENTER WITH A TRAILER - there no place to turn it around!). Drive the 1/4 mile or so to the parking area by the Little Carp River. Park. Continue down the access road to the river. Overlooked Falls is immediately down river. Stay on the near side (south) of the river to view the falls. Hike the short distance back to the road and cross the river on the bridge to pick up the Carp River Trail on the far side of the river. Hike down river (west) to see the falls along the trail. For the last falls on the hike (Little Carp Falls), I crossed the footbridge for the Section 17 Cabin and followed the southern side of the river to the falls. This part of the hike is more rigorous as there is no trail and there are several rolling hills to be traversed on the way.

OVERLOOKED FALLS (LITTLE CARP RIVER)

Private

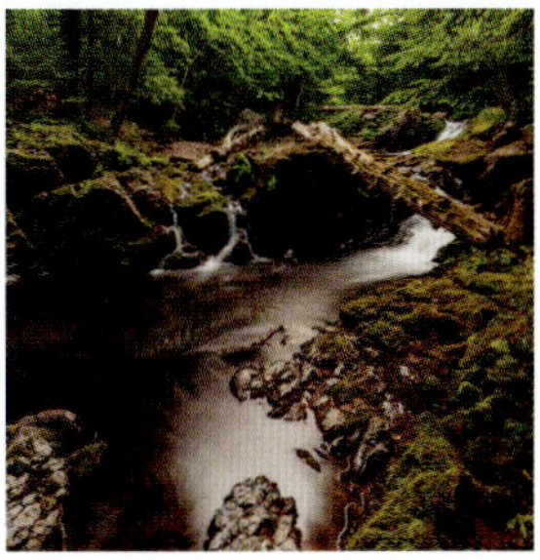

Must See:	7	GPS:	N46 43.215 W89 49.553
Height:	12 feet		
Time:	10-20 minutes	**Hiking Information**	
		Path:	N/A
Driving Information		Length:	100 feet
Signs:	None	Elev. Change:	Slight
Road:	Dirt	GPS:	None
Access:	Somewhat Easy	Danger:	Slight
4WD:	N/A	WP Boots:	None

A split cascade surrounds an outcropping before connecting again in a roundish spill pool. A little further downstream however, a second cascade, narrower than the first, courses over various rocky knobs, spilling into a narrower angled causeway that then turns just in time to leave a rocky bank situated in a prime location for viewing the waterfall!

I prefer to view this waterfall from the southern side of the river. After viewing, head back to the parking lot, cross the bridge, and double back down river on the Carp River Trail to see the rest of the waterfalls on this hike.

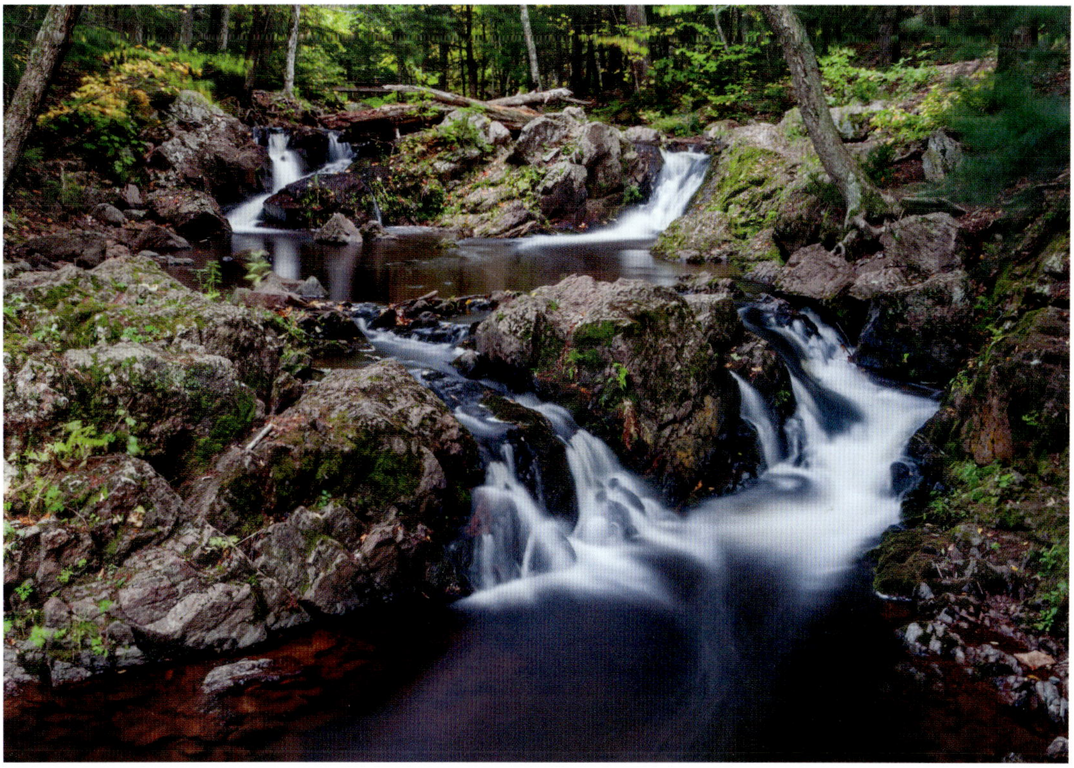

OVERLOOKED FALLS #2 (LITTLE CARP RIVER)

Private

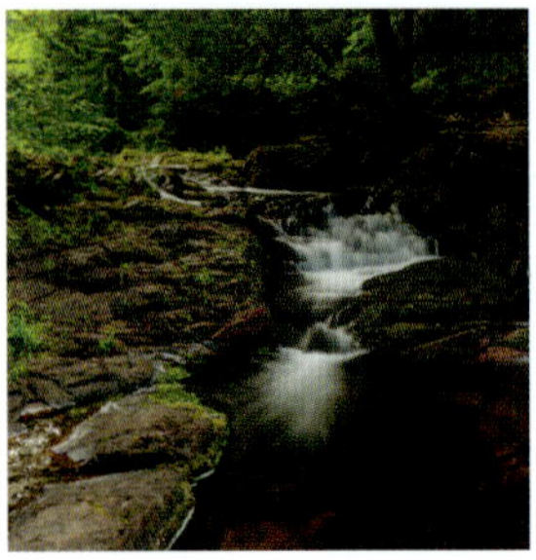

Must See:	5	GPS:	N46 43.261 W89 49.711
Height:	5 feet		
Time:	20-40 minutes	Hiking Information	
		Path:	Footpath
Driving Information		Length:	.27 miles
Signs:	None	Elev. Change:	Moderate
Road:	Dirt	GPS:	Recommended
Access:	Somewhat Easy	Danger:	Slight
4WD:	N/A	WP Boots:	None

Hike downstream on the northern side of the Little Carp River following the Carp River Trail. After about 1/4 mile of hiking head down to the river's edge to view the minor "Overlooked" drops that are about 200 feet apart.

The river sweeps around a slightly higher mass of bedrock and cascades down through a softer section of basalt. The river is channelled down to 2 feet wide at the base of the falls before swelling back out into a 20 by 30 foot pool just before dropping again over the next waterfall.

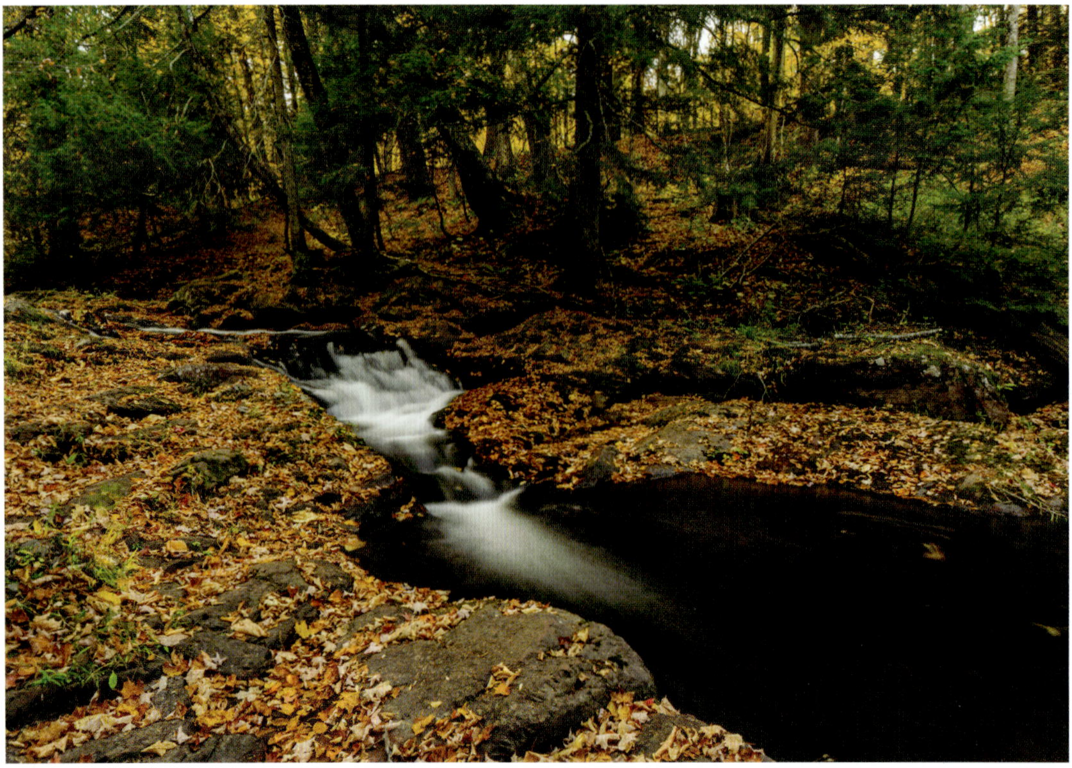

OVERLOOKED FALLS #3 (LITTLE CARP RIVER)

Private

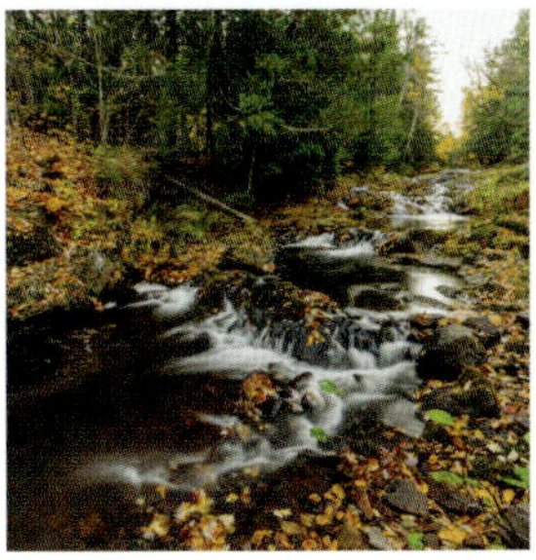

Must See:	5	GPS:	N46 43.266 W89 49.753
Height:	7 feet		
Time:	25-45 minutes	**Hiking Information**	
		Path:	Footpath
Driving Information		Length:	.29 miles
Signs:	None	Elev. Change:	Moderate
Road:	Dirt	GPS:	None
Access:	Somewhat Easy	Danger:	Slight
4WD:	N/A	WP Boots:	None

This gently cascading waterfall stretches out over 100 feet of river length. It begins its descent just below Overlooked Falls #2. These two waterfalls conclude the waterfalls on the Little Carp River until Greenstone Falls - Upper, 300 yards further downstream.

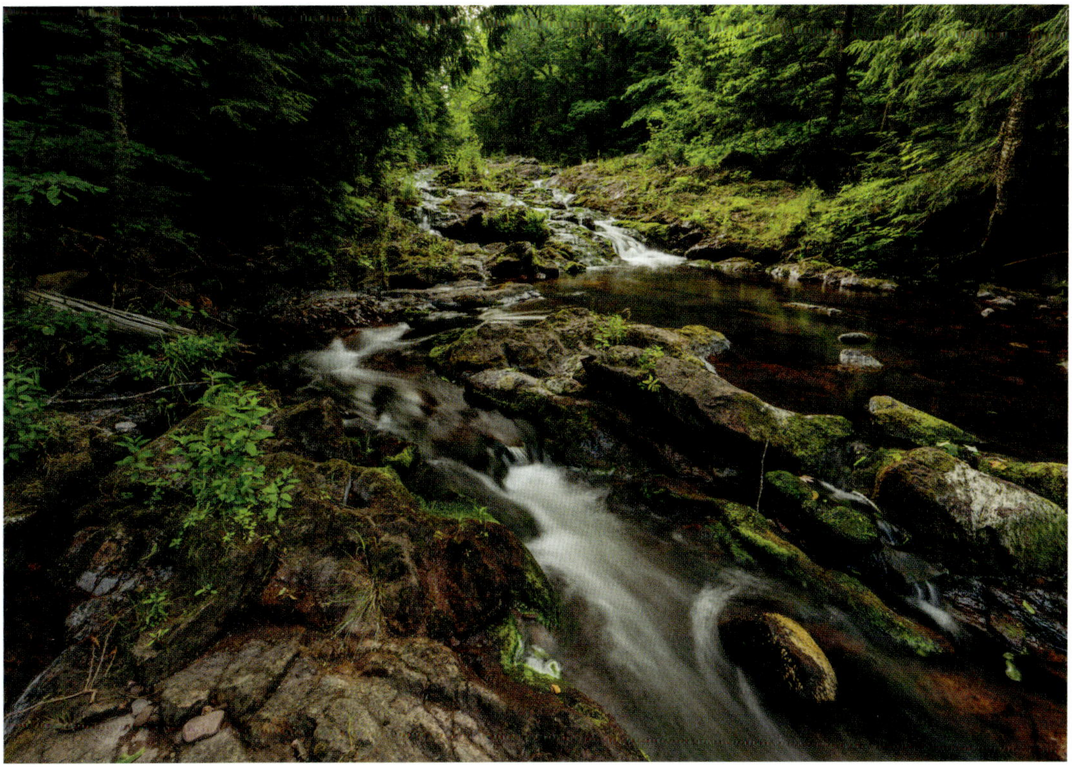

GREENSTONE FALLS - UPPER (LITTLE CARP RIVER)

Private

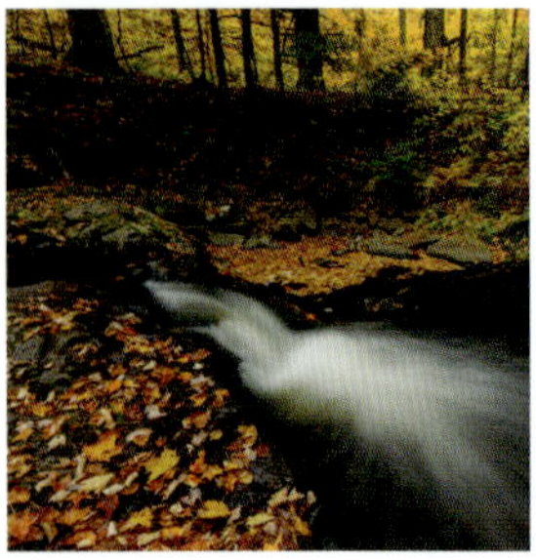

Must See:	4	GPS:	N46 43.384 W89 49.835
Height:	4 feet		
Time:	35-60 minutes	Hiking Information	
		Path:	Footpath
Driving Information		Length:	.45 miles
Signs:	None	Elev. Change:	Moderate
Road:	Dirt	GPS:	Recommended
Access:	Somewhat Easy	Danger:	Slight
4WD:	N/A	WP Boots:	None

Greenstone Falls attracts the lion's share of the attention in this area of the river, and rightly so! But take the time to enjoy this twin drop 200 yards above the much larger waterfall.

Two 2 foot cascading drops are separated by a 20 foot wide spill pool. The lower drop plunges into another pool, aerating it nicely!

As can be seen from the autumn pictures shown, this area is awash in golden leaves in early October. As a bonus, there are rarely any biting insects in the U.P. then!

The drops and twin spill pools.

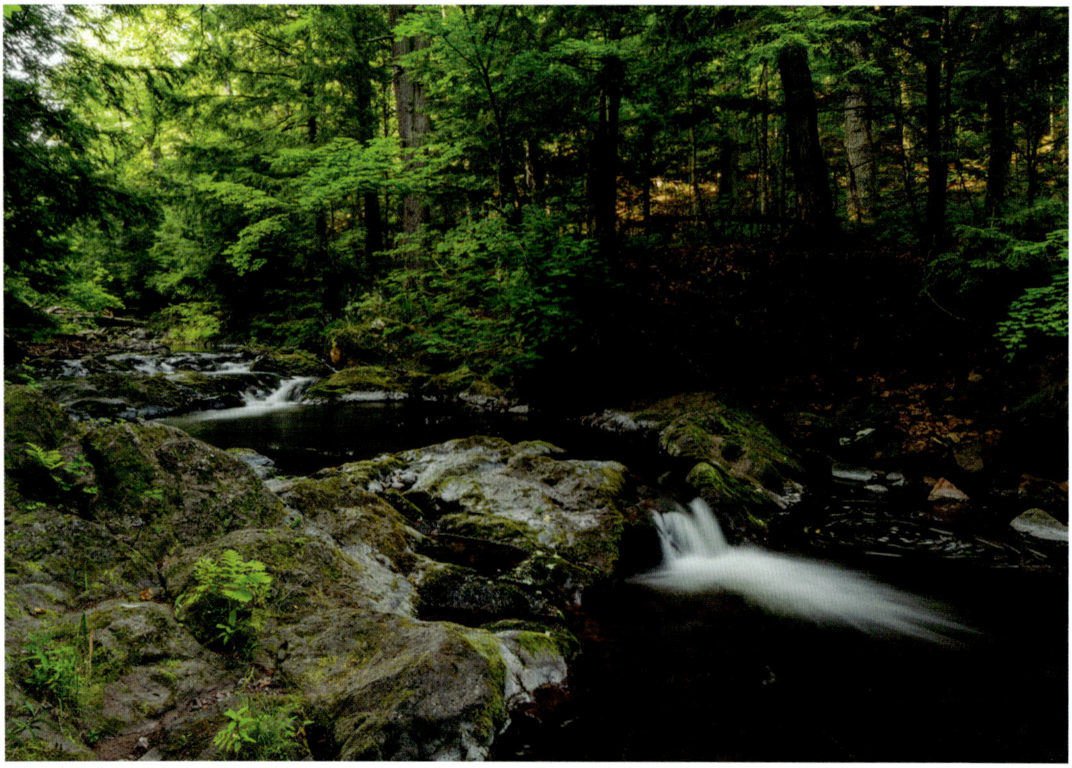

GREENSTONE FALLS (LITTLE CARP RIVER)

Private

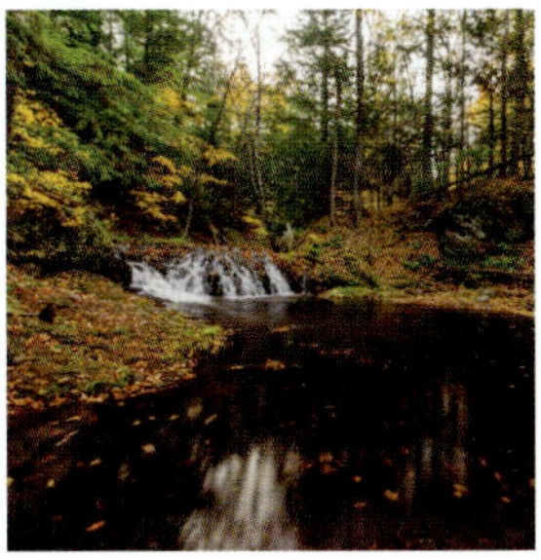

Must See:	7	GPS:	N46 43.429 W89 49.893
Height:	6 feet		
Time:	45-70 minutes	Hiking Information	
		Path:	Footpath
Driving Information		Length:	.51 miles
Signs:	None	Elev. Change:	Moderate
Road:	Dirt	GPS:	None
Access:	Somewhat Easy	Danger:	Moderate
4WD:	N/A	WP Boots:	None

The river flows over a nicely presented conglomerate mass with a nice viewing area along the river's edge. A dark spill pool dominates the area below the falls, the cool waters looking inviting on a hot summer's day!

There is little chance of missing Greenstone Falls. The Carp River Trail runs right by the falls with a sign marking the spot. The river has cut through the sediment down to the bedrock, so be prepared to climb down a steep hillside to get down to the river's edge.

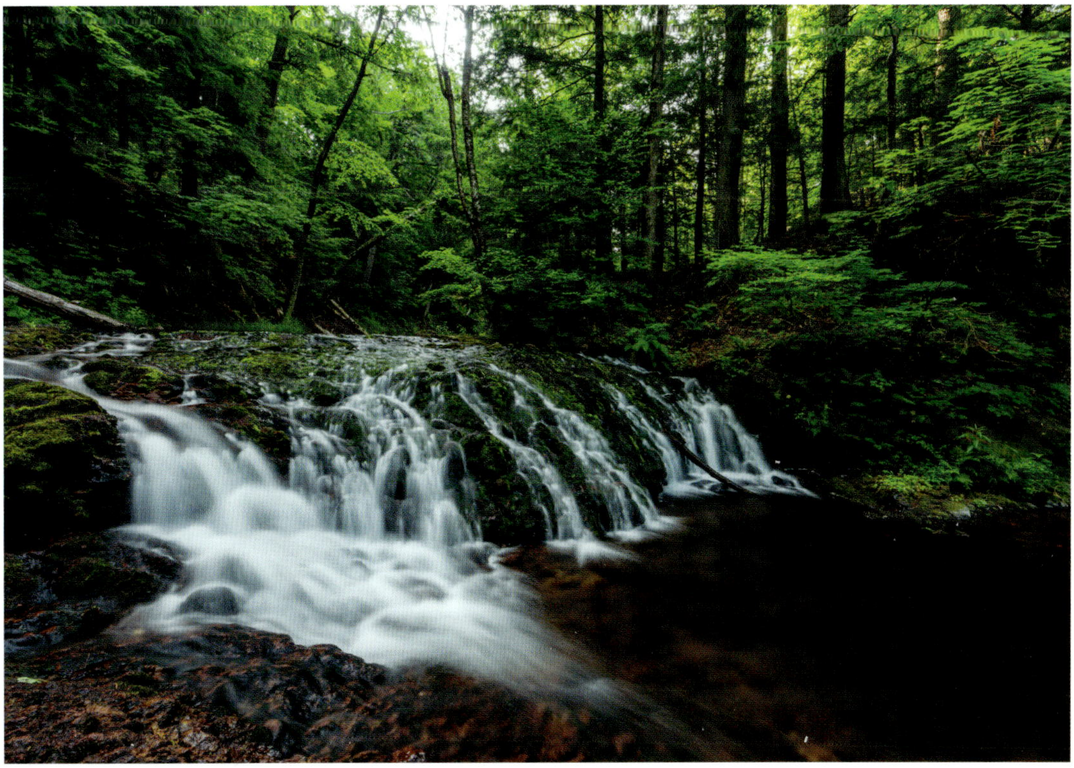

GREENSTONE CABIN FALLS (LITTLE CARP RIVER)

Private

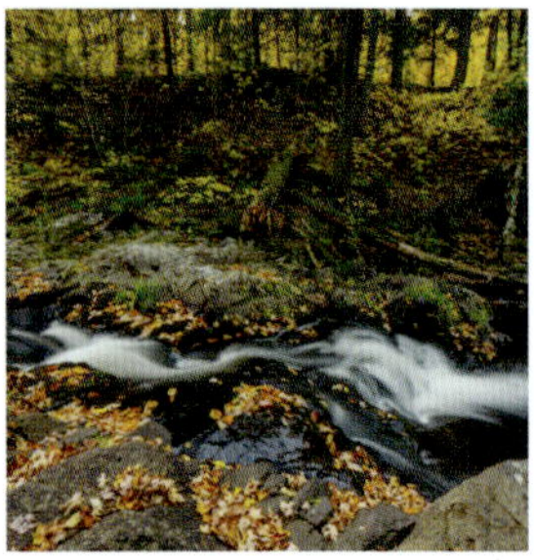

Must See:	4	GPS:	N46 43.456 W89 50.016
Height:	4 feet		
Time:	55-80 minutes	Hiking Information	
		Path:	Footpath
Driving Information		Length:	.60 miles
Signs:	None	Elev. Change:	Moderate
Road:	Dirt	GPS:	Recommended
Access:	Somewhat Easy	Danger:	Slight
4WD:	N/A	WP Boots:	None

Continue down the river for another 200 yards from Greenstone Falls to Greenstone Falls Cabin which is located next to the trail in plain sight. Although the cabin is named after Greenstone Falls, the cabin aptly lends its name to the small cascading waterfall found near it. Hike the 150 down to the river and the falls.

The shallow river picks its way around protruding bedrock and loose rocks centered between banks set back from either side of the typically narrow waterway. The grade suddenly falls, and the river slips away at a bit of an angle while it slides down the chunky basalt. A small rooster tail shoots up toward the base of the falls. At the time of the shot seen above, a strategically placed tree trunk served as a makeshift footbridge immediately below the falls.

An island covered with wild flowers is just downstream from this, the base of the falls.

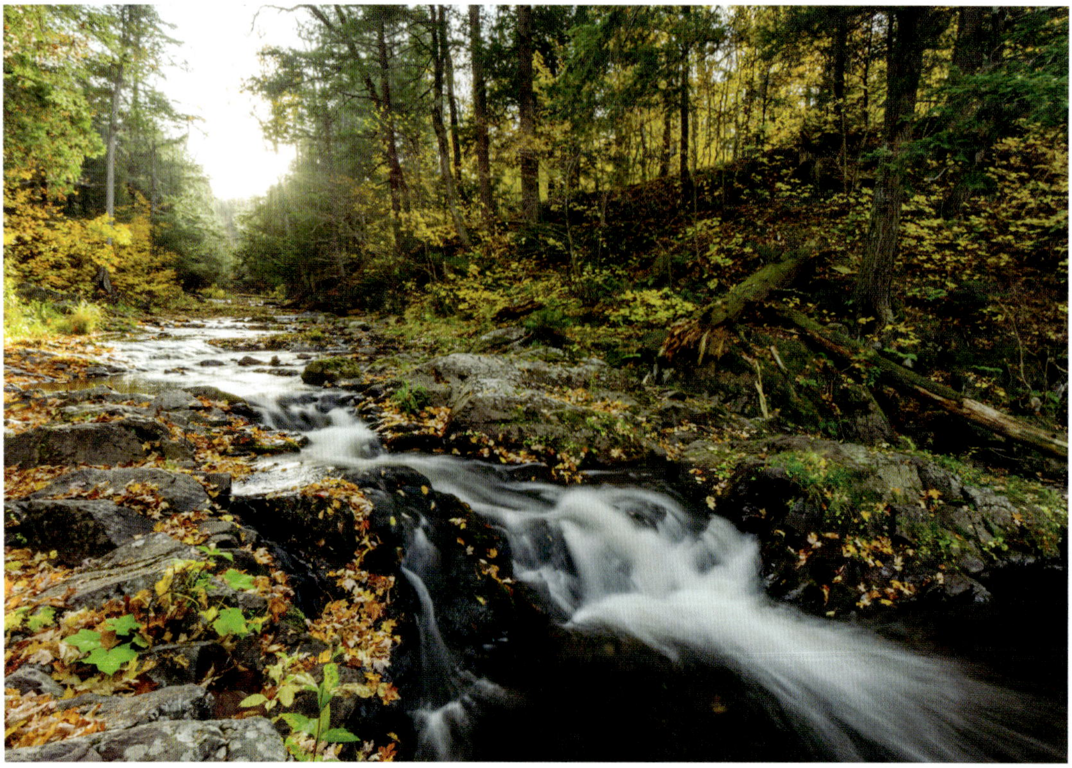

SECTION 17 FALLS - UPPER (LITTLE CARP RIVER)

Private

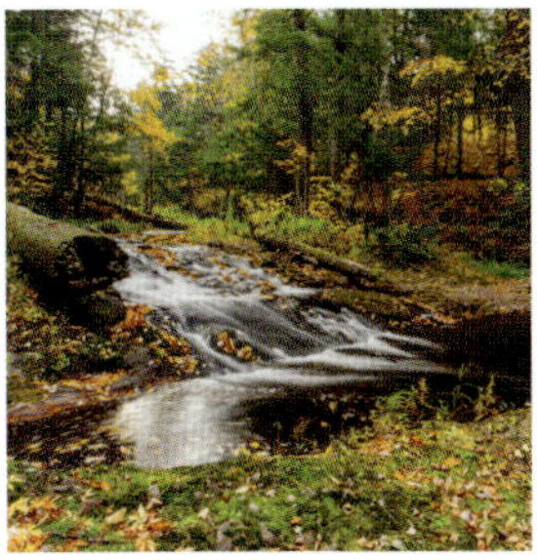

Must See:	4	GPS:	N46 43.474 W89 50.068
Height:	4 feet		
Time:	45-70 minutes	**Hiking Information**	
		Path:	Footpath
Driving Information		Length:	.65 miles
Signs:	None	Elev. Change:	Moderate
Road:	Dirt	GPS:	None
Access:	Somewhat Easy	Danger:	Moderate
4WD:	N/A	WP Boots:	None

The river slides over a rippled conglomerate face, turns hard to the left and then slides down a second, smaller cascading drop before kicking back to the left again as the river widens out. A small wooden bridge spans the river 150 feet downstream.

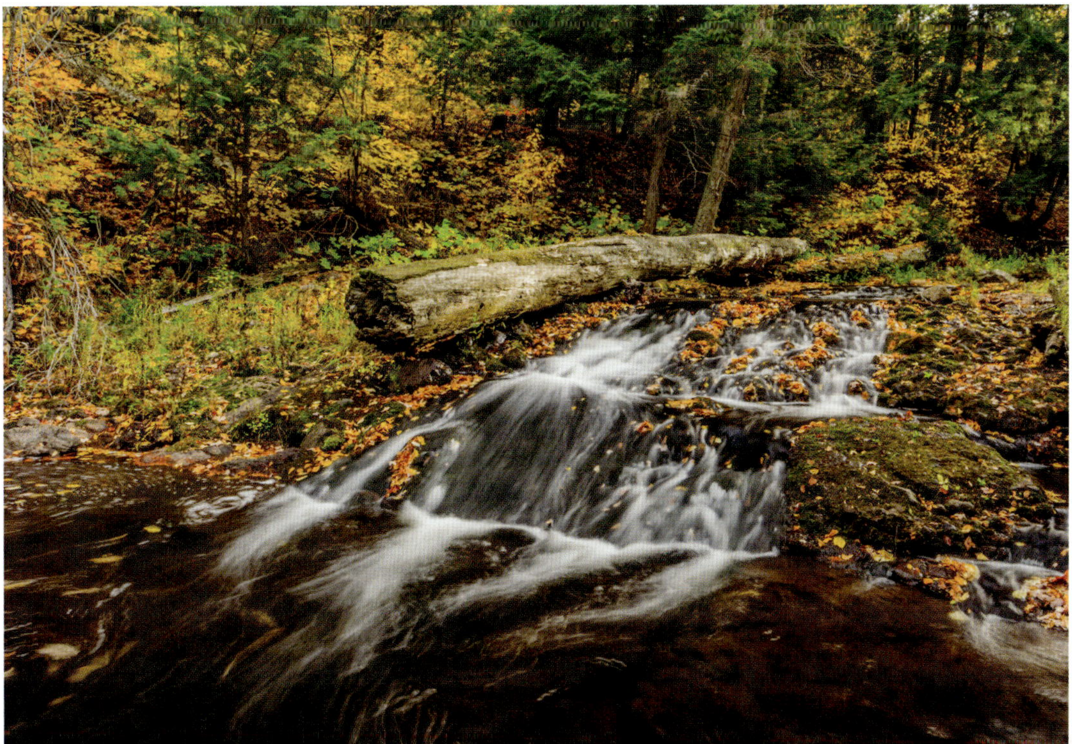

SECTION 17 FALLS (LITTLE CARP RIVER)

Private

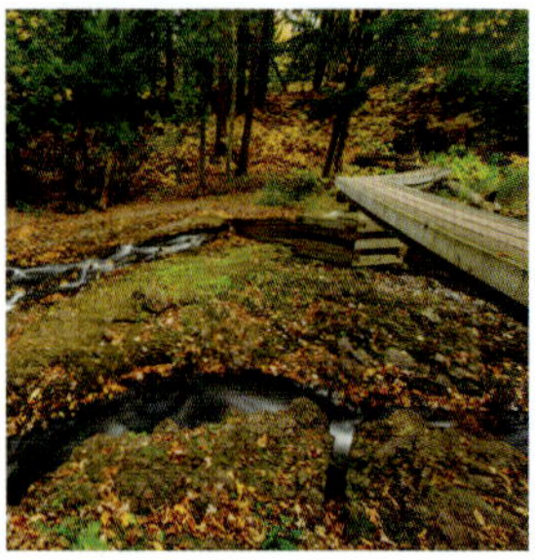

Must See:	3	GPS:	N46 43.476 W89 50.106
Height:	5 feet		
Time:	50-75 minutes	**Hiking Information**	
		Path:	Footpath
Driving Information		Length:	.68 miles
Signs:	None	Elev. Change:	Moderate
Road:	Dirt	GPS:	Recommended
Access:	Somewhat Easy	Danger:	Slight
4WD:	N/A	WP Boots:	None

Section 17 Falls and the Upper Falls are only about 50 yards apart. A narrow, elevated bridge crosses the river to the Section 17 Cabin that is just south of the Little Carp River at the end of a short spur trail. The bridge is built over the top of the short conglomerate slide. Since these two waterfalls are so close together, the Upper Falls can be seen upstream from here.

Section 17 Falls is a split waterfall. A secondary narrow diversion runs along the southern side of the river, splaying down and undercutting the rocky bank before the two streams meet back up at the base of the falls.

The Upper Falls can be seen in the background past the bridge.

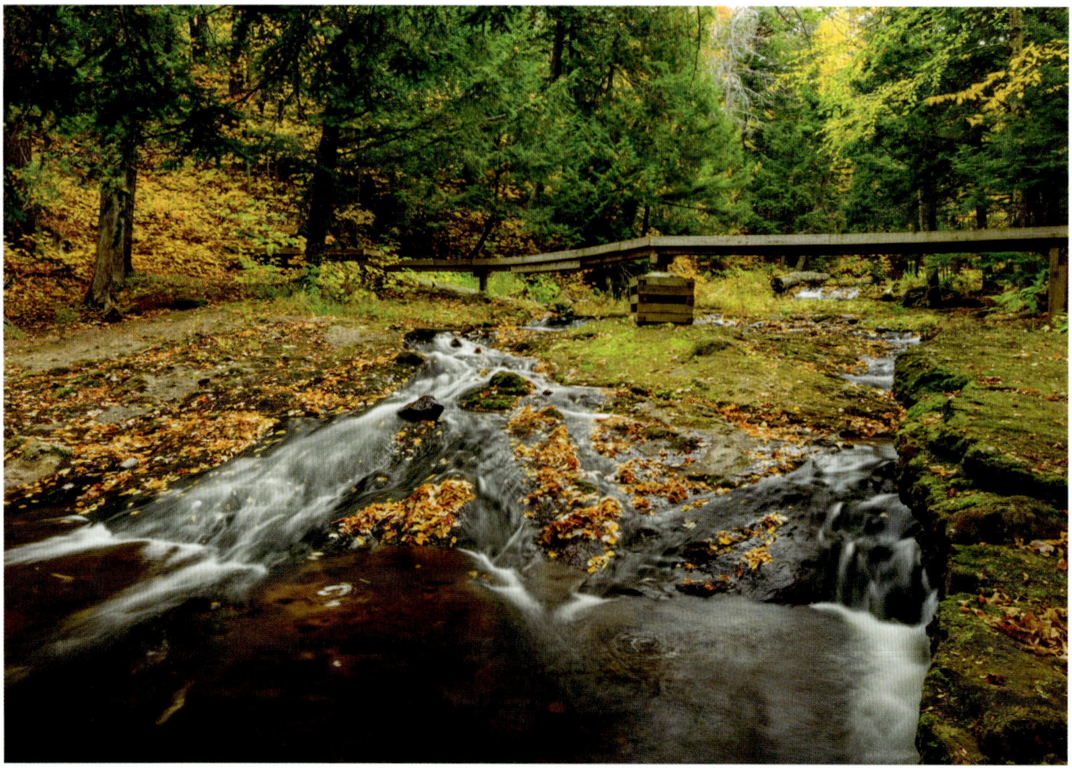

LITTLE CARP FALLS (LITTLE CARP RIVER)

Private

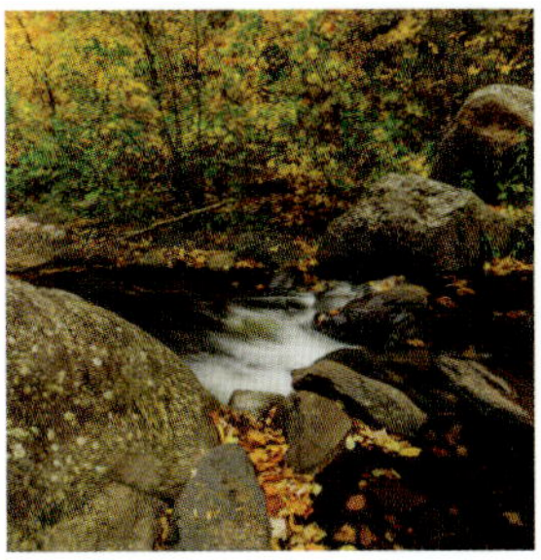

Must See: 4
Height: 2 feet
Time: 70-100 minutes

Driving Information
Signs: None
Road: Dirt
Access: Somewhat Easy
4WD: N/A

GPS: N46 43.515 W89 50.313

Hiking Information
Path: Footpath - None
Length: .88 miles
Elev. Change: Moderate
GPS: Recommended
Danger: Moderate
WP Boots: Helpful

This small, cute waterfall is not near the Carp River Trail. The trail heads northerly, away from the river in this area, so I crossed over to the south side of the river via the footbridge to the Section 17 Cabin and then followed the river downstream. Several ridges run down to the river, so it is necessary to climb up and over these on the .2 mile hike from the cabin to the falls. I feel that this is the most difficult part of this hike along the Little Carp River (It's always more difficult when there is no trail!), so you may want to skip this last little drop unless you are a diehard waterfall hunter!

A 6 foot scramble down the earthen bank is needed to get to the river at the waterfall. There is another small drop about 100 feet upstream as well. Several large boulders sit around the waterfall and a large collection of medium sized boulders litter the river for as far as the eye can see!

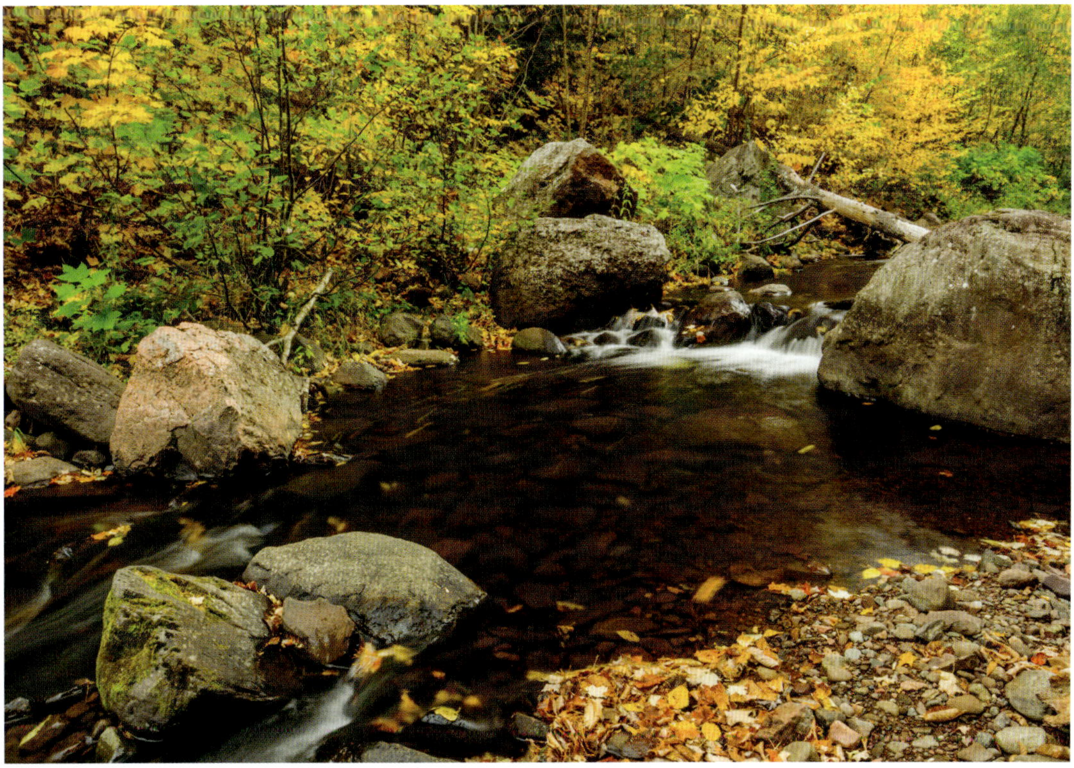

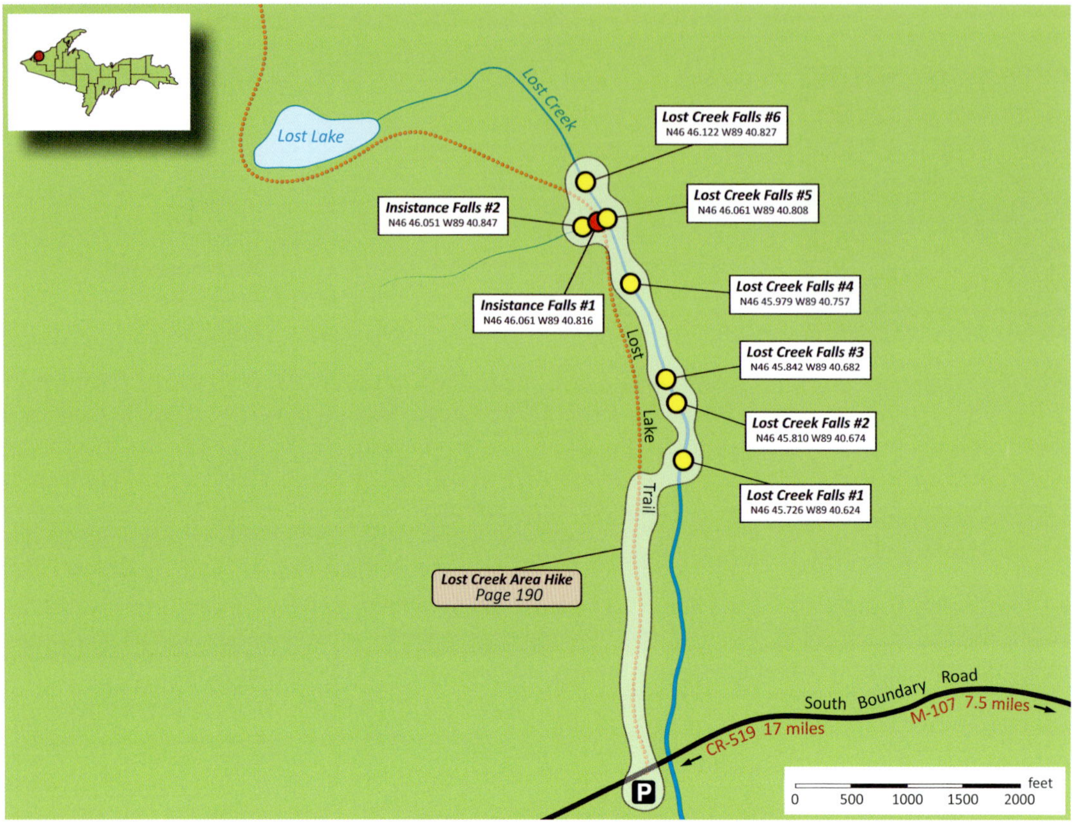

Lost Creek Area Hike

A particularly helpful ranger at the park headquarters clued me in to the drops along Lost Creek. It is a pleasure working with these public servants that show a true concern for this natural treasure and the visitors eager to view it!

Directions: Follow South Boundary Road either 7.5 miles south from M-107 or 17 miles east from CR-519 to Lost Creek Outpost Campground. There is a trailhead here for Lost Lake Trail as well. Park south of South Boundary Road and just west of Lost Creek at the obvious dirt parking area for the trailhead. Hike north, across South Boundary Road, and along the Lost Lake Trail until getting close to the GPS coordinate for the first waterfall. Cut cross country (no trail) to the creek and follow it upstream to the rest of the waterfalls. A slight detour heads west to view the Insistence Falls before continuing north to the last of the Lost Creek Falls.

LOST CREEK FALLS #1 (LOST CREEK)

Private

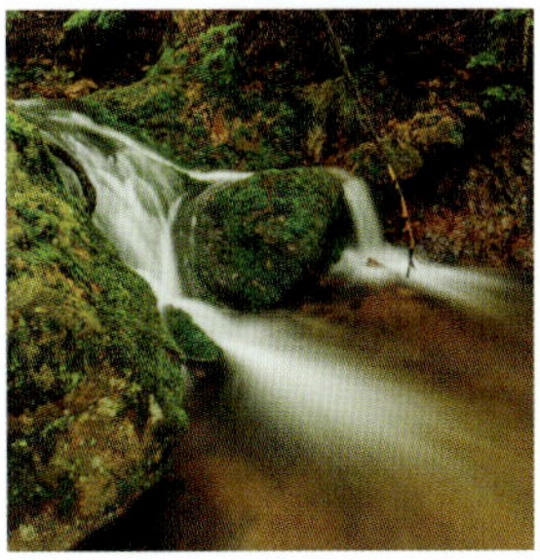

Must See:	4	GPS:	N46 45.726 W89 40.624
Height:	3 feet		
Time:	35-50 minutes	**Hiking Information**	
		Path:	Trail then Nothing
Driving Information		Length:	.54 miles
Signs:	None	Elev. Change:	Moderate
Road:	Secondary	GPS:	Required
Access:	Somewhat Easy	Danger:	Moderate
4WD:	N/A	WP Boots:	Recommended

Porcupine Mountains State Park contains four yurts with three of them strategically placed along back country trails. All of them are found on the eastern side of the park. The easiest to access is the yurt at Union Bay Campground. They are 16 foot diameter cylindrical shaped tent-like buildings looking something like a stubby rocket. Their canvas sides are stretched over a more substantial frame. They are available for rental year-round and accessible by hiking or skiing. A maximum of four persons can sleep on a double set of bunk beds set along the wall across the room from a small wood stove. For more information on the park's yurts check out this page: *http://www.michigan.gov/dnr/0,4570,7-153-10365_24196-158770--,00.html*. Lost Creek Falls #1 happens to be near the Lost Creek Yurt! Climb the steep bank on the far side of the creek to view this yurt up close.

As you can see, Lost Creek is not a major water source. Here the 2 foot wide creek falls down over an edge of bedrock, and then divides around a 3 foot wide, moss covered boulder.

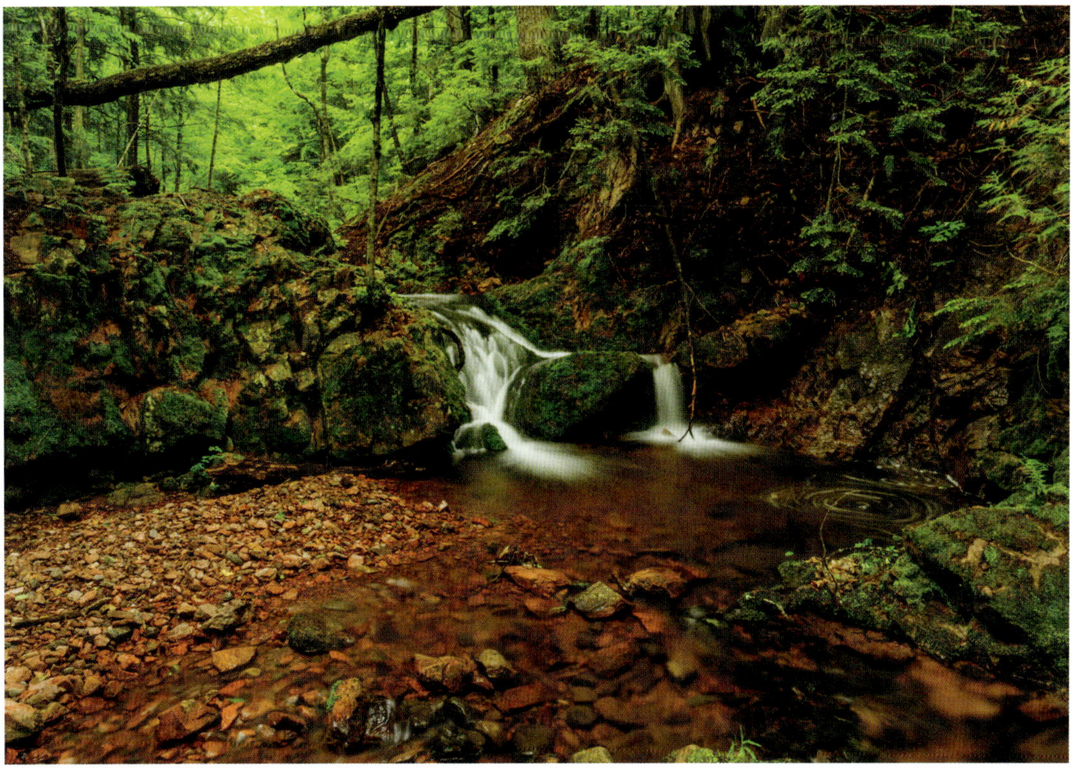

LOST CREEK FALLS #2 (LOST CREEK)

Private

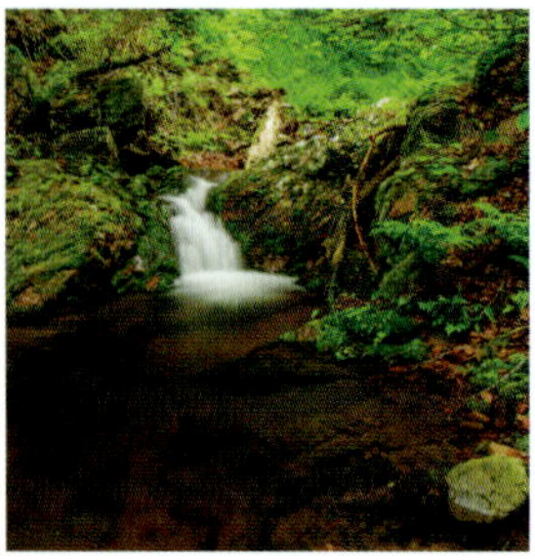

Must See:	4	GPS:	N46 45.810 W89 40.674
Height:	3 feet		
Time:	45-60 minutes	Hiking Information	
		Path:	Trail then Nothing
Driving Information		Length:	.66 miles
Signs:	None	Elev. Change:	Moderate
Road:	Secondary	GPS:	Required
Access:	Somewhat Easy	Danger:	Moderate
4WD:	N/A	WP Boots:	Recommended

The Park is roughly almond shaped, with the tapered ends at the southwest and northeast ends. Three ridges run in parallel bands lengthwise. The northern band sheds water on its northern side directly down to Lake Superior via a dozen or so small waterways. The lowland between this band and the central one is where the Big Carp River runs including the widening of the river known as Lake of the Clouds. The start of the river actually occurs on the southern side of the central band, travels easterly and then cutting to the north through a low point in the middle ridge. It then heads to the west and continues on to Lake Superior. The valley between the middle and southern ridges contains the Little Carp River. This river is shorter and drains a smaller area than its larger sibling to the north. It takes a more direct route, heading to the southwest before turning to the northwest and meeting Lake Superior just a mile down the shore from the Big Carp River. Of the few tributaries and creeks that flow southerly in the Park from the southern ridge, Lost Creek starts the furthest north. Lost Lake, a small lake just 1/4 mile south of the upper reaches of the Big Carp River, empties to the south through Lost Creek, eventually joining the Little Iron River.

Two offset masses of bedrock kick the falls sideways at Lost Creek Falls #2. A 6 foot deep spill pool is featured below the falls.

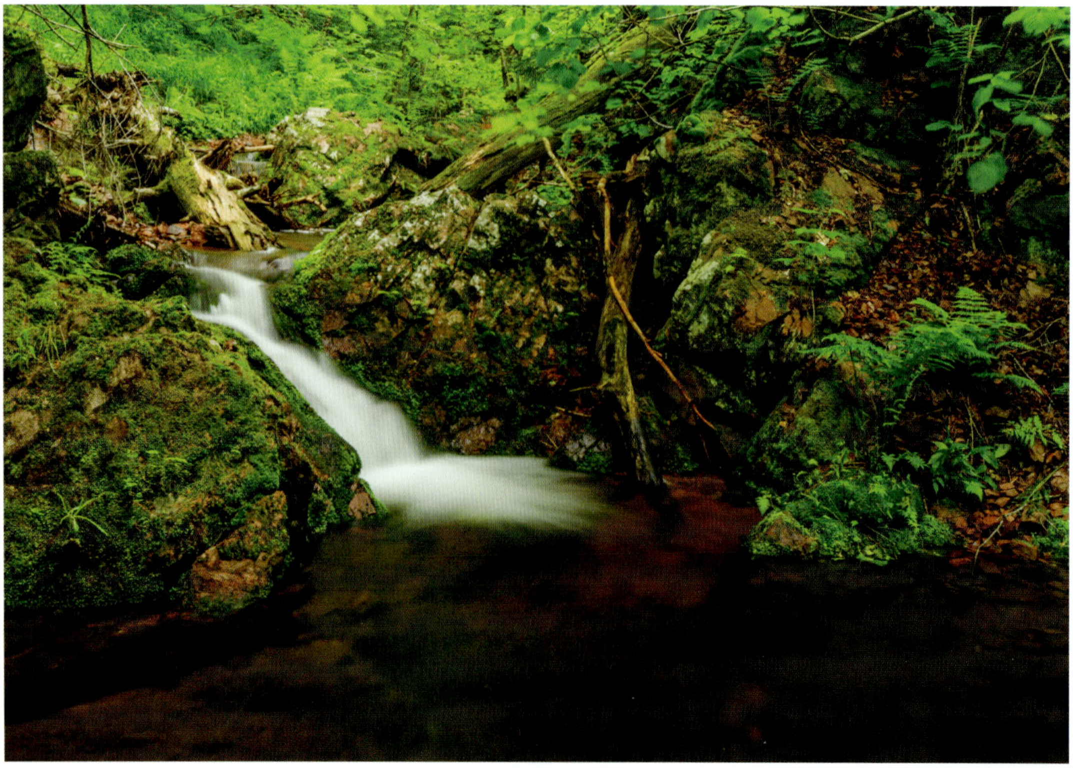

LOST CREEK FALLS #3 (LOST CREEK)

Private

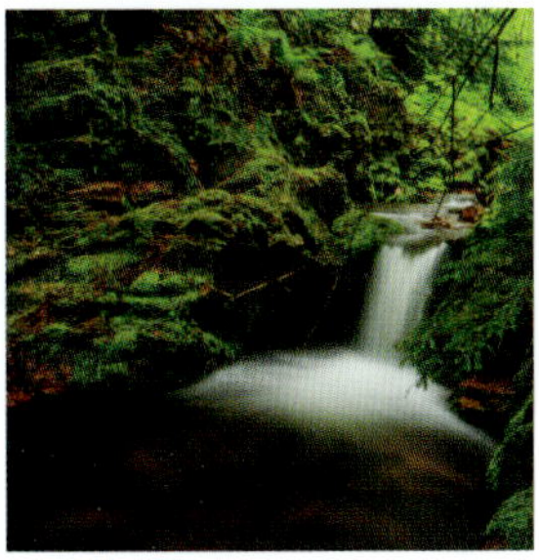

Must See:	4	GPS:	N46 45.842 W89 40.682
Height:	2 feet		
Time:	50-70 minutes		

Driving Information		Hiking Information	
Signs:	None	Path:	Trail then Nothing
Road:	Secondary	Length:	.69 miles
Access:	Somewhat Easy	Elev. Change:	Moderate
4WD:	N/A	GPS:	Required
		Danger:	Moderate
		WP Boots:	Recommended

Impressive 18 foot high canyon walls surround the sides of the waterfall. Moss and lichen cling to these vertical surfaces for a lush green enveloping environment as you stand in the narrows between the walls. Underfoot, red rock chips line the waterway. Although it is but a 2 foot drop, the setting pushes up the "Must See" rating to an OK waterfall. Below the waterfall, the creek expands from a narrow 2' wide stream to a wall-to-wall spill pool.

Lost Creek Falls #3 is just 70 yards upstream from Lost Creek Falls #2. These are the closest 2 drops on Lost Creek. The furthest apart drops happen to be Lost Creek Falls #3 and Lost Creek Falls #4, which have 300 yards separating them.

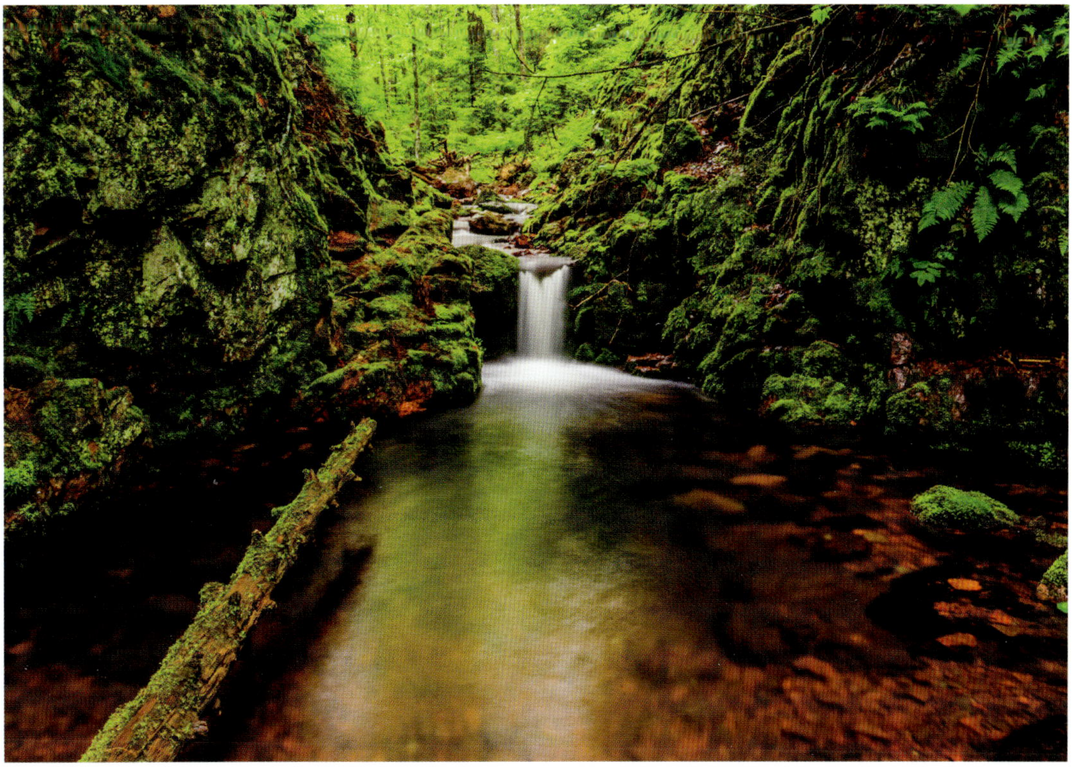

LOST CREEK FALLS #4 (LOST CREEK)

Private

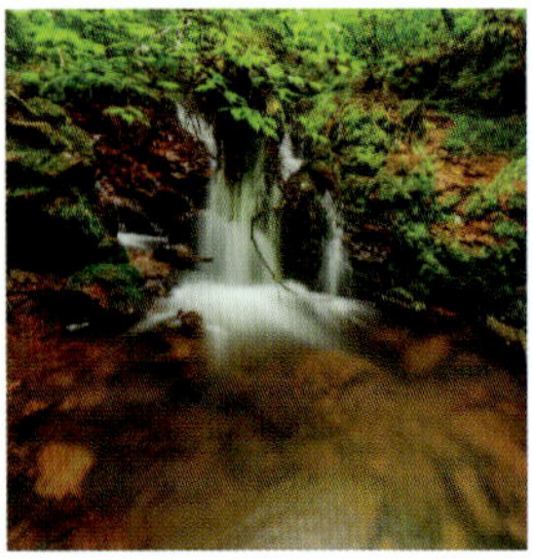

Must See:	4	GPS:	N46 45.979 W89 40.757
Height:	5 feet		
Time:	65-90 minutes	Hiking Information	
		Path:	Trail then Nothing
Driving Information		Length:	.87 miles
Signs:	None	Elev. Change:	Moderate
Road:	Secondary	GPS:	Required
Access:	Somewhat Easy	Danger:	Moderate
4WD:	N/A	WP Boots:	Recommended

Waterfalls seem to be magnets for tree debris! This one had an 18 inch tree trunk laying across the top of the falls when I was there last. Fortunately it was heavily decayed at the time. Hopefully it will be gone soon and the waterfall will be more easily viewed.

Red rock, as is typical with this creek, makes up the steep banks and the creek bed as well. The creek drops five feet through a rough, deep channel. Numerous hardwood saplings are growing along the sides of the creek. This will be a beautiful hike in early October!

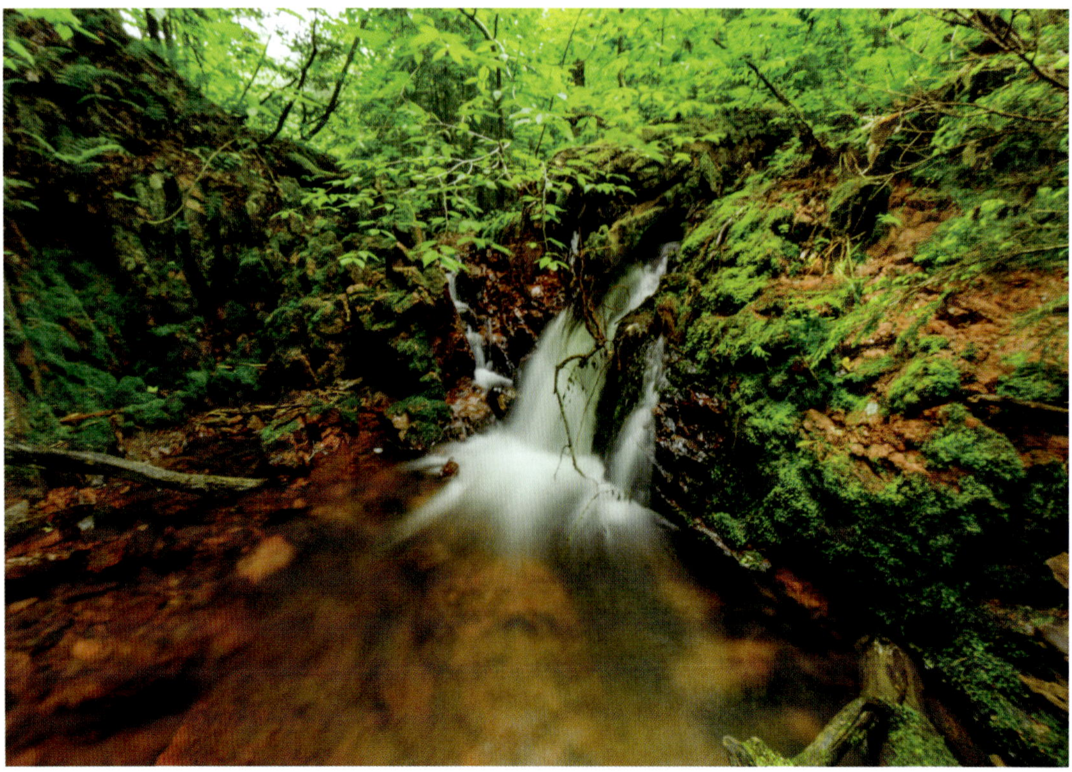

LOST CREEK FALLS #5 (LOST CREEK)

Private

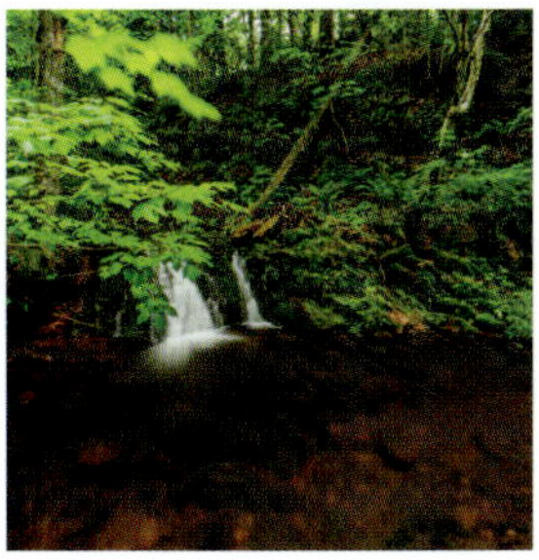

Must See:	4	GPS:	N46 46.061 W89 40.808
Height:	3 feet		
Time:	75-100 minutes	Hiking Information	
		Path:	*Trail then Nothing
Driving Information		Length:	.98 miles
Signs:	None	Elev. Change:	Moderate
Road:	Secondary	GPS:	Required
Access:	Somewhat Easy	Danger:	Moderate
4WD:	N/A	WP Boots:	Recommended

Lost Lake Trail meets Lost Creek for the first time here. Up to this point the trail has paralleled Lost Creek, running to the west of the creek. If you were to hike upstream along the creek starting at South Boundary Road you would travel nearly straight north up to Lost Creek Falls #1. Almost immediately you would turn slightly to the left heading north-northwest past all of the Lost Creek Falls until the creek would make a 90 degree sweeping bend to the left and send you west-southwest for about 1,500 yards to Lost Lake where the creek begins its journey. It is about halfway up the north-northwest leg of the creek that Lost Lake Trail joins up with the creek right here at Lost Creek Falls #5 and Insistence Falls #1.

Lost Creek Falls #5 is a cute little cascade that drops into a perfectly clear, rock based spill pool. Green moss covers the rocks in and around the falls.

**It is possible to follow Lost Lake Trail all the way to this waterfall. You will miss the first 4 waterfalls on Lost Creek, so it is not my recommended route.*

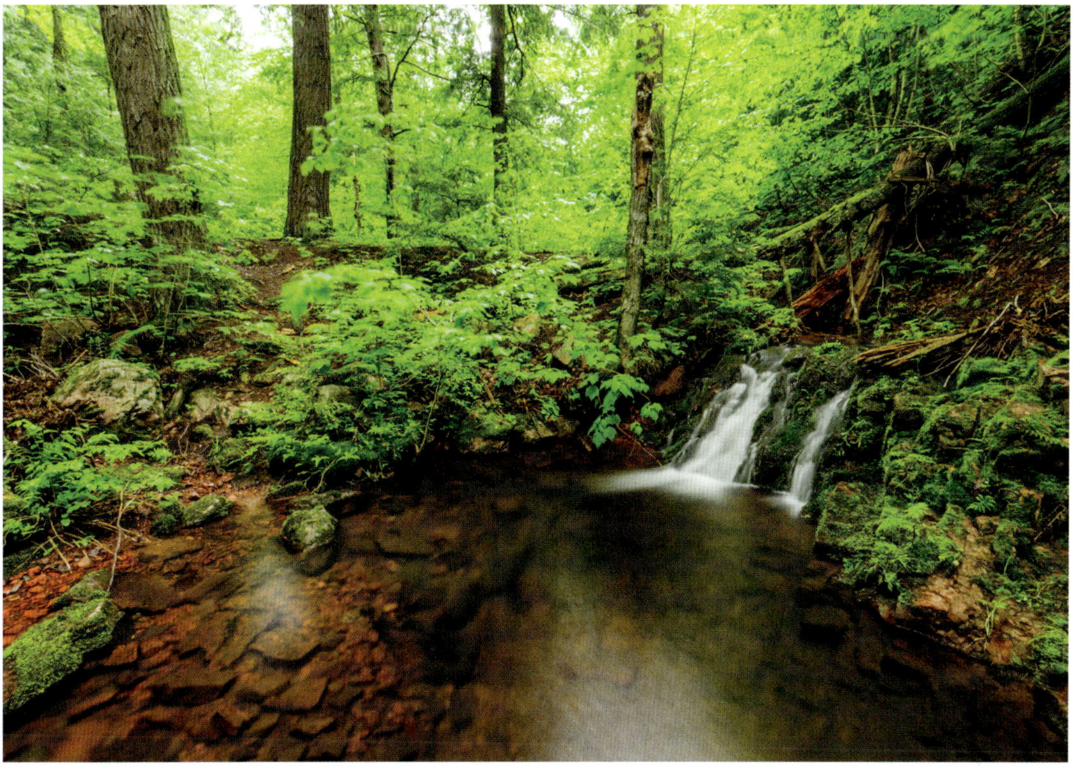

INSISTENCE FALLS #1 (UNNAMED CREEK)

Private

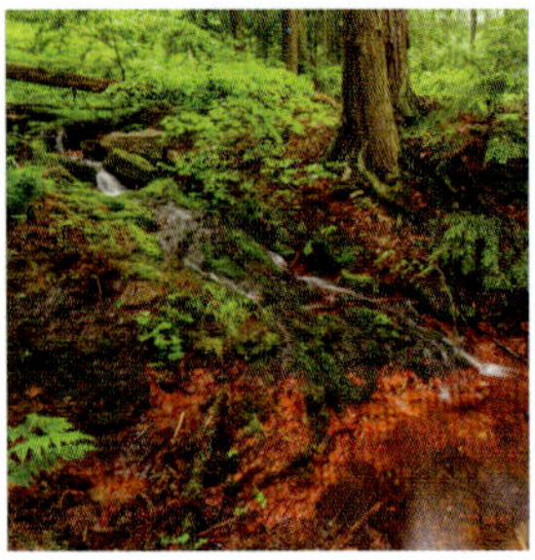

Must See:	3	GPS:	N46 46.061 W89 40.816
Height:	8 feet		
Time:	75-100 minutes	Hiking Information	
		Path:	*Trail then Nothing
Driving Information		Length:	.99 miles
Signs:	None	Elev. Change:	Moderate
Road:	Secondary	GPS:	Required
Access:	Somewhat Easy	Danger:	Moderate
4WD:	N/A	WP Boots:	Recommended

As my son, Kevin, and I hiked Lost Creek in June of 2011, we ran across this little tributary feeding the creek with a small sliding, cascading waterfall dumping into the creek right by Lost Creek Falls #5. As I was photographing the Lost Creek waterfall, Kevin kept insisting that I also include the drop on this tributary. I finally gave in and called it "Insistence Falls"!

The little creek drops 2 feet into a spill pool followed by another 1 foot drop before finishing its descent with a 5 foot long slide into a final spill pool. Lost Lake Trail is only 20 feet downstream from here.

**It is possible to follow Lost Lake Trail all the way to this waterfall. You will miss the first 4 waterfalls on Lost Creek, so it is not my recommended route.*

Look carefully. You may see the blue circles painted on the trees marking Lost Lake Trail.

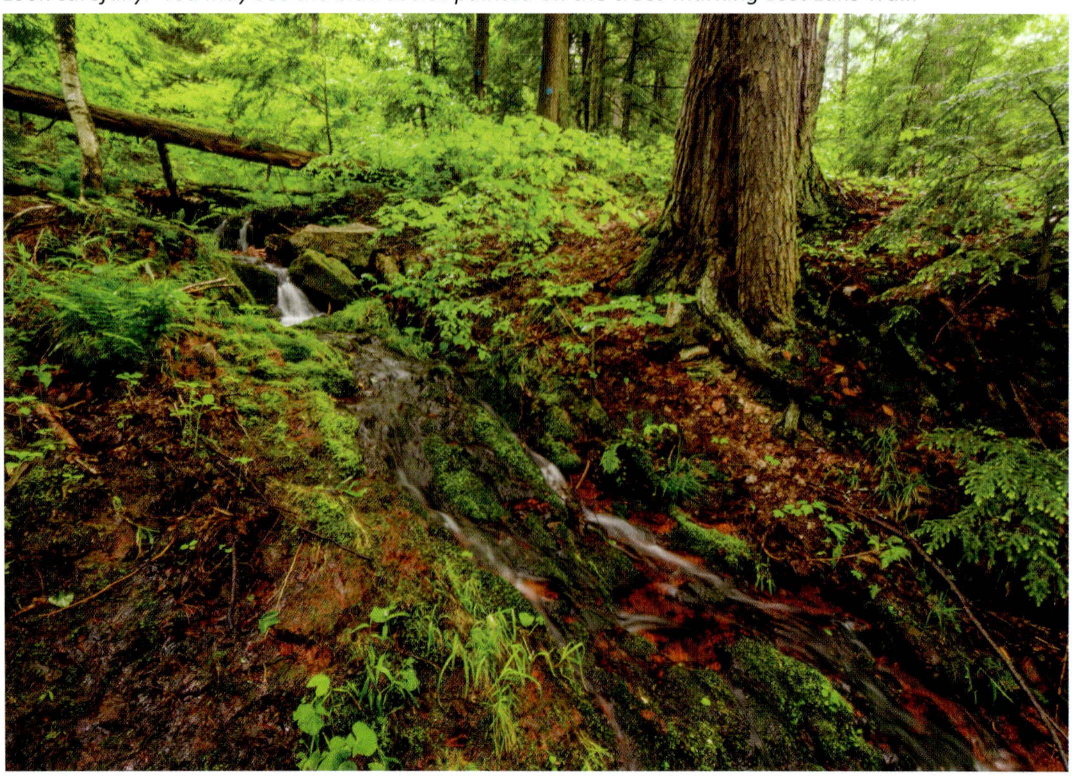

INSISTENCE FALLS #2 (UNNAMED CREEK)

Private

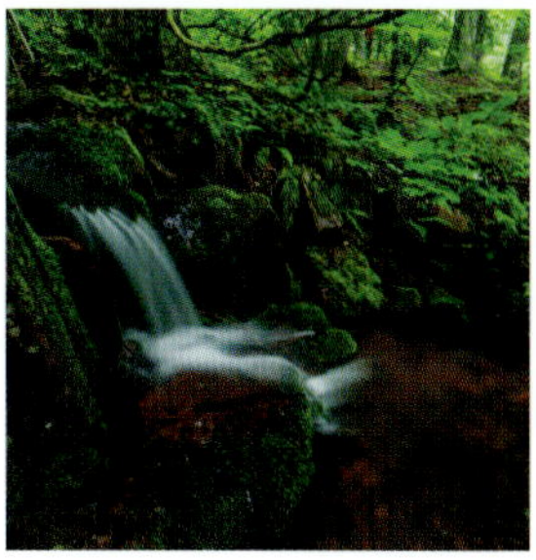

Must See:	5	GPS:	N46 46.051 W89 40.847
Height:	3 feet		
Time:	85-110 minutes	Hiking Information	
		Path:	*Trail then Nothing
Driving Information		Length:	1.02 miles
Signs:	None	Elev. Change:	Moderate
Road:	Secondary	GPS:	Required
Access:	Somewhat Easy	Danger:	Moderate
4WD:	N/A	WP Boots:	Recommended

Kevin was so excited about getting me to include Insistence Falls #1 in my collection that he hiked up the small creek to see if he could find another one! Sure enough, he found one 50 yards upstream. This one has so much character, such a wonderful presentation, that I am very much looking forward to photographing it again!

This cute waterfall is tucked into a rock ringed basin that serves as a calm spill pool. The creek narrows to a chute that falls to a moss covered slab of rock just above the smooth surface below.

**It is possible to follow Lost Lake Trail most of the way to this waterfall. You will miss the first 4 waterfalls on Lost Creek, so it is not my recommended route.*

The overhanging maple branches were so low, I had my camera just a foot or two above the creek.

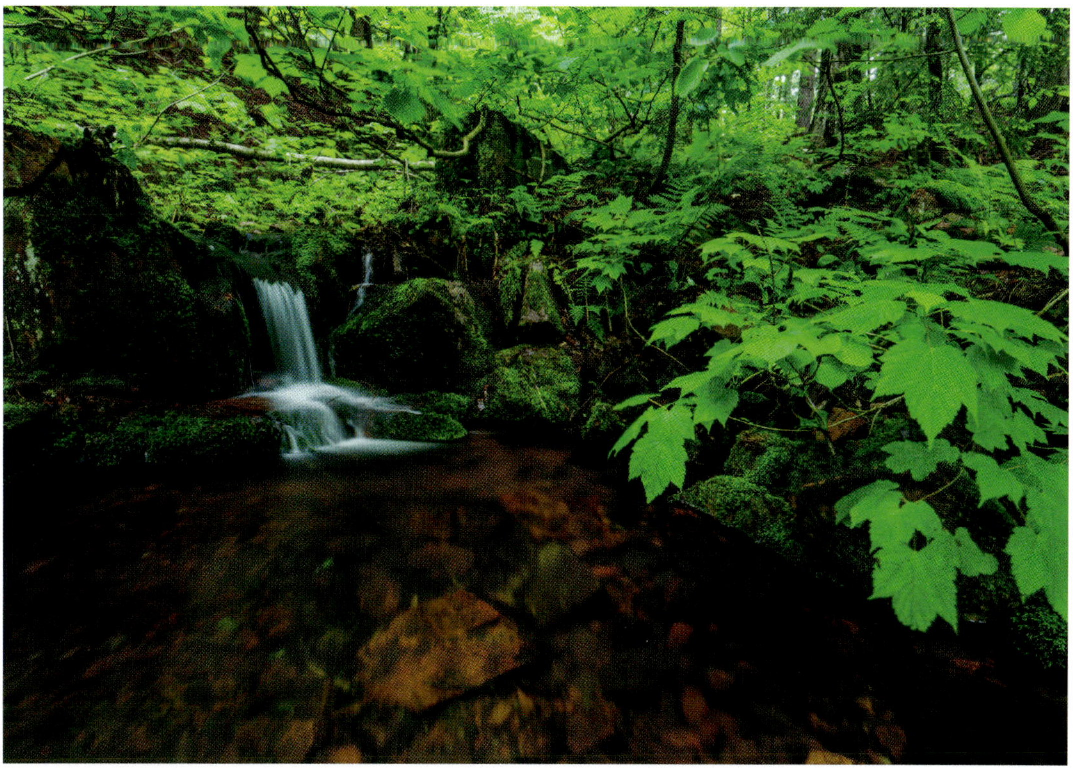

LOST CREEK FALLS #6 (LOST CREEK)

Private

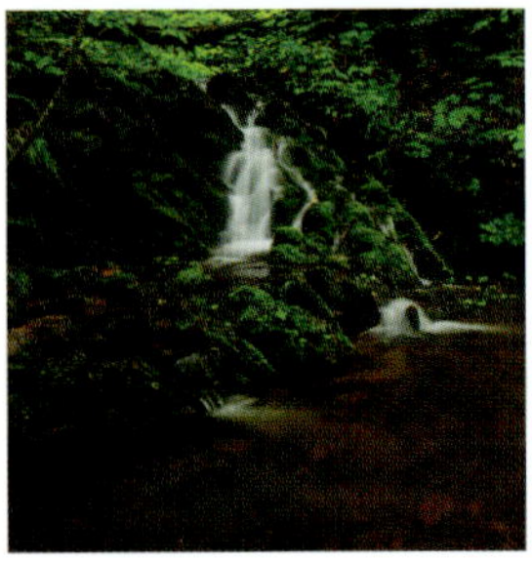

Must See:	5	GPS:	N46 46.122 W89 40.827
Height:	5 feet		
Time:	100-125 minutes	Hiking Information	
		Path:	*Trail then Nothing
Driving Information		Length:	1.06 miles
Signs:	None	Elev. Change:	Moderate
Road:	Secondary	GPS:	Required
Access:	Somewhat Easy	Danger:	Moderate
4WD:	N/A	WP Boots:	Recommended

After taking the short excursion up the unnamed tributary to see the Insistence Falls, head back to Lost Creek and continue up the creek 150 yards to the final drop on Lost Creek. Actually, I am curious about hiking further up the creek. I did search out the next 1/8 mile or so and as the terrain seemed to flatten out I didn't pursue it. After studying a topo map I think that there may be more waterfalls about 500 yards upstream after the creek turns hard to the left (southwest).

The cascading waterfall ends in a somewhat sandy spill pool. A beautiful flat area along the creek is great for viewing the waterfall or having a picnic. Of course, high water would put it under water!

The lush surroundings are so inviting along Lost Creek!

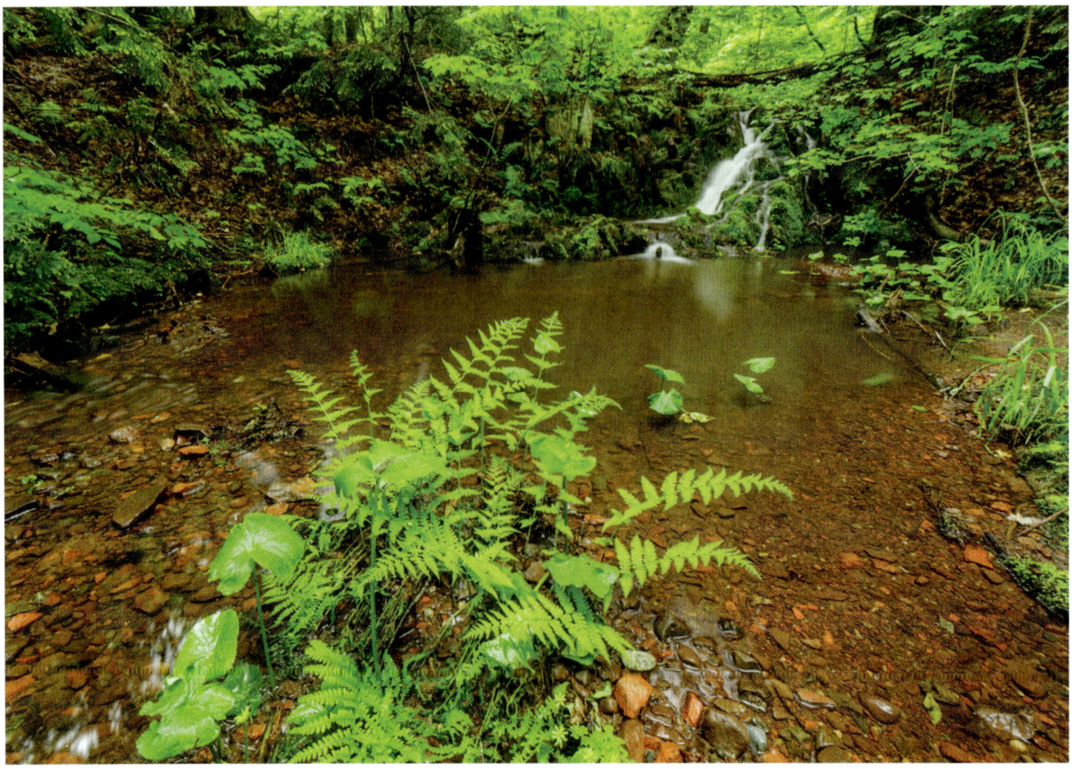

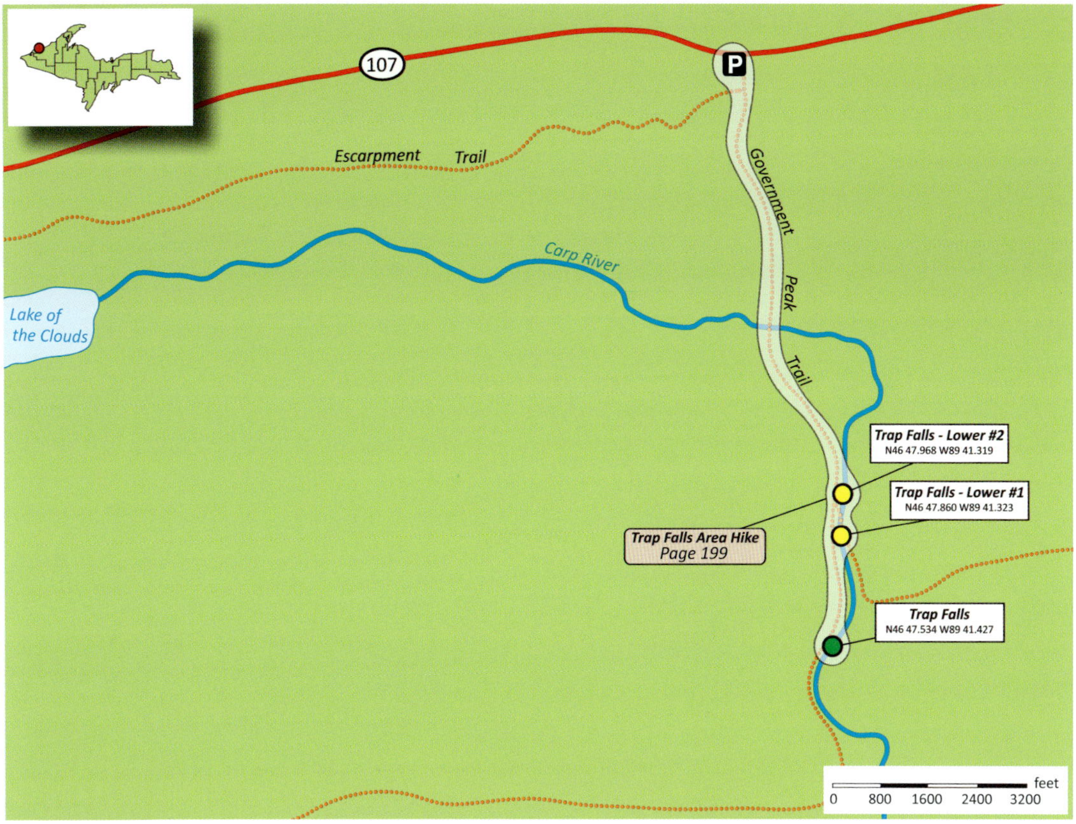

Trap Falls Area Hike

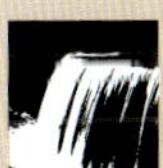

One of my boys went with me on this hike. On our way back from Trap Falls something spooked him and he was sure he kept hearing a wolf as we were photographing the lower falls. He spent so much time looking for the wolf that I'm not sure he ever even took a picture! It is a good reminder that we are not alone in the woods and we need to respect our furred and feathered friends as we enter their environment.

Give yourself some time for this hike. It is a 4 mile round trip hike, but more importantly, the trail winds through an old growth forest with majestic trees on display along the Big Carp River.

Directions: Drive west on M-107 3.5 miles past South Boundary Road. Park at the trailhead for Government Trail. There is a steep climb with rocks underfoot at the beginning of the hike. There are several more climbs toward the end of the 2 mile hike. The trail is well marked and maintained by the Park Service. The hike ends at the falls with a bench for resting and viewing the falls.

TRAP FALLS - LOWER #2 (CARP RIVER)

Private

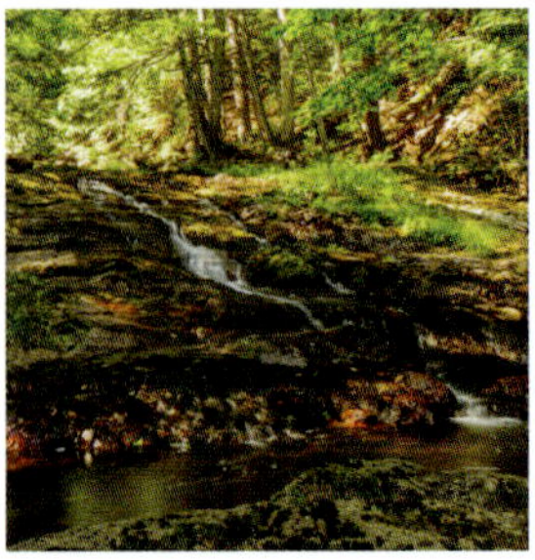

Must See:	5	GPS:	N46 47.968 W89 41.319
Height:	12 feet		
Time:	80-100 minutes	Hiking Information	
		Path:	Semi-improved footpath
Driving Information		Length:	1.42 miles
Signs:	None	Elev. Change:	Moderate
Road:	Secondary	GPS:	Required
Access:	Somewhat Easy	Danger:	Moderate
4WD:	N/A	WP Boots:	Recommended

The river slides down a conglomerate slope, the stones embedded in the rock making rounded protrusions for the water to flow over and around. Three to six foot diameter boulders choke the riverbed downstream. A fallen log at the bottom of the falls offers a great seat for resting - or writing field notes like I am right now!

The river runs down the long slope, looking like there is no riverbed in this low water condition.

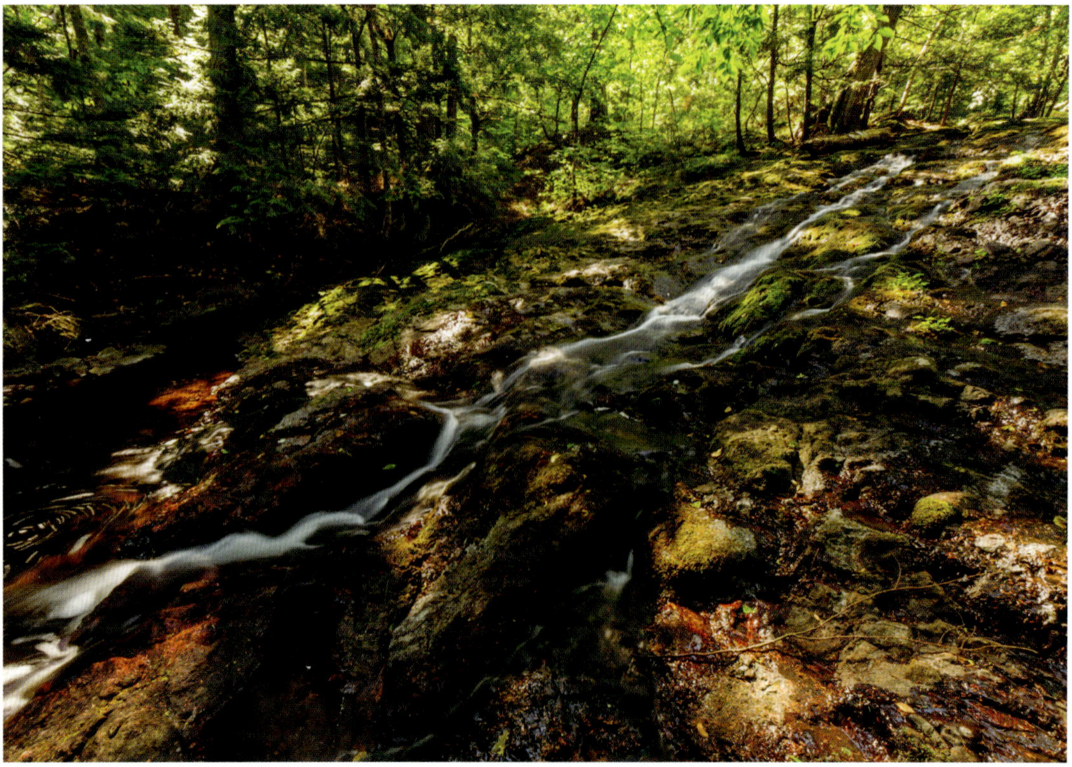

TRAP FALLS - LOWER #1 (CARP RIVER)

Private

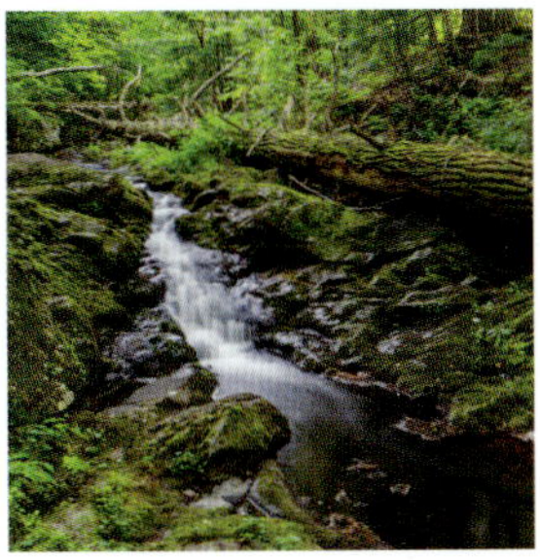

Must See: 5
Height: 4 feet
Time: 90-110 minutes

Driving Information
Signs: None
Road: Secondary
Access: Somewhat Easy
4WD: N/A

GPS: N46 47.860 W89 41.323

Hiking Information
Path: Semi-improved footpath
Length: 1.57 miles
Elev. Change: Moderate
GPS: Required
Danger: Moderate
WP Boots: Recommended

About .4 miles downstream from Trap Falls the river runs through a 6 inch wide channel and cascades down 4 feet over a 15 foot length. Moss covered rocks below the falls offer a great viewing platform.

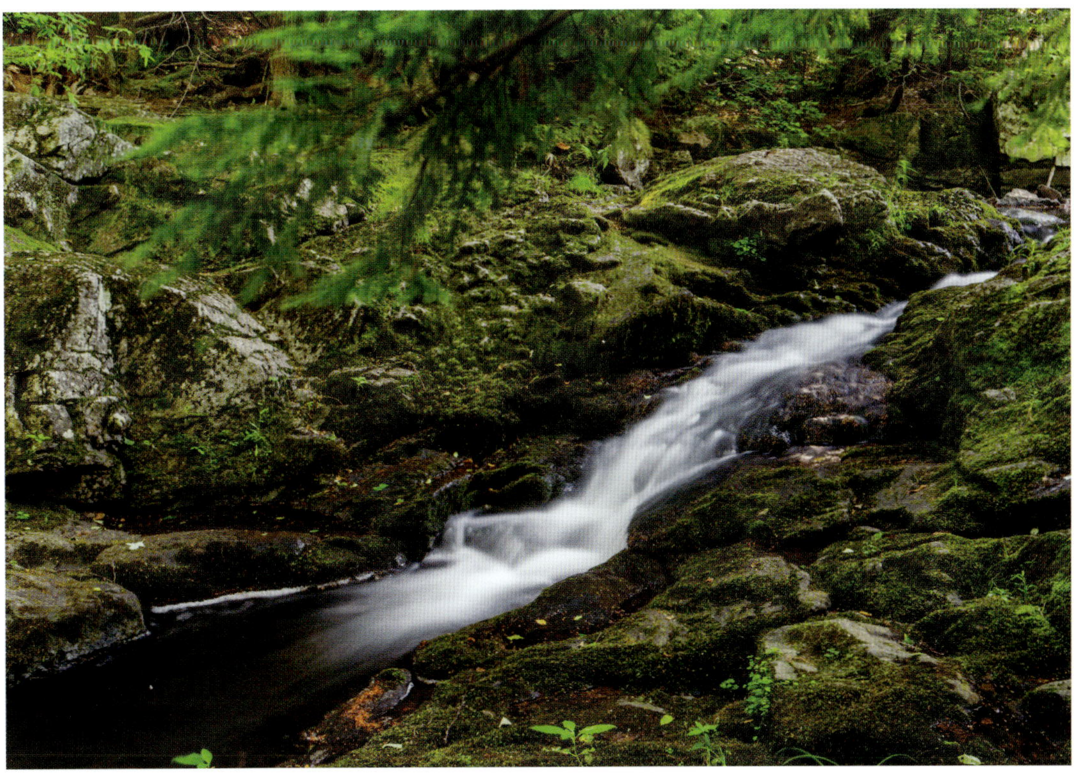

TRAP FALLS (CARP RIVER)

Private

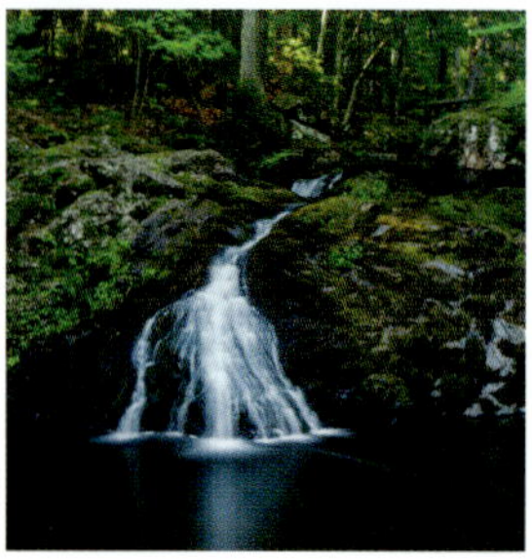

Must See:	8	GPS:	N46 47.534 W89 41.427
Height:	12 feet		
Time:	2-2.5 hours	**Hiking Information**	
		Path:	Semi-improved footpath
Driving Information		Length:	2.01 miles
Signs:	None	Elev. Change:	Moderate
Road:	Secondary	GPS:	Required
Access:	Somewhat Easy	Danger:	Moderate
4WD:	N/A	WP Boots:	Recommended

Government Peak rises to 1850 feet above sea level. Runoff from its slopes gathers in basins on its eastern and western flanks. These open water areas drain to the southeast and combine to form the beginning of the Carp River. After travelling through relatively flat and marshy terrain, the river begins a steeper descent northward through a low point in the middle ridge of the Porkies. About halfway through this descent is Trap Falls. The lower drops occur at the end of this rapid descent. The river then slows down and enters another marshy area extending to Lake of the Clouds and beyond.

Trap Falls is formed when the river narrows down to 1 foot wide as it slides down bedrock, fanning out like a bridal's veil as it makes its way to the bottom of the rock. A wonderful spill pool dominates the area below the falls before returning to the rock strewn river. This is a great picnic area. From this natural viewing area the waterfall presents itself beautifully with a head-on view.

Trap Falls is also known as Epidote Falls

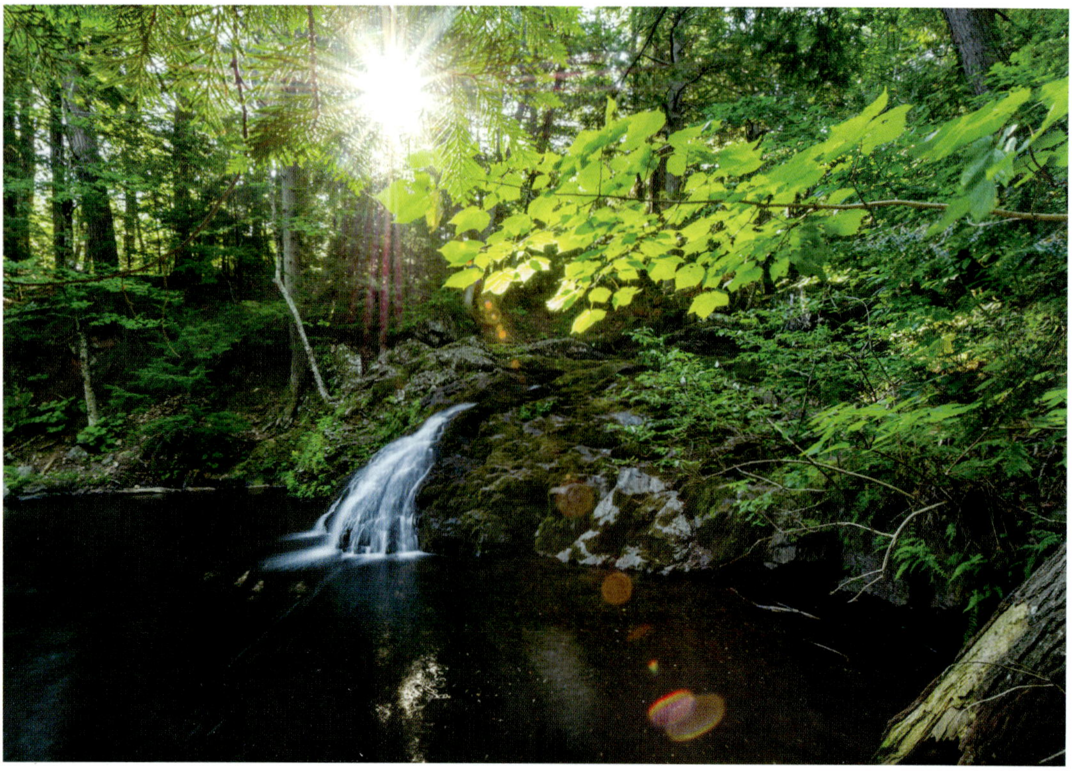

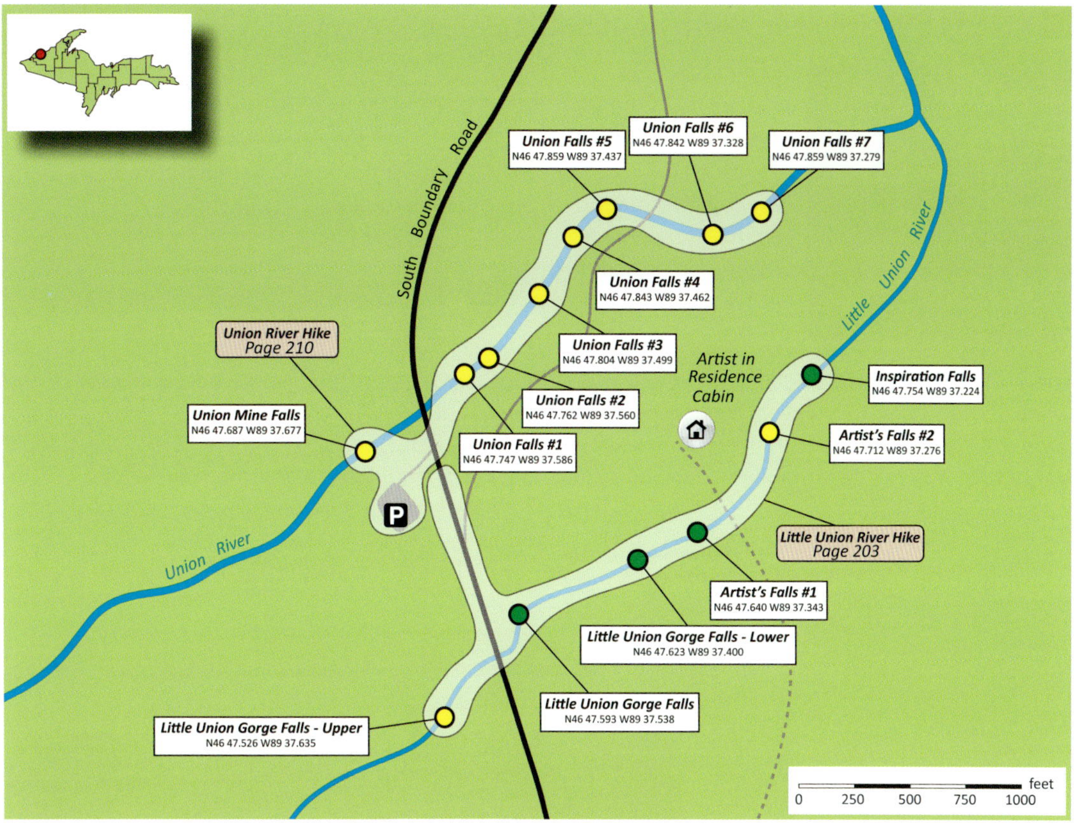

Little Union River Hike

The Little Union River originates between the slopes of the first two mountains on the eastern end of the southern ridge. There is no marshy land along the length of the Little Union River, so as soon as rain falls or snow melts, it rapidly evacuates the slopes, funnels down the river and is gone. Wetlands act as sponges that soak up excess moisture, slowly releasing it back to the waterways and thus moderating the volume of water that flows. Since The Little Union River is lacking this feature, it tends to be a "feast or famine" river. In dry conditions there may be no water at all in the river, the waterfalls looking like stubby rocky cliffs and the riverbed a worn, wide walkway filled with smooth rock. But, in the spring as the snow is melting, or during a rainy season, the waterfalls come to life and transform this river into a waterfall bonanza!

Directions: Turn South on South Boundary Road off of M-107. Drive south for 1.7 miles to the Union Mine Trailhead on the right (west). Pull into the short drive and park in one of the many parking spots. There are often vehicles here, as this is the sole hiking trail access point on the eastern side of the park that leads to the network of trails that crisscross the Porcupine Mountains. Hike back to the road and follow the far side to the south for about 250 yards. A narrow footpath parts the roadside grass and enters the forest. (If the river is running well the Little Union Gorge Falls can be heard distinctly from the road.) The trail leads past the first two waterfalls before cutting across to the Union River. When it veers away from the river leave the path and stay by the Little Union River to see the rest of the falls. After viewing the falls on the eastern side of South Boundary Road don't forget to check out the upper falls on the west side as well. Hike south on South Boundary Road to where the river runs through a culvert beneath the road. Head down through the overgrown ditch and follow the river 150 yards to the falls.

LITTLE UNION GORGE FALLS (LITTLE UNION RIVER)

Private

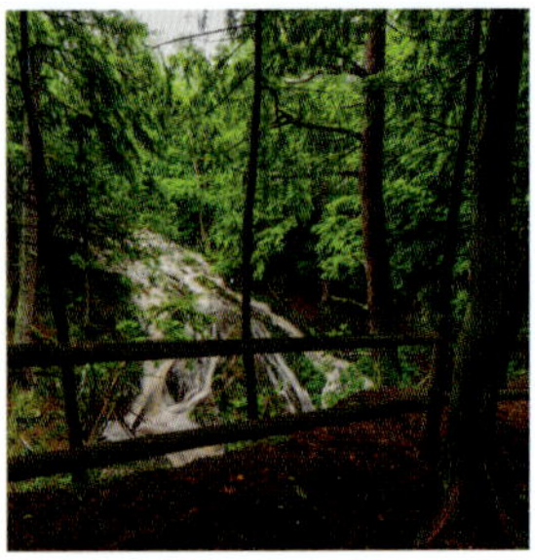

Must See:	7	GPS:	N46 47.593 W89 37.538
Height:	50 feet		
Time:	10-20 minutes	Hiking Information	
		Path:	Semi-improved footpath
Driving Information		Length:	.18 miles
Signs:	None	Elev. Change:	Slight
Road:	Secondary	GPS:	N/A
Access:	Somewhat Easy	Danger:	Slight
4WD:	N/A	WP Boots:	N/A

The 30 foot wide riverbed slides down into the 40 foot deep Little Union Gorge perpendicular to the steep gorge wall. The viewing area with a bench and wooden guard rails is located at the top of the gorge. This works out wonderfully, as the waterfall is viewed head-on as it tumbles down the steeply slanted far wall of the gorge and then turns hard to the left and races along the narrow base of the gorge.

A mature forest maintains a thick canopy overhead. Large hemlock trunks stand tall while soft needles cushion the mostly level ground below.

Note: This is a seasonal waterfall. During dry periods the Little Union River can completely stop running.

When the river flows with a good amount of water, the waterfall is beautiful, fanning out like a peacock displaying its colors!

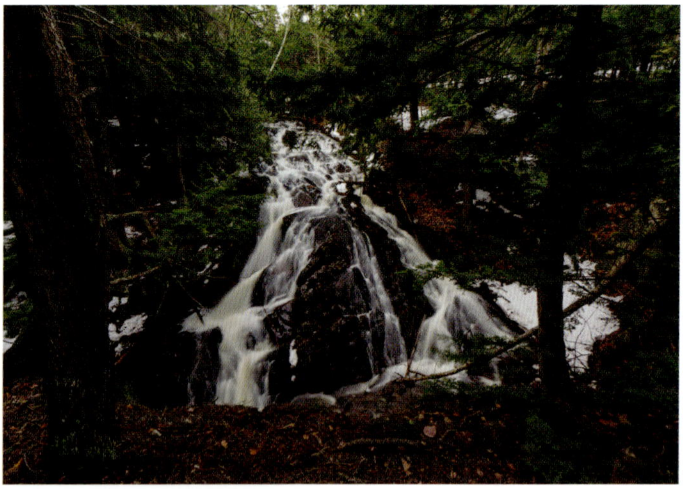

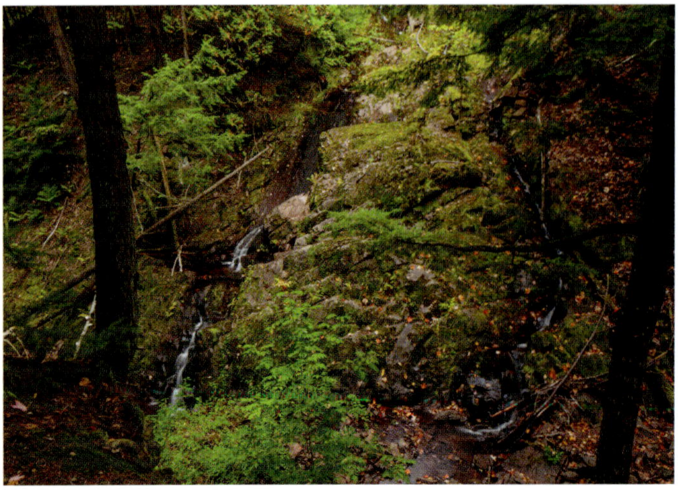

Too often, the Little Union River dries up and becomes a mere ghost of its former self. I have seen this riverbed with no water at all flowing, even less than is shown in this picture which is nearly the same view as the shot shown just above!

LITTLE UNION GORGE FALLS - LOWER (LITTLE UNION RIVER) Private

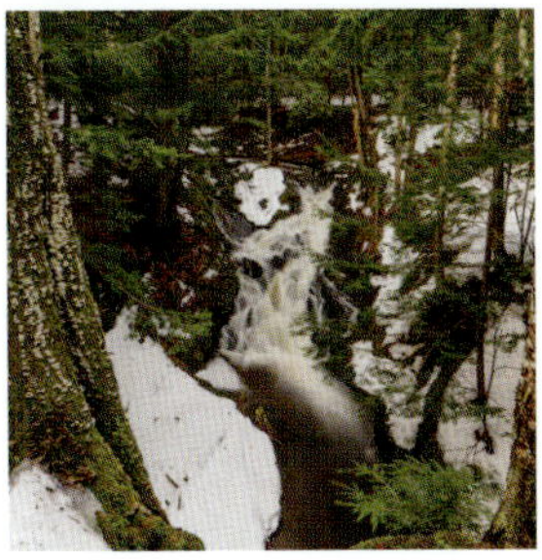

Must See:	7	GPS:	N46 47.623 W89 37.400
Height:	18 feet		
Time:	15-25 minutes	Hiking Information	
		Path:	Semi-improved footpath
Driving Information		Length:	.28 miles
Signs:	None	Elev. Change:	Slight
Road:	Secondary	GPS:	Helpful
Access:	Somewhat Easy	Danger:	Slight
4WD:	N/A	WP Boots:	N/A

The footpath that begins at the road runs along the top of the ravine with the Little Union River down at the bottom. It passes by Little Union Gorge Falls and this, the Lower Falls before cutting to the north to meet up with the Union River and then looping back to the parking lot near the Union Mine ruins. To continue on this hike, follow the riverbed down river. There is undergrowth and uneven footing for the rest of the hike.

The fifteen foot riverbed couched between ten foot rock walls drops down suddenly another eighteen feet before turning hard to the left as it continues downstream. A viewing area with wooden guard rails is situated on top of the vertical cliff that faces the waterfall. A mining shaft from 1846, sunk by the Boston and North American Mining Company, is enclosed by that same guard rail. It is about six by eight feet across and fifteen feet deep. They were attempting to establish a profitable copper mine here. They failed. This is all that remains of that venture. And yet, the same waterfall that greeted those miners of yesteryear with its calming presence continues to bring joy and tranquility to those that seek it out today!

Note: This is a seasonal waterfall. During dry periods the Little Union River can completely stop running.

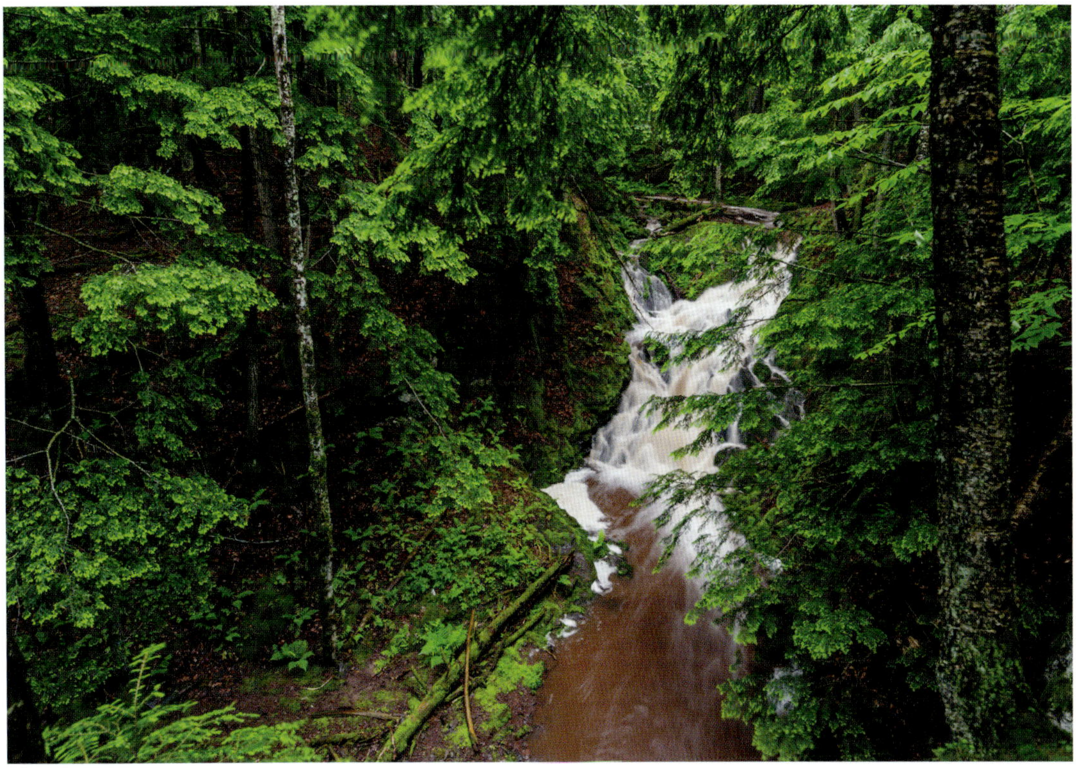

ARTISTS FALLS #1 (LITTLE UNION RIVER)

Private

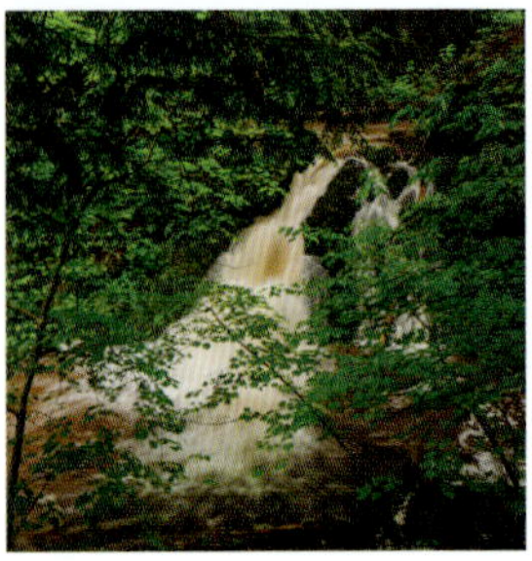

Must See:	7	GPS:	N46 47.640 W89 37.343
Height:	10 feet		
Time:	25-40 minutes	Hiking Information	
		Path:	None
Driving Information		Length:	.34 miles
Signs:	None	Elev. Change:	Moderate
Road:	Secondary	GPS:	Helpful
Access:	Somewhat Easy	Danger:	Slight
4WD:	N/A	WP Boots:	Helpful

After leaving the nice footpath that leads from South Boundary Road to the first two waterfalls on the hike, leave the path and follow the river downstream to the rest of the falls. To view this waterfall more intimately, continue downstream past the waterfall and canyon until it is safe to climb down to the river's edge. Head back up river to the waterfall, this time down inside the shallow canyon!

A narrow crevasse at the top of the falls pours the river down the face of basalt in a slight zig-zag pattern. A spill pool 30 feet wide sits at the bottom of the nearly encircled, oval shaped canyon with fifteen foot walls. The back half of the floor is covered with small stones, making for great picnic and viewing areas.

Thimbleberries in July are working on becoming delicious berries ready to be picked in August! This patch (seen below) drinks up water from the Little Union River below the falls. This fickle river in Porcupine Mountains State Park changes from a wonderful waterfall paradise to a dry riverbed over the course of most summers. Check with the Park Rangers for current conditions.

Note: This is a seasonal waterfall. During dry periods the Little Union River can completely stop running.

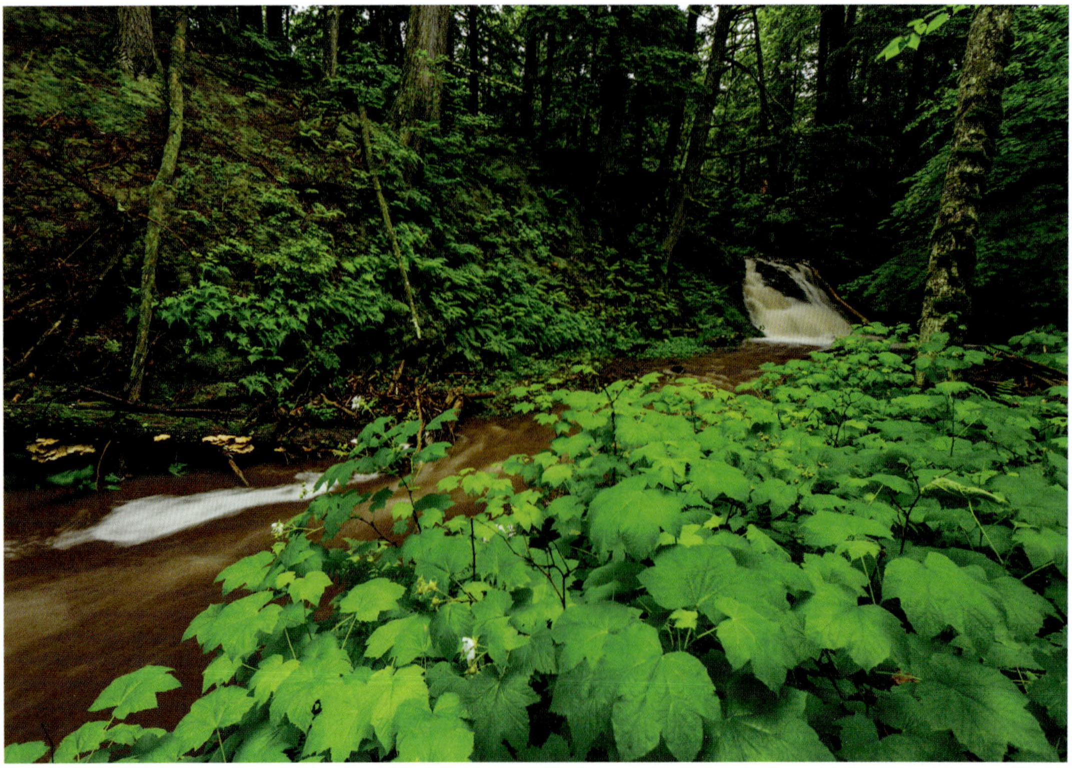

ARTISTS FALLS #2 (LITTLE UNION RIVER)

Private

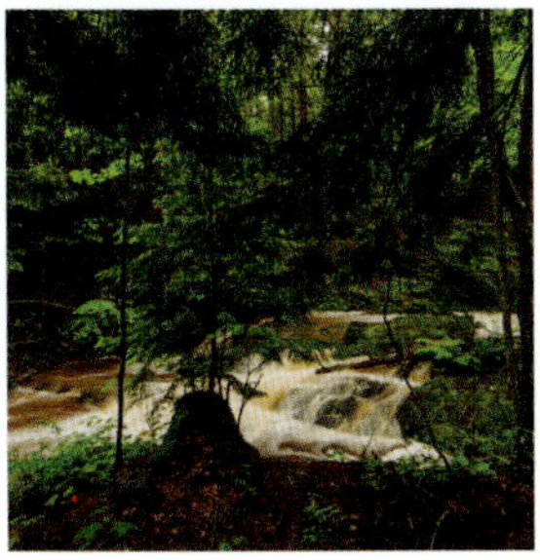

Must See:	6	GPS:	N46 47.712 W89 37.276
Height:	10 feet		
Time:	30-50 minutes	Hiking Information	
		Path:	None
Driving Information		Length:	.44 miles
Signs:	None	Elev. Change:	Moderate
Road:	Secondary	GPS:	Helpful
Access:	Somewhat Easy	Danger:	Moderate
4WD:	N/A	WP Boots:	Helpful

The quaint *Artist in Residence* cabin, the temporary home for artists that have been chosen to participate in the Park's *Artist in Residence* program, is nearby. A charming swing overlooks the falls while the faint smell of wood smoke wafts gently in the breeze.

The narrow, channeled river at the top of the falls broadens out and divides halfway down around a misshapen mass of bedrock. The river then continues in a 20 foot wide riverbed full of smallish, red tinged gray rocks.

Note: This is a seasonal waterfall. During dry periods the Little Union River can completely stop running.

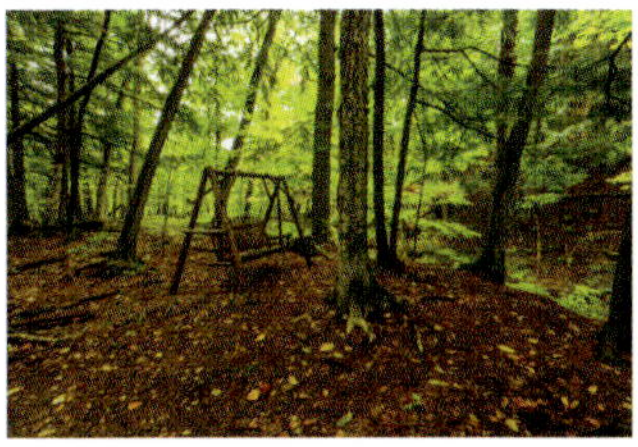

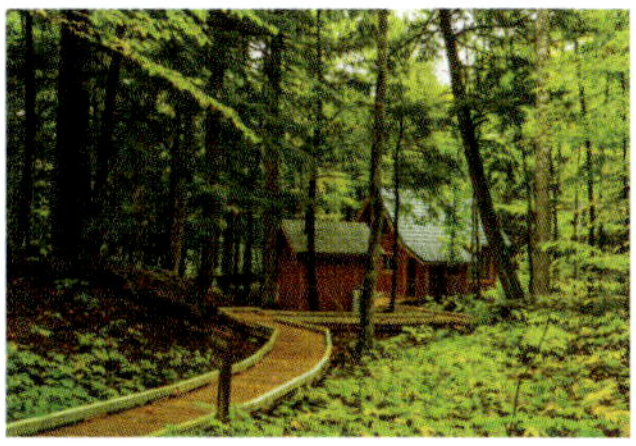

Note the thimbleberries again. I love these tart, delicate red berries! Late August hikes can be delicious. Most thimbleberries are found from Marquette to Ironwood and north up the Keweenaw Peninsula.

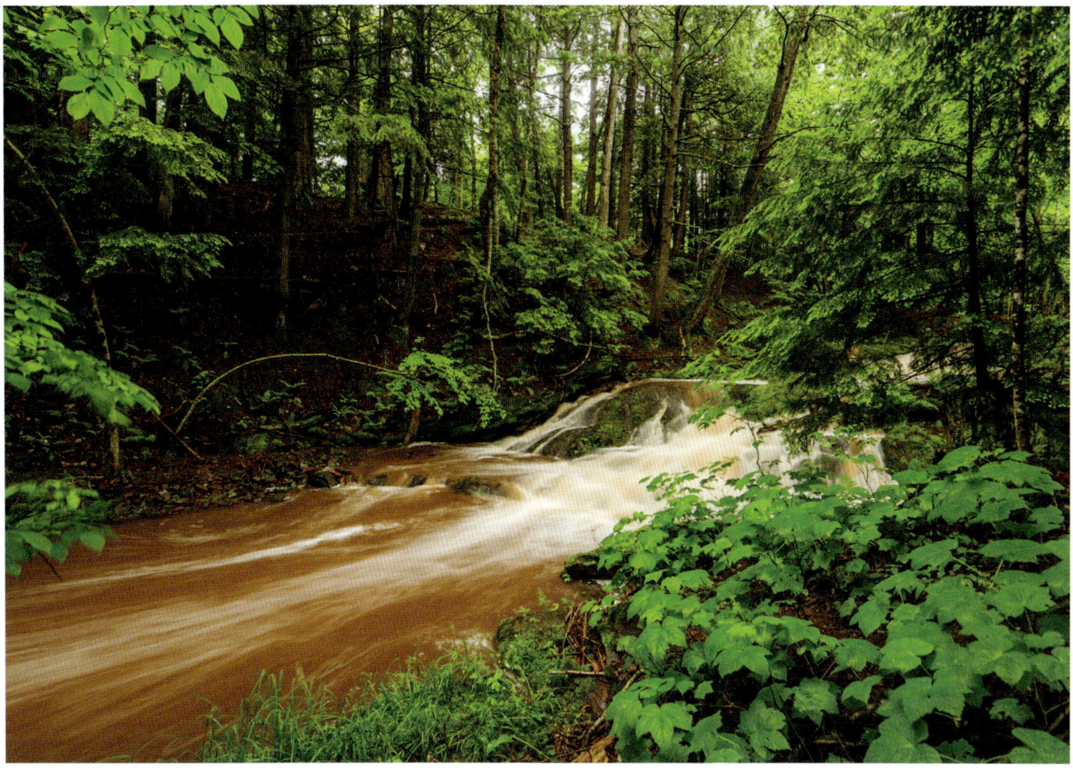

INSPIRATION FALLS (LITTLE UNION RIVER)

Private

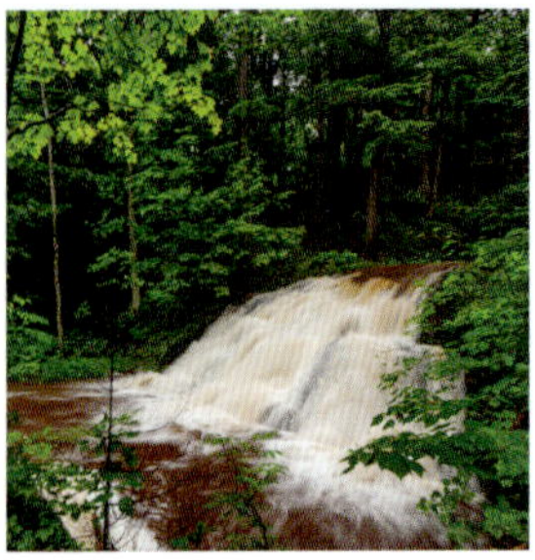

Must See:	9	GPS:	N46 47.754 W89 37.224
Height:	21 feet		
Time:	45-70 minutes	Hiking Information	
		Path:	None
Driving Information		Length:	.51 miles
Signs:	None	Elev. Change:	Moderate
Road:	Secondary	GPS:	Helpful
Access:	Somewhat Easy	Danger:	Moderate
4WD:	N/A	WP Boots:	Helpful

The first time I happened upon this set of waterfalls was August 29, 2011. I had hiked over from Union River and found a dry riverbed. I walked right up the middle of the rock strewn "waterway". When I saw this set of 3 drops I could only imagine what it would look like with water pouring over the ledges! Every time I was in the Porcupine Mountains afterwards I would check the river to see if there was water flowing. Finally, during a surprisingly early spring melt in 2012, I was overjoyed to finally be able to photograph the waterfalls along the Little Union River on March 16, 2012! The photos with lush greenery were taken on July 9, 2013.

The small river slides down a sheet of basalt in a 3-tiered slide. The first slide is 10 feet, the second is 7 feet and the third drops 4 feet. The three are so close together that I have included them together as a single waterfall.

Note: This is a seasonal waterfall. During dry periods the Little Union River can completely stop running.

This is the first of the three drops. Try to imagine it with NO water!

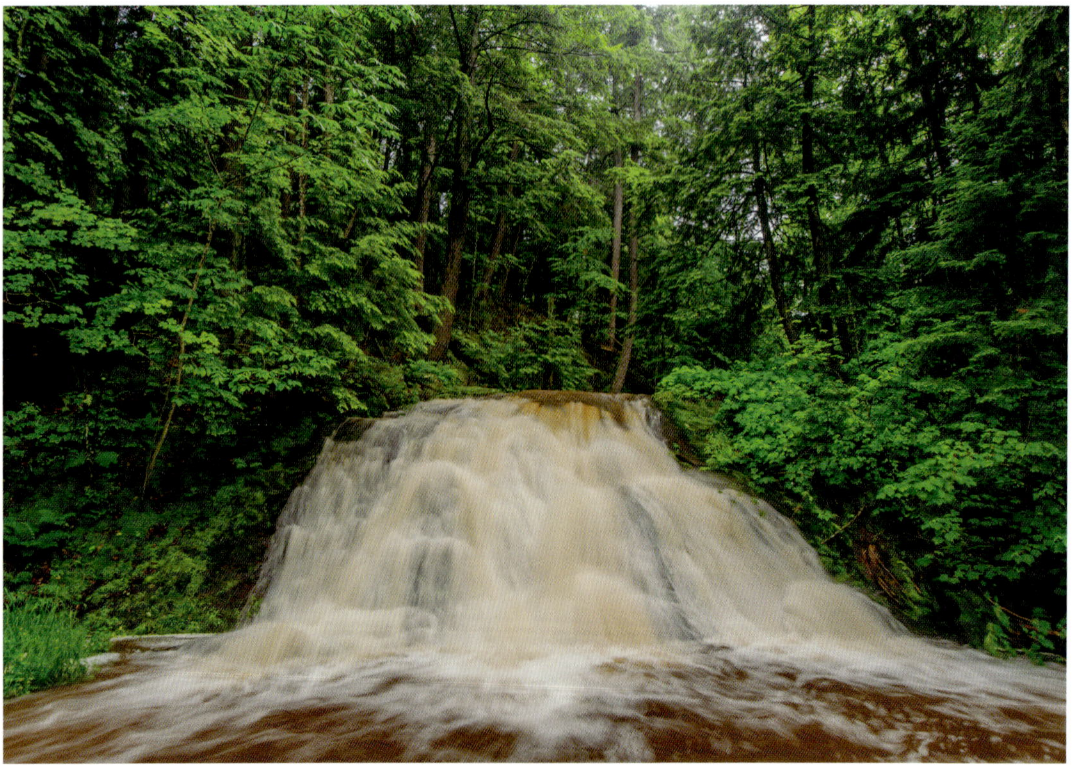

LITTLE UNION GORGE FALLS - UPPER (LITTLE UNION RIVER) Private

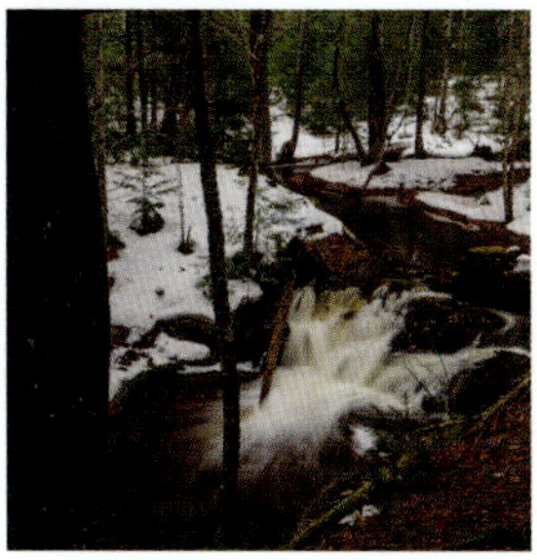

Must See:	6	GPS:	N46 47.526 W89 37.635
Height:	6 feet		
Time:	45-65 minutes	Hiking Information	
		Path:	None
Driving Information		Length:	.27 miles
Signs:	None	Elev. Change:	Moderate
Road:	Secondary	GPS:	Helpful
Access:	Somewhat Easy	Danger:	Moderate
4WD:	N/A	WP Boots:	Helpful

After hiking downstream to the 5 waterfalls on the east side of South Boundary Road, retrace your route back upstream to the road. Follow the road south until finding where the road crosses the river. Climb down through the somewhat steep bank on the west side of the road and hike 150 yards along the north side of the river to the Upper Falls.

The river makes a large, looping S-curve. The falls are in the middle of the second bend and are easily observed from the elevated, undergrowth free, flat bank.

Note: This is a seasonal waterfall. During dry periods the Little Union River can completely stop running.

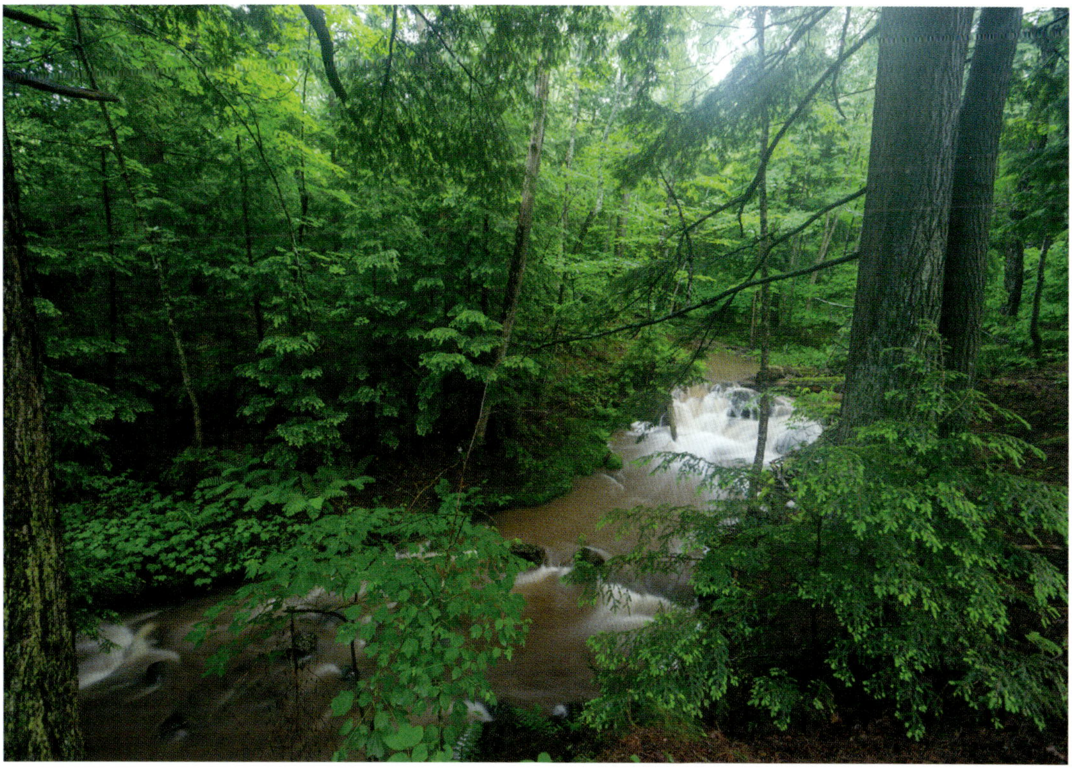

Union River Hike

In 1846 the Union Copper Company began a mining operation along the Union River. Although copper and some silver was mined here, it was not profitable and after a second brief resumption of activities during the Civil war, the mine was closed. In 1908 the Calumet and Hecla Mining Company confirmed the infeasibility of the mine. No further activity has taken place since then.

A one mile self guided interpretive trail beginning near the parking area provides glimpses into the mining activity along the Union River. Hiking along the river to view the waterfalls utilizes some of this trail.

Directions: Use the same driving directions as the Little Union River Hike. Hike northwest to the Union Mine ruins via the interpretive trail. The waterfall here is the only one on the Union River that is on this side of South Boundary Road. After viewing it, follow the interpretive trail to the northeast and across the road. The trail stays on the high ground, offering views of the river and waterfalls running through the gorge below. There are obvious places to climb down to the river's edge along the way. Be careful, as these can be steep and slippery!

(Note: Optional way to include the Little Union River Hike.) After viewing Union Falls #7, hike cross country to Inspiration Falls. There is a trail that connects the two rivers, but it requires a lot of backtracking, so I prefer to just "connect the dots" between these downstream waterfalls. (Remember, the Little Union River is temperamental and may have very little water flowing.)

UNION MINE FALLS (UNION RIVER)

Private

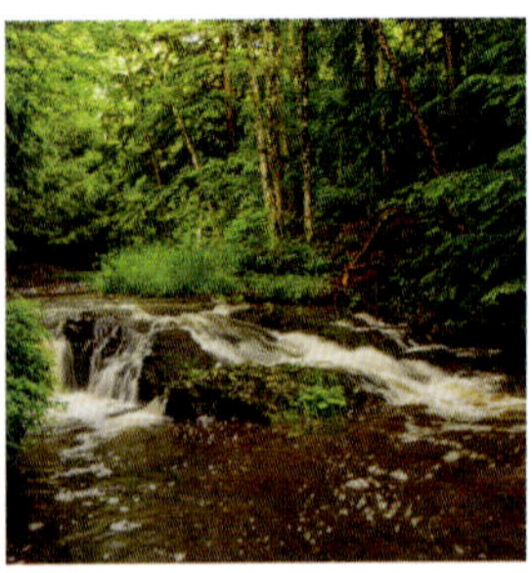

Must See:	4	GPS:	N46 47.687 W89 37.677
Height:	3 feet		
Time:	10-15 minutes	Hiking Information	
		Path:	Footpath
Driving Information		Length:	75 yards
Signs:	None	Elev. Change:	Moderate
Road:	Secondary	GPS:	Helpful
Access:	Somewhat Easy	Danger:	Moderate
4WD:	N/A	WP Boots:	N/A

The Union Mine was started here in 1846. They dammed the river upstream and carved out the left side of the waterfall to fit a paddle wheel into the river. The dam and paddle wheel have long since gone, but the waterfall lives on!

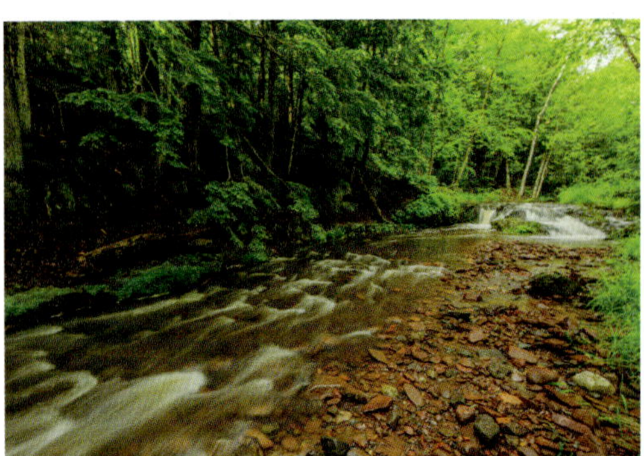

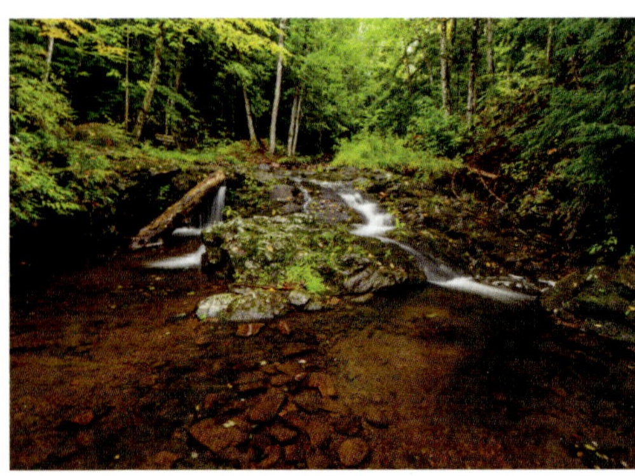

UNION FALLS #1 (UNION RIVER)

Private

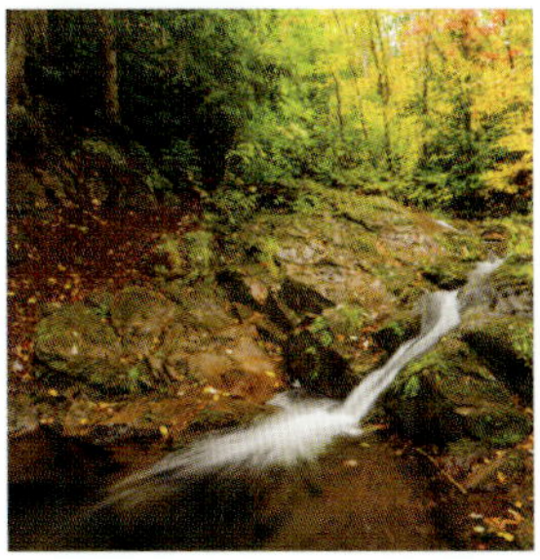

Must See:	4	GPS:	N46 47.747 W89 37.586
Height:	14 feet		
Time:	20-30 minutes	**Hiking Information**	
		Path:	Footpath
Driving Information		Length:	.15 miles
Signs:	None	Elev. Change:	Moderate
Road:	Secondary	GPS:	Helpful
Access:	Somewhat Easy	Danger:	Moderate
4WD:	N/A	WP Boots:	Helpful

Just 200 feet downstream from South Boundary Road, this is the first of the falls that start coming in rapid succession. The interpretive trail follows the top of the ravine above the river. It is an easy hike if staying up there. Plan on a short but steep climb down to the river otherwise!

At first glance these two pictures might seem to be different rivers! Not so. This is the same waterfall as seen in different seasons and with greatly varied water-flows!

The waterfall begins with a 5 foot cascade dumping into an 8 foot long triangular shaped spill pool. It then funnels down to a 1 foot wide channel, sliding down another 4 feet to a second, larger pool. The river divides and cascades down another 4 feet to the river below.

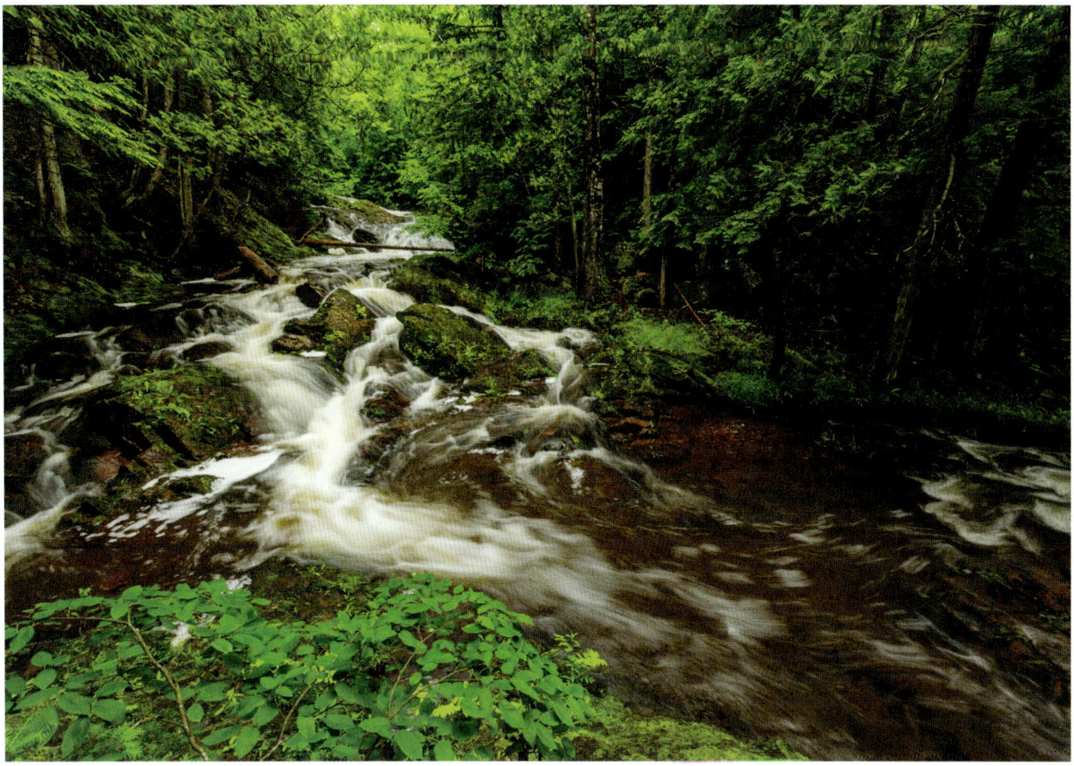

UNION FALLS #2 (UNION RIVER)

Private

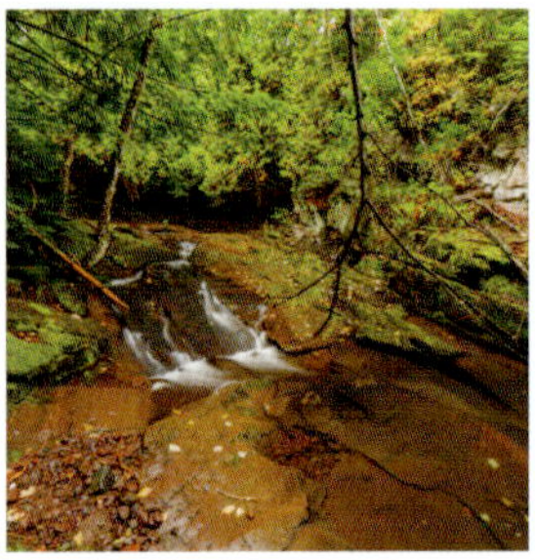

Must See:	5	GPS:	N46 47.762 W89 37.560
Height:	10 feet		
Time:	25-35 minutes	Hiking Information	
		Path:	Footpath
Driving Information		Length:	.19 miles
Signs:	None	Elev. Change:	Moderate
Road:	Secondary	GPS:	Helpful
Access:	Somewhat Easy	Danger:	Moderate
4WD:	N/A	WP Boots:	Helpful

A mere 150 feet downstream from #1, the river drops again in a series of cascades, with the last (and the largest) dropping 2 feet into an almond shaped cavity in the riverbed. A 2 foot slide follows. The river then abruptly turns 90 degrees to the right beneath a 20 foot vertical wall. The falls end with a fanned out 5 foot slide.

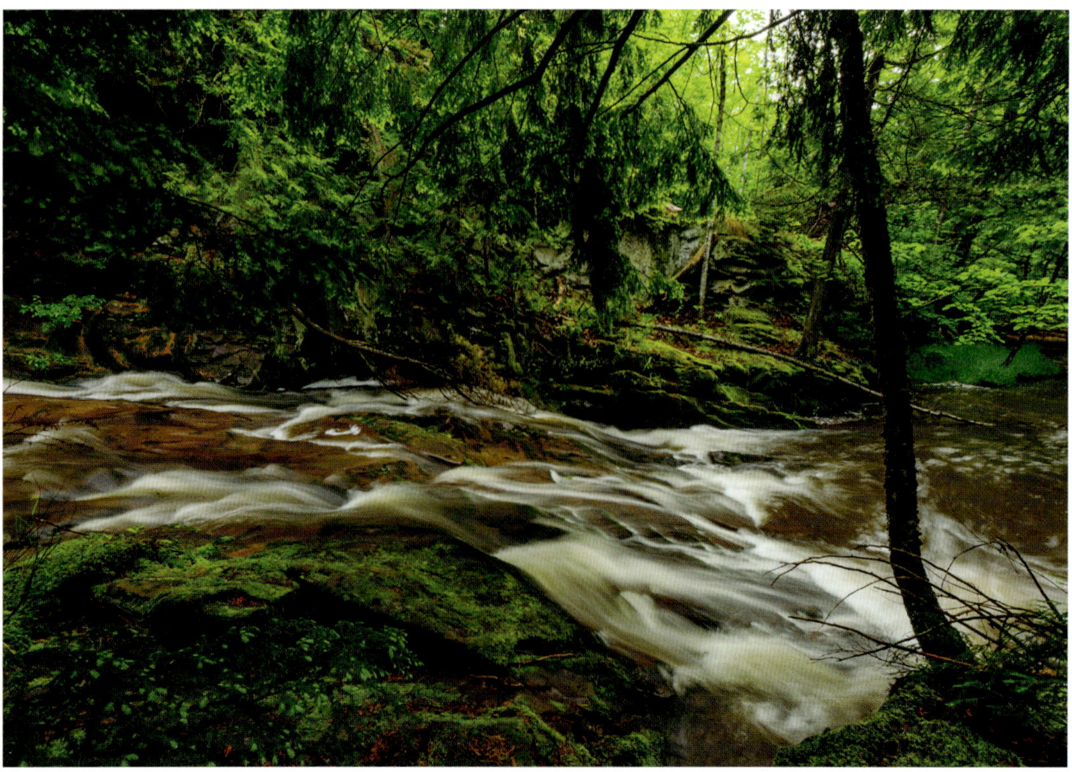

UNION FALLS #3 (UNION RIVER)

Private

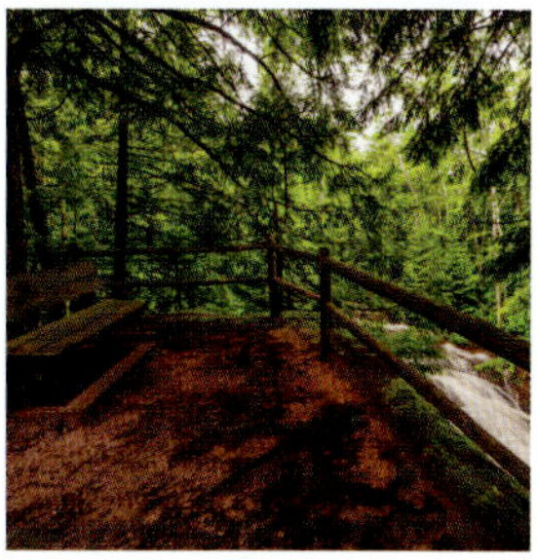

Must See:	5	GPS:	N46 47.804 W89 37.499
Height:	12 feet		
Time:	30-45 minutes	**Hiking Information**	
		Path:	Footpath
Driving Information		Length:	.28 miles
Signs:	None	Elev. Change:	Moderate
Road:	Secondary	GPS:	Helpful
Access:	Somewhat Easy	Danger:	Moderate
4WD:	N/A	WP Boots:	Helpful

Peeled layers of basalt offer a smooth surface for the river to glide down. Several quiet pools, separated by protruding ribs of bedrock provide a safe haven for minnows. The Union Mine Trail overlooks this waterfall from atop a 20 foot high cliff. A strategically placed bench offers a rest for the feet as well as a lovely scenic view before continuing down the trail.

Note the wooden rail at the top of the cliff. The thumbnail shot was taken from up there.

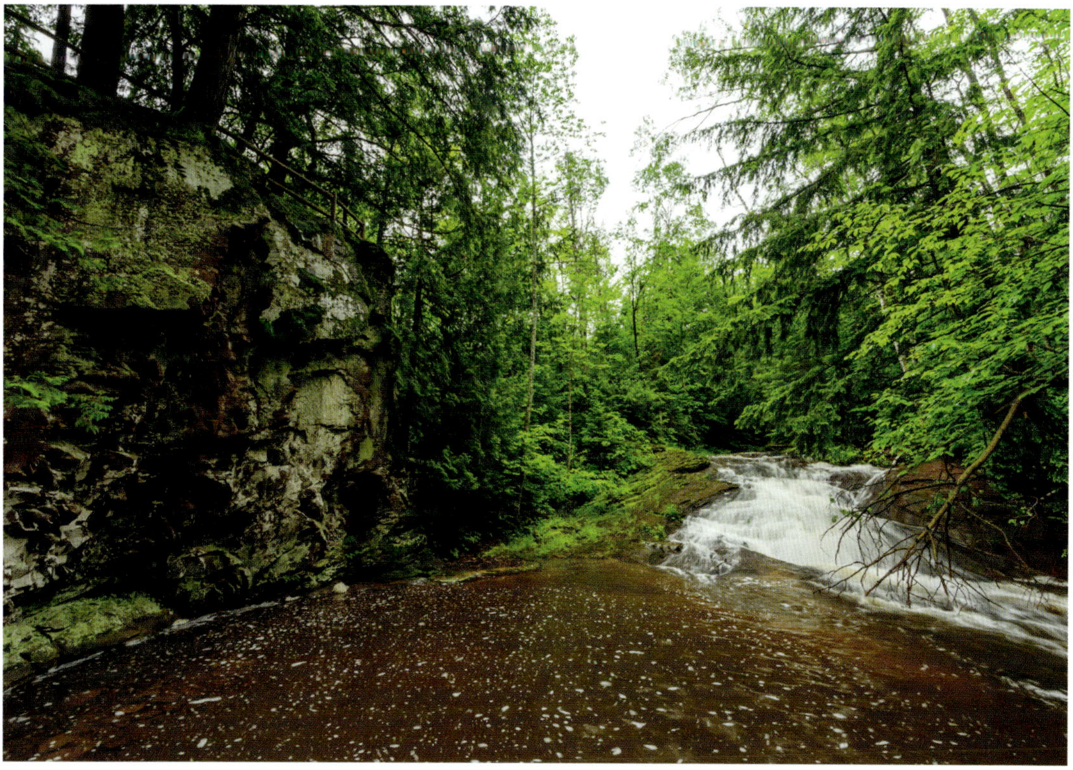

UNION FALLS #4 (UNION RIVER)

Private

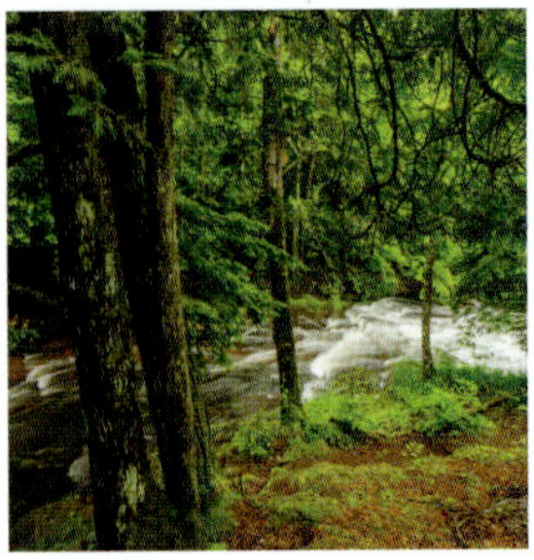

Must See:	6	GPS:	N46 47.843 W89 37.462
Height:	20 feet		
Time:	35-50 minutes	Hiking Information	
		Path:	Footpath
Driving Information		Length:	.33 miles
Signs:	None	Elev. Change:	Moderate
Road:	Secondary	GPS:	Helpful
Access:	Somewhat Easy	Danger:	Moderate
4WD:	N/A	WP Boots:	Helpful

The banks along the river start to lower in this area as the river slowly exits the ravine. The river rushes down a nearly continuous 200 foot long slide, falling about 20 feet in this distance. Access to the riverbed is easier with gentler declines and banks that are widening out a little.

The continuing rapids below Union Falls #4 are beautiful. Be sure to enjoy this waterfall from afar as well as up close!

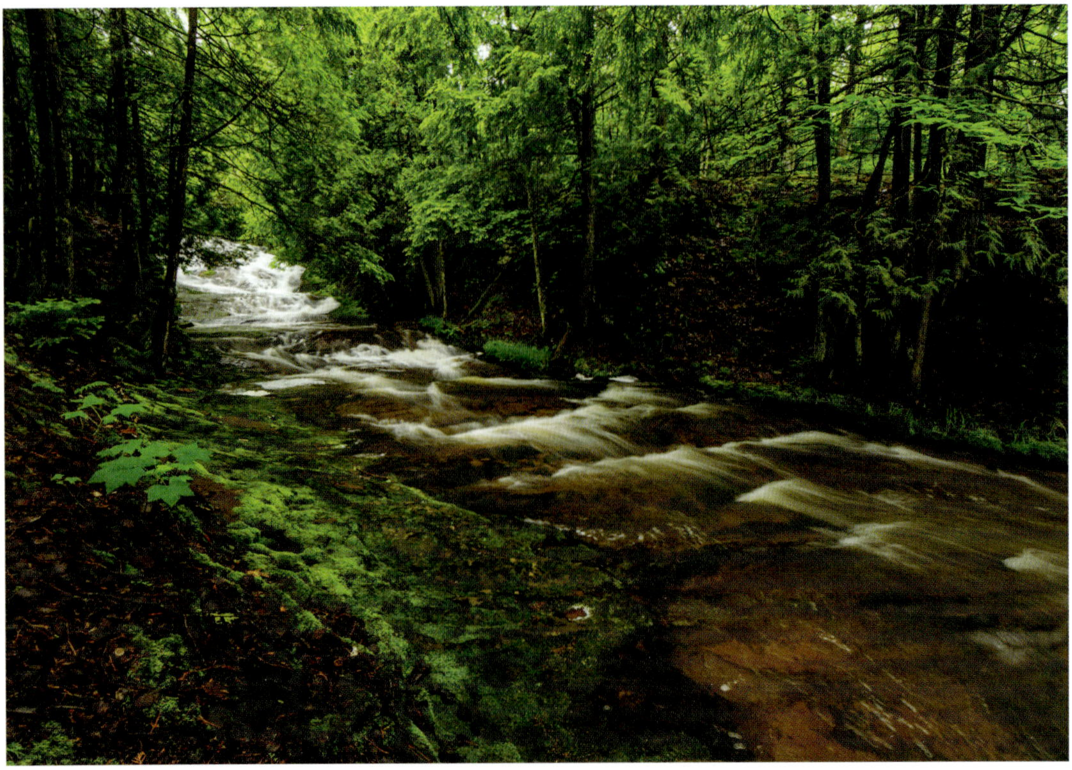

UNION FALLS #5 (UNION RIVER)

Private

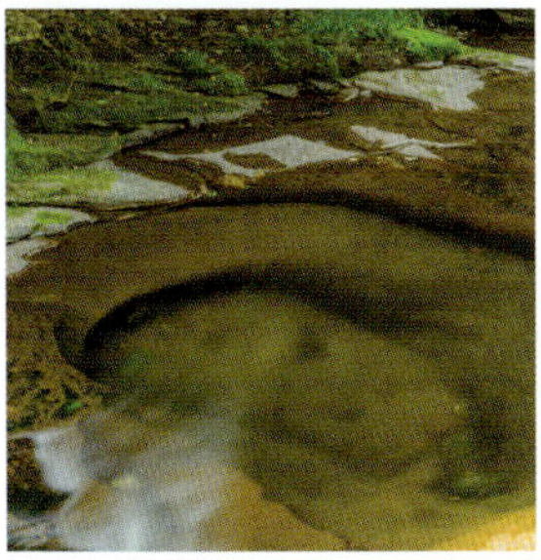

Must See:	5	GPS:	N46 47.859 W89 37.437
Height:	20 feet		
Time:	40-60 minutes	**Hiking Information**	
		Path:	Footpath
Driving Information		Length:	.36 miles
Signs:	None	Elev. Change:	Moderate
Road:	Secondary	GPS:	Helpful
Access:	Somewhat Easy	Danger:	Moderate
4WD:	N/A	WP Boots:	Helpful

This is the last waterfall before the river turns hard to the east/southeast from the northeasterly path it had been on. This waterfall follows closely on the heels of the #4 falls. It is a steeper and shorter slide than #4. A uniquely shaped pool is found at the base of the slide. (See the lower photo) It looks something like a stretched out french curve, with concentric rings in the center of the pool forming a smaller and deeper pool. (See top photo)

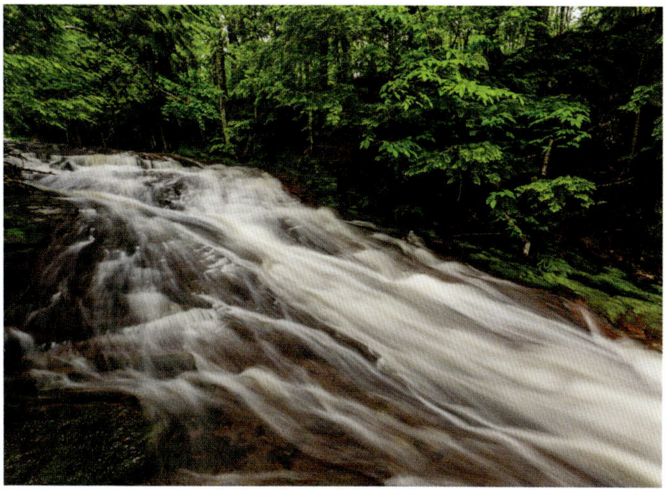

These two lower pictures are good examples of the variability of water flow rates on the Union River.

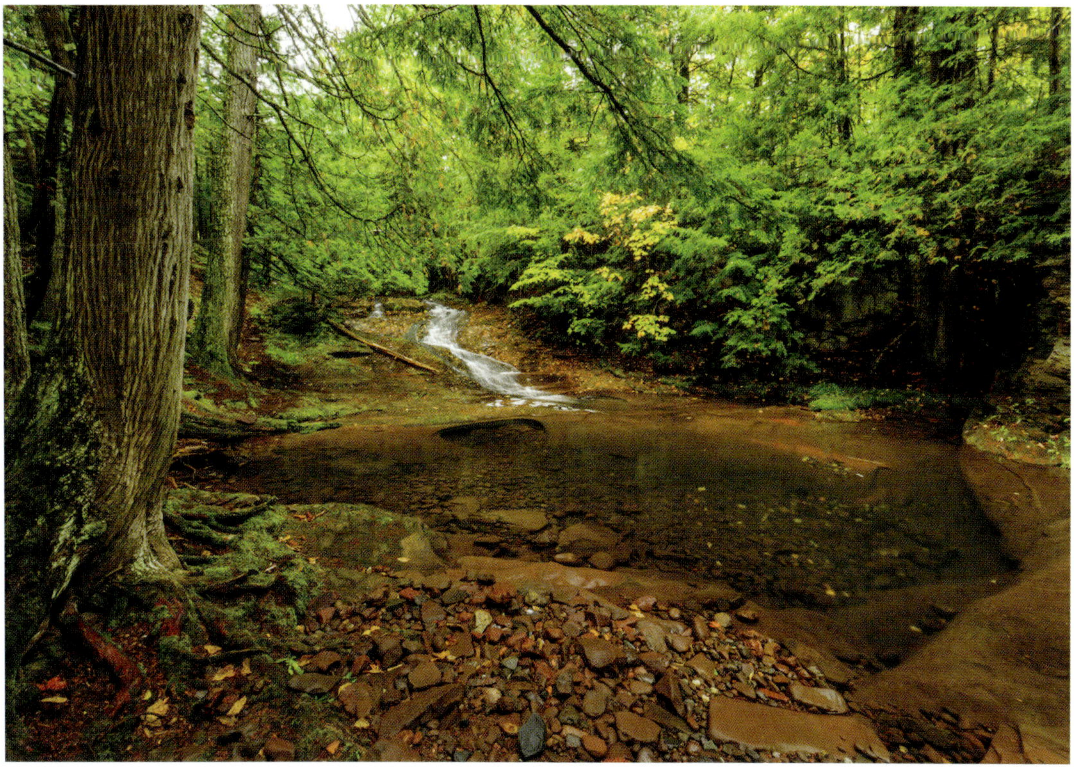

UNION FALLS #6 (UNION RIVER)

Private

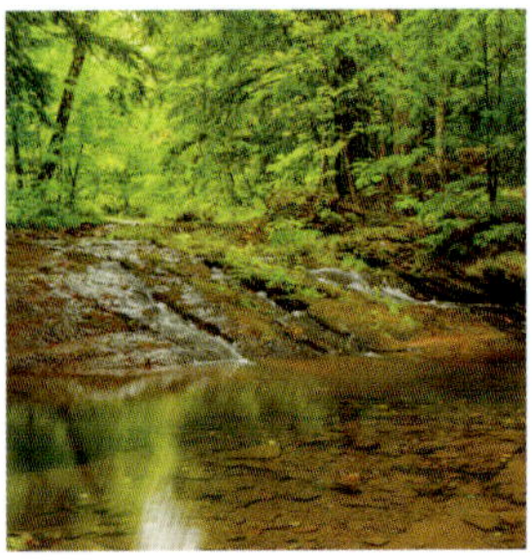

Must See:	5	GPS:	N46 47.842 W89 37.328
Height:	5 feet		
Time:	50-70 minutes	Hiking Information	
		Path:	Footpath
Driving Information		Length:	.45 miles
Signs:	None	Elev. Change:	Moderate
Road:	Secondary	GPS:	Helpful
Access:	Somewhat Easy	Danger:	Moderate
4WD:	N/A	WP Boots:	Helpful

Follow the near side of the river, past the bridge, and through a narrow clearing to the top of the falls. The ravine is now gone, although there is a steep hillside that rises from the river, creating a sometimes slippery hike.

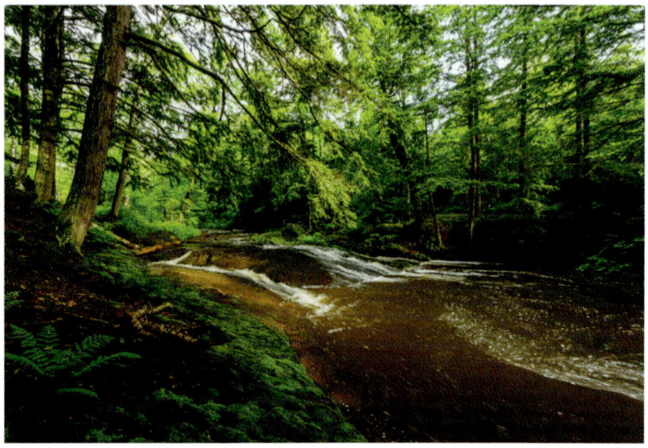

A good sized pool collects the water from this smaller slide. Unevenly surfaced basalt divides the river into sections as it drops into a calm and clear pool that in higher water level times flows around an island that supports a small group of trees.

The island in the river below the falls can be seen in this view from the top of the falls.

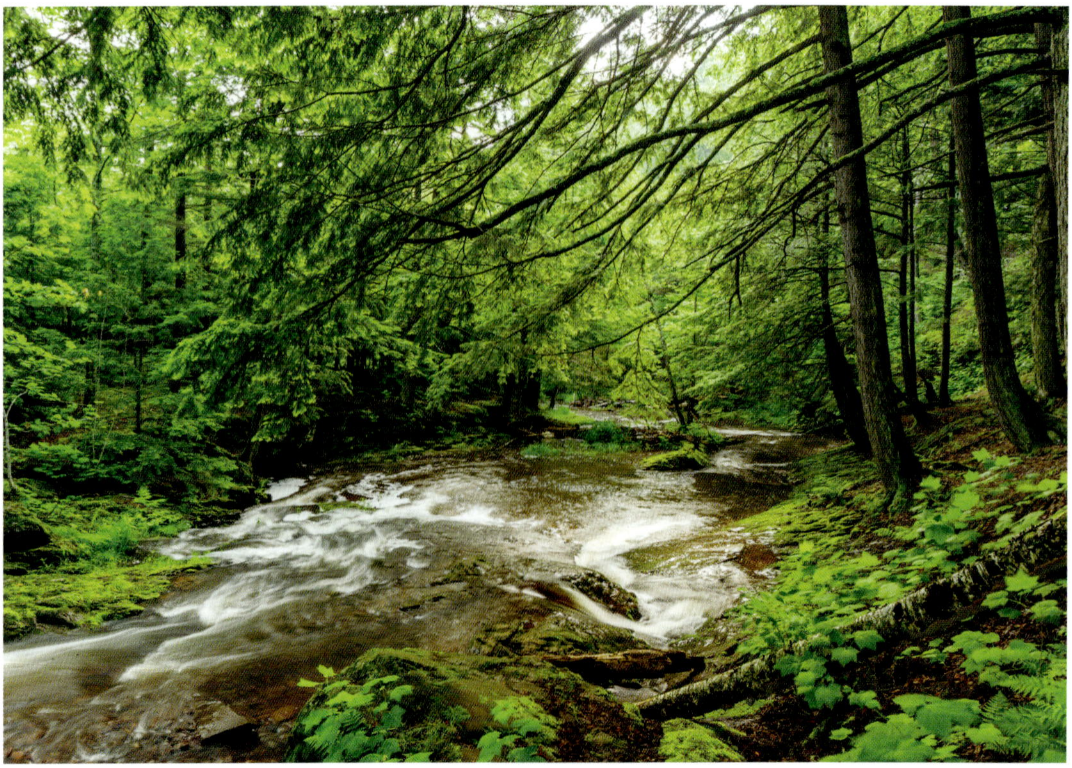

UNION FALLS #7 (UNION RIVER)

Private

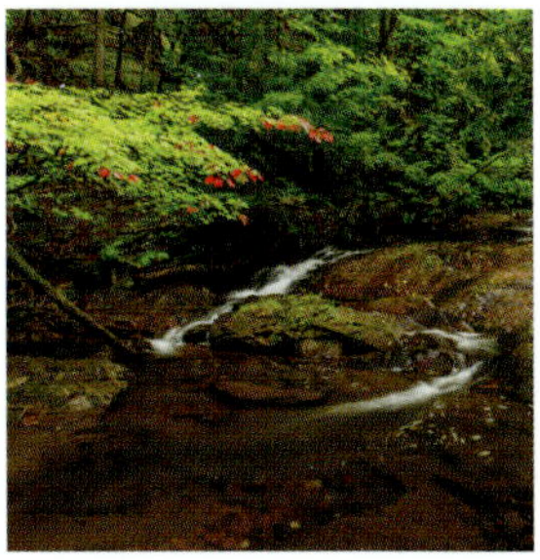

Must See:	5	GPS:	N46 47.859 W89 37.279
Height:	7 feet		
Time:	60-80 minutes		

Driving Information		Hiking Information	
Signs:	None	Path:	Footpath
Road:	Secondary	Length:	.51 miles
Access:	Somewhat Easy	Elev. Change:	Moderate
4WD:	N/A	GPS:	Helpful
		Danger:	Moderate
		WP Boots:	Helpful

Follow the steep hillside along the river as it bends back to the northeast. The viewing here can be a little difficult. The river slides down uneven layers of basalt, ending abruptly at a 2 foot high mass of rock. The falls pour out of both sides of the small natural dam.

About 300 yards down river the Little Union River joins up with the Union River. After joining forces, the river turns again and heads northerly for 1.6 miles to the shores of Lake Superior and empties into the great lake in the middle of Union Bay which sports a wonderfully sandy beach that stretches out along the eastern end of the Porcupine Mountains State Park toward Silver City.

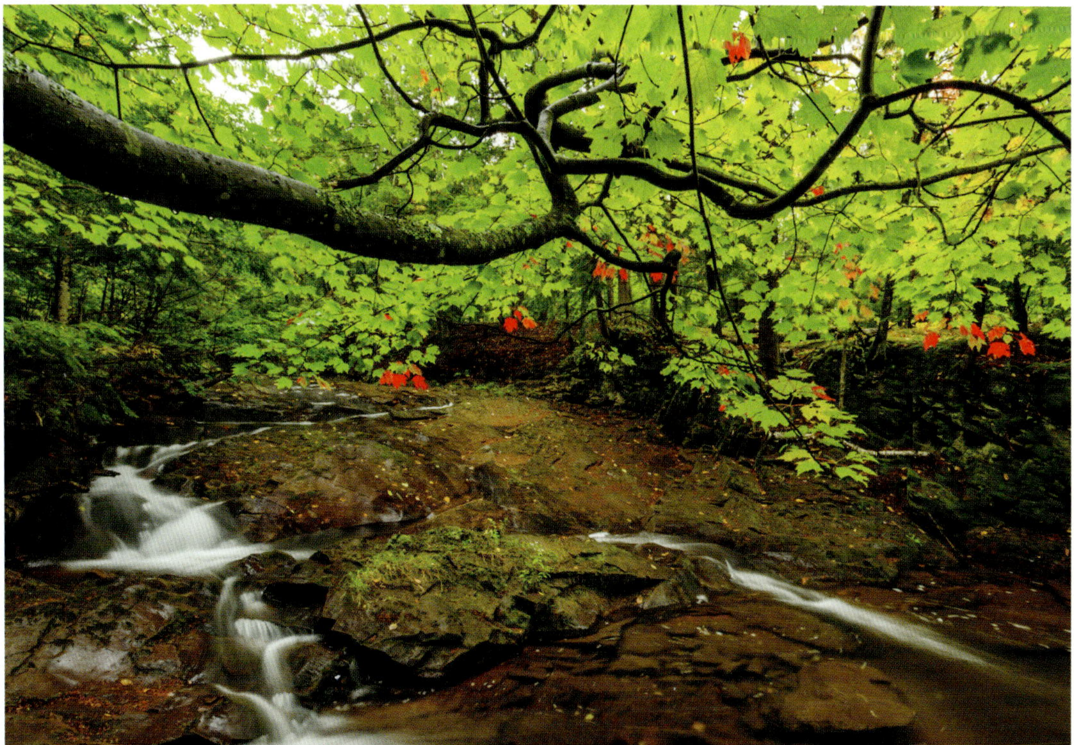

Would you care to seek out more amazing waterfalls in this great state? Then you'll want to check out the rest of the Waterfalls of Michigan Guidebook Series! These will be available soon at a store near you.

To order online, go to *www.mifalls.com*. That's where you'll also be able to browse through Phil's line of postcards, stocked in great retail locations around the state of Michigan.

Do you see an image you'd love to hang in your house or office space? The pictures in this book, and many more, are available as archival quality prints, ready to be framed. They can also be purchased, ready to be hung, as canvas wrapped or aluminum prints. Once again, head to *www.mifalls.com* for more information.

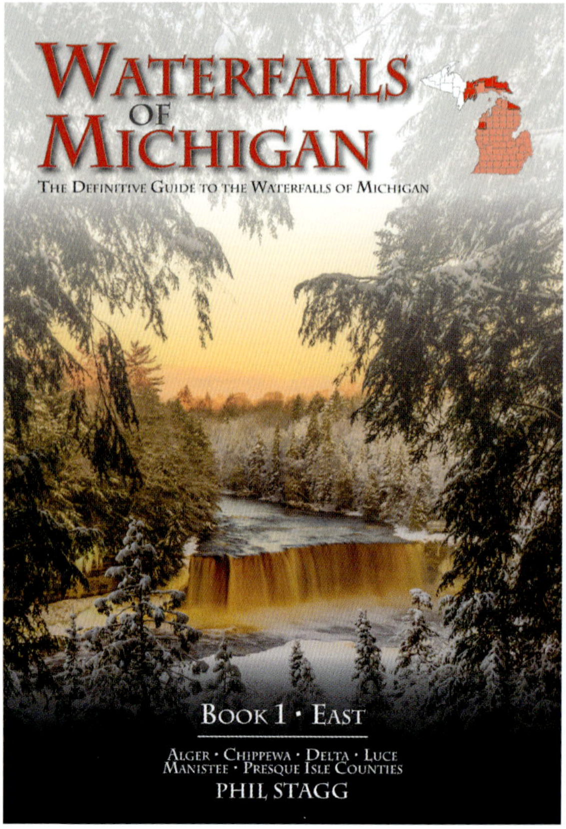

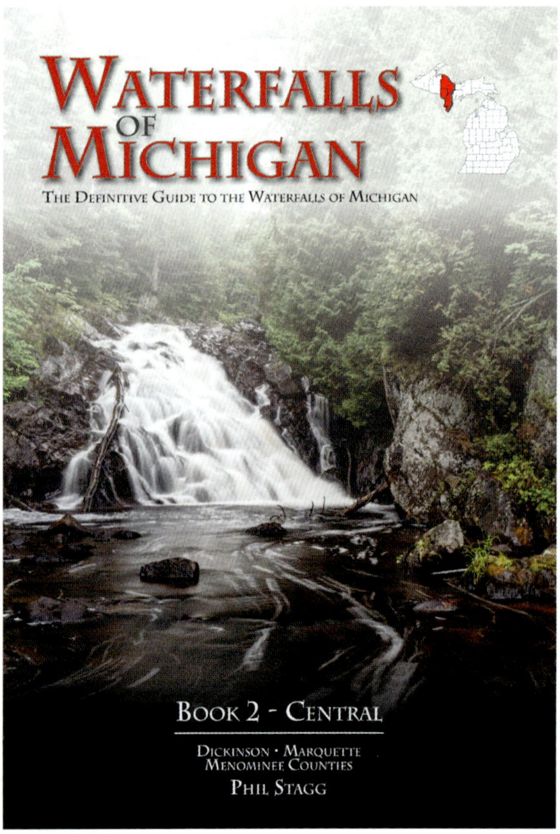

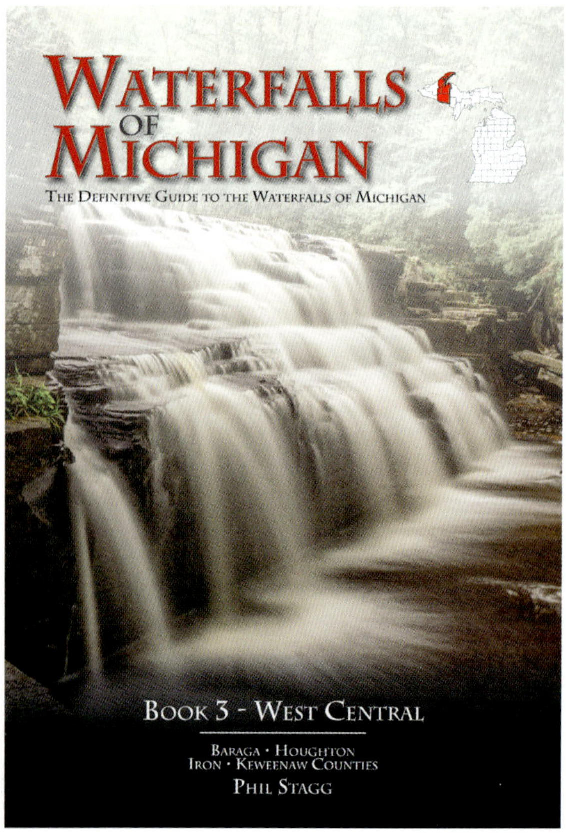